SAM HOUSTON

and the

ALAMO AVENGERS

ALSO BY BRIAN KILMEADE

George Washington's Secret Six

Thomas Jefferson and the Tripoli Pirates

Andrew Jackson and the Miracle of New Orleans

SAM HOUSTON

and the

ALAMO AVENGERS

THE TEXAS VICTORY THAT
CHANGED AMERICAN HISTORY

BRIAN KILMEADE

★ SENTINEL ★

SENTINEL
An imprint of Penguin Random House LLC
penguinrandomhouse.com

First published in hardcover in the United States by Sentinel,
an imprint of Penguin Random House LLC, in 2019.

This paperback edition with a new afterword and updated epilogue published in 2020.

Page 268 constitutes an extention to this copyright page.

ISBN 9780525540540 (trade paperback)

Library of Congress Cataloging-in-Publication Data

Names: Kilmeade, Brian, author.
Title: Sam Houston and the Alamo Avengers : The Texas Victory That Changed American History / Brian Kilmeade.
Other titles: Texas victory that changed American history
Description: [New York] : Sentinel, [2019] | Includes bibliographical references and index. |
Identifiers: LCCN 2019022817 (print) | LCCN 2019022818 (ebook) | ISBN 9780525540533 (hardcover) | ISBN 9780525540564 (epub)
Subjects: LCSH: Houston, Sam, 1793–1863. | Texas—History—Revolution, 1835–1836. | Alamo (San Antonio, Tex.)—Siege, 1836. | Governors—Texas—Biography. | Legislators—United States—Biography. | Texas—History—To 1846.
Classification: LCC F390.H84 K55 2019 (print) | LCC F390.H84 (ebook) | DDC 976.4/04092 [B]—dc23
LC record available at https://lccn.loc.gov/2019022817
LC ebook record available at https://lccn.loc.gov/2019022818

Printed in the United States of America

6th Printing

BOOK DESIGN BY MEIGHAN CAVANAUGH

MAPS BY DANIEL LAGIN

To my mother, my greatest supporter, defender, and inspiration.
May her legacy of toughness, kindness, and loyalty live on
in all those who were lucky enough to know her.

My son, take this musket and never disgrace it; for remember, I had rather all my sons should fill one honorable grave, than that one of them should turn his back to save his life. Go, and remember, too, that while the door of my cottage is open to brave men, it is eternally shut against cowards.

—Elizabeth Houston

CONTENTS

PROLOGUE

The Lessons of Battle

Experience is the teacher of all things.

—Julius Caesar

No small target at six-foot-two, young Sam Houston wasn't thinking about getting hit. He was thinking about getting even. Running through a hail of musket balls, spears, and arrows, he and his fellow soldiers sprinted toward an eight-foot-tall barricade. Behind it was an army of Red Stick Creek American Indians who had massacred three hundred men, women, and children at a Mississippi Territory stockade town called Fort Mims seven months earlier. For months Houston and his fellow soldiers serving under General Andrew Jackson had been attempting to retaliate, only to have the Red Sticks escape them time and time again. But now Jackson and his men had discovered their main camp, here at Horseshoe Bend, and they were not leaving without revenge.

The first man over the barricade took a bullet to the skull and fell back lifeless. Just behind him, Sam Houston never wavered.

On enlisting a year earlier as a private, Houston had immediately attracted notice. Tall and strong, his eyes a piercing blue, he looked every inch a leader. Promoted to drill sergeant, Houston's deep voice rang with authority; in a matter of months, he was promoted twice more. His superiors saw him as "soldierly [and] ready to do, or to suffer, whatever the obligation of . . . military duty imposed."[1] Now that resolution would be tested.

As the second man to top the wall, Houston did not hesitate. Waving his sword, he called for his men to follow. He immediately drew enemy fire, and he leapt to the ground inside the Red Stick fort, an arrow plunged deep into his upper thigh.

Houston refused to be turned aside. Despite the pain, he remained standing, fighting on with the shaft of the arrow protruding from his leg. His platoon, joined by reinforcements, soon drove the Red Sticks back. Only then did Houston look to his wound.

At Sam Houston's order, another lieutenant tried—but failed—to pull the arrow from his thigh. At Houston's insistence, the officer yanked a second time, but still the arrow refused to budge. Houston, sword in hand, demanded a third attempt, saying, "Try again and, if you fail this time, I will smite you to the earth."[2] This time the barbed arrowhead tore free, releasing a gush of blood and opening a deep gash.

Most men would have been done for the day and, after a surgeon field dressed his gaping wound, Houston rested. When General Jackson came to check the wounded, he recognized the young man who had helped lead the charge and honored him for his bravery—but he also ordered Houston out of the fight. Houston objected, but Jackson was firm.

Houston admired Jackson as the sort of father he'd always wanted, but he wasn't about to be kept out of the battle by anyone or anything. A short time later, when Jackson called for volunteers to storm a last Red Stick stronghold built into a ravine, Houston got to his feet and grabbed a musket. Limping and bloodied, he charged. When he stopped to level his gun, musket balls smashed into his right shoulder and upper arm, and his shattered limb fell to his side. Houston barely managed to make his way out of the range of fire before collapsing to the earth.

In the hours that followed, the Red Sticks were finally routed; hundreds of fighters lay dead. Fort Mims had been avenged, and the British deprived of a key ally in their attempt to destroy the young United States.

But Houston had paid a high price for his part in this victory, and he was about to learn that perhaps his drive to be in the action at any cost was not the best way to serve his country.

After Houston was carried from the field, a surgeon removed one of the musket balls but halted the procedure before digging deeper to extract the second lead projectile. In the cold triage of the battlefield, he saw no reason to inflict more suffering. In his judgment, this man would not survive the night. Houston would spend "the darkest night of [my] life" on the damp ground, alone and "racked with the keen torture of . . . many wounds."[3] But he lived to see the dawn.

Houston would carry to his grave the musket ball fragments in his shoulder, and the wound on his thigh never entirely healed. And just a few months later, the wounds tortured him in a different way when, upon arriving in Washington, D.C., he experienced a moment of horror. The British had burned the Capitol and the president's house shortly before. As he looked upon the ruins, he later remembered, "My blood boiled and I experienced one of the keenest pangs of my life in the thought that my right arm should be disabled at such a moment, and while the foe was still prowling through the country."[4]

The wounded and wiser Sam Houston came face-to-face with the limits of bravery. Eager to be a hero at any cost, he had instead become a casualty in a bloody battle, with wounds that left him unable to defend his young country from an even bigger threat. He had recognized how fragile both his own life and the American project were. And he learned a key lesson about war: Courage must be calculated, because courage without calculation could get you killed.

ONE

General Jackson's Protégé

Poor Houston rose like a rocket and fell like a stick.

—Governor William Carroll

am Houston's wounds healed slowly. He underwent several surgeries to repair his arm and thigh. But the young soldier's subsequent rise to power and prominence was surprisingly swift.

By the time Houston returned to active duty in the infantry, General Jackson and his army had won a stunning victory at the Battle of New Orleans, in January 1815, ending once and for all American battles with the British. But even as the war came to a close, Houston's relationship with Jackson continued to grow. Houston became Jackson's protégé—and more, almost a son to Old Hickory—after the twenty-two-year-old, at Andrew Jackson's personal request, was assigned to the general's staff in Nashville, Tennessee.

And Houston needed a father. His own had died when he was thirteen, and he had spent his early teens in frontier Tennessee, with a rocky relationship with his mother. Finally at age sixteen, unhappy with life on his mother's farm, he ran away, finding a home with Chief Oo-Loo-Te-Ka of the Cherokee nation. Houston embraced life with the

Cherokee, since he liked "the wild liberty of the Red Men better than the tyranny of his own brothers."[1]

The Cherokee had trained the restless young man, equipping him for a life of war. Now Houston wanted to be equipped for a life of politics, and he needed someone from his own culture to take him under his wing. Jackson, perhaps perceiving Houston's need and remembering his own fatherless youth, became that man.

When Houston resigned his commission, in 1818, to start a legal career, Jackson continued to support him. Thanks to his mentoring, Houston gained an insider's view of the intricacies of Tennessee politics and was appointed general of the Tennessee militia, a post Jackson once held. And he became a regular visitor to Jackson's beloved plantation home, the Hermitage, where not only Andrew Jackson, but his wife, Rachel, continued to embrace him as if he were a son.

Supported by Jackson, Houston flourished, eventually running, with Jackson's encouragement, to represent Tennessee in Congress. Jackson became a U.S. senator in the same election cycle, and the two men together headed for Washington. Houston's rise didn't stop there. Five years later, he was back in Tennessee as governor and seemed destined for a long and prosperous political career. America was young and growing, and there was much a young man with courage and ambition could do. It seemed that a fatherless child raised in poverty and then by Cherokee was going to make it to the top.

Seeming to cap his success was his luck in love. On January 22, 1829, the thirty-five-year-old Houston and lovely Eliza Allen exchanged marriage vows, by candlelight, in her father's sprawling plantation house. The best of Nashville society toasted to the couple's happiness and to the groom's rise to ever-greater political success.

But the marriage was the turning point in Houston's luck. Just three months later, Eliza abruptly left her husband to return to her father's house. Houston had questioned her faithfulness, and whispers and rumors blossomed into a full-blown scandal. Few details surfaced, but it seems Eliza was vindicated, suggesting Houston to be in the wrong. He disclaimed any accusation, but their relationship was ruined and so was his political career. By allegedly insulting her honor, Houston had violated the social code of the day, leaving him no choice but to resign as governor. As his predecessor, Governor Billy Carroll, observed, "Poor Houston rose like a rocket and fell like a stick."[2]

Houston left Tennessee. He found refuge with the Cherokee once again. Nearly twenty years after he had first asked them for help, the chief welcomed Houston's return.

The man who only weeks before had seemed destined to be president of the United States disappeared entirely from American political life. Tortured, he did all he could to forget his former world. He abandoned his city clothes, the English language, and his birth name, once again becoming known in Cherokee as *Co-lon-neh* ("the Raven"). For months, he attempted to numb his pain with alcohol, admitting later that he "buried his sorrows in the flowing bowl."[3] His huge liquor consumption soon earned him a second name, *Oo-tse-tee Ar-dee-tah-skee*—Cherokee for "the Big Drunk."[4]

TEXAS LOST

Sam Houston's fall from grace was far from President Jackson's only concern. While his protégé was off drowning his sorrows with the Cherokee, Jackson worked hard to undo what he saw as one of the biggest mistakes of the previous occupant of the White House, John Quincy Adams.

To put it bluntly, Jackson hated Adams. First of all, he hated him for having beaten him in the presidential election of 1824. Although Jackson won the popular vote by a solid margin, he got less than the required majority of electoral votes. The House of Representatives had decided in Adams's favor, thanks to the support of Henry Clay. Adams rewarded Clay by naming him secretary of state,* and Jackson accused Adams of making a "corrupt bargain" in accepting "thirty pieces of silver" from Clay, whom Jackson called the "Judas of the West." Despite the outcry from Jackson and others, Adams took possession of the president's house.

But Jackson's dislike of Adams went back further and deeper than the presidential defeat. He thought that the New Englander fundamentally misunderstood the needs of the frontier—and that he had given away land necessary to America's future. Years before, in May 1818, General Jackson and his army, as part of a campaign to protect his fellow citizens from the Seminole Indians, captured the port city of Pensacola in Spanish Florida. The next year Spain agreed to cede Florida to the United States in a treaty negotiated by none other than John Quincy Adams, then serving as James Monroe's secretary of state. This would have been good news for Jackson, had it not been for what Adams gave up in return for Florida.

President Thomas Jefferson had believed Texas to be part of the 1803 Louisiana Purchase. It was a link to the expanse of territory extending to the Pacific, as well as a buffer with Spain's colony, Mexico, to the south. Jefferson had also understood the region's potential value: "The province of Techas will be the richest state of our Union," he told James Monroe.[5] But in negotiating with Spain, Adams agreed to make the Sabine River—rather than the Rio Grande—the new border between American territory and Spanish, effectively handing over all of Texas to Spain.

In Andrew Jackson's mind, that left him with two Adams wrongs to

* In the early nineteenth century, becoming secretary of state was regarded as a stepping-stone to the presidency, the path taken by Jackson's four immediate predecessors, Jefferson, Madison, Monroe, and John Quincy Adams.

right: The first he corrected, in 1828, when he became president, defeating the incumbent Adams in a landslide. The second—the giveaway of Texas—would take longer to fix.

For one thing, the players had changed. Mexico had gained its independence from Spain in 1821. Then, three years later, the new nation south of the border adopted a federal constitution that echoed on the U.S. Constitution. Instead of freeing Texas from a European colonial power, Jackson would now have to coax it away from a democratic republic that had also recently won its freedom. And that was exactly what he hoped to do, sending an emissary to Mexico just a few months after his election.

Jackson wasn't the only U.S. citizen with an interest in Texas: By the thousands, American settlers were flooding over the Louisiana line to homestead in the rich farmland of Texas, which Mexico was making available cheaply to any who wanted it.

Earlier in the century, Americans looking to settle the frontier had been able to buy land on credit. But in 1820, Congress passed a new land act, which made it much, much harder for the average settler to afford it. Now settlers were required to buy a minimum of eighty acres, to be paid for in gold or silver, for $1.25 per acre. That hundred-dollar entrance fee closed the door to lots of people—when, just over the border, a settler could buy land for 12½¢ per acre. For those lacking the cash, the government in Mexico City extended credit, thinking they would have a firmer hold on Texas if they had more people residing in its largely empty expanse. As a result, Americans who wanted a fresh start poured over the border with the blessing of Mexico.

To Jackson, restoring Texas—where his countrymen had rapidly become a majority—to American ownership only made sense, but he knew the bargaining for it would be tough. On Jackson's orders, Colonel Anthony Butler made the Mexicans an offer. The United States would pay $5 million in return for the territory framed by the Sabine

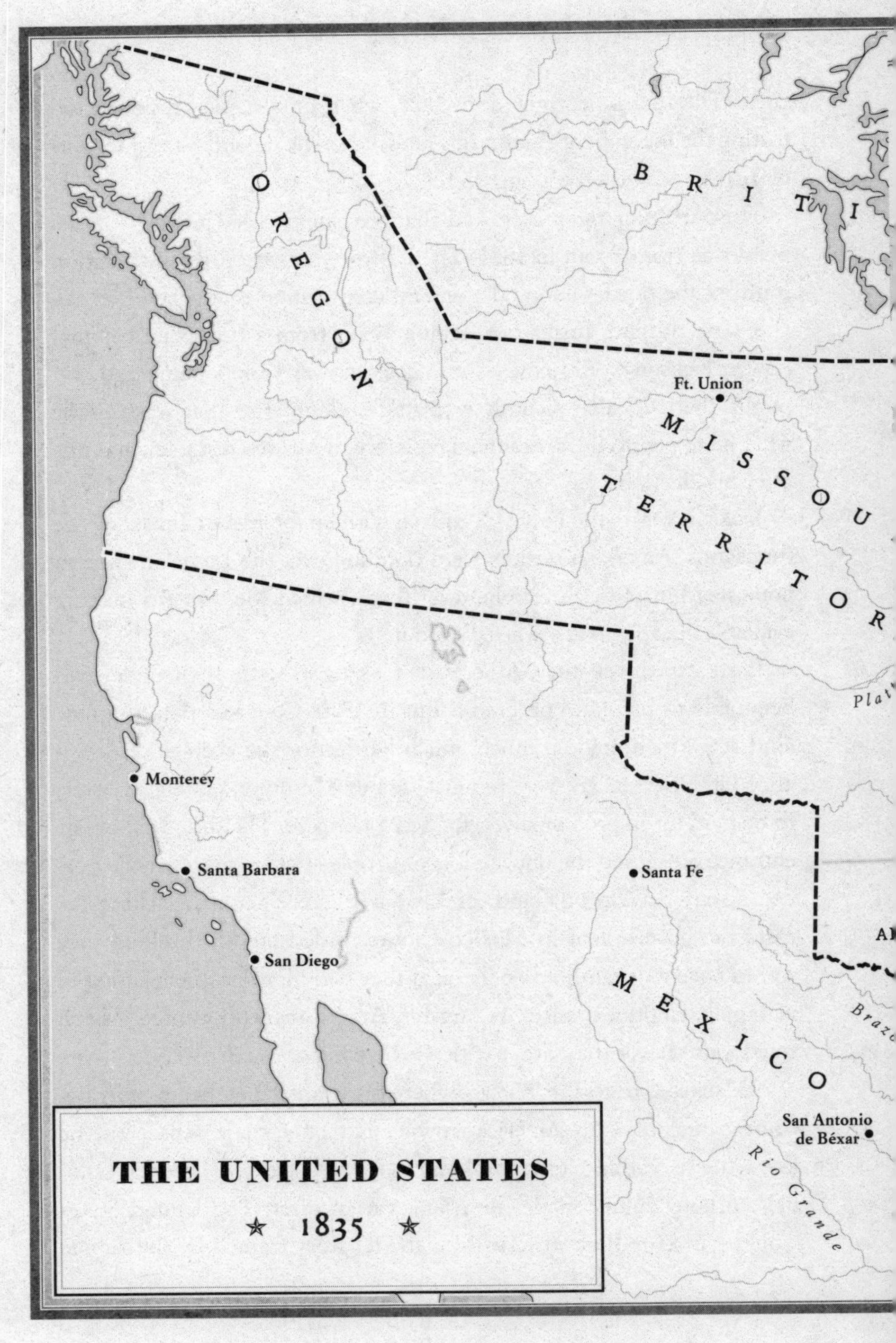
OREGON
BRITI
Ft. Union
MISSOU
TERRITOR
Plat
Monterey
Santa Barbara
San Diego
Santa Fe
MEXICO
Braz
San Antonio de Béxar
Rio Grande
THE UNITED STATES
1835

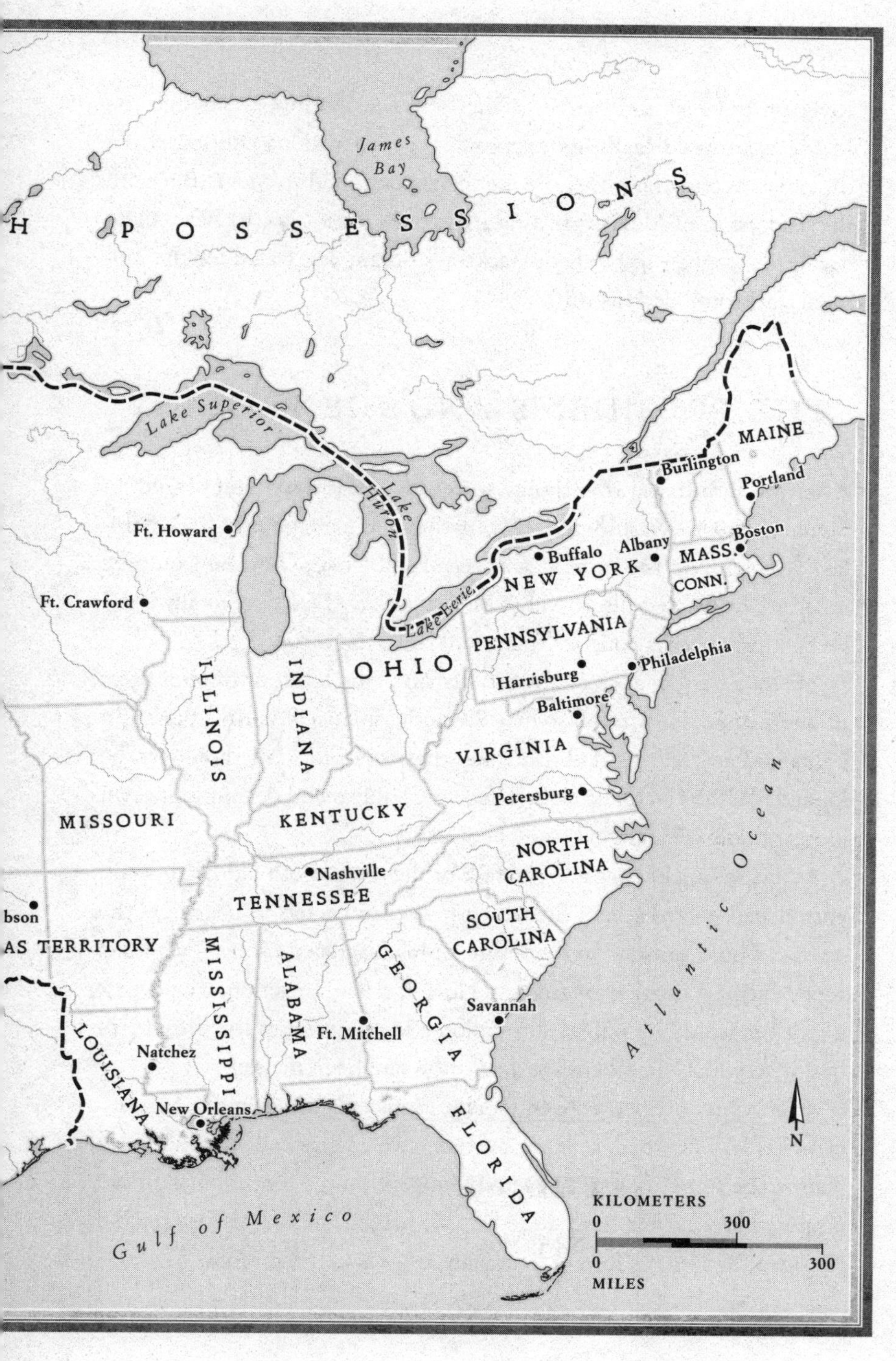

James Bay
H P O S S E S S I O N S
Lake Superior
Lake Huron
Lake Eerie
MAINE
Burlington
Portland
Boston
MASS.
CONN.
Albany
Buffalo
NEW YORK
Ft. Howard
Ft. Crawford
PENNSYLVANIA
Philadelphia
Harrisburg
Baltimore
OHIO
ILLINOIS
INDIANA
VIRGINIA
Petersburg
MISSOURI
KENTUCKY
NORTH CAROLINA
Nashville
TENNESSEE
bson
AS TERRITORY
SOUTH CAROLINA
MISSISSIPPI
ALABAMA
GEORGIA
Savannah
Ft. Mitchell
LOUISIANA
Natchez
New Orleans
FLORIDA
Atlantic Ocean
Gulf of Mexico
N
KILOMETERS
0
300
0
300
MILES

River on the east and the Rio Grande to the southwest. Though the Mexicans refused Jackson's proposal, the two nations continued the diplomatic conversation, and Americans continued to move. But with the leadership of Mexico shifting from one election to the next, there was little progress to be made. Jackson's dream was foiled for the moment. Jackson bided his time.

THE PRESIDENT AND HIS PRODIGY

After his withdrawal from polite society, Sam Houston reappeared, in January 1830, in Washington, D.C., arriving as a member of the Cherokee delegation to the American government. Unsure how he would be received, he wanted his arrival to be a surprise. "Don't say to any one," he had instructed a cousin, "that I will be in tomorrow."[6]

He took a room at an old haunt, Brown's Hotel. But he did not dress in the formal tailcoat of stylish Washingtonians. Wearing buckskin pants and a brightly colored blanket draped around his shoulders, he looked like the Cherokee he had become. Shiny metal decorations sewn loosely to his coat jangled when he walked.

Houston quickly became the talk of the town. Both old friends and entrenched enemies held their breath as they waited to hear how the general would respond to the return of his disgraced protégé, who was representing Cherokee interests, no less. Jackson's reaction, whatever it might be, would be public at a diplomatic reception at the president's house, to which the Cherokee delegation had been invited.

Even when dressed conventionally, Houston's height made him unmistakable. He stood at least six feet, two inches tall, though some claimed he stood six-four or even six-foot-six. At the reception, a turban wrapped around his head added to his height, making it easy for the president to spot his former lieutenant from across the room.

When the president called out to him, the crowd parted. Jackson approached. To the relief of many, the aging, rail-thin president pulled Houston to him, wrapping the younger and taller man in a bear hug. The message was clear: Whatever he had done, and wherever he had been, the general's affection for Sam Houston was undiminished.

For much of the next two years, Houston would remain with his adopted Native American family. In his sober moments, he served as a council leader. He married again, in 1830, this time taking for his wife a Cherokee woman, Tianh, known in English as Dianah Rogers. (Although they were not formally divorced until 1833, Houston and Eliza had already ceased to be man and wife under Cherokee law because they had "split the blanket.")[7] Houston traveled deep into the Arkansas Territory, acting as a Cherokee ambassador, a peacemaker negotiating with the Osage, Creek, and Choctaw. He and Tianh operated a trading store, selling kettles, blankets, soap, and rope to their Native American brethren. Houston represented the Cherokee on trips to Washington, too, arguing that government agents had consistently cheated his adopted people. His former standing in the nation's capital helped him win some small victories. Then, early in 1832, his Cherokee association entangled Houston in a legal case that almost ended Houston's career once again.

During a debate on the Jackson administration's Indian policy, on March 31, 1832, Ohio congressman William Stanbery suggested Houston had been part of a scheme to defraud the government. When Houston read about Stanbery's speech, he was furious. He tried to confront the man who had slandered both him and General Jackson, but for two weeks Stanbery managed to avoid the seething Houston. Then, by chance, Houston spied him as he strolled along Pennsylvania Avenue after dark.

Stanbery was armed with pistols, but Houston was undaunted. After politely inquiring, "Are you Mr. Stanbery?" Houston lit into him with a cane that he had carved from a hickory tree growing at the Hermitage.[8] As Stanbery told the story, "Mr. Houston . . . struck me with the bludgeon he held in his hand . . . repeatedly with great violence."[9]

Stanbery tried to run, but Houston, despite a nearly useless right arm from his Horseshoe Bend wounds, leapt on Stanbery's back and dragged him to the ground, still battering him with his cane. Stanbery tried to fend off his attacker with a pistol, but it misfired. Houston tore the firearm from Stanbery's grip, then delivered a few more licks with his cane. According to one witness, the last blow, aimed below Stanbery's belt, "struck him elsewhere."[10]

At Stanbery's insistence, Houston was arrested and, a month later, tried in Congress on charges of battery and contempt of Congress. Frank Key, a Washington attorney (and the man later remembered by his full name, Francis Scott Key, and as the author of "The Star Spangled Banner"), helped Houston argue his case on the House floor. General Jackson paid for the fashionable suit Houston wore and welcomed Houston to the president's house for updates on the proceedings during the month-long trial. When the case finally drew to a close, Houston, suffering from a brutal hangover after a long night of drinking, gave his own summation. The long speech won the gallery over; it was met with tumultuous applause and calls of *Bravo!* and *Huzzah!* Yet, despite the defendant's persuasive words, the House, after deliberating four days, found him guilty.

The punishment decreed was more symbolic than real—a reprimand from the Speaker of the House—but at Stanbery's insistence, a court case soon followed. Houston was fined the tall sum of $500, along with court costs. But the bizarre events had made him the talk of the town and even the nation, thanks to the newspapers, and he found the attention energizing and redemptive after his long years of obscurity.

"I was dying out," he remembered much later, "and had they taken me before a justice of the peace and fined me ten dollars it would have killed me." Instead, though his reputation was again tarnished, the very public congressional proceeding gave Houston new standing and gained him new confidence. "They gave me a national tribunal for a theatre," he remembered later, "and that set me up again."[11] He was a public paradox, a ruined man *and* a proud hero more famous and admired than ever.

Though reinvigorated, Houston did not try to revive his political career. For one thing, there was little chance of him going beyond his earlier achievements. For another, he needed to come up with the $500 he owed the government. He had been granted a year to pay his fine—to a typical laborer it amounted to roughly a year's wages—and he had an idea of where he might find the money. *Texas* was a place where a man could make his fortune. But it was a place for adventurers, for men like Houston, who might also be called second-chance men.

Some of those who headed for Texas looked to leave past misdemeanors—or worse—behind. Others wanted success and to accumulate wealth. Some were running away; some were seekers, just looking for a chance to prove themselves. Texas had become a place for new beginnings, for men on the make and for families—and for Sam Houston. In Texas, everyone lived in the present and nobody cared about your past.

THE TEXAS ENTERPRISE

"I will ride to the Hermitage this evening, and see the old Chief," Houston wrote to an acquaintance in August 1832.[12] General Jackson was taking refuge from the pressures of Washington politics for a few months back home in Tennessee when Houston arrived on his doorstep. Sadly, "Aunt Rachel" would not be there to join them. Jackson's beloved wife had passed away almost four years before.

On this visit, Houston hoped to secure Jackson's support for his trip. He knew that his mentor's interest in Texas was still strong, that he believed owning it was essential if America was to expand. During Houston's visit to the Hermitage, their conversation inevitably turned to Texas.

This wasn't the first time Houston had proposed to go to Texas. At the time of his first exile three years before, he had boasted of his ambitions for "breaking [Texas] off from Mexico, and annexing it to the United States."[13] This brag had been foolhardy, coming while Jackson and his ambassador to Mexico were in the middle of negotiations. On hearing that Houston, in a drunken state, had claimed "he would conquer Mexico or Texas, and be worth two millions in two years,"[14] Jackson rebuked him. Writing to Houston, the general expressed wonder that Houston would even contemplate "so wild a scheme" and demanded then that Houston pledge "never [to] engage in any [such] enterprise."[15]

In the years since, the two men had corresponded—sometimes on the record, at times off in private letters—and periodically they had met in Washington and Nashville. During that time, diplomacy had produced little progress regarding the acquisition of Texas. Ambassador Butler had suggested to Jackson that they again offer to buy Texas, raising the price from $5 million to $7 million. Jackson had refused, thinking the price too high at a time when he worried about the national debt. When Butler later proposed another tack—a half million dollars or more in bribes—Jackson ran out of patience. He rejected the notion of bribery, writing sharply back to Butler that he must make a deal if he was capable of it. If not, he confided to Colonel Butler, the time might come when circumstances "compel us in self defense to seize that country by force and establish a regular government there over it."[16]

Only a few months later, Houston arrived on the scene. A bankrupt man looking to remake his fortunes, his confidence renewed and his military and diplomatic skills still strong, he was eager to head to Texas. Perhaps he could help win it for America, he thought. In any case, he planned to act upon a deal he had negotiated with New York financiers to acquire lands in the Mexican territory. He believed a Texas venture might prove profitable, confiding in a cousin, "My business in Texas is of some importance to my pecuniary interest, and as such, I must attend to it."[17] But his journey would put him in a place where he could do much more than advance his own finances.

Did Jackson explicitly ask Houston to be his eyes and ears on the ground? Did the two men agree that Houston should seek ways to do what both had dreamed of for years—bringing the territory back into American hands? No record of such orders remains, but the assistance Jackson offered Houston was striking. At Jackson's instructions, the secretary of state issued Houston a new passport, intended to ease his passage through Indian territory, where, officially, Houston would represent Jackson's government in negotiating with the Native Americans. Jackson also loaned him the substantial sum of $500, with which Houston could go much further and perhaps accomplish much, both for himself, for independence-minded settlers in Texas, and in seeking to fulfill Jackson's vision for the United States.

TWO

Gone to Texas

G.T.T.

—A COMMON NINETEENTH-CENTURY TERM, CHALKED ON HOUSE DOORS AND NOTED IN TOWN RECORDS, SHORT FOR "GONE TO TEXAS."

On December 10, 1832, Sam Houston, after crossing the Sabine, planted his boot on Texas turf for the first time. He had stopped en route to bid farewell to his Cherokee wife, Tianh, giving her the trading post, farm, and wigwam they shared. He would not return to her.

Now, entering the territory he'd dreamed of winning for America, he headed for Nacogdoches, just west of the river, where he hoped to make his new home. Perhaps the oldest town in Texas—a Native American settlement for centuries, it had become a Spanish mission town in 1716—Nacogdoches (*Nak-uh-doh-chiz*) seemed to Houston the perfect place to establish a law practice. He needed to find a way to support himself once Jackson's money ran out. He also needed to set about the business of learning Spanish and becoming Catholic, since, according to Mexican law, only Catholics could own land and practice law.

Not that everyone in Texas was a Spanish-speaking Catholic—

although the state of Texas belonged to Mexico, most of those Houston encountered were settlers from the United States. As recently as a dozen years before, the territory had been home to few beyond the fierce, nomadic Comanche, other Native Americans, and wild animals. But now Texas was full of adventurous and ambitious American settlers, thanks to one Stephen F. Austin. And he was a man Houston knew he needed to meet.

Just weeks after arriving, Houston set out from Nacogdoches to the village of San Felipe de Austin on a mission to meet the man who was organizing Texas. Finding him was worth the 180-mile journey, a journey along the old Spanish camino real, a route that Stephen Austin's father had traveled years earlier.

Born in Connecticut before the American Revolution, the young Moses Austin was an entrepreneur at heart. After working as a merchant, he moved to Missouri to invest in mining. Then, after losing his fortune there, he looked west again. In 1821, the fifty-nine-year-old Moses Austin obtained permission from the Mexican governor of Texas, who was eager to populate the sparsely occupied state, for three hundred American settlers to establish a colony there.

Tragically, Moses would not live to settle the land he had negotiated. Just weeks after settling the deal, he died of pneumonia. Not willing to give up his dream, on his deathbed, he pleaded for his son to take up his cause. "Tell dear Stephen," Moses Austin told his wife, "that it is his dieing fathers last request to prosecute the enterprise he had Commenced."[1]

When he took up his father's role as an empresario of Texas, Stephen Fuller Austin, a slender man of twenty-seven, hardly looked like the adventurer type; gentle and genteel, he seemed better suited to the drawing room than an unsettled wilderness. But he spent months in Mexico City, gaining the required seals and signatures to grant him full authority to establish a colony, and then found a suitable site along the

Brazos River, where buffalo and other wild game were abundant, the soil rich, and timber plentiful.

Austin had set about surveying, plotting out land grants, establishing a headquarters, and fulfilling his father's expansive vision. He wanted a port of entry, where goods from outside Texas could be imported and traded. Accordingly, he founded San Felipe de Austin, which served as a capital for his little colony.

By the time Houston arrived in Texas a decade later, Austin's venture had inspired a wave of immigration. Word of his project spread quickly; several hundred immigrants arrived by 1824, and by 1825, the count was over twelve hundred. The promise of more elbow room, a new land of opportunity, a place to flourish, lured some ten thousand more Americans in the late 1820s, people hungry for land. They called themselves "Texians," and in return for taking an oath to the Mexican government, settlers were given large grants of land: 640 acres for each able-bodied man, 320 for his wife, and 160 more for each child. By the beginning of the 1830s, the roughly fifteen thousand Texians outnumbered the Spanish-speaking Tejanos five to one.*

Though an 1830 bill passed by the Mexican congress closed the border, effectively prohibiting further American immigration, a lack of enforcement meant that the ban did less to discourage new arrivals than it did to encourage a sense of solidarity among the Anglo settlers. Immigrants—like Sam Houston—still poured into Texas.

Now, as Houston traveled along the weedy track of the camino, he was eager to learn Austin's plans. Did he hope for independence? Would

---

* The label "Texan" didn't come into general use until after Texas, having been annexed by the United States, gained statehood in 1845. In earlier days, "Texian" distinguished recent arrivals from the United States from the Tejanos, residents of Spanish descent. According to some sources, "Texians" was pronounced *Tex-yans* in the 1830s. J. H. Kuykendall Papers, cited in Huston, *Deaf Smith, Incredible Texas Spy* (1973), p. 5.

he cooperate with Houston's hopes? He was a conservative man, perhaps likely to favor the current state of affairs, but Houston needed to find out.

Houston turned south at the Brazos River, then reached San Felipe, which thirty families called home. He found Austin's homestead without difficulty, but, to his surprise, the hand he shook on the veranda wasn't Stephen Austin's. Austin was traveling elsewhere in the colony. Instead, Houston stood face-to-face with another Texas adventurer, one James Bowie.

WELCOME TO TEXAS

Jim Bowie and Sam Houston even looked like natural allies. A physically imposing six-footer, Bowie was, according to his brother, "about as well made as any man I ever saw." Bowie was as fond of drink as Houston and had also joined Jackson's army during the War of 1812. Born in Kentucky but raised on a hardscrabble Georgia farm, the handsome Bowie—"young, proud, and ambitious"—had, like Houston, left his humble origins behind in order to seek his fortune in Texas.[2]

His light-colored hair tinged with red, Bowie was likable, with an engaging smile and an easy and open manner. His reputation, however, wasn't all sweetness and light; when someone or something set off his hair-trigger temper, it "frequently terminated in some tragical scene."[3] One such moment, in 1827, had left Bowie nearly dead.

In a brawl fought on a sandbar of the Mississippi, Bowie had taken a bullet to his hip and a bloody knife gash to his chest. Neither prevented him from grabbing one attacker by the shirt and pulling him down on the blade of Bowie's long knife, "twisting it to cut his heart strings."[4] The man died quickly, but Bowie fought on, sustaining two more bullet wounds and another from a knife. He survived and always after wore at his side that long and instantly legendary knife as a badge of honor.

In Texas, he mastered Spanish, joined the Catholic Church, and accumulated vast tracts of land. He married Maria Ursula de Veramendi, the striking daughter of the vice governor of the province, and settled into a quieter life.

Upon meeting Houston at Austin's, Bowie volunteered to escort him to San Antonio, the next stop on Houston's Texas tour.[5] Houston eagerly accepted. Always the politician, he wanted to get to know his new place and meet its important people. They traveled in a small group and, at Bowie's insistence, posted a guard each night to watch for Indians.

Bowie was just one of a rapidly growing circle of Houston's connections in Texas. In San Antonio, Bowie introduced Houston to his in-laws, the Veramendis, and other influential Texians, who showed Houston around the adobe homes of the picturesque town. By coincidence, a group of Comanche happened to be in San Antonio at the same time, and Houston fulfilled an obligation to Jackson when he got them to agree to meet with Indian commissioners in U.S. territory.

Heading back east, he stopped in San Felipe, this time finding Austin at home. Houston saw a man of moderate height and sober habits, unmarried but dedicated to Texas (Austin was known to say, "Texas is my mistress"). As for Austin, he recognized in this tall stranger a man worthy of a major land grant in one of his colonies.

By Christmas Eve, Houston became a Texas landowner. For $375 and an American horse, he took ownership of a league of land along the Gulf Coast, a plat of some 4,428 acres. Houston's status as a full-fledged Texian was further affirmed when, on his return to Nacogdoches, he learned that the townspeople had chosen him as a delegate to a convention of Texians. Houston's fame had preceded him, and the Texians had decided they needed his political expertise for the challenge facing them.

The purpose of the convention was to petition that the Mexican government grant Texas statehood status in the Mexican federation, separating it from another Mexican state, Coahuila. Houston and a committee of other settlers would soon draft a constitution for such a new Mexican state, one based on the 1780 charter of Massachusetts. Texians were unhappy at Mexico's restrictions on immigration; even if they had little impact, they felt like an infringement. The linkage to Coahuila felt alien; while Texas was strongly Anglo, the province to the south and west was predominantly Tejano. But the biggest source of concern was actually a single man, a dangerous man, with what appeared to be an insatiable lust for power and wealth.

EL PRESIDENTE SANTA ANNA

Mexico's president seemed to believe that cruelty was usually the best strategy.

General Antonio López de Santa Anna's life story was, in some ways, not so different from Sam Houston's. At about the same time that twenty-one-year-old Houston was defending American independence by fighting the Red Sticks, Santa Anna, one year younger, had also been at war. Unlike Sam Houston, though, he was fighting against his country's independence. In 1813, the young warrior was serving under General Arredondo, a general in the Royal Spanish Army, seeking to put down a rebellion against Spain's control of Mexico.

Like Houston, Santa Anna had risen rapidly in the ranks. Born into a well-to-do family, he had joined the military at age sixteen as a "gentleman cadet." Also like Houston, he sustained an arrow wound early, during a skirmish with the Indians in the Sierra Madre. And, like Houston, his early war experience had formed him.

Where Houston had learned that bravery must be tempered with prudence, Santa Anna had recognized an appreciation of the power of pure brutality. Serving under Arredondo at the Battle of Medina, he was part of the Royal Army that had executed 112 rebels after they surrendered. They pursued more men who fled toward eastern Texas and the United States, putting to death any that they captured. In the end, they killed over a thousand men; only ninety-three managed to escape.

The brutality effectively ended resistance to the oppressive royalist government, but the Mexican desire for freedom from Spain was too strong to stay down forever. Just a few years later, Mexico saw another fight for independence, this time with Santa Anna, a man who could read which way the wind was blowing, on the side of the rebels.

In 1821, sensing a power shift, Lieutenant Colonel Santa Anna switched sides, leaving service to the Spanish king to join the insurgents seeking freedom from Spain. After Mexico gained her independence, Santa Anna's successes helped make him one of the new nation's most powerful military men. In the turbulent years that followed, his power grew. He helped fight off a Spanish invasion in 1829, an attempt by the mother country to recapture its former colony. In the decisive Battle of Tampico, Santa Anna defeated the invaders just as Andrew Jackson had beaten the British at New Orleans, and he was celebrated as the nation's savior and even many in Texas supported him. However, in early 1833, he became more than a general: He was elected president of Mexico. He possessed not only military prowess but the shrewd instinct of a political gamesman and a gift for self-promotion. He did not demure when his admirers described him as the "Napoleon of the West."

Once in control of Mexico, the ambitious Santa Anna consolidated his hold on power. He eliminated all constitutional restraints on his dictatorial authority, explaining that it was foolish to allow the Mexican people to be free. "A hundred years to come my people will not be fit for liberty," he told the U.S. ambassador to Mexico. "They do not know . . . unenlightened as they are [that] despotism is the proper government for them."[6] He thought of his people as children; he believed they needed him to be the adult, to make decisions for them. To Santa Anna, the Texians were ungrateful foreign immigrants.

This was the man who was making decisions about Texas now. His words didn't sit well with all Mexicans—and they certainly didn't sit well with the English-speaking Texians who had come to Texas seeking liberty. Among the newest of those, Sam Houston brought both long experience in reading shifting political tides and a continuing obligation to Andrew Jackson.

Houston soon sent a letter to Washington. He reported on his meeting with the Comanche, but he knew his official duties in regard to tribal affairs would interest his old commander less than an assessment of what he had seen and heard in the heart of Anglo Texas.

"I have travelled near five hundred miles across Texas," he wrote. "It is the finest country to its extent upon the globe," he assured General Jackson, ". . . richer and more healthy, in my opinion, than west Tennessee." He imagined a bright future. "There can be no doubt, but the country East of [the Rio Grande] would sustain a population of ten millions of souls."

The gregarious Houston, in visiting Nacogdoches, San Felipe, San Antonio, and parts in between, in getting acquainted with Bowie and Austin and others, had taken their temperature on independence. "I am in possession of some information," he confided in Jackson, "[that] may be calculated to forward your views, if you should entertain any, touching the acquisition of Texas, by the government of the United States."

That news, too, was excellent. "That such a measure is desirable by nineteen twentieths of the population of the Province," Houston assured Jackson, "I can not doubt."[7]

THREE

"Come and Take It"

We must rely on ourselves, and prepare for the worst.

—Stephen Austin, August 31, 1835

Stephen Austin did everything he could to prevent an uprising. He had gone to Mexico City in the spring of 1833, but, despite his measured manner—and more than a decade of cooperation with the Mexican government—his mission had gone very wrong.

He carried a petition seeking for Texas the status of a state separate from Coahuila, but his firm but reasonable words produced only months of delays and no progress. Austin had despaired. "Nothing is going to be done," he wrote home, his patience exhausted, on October 2, 1833. Unfortunately for Austin, his pen didn't stop there.

Weary and frustrated, he urged the town council of San Antonio to act together with other towns. They should, he wrote, "unite in organizing a local government . . . even though the general government refuses its consent."[1] The runaround he'd faced in Mexico had done nothing to alleviate his worries concerning the future infringement of Texian rights; he knew that his fellow Texians, most of whom had been raised on the principles their fathers and grandfathers had fought for in the American Revolution, were with him.

When Santa Anna's Mexican government got wind of the letter, they arrested Austin. They accused him of sedition and threw him into the Inquisition prison. For a year he would remain in a cell, then he spent more months under house arrest, forbidden to leave Mexico City. He felt lucky when, in late July 1835, he was finally permitted to head home to Texas.

During those same months, Sam Houston kept a low profile, traveling around Texas and, in April 1834, visited Washington—and, undoubtedly, President Jackson. Neither man wanted Texas any less, but they chose to wait and to react as events unfolded—which they soon did.

Once more a free man, Austin made his way north, in the summer of 1835, stopping in New Orleans, where he confided in his cousin Mary Austin Holley, "It is very evident that Texas should be effectually, and fully, *Americanized*." One way or another, a philosophical Austin told Mary, independence would come, just "as a gentle breeze shakes off a ripe peach."[2]

Yet the peaceable Austin still hoped that Santa Anna might listen to reason. Austin feared the odds: After his many months in Mexico City, he fully grasped the size of the enemy; he and his thirty thousand Texian settlers faced a fight with a nation of some *eight million*.

He wanted to believe Santa Anna might be an ally. After all, thought Austin, the man had helped secure his release. His cautious optimism was also fed by a promise Santa Anna had made—"General Santa Anna told me he should visit Texas next March—as a friend." On the other hand, Austin knew that such hopes flew in the face of other actions of El Presidente.[3]

Santa Anna had decreed the Mexican congress powerless and undone earlier liberal reforms. He intimidated his people. When the state of Zacatecas resisted the president's orders to give up their weapons, Santa Anna led the army into the region. In May of that very year, the rebels surrendered, but, according to rumors around the capital, the president permitted his soldiers to run wild, setting fires and pillaging. In fact, more than two thousand civilians in the town had been slaughtered, among them hundreds of women and children. Santa Anna's message was clear: He would be merciless in putting down any who opposed him.

Few doubted that that included Texians and even the United States. In the presence of French and British diplomats, he issued an unmistakable warning. As reported by Jackson's man in Mexico City, he promised he "would in due Season *Chastise*" the United States. He went further, warning that, as the British had done in 1814, "I will march to the Capital, I will lay Washington City in ashes."[4]

Despite Santa Anna's threats, Stephen Austin still wanted to believe he might agree to a solution to pacify the unruly Texians. A strikingly handsome man with deep brown eyes, Santa Anna's quiet willingness to listen had impressed Austin, leading him to hope that, somehow, he could secure the future of his colony without a violent uprising and a bloody fight with Santa Anna. But on returning to America, he wrote from New Orleans to his cousin, admitting that he now could see Santa Anna had no respect for the Texians, that he wanted to make them Mexicans. He wanted to make them bow to Mexicans, to Mexico, and above all to him. What made that suddenly and undeniably clear to Austin was news that Santa Anna had ordered five hundred Mexican troops, commanded by General Martín Perfecto de Cos, onto Texas soil. Santa Anna had decided it was time to teach the Texian rebels a lesson.

Cos and his men, coming from Coahuila, would land at the Texian port of Copano on the Gulf of Mexico. They had been sent to preempt Texian resistance. They would disarm the Texians, peaceably or by force—that didn't matter to Santa Anna. But both sides could see that, with committees of safety springing up in every town—volunteer militias, ready to fight—armed conflict was growing more likely by the day.

The shock of all this, added to his two years in Mexico, altered Stephen Austin's views of Texas's future. Never large or hearty, he looked thin and wan, but the change was deeper. The man who'd departed with an honest allegiance to Mexico had been forced to rethink; now, in a matter of a few September days, Austin would finally abandon his long-held faith in Mexico and in Santa Anna, the man he wanted to believe was an ally to Texas. Like many of the so-called Three Hundred, the first families of Texas, he was reluctant to rebel; he would have been content if Texas were to become an independent state under Mexican authority. But he also wanted the rights restored that Santa Anna's strongman rule had taken away. Now, however, along with the flood of new arrivals who had little patience for the Mexican regime,

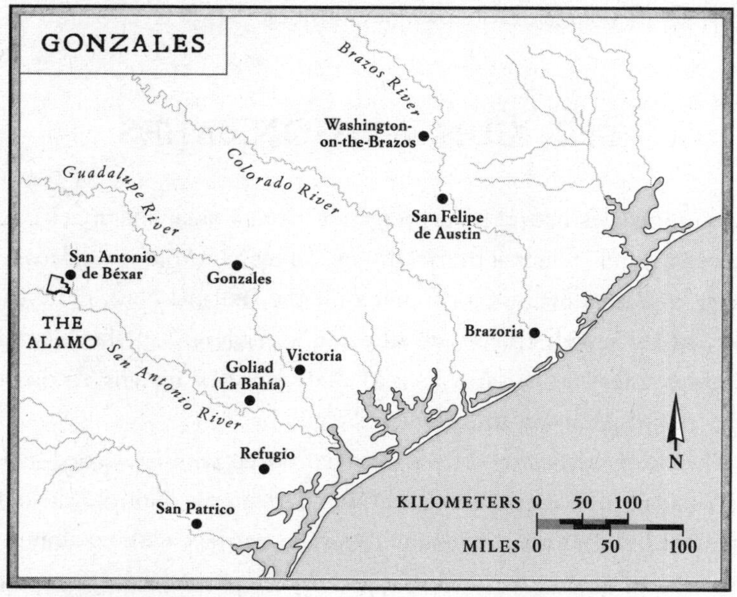

Austin recognized that war was inevitable. If Texas was to achieve its destiny, the Texians must be united in their resolve.

Returning after so many months to his colony at San Felipe de Austin, Austin accepted the chairmanship of the town's Committee of Safety, a volunteer company of rebels mustered in this moment of need, just as the Minutemen in Massachusetts had done in the revolutionary era. On almost the same day, the Committee of Public Safety in Nacogdoches put Sam Houston in charge of its militia. But it was Austin, in San Felipe, who issued a proclamation.

"There must now be no half way measures," Austin decreed as he worried about Cos's march north along the San Antonio River toward San Antonio. It must be, Austin added, "war in full. The sword is drawn and the scabbard must be put on one side until the [Mexican] military are all driven out of Texas."[5]

Little did he know that the war would soon begin a mere seventy-five miles away in the little town of Gonzales.

THE GUN AT GONZALES

When Gonzales had needed protection from Comanche attacks, the Mexican commandant at the nearby and larger San Antonio had loaned the town a small cannon to frighten off the Indians. Now, four years later, in 1835, with rumors of rebellion spreading fast, the Mexican military was eager to disarm any and all disgruntled Texians. As part of Cos's campaign, it was time to take the gun back.

The sleepy settlement of roughly two dozen families settled along the Guadalupe River posed no real threat to anyone. Nor did the half-forgotten little cannon, dismounted from its carriage with no ammunition available. But the Mexicans were determined to squash any opportunities for rebellion before they started, and as the sun-drenched days of September drew to a close, five Mexican soldiers marched into Gonzales to demand the return of the weapon.

The people of the isolated little town had been hearing whispers of Mexican efforts to disarm Texians. A rumor had recently gone around that soon only one man in ten would be permitted to carry a firearm. General Cos and five hundred Mexican troops were said to be coming to Texas to put down any unrest. And President Santa Anna loomed, far away but all-powerful and intimidating, an autocrat who ruled with an iron fist and whose goal of centralizing power and limiting democratic freedom was now clear to all. But whether any of the trouble would reach Gonzales had seemed less sure until the appearance of soldiers ready to confiscate Gonzales's only defensive weapon. Now the larger worries of Texas seemed very local.

Quickly convening a meeting to discuss the demands, the townspeople agreed that the order to hand over the gun made no sense if the Mexicans were looking out for Texian interests. San Antonio possessed at least eighteen better guns to protect it, and now Gonzales would have none. Never mind that they hadn't needed it to drive away Comanche in quite some time—the people of Gonzales correctly discerned that this was a move designed to weaken Texian defenses and destroy Texian morale. They decided to refuse to hand over the cannon. Mayor Andrew Ponton ordered the Mexican soldiers escorted out of town, the oxcart they had brought to carry the cannon left empty.

Their return cargo consisted of only a handwritten note, a message for the Mexican commandant at San Antonio. "The dangers which existed at the time we received this cannon still exist," Ponton wrote. "It is still needed here."[6] His words were half-true. Certainly, a threat remained—only now the biggest danger was not the Comanche, but men in Mexican army uniforms.

Though Ponton had politely offered a seemingly innocent excuse for defiance, it was defiance nonetheless. Everyone understood this would be a temporary standoff. No soldier in Santa Anna's army could let such evident insolence go unpunished. It was only a matter of time before a larger contingent of Mexican soldiers arrived to take the cannon by force.

Ponton looked around him: With just eighteen armed men ready to fight, Gonzales needed reinforcements—and fast. San Antonio was two days' ride away. If the Mexicans responded quickly, their avenging force could arrive in as little as four days, and eighteen Gonzales men would not be enough to fight them off. Desperate for help, one messenger galloped off for nearby Mina, another toward the Colorado River, passing the word to other Texian towns that Gonzales faced grave danger.

THE "OLD EIGHTEEN"

While the messengers were off rallying their fellow Texians, the men of Gonzales prepared to fight.* First, they evacuated the women and children. Some hid in the nearby forest, and others made their way to settlements along the Colorado River.

It was hard for twenty-five-year-old Almeron Dickinson to send away his wife, Susanna. The two of them, though they had been born in Tennessee, had adopted Texas as their native land four years before, settling in Gonzales in 1831. Dickinson tended their farm along the San Marcos River, and just a year earlier he and Susanna had welcomed their first child, a girl they named Angelina Elizabeth. But evacuation was the only sensible option for women and children, and, with Su-

* In later days, the survivors among these men took pride in identifying themselves as members of the "Old Eighteen," defenders of Gonzales. Miles, "Battle of Gonzales" (1899), p. 314.

sanna and Angelina safely gone, Dickinson turned his energy toward defending the home he'd come to love.

The first order of business was repairing the cannon—the truth was that the weapon the Texians were refusing to give up was not in good shape. Fortunately, as a U.S. Army veteran trained as an artilleryman, Dickinson knew a good deal about such guns. As a blacksmith, he knew how to repair them, too.

Dickinson fashioned a new carriage, making rough wheels of tree trunk rounds and inserting wooden axles through holes in their centers. He swabbed and cleaned the gun, and soon it was mounted and capable of being fired. But it really wasn't much of a weapon, Dickinson had to admit, since the cannon had been spiked to disable it years before by a retreating Mexican force. When the nail driven into its touchhole had been drilled out, the operation left an opening the size of a man's thumb. Dickinson did what he could to narrow the hole, but nothing would get this gun into top condition.

With no cannonballs to fire, ammunition had to be prepared. Dickinson and a second blacksmith set about hammering slugs of iron bar into crude balls that, together with pieces of chain and cut-up horseshoes, could be used as grapeshot.

Captain Albert Martin, Dickinson's neighbor, took charge of other preparations. He drilled his little band of men and talked strategy. Their best defense was the Guadalupe River, temporarily swollen by recent rain, which could function like a castle moat between them and enemies approaching from San Antonio in the west. Martin had the newly battle-ready cannon installed in a temporary fortification overlooking the river, and he ordered the ferryboat used for crossing the Guadalupe be moored well out of sight in a backwater hidden by trees upstream. The few remaining boats, too, were tied up on the east bank of the river, out of the reach of any Mexican soldiers.

The men collected the few guns they had—rifles, shotguns, and fowling pieces. Someone suggested a flag was needed, and soon volunteers went to work to make one. Using paint and a sheet of coarse cotton fabric as their canvas, they drew a simple likeness of the barrel of the disputed cannon. Above this symbol, they painted a five-point star to signify the state of Texas. Beneath, they wrote four words in black paint across the length of the six-foot flag. Large enough to be read from enemy lines, they posed a challenge: COME AND TAKE IT.[7]

Now Martin, Dickinson, and the other men waited, hoping that reinforcements would arrive before the enemy.

ONE HUNDRED DRAGOONS

The Mexicans appeared first. On Tuesday, September 29, a column of one hundred soldiers rode into sight. From across the Guadalupe they gazed on little Gonzales.

To these professional soldiers, this was just a routine mission, and their commanding officer, Lieutenant Francisco de Castañeda, had clear orders. He was to demand the cannon be handed over and, one way or another, bring to an end this insolence on the part of the upstart Texians.

Despite the long, two-day ride from San Antonio, the cavalrymen made an impressive appearance astride their horses and dressed in red uniform jackets. They carried nine-foot lances. Sabers and pistols hung from their belts and muskets jutted from their saddlebags.

The eighteen Texians were grateful that the rain-swollen river made crossing dangerous. They were not experienced fighters, but they did not need advanced knowledge of military tactics to understand that if the numbers didn't change—Martin and company were outnumbered more than five to one—this was not a winnable fight.

The Mexicans shouted across the Guadalupe that Lieutenant Castañeda, on behalf of the commander at San Antonio, wished to deliver a dispatch for the mayor of Gonzales. Captain Martin replied that a courier might swim over, and one of Castañeda's men crossed carrying his lieutenant's written demand.

Martin opened and read the dispatch. Its contents were no surprise, consisting of one demand: *The Texians must hand over the cannon.*

With reinforcements not yet there, Martin knew refusal would end badly. But there might be a way to buy time. Thinking quickly, he composed a meek response, saying that, with Mayor Ponton out of town, he lacked the authority to comply. Castañeda and his men would have to remain on the river's west bank overnight. The Mexicans, with an old-world respect for proper procedure, agreed.

As the Mexicans slept on the opposite bank, the men of Gonzales waited and prayed—and their petitions were answered. That evening reinforcements began to drift into Gonzales. Thirty men arrived from Mina; soon another fifty appeared, mustered from homesteads along the Colorado. The rumored arrival of Cos and his army had galvanized many in Texas, and these men came to fight not only for Gonzales but for freedom.

The following morning, the Texians managed to delay matters again; the mayor was still absent, Martin told Castañeda, but having been sent for, certainly he would return soon. Martin proposed scheduling the meeting for four o'clock that afternoon. With any luck, they'd be able by then to organize themselves enough to resist successfully.

At the appointed time, Lieutenant Castañeda returned to the riverbank, expecting to see Ponton crossing over. Instead, he saw a rebellious contingent of Texians gathered on the opposite bank. A Texian read a statement aloud, shouting it across the water. They would not "deliver up the cannon," the voice echoed. "The cannon is in the town and only through force will we yield. We are weak and few in number, nevertheless we are contending for what we believe just principles."[8]

Castañeda must have been shocked. Why would a tiny group of eighteen men think it could hold off one hundred trained Mexicans? Their resistance was irritating but could easily be put down. The day was coming to a close, but the next day he would march his men north to find an easier crossing, then travel south to Gonzales to teach the upstarts a lesson.

THE SKIRMISH

The Mexicans slowly marched north, eventually making camp that evening seven miles north of Gonzales. They occupied the fields of farmer Ezekiel Williams and helped themselves to his crop of watermelons. Secure in what they believed to be their vastly superior numbers, Lieutenant Castañeda and his troopers rested peacefully, blanketed by a deep fog that spread across the Guadalupe River Valley.

The Texians, with their homes and lives on the line, did not rest. As the Mexicans had retreated north, they had been busy accepting further reinforcements and organizing themselves under leaders. Now numbering more than one hundred sixty men, the volunteers elected John Moore as their commander, and Moore decided it was time to act. Martin's delaying tactic had bought enough time for volunteers to arrive from as far away as the Brazos River, and now the Texians outnumbered the enemy. No one knew whether more Mexicans were on the way, and it seemed prudent to act while the numbers were still in the Texian's favor. It seemed even more prudent to make that attack under cover of darkness.

That evening every available boat ferried men and horses across the Guadalupe. Once all the Texians were across, a Methodist preacher named W. P. Smith delivered a "patriotic address," exhorting the brave men to do their duty for God and Texas.[9] Then, on Colonel Moore's order, as one soldier remembered, the Texians moved north "with the greatest order and silence."[10]

The fog slowed progress, but at 4:00 A.M., warned by advance scouts that the Mexican encampment was a short distance ahead, the little army halted. The officers arranged the men into battle formation, with the fifty-man cavalry leading the way. Platoons of infantrymen marched on the right and left, flanking the artillery unit, with the brass cannon on its makeshift carriage and Almeron Dickinson heading its crew. A small guard brought up the rear. Still undetected, Moore's men resumed their advance on the Mexicans in a hushed silence.

A dog's bark broke the silence.

A moment later, a gunshot rang out, a Mexican picket firing into the predawn fog.

With visibility near zero, the Texians took cover in a nearby stand of trees. They waited: Had they been discovered? Or was the Mexican sentinel just jumpy? Either way, the fog was so thick that it would be foolhardy to attack now. They would wait and attack in the morning.

Even after sunrise, visibility remained poor as the fog gradually burned off. The sun slowly revealed that their presence had been discovered. Mexican dragoons stood in a triangular battle formation on a nearby rise, "their bright arms glittering in the sun."[11]

With the element of surprise entirely lost, Colonel Moore agreed to a parley. Meeting on middle ground, Castañeda once again demanded the cannon. The Texians refused. The cannon, they said, was rightfully theirs. Castañeda said his orders required him to remain in the vicinity and await further orders if the Texians refused to hand over the cannon.

Colonel Moore assured his opponent that he spoke for the people of Texas when he promised to "fight for our rights . . . until the last gasp."[12] He invited Castañeda to surrender.

The Mexican replied he must obey orders, and the negotiators returned to their respective lines.

With Mexican reinforcements undoubtedly coming from San Antonio, the Texians were not prepared to wait. Instead, they raised their banner—COME AND TAKE IT—over the cannon that was at the heart of the dispute. When a light was applied to its touchhole, Almeron Dickinson's weapon fired its load of iron shrapnel toward the Mexican line, and the band of farmers and settlers charged across the three hundred yards that separated the combatants.

To the Texians' great surprise, the Mexicans, at Castañeda's order, wheeled their horses and bolted.

"The Mexicans fled," remembered one of the Texians, "and continued to fly until entirely out of sight, on the road to San Antonio." The enemy was out of range before Dickinson's crew could fire off a second blast of iron scraps from the brass cannon.

Why had they fled? The Texians were not sure, but that was no reason not to celebrate the volunteers' victory over the trained forces. One or two Mexicans had been downed by the cannon's improvised ammunition, but the worst injury on the Texian side was a bloody nose suffered by a gunsmith whose horse had thrown him at the sound of the cannon.[13]

Strictly speaking, the Battle of Gonzales was scarcely a battle, and some of its participants would later call it just "the fight at Williams's place."[14] Nonetheless, the tale of the courageous men who'd held Gonzales, who'd defied the Mexicans, spread quickly. The threat of Mexican military action seemed suddenly very real, but in fact Casteñada had orders *not* to bring on a battle to the Texians, but at Gonzales the Texians believed they had defeated an invading army. They had taunted the powerful enemy with their challenge, *Come and take it*.

Gonzales was, quite simply, a moment to savor, a victory, a first victory, over the Mexicans. A wave of confidence spread. More than one account proudly termed the skirmish Texas's "Lexington and Concord moment," but the danger was far from past.

JOINING UP

Where there had been no Texian army, there would soon be one. And some of those who would fight for Texas came together in unexpected ways.

In the darkness at midnight, on October 9, a man on the run through the Texian wilderness listened carefully: Were the men on horseback, their voices barely distinguishable, friend or foe? Fearing they might be Mexican soldiers, he stood frozen, hoping to remain undetected.

He had come hundreds of miles across a desert plain from Monterrey. Despite long years in Texas and a sworn allegiance to Mexico, he had been jailed after Santa Anna became dictator. More than three months elapsed before he managed to slip away during a bathing session in a creek. Riding a fleet horse left him by a sympathetic friend, he raced for the Texas line. Now he could do nothing but wait, half-hidden in the mesquite thicket alongside the San Antonio River.

When one of the silhouetted riders raised a rifle in his direction, his freedom, even his life, might have ended with the report of the gun. But the first sound he heard wasn't the click of a trigger but a harsh demand.

"Who goes there?"

To the stranger's great relief, the rider spoke English.

"A friend," he responded; when he showed himself, some in the company recognized him. The stranger was Ben Milam, an early Texas settler and a man with nearly the status of Stephen Austin. His unexpected appearance was "like finding the dead to be alive."[15]

At forty-seven, Benjamin Rush Milam didn't look much like the soldier boy he once had been. Born in Lexington, he had gone to war with the Eighth Regiment of the Kentucky Infantry and defended his country during the War of 1812. In his late twenties, the restless young man had found a new home in Texas and, along with his friend Austin, encouraged other settlers to move westward, establishing what came to be known as Milam's Colony, located between the Guadalupe and Colorado rivers. He had led a venturesome life, accumulating large landholdings, as well as silver and other mining interests (which twice took him to England), and even investing in a project that led to the opening of the Red River to steamboats.

He had gone to the seat of government to stand up for those "who have built houses, mills and cotton gins, and introduced horses and cattle and hogs and sheep into the wilderness."[16] He had been rebuffed. Now, lined by the years and weathered by his journey, he still wore his tattered prison clothes. A sturdy man who stood six feet tall, Milam felt deeply betrayed by the Mexicans and was willing to fight for the rights of Texians.

When, after his discovery in the mesquite, he heard for the first time that the Texian rebellion had begun, "his heart was full. He could not speak for joy."[17] These men were volunteers, forming one of many bands around Texas who were looking to work together to fight off the Mexicans. Milam immediately volunteered to join the mission he had accidentally interrupted.

Milam and his new associates had a plan: They were looking to meet up with Captain George M. Collinsworth and join the ranks of his volunteer militia.

Hearing the call to arms just days before, Collinsworth, along with fewer than two dozen men, had departed the town of Matagorda near the mouth of the Colorado River. But on the march toward the newly contested heart of Texas, word of mouth brought more men to the cause from the surrounding coastal prairie. Tejanos concerned for their liberty also joined the ranks, bringing Collinsworth's count to more than a hundred men.

His objective was the nearby town of Goliad and its fortified mission building, La Bahía. Population seven hundred, Goliad occupied a hilltop overlooking the San Antonio River. A good, dry road and the navigable river extended south some forty miles to the port at Copano on the Gulf Coast; San Antonio was roughly the same distance north. This was the route General Cos and his troops had just taken, and it made Goliad, with its presidio, a natural base of operations in the region.

If Collinsworth and his volunteers could capture Goliad, the Texians would possess the perfect picket post from which to prevent the Mexicans from using the main supply route into the heart of Mexican Texas. Or, should the Texians persuade the nation of Andrew Jackson to lend assistance to their cause, the allies could land munitions and supplies from the United States.

In scouting the previous day, Collinsworth had gained valuable facts from several local Tejanos. These Spanish-speaking citizens told him the Mexican force holding the fort was small, a garrison of fewer than fifty enlisted men and a few officers. Collinsworth had sent a messenger asking them to surrender, but the mayor had refused.

Seeing no alternative, Collinsworth and his men prepared to attack on October 9. Led by Tejano scouts, three squads, with Milam at the head of one, moved quietly through the streets before midnight that Friday; a fourth band of soldiers remained with the horses outside the town. The mission and the attached imposing stone fortress looked impregnable, but acting on inside knowledge, Collinsworth's men went straight for the north wall.

Using axes, they chopped through a wooden door to reach an interior courtyard. One platoon headed for the quarters of the commandant. A sentinel fired on the attackers, but return fire silenced him. They quickly confronted the surprised Mexican commander, who threw up his hands in surrender. The Mexican defenders shot into the shadows; the Americans took careful aim at the enemy's muzzle flashes.

When a lull in the firing permitted one of Collinsworth's men to call upon the Mexicans to surrender, a Spanish voice agreed.

The short fight left one Mexican dead and three wounded, with a single Texian injured, his wound minor. The victors took two dozen prisoners, the rest of the Mexicans having escaped into the town.

A search of the presidio uncovered valuable weapons, including two brass cannons, six hundred spears, many bayonets, and ammunition. Less valuable were the stands of "Muskets and Carbins . . . the greater part . . . broken and entirely useless."[18] But there were large stores of supplies, including food and blankets and clothing. Ben Milam got a new set of clothes, although they were too small for the large man. Six inches or more of his ankles and arms stuck out like a scarecrow's.

Whatever the spoils, the result was clear: In Collinsworth's words, "I am now in possession of Goliad."[19] As at Gonzales, the Texians had demonstrated to the world—and to themselves—they could come together in common cause and fight effectively. After the news reached the distant East Coast later that year, the *New York Star* had admiring words for the Texians, calling them "mostly muscular, powerful men, and great marksmen; and whether at a distance with a rifle, or in close combat, they will be terrible."[20]

Another clear message had been sent, too: *Santa Anna, beware!*

GENERAL AUSTIN

By 8:00 A.M. on October 10, dispatches from Captain Collinsworth spread the word of Goliad's capture. In a matter of hours, the news reached Gonzales, where the armed force continued to grow by the day, even by the hour. From far-flung settlements, in the interior and on the coast, Texians came to join the fight.

"Recruits were constantly arriving, singly and in squads," remembered one soldier, ". . . [but] we soon had more officers than men."[21] Captain Moore no longer had clear charge of this motley band, the majority of whom hadn't yet arrived when he was chosen. A mix of lieutenants, colonels, and other captains would be required to command these men—but most of all the Texian rebels needed a general. A vote was scheduled for October 11; in keeping with militia tradition, the commander would be chosen by the men.

When Stephen Austin rode into camp early that Sunday afternoon, he didn't look well; "he was so feeble that his servant Simon [had] had to assist him to mount his horse."[22] But that didn't diminish the esteem his fellow Texians held for him and, one by one, the other candidates for the generalship bowed out. When the appointed hour of 4:00 P.M. rolled around, the rank and file unanimously chose Austin commander of the Volunteer Army of the People. He could claim no military experience beyond a few fights with marauding Indians and brief service in the Missouri militia during the War of 1812; still, he was the unimpeachable choice, founder and empresario, a man who'd gone to prison for his belief in Texas. His countrymen knew this citizen soldier would rise to any call to serve Texas.

Austin embraced his new role. Earlier that week he wrote to a friend in San Jacinto, "*I hope to see Texas forever free from Mexican domination of any kind.*" He said it in a private letter—"it is yet too soon to say this politically," he admitted—but he could read Texas's future.[23] The radical idea of *independence*, once held only by Houston and a handful of others, was rapidly becoming the will of the people.

Austin and his staff identified their next target: San Antonio. General Cos held that town; he had been sent to quell the uprising and, together with the five hundred men who had accompanied him from Mexico, the town's defenders were thought to number perhaps 650 men. Cos, a veteran soldier who had risen to the rank of brigadier general, headed a band of disciplined soldiers, fully armed professionals wearing matching blue uniforms with white sashes and tall hats. As Santa Anna had ordered, he was to put down the "revolutionists of Texas."[24]

Austin's officers included Colonel John Moore, commander of the main regiment, which now numbered about three hundred men. The scouts would report to Sam Milam, who had just arrived in Gonzales escorting three prisoners, the Mexican officers captured at Goliad. Responsibility for the artillery fell to Almeron Dickinson. And on October 13, Austin's band began the seventy-mile march, their heading due west.

The Texian "army" that marched out of Gonzales wore no official uniforms. The men, most in their twenties and thirties, wore the clothes of frontier settlers. For a typical volunteer that meant buckskin breeches gathered at the knee with Indian garters. Many wore shoes or moccasins and no socks. Almost none wore boots. Homemade buckskin hunting coats were common, worn atop rough linsey-woolsey shirts. A mix of sombreros and coonskin caps covered their heads.

The weapons included large hunting knives. Not everyone had a gun, but some did, many of them shotguns. The luckiest of them carried deadly accurate Kentucky long rifles. For those with firearms, priming horns and leather bullet pouches hung from their belts.

As his little army marched, Austin worried about the experienced and well-armed Mexican cavalry; most of the men were on foot, but his small mounted force consisted of men carrying homemade lances riding a mix of American horses, Spanish ponies, and mules. Another Austin worry was the hot-blooded nature of his men. Despite having no formal training and poor equipment, many were so keen to fight, so anxious to get into battle, that Austin wondered at his ability to restrain them until their odds improved. In his first official general orders, he warned them: "Patriotism and firmness will avail but little, without discipline and strict obedience to orders."[25]

The enemy outnumbered them, but the Texians were rising to this desperate occasion. Austin dispatched orders by courier for the soldiers from Goliad to join him en route. Two or three dozen new recruits were said to be arriving each day in San Felipe, and the general sent word that they, too, should join him on the march to San Antonio.

Austin also hoped to hear from Sam Houston, who was using his fame to help raise an army in East Texas. As reports of the action in central Texas arrived in Nacogdoches, Houston had, in early October, issued a call for volunteers from beyond the Sabine River, in the United States, appealing to men looking for adventure and a new start. Promising "liberal bounties of land," he implored readers in Arkansas, Tennessee, and Kentucky newspapers: "Let each man come with a good rifle, and one hundred rounds of ammunition, and to come soon." He closed with fighting words: "Our war cry is 'Liberty or death.'"[26] All that high talk was encouraging, but so far Austin had seen nothing of either Houston or his volunteers.

General Cos, a professional soldier with an experienced army, lay in wait, confident he could crush the upstart Texians whenever he wished. His opponent, the wary Austin, marched slowly toward San Antonio, consolidating his growing force. He would order his men into battle with the formidable Cos only when the time was right. Until then, he knew, everything was at risk.

FOUR

Concepción

The morning of glory is dawning upon us.
The work of liberty has begun.

—Sam Houston, *Department Orders*, October 8, 1835[1]

Austin's Army of Texas covered only ten miles a day in its seventy-five-mile march to San Antonio, a slow pace that allowed fresh volunteers to catch up with the force. There was an air of optimism among the men, who were ready to fight for something they believed in—and, judging by the first fights, they were more than up to the task.

Among the new arrivals, together with a handful of his Louisiana friends, was Houston's friend Colonel Jim Bowie. Austin welcomed any and all fresh recruits, but this man's appearance in particular cheered the ragtag army. "Bowie's prowess as a fighter," remembered one who saw him that day, "made him doubly welcome."[2]

Before meeting Houston, Bowie had lived a rambling life. Childhood had taken him from his birthplace in Kentucky to Missouri and Louisiana; his gambling adulthood was spent in Louisiana, Arkansas, Mississippi, and finally Texas. He found a home only upon his marriage to Ursula, in 1831, and with the birth the next year of a daughter, Maria

Elva, and then a son, James Jr. When Houston first met him in Texas, the wanderer had found happiness with his growing family at home in San Antonio—but the next year, in a September 1833 cholera epidemic, Ursula and the two little ones had died. Overnight, Bowie became a childless widower.*

As Sam Houston had done after the implosion of his marriage, Bowie had tried to numb his heartbreak with alcohol. He resumed his iterant ways, traveling to New Orleans and Mexico, pursuing his passion for land. But in late September 1835, on his return to Texas from Natchez, Mississippi, he had heard the call to arms. He and his little company came at a gallop.

Bowie's willingness to fight for his friends was beyond question. After a recent brawl in San Antonio, he scolded a companion who hadn't joined the fight. "Why, Jim," his friend replied, "you were in the wrong." To Bowie, that was no excuse. "Don't you suppose I know that as well as you do? That's just why I needed a friend. If I had been in the right, I would have had plenty of them."[3]

This time Bowie's cause was in the right, though whether he had enough friends to win in the fight against Mexico remained to be seen. When he caught up with Austin's forces, he and his men joined them in the march toward San Antonio, where they would find out.

On reaching Salado Creek, on October 20, Austin ordered a halt to establish temporary headquarters. They were a mere half day's ride from San Antonio, but Austin wasn't ready for the Texians to fight.

Before leaving Gonzales, Austin had issued urgent pleas for supplies. "Send on, without delay, wagons, with what ammunition you can procure," he wrote to his friends back in San Felipe de Austin, "[and] cannon and small-arms—powder, lead, &c.; and also provisions, meal,

---

* Bowie's life story varies from source to source, and some historians now question whether Bowie fathered any of Ursula's children.

beans, sugar and coffee."[4] But delivery was slow and now, after a week's march, the situation at the encampment looked more dire. "The men here are beginning to suffer greatly for the want of bread &c &c."[5]

Another challenge to Austin was the impending battle itself. He and his officers needed a strategy, a plan of attack. He could no longer count on the element of surprise—General Cos already knew the Texians were nearby since, a few days earlier, Ben Milam's scouts had engaged in a brief skirmish with a band of Mexican lancers that ended with the enemy force dashing back to San Antonio, carrying the news of the approaching Texians.

As inexperienced as he was in war, Austin understood he needed to know as much about his enemy as possible. *Did they have the rumored eight hundred or more men?* He knew too little about the town's defenses. *Where had they deployed their dozen or more cannons?* He had a hundred questions and few answers as his men entrenched along the little watercourse.

Austin needed somebody to venture closer to San Antonio, to look for information, as well as find corn, beans, and foodstuffs. He turned to his newest staff officer, Jim Bowie.

Austin recognized the way other men looked up to this fearless man. Having lived for years in San Antonio, Bowie also knew the town and its people very well. Austin assigned a slightly younger man, James Fannin, to be Bowie's co-commander. As the only one in the camp with any real military training (he'd spent two years at West Point), Fannin might be able to think tactically about the assault. Then, too, he might just offset the impulsive instincts of the scrappy Jim Bowie.

Bowie began by smuggling a letter into San Antonio. He learned from friends in the town that General Cos and his men (best estimate: six hundred Mexican troops) had fortified San Antonio with "adobe brick, with Port holes for their infantry." The enemy had mounted at least eight small cannons, some on rooftops. On the other hand, the

Mexicans had limited foodstuffs; "in *five days*," Bowie was told, "they can be *starved* out."[6] Bowie, Fannin, and company had also gone on small scouting missions and twice been "attacked by the enimy." But those skirmishes consisted of little more than brief exchanges of gunfire. Bowie asked Austin for fifty more men to assist him—*and* recommended that the Army of Texas move on San Antonio. He was confident of success.[7]

But Stephen Austin wasn't ready. He ordered the reconnoiterers back to camp. He wanted this fight to be on his terms, at a time he thought right. He also had to confront an immediate problem of Texian politics.

THE CONSULTATION

From a distance, the rider looked like just another volunteer. But as the stranger neared the temporary Texian camp, some thought they knew the identity of the man astride the little Spanish stallion. Soon the happy news began to ripple through the Army of Texas. The tall man on the little yellow horse, his feet almost touching the ground, was General Sam Houston.

The famous man arrived alone but instantly drew a crowd. Spontaneously, he delivered a speech to the excited men, "urging the necessity of concerted action among the colonists," as Noah Smithwick remembered it, and, "arguing that it should be for independence."[8] His audience needed no convincing and were thrilled to rally to the charismatic Houston. They cheered, heartened to have the great man on their side.

Oddly, though, Houston hadn't come to fight. His purpose was different: The new Texas needed a government. With Santa Anna having dissolved the legislature for the state of Coahuila y Tejas more than a year earlier, no form of representative government existed; in short,

Texas was "without a head."[9] And the rebellious Texians needed not only to stick together but to do it in an organized way.

The timing of Houston's appearance was no accident. In a matter of days, the Council of Texas, a body consisting of men from far-flung districts, planned to gather to sketch out a plan for governance. Delegates were already gathering in San Felipe de Austin, which had been chosen to take advantage of the just-arrived printing press and the newspaper it produced; the *Telegraph and Texas Register* could spread the word. But before beginning a formal session, the council needed a quorum. The purpose of Houston's visit was to corral the men already in the Army of Texas who had been chosen by their friends and neighbors to be delegates to the San Felipe Consultation.

That put Houston and Stephen Austin in direct conflict. Austin grasped the importance of the council's work, but he also knew, as general of this little army, he could hardly afford to lose a man. And he worried that the departure of some might lead to the departure of many. Instead of arriving to help in the fight, Houston would rob the army of fighters. Austin wasn't happy, but, always fair-minded, he looked for a solution.

On Sunday morning, October 25, he convened a meeting at the encampment. A number of other men spoke their minds, but Austin and Houston anchored the discussion. The central issue: *Stay and fight* vs. *Depart and debate.*

Houston made his case for the Consultation, arguing that they needed to organize a government for Texas and must do it swiftly. Then he spoke his mind about the ragtag band he saw before him. They needed more training, he told the troops. They were ill-equipped and, as Houston saw it, a lack of artillery doomed any assault on the well-barricaded town of San Antonio and its cannons. Rather than battling the well-armed and well-drilled regulars in the Mexican army, Houston told the assembled men, they would serve the cause of Texas better if they withdrew to Gonzales for winter camp, where they could make themselves into a real army.

These didn't sound like fighting words, but they were spoken by a fighter who, from harsh experience, knew the importance of prudence—and the costs of foolhardy courage.

When General Austin in his turn spoke to the crowd, he looked like the sick man he was; as one observer reported, he was "just able to sit on his horse." But despite the dysentery that caused him intense intestinal distress, he found the energy to deliver a deeply felt plea on behalf of his adopted land.

While he favored the purpose of the Consultation—*yes, certainly Texas needed a functioning government*—he passionately disagreed with Houston's plan to retreat back over hard-won ground; that would simply squander their first successes. The general promised his soldiers that he "would remain as long as 10 men would stick to [me], because the salvation of Texas depends on the army being sustained and at the same time the meeting of the convention."[10]

Houston and Austin, at odds with each other, had made their cases. The jury would be the fighting men, and a vote was taken. The vast majority of the men were angry and eager. They rejected retreat—but also recognized the need for the Consultation. The thorough airing of the matter permitted both a renewed commitment to the fight and an endorsement of a meeting of the council.

Despite their differences, Houston and Austin put their heads together; honoring the vote, they came to a compromise. Houston would go to San Felipe accompanied by the essential delegates, a total of fewer than twenty men. And he would carry a memorandum from Austin, who, understanding how critical the deliberations would be to the future of the region, wanted his opinions heard.

The debate in San Felipe would pit the radical faction, which some called the War Party, against the Peace Party, with the key tension between them whether they were fighting, on the one hand, for Texas's complete independence from Mexico or, on the other, for Mexican statehood and assurances of its citizens' rights under the Mexican Constitution of 1824, which Santa Anna had violated. In his letter, Austin made the case for remaining a Mexican state. But that would have to be resolved at the Consultation.

The next morning, Houston rode out the way he'd come, leaving Austin and the army to pursue a fight he thought misguided. As the big man departed, Austin was buoyed by the arrival of more than a hundred Tejano reinforcements, including a contingent of thirty-eight men led by Juan Seguín, the son of Austin's oldest Mexican friend. The army was growing more diverse, and it no longer looked like an entirely Anglo-versus-Mexican fight, but an uprising by all sorts of settlers resisting Santa Anna's iron rule.

With Houston gone, Austin issued the order for his troops, consisting of roughly four hundred effectives, to march west at last, moving closer to San Antonio. He had had enough waiting. As he'd promised the Council of Texas in the letter Houston carried, he would "press the operations as fast as my force will permit."[11]

"THE MOST ELIGIBLE SITUATION"

Barely a day after Houston left, Jim Bowie headed out toward San Antonio.[12] "You will select the best and most secure position that can be had on the river," General Austin ordered. The army needed a campsite close to San Antonio, one with pasturage for horses that was safe "from night attacks of the enemy."[13] And the general wanted it in time for the Army of Texas to make camp by nightfall.

Bowie and his division of ninety-two mounted men headed north from their base of operations at Mission San Francisco de la Espada.

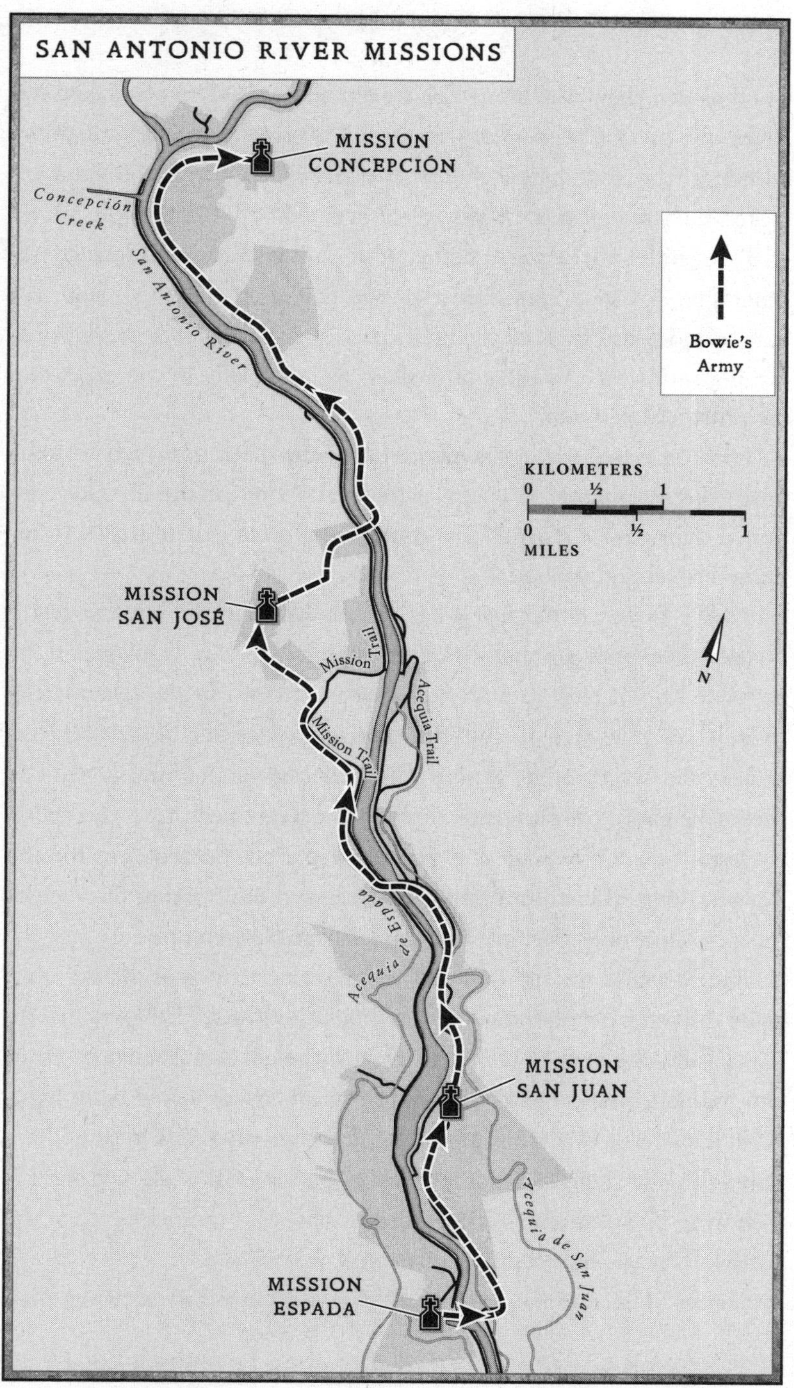

SAN ANTONIO RIVER MISSIONS
MISSION CONCEPCIÓN
Concepción Creek
San Antonio River
Bowie's Army
KILOMETERS
0
½
1
0
½
1
MILES
N
MISSION SAN JOSÉ
Mission Trail
Mission Trail
Acequia Trail
Acequia de Espada
MISSION SAN JUAN
Acequia de San Juan
MISSION ESPADA

They picked their way along the tree-lined bank of the San Antonio River and, two miles upstream, inspected Mission San Juan Capistrano. Although the abandoned church overlooked the river, the situation lacked the strategic advantages Austin wanted.

Three miles on, Bowie, together with Captain Fannin, inspected another site, but soon dismissed this one, a church called Mission San José, as indefensible. With the hours passing rapidly and Austin's words ringing in his ear ("with as little delay as possible"), Bowie urged the men further upstream.[14]

They encountered an enemy cavalry patrol, but after a brief skirmish, the outnumbered enemy withdrew. None of the Texians sustained injury, but General Cos would soon hear of their arrival in his immediate neighborhood.

Finally Bowie found just what he was looking for. Located just a quarter mile from another one-time Spanish mission, Concepción, he happened upon high ground at a U-shaped bend in the meandering river. It was a flat area, surrounded by stands of timber and scrub brush around the water's edge, behind which the men could take cover. The Mexicans could only advance through a narrow neck, and the nearly enclosed meadow would also provide a perfect field of fire for the Texians' long rifles. Best of all, the site lay within striking distance of their ultimate objective, just three miles from San Antonio.

They'd found the right place to camp, but one look at the sky indicated the short October day was drawing to a close.[15] There was no way Austin and the main force could reach Mission Concepción by dark, and that left Bowie a hard choice. The safest course would be to hightail it back to the main encampment. The alternative was to camp here to hold this strategic site, but that would be both risky—Bowie and his men would be outnumbered by Cos's troops, who were closer than the Army of Texas—and counter to Austin's orders.

Colonel Bowie, a man possessed of an independent streak wider than the Mississippi, never made decisions out of fear of friend or foe. Back in Louisiana, he'd won a reputation not merely for his knife fighting but as a tamer of wild horses and even for riding alligators. ("The trick was to get on [the alligator's] back, at the same time grasping his upper jaw firmly while gouging thumbs into his eyes. He couldn't see to do much and the leverage on his jaw would keep him from ducking under the water with the rider.")[16] He decided to ignore Austin's command.

Bowie's division would stay the night right where they stood, but, recognizing the possibility of attack, Bowie and Fannin established defensive positions. Forty-one soldiers under Bowie's command made camp on the north side of the roughly semicircular field, while Captain Fannin's company occupied the south side. Pickets were assigned to keep watch, including a detachment of seven men who occupied the cupola of the nearby mission with its broad view of the surrounding countryside.

Although the Mexicans lobbed a few cannonballs in the darkness from their camp on the other side of the river in the early evening, the Texians passed a quiet night, and the sentries raised no alarm. Bowie drank his share of a bottle of mescal before lying down to rest. This veteran of many fights had no great fear of what was to come. As one companion reported, "I never saw a man sleep more soundly than he did."

Back at the main camp, an anxious Austin waited. When a courier from Bowie finally arrived after dark, the general, already deeply worried about the fate of Bowie and his men, was frustrated. His army divided, he could do nothing until morning. Even then reinforcements would need two hours to reach Mission Concepción. After ordering his officers to prepare for a dawn march, Austin, unlike Bowie, spent a sleepless night, anxiously awaiting morning. He worried that he was about to lose what amounted to a quarter of his army.[17]

ACTION!

Shortly before dawn, Henry Karnes, one of Bowie's sentinels, heard hoofbeats. Tennessee born, the short, stocky Karnes rarely swore—but at that moment he must have been tempted. In the predawn light, speaking softly in his high-pitched voice, he urged the rifleman at his side to keep silent.

While Bowie slept, Austin's worst fear had been realized. General Cos, told by his spies that he outnumbered the ninety or so Americans camping in the horseshoe bend, had ordered one hundred troopers to slip across the river in darkness. Downstream from the Texian camp,

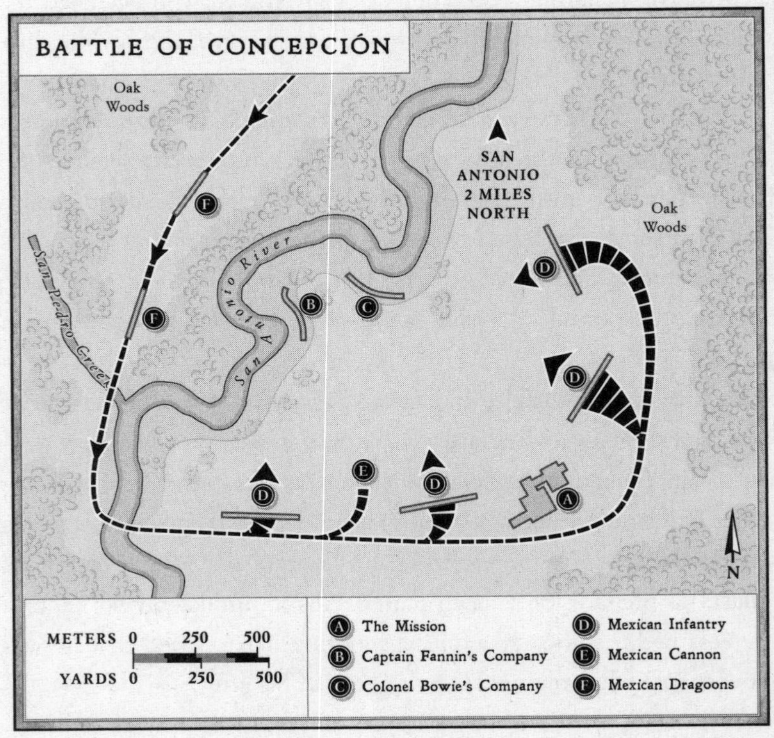

the Mexican dragoons had waded ashore undetected, together with several companies of infantrymen and artillery detachments, totaling another two hundred, hauling a pair of field cannons.

The two Texian sentinels squinted into the mists, looking to see what they had heard. Then, just as Karnes glimpsed the legs of a horse in the middle distance, the report of a musket ripped the watchful silence.

The Texian rifleman quickly returned fire, and Karnes charged into the gloom, firing his pistol at the dim silhouette. But the Mexican horseman disappeared into the bank of fog, and again they heard the sound of hoofbeats, this time in rapid retreat. With that, the two lookouts fell back to their camp, where the other volunteers, their sleep shattered by the gunfire, leapt into action.

As the Texians scrambled for their guns, more unseen Mexicans opened fire. For a time, Jim Bowie later reported, they "kept up a constant firing, *at a distance*, [but] with no other effect than a waste of ammunition of their part."[18] Waiting for the morning fog to clear, the enemy didn't show themselves, and the firing soon ceased.

Meanwhile, the Texians prepared for an imminent attack. Some herded the horses to the riverbed below and tethered them to trees. At the edge of the clearing men hacked at bushes and vines with their hunting knives. Along the surrounding banks that descended to the river, they cut footholds, enabling them to step up and shoot before falling back and below the protective embankment, then reload and rise to fire again. Their defensive position, with the left flank angling away from the right, would put Mexicans who charged into the open ground in between and at the mercy of deadly raking fire.

"Keep under cover, boys," Bowie ordered, ". . . we haven't a man to spare."[19]

As the fog burned off, a battle line of Mexicans slowly became visible, two hundred yards away but ready to attack. The uniformed men filled the breadth of the hundred-yard-wide neck that provided the only land access to the horseshoe-shaped field of battle. At the center stood one hundred infantrymen, flanked on both sides by cavalry. Cannoneers brought up the rear. For any Texian considering retreat, a look over his shoulder revealed another two companies of Cos's dragoons on the opposite shore of the San Antonio River. Though it was a shock to the Texians to realize they were effectively surrounded, a gunsmith and Gonzales veteran named Noah Smithwick no doubt spoke for Bowie and Fannin and the rest when he said, "Retreat formed no part of our programme."[20]

At eight o'clock, a rifle shot signaled the Mexican attack.

The Mexican infantry marched forward as the field became a blaze of gunfire and billowing smoke. As they had been trained to do, the Mexicans fired their muskets in volleys while the Texians operated as individuals. Bowie's men fired less often—"but with good aim and deadly effect."[21] The ranks of the oncoming infantry thinned as the Texian marksmen dropped Mexicans, some dead, others wounded, to the ground.

Ten minutes into the fight, a Mexican cannon boomed. The four-pounder fired canister and grapeshot, which crashed harmlessly into the trees overhead. The only effect upon the crouching Texians was a shower of ripe pecans that rained down from above.

As the Mexican artillerymen worked to adjust the cannon's angle of fire, the Texians began shifting their position behind the bluff. After taking his shot each man would, as usual, step back and below the protective embankment to reload. But now, before rising to fire again, he would shift a few steps around the curve of the embankment, working closer to the position of the cannon.

One by one, the Texian fire brought down the exposed Mexican artillerymen. Although fresh gunners took their places, those, too, became the most-favored target of Bowie's men. When the second crew fell, a third took their place.

Slowed by their enemy's persistent and deadly marksmanship, the Mexican infantry regrouped, preparing to charge again. But Bowie issued his order first. Clambering out from behind their riverbank barricade for the first time, his men surged toward the brass cannon; in a matter of seconds, it was theirs. Finding the gun loaded and ready to fire, Bowie's men pivoted the weapon and emptied its load of iron at the Mexican infantrymen.

To their surprise, the cannon fire produced an immediate result. As the Texians observed in delight, the enemy was suddenly in full retreat. Stunned at the losses the Texians had inflicted, the Mexicans turned and fled back to San Antonio. In that moment, the battle was decided.

The Battle of Concepción ended in another decisive win for the Texians; as they had at Gonzales, the upstart settlers had taken on an impressive uniformed force, and again won a significant fight. Bowie's division sustained only two casualties, with two men wounded in the fighting. But as the guns went quiet, the screams of a soldier named Richard Andrews echoed across the battlefield.

Despite Bowie's orders, Andrews had ventured out from behind the bluff in the heat of the battle. An easy target, he had been quickly cut down when a shot tore into his left side; the iron ball exited his abdomen on the other. One of the first men to reach him had been Noah Smithwick.

"Dick, are you hurt?"

Andrews managed to reply to his friend, "Yes, Smith, I'm killed." Prone, in unbearable pain with his bowels protruding from his wound, Andrews would die hours later.[22]

The violent and public passing of their fellow soldier would be a reminder of what was at stake. Every man's life was on the line in the fight—but in just two hours, the Texians gained a clear victory in their first full-scale battle with Santa Anna's army.

"THE BRILLIANCY OF THE VICTORY"

Thirty minutes after the Mexicans fled, General Austin arrived. On hearing distant gunshots, his army had quick-marched; when the firing had stopped, Austin, still at a distance, feared the worst. But on reaching Concepción, he saw the Mexican rear guard just visible in the distance, bound for San Antonio.

After being told of the rout of the Mexicans, Austin's first instinct was to order a pursuit of the fleeing and disorganized enemy: "The army must follow them right into town!"[23] Wouldn't San Antonio itself, with its defenders shocked and in disarray, be vulnerable?

His officers counseled caution. The town was fortified. According to Bowie's sources inside San Antonio, at least six cannons had been mounted on the walls of the church, a solid masonry building known as the Alamo. The artillery included an eighteen-pounder, and a handful more defended squares within the town. As for the Texians, their artillery trailed well behind. Attempting a frontal assault would expose Austin's army to deadly artillery fire and a spray of bullets from riflemen well protected by the adobe walls of the town. To storm San Antonio would put the entire army at risk.

Reluctantly, Austin contented himself with Bowie's morning success. Some three hundred Mexicans had surrounded a mere ninety-four Texians, but Bowie and Fannin's defensive strategy worked. Although the enemy's advance guard had come within eighty yards of their line, the Texians' guns had taken a terrible toll; the outnumbered defenders repulsed their attackers. Even without Sam Houston, they had prevailed.

In contrast to the Texian losses (one wounded, one dying, a few horses lost), downed Mexicans lay across the field of battle. At least sixteen were dead or dying; perhaps twice as many had been wounded.

That afternoon, the parish priest arrived from San Antonio, and after a parley with Austin, a long line of wagons and attendants carted the Mexican dead and wounded back to the town. In the evening, the Texians buried Dick Andrews. Over his grave, located at the foot of a pecan tree, they fired a rifle volley, as well as a cannon salute—using the captured Mexican cannon.

The difference between the kinds of guns used by the two sides had been one deciding factor in the battle. The Mexican smoothbore muskets had an effective range of roughly seventy-five yards; that was perfectly adequate for a European-style battle in which two armies marched toward each other in battle formation on open ground. But General Cos's infantry had marched on a largely hidden enemy, one armed with long rifles with more than double the effective range of the muskets the Mexicans carried.

In the hours after the battle, the Texians discovered they had possessed another—and unexpected—strategic advantage. As they helped themselves to the cartridges and cartridge boxes abandoned by fleeing Mexicans on the field, they examined the salvaged ammunition. To their surprise, they found the enemy had been using "by far the poorest powder" they'd ever seen. As one soldier reported, "Compared with the double Dupont, with which we had been furnished, it was evident that we had vastly the advantage over our enemy in this particular. We therefore emptied all the [Mexican] cartridges, and saved only the bullets."[24] The discovery explained why so many enemy musket balls had fallen well short of the Texian line.

Texian marksmanship and poor Mexican powder helped win the day, but so had their tactics. Having positioned his men wisely, Bowie's order to attack the Mexican artillery position could not have been better timed.

Despite his sleepless night and frustration at Bowie's insubordination, Austin admired the accomplishments of Bowie and Fannin's band

and reported proudly to the conventioneers at San Felipe on the "brilliancy of the victory gained."[25] Perhaps more than anyone else in the Texian camp, Austin also understood the larger military calculus. Whatever their success that Wednesday morning, the rebels remained clear underdogs.

Yet he and his expatriate Americans also knew precisely what they were fighting for. They were raised on the stories of the revolutionary generation. Austin and his Texians were colonists, too, resentful of taxes and other restrictions imposed by European masters. The success at Concepción only served to boost their confidence.

If they had to reprise the War of Independence right there in Texas, then so be it.

FIVE

A Slow Siege at the Alamo

This force, it is known to all, is but undisciplined militia and in some respects of very discordant materials.

—Stephen Austin, November 4, 1835

General Martín Perfecto de Cos possessed what General Stephen F. Austin wanted: The Mexicans occupied the town of San Antonio. Cos had roughly twice the men Austin did plus a dozen-odd cannons with which to defend the town. Quite simply, if Austin wanted San Antonio de Béxar, he would have to come and take it.

From his encampment north of San Antonio, Austin eyed the village of some two thousand people just downstream on the west bank of the lazy San Antonio River. The provincial capital consisted of a small grid of streets that radiated from the San Fernando church and the Plaza de Armas and Plaza de las Islas, the military and main squares on either side of the church. Stone buildings surrounded the two squares, but quickly gave way to flat-roofed adobe and mud huts. Where the dwellings ended, fertile fields of corn began.

From his vantage, Austin could also see the single bridge that crossed the shallow and meandering river, linking the town to an array of crumbling structures on the other side. The Mission San Antonio de Valero had been home for much of the previous century to Franciscan missionaries and their Native American converts. More recently, its abandoned church, now occupied by Mexican troops, and a walled courtyard had been armed with cannons now pointing north at Austin and his men. It had also gained the name *El Alamo*, after the Coahuila town that was home to some of the first soldiers stationed there. It looked like whoever held the Alamo would hold the town.

When General Cos looked out from San Antonio, he could see the Old White Mill surrounded by the sprawling encampment of Texian troops, roughly a mile away. To the south of San Antonio, Bowie and Fannin remained in place with a smaller force near Mission Concepción.

From the safety of the Alamo, the Mexicans watched as two hundred fresh volunteers arrived from Nacogdoches, passing within sight of San Antonio; these East Texas "Redlanders," commanded by a South Carolina–born Texian named Thomas Jefferson Rusk, brought the troop count in Austin's camp to six hundred. Cos's spies reported on a dozen supply wagons that arrived from Goliad, carrying much-needed foodstuffs, including forty-three barrels of flour, six sacks of salt, two boxes of sugar, and coffee, as well as soap, candles, and tobacco.[1] Another early November delivery added three light artillery to Austin's small array of cannons.

Austin's first gambit that November was to send two colonels under a flag of truce to invite General Cos to surrender. The Mexican commander refused, sending the town priest, Padre Garza, to explain that his orders required him "to defend the place until he died."[2] Any talk of peace, Cos said, was entirely pointless.

During the early days of the month, the Mexican artillery at the Alamo fired upon the Texian camp; though the Texians fired back, Austin and his gunners soon decided that the effect on the walls of the mission accomplished little beyond sending clouds of dust into the air.

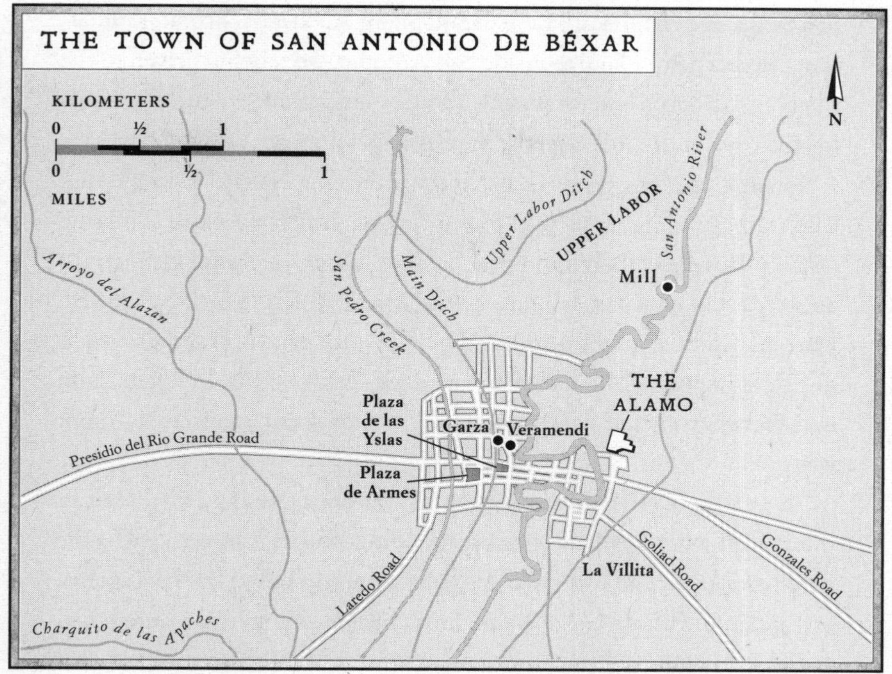

Occasional firings would continue throughout the month, but Austin understood that the Texians needed to soften up the town with bigger guns—an eighteen-pounder was on the way—before attempting a land assault.

Both sides scouted the other, with Austin's cavalry circling the town daily, and one small skirmish did accomplish something. On November 8, a former militiaman named William Barret Travis rode south at the head of a small company of Texian cavalry. A sometime lawyer who had also founded a newspaper back in the Alabama Territory, Travis had come west after his marriage collapsed; at twenty-one he left his son and cheating wife behind, becoming another of Texas's second-chance men. On this day, as he and his men rode along the Laredo road, Colonel Travis spotted what he had been looking for: unmistakable evidence of a large herd of horses. These had to be the Mexicans' surplus animals that, according to a source inside San Antonio, were being driven to the safety of Laredo. General Austin wanted—and needed—these animals for the cavalry, to pull wagons, to position cannons.

Picking up their pace, Travis and his dozen men set off in pursuit. The trail grew fresher as they found first one, then a second campsite. As they closed on their still unseen target, Travis deployed his men for an attack, but darkness fell rapidly and forced Travis to order a halt. He worried his force might be outnumbered by the enemy and didn't want to risk stampeding the horses in the dark. With no fire to warm them nor shelter from the cold rain, Travis's team spent a miserable night waiting for dawn.

At first light, they made a stealthy approach. Seeing two Mexican riders well away from their camp rounding up stray horses, Travis ordered a charge. The surprised Mexicans, outnumbered by the Texians, surrendered without a shot being fired. Five enemy soldiers were taken prisoner, though the two riders rounding up the horses escaped. But Travis reported a haul that included six muskets, two swords, and "300 head of gentle Spanish horses including ten mules."[3]

Travis's success was welcome. "I have to thank you and express my approbation of your conduct and that of your men in this affair," Austin told him. "It has been creditable to yourselves and useful to the service."[4] But the victory proved a small one since the captured horses, underfed and in poor condition, had to be put out to graze before they could be put into daily use.

November would not be a month of big victories, and Austin struggled to maintain discipline in his camp as he waited for the right moment to attack. Some volunteers, unhappy with the weeks of inaction or worried about their farms and families back home, simply packed up and headed for home. His men's behavior could be troublesome, especially when they were drinking, Austin admitted, writing to San Felipe and requesting, "In the name of Almighty God . . . send no more ardent spirits to the camp." The last thing his army needed was more "whysky."[5]

What the Texians *did* need was a little spontaneous leadership—and in the persons of "Deaf" Smith and Old Ben Milam, they would soon find it.

When the rumors of revolution reached him back in September, Erastus Smith wanted no part in the fight. Known as "Deaf" (he'd been hard of hearing since childhood), the red-headed Smith had spent years wandering and tended to keep to himself.

Born in New York's Hudson Valley, he lived in Mississippi before coming to Texas, in 1821, where he married a Mexican widow. For years he had lived a happily settled life in San Antonio with Guadalupe and a family that now included four children. But on his return from a hunting trip early that October, the forty-eight-year-old Smith experienced an event that prompted a change of heart.

One of General Cos's officers stopped him at the edge of town. As the two men talked, Smith observed a group of other soldiers approaching quickly. Smith grew instantly suspicious: In a town of divided allegiances, he had tried to keep his head down, but these men seemed to be coming for him. Then the officer grabbed for the bridle of his horse; Smith reacted, wheeling his horse, but, before he could spur his mount to escape, the officer raised his saber and swung. Smith took a glancing blow to the head.

His hat gone and his head bloodied by the blow, Smith broke for the Texian line. Pursued by Mexican troopers, a storm of shotgun pellets peppering him, Smith returned fire over his shoulder. He won the race and, a mile later, his red hair and unshaven cheeks stained with blood, an angry Deaf Smith presented himself to General Austin.

"I told you that I would not take sides in this war," he explained. "But, Sir, I now tender you my services as the Mexicans acted rascally with me."[6] Like Ben Milam, Austin himself, and others, Smith's sense of justice had been pushed beyond endurance. He, too, would take up arms in this fight.

A GENERAL FADES AWAY

As November passed, Austin's days as a general also neared an end. From the start, he had resisted becoming commander in chief; he was not a natural military leader and had accepted the role only because as the senior leader of the colony he hoped he could be a unifying figure among the motley mix of Texian volunteers. Now with the fight stalled and his health still poor, he dispatched an express rider to San Felipe carrying a note to the Consultation.

He made two plainly stated requests. First, he asked yet again that more artillery and ammunition be sent to the front, along with blankets, shoes, socks, and appropriate clothing for his men now that nighttime temperatures dipped into the forties.

Second, he asked to be relieved of duty. He urged the council "earnestly and pressingly" to organize "a *regular army* and invit[e] a Military man of known and tried Talents to command it."[7]

Now that they had a quorum with Houston and the delegates he had taken with him a few weeks before, the Consultation faced many pressing matters, including whether or not to issue a declaration of independence. (They decided against, settling instead on a pledge to create a provisional state government within the nation of Mexico; to do otherwise, they reasoned, would risk turning Tejano allies against the rebels.)

The nearly sixty delegates moved on to authorize the organization of a civil administration for Texas. They chose a governor (Kentuckian Henry Smith, an early Texas settler) and a legislative body, the General Council, to be manned by one delegate from each district.

Finally, they acted on Austin's recommendation, resolving to establish a "regular army," one modeled on the rulebook of the U.S. military. But they made no provision for the existing volunteer army; they chose a commander for the new army, which then existed only on paper. And they named Sam Houston to be its major general.

Houston had been lobbying for a change to Texian military plans ever since he'd arrived in San Felipe in October. This had less to do with his personal feelings toward Austin and much more to do with his strongly held opinion that the Army of Texas should abandon the siege of San Antonio until spring. So convinced was he that the siege was a mistake that he had even worked to influence his friend Jim Bowie and others under Austin's command to argue with their commander.[8]

Houston's well-known opinions probably contributed to the Consultation's choice of him as general, but it's likely they would have selected him anyway. There was something reminiscent of George Washington's appearance at the 1775 Continental Congress in Houston's presentation of himself for service. His imposing stature, his military service in the War of 1812, his generalship of the Tennessee militia, and his status as a well-known former Tennessee governor made him an easy choice.

Now Texas had two armies and little meeting of the minds: Austin, at least for the present, headed the citizen militia, while Houston was charged with creating an official force.

But the Consultation had a plan for Texas's elder statesman once he left his command. They named Austin the new government's emissary to the United States, instructing him to negotiate a million-dollar loan to get the new state up and running.

As for Austin, he had one more military maneuver left in him.

. . .

When informed of his new, nonmilitary role, on November 18, Austin chose to keep the news to himself. Four days later, he ordered his officers to prepare their men for a dawn attack the next morning. Although officially he had been relieved of duty, no one had arrived to take his place—and Austin wanted to capture San Antonio before his generalship ended.

Austin's wish would not come true, but not because of any failure on his part. At 1:00 A.M. that night, one of his divisional commanders awakened him. He reported that his officers and men refused to obey orders. Some of them, undoubtedly influenced by Houston, opposed the order of attack and were "unwilling to attempt it." Though "greatly astonished and mortified," Austin had little choice but to withdraw the command.[9] There would be no November assault on San Antonio.

The day after, a disappointed Stephen Austin took his leave. He bade the troops farewell, urging them to be "true to Texas and obedient to their commander."[10] Austin would not miss the challenge of instilling discipline among this wild bunch of independent men. He did not question the frontiersmen's toughness, but he felt frustrated by their unwillingness to submit to normal military discipline. It was apparent even at reveille. As one recent recruit reported, the troops at morning roll call stood before their sergeant half-dressed, most without their guns. Some didn't join the ranks at all but remained at nearby fires preparing their breakfasts. "Once a sleeping 'here!,'" the newcomer reported, "[coming] from under the canvass of tent, caused a hearty laugh among the men."[11] Despite the call to attention, the man couldn't be bothered to rise from his bed. This assemblage of Texians could barely be called an army. It survived on rationed supplies, fought for no pay, and lived in the cold. That very morning the temperature had dropped to thirty-one degrees.

Yet as he took his leave, the volunteers understood that Austin, whatever their doubts about his generalship, was one of Texas's finest. "The men came up and shook hands with him in tears and silence," his nephew and aide Moses Austin Bryan reported, "for many thought they would never see him more."[12]

With Houston off raising the new official army, a Texian named Edward Burleson was elected general of the militia. Like Houston, he had fought in the War of 1812, and the troops identified with his personal history. His family had moved from North Carolina to Alabama during his childhood; after his marriage, he'd taken his own family to Missouri and Tennessee before coming to Texas, in 1829. He, too, was a second-chance man. With Burleson now in charge, Austin, together with his nephew and a manservant, headed out for San Felipe de Austin, the first step in his journey back to the United States.

THE GRASS FIGHT

When Deaf Smith had come into camp, Austin recognized he was a natural scout. He was a skilled horseman. He knew the region well, and the solitary nature of the task suited him. His neighbors reported that Smith was afraid of nothing. Austin sent him on regular patrols, since the Texians needed intelligence regarding Mexican supplies and troop movements. He had become "the eyes of the army."

Smith, Bowie, and Burleson, in small bands or, sometimes, in mounted companies of fifty or a hundred men or more, looked to intercept Mexican dispatches, disrupt convoys, and drive off Mexican reinforcements coming from the Rio Grande. Teams of Texians lit prairie fires to burn off grasses that the Mexicans might use for forage to feed their animals. The result of these November forays had been a series of small skirmishes, but the fighting, mostly limited to small-arms fire, did little harm to either side. On several occasions, large bands of Texians tested the Mexicans, advancing to within a quarter mile of the town, but Cos refused to be drawn out into the open.

Then, at 10:00 A.M. on November 26, Deaf Smith returned to the main encampment at a full gallop. He brought news: A Mexican cavalry column, roughly five miles southwest of San Antonio, was headed toward the town. Smith's sighting, coupled with recent rumors of a shipment of silver coin for an overdue Mexican payroll, got everyone's attention. The new camp commander, General Burleson, ordered Jim Bowie and a squad of forty men to saddle up and intercept the Mexican troops. In minutes they rode out of camp, followed by one hundred infantrymen on foot.

The Texian cavalry caught up with the 150 Mexicans a mile from San Antonio as they crossed a dry creek bed. Among the volunteers were both Deaf Smith and Henry Karnes, the picket who first spied the Mexican attackers at Concepción.

Despite unfavorable numbers, Bowie charged into the midst of the enemy, guns blazing. The return fire was intense, but Bowie drove his men into the enemy ranks a second and a third time before both sides took cover in "Muskeet Bushes."[13] Bowie and the Texians kept up their fire, awaiting the arrival of the infantry.

Then the Mexicans attacked. The Texians, now able to aim their long rifles with precision at the uniformed men surging toward them, forced the Mexicans to retreat. An enemy wave came again, but the Texian infantry, moving in double-quick time, arrived, and the Mexican attackers were driven back.

An enemy relief party arrived from the town towing a single cannon. The field piece was quickly positioned, its barrel aimed at the Texians. But the grape and canister shot that arced its way toward Bowie's line did little harm.

Within the larger confusion of battle, several skirmishes were fought.

In one, James Burleson, the general's father, led a cavalry charge, urging his men, "Boys, we have but once to die!"[14] The momentum of the battle favored the Texians, and after repeated cannon firings failed to dislodge the Texians, the Mexicans, under covering artillery fire, retreated to the town. Except for a few cannon booms and sporadic musket and rifle fire, the fight was over.

For the Mexicans, the price had been high. Burleson claimed fifteen dead Mexicans lay in the creek bed and that other casualties had been carried from the field; Bowie estimated the Mexican losses at more than fifty.[15] The price for the Texians was much smaller, amounting to several wounded, none seriously.

In their hasty retreat, the Mexicans had also abandoned a pack train of forty heavily laden mules and horses. In the quiet after the tumult of battle, the Texians examined their captured spoils, hoping to find a wealth of silver. Or perhaps ammunition and food. They found nothing so precious. Rather than silver—or even flour, sugar, and salt—the Texians discovered they had fought for fodder. The animals carried only fresh-cut grass, gathered to feed the horses within the besieged town.

The fight—a "ludicrous affair," in the judgment of one soldier—was mockingly called the "Grass Fight," but Burleson's men had fought well.[16] Finally they had managed to confront a contingent of Cos's men outside of San Antonio. But the anticlimactic battle over grass cuttings seemed oddly apt: The month of November, which opened with Austin's high hopes for capturing San Antonio, drew to a quiet close.

DECEMBER

Far from the front and looking to find recruits for Texas's new regular army, Houston still grumbled; he remained convinced the Texian militia would never take San Antonio without larger cannons. He pressed for withdrawal, trying to enlist Bowie and others in opposing an attack. *Why not wait?* he argued. As he wrote to James Fannin, "Remember our Maxim, it is better to do well, *late:* than never!"[17]

On the night of December 3, the tide looked to be turning Houston's way.

That day three Anglo Texians fresh from San Antonio had brought both encouraging news and invaluable intelligence. Mexican morale was low, they said, and they were able to map out the city's gun placements and the locations of the Mexican troops. The storming of San Antonio seemed suddenly feasible. Armed with this knowledge, at first General Burleson ordered the troops to be ready at 4:00 A.M. for an attack to begin at dawn. Then, at midnight, a shadowy figure was reported near the Texian lines, crossing to speak to a Mexican sentry.

Had he been a spy? Did Cos now know they were coming?

Fearing his plans had been discovered, Burleson, as Houston himself would have wished, withdrew his orders. Seeing the wisdom of waiting until they had full strength, the Texian leadership supported him. His officers, almost to a man, had voted at a council of war against moving on San Antonio.

The reaction was different among the rank-and-file volunteers. These men were exhausted by the seven-week siege, wound tight by waiting for the fight, and staying constantly ready to risk their lives. As they got word that there would be no fight, their tense quiet gave way to a clamor of outraged shouts. Some indignant volunteers openly cursed their leaders.

These settlers had come to fight for their adopted homeland: "[We] preferred Death in the cause," one soldier wrote to his brother and sister, "than such a disgraceful defeat."[18] Marching for a winter camp—at Gonzales, at Goliad, it didn't matter—made no sense to them. That would be to retreat. "All day we [got] more and more dejected," one Texian wrote in his diary.[19]

Furious at having their time wasted and not willing to stay and serve as winter came on, disgruntled groups of weary and frustrated Texians collected their gear and headed for home. By one count, between 250 and 300 men marched out of camp.

Looking to stem the flow of departures, Burleson mustered the men. As the commander prepared to issue orders to abandon camp and march for Goliad, big Ben Milam returned from a scouting mission south of San Antonio. He read the faces around him—the anger, the disappointment—and decided immediately that this humiliation was wrong. He wasn't a man to give up.

As the troops gathered, Milam stepped forward and offered a challenge.

"Boys, who will follow Ben Milam into San Antonio—let all who will form a line right here."[20]

A thunderous chorus of voices responded: *I will! . . . I will! . . . I will!* Deaf Smith was among the first to step up, but many other men followed. Though most were Texians, more than a hundred were members of the New Orleans Greys, one of the first companies of troops from the United States, who had marched into camp two weeks earlier. The men in the fresh gray uniforms arrived well armed and well supplied, thanks to generous citizens back in the Crescent City. These soldiers were a mix, with more than two dozen Americans from the North plus men who were French, Canadian, German, English, and Irish. They quickly melded into the three-hundred-man army of self-selected men. With the unexpected demonstration of a willingness to fight, Burleson made the case to the remaining volunteers, several hundred in number, to remain at the White Mill as a reserve force.

Milam laid out a bold but simple attack. First, a small company of gunners would, under the cover of night, position their cannons within range of the Alamo. At 5:00 A.M. they would begin firing, bombarding the mission buildings. Milam expected the Mexicans to rally. They would seek to defend the Alamo—but against an anticipated onslaught from the east that would not materialize.

The shelling would be a classic diversion: Milam's real objective was the town itself. The new arrivals from San Antonio had offered an invaluable tactical fact: A number of buildings at the edge of town stood unoccupied. Milam's plan called for the Texian invaders to breach the village perimeter from the northwest. If they could gain a foothold in the empty houses, they could move on the squares at the heart of the city. With Mexican defenders otherwise occupied on the other side of town with the incoming salvos, many fewer men would be in position to oppose the assault.

The plan made sense, and in a few hours the long-awaited attack would begin. An entirely new mood suddenly prevailed among the Texians. Milam's bold leadership lifted morale: These men had come to fight, not to run, despite Houston's cautions. As they waited for the order to march, according to one fifteen-year-old soldier, "the boys were as joyous as if waiting a festive affair."[21]

A QUIET NIGHT, INTERRUPTED

In the predawn quiet, the rebels moved through the corn stubble north of San Antonio. Forbidden by their officers to speak, the two divisions of men listened to the whistle of a cruel north wind and the routine shouts of "All is well!" that echoed along the line of Mexican sentries. So far, the town's defenders knew nothing.

The artillery crew, escorted by a small band of infantrymen, positioned, loaded, and primed a field piece within range of the Alamo.

Across the river, at the head of one division, Milam brought his hundred-odd troops to a halt. He hoped to enter the town via a quiet back street, leading his half dozen companies toward an empty house within musket range of the town square. The other division, guided by Deaf Smith, would follow the river to Soledad Street and occupy the empty Veramendi house, once the home of Jim Bowie's wife and in-laws, all taken by cholera.

A fog rose off the river as daylight approached, offering a welcome shroud for the break-of-day surprise to come.

When the boom of the single cannon fractured the silence at 5:00 A.M., the waiting Texians listened. Within moments they heard "the brisk rattling of drums and the shrill blast of bugles."[22] Judging by the direction of the trampling feet, many Mexicans soldiers were headed toward the river to help defend the Alamo. "Our friends," said one of the New Orleans Greys of the gunners, "had done the trick."[23]

Then came the firm but quiet order to march. "Forward, boys! We're going to town."[24]

The Texians closed on San Antonio as planned, and Milam's men reached their objective without incident. But a Mexican sentry spotted Deaf Smith as his team approached Casa Veramendi. The enemy picket fired once before Smith silenced him, but the report of the gunshots led to a general alarm. The artillery diversion had worked, getting Milam and his men close to the central plazas without a single casualty. But now the enemy knew they were there.

Suddenly the world was shooting at them as a storm of musket fire came their way. The main plaza at the town center had been closed off with barricading, and the muzzles of cannons protruding through portholes were soon spitting fire, too. With the narrow streets raked with canister shot, the invaders turned to the nearest houses, breaking through their doors to find cover. Some of the homes they entered were very much occupied. "Men, women and children began to run out," reported one of the invaders, "in their night clothes and unarmed."[25]

When and where they could, the Texians returned fire. Again their Kentucky long rifles and superior powder proved lethal, effective at

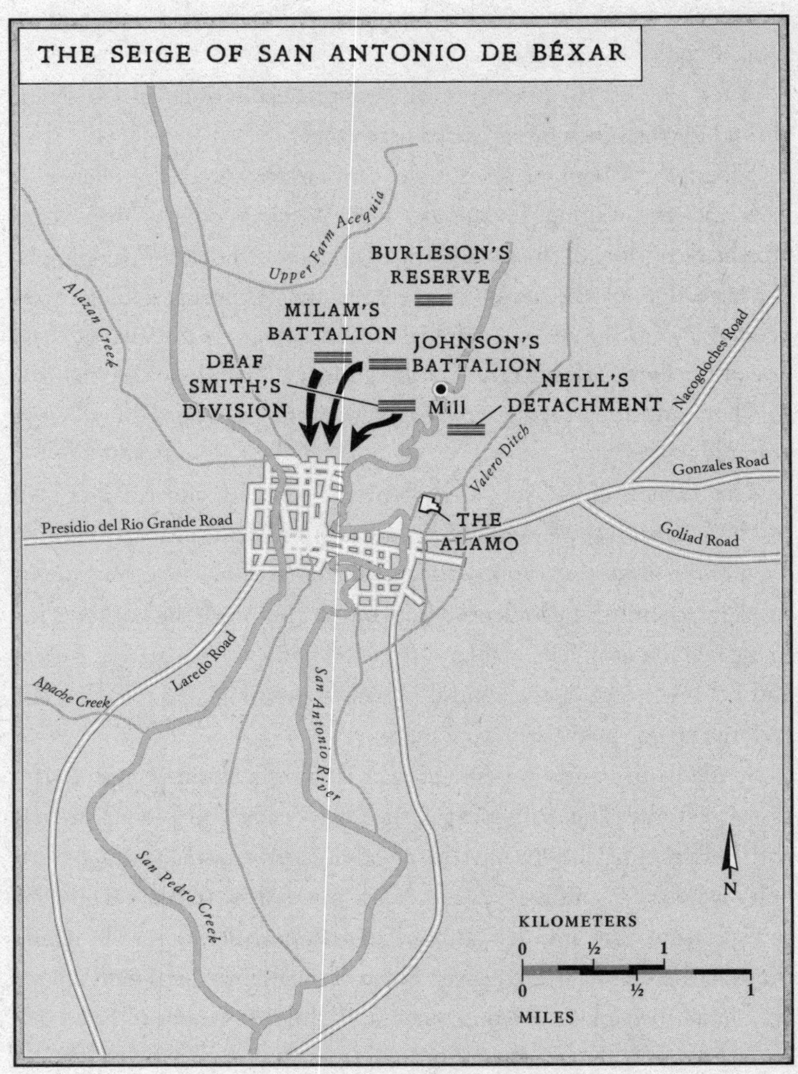
THE SEIGE OF SAN ANTONIO DE BÉXAR
Upper Farm Acequia
BURLESON'S RESERVE
Alazan Creek
MILAM'S BATTALION
JOHNSON'S BATTALION
DEAF SMITH'S DIVISION
NEILL'S DETACHMENT
Mill
Nacogdoches Road
Valero Ditch
Gonzales Road
Presidio del Rio Grande Road
THE ALAMO
Goliad Road
Laredo Road
Apache Creek
San Antonio River
San Pedro Creek
N
KILOMETERS
0
½
1
0
½
1
MILES

two hundred yards. "No sooner did a head appear above the walls than it served as a target for a dozen hunting rifles, and there was always another dead Mexican."[26] But as the sun rose, the "heavy cannonading from the town was seconded by a well directed fire from the Alamo."[27] General Cos, no longer deceived by the lone gun firing from the east—which the Texians had already withdrawn—had pivoted his array of cannons to bombard the rebel position in the town.

At midday the firing slowed as both sides considered the new terms of the fight. The two field pieces the invaders had brought with them had been of little value; although the Texians had finally taken the fight to the streets of San Antonio, the Mexicans, after weeks of preparation, still held a strong defensive position. Pinned down, the invading force of Texians could clearly see that unlike their battlefield successes at Gonzales and Concepción, this fight wouldn't be over in a matter of minutes or even hours.

From their new headquarters, in town but also inside a set of Spanish-style houses, the rebels would face five days of overcoming the enemy's "obstinate resistance" to decide this first battle for San Antonio.[28]

DOWNTOWN SAN ANTONIO

Out of fear of Indian attack, the founders of San Antonio de Béxar had arranged their streets for easy defense. The town's homes were fortress-like, consisting of thick adobe or limestone walls with iron grates on the windows and solid oak doors. The Texians, once inside the dwellings, set about further adapting them to their purposes. "With crow bars we perforated the walls of the houses," remembered physician Joseph Field, "making port holes, through which we kept up a constant fire."[29]

The sightlines weren't perfect, so ten of the Texians, led by Deaf Smith, climbed to the roof of the Veramendi house. They made their way to the parapet that surrounded the roof but were quickly spotted by Mexicans in the tower of the San Fernando church. The Texians soon paid a heavy price. Half the men were hit, including Smith. His wound was serious enough that a hole had to be chopped in the earthen roof so that he could be lowered back into the house using an improvised sling made of blanket.

To ease communications between their two divisions, the Texians had spent the night hours trenching the nearby street. Using the excavated dirt, they raised a breastwork of dirt, stone, and sandbags. Meanwhile, Burleson consolidated the reserves back at the White Mill and dispatched a messenger to San Felipe, urgently requesting more troops and ammunition. "Considerable reinforcements" were said to be on the way to aid the Mexicans—and the Texians needed all the help they could get.[30] Artillery at the Alamo was steadily firing into their midst, and the Mexican small-arms fire persisted.

When day two of the fight ended with no notable gains, the Texians realized that if they wanted to more than hold their ground, they needed to dislodge the well-entrenched Mexicans; in short, they needed to advance on the square where they could mount a direct offensive. At midday on day three, December 7, Henry Karnes led one such raid.

Eyeing a large stone house across the street, Karnes instructed his fellow soldiers, "Boys, load your guns and be ready." Indicating his destination, he explained, "I am going to break open that door, and I want you to pour a steady hot fire into those fellows on the roof and hold their attention. . . . When I break [the door] in I want you boys to make a clear dash for that house."[31]

With an iron bar in one hand, his rifle in the other, he sprinted across to the doorway and made short work of bashing in the door. When he and his company burst in, they saw Mexicans escaping into another room. Some Mexicans fired back, but the invaders knew what they had to do. Using bars and axes, they pounded through interior walls, moving room by room, gradually getting closer to the square.

The Texians scavenged food where they could, including slaughtering and butchering an ox and cooking it over open fires. But the Mexicans peppered their fires with musket fire, making food preparation a dangerous occupation.

Late on the afternoon of December 7, the Texians sustained a major loss.

Their leaders met at Casa Veramendi to lay out the plan of attack. Colonel Ben Milam crossed Soledad Street to join the conference, where he and the others sat down to plot out an after-dark surprise attack on the Mexican position on the plaza. In order to better understand the topography, Milam stepped out into the courtyard of the Veramendi house. All day gunfire had echoed around the square, but Milam ignored it. Protected by the garden wall, he wanted to get a better view of the enemy guns and command post.

Before departing two weeks earlier, Stephen Austin had given Milam a field glass. The big man held the telescopic lenses to his eyes, scanning the enemy stronghold. As he took in the view, planning the Texians' next step, he caught the attention of a Mexican positioned in a tree by the river. The Mexican aimed. He fired. And Ben Milam collapsed to hard ground. The ball that entered his brain killed him on the spot.

One soldier who turned in the direction from which the shot had been fired saw a telltale puff of smoke amid the thick greenery of a cypress tree near the river. Texian rifles were quickly readied, aimed, and fired; the report of the rifles was followed by the fall of another corpse, as the rifleman tumbled through the evergreen branches before crashing to the ground and rolling into the San Antonio River.[32]

The day's casualty list for Texians was small—one dead, two slightly wounded—but the loss of Milam weighed heavily on Texian morale. He had inspired this assault on the town; now he was dead. Adding to a sense of alarm, the enemy raised a black flag.[33] Though this was the rebels' first sighting of the dreaded pennant, they knew its message. The enemy would give no quarter; the Mexicans would offer no mercy and take no prisoners. To be captured would likely mean being put to death. This was Santa Anna's way.

Everyone knew, as one captain put it, "This army is in danger—Texas is in danger."[34]

"THE ENEMY GAVE WAY INCH BY INCH"[35]

The battle had become a struggle for survival. The dogged, rugged fighting continued on the streets, but, out of reach of the raking musket and cannon fire, the rebels advanced, house by house. Like moles tunneling unseen, the Texians broke through the interior adobe walls that separated one house from the next. "Using battering-rams made out of logs ten or twelve feet long . . . stout men would punch . . . holes in the walls through which we passed."[36]

They worked toward the plaza, but time was tight with the arrival that day of a convoy of Mexican troops, which had eluded Burleson's scouting parties, and the prospect of more. The Mexican reinforcements were a mixed bunch, experienced infantry, cavalry, and artillery men, along with untrained conscripts and even convicts. One Texian soldier expressed his worry: He reported that he and his fellow fighters feared that they would be "sweap of [swept off] by a general charge."[37] The new arrivals—they numbered about six hundred—could tip the balance.

Then, during the night of December 8, the Texians captured an important prize: They gained control of the priest's house; from there rebel riflemen could sweep the Plaza de las Islas—and the Mexican gun emplacements—with direct and deadly fire. They set about cutting portholes to make the most of this commanding vantage. Despite the loss of Milam, this new development gave hope to the tired men.

Even before firing could begin at first light, the Mexicans recognized they had no choice but to pull back. In the middle of the night, hundreds of soldiers began hauling nine of the ten artillery pieces, munitions, wounded soldiers, and everything of value to the Alamo. The sudden retreat inspired numerous officers and their companies—some two hundred Mexicans—to set out in the direction of the Rio Grande. They deserted rather than stay and face defeat.

The Mexicans had managed to get out of the town, but the scene across the river at the Alamo was chaotic. The mission enclosure was simply too small to accommodate all the men, along with the women and children, not to mention the horses.

Cos was in deep trouble and he knew it. His supply line had long since dried up; the six hundred arrivals had brought no supplies, only more hungry mouths to feed. There was insufficient firewood and water inside the Alamo, and replenishing the supplies required venturing out to face Texian rifle fire. The days of fighting had taken a toll, too, with wounded officers and men to care for. And the cannoneers were running short on ammunition.

At 6:00 A.M., General Cos, still in his bed, rose to a sitting position and issued the order to surrender. "I authorize you to approach the enemy and exact of him whatever may be possible."[38] Three officers, accompanied by a trumpeter, rode into town.

The trumpeter sounded the call for a parley; the Texians did not reply. They now occupied all the houses that lined the north side of the plaza, and their rifle barrels were visible protruding through windows and holes cut into the walls. Cos's emissaries resorted to a handkerchief, mounted on a pole. Raising the white flag got a reaction: Thirty Texians emerged from the priest's house. The Mexican officers asked to see the Texian commander; Burleson was duly summoned. After a delay, he arrived and immediately agreed to a suspension of fighting.

Only the terms of the surrender remained to be settled; the fight for San Antonio de Béxar was over. Unlike the Mexicans and their flag of no quarter, however, the Texians would be fair and merciful. An honorable fight would conclude with honorable terms.

THE END OF THE BEGINNING

More than a dozen hours of negotiation concluded, at 2:00 A.M., Thursday, December 10, 1835. The terms of surrender permitted the defeated army to depart with arms and private property. They would take one cannon, a four-pounder, for protection in the event of Indian attack. The sick and wounded would remain and be cared for. Most important, General Cos and his officers gave their word of honor that they would not "in any way oppose the reestablishment of the federal constitution of 1824."[39] They were not to rejoin the fight to suppress the uprising.

Not every Texian was happy with the terms of surrender. Many thought the Mexicans had been let off easy. Lieutenant William R. Carey probably spoke for many when he called it a "disgraceful treaty" and a "childs bargain."[40]

Nonetheless, on December 14, General Cos led an ignominious march toward the Rio Grande. He departed with 1,105 men, a count that did not include hundreds of troops who had deserted the day before or the wounded who remained in San Antonio. They left to the victors twenty-one artillery pieces, five hundred muskets, and other supplies.

The Texians had defeated a well-entrenched foe with substantially more manpower. The cost had been the life of Ben Milam, buried with his boots on in the dooryard of Casa Veramendi. Another five rebels died; though one man lost an eye and another a leg, fewer than three dozen were wounded. That seemed a small price to pay for a large prize in the fight for freedom. The Mexican losses were harder to calculate, but their casualty count was in the hundreds.

This felt like victory. When, on Christmas Day 1835, Cos and his army arrived at the Rio Grande, they were the last Mexican troops in Texas. They had vowed never to serve again against the rights of the Texians, and most of the Texian fighters felt safe in returning to their homes and families, where they could bask in the glory of their accomplishments. As the Texas General Council proclaimed, "You are the brave sons of Washington and freedom."[41]

The victory at San Antonio appeared to be a giant step closer to independence. The capture of the Alamo was a triumph, and the retreat of the Mexican force cause for great rejoicing. Could the war even be over? Sam Houston didn't think so. He suspected it was a fight they should not have had, and the Alamo a fort that could not be held: Preparing for the worst, he kept busy trying to raise an army, offering a cash bonus, eight hundred acres of land, and immediate Texas citizenship to fresh volunteers.

Yes, the Texians had proven themselves on some level, but now they would have to confront a profoundly angry and vengeful enemy in the person of His Excellency Santa Anna. Houston would see that they were prepared.

SIX

The Defenders

[We have] no remedy but one, which is an *immediate declaration of independence.*

—Stephen Austin, January 7, 1836

The new year brought bad news. On January 4, 1836, the *Telegraph and Texas Register*, the San Felipe newspaper launched three months before as "a faithful register of passing events," published a chilling warning. President Santa Anna, along with a reported ten thousand troops, was bound for Texas to do battle with the rebels, to avenge their victory over General Cos. His stated intention? To leave nothing of the rebels "but the recollection [they] once existed."[1]

Major General Sam Houston felt ready to seize the moment. Focused on his duties in Texas's newly designated capital, Washington-on-the-Brazos, the usually hard-drinking commander in chief had even set aside liquor. "I am most miserably cool and sober," he assured a member of the General Council, "instead of Egg-nog; I eat roasted Eggs in my office."[2] He ordered clothes sent from Nacogdoches to his new headquarters, now located in Washington-on-the-Brazos. His personal library came, too, including Thucydides' *History of the Peloponnesian*

War, a history of Texas, and a volume of army regulations. He would need all the knowledge and wisdom he could find as he confronted the many obstacles facing the Texian army.

The deeply divided provisional government of Texas posed one large challenge. Governor Henry Smith and the General Council seemed unable to agree on anything, including the very goal of the present war: Was Texas fighting to be a Mexican state or a "*free,* sovereign" republic?[3] The two branches of the young government differed on military matters, too, starting with whether Houston was commander in chief. Governor Smith thought he was, but the General Council regularly ignored the chain of command, issuing orders directly to various officers in the field.

By mid-January, the divide was so great that the governor proclaimed the General Council dissolved (he called its members "scoundrels") and the council, dismissing him as a "tyrant," impeached Smith.[4] That left Texas governance effectively paralyzed until the next meeting of Texas's delegates, scheduled to convene on March 1.

Caught in this political crossfire, Sam Houston looked for the best strategy to defend Texas. But the military situation was no less chaotic.

In the weeks after the capture of San Antonio, the Army of Texas splintered. Many Texians headed home, thinking the war had been won. Then, on January 3, 1836, two hundred of those who stayed to defend San Antonio packed their bedrolls, grabbed their guns, and headed for Goliad. The General Council, ignoring Houston, had decided to take the fight to the border; headed for Matamoros, Mexico, they hoped that by capturing the port town on the south bank of the Rio Grande, they might take the action out of Texas and into Mexico. James Fannin, veteran of the successful fight at Concepción, worked to raise an auxiliary corps for an expedition to "reduce Matamoros." With no money in the treasury, the Texian soldiers were promised they could ravage the town if they took it, collecting "the first spoils taken from the enemy."[5] Fannin and his men departed with the bulk of the provisions, horses, and medicines, leaving a mere 104 soldiers at the Alamo. The Texians who stayed, some of them sick and wounded, faced "all the hardships of winter"—*and* the task of defending the town.[6]

"Oh, save our poor country!" Houston exclaimed when he heard what had happened. "[We must] send supplies to the wounded, the sick, the naked, and hungry, for God's sake!"[7]

He recognized the Matamoros plan for what it was—an "absurdity."[8] He regarded the Texas Revolution as a fight for right, and to give the men license to loot the Mexican town? That would make the Texians pirates and predators.[9] The planners believed that the Mexican inhabitants of the town would rise up, embrace the invaders, and join their rebel ranks, but that sounded like wishful thinking to Houston. So he set off to meet the men at Goliad, hoping to lead the army in a different direction.

When he got there, on January 14, Fannin was off recruiting soldiers. In his place, Houston found a pretender to his own role, a man named Dr. James Grant, who styled himself "Acting Commander-in-Chief." Wounded in the fight at San Antonio, the educated Scotsman had won the respect and admiration of many of the soldiers as a man who had fought for Texas, something Houston had yet to do.

Houston thought the plan was bad, but he now saw the motivations were even worse: Grant's main interest was to use the volunteer army to fight for *his* personal land claims south of the Rio Grande. Plus the proposed invasion of Matamoros, now discussed publicly for a month, was no longer a Texas secret. "The Mexicans," as one soldier in the little army noted, "aware of our plans, were strengthening the defenses of their city and every day making it more nearly impregnable."[10] *And* Santa Anna and his men, though still far away in central Mexico, were mile by mile making their way north.

Two decades before, Houston had selflessly thrown himself into battle, risking his life at Horseshoe Bend. For that, he paid dearly, sustaining devastating wounds to his shoulder and upper thigh that still tormented him more than twenty years later. This time, Houston counseled caution.

He spent several days with the army as it marched to Mission Refugio, listening, getting to know the men, and getting known by them. As they talked, Houston, older and wiser at age forty-three than most of the troops, made a lawyerly case for holding back. Then, on arrival in Refugio, he addressed the assembled troops. After years spent under Andrew Jackson's tutelage, he knew how to work a crowd of soldiers.

"We must act together," he told the Army of Texas—"*United we stand divided we fall.*"

He argued that to invade Mexico was pure folly. "[Though] I praise your courage," he told them candidly, "my friends, I do not approve of your plans."[11]

Houston believed the Texian army might be destroyed in such a fight. Just two hundred men, marching two hundred miles through strange and potentially unfriendly territory? "A city containing twelve thousand souls," he believed, "will not be taken by a handful of men who have marched twenty-two days without bread-stuffs, or necessary supplies for an army. If there ever was a time when Matamoras could have been taken by a few men, that time has passed by."[12] With that, Houston again mounted his horse and rode away. As head of the regular army, he could not order these militiamen; he could only plant doubts in their minds.

But he departed disheartened. He worried about the cause of Texas and, seeing him lost in thought, Houston's staff left him to his thoughts as they headed north.

That night and the next day, Houston pondered. He later admitted he considered "withdraw[ing] once more from the treacheries and persecutions of the world" to return to the Cherokee to "bury [myself] deep in the solitude of nature, and pass a life of communion with the Great Spirit."[13] And, very likely, once again drink deeply from the "flowing bowl."

When Houston and company reached San Felipe de Austin, Governor Smith, trying vainly to hold on to power, granted the unhappy Houston a few weeks' furlough to carry out an assignment. The task would take him back to the Cherokee, but very much in service to the Texian cause. Houston would become an ambassador for Texas. He would stay true to the cause, since Governor Smith wanted to be sure that a large band of some four hundred Cherokee in East Texas remained peaceable—the last thing the Texians needed was a second formidable enemy. Houston headed east to make peace at the council fire of Chief Bowl, warlord of the Texas Cherokee, hoping to return with a treaty in time for the next gathering of delegates. With a new duty, he again aimed his gaze "with enthusiasm upon the future prospects of Texas."[14]

During Houston's weeks of absence, the Texian plan to move on Matamoros collapsed, in part because Houston's words had persuaded many soldiers such an attack would be a fool's errand. Instead, the next Texian fight would unfold back in San Antonio. Only this time, the roles were reversed: The Texians, now inside the Alamo, would face a siege by the Mexican army now making its way north.

FIGHT OR FLIGHT?

On January 18, Jim Bowie rode hard for the Alamo. After a long day in the saddle—he and his thirty men covered more than seventy miles—he saw a bittersweet sight. In the middle distance he spied the silhouettes of the mission and the bell tower of the San Fernando church.

They would never fail to bring to mind his wife and children, now more than two years dead.

For Bowie, San Antonio de Béxar remained a place of homecoming, but this time he arrived with a purpose. Sam Houston admired the man's "promptitude and manliness" and respected his "forecast, prudence and valor."[15] Just the day before, freshly back from his mission to the Cherokee, he'd entrusted Bowie with orders for the garrison at San Antonio.

In recent weeks, the Texian commandant in San Antonio, Lieutenant Colonel James Clinton Neill, had written repeatedly to the government, pleading for reinforcements. Like Houston, he had fought and been wounded in the Battle of Horseshoe Bend. Like the men around him, he saw this fight as an extension of his father's and grandfather's fight back in North Carolina in the Revolution.

On arrival, Bowie saw an undernourished, ill-clad, and unpaid garrison. In the new year, Neill's company had continued to dwindle, falling to 114 men, three dozen of them sick or recovering from wounds. And this contingent was supposed to fight off a thousand-man Mexican force that, according to Neill, was already "destined for this place" from central Mexico?[16]

Yet morale remained surprisingly high, further buoyed by the sight of braveheart Bowie and his men. But the situation was not as it at first seemed to Colonel Neill. When he read Houston's written directive, Neill found Bowie hadn't come to fight Mexicans: Houston's orders called for dismantling the San Antonio outpost. The commander in chief instructed that the barricades in the streets of San Antonio be destroyed; the Alamo blown up, demolished, rendered unusable; and the artillery and stores removed to Gonzales. He didn't want to lose good men fighting to hold a fort he believed they couldn't defend.

Colonel Neill had requested relief—and this notion of abandoning and obliterating San Antonio was something else altogether. Like Ben Milam's back in December, Neill's first instinct was to rebel.

He was an artillery officer by training, and together with one of his junior officers, Lieutenant Almeron Dickinson, Neill had fired the first cannon at Gonzales. As they absorbed Houston's orders, Neill and Dickinson quickly realized that removing the artillery and ammunition simply was not possible. When Dr. Grant departed in December with the bulk of the troops, he had taken virtually all the horses and wagons; without draft animals, the array of captured cannons, many of which were in good firing condition, were going nowhere. To the cannoneers, the notion of abandoning the guns, the largest array of Texian artillery, made no sense at all.

Houston's orders arrived without President Smith's authorization, so the men in Neill's command decided to carry on with the work of stiffening the defenses at the Alamo; they would await confirmation. As he waited, Bowie began to weaken in his commitment to Houston. After all, Bowie recognized a good defensive position when he saw one, and here was a town that had been his home and that was defended by men whose bravery and commitment were contagious. Unable to resist helping, Bowie pitched in with the rebuilding, "laboring night and day."

Bowie soon communicated his change of mind to the Texian government. "I cannot eulogise the conduct & character of Col Neill too highly," he wrote to Governor Smith two weeks after his return to San Antonio. "No other man in the army could have kept men at this post, under the neglect they have experienced."[17]

Jim Bowie, widower and wheeler-dealer, fortune hunter and fighter, also confided how much the forthcoming fight at the Alamo now meant to him. An uncomplicated man, Bowie, together with Neill, had reached a joint resolution.

He wished to help the people of San Antonio. "We will rather die in these ditches than give it up to the enemy."[18]

But if they were going to keep the Alamo in Texian hands, they were going to need more help.

WILLIAM BARRET TRAVIS

For a man of twenty-six, Lieutenant Colonel William Barret Travis brought wide experience to the fight for Texas. A teacher, lawyer, and militia officer, he appeared to many as a fine man and good citizen, despite rumors of a checkered past. Travis was said to have blown up his promising law career when at age twenty-one he suspected his wife of infidelity and murdered the man he thought was her lover.

Having settled in Texas in 1831, Travis officially became a landowner and Texas settler, making a new home in the land of men looking for second chances. He practiced law in San Felipe de Austin and lived alone in a rooming house. His success permitted him to hire a law clerk and own several horses. A literate man, he read widely, noting in his diary the borrowed books of Greek and English history, as well as fiction.

By 1835, he wanted a more settled life. He had found a woman he wished to make his second wife, and to make that possible, a formal divorce from his first wife was begun. Travis also addressed the matter of the children left behind in Alabama when, in May 1835, he signed his last will and testament. He designated Charles Edward, five years of age, and Susan Isabella, the daughter he had never seen, as his sole heirs.[19]

When the Texas rebellion began, Travis immediately committed himself to the fight. He remained with Austin during the siege at San

Antonio, proving himself both as a scout and as a field commander in the skirmish where he and his men captured the Mexican horses in November 1835. He offered detailed advice to the governor and the council, giving them recommendations regarding the organization of the new army. His reward, on December 21, 1835, was elevation to the rank of lieutenant colonel, commandant of the cavalry.

Then, on February 3, 1836, Lieutenant Colonel Travis, dressed in homemade Texas jeans (a formal uniform he'd ordered hadn't arrived), crossed the San Antonio River. In response to Neill's repeated pleas for help from San Antonio, the governor had ordered Travis to the town's defense.

Along with his platoon of thirty men, Travis brought the total defenders to barely 150.

FORTRESS ALAMO

"You can plainly see," observed Ensign Green B. Jameson, "that the Alamo never was built by a military for a fortress."[20] Jameson, the chief engineer at the Alamo, spoke truly as the mission, established in 1718 and after, began as a place of faith, where Franciscan friars taught Native Americans the tenets of Roman Catholicism.

The Franciscans chose the site of their church with care. The little community required a reliable source of water, fuel for warmth and cooking, and surrounding acreage for grazing and cultivation. Over the decades, the church with its enclosed village developed, rectangular in shape, with tall walls of rough stone that bounded an open plaza on three sides. Lining the enclosure were rambling adobe living quarters for Indians, soldiers, and servants, as well as kitchens and shops, all of which faced into the courtyard.

Green Jameson wanted to transform the rambling structures into

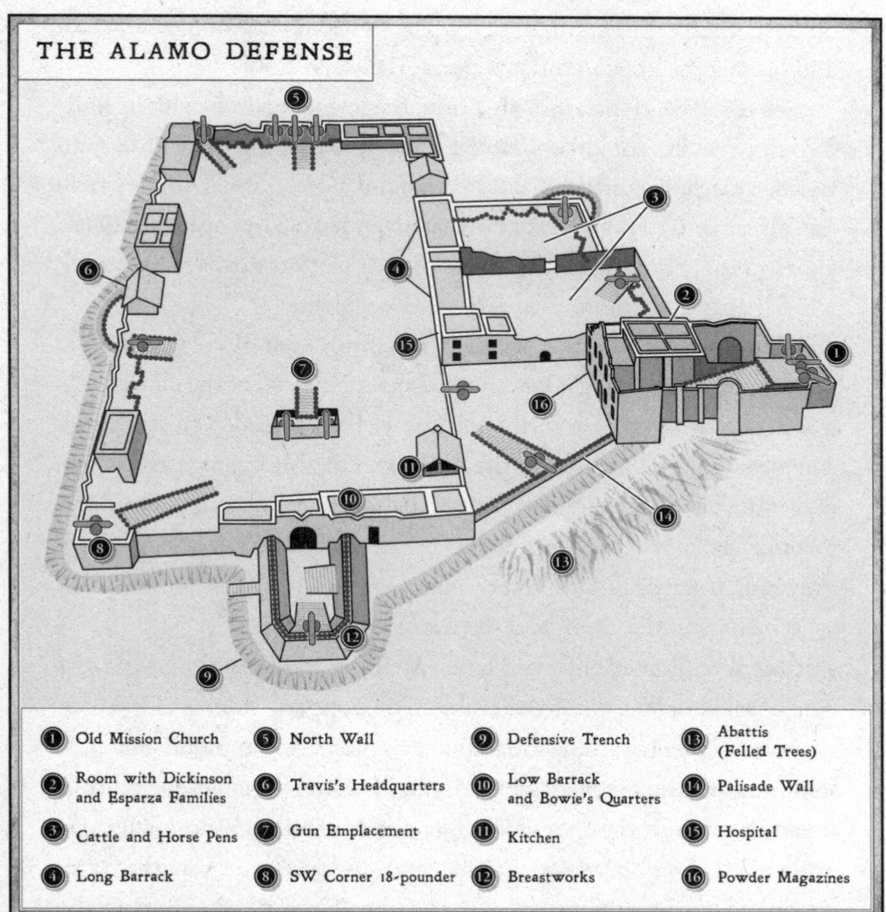
THE ALAMO DEFENSE
1 Old Mission Church
2 Room with Dickinson and Esparza Families
3 Cattle and Horse Pens
4 Long Barrack
5 North Wall
6 Travis's Headquarters
7 Gun Emplacement
8 SW Corner 18-pounder
9 Defensive Trench
10 Low Barrack and Bowie's Quarters
11 Kitchen
12 Breastworks
13 Abattis (Felled Trees)
14 Palisade Wall
15 Hospital
16 Powder Magazines

what he thought of as "Fortress Alamo." He hadn't trained as an engineer—just weeks earlier he had been practicing law in San Felipe de Austin—but he drew a rough plan of the Alamo. The church had been secularized in 1793, and the mission had become barracks for the Spanish, then the Mexican military. The previous autumn General Cos and his men had begun fortifying the Alamo.

Cos recognized that, though a ruin, the former church, with its four-foot-thick walls, could be adapted for military purposes, with a gunpowder magazine, officers' quarters, and a storehouse. The Mexicans had also erected a ramp of rubble that extended nearly the length of the church nave, rising from the entrance to a platform over the chancel, which became an improvised gun emplacement.

Now, however, Jameson faced the daunting task of completing the fortifications and doing it with limited manpower. Near the church was a yawning fifty-yard gap in the mission wall that needed to be closed. There were no parapets atop the walls, and the Mexicans had left several unfinished semicircular earthen batteries at intervals around the exterior walls. Jameson wanted perimeter ditches dug, too, one with a drawbridge across it. Most important, there were cannons to install "so as to command the Town and the country around."[21]

Even with limited time and labor, Jameson was bullish on the prospect of making the Alamo defensible. The rumored "1000 to 1500 men of the enemy being on their march to this place" left him undaunted. If they continued their work of fortifying the Alamo, Jameson felt confident that the Texians would "whip [the Mexicans] 10 to 1 with our artillery."[22] Confidence (or was it overconfidence?) rose as the work continued, despite the fact that no one knew the whereabouts of the enemy, near or far. Nor did the Texians know they were about to get a much needed boost to their morale.

COLONEL CROCKETT

Back in early November, a Tennessean in a coonskin cap headed for Texas. For the next three months, walking all the way, David Crockett got the lay of the land in rebellious Texas.

He was another of the many lured by the fight for liberty. Word of the conflict had reached Boston, New York, and Philadelphia. Crowds gathered in Mobile, Macon, New Orleans, and Nashville to raise their voices and raise money for the cause. Men from Pennsylvania, Virginia, Alabama, Kentucky, and Louisiana, inspired by rousing speeches, went west. Like many who had gone to Texas in previous years, these volunteers could be called second-chance men. Certainly Crockett, not so many months from his fiftieth birthday, was looking to start again.

Born on the Virginia frontier in 1786, he spent most of his teenage years away from his perennially penniless family (he had eight siblings), sometimes to avoid his father's beatings, at other times to work off his father's debts.[23] Married at nineteen, David soon fathered three children of his own and migrated west, reaching West Tennessee. He built a log cabin and set out to make a life for himself and his family.

With the outbreak of the War of 1812, he joined up to fight the Creek Indians, serving as a scout for Andrew Jackson. Though a mere private, he once met with the general in person and left the encounter impressed. On witnessing Old Hickory's resolution of a dispute, Crockett adapted Jackson's words, which became the frontiersman's motto: "Be always sure you are right then Go, ahead."[24]

The necessities of backwoods life made hunters of many men, but Crockett "got to be mighty fond of the rifle" and gained superb skills as a marksman and tracker.[25] He regularly won shooting matches and at times made his living as a hunter. Once he shot forty-seven bears in a single month; he killed another on a moonless night by stabbing the animal in the heart. People said he could "whip his weight in wildcats, and was so tough he could climb a thorn tree with a panther under each arm."[26] By his own account his eyes were "as keen as a lizard's."[27]

When his first wife died, he remarried and moved to Tennessee's Alabama border. Likable and entertaining, Crockett leveraged his local popularity into an appointment to serve as magistrate, a position where he continued to display the homespun humor and straightforwardness for which he was beloved. In executing his judicial responsibilities, he said, "I gave my decisions on the principles of common justice and honesty between man and man, and relied on natural born sense . . . for I had never read a page in a law book in all my life."

His neighbors approved, sending him to the Tennessee General Assembly, where he displayed a deep distrust of "ready money men." These speculators, with cash in their pockets, would buy lands that Crockett thought ought to be distributed to "poor people" who would establish homesteads.[28] Helping people with very little was a theme he would return to throughout his political life and, whatever his circumstances—over the next decade his fortunes rose and fell—Crockett always thought of himself as "a poor man." That status brought with it a sympathy for others in need. "Whenever I had any thing," he would write late in his life, "and saw a fellow being suffering, I was more anxious to relieve him than to benefit myself. . . . It is my way."[29]

By December 1827, he was on his way to Washington City, where he served for three terms in the U.S. House of Representatives. Despite an unremarkable record as a legislator, he emerged as a national character. More than a few politicians resented his candor, sharp tongue, and independence. One of those was Andrew Jackson, and Crockett, defying both President Jackson and his party, lost his reelection campaign in 1831, only to regain his seat in 1833. Then, in 1835, when he faced another close race—and the very determined opposition of Jackson—he offered a plainspoken platform. "I told the people of my district that I would serve them as faithfully as I had done; but if not, they might go to hell, and I would go to Texas."[30] After losing by 252 votes, Crockett, true to his word, lit out on the Southwest Trail.

On his trek across Texas, the famous hunter, raconteur, congressman, and author had been fêted at every stop. Cannons were fired in his honor; he was toasted at banquets.

He was a folksy man of the people who spoke truth to power but on leaving home the previous November, he claimed no commitment to the cause of Texas, saying only, "I want to explore the Texes well before I return."[31] But by January, he reported, "I must say that as to what I have seen of Texas it is the garden spot of the world [with] . . . the best land and best prospects of health I ever saw." And he ended his letter with a few words of reassurance. "Do not be uneasy about me," he wrote. "I am among friends."[32]

When Crockett came through the Alamo gates, on February 8, 1836, he led a merry band of a dozen soldiers. He called them the Tennessee Company of Mounted Volunteers, although just three of them had begun the trip with him back in Tennessee. The men in the old mission certainly welcomed any and all volunteers—but a man like Crockett doubly so.

Crockett's fame preceded him and the defenders of the Alamo called upon the new arrival to give a speech. Climbing atop a wooden box, Crockett happily obliged the cheering crowd. As one Texan lad recalled, Crockett, at age forty-nine, remained "stout and muscular, about six feet in height, and weighing 180 to 200 pounds." Though his florid complexion suggested his fondness for drink, he "had an ease and grace about him which . . . rendered him irresistible."[33]

No one told a story like Crockett, who had published a memoir that had partly been key to his fame, and he regaled the men with his best stories, events from his own life, quickly winning their rapt attention. There were hunting yarns and stories of highfalutin politicians whom

Crockett expertly humbled. He told them of his promise to his constituents in Tennessee, that if they didn't want him to represent them in Washington, he would go to Texas. And here he was!

As if he hadn't already won their admiration and respect, Crockett refused an offer of an officer's commission; despite his military experience and seniority, he was content to be a simple soldier: "[A]ll the honor that I desire," he told them, "is that of defending as a high private . . . the liberties of our common country."[34]

Crockett would be a welcome soldier, valued for his wit, as well as his fiddle playing, and counted upon for the deadly accuracy of his famous rifle, Betsy. He was doubly welcome because he wasn't above picking up a shovel, working to improve the Alamo's defenses.

WHO'S IN CHARGE HERE?

No one sat still at the Alamo. Following the orders of engineer Green Jameson, men worked at getting the twenty-odd cannons mounted on the parapets, and by midmonth Almeron Dickinson and the other artillerymen had positioned all but three.

Colonel Neill watched the work—and waited for reinforcements. One by one, Jim Bowie, William Travis, and David Crockett had arrived, each accompanied by his own squadron. Even with the added troops, counted only in the dozens, the total number of ready fighters still remained at fewer than roughly 150. With Tejano volunteers, the defenders reached barely 175 men.

When, on February 11, Neill departed unexpectedly—an urgent summons prompted by a family illness led him to take a leave—the chaotic divide in the new Texian government began to play out in San Antonio, too. Before leaving, Neill asked Travis, whose rank made him the obvious choice, to take command of the post. But volunteer Texians, as Austin had found to his frustration the previous fall, insisted upon voting their preferences. Travis had no choice but to permit an election and Travis, as the newcomer, got fewer votes than Jim Bowie, who, despite his lack of a formal officer's commission, had led many of these men at Concepción. Lieutenant Colonel Travis might have the ear of the governor and the authority of the commander in chief, Sam Houston, but the famously daring Jim Bowie remained the volunteers' favorite. There was no firm hand to settle the dispute since Houston, still far afield conversing with the Cherokee, was in no position to intervene.

Worried about the chain of command, Travis dispatched a private letter to Governor Smith. "Since his election [Bowie] has been roaring drunk all the time . . . turning everything topsy turvey."[35] But soon Bowie, sobering up after a two-day binge, apologized to Travis, and the two came to an understanding. They would sign orders jointly, with Bowie in charge of the volunteers and Travis commanding the regulars and the cavalry.

Meanwhile the work of strengthening Fortress Alamo continued, and Travis dispatched men to scour the countryside for provisions. Wells were dug to assure a supply of water within the walls. But the men needed a respite and on the occasion of George Washington's 104th birthday, Travis and Bowie granted their soldiers permission to set aside their work at the Alamo.

On San Antonio's Soledad Street, Texians and Tejanos alike ate tamales and enchiladas. They drank and they danced the fandango with the women of the town, to the accompaniment of fiddles and guitars. The carefree carousing, which extended into the night on February 22, seemed less a celebration of the Founding Father's life than a release of tension built up over weeks of preparation and anticipation.

By the next day, however, the simple pleasures of the celebration returned to worries about the Mexican army. Travis's best guess had been that Santa Anna would not arrive until mid-March, but with too few men to perform too many tasks, he was forced to rely on friendly Tejanos for scouting reports. One Tejano resident of San Antonio, freshly returned from the Rio Grande, reported that the Mexican army, numbering some thirty-five hundred on foot, accompanied by fifteen hundred cavalrymen, was crossing the river. If true, that meant the estimated time of arrival was a matter of days. But some Texians scoffed at the Mexican intelligence.

Travis took a wait-and-watch approach, until the afternoon of February 23, when he heard five ominous words: "*The enemy is in view!*"[36]

Accompanied by the pealing of bells, the voice came from a lookout, high in the belfry of the San Fernando church. A crowd gathered as several soldiers quickly ascended the bell tower. But they saw no enemy army. They "halloed down that it was a 'false alarm.'"

The crowd dispersed, but Travis wanted to be certain that the Mexicans weren't simply hiding "behind a row of brushwood," as the sentinel who'd seen them insisted. He dispatched two men on horseback to investigate, instructing them to return at speed if they spied the enemy. Travis himself then climbed the tower stairs to watch as Dr. John Sutherland and another scout, John W. Smith, departed.

The men rode out on the Laredo road, which was muddy and slick from recent rainfall. And minutes later Lieutenant Colonel Travis got his answer: Barely a mile from the town, topping a low rise in the terrain, the scouts wheeled, spurred their horses, and made for the fort. They had seen the glint of armor of what they guessed to be fifteen hundred men on horseback.

Sutherland's horse lost its footing on the sloppy track, throwing its rider to the ground. But the doctor's companion helped him back into the saddle, and together they galloped back to San Antonio. There, when Sutherland dismounted, his knee gave way beneath him, and he needed David Crockett's shoulder to lean on as he reported to Travis.

Sutherland and Smith told Travis what they had seen—and at the speed of sound the news spread around the town. By three o'clock, on February 23, Commandant Travis had penned a short but imperative dispatch. Dr. Sutherland, despite his painful knee, could still ride a horse; since he would be little use as a defender, the doctor played the messenger, carrying the news of Santa Anna's arrival to Gonzales.

The note, in Travis's script, put the situation plainly.

> *The enemy in large force is in sight. We want men and provisions. Send them to us. We have 150 men and are determined to defend the Alamo to the last. Give us assistance.*[37]

The countdown had begun.

SEVEN

Twelve Days of Uncertainty

You know that in this war there are no prisoners.

—General Antonio López de Santa Anna, February 27, 1836

El Presidente—General Antonio López de Santa Anna—mounted his horse. He led from the front, mimicking a portrait he once saw of his idol, Napoléon Bonaparte, at the head of his troops. This time Santa Anna's advance corps consisted of staff officers, three companies each of light infantry and grenadiers, and artillerymen with two mortars. As the line of march snaked out from behind the low San Alazán Hills, the sun glinted off the Mexicans' silver helmets and breastplates. Less than two miles away, Texian lookouts watched from San Antonio.

Tall for his time—he stood five-foot-ten—Santa Anna looked lean and hungry. At forty-two, his hair remained dark, his skin olive toned. A man of little education, he spoke only Spanish, but his manners were practiced, and he had the carriage of a nobleman. He was here to put down a rebellion, but his greatest desires remained money and luxury. He flaunted a gold snuffbox and wore epaulets fringed with silver. He reveled in the attention and admiration of his people. A man of no fixed principles, his politics remained fluid—after fighting for Spain, then for Mexican independence, he fought now for himself, his comforts, and his own wealth and power.

Santa Anna did not reserve his cruelty for the enemy. Though he slept in a luxurious tent and dined on monogrammed china, his two-month march north had been an ongoing ordeal for the troops, with frigid rivers to cross and a shortage of food and water. Santa Anna himself had spent two weeks sick in bed en route, but he was luckier than many. His army lost about a man a mile, with more than four hundred of his 6,119-man force dying of dysentery, fevers, and exposure to cold and snowfalls of a foot and more. Occasional Indian raids also took a toll.

He arrived with a mission. Ten weeks before, the honor of his country had been sullied, at this very place, by the surrender of General Cos. For that, he would punish the Texians at Gonzales, Goliad, and Concepción.

He wasn't intimidated by the rebels. To Santa Anna, the Alamo was no more than "an irregular fortification hardly worthy of the name." He saw opportunity: Capturing the dilapidated mission would, he believed, "infuse our soldiers with that enthusiasm of the first triumph that would make them superior in the future to those of the enemy."[1] He anticipated only weak opposition, merely "mountaineers of Kentucky and the hunters of Missouri . . . an army ignorant of the art of war, incapable of discipline."[2]

He was a cruel and driven man, yet women found this man attractive, despite the fact that he rarely smiled, his expression perpetually unhappy, even gloomy. That inscrutability left some people wondering, but as one lady of the day would soon say of him, "It is strange . . . how frequently this expression . . . of placid sadness is to be remarked on the countenances of the most cunning, the deepest, most ambitious, most designing and most dangerous statesmen."[3]

The men of the Alamo would soon discover how utterly ruthless Santa Anna could be.

THE ENEMY APPROACHES

This time, no one doubted the meaning of the clanging bell. On Tuesday, February 23, the lethargy of a morning-after in San Antonio quickly gave way to furious activity as the bell tolled. Travis ordered the soldiers to withdraw to the Alamo, and double-quick the Texian fighters grabbed their guns, ammunition, whatever they could carry, and headed for the bridge.

Time was tight: Mexican troops, now in full sight and less than two miles away, marched toward them. No one knew when the first shots would be fired, but the Texians corralled the horses, penning them in what, during the Alamo's days as a mission, had been the convent garden. Still in the town, Jim Bowie went about San Antonio, searching for foodstuffs, ransacking deserted houses. He found some of what he was looking for, and the stores of corn at the Alamo went from three bushels to more than eighty.[4] Other defenders confiscated a herd of thirty beef cattle and drove the animals into a pen within the mission walls. Wounded and sick men were transferred to the safety of the walled compound.

The Texians' refuge, consisting of about four acres enclosed by the makeshift ramparts, became home to not only the men sworn to defend the Alamo but a mix of Anglo and Tejano families. Bowie collected members of the Veramendi clan, including his late wife's sister and her husband. In the hustle and bustle of the evacuation, Captain Almeron Dickinson reacted not as an artillery officer but as a husband and father.

Riding bareback, he galloped to the house he shared with wife Susanna at the corner of Commerce Street and the main plaza. Without dismounting, he called to her, "Give me the baby! Jump on behind and ask me no questions." With fifteen-month-old Angelina cradled in one arm, he helped swing Susanna up behind him.

There would be no fight this day: The Texians conceded the town as indefensible and, by late afternoon, the Mexicans took possession of San Antonio. Mounted grenadiers and foot soldiers dispersed to scout the nearly deserted streets. A Tejano boy of the town who had been playing nearby watched as Santa Anna and his staff dismounted near the church. For twelve-year-old Enrique Esparza, the sight of the general was indelible. "He had a very broad face and high cheekbones. He had a hard and cruel look and his countenance was a very sinister one."[5]

As the Texians watched from behind the Alamo's west wall, a distance of less than a half mile, a flag rose above the bell tower of the San Fernando church, previously the site of a Texian lookout post. Once again, Santa Anna's men would take no prisoners and show no mercy in dealing with these rebels.

But the Texians would not be intimidated: In response, they fired their biggest cannon, an eighteen-pounder, with a great, resounding boom.

After the Mexicans returned fire, lobbing a few shells from their field pieces, the guns on both sides went quiet. When a white flag was raised, the Texians sent messengers under a flag of peace to parley. With the odds as they were, an honorable retreat like the one Neill had granted to General Cos in December might be worth considering. But Santa Anna refused to negotiate. An aide, responding on his behalf, stated that "according to the order of His Excellency, the Mexican army cannot come to terms under any conditions with rebellious foreigners."[6]

The flag of no quarter and Santa Anna's unwillingness to talk left the Texians with no alternative. Travis and Bowie drafted a joint letter to Colonel Fannin, pleading for help. The commander of Goliad seemed their best hope—Fannin and his four hundred troops weren't so far away, a hundred miles distant. The two Alamo commanders told Fannin that their garrison, as of that morning's muster, amounted to just 146 effectives. They urged Fannin to send help—and assured him that they remained "determined *never to retreat.*"[7]

As for Santa Anna, he received no plea from the Alamo. Travis gathered the men of the Alamo; they agreed to swear a collective oath to "resist to the last."[8] That day the Texians responded to Santa Anna's threats with gunfire, as the report of their biggest gun once more echoed over San Antonio. The rebels would stand their ground.

THE SIEGE

The concussion of cannon blasts was almost constant. A five-inch howitzer and several field pieces bombarded the Alamo throughout the day. Though the cannonballs and shards of flying stone injured no one, the Texians did find themselves one man down when Jim Bowie fell ill, deathly ill.

Bowie's sister-in-law, Juana, cared for the fevered man in an upstairs room in the Alamo chapel. But the nature of his ailment could only be guessed. Cholera or typhoid? Pneumonia? Perhaps some long-lingering ailment like tuberculosis that had grown suddenly grave? Whatever it was, it was serious, keeping Bowie confined to a cot that, some feared, might become his deathbed.

The illness meant that Bowie, weak and delirious, could no longer lead the volunteers. That put William Travis in charge of both Bowie's men and the regulars. The responsibility for saving the lives of those around him, much less winning a battle against Santa Anna's vastly larger army, had become Travis's heavy burden.

He considered the situation. Sam Houston's worst fears seemed to be coming true. The enemy was near—but help far away. Windswept San Antonio sat amid a Texas wilderness. No help would come from

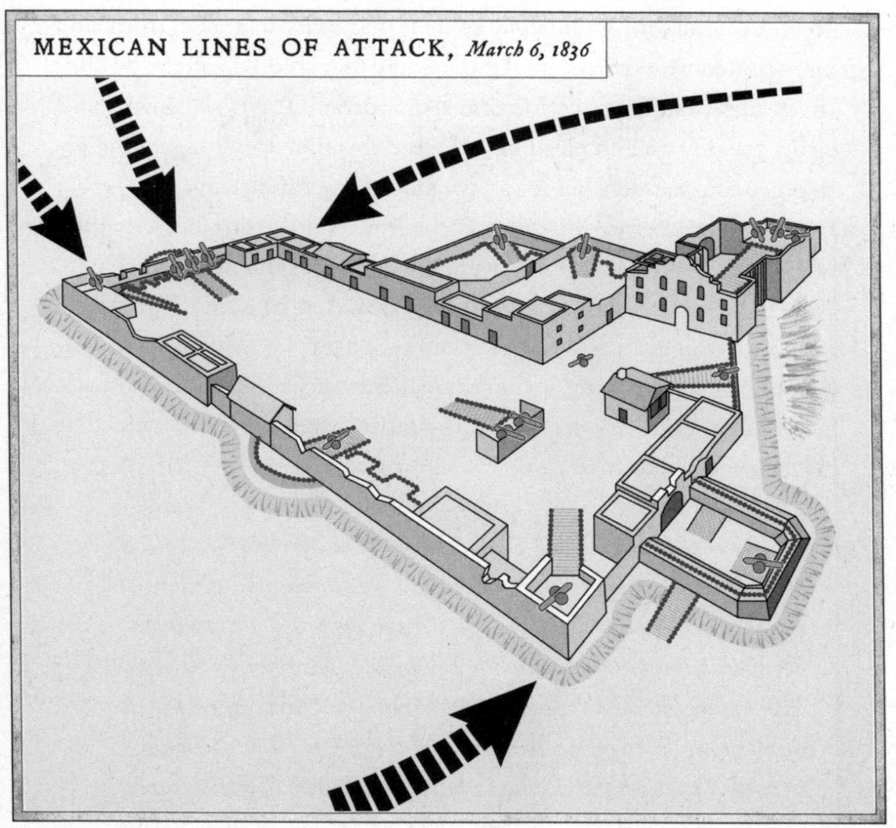

the north, where the hills and plains were home to few settlers and many unfriendly Indians. Travis hoped reinforcements would arrive from Gonzales to the east and Goliad to the south, but the enemy now entirely controlled the territory west of the city. Santa Anna and his men occupied the nearby streetscapes, and scouting reports warned of other large Mexican forces on the march.

Although the Texians had worked for weeks to make the Alamo battle-ready, the defenders, now withdrawn inside the fort's walls, could see more clearly the weaknesses of their position. More men, rifles, and ammunition would be needed if they were to fend off an attack by hundreds upon hundreds of Mexicans. A worried Travis sat down once again, pen in hand, to plead for help, but this time he wrote not merely to other commanders but for a very much larger audience.

Two weeks before, his instinct for leadership hadn't been evident when he and Bowie bickered over which of them should be in charge. Now as the sole commander, suddenly boxed in by a merciless opponent, he found his true voice. He possessed a gift for words, one he had polished in his days writing for the small newspaper he'd founded back in Alabama, the *Claiborne Herald.* In drafting a public letter, he blended his fears with a steely resolve.

> *To the People of Texas & all Americans in the world—Fellow citizens & compatriots—I am besieged, by a thousand or more of the Mexicans under Santa Anna—I have sustained a continual Bombardment & cannonade for 24 hours & have not lost a man—The enemy has demanded a surrender at discretion, otherwise, the garrison are to be put to the sword, if the fort is taken—I have answered the demand with a cannon shot, & our flag still waves proudly from the walls—*I shall never surrender or retreat. *Then, I call on you in the name of Liberty, of patriotism & every thing dear to the American character, to come to our aid with all dispatch—The enemy is receiving reinforcements daily & will no doubt increase to three or four thousand in four or five days.*
>
> *If this call is neglected, I am determined to sustain myself as long as possible & die like a soldier who never forgets what is due to his own honor & that of his country—Victory or Death.*
>
> *William Barret Travis*
> *Lt. Col. comdt*[9]

Travis knew that he and the men around him, captive as they were, faced the fight of their lives. He understood, too, that defending the Alamo represented something larger. He and his Texians might occupy an obscure frontier town, but he wrote as if their story, their cause, transcended time and place, his a voice for the cause of liberty everywhere.

THURSDAY, FEBRUARY 25, 1836

No friend of liberty, Santa Anna tested his tactics. In the night his men planted batteries north and south of the mission, roughly four hundred yards from the Alamo. From these new positions, they maintained their fire.

Conserving their powder, the Texians fired back only intermittently.

From his headquarters, Santa Anna supervised the distribution of shoes. He left the town to scout with a cavalry unit. Then, at ten o'clock that Thursday morning, he ordered a force of more than two hundred Mexicans to march on the Alamo. The uniformed men crossed the shallow river and marched toward the scattering of nearby buildings south of the Alamo's main gate.

The Texians held their fire until the enemy arrived "within point blank shot." Then the Alamo's defenders opened with a full fusillade, their cannons unleashing grape and cannon shot. The Texians' long rifles—with David Crockett cheering his boys on—and the artillery took a deadly toll on the approaching fighters. The Mexicans still standing scrambled back into the shelter of the abandoned houses, and the two sides exchanged fire for two hours before the Mexicans finally withdrew. When they retreated, they carted with them at least eight dead and wounded.

Travis reported on the morning's action, writing to Major General

Sam Houston. Houston was far away, still on his journey to and from the Cherokee, blithely unaware of the turn of events at the Alamo, having ordered its evacuation the month before.

"Many of the enemy were wounded," Travis wrote, "while we, on our part, have not lost a man. . . . I take great pleasure in stating that both officers and men have conducted themselves with firmness and bravery." He cited Captain Dickinson in particular for his gallantry, as well as "the Hon. David Crockett" for "animating the men to do their duty."

Proud as he was of the first exchange of fire, Travis remained deeply worried. "Do hasten on aid to me as rapidly as possible, as from the superior number of the enemy, it will be impossible for us to keep them out much longer."

Without apology, Travis also spelled out the stakes once more: "If they overpower us, we fall a sacrifice at the shrine of our country."[10]

Travis's call for help had reached Colonel James Fannin. Goliad's commander speedily divided his garrison, ordering all but one hundred of his four-hundred-some men to prepare to march. As they readied for departure, Fannin reported via letter to army headquarters in Washington-on-the-Brazos that he felt a brotherly obligation. "The appeals of Cols. Travis & Bowie cannot . . . pass unnoticed—particularly by troops now on the field—Sanguine, chivalrous volunteers—Much must be risked to relieve the besieged."[11]

Fannin and company headed out for San Antonio, a hundred miles away, that very afternoon. But then, just two hundred yards from Goliad's gate, they faced their first obstacle. A wagon broke down.

After a delay, with pairs of yoked oxen pulling each cannon, Fannin and his men managed to cross a nearby river. But, as more wagons failed in the process, their progress slowed again. With darkness falling, the little army made camp for the night, still within sight of the Goliad mission.

In the morning, Fannin's officers requested a council of war. They were having second thoughts about their immediate urge to go to the aid of their fellow Texians. The three-hundred-man contingent had no bread or beef and little rice; as Fannin's aide-de-camp Captain Brooks put it, "We are almost naked and without provisions and very little ammunition." Fannin himself now doubted whether the artillery could be gotten to the Alamo. Others expressed concern that the hundred men left behind would be unable to defend Goliad, the place they had recently renamed Fort Defiance. And even if Fannin's contingent made it to the Alamo, wasn't the mission likely to fail? In Captain Brooks's words, "We can not therefore calculate very sanguinely upon victory."[12]

Fannin, Brooks, and the other commissioned officers deliberated before reaching a unanimous decision. As Fannin, seeming to forget that he had just said that much should be risked for the sake of the Alamo, soon decided, "It was deemed expedient to return to [Goliad] and complete the fortifications."[13]

Travis's request that Fannin send men would go unanswered. Fannin's resolve had wavered and broken; the proposed mission to aid the Alamo had come to nothing.

A **STRONG WIND** came up that evening, but Santa Anna and his men ignored the temperature as it dropped below forty degrees. The Mexican guns not only maintained their fire, but the Texians awoke to the sight of cavalry encamped on the hills east of the Alamo. The enemy was now poised to block a retreat or to intercept reinforcements from Gonzales. The noose was tightening.

In the night, a small band of Texians had quietly left the Alamo and set fire to the houses close by. The shanties, which had provided the enemy cover during the previous day's skirmish, went up in smoke. Burned to the ground, the ash and rubble of the humble buildings left an open field for the men with long rifles.

The terms of the battle grew clearer. From the safety of Fortress Alamo, the Texians could hold off a much larger army, with their artillery and rifles throwing lead at any attackers who approached within two hundred yards. If the enemy chose to make an all-out assault, Travis felt confident that his gunners and riflemen would inflict staggering casualties. Santa Anna might risk such a bloodbath—and with his superior numbers, he could prevail—but surely His Excellency recognized that such a victory would seem more costly than a defeat?

On the other hand, the Alamo enclosure, Travis knew well, was simply too large for his 150 men to defend indefinitely in the face of constant artillery fire. Not that he had a choice: Until more Texians came to their aid, the Alamo defenders would have to occupy themselves with improving their fort. That wasn't easy: Moving about the Alamo, they had to be constantly wary, dodging shells and cannonballs that regularly whistled in from the sky.

LONG DAYS, LONGER NIGHTS

Travis ordered more sorties to demolish all the remaining shacks near enough to the Alamo to provide enemy cover. In the process, his men salvaged bits and pieces for firewood, an increasingly precious commodity.

Engineer Green Jameson and his construction detail dug trenches; one shovelful at a time, the excavated earth added to the bulk of the walls and shaped parapets atop them.

Riflemen found the best spots from which to pick off any Mexican foolish enough to raise his head within range. From the opposite side of the line, a Mexican captain observed one shooter whose flowing hair distinguished him from the rest. The tall man fired from a favored spot, dressed in a buckskin suit and patterned cape.

"This man," Rafael Soldana reported, "would kneel or lie down behind the low parapet, rest his long gun and fire, and we all learned to keep at a good distance when he was seen to make ready to shoot. He rarely missed his mark, and when he fired he always rose to his feet and calmly reloaded his gun seemingly indifferent to the shots fired at him by our own men."

The independent figure sometimes crowed over his well-aimed shots, taunting the enemy in "a strong, resonant voice." The Spanish-speaking Mexicans could not understand his words, spoken in English, but would later learn his identity. As they rendered his name, he was "Kwockey."[14] To the Americans, he was the man known as Crockett, who was defending the biggest gap in the Alamo's perimeter, where, on the south side, the wall ended short of the chapel. Although the space was now lined with a palisade of sharpened stakes angled toward potential attackers, it remained a likely Mexican route of assault.

General Santa Anna, on the outside looking in, bided his time. He would wait for an oncoming brigade to add to his forces, but he harbored no doubts as to the outcome of the eventual fight.

"After taking Fort Alamo," he wrote confidently to his minister of war, "I shall continue my operations against Goliad and the other fortified places, so that before the rains set in, the campaign shall be absolutely terminated up to the Sabine River, which serves as the boundary line between our republic and the one of the North."[15]

He ordered the installation that night of another gun battery, this one near the old mill. With first light, cannonballs began to rain in from yet another direction, almost due north of the Alamo. When one of his scouts reported, on February 29, that a two-hundred-man Texian force was on the road from the Presidio La Bahía, the fortress at

Goliad, Santa Anna ordered one of his generals to lead a force of cavalry and infantry to intercept the Goliad men. When they found no sign of a Texian force, they returned to Santa Anna's camp at San Antonio.

Wondering at the whereabouts of Fannin and company, Travis asked Austin's old friend Juan Seguín, a trusted Tejano, to carry another plea for help to the outside world. Needing a good horse for the mission, he went to ask the bedridden Bowie if he might borrow his.

Seguín found the aging fighter "so ill that he hardly recognized the borrower."[16] But Bowie agreed to lend his mount, and the messenger left that night through the north gate.

Nearing the Mexican cavalry camp, he approached at a leisurely pace as if reporting in. He spoke Spanish, lulling the Mexican sentinels into lowering their guard—but, as he neared, he suddenly spurred his horse and dashed past, disappearing into the night before the dragoons could react.

Back at the Alamo, Travis and his men waited and hoped. Crockett distracted them with his fiddle, accompanied by the droning bagpipes of Scotsman John McGregor. These were evenings of drink, of cards and talk, but little seemed to change except the weather. One night Crockett and McGregor faced off in a musical competition to make the most noise; it was a fine distraction as a brutal norther finally blew past, its bitter cold winds giving way to milder air.[17] The Texians welcomed the change—it occurred at a moment when nothing whatever seemed to be going their way.

DON'T SHOOT!

In the early morning hours of March 1, the Alamo sentinel shot first. Noises in the dark, nearby but outside the walls, drew his fire—but no one shot back. Instead the lookout heard voices, hissing in English.

Don't shoot! We're friends!

They were men from Gonzales, the place where, with the second shot heard 'round the world, the war had begun. Their neighbors had come to the aid of Gonzales and, summoned by a Travis alert, they had come here to do the same. Circling north, they had managed to skirt the Mexican dragoons guarding the road.

Ushered into the Alamo, the reinforcements were welcomed with cheers. But the defenders' sense of relief at the newcomers' arrival quickly faded. The company of volunteers, one of them wounded in the foot by the guard's gun, numbered just thirty-two men. That brought the total to 180 fighters; the Mexicans, depending upon which estimate one believed, numbered fifteen hundred. Or twenty-five hundred. Or even six thousand men.

For the rest of the defenders, the arrival on March 1 was a sort of anniversary: One week had passed since the appearance of Santa Anna forced them to withdraw into the Alamo. There had been no major attack. The only thing that seemed to change was still the weather, which was turning cold again, but every man understood the situation could explode at most any time.

WHERE IS SAM HOUSTON?

While the men in the Alamo waited and worried, the missing general reappeared: Houston had returned from Cherokee country, riding into Washington-on-the-Brazos on February 28. He brought good news: He'd signed a treaty of peace with the Cherokee. On arrival, however, he encountered some very bad news, in a just-arrived dispatch addressed to "Sam Houston, Commander-in-Chief of the Army of Texas."

The report, written in Colonel Travis's slanting and hurried hand, was enough to make Houston's head spin. He learned for the first time of Santa Anna's early arrival. He read of the initial skirmish between the desperate defenders of the Alamo and the Mexican army. He didn't have to read the closing line—*"Give me help, oh my Country! Victory or Death"*—to know Travis and troops were in terrible trouble, trouble they might have avoided had they followed Houston's earlier instructions to evacuate the mission.

Houston immediately began planning his response, but before he could take military action, he had to help complete the writing and signing of a Texas declaration of independence, an action that had been a long time in coming.

On March 1, in a makeshift building overlooking the Brazos River, forty-one delegates to a new convention came to order to reorganize revolutionary Texas into a republic.

In a simple structure with cotton cloth and animal skins for doors, the delegates suffered in bitter wind and cold, but they produced what they had come for: "The Unanimous Declaration of Independence made by the Delegates of the People of Texas." One statement summed it up: "We do hereby declare, that our political connection with the Mexican nation has forever ended, and that the people of Texas do now constitute a free, sovereign, and independent republic."[18]

On March 2, which just happened to be Sam Houston's forty-third birthday, the delegates signed the declaration. The day after, the delegates designated him commander in chief, this time with full and absolute authority over all the troops, be they volunteer, regular army, or militia.

Now could he address the task of facing down Santa Anna.

BACK AT THE ALAMO

On Thursday, March 3, a lone rider slipped through the ever-tightening enemy perimeter to enter the Alamo. He told of sixty volunteers en route from San Felipe, with another three hundred to follow. To Travis and his officers, the arithmetic looked suddenly better. With these fighters—along with, they hoped, Goliad's three hundred—Travis's command could grow to eight hundred men. *That* would make for a much fairer fight. But before more Texians could arrive, raucous cries of celebration sounded across the river.

A glance over the west wall revealed the reason. A long ribbon of troops entered San Antonio. There were a thousand or more men marching in from the west, a mix of experienced sappers (military engineers) and fresh conscripts. These new troops raised the total under Santa Anna's immediate command to at least twenty-five hundred men, a force more than a dozen times greater than that inside the Alamo.

Travis could wait and hope for help to arrive from somewhere, from anywhere; or he could try writing yet again. This time he addressed the top man, the president of the Texas convention.

He reported in full, describing the enemy's gradual encroachment, the arrival of the small Gonzales force, and the near doubling of enemy ranks. Despite the fact that "at least two hundred shells have fallen inside of our works," Travis reported proudly, "the spirits of my men are still high." He again appealed for troops, ammunition, and supplies, requesting the immediate dispatch of "at least 500 pounds of cannon powder, 200 rounds of six, nine, twelve, and eighteen-pound balls, ten kegs of rifle powder, and a supply of lead." If they were better equipped for battle, the fight could be "decisive," he promised. His men could be trusted to "fight with desperation and that high-souled courage that characterized the patriot, who is willing to fight in defense of his country's liberty and his own honor."[19] He sealed the letter with wax.

Within hours, however, Travis's hopeful house of cards began to collapse when word came of Fannin's decision to turn back. No help would be forthcoming from Goliad.

With that news, a fatalistic frame of mind came over William Travis.

He understood perhaps better than any in the garrison that, as he ominously admitted, they were probably engaged in their "last struggle." With the call for outgoing mail announced, the messenger readied to depart with the fall of night. He would carry letters from several Alamo defenders, but Travis at this late hour felt the need to scribble down one more note. This he composed as a private citizen, not a commanding officer. It was a letter to his son's schoolteacher.

> *Take Care of my little boy. If the country should be saved, I may make for him a splendid fortune; but if the country be lost and I should perish, he will have nothing but the proud recollection that he is the son of a man who died for his country.*[20]

It would be Lieutenant Colonel William Barret Travis's last letter.

MARCHING ORDERS

As the courier carried his pouch full of letters toward their intended recipients, Santa Anna called a council of war on March 4.

Some of his officers advised patience: The Texians could go nowhere and, with a pair of twelve-pound cannons only two days out, why not wait and reduce Fortress Alamo to rubble? Other generals expressed eagerness to attack right away.

Santa Anna himself had grown impatient. He wanted a plan of attack, an immediate plan for ending the rebel resistance with a direct assault. He ordered one be prepared.

The preliminaries were in place. Just the previous afternoon, the Texians had observed Mexicans, in the plain light of day, sawing and hewing lengths of wood for the legs and rungs of scaling ladders. At varying distances, Santa Anna's men had dug entrenchments and gun batteries on all sides of Fortress Alamo. The most recent, north of the fort, was closest, now firing from within two hundred yards.

At two o'clock on the afternoon of Saturday, March 5, detailed orders from Santa Anna circulated. "The time has come," they began, "to strike a decisive blow upon the enemy occupying the Fortress of the Alamo."[21] The soldiers were to retire at dark, then, at midnight, form into four columns of foot soldiers, each assigned a point of attack—the northwest and northeast corners, the east wall, and the Alamo's most evident vulnerability, the palisade in the gap of the south wall. A cavalry regiment deployed to the east would crush any Texians seeking to escape. A fifth column would lie in wait at the new north battery; commanded by Santa Anna, the reserves could be ordered into battle whenever and wherever the need arose. Everything was to be in readiness by four o'clock on Sunday morning.

Although wholly ignorant of how soon their fate would fall, the Texians would have to endure only one more bitter night, with a wet north wind and temperatures near freezing.

CROSSING THE LINE

On Saturday afternoon, the Mexican cannonade went silent two hours before sunset. In the welcome but unfamiliar quiet, William Travis summoned his men to parade in the Alamo's central plaza. Several soldiers carried Jim Bowie, still on his cot, feverish and on the edge of delirium, from his confinement.

Travis addressed the garrison.

"My soldiers, I am going to meet the fate that becomes me. Those who will stand by me, let them remain, but those who desire to go, let them go."[22]

The men cheered his words.

Travis drew his sword. Using its tip, he scribed a line in the dirt in front of the men in formation. He invited all those who would stand with him, who would die with him, to step across the line.

As one, the able-bodied men stepped forth; Jim Bowie, despite his fevered state, requested that he be helped across. Just one man remained behind; he was permitted to depart. He would survive to recount this story.[23]

Travis and his men worked into the night, further stabilizing the fortifications. Many of the eight hundred muskets and rifles on hand were made ready: With more than one gun per man, the Texians could deliver a rapid initial rate of fire without reloading. The artillerymen had at least five hundred loads of canister and grapeshot.

The commander made one other parting gesture before retiring for what would prove to be an abbreviated night's sleep. Visiting the Alamo church, Travis noticed little Angelina Dickinson. From his finger, Travis removed a ring of hammered gold; it was inset with a large agate stone. He strung it on a loop of string, which he then slipped over the head of the fifteen-month-old like a necklace.

The child's mother, Susanna, stood nearby. She promised Travis that if anything happened to him she would be sure that the keepsake was delivered to Travis's son, Charles.

EIGHT

The Massacre

A desperate contest ensued, in which prodigies of valor were wrought by this Spartan band.

—MARY AUSTIN HOLLEY, *Texas*

The Texians' day began at 5:30 A.M. with the sound of distant shouting. As the sun came up, the Alamo defenders heard calls of *Viva Santa Anna!* and *Viva la republica!*

Blaring bugles then made the attack official, and the Mexican troops, less than two hundred yards away, leapt to their feet. Having lain quietly for two hours, on their stomachs and unseen in their blue uniforms, they hoisted their guns and swords and ran toward the Alamo.

At last, on Sunday, March 6, 1836, the real fight began.

For the Alamo's sleeping commandant, insulated by the adobe brick of his room in the middle of the west wall, his officer of the day put the news plainly. Banging open the door of Travis's bedchamber, he shouted, "Colonel Travis! The Mexicans are coming!"

Rising quickly from his bed, Travis grabbed his gun and sword. He ran out into the open plaza, yelling, "Come on boys, the Mexicans are upon us and we'll give them *Hell.*"[1]

Heading for the gun battery in the Alamo's northwest corner, he could hear his riflemen atop the walls as they began firing at the on-coming Mexicans. The cannon were not yet booming, though Travis needed the big guns to prevent the much larger Mexican force from reaching the Alamo's wall. He sprinted up the ramp that rose to the gun emplacement.

On reaching the top of the rampart, he, too, discharged his shotgun, one barrel first, then the other. Moments later, the cannons at last started firing. Standing nearby, silhouetted by stop-time powder flashes, Travis made a fine target from the darkness below. Some unnamed Mexican sighted in and fired.

Travis took a hit: A lead ball smashed squarely into his forehead. He went down, his hand still clenching his gun, collapsing into a strangely lifelike sitting position. In the opening minutes of the fight for the Alamo, the Texians lost their battle leader, the man whose words would forever frame the events of the fight that was unfolding around his lifeless form.

THE FIRST WAVE

Santa Anna employed Napoléon's tactics. With his overwhelming man-power advantage and little regard for casualties, he threw the four columns of infantry at the four corners of the Alamo. He remained well back, an observer, astride his fine steed.

The general had surprise on his side: After weeks of bombardment, in the wee hours of a Sunday, he caught the Texians unawares and unready. His advance guard had overwhelmed the rebels' pickets on the perimeter, slitting throats or running them through with bayonets before they could sound the alarm.

Inside the Alamo, the surprised Texians moved to their assigned posts as quickly as they could and began delivering a murderous fire at the attackers approaching the Alamo's perimeter walls. Their rifles damaged the Mexican wave, "leaving a wide trail of blood, of wounded, and of dead."[2] Each rifleman, having emptied one loaded gun, reached for the next.

The Texian artillery added to the deafening din of the battle. In the absence of standard-issue canister and grapeshot, Almeron Dickinson and his fellow artillerymen had packed their cannon barrels with metal fragments, such as nails, horseshoe pieces, and chain links; the more jagged the scrap, the better. Powered by superior American-made gunpowder, the hail of deadly debris added to the numbers of fallen men on the field, taking down officers as well as foot soldiers. One stunned Mexican colonel watched as "a single cannon volley did away with half [a] company" of his men.[3]

The officer who had surrendered San Antonio back in December, General Martín Perfecto de Cos, ignoring the promise he had made not to return and fight in Texas, led his three hundred infantrymen as they charged Travis's battery. Having lost once to the Texians, Cos needed to redeem his tarnished reputation in Santa Anna's eyes. Some four hundred men under Colonel Duque advanced on the other corner of the Alamo's north wall. Three hundred soldiers commanded by Colonel José María Romero attacked the strong east front, where Captain Dickinson's three twelve-pound cannons, mounted high on the rear wall of the ruins of the Alamo's chapel, appeared to its attackers to be "a sort of high fortress."[4] Colonel Juan Morales's one hundred men moved on the south wall, looking to capture the main entrance and penetrate the palisade guarded by Crockett and his company.

The "terrible shower" that burst from the Texian cannons opened gaps in the Mexican ranks on all fronts. Colonel Duque went down with a thigh wound, but the swarm of Mexicans kept coming. These were soldiers trained to "scorn life and welcome death," to seek "honor and glory."[5]

On approach, some light infantrymen had fanned out and, armed with accurate Baker rifles, they targeted the Alamo defenders on the roofs, exposed with no parapets to protect them. At closer range, the short-barreled guns the troops carried—the Texians dismissively called them "blunderbusses"—gained effectiveness yard by yard. The Texians' earlier advantage of preloaded guns ended; each rifleman had to resort to reloading, costing him precious time.

On reaching the foot of the wall, however, the attackers discovered that next to none of the scaling ladders had made it across the killing field. Inside the Alamo the thuds of Mexican axes could be heard on the thick wooden doors; some Mexicans wielded crowbars, struggling to pry open the boarded-up windows. But the attackers were suddenly stymied.

Acutely aware of their losses—according to one Mexican soldier, "it seemed every cannon ball or pistol shot of the enemy embedded itself in the breasts of our men,"[6] the north wall attackers wavered. With gunfire still raining down from above—one cannon now raked the attackers in the lee of the wall—Santa Anna's men fell back.

From a distance, a noncombatant, José Francisco Ruiz, mayor of San Antonio, called it as he saw it. The Mexican army's initial assault, he observed, was "repulsed by the deadly fire of Travis's artillery, which resembled a constant thunder."[7]

The Texians were holding strong.

HIS EXCELLENCY

For Santa Anna, no glory could be claimed without bloodshed. Watching the attack on the Alamo, he took grim pleasure in the dirge-like notes of the "Degüello," the rhythmic march that, on his orders, accompanied the assault. Sounded by his buglers, it signaled to his men that no quarter would be given.* To their enemy, it was "the music of merciless murder."[8]

Standing with the reserve troops just fifteen minutes into the battle, Santa Anna looked on as dozens and dozens of his own men lay slaughtered after the first assault. His officers, aware that a full attack would result in a "great sacrifice" of men, had wondered at the timing of the attack: *Why not wait? The siege was working. More big guns were due any day.* But such niceties were wasted on Santa Anna, who remained firm. The generals and colonels had no choice but to obey His Excellency's orders, "[choosing] silence, knowing that he would not tolerate opposition, his sole pleasure being in hearing what met with his wishes."[9]

Dressed as usual for a campaign—he wore a green frock coat—Santa Anna got his bloody battle. To prevent any Texians from escaping the Alamo, he had taken the precaution of positioning a squadron near the Gonzales road and ordered a veteran cavalry unit to run down any rebels who tried to flee. He wanted to obliterate the defiant Texians, no matter what the cost.

But the fight wasn't going as he had hoped. He studied the Alamo, where, in the morning's first glimmer of daylight, he could still see the bright blasts of flame from the mouths of the Texian cannons. Two of his columns had slowed in the face of the artillery fire; another veered off its course; and the fourth, attacking the main gate, had been forced to take shelter behind a few remaining huts near the Alamo's southwest corner.

The initial attack failed to penetrate the Alamo's defenses.

His reserves were among the best men in Santa Anna's army, consisting of four hundred men. Now, he decided, was the time to order them into battle. This second wave would penetrate the wall, he hoped, ending Texian resistance once and for all.

---

* Derived from the Spanish *degollar*, "Degüello" literally means throat-cutting.

THE SECOND WAVE

Inside the Alamo, Travis lay dead. His second in command, Jim Bowie, could not take his place. Weak with disease, sweating feverishly, he lay in his bed, only dimly aware of the firefight. But the Texians kept fighting.

At the southwest corner of the Alamo enclosure, the biggest of the Alamo's guns pounded the Mexicans. On the platform at the rear of the church, three smaller cannons looked east. But nowhere were there enough Texians to man all the guns properly. Instead of a usual crew of a half dozen per gun, the Texians depended on skeleton crews half that size.

The gunners along the north wall aimed at the army of attackers as they regrouped. Despite the losses sustained on the first attack, this force grew larger as the Texians watched. Along with Santa Anna's reserves, the third column, deflected by the big guns in the chapel, now joined in a full-frontal assault along the length of the northern exposure. This time, on reaching the base of the wall, they took a determined new approach.

Green Jameson and his men had worked to stiffen the northern defenses, facing a once-crumbling stone and adobe wall with a layer of timber and stone. Though as high as twelve feet in places, the earthworks were not yet finished—and the exposed beams and stacked stones made the wall vulnerable. General Juan Amador grasped the opportunity: He began to climb and ordered his men, their guns slung over their shoulders, to follow. They found footholds and handholds, with one soldier helping the next, despite the continued Texian fire from above. Before long they had breached the Alamo's walls.

Some of the agile ones who cleared the wall first met with the bayonets and rifle butts of Texian fighters who stabbed and bludgeoned them. At other places along the expanse of the wall, the appearance of a Mexican head was greeted with lead fired by nearby Texians or riflemen on top of a central building within the Alamo, the Long Barracks. Despite the falling dead and wounded, one Mexican officer reported, "the courage of our soldiers was not diminished . . . and they hurried to occupy their places, . . . climbing over their bleeding bodies."[10]

This time, despite the casualties, there would be no Mexican retreat. "We could hear the Mexican officers shouting to the men to jump over," the Tejano boy, Enrique Esparza, later remembered.[11] That moment—it was a shift in the tide of battle—would stay with him forever. The fall of the Alamo became inevitable when the first uniformed men of Mexico climbed over the wall. The few were followed by the many, as a surge of attackers cleared the parapet and, one by one, dropped to the plaza below.

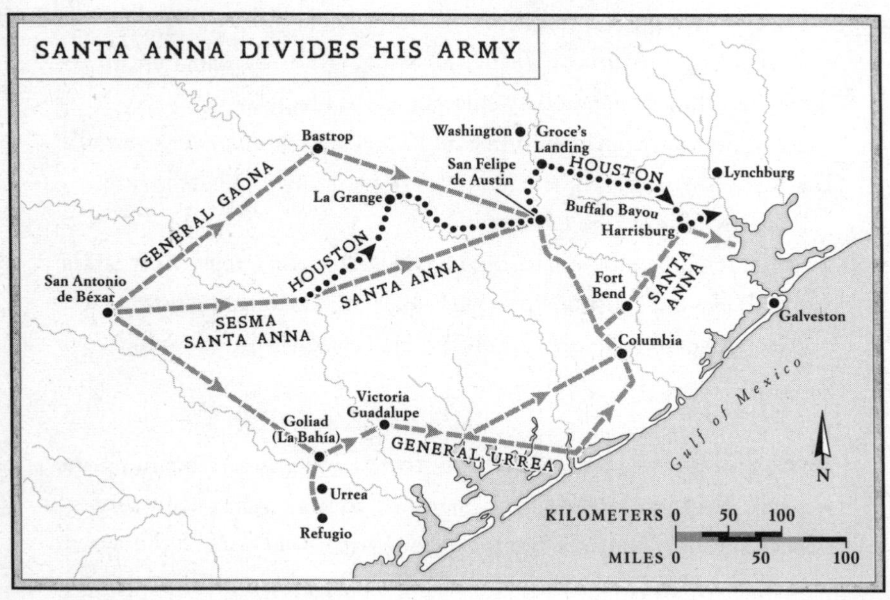

This time the Texians were the ones to retreat, withdrawing the soldiers who were at the perimeter wall to the Long Barracks in hopes of one final holdout.

Captain Almeron Dickinson manned the chapel's big guns. Bunked down in the church, he and his gun crew had slept close to their post, and in the early moments of the battle, one of his cannons had been the first to fire. The intimidating cannon had done its work, raking the left flank of the oncoming Mexican third column, causing Colonel Romero's command to veer away from the church and head northward, seeking a new point of attack unprotected by cannons.

As the battle continued, however, the artillery captain read the changing situation. With the Mexicans entering the Alamo compound, he knew the Alamo defenders lost ground they couldn't afford to lose. With the tumult still raging hottest along the north wall, Dickinson left his post, stealing a few moments for words he had to say.

He managed to find his wife, Susanna, and their daughter, in the family quarters in the sacristy adjacent to the chapel.

"My dear wife," Almeron began. "They are coming over the wall." But that didn't say it all, and she deserved to know the harsh truth.

"We are all lost," he told her.

More remained to be said, but he needed to return to his post on the scaffold. He made just one parting request of Susanna Dickinson.

"If they spare you, love our child." He kissed her in farewell.[12]

With the north wall breached, the Alamo gunners manning the southwest cannon turned their gun inward to fire on the enemy soldiers flooding the Alamo plaza. But the cannon fire would not halt the swarm of attackers; Santa Anna's men opened the northern gate, permitting many more Mexican soldiers to rush in. From the west, the Mexicans pried and hacked open the boarded-up openings and climbed through.

Now members of the fourth column, until then pinned down by the Texians' southern cannon, charged the south wall. Within moments, they overran the artillery position, killing the gunners and capturing their weapons. With possession of the largest gun, the Mexicans set about turning it on the Texians.

At the palisade, the riflemen, led by David Crockett, watched the battle turn. They saw no alternative: Crockett and his Tennessee boys withdrew, taking cover in the church.

Barely a half hour into the battle, the fight had been redefined, the perimeter walls lost and Texian territory reduced to two buildings. The Texians, deprived of most of their cannons, were effectively caged inside the adobe walls of the Long Barracks and the Alamo church.

THE END

Many of the Texians, now truly trapped, had no means of escape from the two-story, brick-and-adobe Long Barracks. For the moment they remained safe inside its solid walls and behind the heavy wooden doors. From windows and loopholes, the Texian sharpshooters could pick off Mexican soldiers in the plaza with impunity, forcing the attackers to take cover where they could. But the Mexicans soon pivoted the captured cannons and sent their cannonballs crashing through the adobe walls.

Once the guns turned, it was only minutes before the first of the Long Barracks doors had been blasted open. Firing as they surged through, the Mexicans met with a hail of gunfire from the Texians. "The tumult was great, the disorder frightful," according to a Mexican officer. "Different groups of soldiers were firing in all directions, on their comrades and on their officers, so that one was as likely to die by a friend's hand as by an enemy's."[13] The fight became room-by-room as the Mexicans broke down doors. "The struggle," one Mexican sergeant remembered, "was made up of a number of separate and desperate combats, often hand to hand."[14]

Even the inmates of the so-called hospital—men still recovering from wounds sustained in December or from illness—fought valiantly. Despite being confined to their beds, they shot at the attackers from where they lay. According to one Mexican sergeant, he and his soldiers rolled a small cannon into the hospital doorway and fired canister shot into the room, killing fifteen sick men.

Although, according to one Mexican sergeant, "the Texians fought like devils," in just a few more minutes, no Texians were left alive in the barracks.

Meanwhile, along the south wall, the Mexicans burst into one of the small dwellings. At first, in the near darkness, the Mexicans saw no one. Then they spied something, someone, a human form that lay motionless on a makeshift bed, mostly obscured beneath a blanket. In the heat of the bloody battle, they assumed that, out of terror, the man hid himself beneath the covers "like a woman."[15]

Then he moved. Awakening to a nightmare, Jim Bowie struggled to reach a seated position. But the attackers moved quickly toward him. Though he reached for his notorious knife, for the first time Jim Bowie's instinct for self-preservation fell short and, before he could defend himself, he was "butchered in bed."[16]

Whether his killers knew the identity of their famous victim isn't clear, but, later, one of the Mexican generals acknowledged that the troops had skewered "the perverse and boastful James Bowie" with their bayonets.[17] The end of his life had been a brutal one: Dying or perhaps already dead, his body had been raised on enemy bayonets and tossed about until his killers' uniforms were soaked with his blood.

Another fifty or sixty Texians, looking to retreat but unable to reach either the church or the barracks, had gone over the mission wall to make a run for freedom. Taking cover in a drainage trench, they ran for the Gonzales road. But Santa Anna's cavalry stood ready, stationed, as instructed, "to scout the country, to prevent the possibility of escape."[18] The skilled horsemen made short work of running down the fleeing men, and none of the defenders survived the slaughter.

Now only the church remained in Texian hands. The Mexicans once again pivoted the Alamo's biggest cannon, directing its fire upon the church, barely a hundred yards away. The piles of sandbags that protected the church facade were blasted into a cloud of sand, and Santa Anna's men shouldered through the entrance doors.

In those minutes of desperate chaos, Almeron Dickinson fell. Only Crockett and the diminished ranks of his men remained to fight on, but they no longer defended the Alamo; theirs was a matter of survival. As the enemy flooded every space in the Alamo, these last remaining defenders no longer had time to reload their muzzle-loading rifles, and there weren't enough bowie knives or bayonets to defeat Santa Anna's hundreds.

The Mexicans had their orders—none but women and children were to be spared—but the last men standing surrendered to General Castrillón. The Mexican officer respected their honorable plea for mercy, and seven men, led by David Crockett, put down their weapons, trusting the Mexican general would treat them honorably as prisoners of war.

By 6:30 A.M., a strange half silence fell as the sun rose over the horizon. The firing had ended, permitting the "groans of the wounded and the last breaths of the dying" to be heard.[19]

NINE

Bring Out the Dead

> The gallantry of the few Texans who defended the Alamo was really wondered at by the Mexican army. Even the generals were astonished at their vigorous resistance, and how dearly victory was bought.
>
> —José Francisco Ruiz

With the fight over, Santa Anna made his way across the field of battle. At a distance of a hundred yards, he saw a few scattered bodies of his soldiers. By the time he reached the Alamo's main gate, the number of dead Mexicans lying on the ground was shocking.

Inside the old mission walls, the bloodletting had been even worse. Intermingled on its central plaza were dead Mexicans in blue uniforms and Texians dressed in stained deerskin and filthy homespun.

Santa Anna, a veteran of many bloody battles, expressed no regrets. "These are the chickens," he remarked to one of his captains, dismissing the dead. "Much blood has been shed; but the battle is over. It was but a small affair."[1]

His lack of compassion extended to survivors in his own army. No hospital tents or field surgery had been readied, and the lack of adequate medical corps and supplies would, in the days and weeks to come, cost many a wounded Mexican his life.

Hearing no more than an occasional stray gunshot outside the mission—the dragoons still hunted down the last of the escapees, who hid in gullies and underbrush—Santa Anna wanted only to be able to report with finality his great victory. Before writing to his minister of war, he ordered the dead bodies of Travis, Bowie, and Crockett identified. The first two were easily found: Travis's remains rested just where he had fallen, on the northwest battery, and Bowie's body, crudely torn by bayonets, lay in a bloody heap in what had been his sickroom.

Despite his orders that no quarter be given any Texian fighter, Santa Anna discovered that David Crockett wasn't dead. When brought before him, Crockett stood tall, unwilling to grovel.

The man who'd captured him, General Castrillón, counseled generosity toward "*Coket*," whom he described as a "venerable old man."[2] But Santa Anna scolded Castrillón for sparing the Texians. "What right have you to disobey my orders? I want no prisoners."[3]

Personally affronted by Crockett's survival, the indignant Santa Anna chose mercilessness. True to his word, he ordered the immediate execution of Crockett and the handful of survivors.

After a moment of shocked hesitation—the officers engaged in the previous hour's action thought such a step dishonorable—Santa Anna's own staff officers, men who had remained out of the fight, "thrust themselves forward, in order to flatter their commander, and with swords in hand fell upon these unfortunate defenseless men just as a tiger leaps upon his prey."

Not killed in battle, but murdered, Crockett was thus among the last to die at the Alamo. At least one of the Mexicans, appalled at the dishonorable mutilation of defenseless men, turned away so as not to witness the final annihilation of the Texians.[4]

. . .

SANTA ANNA DICTATED his report, addressed to His Excellency the Secretary of War and Navy.

"Most Excellent Sir—Victory belongs to the army, which, at this very moment, 8 o'clock A.M., achieved a complete and glorious triumph that will render its memory imperishable."

Not content to claim victory, Santa Anna went on to improve upon the facts. He exaggerated the strength of the Texians, more than tripling their numbers, to make his success sound all the greater.

"Among the corpses are those of Bowie and Travis, who styled themselves colonels, and also that of Crockett," his report said. That much was true, but when he cited Mexican losses—"70 men killed and 309 wounded"—he told less than the truth.[5] The Texians had actually killed or wounded 521 Mexicans, wiping out more than a third of Santa Anna's finest fighters.

Santa Anna's claim that the victory was glorious may have fooled his superiors, but his men knew better. As one of his officers remarked, "With another victory such as this, we'll go to the devil."[6]

MRS. DICKINSON, WITNESS

Captured and watched over by an armed Mexican guard, the women and children of the Alamo huddled in a corner of the chapel. Susanna Dickinson held her terrified daughter, Angelina, to her breast. When a Mexican officer came looking for the lone Anglo woman in the Alamo, he spoke to her in English.

"Are you Mrs. Dickinson?"

Though in shock from the carnage of the preceding hour and mourning her husband, she managed to acknowledge that she was.

"If you wish to save your life," the officer commanded, "follow me."

She limped along behind him, her leg bleeding from a wound sustained when a bullet fragment ricocheted and struck her calf.

She would remember that walk the rest of her life. "As we passed through the enclosed ground in front of the church," she told an interviewer many decades later, "I saw heaps of dead and dying." One had been her friend, a man "frequently an inmate" in her home.[7] That was the great Crockett—and here he was, beside her path, mutilated but recognizable, his "peculiar cap" on the ground beside him. She had enjoyed his fiddling, and just days before, contemplating the coming battle, he had confided in the pretty, black-haired lady. As a man of the great wide open, Crockett never expected his life to end penned up like cattle. "I don't like being hemmed up," he told her.[8]

The guard escorted her to Santa Anna himself.

Despite being afraid for her life, she unexpectedly met with something like kindness. The general ordered the woman's wound dressed while the two spoke through an interpreter. As he asked her mother questions, the fifteen-month-old daughter, blithely unaware of who the dark-eyed man in the uniform was, engaged the hard-hearted general.

Utterly charmed by the pretty child who climbed onto his lap, Santa Anna decided she should be taken back to Mexico. She would be educated properly, he told her mother. He promised to provide generously for the child; she would be raised like the heir of a nobleman.

Yet even the shock of all that had happened wasn't enough to persuade Susanna Dickinson to hand over the care of all she had left in the world to the man responsible for the death of her husband. Though barely into her twenties, having lived the hard life of a frontier settler, she held her head high. She found the courage to refuse and waited to hear how Santa Anna would respond.

To her surprise, he did not react with the cruelty she'd expected. To the other women, Santa Anna gave a blanket and two silver dollars each before dismissing them.[9] But Mrs. Dickinson, who had outright rejected his larger gesture of charity, got different treatment, not violence, but a kind of psychological punishment. Summoning a servant, he ordered him to accompany Susanna Dickinson, taking Angelina with her, to carry a message to her fellow Texians.

The letter—though addressed to "the inhabitants of Texas," the true addressee should have been Sam Houston—would justify what his army had done to the "parcel of audacious adventurers" at the Alamo.[10] But the messenger herself would underscore his message. Santa Anna forced the widow of a man he had killed to do his bidding, to carry a message justifying his actions.

BURYING THE DEAD

That afternoon, Santa Anna dealt with the dead. His men collected the remains of the Mexicans killed in the battle. They would be buried in the Catholic burial ground.

For the Texians, Santa Anna had in mind only desecration.

He ordered his cavalrymen to drag the corpses of the defeated defenders away from the Alamo. Taken to the east of the town, they were piled with the remains of the Texian fighters who had attempted to make their escape on the Gonzales road.

The mayor of San Antonio led a company of dragoons to collect firewood and dry branches from nearby stands of trees. When they returned, the first of the Anglo dead had been dragged into a heap; the freshly collected mesquite and cottonwood was piled on top. Another layer of the dead came next and, on the return of the dragoons with a second load of wood, the pile grew higher as more fuel was added. By the time the job was done, there were three large bonfires containing layers of wood and some sixty bodies each.

At five o'clock that evening the Mexicans lit the funeral pyres. By Mayor Ruiz's count, "the men burnt numbered one hundred and eighty-two. I was an eyewitness."[11]

As fire blazed that evening, a small company of cavalrymen escorted Susanna and Angelina, along with the servant, out of San Antonio. From her seat on a mule, Mrs. Dickinson left the ruin of the Alamo behind. The little party passed the pyres and the unmistakable smell of burning flesh. In the wan light of the setting sun, vultures circled overhead.

TEN

Houston Hears the News

The capture of the Alamo . . . gave us a prodigious moral prestige. . . . The attainment of our goal [is] now almost certain.

—General Antonio López de Santa Anna

In the year 1836, news traveled across Texas only as quickly as an express rider could carry it. That meant Colonel Travis's appeal for help, written on Thursday, March 3, arrived in Washington-on-the-Brazos three days later. The courier interrupted breakfast in the newly designated capital on the same Sunday morning that the Alamo had awakened to an overwhelming assault.

Though the new government of Texas had adjourned until Monday, a special session was immediately called to order to hear what the chair called "a communication of the most important character ever received by any assembly of men."[1]

Travis's letter was read aloud. "At least two hundred shells have fallen inside of our works. . . . The spirits of my men are still high. . . . We have contended for ten days against an enemy whose numbers are variously estimated from fifteen hundred to six thousand men. . . . I look to the colonies alone for aid . . . unless it arrives soon, I shall have to fight the enemy on its own terms. . . . Our supply of ammunition is limited."[2]

No one in the room knew these lines had been written by a man now dead. But his closing words—*"God and Texas—Victory or Death"*—inspired delegate Robert Potter to get to his feet. Another second-chance man—a North Carolinian by birth and former U.S. congressman (he had fled west after castrating two men he suspected of consorting with his wife)—Potter made a motion that "the Convention do immediately adjourn, arm, and march to the relief of the Alamo."[3]

The new nation's commander in chief of the Armies of the Republic, Sam Houston, rose to disagree. Houston's instincts told him that this moment meant everything: "The next movement made in the Convention," he believed, "would be likely to decide the fate of Texas."

Major General Houston had the floor and, with all eyes on him, he denounced the idea as "madness, worse than treason." Having just declared Texas independent, he argued, if the convention went to war before setting up a structure for the new country, they would set themselves up for disaster. "There must be a government, and it must have organic form," he argued; "without it, they would be nothing but outlaws, and could hope neither for the sympathy nor respect of mankind."

At his eloquent best, Houston spoke for an hour—and made the men around him a promise. The delegates should "feel no alarm," he advised. He pledged that he himself would head to Gonzales to rally the militia, that he would defend Texas, and that the enemy would have to march over his "dead body."[4] If Santa Anna wanted to destroy rebel Texas, Houston saw his job as ensuring it survived.

One hour later, dressed in a Cherokee coat, he mounted his horse, a saber hanging at one side, a flintlock pistol jammed into his belt on the other. Together with his aide-de-camp and three volunteers, Houston headed out on the open prairie. Though he was a general without an army, the fight had just become Sam Houston's.

When General Houston arrived in Gonzales, at four o'clock on the afternoon of March 11, he found 374 men, many without guns or ammunition; two usable cannons; and rations for just two days. Before dark the news got worse: Two Mexicans appeared telling a terrible tale, reporting the Alamo captured, its defenders all dead.

Wanting to avoid panic in the town, Houston publicly dismissed the report and took the two men into custody. But the word had already spread and, on hearing of the slaughter, twenty volunteers deserted. To quell the alarm, Houston ordered his officers to mix with the volunteers and pass the word that the two Mexicans were spies.

Privately he believed the story to be true. The day before, drawing on his Cherokee training, he had paused to put his ear to the ground on the way to Gonzales. He expected to hear the reverberation of guns, which for days had been "a dull rumbling rumor . . . booming over the prairie like distant thunder." When he rose from the ground, Houston had heard "not the faintest murmur" from the hard-packed prairie soil.[5]

He wrote immediately to Colonel Fannin; if the Alamo was gone, then the only other organized military force of any size was Fannin's Goliad garrison. Informing Fannin of the reported fate of the Alamo, Houston admitted he worried the "melancholy [report]" was true. He ordered Fannin to retreat, to move his force to the town of Victoria.[6]

Houston, on the morning of March 13, dispatched the reliable Deaf Smith, who knew the territory well, to "proceed within sight" of San Antonio. He wanted the facts of what had happened at the Alamo, and Smith, along with Henry Karnes, promised Houston they could make it to San Antonio and back in three days.[7]

. . .

Only hours were required. Returning at twilight, the entourage led by Deaf Smith made a strange sight emerging from the darkness. He rode in with a child in his arms, a woman riding alongside.

Just twenty miles west of Gonzales, Smith had met up with Mrs. Dickinson; she was, in Houston's words, a "stricken and bereaved messenger." Taken to his private tent, where Houston took her hand, she recounted "her fearful narrative of the butchering and burning." The earlier reports about the "dark tragedy" at the Alamo were true.[8] Houston himself "wept like a child" as he listened to Mrs. Dickinson's narrative.[9]

To the people of Gonzales, the news hit very close to home. Two weeks before, thirty-two village men and boys had gone to the Alamo's aid; this report of their loss left twenty widows keening and many children fatherless. As one of Smith's fellow scouts reported, "Here the public and private grief was alike heavy; it sunk deep into the heart of the rudest soldier."[10]

Santa Anna had succeeded in striking fear in the hearts of those who opposed him. But he had also provoked rage. Not just Texians, but Americans in the states were appalled at the way Mexico had treated not just men fighting for liberty, but also women and children. Many of the dead had been imperfect, yet by dying they became heroes. And people who loved freedom wanted their deaths avenged.

Santa Anna had overplayed his hand. His brutality at the Alamo hadn't left Texians shaking in their boots; instead of intimidating the population of Tejas, the news brought to a boil anger and outrage even in Texians reluctant to declare for revolution. He had provided a cause that would unite the undisciplined troops, and had even caused more Americans to flow to the aid of the Texians.

He hadn't put out a fire: He had lit one.

But the fire was going to take some time to reach him, and in the meantime there was more bad news for more than the people of Gonzales. Mrs. Dickinson reported that five thousand men marched toward them. According to very recent "disagreeable intelligence," Goliad was a primary target of the large Mexican force crossing the Rio Grande. Santa Anna aimed to live up to his sworn promise "to *Take Texas or lose Mexico.*"[11]

With the Alamo no longer an obstacle in Santa Anna's path, Houston believed the Army of Texas had no choice: They would not march forward to engage the enemy but would retreat, staying alive to fight another day. Fannin's men at Goliad would have to fend for themselves.

ELEVEN

Fort Defiance

[Fannin] is an ill-fated man.

—Sam Houston to Thomas J. Rusk, March 23, 1836

On Saturday, March 12, James Fannin, commander of Goliad, received General Sam Houston's order to withdraw. The young colonel had a mixed past, having come to Texas to escape debts and the shame of flunking out of West Point. But he wanted to redeem himself, and after his success with Bowie at Concepción, he had worked hard to get what he called this "post of danger."[1] To Fannin, this reversal of plans came as a surprise.

Only a month before, he'd been instructed to fortify Goliad against the Mexicans and, at first, all had gone well. He and his men shored up the defenses of the old Spanish fort, built on the highest hill in the vicinity. Three-foot-thick stone walls, standing eight to ten feet in height, enclosed some three and a half acres that held a church, a barracks, and a handful of other buildings. They rebuilt the fort's gate and secured its water supply. The Mexicans had called it La Bahía, but the Texians renamed it Fort Defiance, and here Fannin martialed the men who had marched from all over the United States to fight for Texas, happy to consider himself the main obstacle to the Mexicans.

But things had gone wrong, too. First, there had been the indecision at helping the men trapped in the Alamo. When Travis had called for help ("In this extremity, we hope you will send us all the men you can spare promptly"), Fannin's immediate instinct had been to go to the rescue of his brothers-in-arms.[2] Then the march to San Antonio had ended prematurely, just one day in, with wagon failures and a vote by

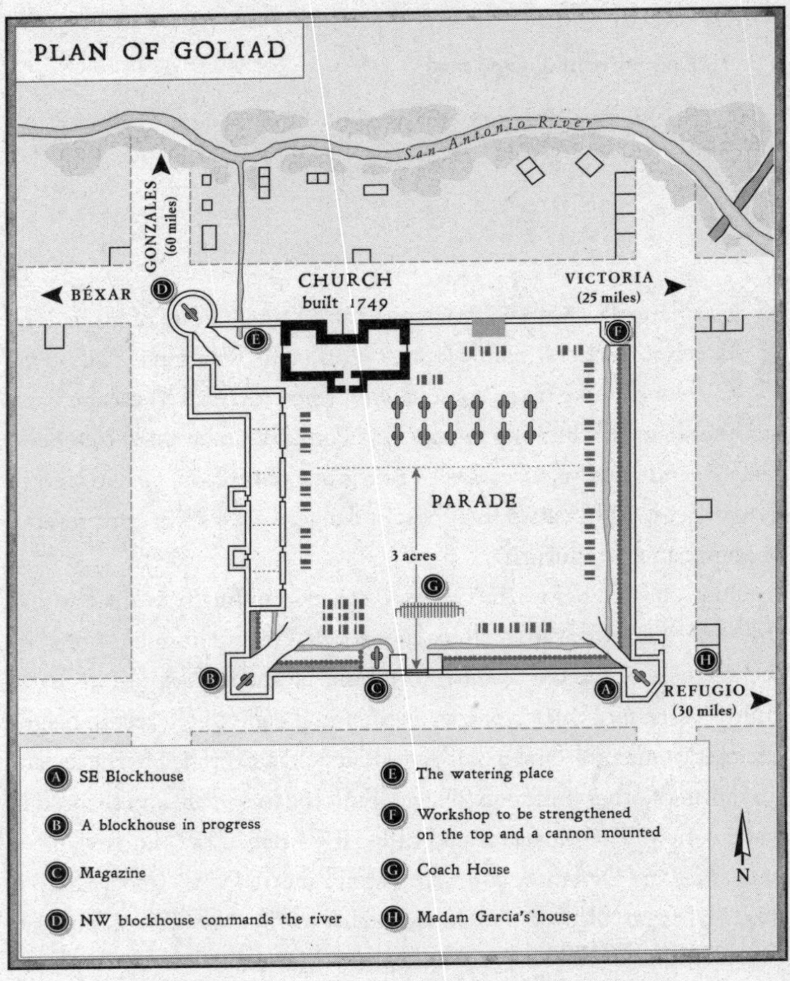

Fannin's officers to abandon the mission. They had returned to Fort Defiance in the freezing rain, leaving Travis and his men to prepare to fight their own battle.

Soon after, Fannin began to run out of supplies. He spent many hours writing long letters to the new government. Like Travis, he begged for promised supplies. He reported his men were hungry and ill clothed, but got little response. He had difficulties disciplining his men—some refused to obey him. But he put the best face on things when he wrote to his sometime business partner, on the last day of February, immediately after the aborted rescue trip to the Alamo. "I will never give up the ship," he wrote. "If I am whipped, it will be *well done*—and you may never expect to see me. . . . I am too mad . . . to do—any thing but fight."[3]

Now, as Fannin read Houston's orders—and as Mexican general Urrea and his army approached—he harbored doubts. Humbled and now hesitant, Fannin wondered if perhaps his strengths "[do] not constitute me a commander."[4] The man who had sworn never to leave his post was now ready to retreat, but there was a practical obstacle.

RETREAT

Houston expected him to move, but the previous day, Fannin had sent a small force of two dozen men, along with most of Fort Defiance's wagons, to Refugio, a village thirty miles away, to help evacuate settlers before the Mexicans arrived. Concerned for his men and settlers, Fannin decided the soldiers at Goliad would have to wait for the party's return.

Then two more couriers arrived from Gonzales. Exhausted from their thirty-hour ride, they handed over another letter from Sam Houston, informing Fannin that the Alamo had fallen.

Reading that "the bodies of the Americans were burned after the massacre" was a body blow.[5] He had failed to help Travis, Crockett, Bowie, and the rest. He had done nothing and now some of Texas's greatest fighters were dead.

Just after midnight on Sunday morning, March 13, still another messenger interrupted the quiet night, this one from Refugio. He brought more bad news: The wagons full of retreating settlers had run into Urrea's advance cavalry. Though they'd managed to escape capture and take shelter in an old church, they were trapped and desperately needed reinforcements. Before daylight, at Fannin's order, reinforcements galloped south to help.

They did their job well, driving off the outnumbered Mexicans by three o'clock that afternoon. But Fannin, back at Fort Defiance, could only watch the horizon, seeing no messenger with news of his troops' fate. And a second travel day was lost, one that might have been spent obeying Houston's orders to move what had become a key part of his army out of harm's way.

On Monday, Fannin sent a scout to Refugio to learn the fate of the men he'd sent. What he couldn't know was that, defying Fannin's order to return, one of his officers had chosen to attack a nearby encampment of Spanish settlers rumored to be spies. All Fannin knew was that his courier did not return and, with the setting sun, three days had passed since the order to retreat.

Tuesday brought no news so, on Wednesday, now four days after receiving Houston's order, Fannin sent one last messenger, this one a Captain Frazer, who pledged that, given "a good horse . . . if alive, [I will] return in twenty-four hours, with intelligence." True to his word, Captain Frazer reappeared at four o'clock the following day—with the worst news possible. Their powder soaked by an attempt to cross the river, a contingent of Fannin's men had surrendered. The Mexicans, ignoring the rules of war, did as they had at the Alamo, massacring the captives on the open prairie.

In the absence of commanding general Houston, Fannin held a council with his officers. They had no clear sense of their enemy—were they facing two hundred or four hundred or a thousand men? Now that their pointless wait for the return of the others was over, they decided the best course was to evacuate Fort Defiance the next day, an action, in looking back, he probably should have taken in the first place.

But, as they prepared to head out the next morning, Fannin delayed yet again. After spotting a Mexican cavalry patrol, a cat-and-mouse fight unfolded with Texians and Mexicans playing a deadly and time-consuming game of pursuit-and-retreat. The result was another day lost.

Finally, at nine o'clock on Saturday, March 19, after a full week's delay in following orders, a line of three hundred troops marched out of Fort Defiance. Oxen pulled heavily loaded wagons and carts carrying baggage and the sick, as well as a half dozen cannons, a brass howitzer, and hundreds of spare muskets. As a parting gesture, the Texians put the torch to the town, leaving "the half-destroyed buildings of the fort, still overhung with dark clouds of smoke from the smouldering flames."[6]

RETREAT FROM GOLIAD

The San Antonio River presented the first obstacle to the fleeing Texians. The horsemen and infantry crossed the shallow water easily. But some of the draft animals balked at climbing the muddy east bank, and one of the largest of the cannons tumbled into the river.

The Alabama Red Rovers in the vanguard turned back. Putting down their guns, they waded into the water; putting their shoulders to the wheels, they helped push the rest of the cannons up the steep and slippery slope. But forward progress slowed to a halt and the men's determination flagged—just as had happened on the aborted mission to the Alamo weeks earlier.

Despite the delay, advance scouts reported that the due-east escape route was still clear. General Urrea apparently remained unaware of the Texian evacuation. On clearing the river, the Texians trudged on. But men and officers alike recognized that the large quantities of goods they carried held them back and began to jettison their supplies. "Before we had gone half a mile," reported one of the New Orleans Greys, "our track was marked by objects of various kinds scattered about the road, and several carts had broken down or been left behind."[7]

Six miles on, Colonel Fannin decided to rest the oxen, which showed signs of becoming "wild and contrary."[8] While the animals grazed on a patch of green grass, the men rested—and the officers argued.

Several took exception to Fannin's order to halt the line of march in the middle of open prairie. Coleto Creek lay less than five miles away, its banks lined with trees, which offered a defensive situation quite like that at Concepción. *Better there than here,* some thought. *We should press on.* One Alabama captain, Jack Shackelford, argued vehemently for "the necessity of getting under the *protection of timber*" as soon as possible.[9] But Fannin rejected Shackelford's pleas. Having prevailed once in a fight with the Mexicans, he clung to the desperate belief that he could beat them again. Shackelford was overruled, and an hour elapsed before the march resumed at one o'clock.

Fannin's little army crossed another stream, the Manahuilla Creek, and three miles further on, with the tree line at Coleto Creek now in plain view, several soldiers in the rear guard noticed "something that resembled a man on horseback."

When the silhouette remained motionless, the scouts decided the object "must be a tree or some other inanimate object."[10]

Some minutes later, they squinted hard at a barely distinguishable thin black line along the horizon. Again the lookouts decided there was nothing to fear, maybe just a herd of cattle. But soon a black mass, growing larger by the moment, took on the unmistakable shape of men on horseback. It was Urrea's cavalry.

Fannin reacted immediately, ordering artillerymen with a six-pound cannon to move to the rear of the column and fire on what the Texians could now see were two companies of Mexican cavalry and one of infantry. The cannon fire fell short, and Fannin, convinced the Mexicans planned only to skirmish and plunder the Texian supplies, ordered his men to keep marching toward the cover offered by the wooded riverbank, now less than two miles ahead. As ordered, the Texians "marched onward, cool and deliberately," so as not to spook the oxen.[11]

Once again, however—this time for the last time—an equipment failure brought Fannin's column to a standstill. An ammunition cart broke down, and with no time for repairs, Fannin saw no alternative. The fight would have to happen here.

He tried to make the best of a bad situation, and he ordered his men to establish a perimeter. Unable to move to higher ground, the Texians occupied a small depression, several feet lower in altitude than the surrounding prairie. Stands of trees were within sight but unreachable.

The Texian defense took the shape of a hollow square. Needing cover, they arranged piles of cargo and the wagons around its perimeter, then shot some of the oxen, using the carcasses to fill some of the gaps in an improvised breastwork. Fannin had cannons positioned in the corners of the square, manned by four artillery companies. They finished setting up their improvised defense not a moment too soon; by this time a second Mexican force was in sight to the north, maneuvering into a position to prevent the Texians from reaching the creek.

Left outside the defenses were several hospital wagons full of wounded. Frightened by the oncoming army, Mexican wagon drivers, who had been working for the Texians, had abandoned their carts and headed for the Mexican line, leaving the frightened steers to run where they would. Now the wagons were stranded, about fifty yards outside the defensive square, vulnerable to the approaching Mexicans.

There was no time to bring them back, but one of the orderlies assigned to caring for the wounded, Abel Morgan, refused to abandon them. He got himself a musket from a munitions wagon inside the defensive square and sprinted back to his wagon, along with four other volunteers. They positioned themselves to defend the wounded in the fight that, everyone knew, was only minutes away.

In the moments before the battle began, the Texians gazed out on an intimidating array of the enemy, which now virtually surrounded their improvised defensive position. The rules of engagement had changed in one major way: With many of their oxen now dead, the Texians were going nowhere. They had no choice but to make their stand.

THE BATTLE OF THE PRAIRIE

As the Mexican army approached, Colonel Fannin ordered his troops to hold their fire. He didn't want to hear the report of a Texian rifle until the enemy was in point-blank range—there was no ammunition to spare.

The first of General Urrea's men moved on what had been the front of the advancing Texian column. Mexican cavalrymen, now dismounted, marched forward and, from a distance of some two hundred yards, unleashed their first volley. No men fell, but the Mexicans continued to advance. When their second volley went "whizzing over our heads," Captain Shackelford ordered his men to sit down for cover. The third volley drew blood, with several Texians hit by musket balls.

Fannin issued "orders . . . in a calm and decided manner," despite

Serving under General Andrew Jackson at the Battle at Horseshoe Bend in 1814, Sam Houston famously ordered another officer to pull a Creek arrow from his thigh. Jackson's army won the battle, but hundreds of lives were lost—and Houston paid a high price for his drive to win.

General Andrew Jackson was a mentor and father figure to young Houston. Even after Jackson's victory at New Orleans ended America's years-long war with Britain, he remained a mentor to Houston, encouraging him in his quest for Texas.

When President Thomas Jefferson made the Louisiana Purchase in 1803, he thought Texas was part of the deal. He later predicted, "The province of Te[x]as will be the richest state of our Union."

John Quincy Adams was the man who, in Andrew Jackson's judgment, gave away Texas.

Sam Houston spent some of his childhood years with the Cherokee nation, and he found refuge with them again as an adult when he fell from grace in Washington. To his Indian friends, he was known by the name Co-lon-neh ("the Raven"), and he is shown here wearing a turban after the Cherokee custom.

When Houston first arrived in Texas in the hopes of winning it for America, he knew he had to meet Stephen F. Austin, the "Father of Texas." In this mural, which is now unfortunately destroyed, Austin is shown distributing land deeds to new, ambitious Texas settlers from the United States.

William Howard painted Stephen F. Austin, in 1833, as a settler, Empresario, hunter, and statesman. The open book at Austin's feet is a copy of the Law of Mexico.

Mexican general Antonio Lópes de Santa Anna liked to be thought of as the "Napoleon of the West," and his attempt to consolidate his power once he rose to prominence in Mexico was partially responsible for the Texians' rebellion.

General Martín Perfecto de Cos, as pictured in this contemporary woodcut, was one of the first of Santa Anna's commanders to attempt to suppress the Texian rebels. After hearing that Santa Anna had dispatched Cos and his army of 500 to march along the San Antonio River to preempt Texian resistance, Stephen Austin declared "war in full."

The Texas Revolution's "Lexington and Concord" moment took place at Gonzales, as pictured here in a modern reimagining. During this first battle of the Texas Revolution, the Texian army collected the few guns they had and hung a six-foot flag large enough to be seen from enemy lines that read, "COME AND TAKE IT." Even though outnumbered and outgunned, the Texians won their first victory over the Mexicans at Gonzales.

A major landholder and a man with nearly the status of Stephen Austin, brave Ben Milam had a long history in Texas. When he heard that the Texian rebellion had finally begun, "his heart was full" at the thought of a band of volunteers working together to fight off the Mexicans. His life ended prematurely at the Siege of San Antonio.

Like Houston, James Bowie was a "second chance man" who came to Texas searching for a new life. Known for his knife-fighting and alligator-riding abilities, Bowie led his men to victory at Concepción, but perished at the Battle of the Alamo.

William Barrett Travis, commander of the Alamo, pictured here as sketched by fellow soldier Wiley Martin in December 1835, also perished at the Battle of the Alamo—after pledging to fight until the very end.

Known as "Deaf," Erastus Smith was a resident of San Antonio before proving invaluable to Sam Houston as a spy and messenger. After he became president of Texas, Houston acknowledged Smith's contribution, commissioning T. Jefferson Wright to paint this portrait.

For Colonel James W. Fannin, a West Point dropout, Texas held the promise of a new life—one where he could pay off his debts and renew his reputation. As commander at Goliad, he displayed his bravery and conviction for the cause of Texian independence—but also a lack of decisiveness that would have a deadly cost. Here, Fannin poses for a portrait that was likely painted during his days at West Point.

Like Houston, Bowie, and Fannin, David Crockett came to Texas looking for a second chance. The former Congressman, known for his back-country character and for his tall tales, was among those killed at the Alamo.

Despite Houston's wishes, a small crew of Texians attempted to defend San Antonio from Santa Anna's army of 3,500. The odds were against them, but they agreed to fight to the death—a fight that later would be memorialized by many artists.

Perhaps the best of the Mexican generals—unlike Santa Anna and Cos, he lost none of his battles in Tejas—José de Urrea was the victor at the Battle of Coleto, the fight that led to the execution of the hundreds captured at Goliad.

Even though they were far outnumbered by Santa Anna's army, the Texians were not intimidated. When they saw the Mexicans approaching, they immediately fired their biggest cannon, an eighteen-pounder, with a great, resounding boom. This image of the fight at the Alamo suggests something of the furor of the battle.

During the massacre, Santa Anna employed Napoleon's tactics. While his army overwhelmed the Texians in manpower and artillery and surrounded the Alamo, Santa Anna remained an observer. Even with Colonel Travis dead and Bowie weak with disease trapped inside the mission, the Texians fought until the end. The mythologizing of the Alamo has resulted in many later images like this one, which pictures the Alamo in flames. The artist in this case took many liberties, among them a burning building that little resembles the Alamo as it looked in 1836.

Susanna, the young wife—and widow—of Almeron Dickinson was among the few Texian survivors of the Alamo Massacre. Wounded during the battle, she refused Santa Anna's offer to take her and her daughter back to Mexico and instead was tasked with carrying a message from Santa Anna to the Texians. Here, she's pictured late in life.

Not long after the massacre at the Alamo, General Urrea's army perpetrated another massacre of Texians at Goliad. After promising their safety, Urrea's men marched the unsuspecting Texian prisoners from Goliad to their execution.

Not long after the slaughter of his men, Goliad commander James Fannin faced a Mexican firing squad.

In the weeks leading up to the final battle of America's fight for Texas, Houston employed a strategy of retreat—nearly losing the trust of his army. The strategy kept the Texian army safe until they attacked Santa Anna's army in the Battle of San Jacinto.

Houston delivered the most rousing speech of his lifetime before the Battle of San Jacinto, declaring: "We will meet the enemy. Some of us may be killed and must be killed; but soldiers, remember the Alamo*, the Alamo, the Alamo*!"

During the battle, Houston twice had his horse shot out from under him, as depicted in this detail from McArdle's *Battle of San Jacinto*. The second time, Houston himself was also shot, taking a musket ball to his ankle.

After the defeat of the Mexicans in just eighteen minutes and their subsequent capture, Houston, shown here nursing his wounded leg, negotiated terms of surrender in the shade of a tree hung with Spanish moss.

A late-in-life photograph of Santa Anna, who survived his defeat at San Jacinto to take power again (and again) in Mexican politics. He lived to age eighty.

A Mathew Brady photograph of the sixty-eight-year-old Houston. By 1861, he had once again become a national figure, having served in the U.S. Senate after his short-lived nation became the state of Texas. A city had been named for him, too. He died in Huntsville, Texas, in 1863.

Few men remained in the ranks of the Old Texian Veterans when, in 1906, they gathered at Goliad to commemorate the seventieth anniversary of the battle. Just six survivors attended what would be the last reunion.

the tension.[12] As he stood just behind the front line, reminding his men to hold their fire, he narrowly missed death. A musket ball blasted away the hammer of his rifle, disabling the gun but leaving him unhurt.

At a distance of a hundred yards, the enemy halted to reload their guns. Fannin saw his moment: At last, he ordered his men to open fire.

Despite a hail of bullets, balls, and cannonballs, the Mexicans, some of whom had fought at the Alamo, charged. With their officers prodding and directing, they advanced in the face of the musketry and the crack of the Texian rifles. Many Mexicans fell, dead and wounded, but to the Texians, uncertain of how many attackers there were—some thought five hundred, others a thousand or more—the tide of Mexicans never seemed to stop.

The firing took a toll on the Texian defenders, too. A ball struck Fannin in the thigh; though it missed the bone, it opened a serious flesh wound. But he remained standing, issuing orders.

To the rear, a second front opened when an even larger body of Mexican infantry swarmed forward to fire their first volley. Once the smoke cleared, the Texians defending the rear fired back with both rifles and cannons, "mowing [the enemy] down with tremendous slaughter."[13] The Mexican infantrymen left standing went down on their bellies, rising only to shoot at—and be shot at by—the defender's marksmen.

The orderly Abel Morgan found himself in the middle of the intense fight "where balls were whizzing about like bees swarming." Of the four men who'd joined him at the hospital wagons, one took a musket to the skull; it opened a hole in the man's head but didn't kill him on the spot; he handed his rifle to Morgan. Another rifleman went down, a bone in his upper leg smashed by a musket ball. One of the doctors, Joseph Barnard, came from inside Fannin's square to help defend the hospital wagons, and with his help the men held off the Mexicans.

A cavalry charge to the Texians' rear came next. More than two hundred strong, the Mexicans raced forward, lances gleaming, issuing war cries as they came. At a distance of sixty yards, they met with a barrage of rifle fire. Two loads of canister fire ripped into their ranks, and the survivors who could retreated. It would be the last cavalry charge of the day. "Many were the Mexicans I saw leave their horses that day," remembered one Texian, "who never were to mount them again."[14]

But the Texians couldn't maintain their fire. Mexican sharpshooters had targeted the artillerymen, and many lay dead or wounded. The cannons grew overheated; with no source of water to cool and swab them, their touchholes clogged. The artillery gradually went silent, leaving the Texians to rely on muskets and rifles alone.

The Mexicans made repeated charges; in the face of Texian gunfire, still doing damage without the cannons, they retreated each time. Only when darkness began to fall, more than two hours into the fighting, did the firing cease. The Mexicans withdrew, making camp in the trees at Coleto Creek a mile away.

Men and horses, wounded and dead, lay on a battlefield littered with abandoned guns and other weapons. The outmanned Texians, even without natural cover, had made the Mexicans pay dearly.

SURRENDER

With the quieting of the guns, the terrible aftersounds of battle grew audible, with the groans of the dying accompanying the cries of the wounded calling for water. There was no water to be had in the middle of the prairie, and, as one doctor reported of the injured, their "misery was greatly aggravated" by the lack of water.[15] Then the word went around there was no food. In the rush to render Goliad unusable, the food supplies had accidentally been burned in Fort Defiance.

The wounded Fannin, barely able to stand, took the counsel of his officers. There were nine Texians dead and more than fifty wounded.

Many of the oxen had wandered off and others shot by Texians and Mexicans. There were simply too few teams to transport the wounded disabled by their injuries. That made a full retreat impossible.

One option called for abandoning the wounded, spiking the guns, and taking the fight directly to the Mexican line, hoping to break through, find cover in the woods beyond, and eventually gain the road to Victoria. "Better to sacrifice a part than the whole," the argument went, better to avoid "plac[ing] ourselves at the mercy of a foe in whose honour and humanity no trust could be reposed."[16] The massacre at the Alamo taught them that.

But Fannin and most of his officers rejected the desperate plan. They refused to leave the wounded, men whose lives might be saved; if left behind, he was certain, they would face only death by bayonet. Instead, they decided, the Texians would dig in and fight on.

Fannin ordered his men to make a trench around the perimeter, and for hours men wielding shovels worked to dig a two-foot-deep ditch around the one-acre Texian camp. The carts and more animal carcasses were rearranged to provide better cover. And then the men attempted to sleep, though the night was cold, the blankets few.

The long and starless night also offered the Mexicans cover, and they could be heard retrieving the dead and wounded; their casualties far exceeded Texian losses. But the Mexicans also busied themselves in other ways. They peppered the Texian camp with occasional sniper shot from what seemed like every direction. Buglers accompanying patrols played Mexican battle songs to disrupt the sleep—and the nerves—of the Texians. General Urrea wanted to rattle his enemy.

At daylight, the Mexicans presented a new and impressive military front. Reinforcements had arrived, bringing with them two four-pound cannons and a howitzer. The artillery now stood poised, ready to fire, two hundred yards away between the Texians and the timberline, fronting a long line of Mexican troops. Fannin and his men had known they were greatly outnumbered, but this display led some to estimate the disparity was seven to one, or more, now that the Texians' effective force had been reduced to some two hundred men.

At seven o'clock the Mexican cannons roared, sending cannonballs arcing toward the Texian camp. But the firing stopped as suddenly as it had begun and, during the quiet that followed, the Mexicans did not charge. Instead, they raised a white flag, indicating not surrender, but a request for parley.

The Texians responded with a white flag of their own.

Despite his painful leg wound, Fannin limped to a midpoint on the empty prairie, accompanied by two officers. Met by three of Urrea's officers, the Texian colonel listened to their terms of surrender. The Mexicans promised the lives of the Texians would be spared, and that those who surrendered would be treated in all respects as prisoners of war consistent with the practice of civilized nations. The victors further promised to return the wounded to Goliad, where they would be properly tended, and the healthy prisoners would, in eight days, be permitted to sail from a nearby port back to the United States. In return, the Texians must lay down their guns and promise not to raise arms against Mexico in future.[17]

Houston was too far away to consult, but Fannin, his officers, and his men saw little alternative: They accepted Urrea's terms. In the face of annihilation, they opted for what they understood would be survival.

RETREAT UNDER GUARD

At first, the Mexicans remained true to their word. That afternoon—the date was March 20—they marched the Texian prisoners who were well enough to walk back to Goliad, where they arrived shortly after sunset.

At Fort Defiance, the Texian force was confined to the church.

There wasn't enough room in the small space for the hundreds of men, many of them wounded, to lie down. They huddled together, with armed Mexican guards occupying the center of the church that had become a prison.

The next day, carts ferried more wounded, including Colonel Fannin, from the field of battle back to Goliad. Meanwhile, the men shut up in the church received no food or water.

On Wednesday, the prisoners were permitted to leave their cramped quarters to sleep outdoors, and the Mexicans moved their own wounded men into the shelter of the church. The men breathed a sigh of relief in the open air and were cheered to hear that Colonel Fannin had been sent to the port of Copano to charter a schooner, the *William and Francis*, for their return.

While Fannin was gone, the Mexicans marched in more prisoners. Some of those who had gone to Refugio had been captured after their attempt to aid the settlers. The prisoner head count now exceeded four hundred men.

When he returned on Saturday, Fannin's good spirits cheered the men. He expressed confidence in their imminent release. Although the *William and Francis* had sailed, he expected another ship would soon be found to carry them to New Orleans.

On the Mexican side, however, a different end of the drama at Goliad was being discussed. General Urrea respected Fannin. He recognized that the Texians had surrendered because they trusted him; "under any other circumstances they would have sold their lives dearly, fighting to the last." Despite being under orders to take no prisoners, he had done so, and now had written to Santa Anna, seeking to use "my influence with the general-in-chief to save them if possible, from being butchered, particularly Fannin."[18]

It seems Santa Anna was not persuaded. On the morning of March 27, the eighth day of captivity, a Mexican officer summoned two of the

Texian doctors to his tent, pleasantly located in a peach orchard several hundred yards from the fort. "He was very serious and grave in countenance," one of the doctors later wrote, "but we took little notice of it at that time."[19] His purpose unclear, the officer left the doctors to wait, though they wished to get back to their patients in the fortress.

While the doctors waited in puzzlement, the Mexican soldiers, acting under orders from Santa Anna, divided the prisoners into three companies and marched them out of the fort in different directions. Reassured by rumors that a ship awaited them and they were being evacuated for the coast, some of the men departed Fort Defiance singing "Home Sweet Home," assuming they were going to freedom.

Flanked on both sides by armed soldiers, the unsuspecting Texians marched perhaps a half mile before being ordered to halt. The Mexicans then formed a line across from them, revealing themselves to be a long and efficient firing squad.

Before the Texians could react, the soldiers raised their rifles and muskets and shot their prisoners at short range. Mexican lancers and infantrymen armed with bayonets pursued any Texians who managed to survive the gunfire to turn and run.

Back at the fort, Colonel Fannin was imprisoned in a small room inside the church. He heard the executioners' volleys and was told that he, too, would be shot. His captors took him into the church courtyard, assisting him in this final walk, as the wound in his right thigh left him lame. Knowing he would soon die, he handed over his watch to the officer in charge, asking that, in return, his body might be buried. He gave the officer all the money he had and asked that the executioners not "place their muskets so near as to scorch his face with powder." The officer, in broken English, promised that Fannin's remains would be interred "with all necessary formalities."

Seated on a chair because of his leg wound, his own handkerchief covering his eyes, Fannin unbuttoned his shirt, accepting his fate. Yet, once again, the Mexicans broke their word. The firing squad shot him from a distance of two feet, and Fannin's remains were unceremoniously added to a funeral pyre with other Texians.[20]

Two dozen Texians lived, among them orderlies and doctors the Mexicans needed to care for their wounded and a few carpenters and other artisans. Some survived thanks to the intervention of a Mexican woman, Francita Alavez. The wife of a cavalry captain, she used her influence—and the unspoken approval of some Mexican officers disgusted at the needless slaughter of the Texian prisoners—to save some of the soldiers. Having secured their release the previous night, she kept them hidden.[21] Alavez would be remembered as the Angel of Goliad: As one survivor put it, "Her name deserves to be recorded in letters of gold."[22] But more than four hundred men had been murdered in cold blood.

The fortress that was Goliad now belonged to Santa Anna's army. Another atrocity had been committed in the name of El Presidente. And the ranks of Sam Houston's already small army had just become significantly smaller.

TWELVE

The Texian Exodus

> There was not a man in the Alamo but what, in his death, honored the proud name of an American.
>
> Let the men of Texas avenge their deaths.
>
> —Sam Houston to James Collinsworth, March 17, 1836

After he had issued his orders to Fannin, Sam Houston, then in Gonzales some sixty miles north, worried and wondered. "I am fearful Goliad is besieged by the enemy," he confided to a fellow officer.[1] It would be weeks before he learned of Fannin's fate, and in the meantime, more immediate worries occupied his mind.

In mid-March, with the Alamo gone and the status of Fannin and his men uncertain, Houston understood that the survival of the republic depended on the few men he still had at his command. When Mrs. Dickinson told him of the fall of the Alamo, she warned that as many as *five thousand* Mexican troops were on the march; with a force of less than a tenth that size, there was no way the Texians, at least for the moment, could afford to face down the enemy. In short, Houston and his troops needed to get out of the reach of Santa Anna's army. For the moment, at least, there was only one wise strategy: Retreat.

No time could be wasted. The army would travel light, he decreed, telling his troops to take only what they could carry on their persons. He had the men sink two unwieldy cannons—his only artillery—in the Guadalupe River. Extra clothing and supplies were ordered left behind.

Left without army protection, the civilians had no choice but to retreat, too. Knowing the Mexicans could not be trusted not to punish civilians, Houston ordered that most of the army's baggage wagons and oxen be given to the citizens of the town to aid in their escape.

The caravan of troops and tagalong civilians, including women and children, was on the march by midnight on Wednesday, March 16. They kept moving through the night; not until near morning did Houston order a halt for an hour's rest. As his men ate breakfast, they heard explosions from the direction of Gonzales.

Deaf Smith, along with red-headed Captain Henry Karnes and a handful of other men, had been instructed by Houston that "not a roof large enough to shelter a Mexican's head was to be left, [along] with everything else that could be of any service to the enemy." Staying behind, Smith and his men had placed canisters of gunpowder in the houses before lighting the town on fire.

All of Texas was at stake and Houston didn't want to leave *anything* that would be of use to Santa Anna.

Marching toward the Colorado River, which he wanted to put between his army and the Mexicans, General Houston worked hard to keep morale up. He made sure the men saw him, riding slowly from the front to the rear of the column, wagging his forefinger as he went, counting his troops. On the way to the rear of the column, he was heard to say, "We are the rise of eight hundred strong, and with a good position can whip ten to one of the enemy."[2]

By sundown on March 17, the caravan reached the Colorado, and the Army of Texas camped at Burnham Crossing. As the moon rose,

Houston sat before a flickering fire. He held a knife in one hand, an oak stick in the other, nervously whittling and talking quietly with an aide, George Washington Hockley, a friend from Tennessee days.

When he had let his head count be overheard, Houston had exaggerated; his numbers and his confident words, he hoped, would keep spirits up. In fact, his army numbered more like six hundred men, including a hundred-odd new volunteers who'd joined the march that day.

Houston had also exaggerated when he had said that his Texians were ten times the fighters the Mexicans were. Most of his men were raw recruits. "It would have been madness to have hazarded a contest," Houston believed. "The first principles of the drill had not been taught the men."[3] He also needed to rein in the overeager men who were outraged at the retreat, those who wanted to fight the enemy at the first opportunity. They wanted revenge for the Alamo; he wanted to win the war. Fighting too soon could risk everything.

To shape a disciplined fighting force, he needed, above all, time. He needed to establish discipline, to practice formations, to teach his troops how to attack and withdraw. He must rely on speed and mobility—and surprise—and that required practiced coordination. "Our forces must not be shut in forts," Houston believed.[4] Even before Travis and his men had met their end at the Alamo, Houston had learned that lesson at Horseshoe Bend fighting with Andrew Jackson. Even a good fortification is not impregnable.

In the morning, the river crossing began in a heavy rain; with Mexicans in pursuit, the Texians couldn't afford to wait for the sky to clear. Families first, Houston ordered, and the fleeing citizens, numbering more than a thousand, carrying what little they could, took turns going aboard the flat-topped vessel to be poled to the Colorado's east bank. Next Texian troops crowded onto the ferry's broad deck, which shuttled back and forth all day.

The rain swelled what was already a wide, deep, and fast-moving watercourse; no Mexican army could get troops and supplies across by crossing the Colorado under these conditions. And Houston, his entourage safely on the river's left bank, made sure. He ordered the ferry set afire. With its useless remains on the bottom of the Colorado River, he had just bought his army some time.

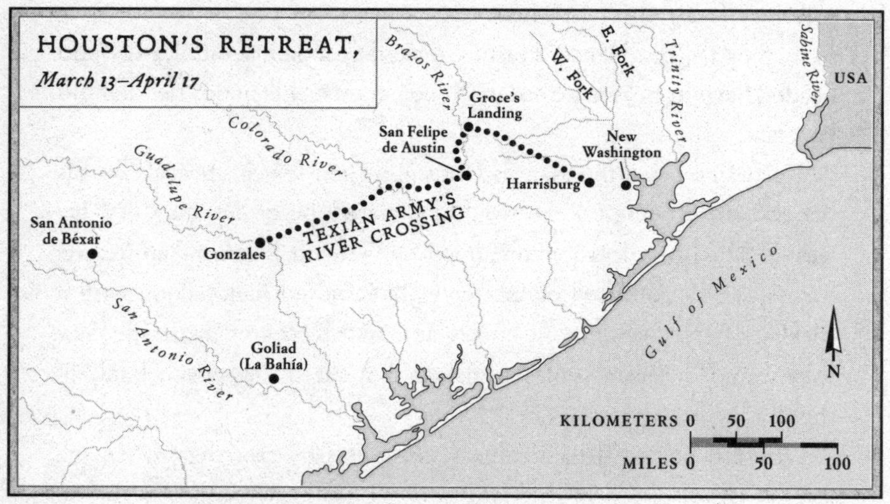

THE ENEMY ACROSS THE WATER

Two days after Houston's army established camp on the other side of the river, Deaf Smith caught up with Houston. Dressed in his battered hat, ragged shoes, and oversized pantaloons he could hardly have looked less military. But he had done his job and more: While the army's officers marched and drilled the army, Houston's little spy company, led by Smith and Henry Karnes, had been on the move, constantly on the lookout for the enemy. When they observed fresh horse tracks in the saturated sandy soil a few miles from the camp, they guessed a band of enemy scouts had passed within the hour.

After checking their guns, they set off in pursuit. The Mexicans tried to flee, but in an exchange of fire, one enemy rider was killed, a horse was lamed by a pistol shot—and the Texians got themselves a prisoner. The rest of the Mexicans got away, but the Texian scouting party took the dead lancer's pistols, picked up a pair of saddlebags, and headed back to Beason's Ford with their captive, his hands tied behind his back.

Karnes escorted the man to Houston. The Mexican begged for his life and, after being told he would be spared, he spilled his story. He was attached to a force commanded by General Joaquín Ramírez de Sesma, which consisted of "six or eight hundred men" along with a cavalry of sixty or seventy horses and two pieces of artillery. They were camped several miles upstream but on the opposite bank of the Colorado.

Houston posted detachments at three nearby crossings; when the level of the river fell in the days to come, his army would be able to cross it. Meanwhile, the usual hot-blooded officers were keen to take the offensive. Some men who had eagerly awaited a strong leader to take charge of the army began to doubt whether Houston was the right man after all, and a few quiet voices questioned his bravery, asking aloud whether Houston wasn't a coward for not immediately engaging Sesma's force. But cooler heads understood, as one captain put it, that "there are times when it requires more courage to retreat than to stand and fight."[5] A few soldiers deserted in frustration, but, since Houston held the reins, for the next several days his army made no major moves.

Couriers came and went, bringing disheartening news. To Houston's shock, he learned that the government of the Texas republic had also retreated. When word of the Alamo debacle reached Washington-on-the-Brazos, some delegates immediately saddled their horses and rode out of town. Others got blind drunk. The good men who stayed got down to business, convening a session of the convention that lasted until 4:00 A.M. the next morning. David G. Burnet, a transplanted New Yorker, emerged as president. Thomas Jefferson Rusk, a veteran of the Come-and-Take-It fight at Gonzales, became secretary of war. Once elected, however, the new officeholders' first order of business had been to organize a removal eastward to Harrisburg.

Houston took the government's decision as a personal insult. "It was a poor compliment to me," he wrote to Rusk, a sometime legal client of Houston's back in Nacogdoches, "to suppose I would not advise the convention" when the need arose to move.[6] If the nation's leading officers ran in panic, then wouldn't every settler do the same? Houston had seen the hardships of the Gonzales families in his party, and now he feared the panic would spread quickly.

The scenes of civilian retreat varied little, as one witness reported. "The road was filled with carts and wagons loaded with women and children, while other women, for whom there was no room in the wagons, were seen walking, some of them barefoot, some carrying their smaller children in their arms or on their backs, their other children following barefooted; and other women were again seen with but one shoe, having lost the other in the mud; some of the wagons were broken down and others again were bogged in the deep mud. Taken all in all, the sight was the most painful by far, that I ever witnessed."[7]

A Gonzales man brought more ill tidings: Fannin had surrendered. Though the ultimate fate of Goliad's defenders remained unknown to Houston, he was certain Fannin and his four hundred men could no longer be counted on to fight for Texas, imprisoned as they were in Fort Defiance. That meant not only had his army lost one wing at the Alamo but the other had been captured. Appointed commander in chief of the Armies of the Republic, Houston now had just his own command, some hundreds of men living in the cold without tents, drilling along the Colorado. It had become Texas's last best hope.

THIRTEEN

An Army Assembles

> It were perhaps hyperbolical to say "the eyes of the world are upon him," but assuredly the people of Texas . . . regard his present conduct as decisive of the fate of their country.
>
> —President of Texas David Burnet on Sam Houston

"You know I am not easily depressed," Sam Houston admitted in a letter to Secretary of War Rusk, but "I have found the darkest hours of my life! . . . For forty-eight hours, I have not eaten an ounce, nor have I slept."[1]

The widespread fear that swept across Texas did produce one positive result: Houston's army began to grow rapidly. His considered strategy of retreat was beginning to win converts, as men from the more populated region of East Texas saw the risks expanding toward them; they flocked to save their homes, to fight for their families, and to stand up for the fragile new republic. The Army of Texas camped at Beason's Ford grew to eleven hundred, then twelve hundred, and the ranks continued to swell. "Men are flocking to camp," reported Houston. "In a few days my force will be highly respectable."[2]

If his wasn't yet a true fighting machine, these green volunteers, with a smattering of former American soldiers, did show signs of learning how to obey orders. One night Houston discovered for himself that the training had begun to take.

After an inspection of the camp perimeter, Houston returned well after dark. An armed sentry spied him in the gloom and demanded, "Who comes there?"

"I am General Houston," he replied. "Let me pass on."

The guard would have none of it. His orders forbade him to permit any stranger to enter the camp.

"I don't know you to be General Houston," he said, raising his gun. "Don't you move or I'll shoot."

Houston swallowed his surprise—and he couldn't help but be pleased.

"Well, my friend," Houston allowed, "if such were your orders, you are right." Houston took a seat on a nearby stump and waited patiently. Only after the officer of the day was summoned and the visitor's identity confirmed was Major General Houston permitted to reenter the camp.[3]

With boys like this one—many of Houston's soldiers were teenagers, very few aged thirty or more—he might yet lead a fine fighting force into battle with Santa Anna. Still, just as new men were coming, others were going, impatient and tired, returning to their homes. Somehow Sam Houston had to hold this army together. He had to keep his volunteers with him—and avoid confronting his larger and more experienced enemy.

THE ENEMY

Santa Anna expressed no regrets. "The capture of the Alamo," as he saw it, "gave us a prodigious moral prestige. Our name terrified the enemy, and . . . they fled disconcerted."[4]

The victory also made the Mexican want to go home, believing he had accomplished his goal of suppressing the uprising. But after consulting with his generals—some of whom argued the fight had only begun—His Excellency accepted that he had business to finish in Texas. And a tricky business it was.

On the one hand, he wanted to avoid provoking a fight with Andrew Jackson and the United States. That the American president coveted Texas was hardly a secret, and the longer Santa Anna stayed and the closer he got to the Louisiana border, the greater was the risk of escalating what, in his opinion, was a matter for the Mexican nation. Although he hoped that many of his troops would settle in Texas after the war, he would bring the fight to a rapid and, if necessary, brutal close.

Santa Anna wasn't wrong to worry about President Jackson: Sam Houston's mentor still shared his interests in Texas's independence. In not-so-far-away Washington, as news of the fighting in Texas reached him, Jackson considered his country's western boundaries, looking down his hawk-like nose at the map of the country he wanted to expand. If Texan refugees—most of them American—began to pour into the United States, he might well have the excuse to engage Mexico and wrest control of Texas on the battlefield. And maybe more than Texas? Jackson's generals—one of whom was poised very near that border—kept him in the picture and, though his on-the-record instructions were measured, General Jackson and his former aide-de-camp Sam Houston understood one another as only old friends can.

Santa Anna had spent weeks at San Antonio after the fight at the Alamo. It was a civilized place, where he found a young woman for company and he contented himself with shaping a plan. Three divisions of his army would march on the enemy. In order to drive the rebels out of Tejas, he aimed at the more populous East Texas. One force would take a northern route. The second, led by General Urrea, would veer south to capture Goliad before continuing toward the coast to take control of the port towns and shut off Texian sources of supply. The third and largest expeditionary force, led by Santa Anna himself, would be the tip of the arrow. Then the separate forces would reunite along the Brazos River and pursue the rebel army to its end.

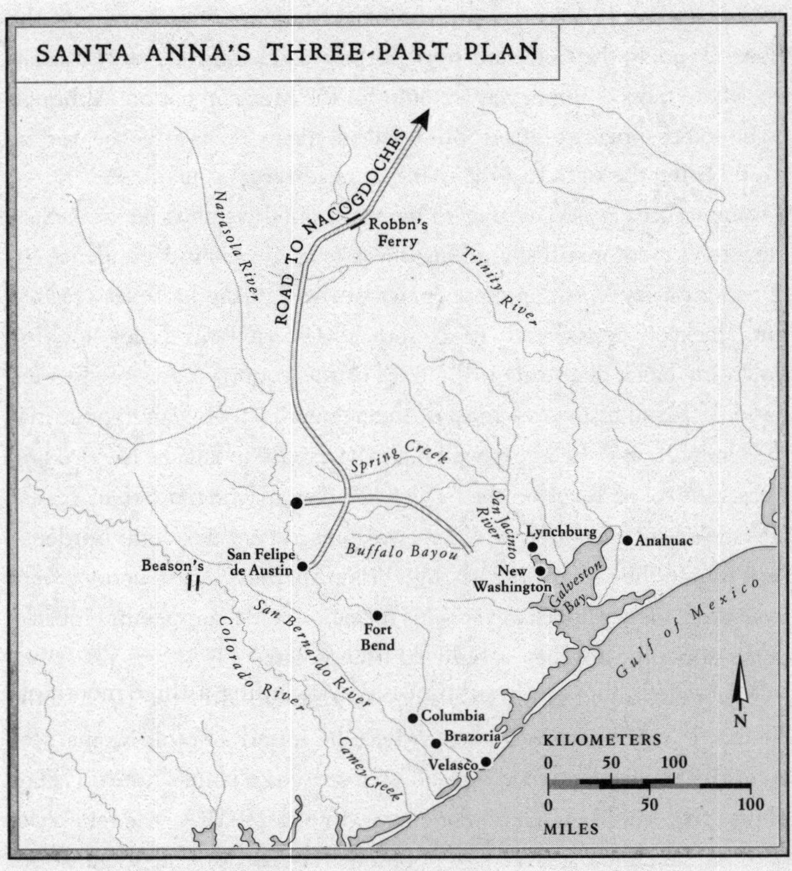

A MISERY OF MUD

Fearing the Mexicans now knew his whereabouts and might destroy his army before they were ready, Houston and his army stole into the night on March 26. To mislead any Mexican scouts keeping watch at a distance, the Texians lit blazing campfires before they slipped into the shadows. A few infantry sentinels remained behind as the rest of the army began the trek toward San Felipe de Austin. Five miles later the troops rested, waiting while the pickets caught up, then resumed the march.

But the tide of soldiers had turned again in recent days. The ranks of the army now shrank, with more men drifting away than arriving. Fannin's capture hadn't helped, and a growing number of men wondered at the prospects of the campaign in the face of Santa Anna's army; some reported the enemy force numbered in the tens of thousands. Worse yet, Houston was still falling back, meaning more families would be left exposed as the battle line shifted east. Many of the departing soldiers left to return to their homes to help loved ones. Noah Smithwick, veteran of the Battle of Gonzales, described the abandoned homesteads he saw. "Houses were standing open, the beds unmade, the breakfast things still on the tables, pans of milk moulding in dairies."[5] Countless settlers up and ran for their lives.

For the families, the journey posed immense dangers and hardships. Just ten at the time, one girl later recalled her father piling the family into a wagon. She and her three sisters, including a three-month-old baby, left almost everything behind, including the ten-year-old's treasured books. On the journey they witnessed death and illness, experienced dangerous river crossings and all-night travels, and ended up with nothing but "what clothes we were wearing." Fear was a constant; in the midst of the trip, they learned of the terrible events at Goliad. One night her father, a veteran of the War of 1812, recognized the boom of cannon fire not so far in the distance. By early April, she later wrote, "we were as wretched as we could be; for we had been five weeks from home, and there was not much prospect of our ever returning."[6]

For families and soldiers alike, the retreat wasn't easy. No true roads existed in Texas, only paths through undeveloped lands made by travelers on foot, horseback, and cart. The name by which many such routes were commonly known—"trace"—was accurate. A journey of any distance was a slog, since the traces were frequently interrupted by rivers, creeks, and bayous, few of which were spanned by bridges.

Despite the difficulties, Houston persisted in drawing the men back. Perhaps he considered the Alamo proof that his strategy of waiting until he was strong enough to fight was correct. Perhaps he remembered his own youthful insistence on fighting while wounded—a fight that had hurt more than helped the cause. Whatever his reasons, one thing was clear: no matter how eager his men were to face their enemy, Houston's strategy was to play keep-away for now.

When he reached the Brazos River, Houston faced a new challenge to his authority: Some of his men now threatened to defy his orders. One of the mutinous voices belonged to Captain Moseley Baker, another second-chance man. He had left large debts behind in Alabama (and an accusation of defrauding a bank). More recently, having established himself in Texas as a lawyer, he was quick to join the rebel cause. He had fought at Gonzales, and when he gathered a group of volunteers together in his adopted town of San Felipe de Austin, he took a hard line. "Let us all, with one accord, raise our hands to heaven and swear," he insisted. "The Texas flag shall wave triumphant, or we shall sleep in death."[7]

Baker took it personally that Houston was leading the army away from central Texas. As a married man with a daughter, he understood the hardships of the settlers as they left their homes and marched to who-knows-where; as a fighter, he accused Houston of avoiding a battle. "You had before you the example of Fannin, of Burleson and Milam

[but] . . . you determined that your first military act should be a retreat." Instead of attacking, as Baker saw it, Houston was "content to hear yourself spoke of as the Patrick Henry of revolution."[8]

In order to deflect the rumblings in the ranks, Houston ordered Baker and Major Wyly Martin—the latter was a veteran of Horseshoe Bend who, like Baker, also wished to take an immediate stand—to defend the Brazos River. The two men could hardly say no when asked to prepare for the action they said they wanted. Baker and his men took up a position on the east bank, ready to slow the advance of any enemy force near San Felipe de Austin, while Martin and company were to defend the Fort Bend crossing a short distance downstream. Houston thus defused the ire of the unhappy fighters and also managed to avoid a premature confrontation with the Mexican troops on his trail.

Secretary of War Rusk had become Houston's main confidant within the government. Like so many others, Rusk came to Texas as a seeker; in his case, he was in pursuit of men who had embezzled a small fortune from the Georgia mining company that had been his business. The son of an Irish immigrant stonemason, the broad-shouldered Rusk had stayed and made a place for himself. Though just thirty-two, he had a native authority about him, and believing fervently in a free Texas, he had organized a company of volunteers in Nacogdoches to join the fight.

Houston explained his actions concerning Baker and Martin in a letter to Rusk. "Had I consulted the wishes of all, I should have been like the ass between two stacks of hay. Many wished me to go [downstream], others above. I consulted none—I held no councils of war. If I err, the blame is mine."[9] Houston's thinking put him at odds with his men, but he saw no alternative. He would have to square his shoulders and tough it out. Texas's survival depended on him, and he was not going to let a desire for revenge lead to a premature fight and defeat.

The army's retreat resumed. Leaving Martin and Baker behind, Houston and his troops headed upstream along the west bank of the

Brazos River. Houston was continuing to play his cards close to his vest: The only certainty was that the army needed to stay ahead of the Mexicans—until the time (and no one knew when that would be) that Houston chose to turn and fight.

BORROWED TIME AT BERNARDO PLANTATION

Was this trek across Texas an act of cowardice? More and more of Houston's young detractors had begun to think so. But people old enough to recall the American Revolution discerned a method where others saw madness.

The elders could remember that General George Washington, fearful of losing his army, retreated out of enemy range more often than not. Washington wished to fight battles he could win, to wait for the days when the odds favored him. Might General Houston be thinking the same way?

Some wise men also recalled that Baron Von Steuben, Washington's Prussian-trained inspector general, introduced a rebel rabble to the essentials of order and discipline, to drills and tactics. Perhaps at their April encampment, just across the Brazos River from a place called Groce's Landing, Houston could finally shape this haggard, rain-soaked, underfed, and undisciplined bunch of stragglers into a fighting force.

The man who welcomed Houston and his army, Jared Groce, was among the richest settlers in Stephen Austin's district. He grew cotton and owned Texas's first cotton gin, as well as a sawmill and land as far as you could see. From the columned porch that ran the length of his rambling plantation home, called Bernardo, he took in a panoramic view of the Brazos River. But his plantation amounted to much more than a homestead. When the army pitched its camp, twenty miles north of San Felipe, on April 1, Groce had the fields, flocks, fodder, and livestock to provide for a hungry army.

The weather refused to cooperate, and with nearly constant rain, the "camp became extremely muddy and disagreeable."[10] But the sickest soldiers recuperated in the Bernardo mansion house, which became a hospital. After weeks of exposure and tainted water, many men suffered from colds, whooping cough, or persistent diarrhea. This period of rest at Groce's permitted a reorganization of the medical staff, too, consisting of a half dozen physicians, and the installation of the medicine chest into a designated cart for transport in the battles to come.

As the Texians settled in, however, Santa Anna's army was never far from Sam Houston's mind.

SANTA ANNA ON THE MOVE

On the last day of March, Santa Anna had begun to march his force eastward, leaving San Antonio for the first time since the fall of the Alamo. He reached Gonzales on April 2. His troops crossed the prairie, passing small wooded areas—"a vast garden," according to one of his officers, "beautifully interrupted by woods."[11] They saw lilies and poppies coming into spring bloom, a stark contrast to towns burned beyond habitation. Many fields and pastures had been torched by departing citizens or Houston's army, in keeping with the American commander's wish that nothing be left behind that might be of use to the enemy army on his trail.

Rains slowed the march, but by Easter Sunday, April 3, Santa Anna led an advance force consisting of five hundred infantry, fifty cavalry, and scouts. The rest of his army would follow after a barge got the heavy loads of baggage and ammunition and the pair of eight-pound cannons safely across the Guadalupe River.

On April 5, His Excellency's force crossed the Colorado, a few miles downstream from the Texians' recently abandoned camp at Beason's Ford. Houston's trail was far from cold—he was still at Groce's Landing—but when the main Mexican column reached San Felipe on April 7, Santa Anna found that "the town . . . no longer existed, because the enemy had burned it and sent the inhabitants into the interior." Baker's company had burned the place and, by coincidence, three of his men had returned to inspect the ruins the day the Mexicans arrived. Caught by surprise, two of them got away—but the third got caught. When interrogated, the captive revealed he knew Houston's whereabouts (a few miles upstream at Groce's crossing) and the size of his force (he said eight hundred men), and "that [Houston's] intention was to retire to the Trinity river, in case the Mexicans cross the Brazos."[12]

Santa Anna was gaining on the Texians. But first he had to cross the Brazos and that, he found, would take some time. He confronted two problems. One, Houston had ordered every vessel in the vicinity destroyed; and two, Captain Moseley Baker and his skilled riflemen awaited across the water, ready to pepper anyone who tried to come ashore at the landing with deadly rifle shot.

LITTLE MORE THAN a dozen miles north, Houston's officers drilled the healthy troops almost nonstop. He reorganized the regimental command structure. The infantry learned military basics, including line tactics, in which two or more ranks of soldiers march in close alignment toward the enemy, then fire in unison for maximum effect.

Houston spent much time in his tent, studying maps and tending to his correspondence. He dispatched letter after letter to East Texas and to the government, seeking supplies and more manpower. He addressed one "to the Citizens of Texas," assuring them that "the enemy . . . are treading the soil on which they are to be conquered."[13] He issued orders to Baker and debriefed his scouts, who were constantly coming and going, doing their best to keep him apprised of enemy movements. "Mr. E. Smith is out, and, if living, I will hear the truth and all important news," Houston told Rusk.[14]

Bad news arrived: Three survivors of Goliad, "wounded, barefoot, and ragged," staggered in with the first word of the slaughter.[15] Houston learned the details of a demise he had feared, when the Texians who surrendered as POWs had been divided into groups, marched out of town, and shot like dogs. To an army preparing to fight, the news was a terrible shock; the manpower would be missed. According to the rolls, Houston's army now numbered nearly a thousand men. But that included substantial detachments that remained under the command of Baker and Martin; by Houston's calculation, the Army of Texas at Groce's land barely exceeded five hundred effectives.

The politicians felt the reverberations, too. Commander in Chief Houston got a desperate letter from the Texas president, David Burnet. "Sir: the Enemy are laughing you to scorn. You must fight them. You must retreat no farther. The country expects you to fight. The Salvation of the country depends on your doing so."[16] Secretary of War Rusk arrived in person, looking to encourage Houston to take on the enemy but also adding his gravitas and support to Houston's leadership. Eighty volunteers arrived from East Texas, regulars from the U.S. Army, some of them still wearing their uniforms. Then cannon fire in the distance, on April 7, announced the presence of Mexican troops in San Felipe de Austin, though Houston did not know whether or not Santa Anna was in command.

DIG THE GRAVES

Discontent remained common in the ranks. Many an impatient soldier was heard grumbling that "it was time to be doing something besides lying in idleness and getting sick." No longer ignoring the rising volume of complaints, Houston ordered two graves dug and issued a notice, which appeared on trees around the camp. The first man who called for volunteers to strike out on their own would be court-martialed and shot. The threat—together with a rumor that the army would break camp in a matter of days—defused the situation.[17] Houston was walking a delicate line, weighing matters of discipline even as he worried about his soldiers' devotion to the cause. They needed to be together to right the wrongs perpetrated by Santa Anna.

The appearance of a gift from the people of Cincinnati lifted plummeting morale. On hearing of the uprising in Texas the previous fall, citizens of the Ohio city commissioned the manufacture of two cannons. Shipped via New Orleans, the cannons arrived at Groce's on April 11. Colonel James Neill took charge of a new artillery battery, with nine volunteers manning each of the cast-iron guns, which were christened the "Twin Sisters." Blacksmiths set to work cutting up horseshoes and other available iron scrap for use as canister shot.

The blacksmiths shared Groce's shop with gunsmiths. Both groups kept busy. Groce had donated his plantation's plumbing pipes—they were made of lead, an expensive import in frontier Texas—and the smiths melted the lead to cast as bullets.

It was with the blacksmiths—for barely a moment and for the first time in a month—that Houston relaxed enough to allow his lighter side to show.

When a new volunteer arrived carrying an old flintlock rifle in need of repair, some wag in the ranks pointed. "The blacksmith is there," the recruit was told; looking up, he saw a man dressed in a well-worn leather jacket, watching the other smiths at work.

The new recruit approached. "I want you to fix my gun," he began, speaking to Houston, whom he did not recognize. "The lock is out of order, it won't stand cocked."

The general played along. "Very well," he said. "Set her down there, and call in one hour and she will be ready."

When the owner learned—to his horror—Houston's identity, he returned. Afraid he might be punished for insubordination, he approached the commander, hat in hand, asking for forgiveness.

The general just laughed. "My friend," he reassured the soldier, "they told you right, I am a very good blacksmith." He handed over the gun, which he had dismantled and cleaned. "She is in good order now, and I hope you are going to do some good fighting."[18]

Houston had learned much from his mentor. Jackson was a master at winning his men's allegiance on the march; part of that was to maintain his authority and yet become one of them.

THOMPSON'S FERRY

Santa Anna looked across the Brazos River from San Felipe de Austin. His first attempt to get his army to the opposite shore had failed when a flatboat, manned by a squad of his men, had returned, rebuffed by a hail of bullets from Moseley Baker's riflemen. Baker got his wish: He got to mix it up with the enemy, and he and his men acquitted themselves honorably. The Mexican general had ordered his artillerymen to return fire, but two days of bombardment—booms were heard at Groce's—hadn't cleared the nest of snipers.

Santa Anna decided to leave General Sesma to continue the fight, while he headed downstream to find another crossing.

At Thompson's Ferry, on April 12, he tested his luck again, only this time he resorted to trickery. Before being observed by anyone on the opposite bank, the general and his men concealed themselves in the bushes. Then Colonel Juan Almonte, who spoke fluent English, showed himself on the shore.

He hailed a boatman standing across the Brazos.

Thinking the lone figure calling to him was a Texian looking to join the exodus, the ferryman poled over. The Mexicans quickly overpowered the unsuspecting boatman (by one account, Santa Anna himself wrestled him to the ground), and his vessel soon began shuttling Santa Anna's force—seven hundred infantry, fifty cavalry, and a cannon—to the opposite bank.

Santa Anna wondered about Sam Houston. He held the Texian army in contempt after the Alamo and Goliad and saw no reason to think his present opponent any more dangerous than Travis or Fannin. His campaign, he believed, had become little more than "a military parade," in the face of an opponent who "was not undertaking a retreat but was in full flight."[19]

A new piece of intelligence inspired a new plan. From a Mexican colonist, Santa Anna learned that the "so-called government of Texas" was within striking distance at Harrisburg. He saw a clear way to end this fight: If he could capture the leaders of the revolution, he would strike "a single blow . . . mortal to their cause." His first objective wouldn't be to snare Houston but, rather, to capture the entire rebel government. If he moved quickly, Houston couldn't—or wouldn't—interfere, since the Texians were camped well to the north, out of Santa Anna's direct line of attack, and reportedly heading east.[20]

Santa Anna measured the odds. Tradition was not with him—most military planners regarded keeping an army together of paramount importance—but he was certain he saw the opening he wanted, an easy and major win in an immediate strike. And on April 14, Santa Anna led his contingent of dragoons, grenadiers, and riflemen toward Harrisburg, planning to end this rebellion once and forever.

FIGHT OR FLIGHT

Two days before, plumes of thick black smoke from the twin stacks had signaled departure time for Houston's army. Fired by green wood, the steam engine of the *Yellow Stone* began the work, at ten o'clock on the morning of April 12, of carrying the Army of Texas across the Brazos. The retreat east resumed.

On seeing the steamboat docked at Groce's wharf ten days before, Houston had impressed the side-wheeler into service "for the benefit of the Republic."[21] Having the ship meant that the high waters of the rising river no longer posed an obstacle.

Captain John Ross and his crew ferried the men across. With the 120-foot-long deck stacked with bales of cotton to protect her boilers and pilothouse from enemy rifles, the *Yellow Stone* required seven trips to carry the seven hundred soldiers (including more than a hundred sick and wounded), two hundred horses, and ten ox-drawn wagons loaded with ammunition and baggage to the left bank.

Houston went across with the first load of men and cargo; Rusk came last after supervising the loading. Secretary of War Rusk had emerged as an invaluable Houston ally, rebutting criticisms from the government and soldiers alike.

On April 13, Houston and his army marched along Cypress Creek—but away from Santa Anna's forces. Again the dissention in the ranks grew louder—*Did Houston intend to retreat all the way to Louisiana, to seek the direct military aid of Jackson and the United States?*[22] It didn't help that Moseley Baker and Wyly Martin, together with more than three hundred men, had retreated from the Brazos and rejoined Houston's force. Their voices only added to the discontent.

By April 16, the Texians marched through Cypress City; a few miles later they reached a fork in the road. There a local landmark, the Which-Way Tree, stood like a scarecrow with its arms raised. One craggy limb indicated the road to Nacogdoches; to tread that path meant further retreat, perhaps to the Sabine River and beyond. Another gnarled branch pointed due south, toward Harrisburg and—very likely—the long-awaited fight. The tree remained silent, but, according to Dr. Nicholas Labadie, a physician riding with the advance guard, a local man named Roberts did the talking.

He stood near the gate to his farm. Just as Houston rode up, Roberts was asked, *Which way to Harrisburg?*

"The right hand road will carry you," he replied, "just as straight as a compass."

Before Houston could say a word, a shout came from the ranks. "To the right, boys, to the right." The cry was repeated by others—"loud and joyous shouts followed in succession." The army's band made the turn, too, following the right arm of the Which-Way Tree.

Houston had kept his plan to himself, issuing no standing orders regarding which way to turn. Would Houston rather have had the army head straight for the Sabine—the cowardly way out, his skeptics thought—or turn south and fight? Suddenly, though, Houston's preference no longer mattered. As one soldier remembered, "the head of the column . . . took the right-hand without being either bid or forbid."[23]

The soldiers may have been pleased, but not everyone liked the southward turn.

Mrs. Pamelia Mann, for one, was miffed. An inn operator fleeing Washington-on-the-Brazos, she had recognized there was safety in numbers and had reached an understanding with the Texian army when the army left Groce's landing. "If you are going on the Nacogdoches road," she had said, "you can have my oxen." Yoked to the Cincinnati cannons, the sturdy animals pulled the heavy equipment along the muddy route and Pamelia Mann had joined the caravan.

Now the deal had changed. When she realized the destination had shifted with the turn toward Harrisburg, Mrs. Mann, well-known for her hot temper, galloped to the head of the column. She was said to have "fought everyone except Indians,"[24] and now she confronted the commander in chief.

"General, you told me a damn lie," spat out the angry woman. "Sir, I want my oxen."

"Well, Mrs. Mann, we can't spare them," Houston replied as reasonably as he could. "We can't get our cannon along without them."

"I don't care a damn for your cannon," she replied, brandishing a pistol. She soon headed north, away from the army, trailed by the oxen she had unharnessed herself, cutting the rawhide tug with her knife as the men looked on wordlessly.

Captain Rohrer, one of the wagon masters charged with delivering the cannons, remonstrated with Houston. "We can't get along without them oxen, the cannon is bogged down."

Houston, caught in the middle, offered a noncommittal reply. "Well . . ."

Rohrer, determined to get the draft animals back, turned and rode off with another soldier in pursuit of Mrs. Mann. He was a hundred yards away when Houston, rising up in his saddle, hollered a warning. "Captain Rohrer, that woman will fight."

"Damn her fighting," was the reply.

Nothing more was heard on the matter until nine o'clock that evening, well after the army had made camp for the night. Rohrer returned, his shirt badly torn—without the oxen.

"Hey, captain, where is your oxen?" someone hollered.

To the amusement of many, Captain Rohrer's abashed reply was, "She would not let me have them."

Mrs. Mann had won her fight, and it seemed the soldiers had won theirs, too. Houston had kept them fighting battles they could not win—now he would find out if he had held them back long enough.[25]

FOURTEEN

The Battle at San Jacinto

We go to conquer. It is wisdom, growing out of necessity, to meet the enemy now; every consideration enforces it. No previous occasion would justify it.

—Sam Houston to Henry Raguet, April 19, 1836

The heavy spring rains meant misery to every soldier, Mexican and Texian, as the confrontation between the mismatched armies drew closer. Drenched clothing never seemed to dry, and the mud on what passed for roads grew deeper by the day. Streams swelled into rivers and rivers looked like lakes. The challenging conditions also revealed something about the characters of both generals.

General Sam Houston—seemingly now committed to confront Santa Anna—won new respect from some of his troops when, in the course of the demanding, two-and-a-half-day, fifty-five-mile march to Harrisburg, he dismounted his horse to help the wagon drivers when their carts bogged down in the mud. Despite his high rank and old war wounds, again and again he leaned his good shoulder into wagon wheels. His men took note.

On Santa Anna's trip to Harrisburg, he grew impatient at the progress of his column. When a fallen tree bridged one creek bed, its broad trunk easing the passage for men on foot, Santa Anna stepped carefully across, and a dragoon swam his horse through the rushing waters. But rather than wait for his soldiers to help carry the baggage and commissary stores safely across, His Excellency ordered the fully loaded mule train to cross the swollen stream. Up to their withers in water, several mules lost their balance. There was a "terrible jamming of officers and dragoons, pack-mules and horses," one of his officers noted in his diary. Several animals drowned "in a scene of wild confusion."

Santa Anna's reaction to the dangerous situation? "His Excellency witnessed [it] with hearty laughter."[1] The lives of men, Mexican or Texian, meant little to His Excellency.

Santa Anna had a particular reason for hurrying to Harrisburg. He was keen to arrest the Texas government and especially its vice president. Previously a provincial governor and Mexico's ambassador to France, Lorenzo de Zavala had opposed Santa Anna's power grab in Mexico City and His Excellency's reversal of democratic reforms. Santa Anna regarded the exiled Zavala as a sworn enemy and a traitor to his country; he wanted to make Zavala his prisoner.

As far as Santa Anna was concerned, Houston's army could be dealt with later. His exact location wasn't clear, but scouts reported that the retreating Texian general aimed for Nacogdoches and the Sabine. "Since he is escorting families and supplies in ox-drawn wagons, his march is slow," Santa Anna noted. He believed that if he could promptly capture the government, he would still have time to subdue Houston. "The Trinity River, moreover, should detain him many days."[2]

On April 15, the morning after the hazardous crossing, Santa Anna headed for Harrisburg. Despite marching at double-time pace, per Santa Anna's orders, the Mexicans remained far from the town at sunset. But their commander, accompanied by an officer and fifteen dragoons, rode on. The midnight hour approached before they finally reached their destination.

Harrisburg's streets were desolate. The only sign of life the Mexicans managed to find was in a printshop, the new offices of the *Telegraph and Texas Register.* At gunpoint, three ink-spattered men told Santa Anna he had arrived too late. The government had departed hours before, boarding the steamboat *Cayuga*, along with most of the inhabitants of Harrisburg. The vessel had steamed for New Washington, a town some twenty miles southeast on a river known as Buffalo Bayou.

Angry that his prey had eluded him, Santa Anna ordered the printing equipment destroyed, the ruined press parts and type cases thrown into the river. Only weeks earlier this same press had inked the first impression of the Texas Declaration of Independence.

HARRISBURG

Three days later, when General Houston looked across Buffalo Bayou, Santa Anna's army had come and gone, leaving the river town unrecognizable. "We arrived at Harrisburg about noon," one Texian private reported, "[and] the smoke at the town told us too plainly . . . that the enemy had been there before us, and set fire to its buildings."[3]

Exhausted after the long march, the Texians made camp. Deaf Smith and his team departed on another mission. Houston wanted to know the exact whereabouts of the enemy that had burned Harrisburg. Tired as they were, the Texians felt ready to engage. "They were of one mind," one colonel remembered, "to march down and fight the enemy."[4]

Smith, Henry Karnes, and their scouting party swam their horses across the wide, slow-moving Buffalo Bayou. A dozen miles downstream, they met—and promptly took as their prisoners—three men. One was a Mexican captain; his companions were a guard and a Tejano guide. A search of their belongings revealed that the captain was a government courier, and his saddlebags contained for-his-eyes-only dispatches addressed to Santa Anna.

On the little party's return to Houston's camp at eight o'clock that evening, the captives' arms were bound behind their backs. The general summoned Sergeant Moses Austin Bryan, nephew of Stephen Austin and fluent Spanish speaker, to help question the prisoners.

The guide claimed he had been detained by the Mexicans in San Antonio while on a furlough from the Texian army. His commanding officer was summoned and confirmed both the man's identity and his commitment to the rebel cause.

How many men had been in the force that burned Harrisburg? Houston wanted to know.

The Tejano wasn't certain, but he had "heard some of the officers say . . . that there were 500 infantry and 100 cavalry and one twelve pound cannon."[5]

The numbers reassured Houston and Secretary of War Rusk. At least for the moment, the Mexican force in the vicinity was smaller than the Army of Texas, which now hovered around a thousand men.

Major Lorenzo de Zavala Jr., son of the republic's vice president, and a team of Tejanos speedily translated the documents the courier carried. They found some were letters home, addressed to loved ones back in Mexico, and of no strategic value. But others offered invaluable intelligence.

One revealed that General Cos and 650 soldiers would soon arrive to reinforce the men who had burned Harrisburg. It also became clear that the Mexicans didn't know where Houston's army was or that it was following in their footsteps. Still another fact emerged, one that galvanized Houston's interest: "I learned," he noted, "that General Santa Anna, with one division of his choice troops, had marched in the direction of Lynch's Ferry, on the San Jacinto."[6]

The man who had ordered the slaughter at both the Alamo and

Goliad was in striking distance, just downstream on the Buffalo Bayou. As they reviewed the documents together, Houston and Rusk reacted as one.

"We need not talk," said Houston, turning to Rusk. "You think we ought to fight, and I think so too."[7]

FROM HUNTER TO HUNTED

The capture of the courier changed everything. The roles that Houston and Santa Anna played suddenly reversed: Houston became the hunter, His Excellency the hunted. Thanks to Deaf Smith's brilliant intelligence gathering, Houston, now armed with the who, what, where, and when, could plan a surprise attack. Here was his chance to steal the initiative from Santa Anna; the enemy commander, by making his impulsive move to capture the government, had given Houston an opening. Santa Anna had isolated himself with a fraction of his forces at hand.

At the same time, Houston's army showed signs of finally coalescing. The time at Groce's had helped. By retreating across Texas, Houston had bought time for these men to grow together, to gain experience, to learn military tactics. He had identified who among his officers were to be trusted in battle. Now Houston saw an army that showed its readiness to act in unison: He'd seen that when, spontaneously, the rank and file had chosen to move toward the fight at the Which-Way Tree crossroad.

But time was suddenly of the essence. If the Texians could move quickly—that is, if Houston could strike before the larger Mexican army reassembled—he might be the one doing the capturing. This war was about revolution, about freedom, but it was also about avenging the annihilation at the Alamo. And at Goliad. For the first time since Houston had taken command of the Army of Texas, a big battle loomed in his immediate future, suddenly inevitable, perhaps only a day or two away. After a long reluctance to engage until the right moment, Houston now foresaw a battle he was ready to fight.

Houston and his men may have needed no further motivation to carry this fight to the Mexicans, but, on close inspection, another grim reminder emerged of the savagery of their enemy. Only weeks before, the saddlebags containing the Mexican documents had been the property of a fellow Texian. There, on the underside, the name *W. B. Travis* had been inscribed. Travis's bags had become a battlefield souvenir, scavenged by the murderous victors at the Alamo.

A NARROW ESCAPE

Santa Anna's impulsive pursuit of the Texas government wasn't accomplishing what he'd hoped it would. On Sunday, April 17, he again missed a chance to roll up the rebel officials.

His advance guard galloped into New Washington just in time to watch a rowboat, with President David Burnet and his party aboard, make for the schooner *Flash.* Though the retreating Texians remained in rifle range, the chivalrous colonel Juan Almonte, commander of the Mexican cavalrymen on the shore, spotted a woman in the boat—she was Mrs. Burnet—and ordered his men to hold their fire. The Mexican horsemen watched helplessly as the Texians boarded the *Flash*, a riverboat outfitted as a privateer in service to the newly founded Texas navy. Riding the tide, the little vessel sailed downstream toward Galveston Island.

When he got the news of Burnet's escape, Santa Anna chose not to countermarch; he would not rejoin the rest of his army but instead pushed on to New Washington. When they reached the town the next day, most of his men enjoyed the considerable stores in its warehouses, including flour, soap, tobacco, and other goods. Santa Anna would make the Texians pay once more—he planned to burn this town on departing—but first he dispatched a squad of scouts to locate Houston.

In his mind's eye, His Excellency saw a new main objective, Houston's army. If it was within striking distance, he would, he decided, "intercept Houston's march and . . . destroy with one stroke the armed forces and the hopes of the revolutionists."[8] That goal seemed suddenly close at hand when his scouts returned, bringing word that Houston was less than a day's march away. With opportunity near, a plan was made.

Thus, both armies aimed for a point of convergence. Their common destination was a place called Lynchburg, yet another river town. This one overlooked the watery intersection where the Buffalo Bayou joined the San Jacinto River.

Believing Houston to be in full retreat, Santa Anna expected the Texian commander to make for Lynch's Ferry, where ferry service connected the open prairie on the west bank of the San Jacinto with Lynchburg and the rest of East Texas; this was Houston's best and probably only escape route. Santa Anna planned to surprise the Texian army before it crossed and, at last, finish the job of crushing the rebellion.

Meanwhile, Sam Houston was doing everything in his power to get there first. He, too, hoped for the element of surprise, when his men, now more than ever ready to fight for their freedom, turned and made their stand.

Just two roads led to Lynch's landing. With the Texians coming from the west and the Mexicans from the south, the armies were on a collision course. Their now inevitable meeting would decide the future of Texas.

A CHANCE TO SAVE TEXAS

General Houston's orders worked their way down the line. Leave the baggage behind, the men were told; pack just three days' worth of rations for a quick march. A small contingent of some seventy-five healthy men would be staying in Harrisburg to safeguard the two hundred or so sick and wounded. If attacked, these guards were to shoot the two Mexican prisoners and blow up the ammunition wagon. For everyone else, as one soldier put it, "The long cherished wish of our men to meet the enemy seemed likely to be speedily gratified."[9]

Whatever the skepticism of a few officers and soldiers who still held deep reservations concerning Houston's leadership, more of his men had warmed to him—and to the *cause*. On the eve of the battle, they fell into line, ready to face up to the cold cruelty of Santa Anna.

Before the army broke camp, Houston, seated in the saddle on his tall white horse, addressed his army, which surrounded him in an open square formation. After weeks of revealing little of his strategy, in the speech of a lifetime he told his soldiers that the time to fight now approached. Houston spoke of glory, of a great victory. But as he reached the conclusion of his address, he minced no words.

"We will meet the enemy. Some of us may be killed and must be killed; but, soldiers, remember the Alamo, *the Alamo! The Alamo!*"[10]

The men heard his passion—and they shared it. "The watchword had no sooner fallen from his mouth, then it was caught up by every man in the army, and one simultaneous shout broke up into the sky—*Remember the Alamo.*"[11] They were ready to fight in memory of their brother Texians, fallen for their cause. As one colonel observed, "After such a speech, but damned few will be taking prisoners—that I know."[12]

A private in Captain Moseley Baker's company spoke for many, if not all, the soldiers when he remarked, "Had General Houston called upon me to jump into the whirlpool of the Niagara as the only means of saving Texas, I would have made the leap."[13] With a battle imminent, the disgruntled rumblings diminished with the rise of the primal urge to avenge the deaths of Travis's and Fannin's forces.

Privately, Houston was philosophical. As he wrote in a letter to his friend Henry Raguet in Nacogdoches, "This morning we are in preparation to meet Santa Anna. It is the only chance to save Texas. . . . We will only have about seven hundred to march with [and] . . . the odds are greatly against us. I leave the result in the hands of a wise God."[14]

At least his men would proceed with full stomachs. After many meals of half-cooked meat from beeves slaughtered along the route, the men ate corn bread. A flatboat loaded with supplies for the enemy—confiscated from a Tory Texian—provided cornmeal, out of which the men improvised crude dough cakes on sticks, cooked over their open fires. And then they marched.

Two miles downstream from Harrisburg, they met their first obstacle, but the scouts and the cavalry led the way, swimming their horses across Buffalo Bayou, twenty feet deep and flooding its banks. The infantry followed aboard a leaky ferryboat. Houston went across first and helped rig a makeshift cable of rope "fastened to both sides of the stream, which enabled the boat to make more rapid trips, and kept it from floating down the stream."[15]

Lookouts maintained a vigilant watch: General Cos and the Mexican reinforcements, coming from the rear, could be expected to be following the same route. A delay for repairs to the boat using the floorboards from a nearby house meant the process took much of the day. The men already across took cover in bushes beside the road, but no enemy sightings occurred before Rusk stepped back onto solid ground with the last of the soldiers. He had stood ankle deep in water as the ferry rode lower and lower, but the men, along with the two heavy cannons, the Twin Sisters, were now safely across.

Reunited on the same side of the Buffalo Bayou, the army resumed its advance, following along the right bank. Only after midnight did Houston call a halt, "for a short time, and without refreshments."[16] The

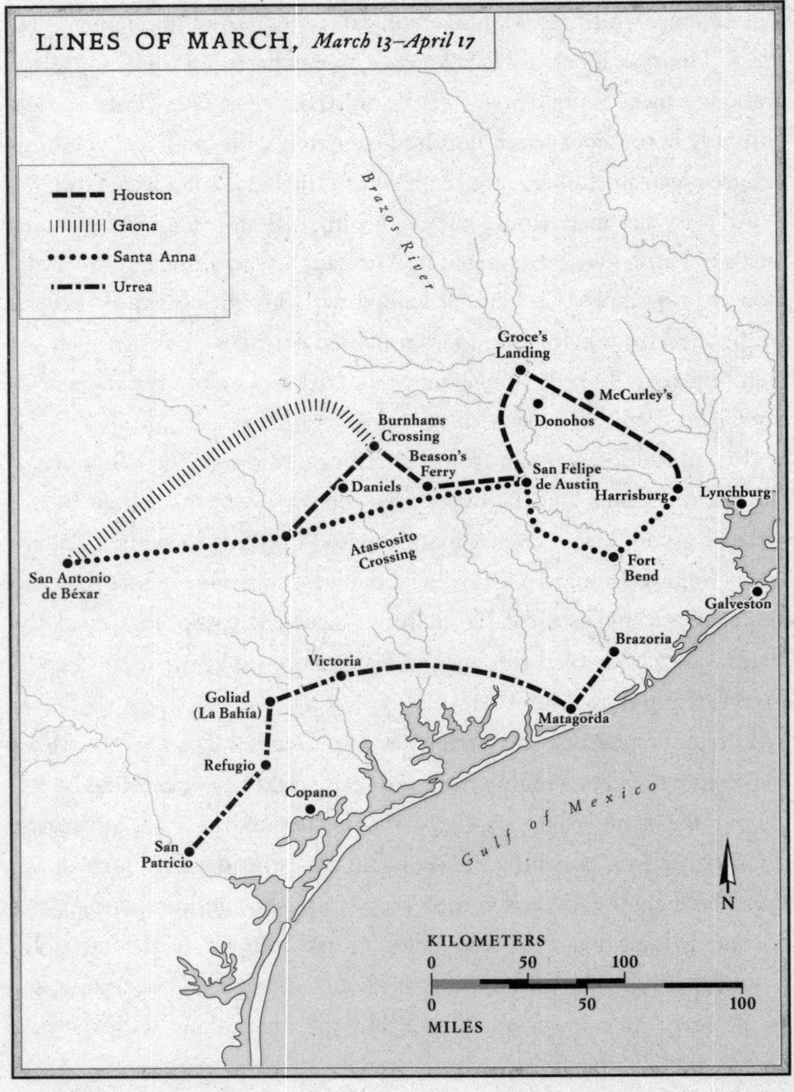

army passed a tense night, sleeping on the cold and soggy ground, rifles within reach.

As the Texians moved along the Buffalo Bayou, the Mexicans, barely a dozen miles away, set fire to New Washington, torching "a fine warehouse on the wharf, and all the houses in town." Even as the smoke filled the sky, a messenger arrived in a rush: Houston and his force had been sighted.

When the news reached Santa Anna, still in the town, he leapt onto his horse. He spurred the animal toward the front of the column. "The enemy are coming!" he yelled. "The enemy are coming."[17]

A column of attack was soon formed, and Santa Anna's army headed north. The fight for Texas loomed closer yet, now mere hours away.

A SMALL SKIRMISH

On April 20, the Texians moved out at daybreak. After crossing a timber bridge over another watercourse, Vince's Bayou, they filed past the remnants of campfires. The rain-soaked ash was a reminder that Santa Anna's army recently walked this route, before veering south toward New Washington.

After two hours of trudging through mud, Houston ordered a halt for breakfast. But before the food could come off the fires, a scouting party brought news that the Mexicans were also within striking distance of Lynch's Ferry.

General Houston knew one thing above all: His Texians had to get there first, and following a flurry of orders, the hungry men, bolting half-cooked meat, hustled on. The morning became a race for strategic

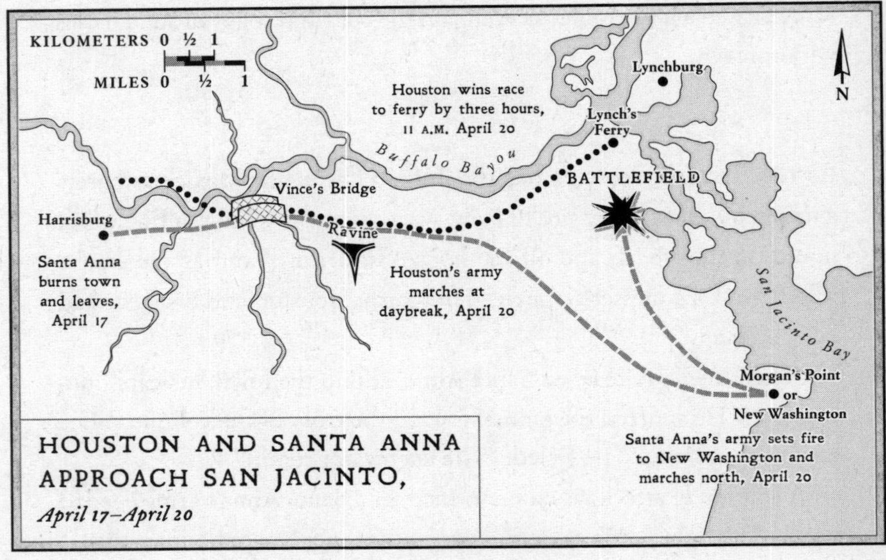

HOUSTON AND SANTA ANNA APPROACH SAN JACINTO,
April 17–April 20

ground, and by midmorning, the Army of Texas reached their destination. To the relief of all, no Mexicans were within sight.

Looking to establish his line of defense, Houston and his officers surveyed the likely battlefield. It consisted of open prairie, two miles wide east to west. Thickets of trees dotted the perimeter, and the field was bounded on three sides by water. The Buffalo Bayou formed the north boundary, the San Jacinto River the east, with the ferry crossing at their joining. A small body of water, Peggy Lake, occupied the southeast corner of the field. After one of the wettest springs in Texas memory, all the shorelines had broadened into swamps.

Houston selected a grove of live oaks for his army. The immense trees, their branches curtained with low-hanging Spanish moss, would provide ideal cover for his riflemen. Before them lay the broad prairie, covered with tall grasses. Houston posted his cavalry on his right flank, half-hidden by a copse of trees. At the center, the Twin Sisters would anchor the Texian line.

The men were well fed and their guns stacked when, shortly after midday, the first of Santa Anna's force came into view. Mexican cavalrymen appeared atop the low rise that divided the prairie, a line of infantrymen in their wake.

From his vantage a mile away, Santa Anna could see little of Houston's force, obscured as it was in the shadows of the trees. His scouts advised him that the enemy had two cannons, but that did not deter him. The Mexican leader ordered a company of troops to advance on the rebels while he moved closer and took cover in a stand of trees. He hoped to lure these backwoodsmen from their lair; in the open field, the trained Mexican horsemen would have the enemy at their mercy.

On the Texian side, the music of blaring trumpets grew audible as a company of Mexican cavalry approached. "Houston showed himself restless and uneasy," remembered one Texian, "casting his eyes towards the cannon and toward the advancing enemy."

The general ordered most of the men to lie flat on the grass; the less Santa Anna knew about the size and arrangement of the Texian force, the better. Then he issued the order all had been waiting for. "Clear the guns and Fire!"[18]

His artillerymen had no practice firing the Twin Sisters—they had neither powder nor cannonballs to spare—so the great booms at that moment were the first heard from the Cincinnati cannons. The shots wounded no Mexicans—the angle of fire was too high—but the dragoons halted, then wheeled, reversing their course back to Santa Anna's ranks.

Next His Excellency ordered his own cannon brought forward. Once it had been hauled under the cover of a dense wood within range of the Texian camp, the Mexican twelve-pounder opened fire. The first round fired by the brass cannon known as the Golden Standard ripped through the treetops, soaring into the Buffalo Bayou beyond. Only a few branches fell harmlessly among the Texians.

In response, Houston ordered the Twin Sisters advanced to the edge of the prairie. When the Texian six-pounders resumed firing, their loads of iron balls and scrap drew the first blood of the afternoon. A Mexican captain was badly wounded, his horse and two mules killed. As the exchange of fire continued, the Texians, too, sustained a casualty when a copper ball struck their artillery commander, Lieutenant Colonel Neill, smashing his hip.

The action slowed, but some of Houston's officers urged a major attack, arguing they might gain the upper hand if they could seize the single Mexican cannon. The general had his doubts, but at about four o'clock Colonel Sidney Sherman rode up and proposed a mission to capture the Mexicans' gun. Houston at first resisted. But Sherman, a Kentucky volunteer who had sold his cotton business to come to Texas to join the fight, persisted. He wasn't alone and, in the face of many men eager to carry the battle to the enemy, Houston agreed to permit one foray onto enemy ground.

Though Houston authorized only a reconnaissance mission, almost seventy Texian cavalrymen rode out. Deaf Smith and Henry Karnes were among those who joined Sherman's ranks, as was Mirabeau Lamar, a Georgian who rode a borrowed horse. But in midexecution, the mission changed: Upon seeing the Mexican cannon being withdrawn from its advance position, the Texians charged into a nest of Mexican horsemen.

A brutal fight ensued. It nearly ended in disaster, since the improvised Texas cavalry—they were merely riflemen on horseback—needed to dismount after discharging their unwieldly long rifles if they wished to reload. But Mexican cavalry, armed with sabers and lances, just kept coming.

It was a near thing. Secretary of War Rusk had joined in—and he was lucky to survive the episode. Surrounded by enemy lancers, Rusk made it back to the Texian camp only after Private Mirabeau Buonaparte Lamar (a future president of Texas) came to his rescue, driving his stallion into a circle of Mexican dragoons about to capture Rusk, creating an opening for both men to escape. The Texians scampered back to their defensive line, having lost several horses and sustained two casualties. With the Twin Sisters firing on them, the Mexicans also retreated.

Houston wasn't happy: Even on the eve of what he thought might be the biggest battle of the war, his overeager men only half listened to his orders. Tomorrow, he thought, they would have to do better.

Like two Texas bull elks circling one another before locking horns, Houston and Santa Anna were each getting the measure of the other, assessing and gauging. They had traded cavalry charges and artillery fire; both sides suffered a few casualties. As darkness fell, neither army occupied an enviable position, with the Texians boxed in by a bayou behind and a bottleneck at the Lynchburg crossing. They had no line of easy retreat. Santa Anna's camp was no better, situated on a small rise with the San Jacinto River on one flank and Peggy Lake to the rear.

Yet the terms of battle had been established, as two armies and two commanders regarded each other, separated by fewer than a thousand yards of prairie grass that swayed peacefully in the evening breeze.

FIFTEEN

"Remember the Alamo!"

We are nerved for the contest, and must conquer or perish.

—SAM HOUSTON, APRIL 19, 1836

Sam Houston slept late on April 21. For the first time in days, he lay until full daylight, eyes closed, his head on a coil of rope. As he remembered later, he rested "calmly and profoundly," newly confident that his "soldiers had eaten the last meal they were to eat till they had won their independence."[1] In a report penned the night before to President Burnet, he dubbed their bivouac "Camp Safety."

Around the sleeping general, however, "a restless and anxious spirit pervad[ed] the camp."[2] Some men rose at 4:00 A.M., still believing an all-in encounter the day before would have won the day for Houston's army. That air of discontent heightened when, at eight o'clock, a Texian scout spotted a column of men approaching from the direction of Harrisburg. Karnes and Smith investigated and reported—as the intercepted dispatches had warned them might happen—that Mexican reinforcements had arrived. General Martín Perfecto de Cos, accompanied by some four hundred men and two hundred supply mules, had marched into Santa Anna's camp to drumrolls and shouts of joy.

At that moment, Deaf Smith, always a man of few words, spoke for many. "The enemy is increasing," he said simply. "Today we *must* fight, or never."[3] The head count of Houston's Texian force numbered roughly eight hundred.

As for the enemy across the field, the Texian scouts reported that Santa Anna's force had not only grown in number but had spent much of the night constructing a breastwork. Their defensive line, set back from the midfield ridge, now had a five-foot-high mass of luggage, crates, barrels of grain, sacks of corn, and hastily cut brush protecting

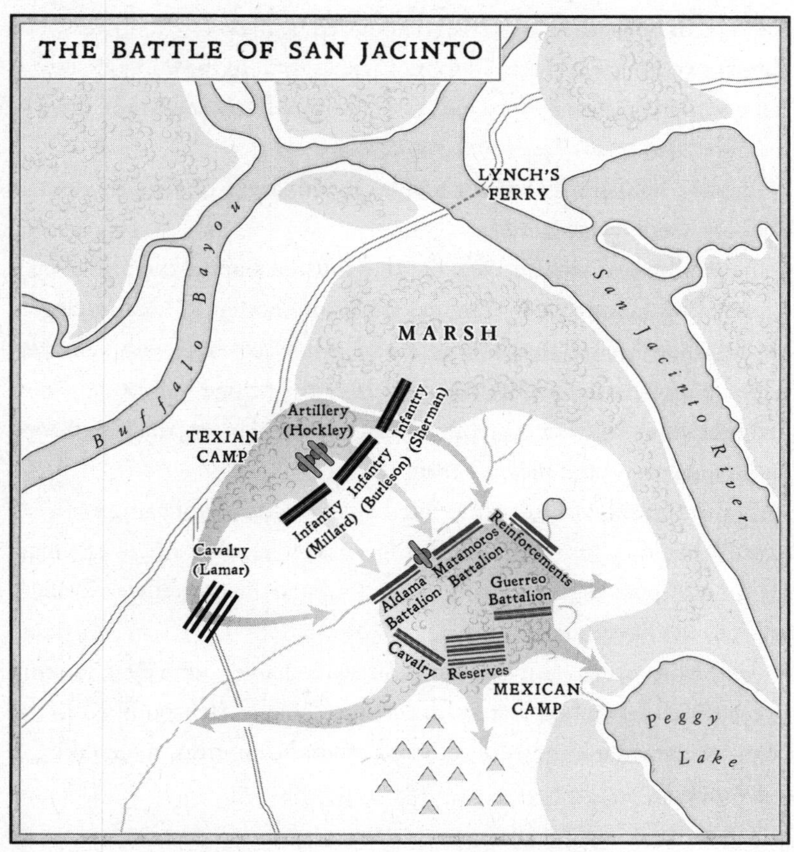

its left side. The breastwork was flanked by cannons and infantrymen on the river side and cavalry on the other.

As the sun rose toward its zenith, so did the frustrations of the Texian volunteers. By some accounts, every man was ready to fight and impatient of further delay. But Houston was biding his time one last time. He dispatched Deaf Smith to estimate the size of the enemy force. Ignoring the bullets that whistled past, Smith held his glass to his eyes, counting. The numbers were not encouraging: By this latest count, Houston's army consisted of 783 men, the enemy's more like fifteen hundred.[4]

Aware of the impatience in the ranks, Houston called a council of war. He sat beneath an oak tree surrounded by his six field officers. For almost two hours, he listened to their views, but, in the end, one essential question occupied everyone's attention: *Shall we attack the enemy in their position, or shall we await his attack?*

Finally, Houston called for a vote. By a margin of two to one, the decision was to wait.

Next Houston sent for Deaf Smith. Houston wanted the bridge over Vince's Bayou destroyed. This region was unfamiliar to him, relying as he did upon his scouts and a crude map now covered with smudged pencil annotations. But the destruction of the bridge that both armies had used might slow or even prevent the arrival of more Mexican troops and it also prevented his men from retreating.

Smith and six volunteers mounted up and rode out of camp carrying axes. When they returned—the bridge was eight miles away—the master scout reported that cutting a few timbers "made [Vince's Bridge] fall into the bayou."[5]

In the meantime, General Houston walked among the men, looking to measure their mood just as his mentor General Jackson liked to do. Many of the volunteers were gathered around campfires, some taking a late lunch.

"[He] asked us if we wanted to fight," remembered Private James Winters. "We replied with a shout that we were most anxious to do so."

Houston's response was unambiguous. "Very well," he told them, "get your dinners and I will lead you into the fight, and if you whip them every one of you shall be a captain."[6]

At 3:30 P.M. the order finally came down the line. "PARADE AND PREPARE FOR ACTION!"

REST FOR THE WEARY?

On the other side of the line, Santa Anna was taking a siesta.

That morning he had risen early. He watched the approach of Cos and his men; their arrival gave the Mexican commander added confidence, but, since they had marched all night, he permitted the exhausted soldiers to stack their arms and bed down in a nearby grove of trees. He personally made a foray into the field to appraise the Texian line through his spyglass. But by midafternoon, with no sign of action from the Texian side, Santa Anna relaxed his guard and permitted the rest of his men to stand down and stack their guns. The Texians showed no signs of attacking and, with their backs to the bayou, Houston's army certainly wasn't going to slip away.

Santa Anna decided upon a rest and, like him, many officers and soldiers lay down. Others in his army ate, took their horses to the water, or wandered into the woods to harvest tree branches for shelter. The officer in charge, General Fernández Castrillón, took the opportunity to shave, wash, and change uniforms. He paid little or no attention to the sentries who remained on duty.[7]

THE PLAN

The rise between the armies, as well as the trees overhead, helped mask Houston's battle array. Unseen by the Mexicans, he positioned his infantry divisions in two lines, with his men divided in half on either side of the cannons, which were now commanded, with Neill wounded, by his aide Colonel Hockley. The cavalry, led by Mirabeau Lamar, newly promoted by Houston to the rank of colonel, waited on his extreme right, largely hidden by a stand of trees.

His battle plan could hardly have been simpler. First, the sixty-one men on horseback would move on the Mexicans' left, "for the purpose," said Houston, "of attracting their notice." Thus distracted, the enemy might remain unaware of the infantry—shoulders hunched, half-hidden by the topography and the grasses—trotting across the prairie that separated the armies. At the same time, the Twin Sisters would be wheeled to a station within two hundred yards of the enemy's breastwork.[8]

From the treetops, lookouts reported that no Mexicans seemed to be standing sentinel.

While the uniformed Mexicans the previous day had, according to one Texian captain, looked "exceedingly grand in the[ir] picturesque costume," no two of the Texians waiting to fight looked alike.[9] They could lay no claim to being a proudly uniformed army; they remained, in looks and origin, a diverse blending of men. Frontiersmen in buckskin lined up with merchants wearing waistcoats and cravats; Stephen Austin's nephew Moses Austin Bryan wore a claw-hammer-tailed frock coat. On their heads they wore top hats, sombreros, fur caps, or round hats of wool or velvet. A few wore remnants of military uniforms, but, mud stained and tattered, none met West Point standards. The troops looked unkempt and unwashed, with matted hair and beards. There were Tejanos and Yankees, Georgians and Kentuckians, Alabamians and Virginians, Americans of all sorts with a smattering of immigrants from Europe. Houston's army shared little but a deep desire to avenge the needless slaying at the Alamo and Goliad—and to defend a free and sovereign Texas.

Houston, riding a gray stallion named Saracen, moved along the lines, which extended some twenty-five hundred feet end to end. He spoke to all the captains. He conferred with Secretary Rusk. And at four o'clock, he raised his sword.

"Trail arms!" he ordered. "Forward!"

As instructed, the men began to move through the grass carrying their guns butt down, with muzzles inclined upward. The cannoneers pulled the pair of guns forward, their low-angled barrels almost invisible in the tall grass. As the army advanced, Houston patrolled the line. "Hold your fire, men," he ordered, "hold your fire."[10]

One of the older soldiers on the field, fifty-seven-year-old Jimmy Curtis—known as "Uncle Jimmy"—carried two guns. When Secretary Rusk asked why, the settler (he had been among Stephen Austin's original Three Hundred) replied, "Damn the Mexicans; they killed my son and son-in-law in the Alamo, and I intend to kill two of them for it, or be killed myself."[11]

The men on the far left, who remained partly hidden by the thicket of trees that lined the San Jacinto River, moved quickly. They were the first to fire.

"THE ENEMY! THEY COME!"

"The enemy!" the call rang out. *"They come! They come!"*

When, shortly after four o'clock, a single Mexican bugler sounded the alarm, an officer climbed atop a stack of ammunition boxes. He saw a long line of determined men approaching.

"We marched upon the enemy," one Texian private noted, "with the stillness of death."[12]

The bloodletting had begun moments before with gunfire in the woods, followed by cannon fire from the Twin Sisters. For most of the Mexicans, the ominous booms had been a complete surprise. Hunks of deadly, high-flying horseshoe scrap and grapeshot suddenly fell from the sky into their camp.

Soon a few muzzle flashes could be seen from along the Mexican line, but the disorganized defense managed only an erratic counterfire before the Texian cavalry charged the Mexicans' left flank. And the main army kept coming.

Moments later, Houston, atop his horse some twenty yards in front of his infantry battle line, brought Saracen to a stop. He ordered the army to halt. On his command, the men, now melded into one line, knelt on one knee, raised their guns, and, as one, fired their first musket and rifle volley at a distance of sixty yards.

Through the blue haze of gun smoke, Houston ordered the men to reload, but Secretary Rusk overruled his commander in chief. "If we stop," he yelled, "we are cut to pieces. Don't stop—go ahead—give them hell."[13]

Behind the Mexican lines, chaos and confusion reigned. Men awakened from their siestas were racing for their guns. Officers screamed contradictory orders.

Suddenly the earth seemed to rise up to meet General Houston. His big stallion collapsed beneath him, the animal's hide pierced by five balls. Houston kept his feet as Saracen sank to the ground, and a soldier corralled a riderless horse for the commander. Swinging his leg over the shorter horse, Houston found his feet dangled well below the stirrups.

The Texian infantry surged forward and, as the attackers came within earshot, the Mexicans heard another terrifying sound rend the air: Houston's men unleashed bloodcurdling war cries: *"Remember the*

Alamo! Remember La Bahía! Remember Fannin!" The chorus of angry men, bent on revenge, now came at such speed that few of the surprised Mexicans had time to man their proper positions.

The infantry on their right flank surprised a division of Mexican soldiers in the trees. After an exchange of fire, Santa Anna's men retreated quickly, and the Texians moved relentlessly on.

With shocking suddenness—few of the men had stopped to reload—Houston's army was vaulting the Mexican barricade.

One regiment of attackers made the artillerists manning the Golden Standard a particular target. The Mexican gun had fired on the Texian cavalry but had turned in the direction of the Texian infantry when a rifle shot took down the man who, match in hand, was about to fire the next volley. Most of the members of the gun crew soon fell to well-aimed bullets or to charging Texians clambering over the breastwork; the surviving gunners, outmanned and overwhelmed, abandoned their station, "commenc[ing] an immediate and disorderly flight." Their commander, General Castrillón, who had stood resolutely behind the gun, urging his men to fight on, "folded up his arms, stood and looked on sullenly" before walking off. With the posture of a proud military man, Castrillón made an excellent target and soon fell, mortally wounded, his body riddled by rifle balls.[14]

The battle had barely begun when Houston, a highly visible target as he patrolled the battlefield, had another horse shot from beneath him. But this time, as the horse went down, the general himself felt a sudden pain in his left ankle. A musket ball, fired from a Mexican gun, smashed into his ankle, fracturing his leg. Houston staggered as he came off the dead horse but, leaning on a soldier who came to his aid, remained upright. Another Texian gave up his mount, and the men helped General Houston into the saddle.

Once behind the Mexican line, the attackers used their rifles as clubs; few had bayonets. Some long guns fractured, and the fighters resorted to using "heavy hunting knives as cleavers [and] their guns as clubs to knock out the brains of the Mexicans."[15] Early in the battle, Deaf Smith, thrown from his horse in the melee at the breastwork, found himself amid the enemy. "Having dropped his sword in the fall, he jumped up, drew one of his belt pistols, presented it at the head of a Mexican who was attempting to bayonet him, and the percussion-cap exploded without the pistol's going off. Upon which, Smith threw the pistol at the head of the Mexican, staggered him back, seized his gun . . . and defended himself with it."[16] Smith lived to tell the tale.

"A BEWILDERED AND PANIC STRICKEN HERD"[17]

Many, many Mexicans soon lay dead or wounded, but some Texians fell, too. One company of nineteen men sustained four casualties in the charge as the rest fought on. Another wounded man who kept fighting, despite a boot filling with blood, was General Sam Houston.

Terrified Mexican soldiers made for the trees, looking for shelter. Santa Anna himself proved unable to rally the men; he was observed "running about in the most excited manner, wringing his hands and unable to give an order."[18] Just one battalion had managed to confront the oncoming Texians when a desperate recognition struck one of Santa Anna's generals as he attempted to organize a counterattack. "In a few minutes [the Texians] won the victory that could not even be imagined."[19]

"In ten minutes after the firing of the first gun," Secretary Rusk reported the next day, "we were charging through the camp, and driving them before us."[20] In eighteen minutes, they had won.

The fight deteriorated into a one-sided rout. The Texians' blood was up as they avenged the loss of so many at the Alamo and Goliad. Some

Mexicans asked for quarter, kneeling and pleading for mercy. *"Mi no Alamo! Mi no La Bahía,"* claiming to have fought at neither the Alamo nor at Goliad.[21] The Texians were beyond hearing the enemy's denials or even the orders of Houston and his officers for the men to fall back, "to take prisoners, not to kill anyone." One lieutenant interpreted such directives for his men: "Boys, take prisoners. You know how to take prisoners: take them with the butt of your guns."[22]

Many retreating Mexicans, on reaching the shore of Peggy Lake, abandoned their guns and dove in, hoping to swim to safety. The Texian riflemen in pursuit raised their guns and commenced a deadly target practice, picking off the fleeing soldiers "as fast as they could load and shoot." The waters of the lake turned blood red.[23]

When an officer ordered them to stop, one soldier turned on him. "If Jesus Christ would come down from Heaven and order me to quit shooting yellow bellies I wouldn't do it, Sir!"

The officer reached for his sword. The soldier countered by cocking his rifle, and the officer "very discreetly . . . turned his horse and left."[24]

Some of the Mexican cavalry took to the prairie, making for Vince's Bridge, only to find it collapsed into the river and impassable. Men and horses alike drowned attempting to cross; still more men died when the Texians in pursuit caught up and "pour[ed] down upon them a deadly fire, which cut off all escape."[25]

With victory assured, Houston rode slowly back to the stand of live oaks, blood dripping from the bullet hole in his boot. On reaching the tree beneath which he'd slept the night before, he collapsed; his friend and chief of staff, Colonel Hockley, caught the half-unconscious general as he slid off his horse.

A surgeon was summoned. Once he cut the boot off Houston's badly swollen leg, bones could be seen protruding from the flesh. Dr. Alexander Ewing cleaned and dressed the wound.

Only twilight brought an end to the slaughter, and Secretary of War

Rusk accepted the surrender of Mexican colonel Juan Almonte and some two hundred men. As the shooting slowly stopped, the wounded were cared for. Guns, ammunition, horses, mules, and sabers were collected by the hundreds, and a lockbox of some $12,000 worth of silver pesos was uncovered in the Mexican camp.

The Texians had fewer than a dozen men dead or dying, another thirty or so wounded. But virtually all of the men under Santa Anna's immediate command were either dead, wounded, captive, or soon-to-be-captured. Under the watchful eyes of more than two dozen guards, the prisoners huddled around campfires they themselves built although, at first, when ordered to cut wood to build the fires, more than one Mexican worried that "we were to be burnt alive in retaliation for those who had been burnt in the Alamo."[26] Though casualty estimates varied widely, almost certainly some 630 Mexicans died in the battle, with more than two hundred wounded. The total prisoners would in the coming days exceed seven hundred.

The Texians had outperformed everybody's expectations. As Houston put it, "Every officer and man proved himself worthy of the cause in which he battled."[27] To many, the overwhelming victory brought to mind the stunning success of Andrew Jackson's army at New Orleans two decades earlier.

But as night fell, one large question remained unanswered: Where was His Excellency, Santa Anna? Additional Mexican troops were not all that far away, and if he reached them he might return for revenge.

SIXTEEN

Old San Jacinto

The 22nd day of April was the first *free* day in Texas. Before then, her people had declared their independence, but now they had won it in a noble contest. The victory was physically and morally complete [and] . . . the Texans had their revenge.

—H. Yoakum, *History of Texas*

The morning after the big battle, a detachment of Kentucky volunteers swept the prairie looking for Mexicans on the run. Near the bridge that Deaf Smith downed, Captain James Sylvester rode alone when a movement in the ravine caught his eye. He turned to call out to his squad, scouting for game in nearby woods. By the time Sylvester looked back, the figure seemed to have vanished.

The Texian captain rode closer. At first, he saw only a Mexican blanket on the ground, almost obscured by the vegetation. Then he noticed that the blanket, worn as a serape, covered a man lying motionless.

Sylvester ordered him to stand, and the stranger—certainly a Mexican—rose reluctantly. The Kentuckians surrounded him. "He was tolerably dark skinned," noted one of them, "weighed about a hundred and forty-five pounds, and wore side whiskers." Dressed in a plain cotton jacket and an old hide cap, he appeared to carry no weapons.

Despite the language barrier, they managed to learn he was a soldier and that, no, he didn't know where Santa Anna was. But Sylvester's sharp eye saw something amiss. Beneath his plain outer garments, the Mexican wore a fine shirt with studs that glimmered like precious stones.[1]

Accused of being a liar—no mere soldier would possess such a garment—the man then admitted he was an aide to Santa Anna. To prove it, he showed them a letter in his possession from one of the Mexican generals. Sylvester and his men decided Houston might wish to interrogate this man.

Once they returned with their prisoner to their battlefield camp, however, the Mexican prisoners they passed did something unexpected. On seeing the man in the humble serape, they leapt to their feet and saluted or lifted their caps. Some clapped and cheered.

"El Presidente!" they called out to him. *"General Santa Anna!"*

Captain Sylvester and his men had captured not an aide to Santa Anna but His Excellency himself.

GENERAL MEETS GENERAL

After a night deprived of sleep due to the pain, Houston lay dozing on the ground at midday. He stirred with the approach of the company and their captive. Colonel Hockley escorted Santa Anna to Houston, where the enemy commander, his plain clothing spattered with mud, stepped forward, "advancing with an air of one born to command."[2]

He announced, in Spanish, "I am General Antonio López de Santa Anna, President of Mexico, Commander-in-Chief of the Army of Operations. I place myself at the disposal of the brave General Houston."

The surprised Houston, according to one account, replied, "Ah! Ah! indeed, General Santa Anna. Happy to see you, General." He gestured toward a nearby toolbox. "Take a seat, take a seat." General Almonte, who spoke English, was summoned into the circle.

Half sitting, Houston listened. With his officer translating, Santa Anna began with flattery. "That man may consider himself born to no common destiny, who has conquered the Napoleon of the west."

Then he added, "And it now remains for [you] to be generous to the vanquished."

Houston stared at the man, then shot back, "You should have remembered that at the Alamo."

A crowd had begun to gather as word spread around the camp of the prisoner's identity.

Houston waited, but Santa Anna offered his justification.

"I had summoned a surrender and they had refused," he explained. "The place was taken by storm, and the usages of war justified the slaughter of the vanquished."

Though Sam Houston's anger was rising, his response was measured.

"That was the case once but it is now obsolete. Such usages among civilized nations have yielded to the influences of Humanity."

As the generals' exchange grew more heated, a growing undertone of voices became audible. Among the men outside the circle of officers there were "demands for the captive's blood."[3] Some called for "the butcher of the Alamo" to be shot; others wanted to hang the man.

Santa Anna, now entirely surrounded by hostile faces, asked that his medicine box be brought to him. From it he withdrew a wad of a tincture of opium, which he swallowed, to calm his nerves. For a man accustomed to complete deference from any and everyone he met, these jarring calls for his head, even if only half understood, intimidated His Excellency.

Houston pressed him on Goliad. "If you feel excused for your conduct at San Antonio, you have not the same excuse for the massacre of Colonel Fannin's command." As if twisting the sword, he went on. "They had capitulated on terms proffered by your General. And, yet, after the capitulation, they were all perfidiously massacred."

Again, Santa Anna deflected, refusing responsibility. "I was not apprised of the fact that they had capitulated," he claimed, then he blamed General Urrea. "And if the day ever comes that I can get Urrea into my hands, I will execute him for his duplicity in not giving me information of the facts."

Aware of his men and their angry murmurs, Houston realized that pursuing these questions would only fire their fury. They already wished to exact retribution. Another thought surfaced: He must keep His Excellency alive. As a matter of honor, he could not execute this man. Furthermore, his corpse would be of little value, but alive, Santa Anna carried authority with his troops. He could be an instrument, useful in negotiating a formal armistice and in securing the surrender of the other Mexican forces in Texas.

With that, Houston veered the conversation away from confrontation.

He ordered Santa Anna's tent be set up nearby, that his trunks be brought to him. The time had come for negotiation, and Secretary of War Rusk entered the conversation; the exchange that day would last nearly two hours. Rusk would ask His Excellency to order his other generals "to evacuate the country." Santa Anna, according to one of Houston's aides, "displayed great diplomatic skill in the negotiation." He refused at first, but eventually he agreed to do as asked.[4]

The agreed-upon terms would bring a complete stop to the fighting. Santa Anna would order his generals to retreat the way they had come. In time, a treaty would be negotiated and signed (neither Houston nor Rusk could speak for the Texas government), but an armistice had been reached between these men. Provided with his own writing desk, Santa Anna wrote out orders.

Once the letters were done, Deaf Smith stowed them in his saddlebags. He would gallop that night toward the banks of the Brazos River, where Santa Anna's orders would be delivered into the hands of General Filisola.

"I am a prisoner," His Excellency wrote to his generals, "in the hands of the enemy." More important, he informed them, "I have agreed with General Houston for an armistice." Then he issued a command: The other Mexican regiments in Texas were to countermarch to San Antonio. All prisoners were to be freed. No inhabitants of Texas were to be interfered with. "Negotiations are under way to bring the war to an end for ever."[5]

The fight for Texas's freedom had been won.

SEVENTEEN

President Sam Houston

My venerated friend, you will perceive that Texas is presented to the United States as a bride adorned for her espousal.

—Sam Houston to Andrew Jackson

Two weeks after the battle, infection threatened Houston's leg. He rested on a cot, a mile or so from the battlefield but within range of the stench of unburied and rotting Mexican corpses. Without proper medicines and treatment, Dr. Ewing warned, lockjaw might kill him. Houston agreed to travel to New Orleans to seek the medical care he needed after handing off his duties to Secretary of War Rusk.

Several days earlier, the *Yellow Stone* had returned to Lynch's Ferry. The riverboat's passengers included President Burnet and the cabinet, who arrived to take charge of the peace. Never an admirer of Houston and jealous at his success, Burnet was angered that a preliminary treaty had been signed without his consultation; he had few good words for the victorious general. He held Houston in low regard, despite the events of April 21, blaming him for the long campaign, for the plight of the fleeing settlers—the "Runaway Scrape," as it would be known—

and even the failure of the Texian army to capture the entire Mexican force.

On May 5, the feverish Houston bade his soldiers farewell. Unlike Burnet, the troops now revered their general, and he returned their esteem. "Your valor and heroism have proved you unrivalled," Houston told them. "You have patiently endured privations, hardships, and difficulties." He promised them that, one day, they would be justly famous and would proudly say, "I was a member of the army of San Jacinto."[1]

When Rusk and his brother brought Houston, still prone on a cot, to the dock, President Burnet refused Houston passage on the *Yellow Stone.* The ship was to carry the president and his cabinet, along with Santa Anna, back to Galveston, where they planned to complete the peace negotiations. According to Burnet, Houston, having resigned his commission, was no longer welcome aboard the vessel.

The ship's captain disagreed. "This ship is not sailing," he said firmly, "unless General Houston is on it."[2]

Captain John Ross knew and admired Houston; Ross's ship had played a crucial role earlier in the fight, ferrying Houston's army across the Brazos River at Groce's Landing. In the face of Ross's insistence, Burnet had no choice but to watch Major General Rusk and his brother, David, carry the ailing Houston aboard.

When the *Yellow Stone* reached Galveston, the parties went in separate directions. Burnet and his cabinet, together with their prisoner, Santa Anna, proceeded to Velasco, where they negotiated what would become known as the Treaty of Velasco. The terms were much as Houston and Rusk had suggested in the articles of understanding they prepared: Santa Anna pledged not to attack Texas and, on his return to Mexico, to use his influence on his government to agree to the peace. Santa Anna also signed a second, secret document in which he agreed to try to persuade his fellow Mexicans to recognize the Republic of

Texas as an independent state and to accept the Rio Grande as the international boundary.

As for Houston, he found passage aboard the schooner *Flora*, and lay semiconscious on the narrow deck. The ship's captain believed his famous passenger, his leg loosely wrapped in a bloodstained shirt, to be a dying man. But word of Houston's imminent arrival preceded him, and on May 22, when the *Flora* arrived in New Orleans, a cheering throng lined the levee. Some of the crowd surged aboard the little merchant vessel, nearly swamping the two-masted merchantman. All had come to see the general.

With a great effort, Houston rose to his feet to greet them. The man that many Texans now thought of as "Old San Jacinto" had become a hero, but the crowd fell silent when, after briefly bracing himself against the gunwale to greet them, he collapsed onto a litter. As she would recall years later, the sight of the great man so perilously ill caused a seventeen-year-old named Margaret Lea to burst into tears.

The same surgeon who, twenty-one years before, treated the wounds Houston sustained at the Battle of Horseshoe Bend removed twenty shards of bone from Houston's ankle. The patient improved slowly, recuperating in the home of a friend, a fellow soldier with whom he had marched into battle during the War of 1812. A week passed before he felt able to sit up for more than a few sips of water.

Although still weak, he began the trip back to Texas in mid-June. He regarded Nacogdoches as his home, but the ambitious Houston, a veteran of more than a few political battles, understood he now possessed real clout in Texas—and in these formative weeks in Texas's quickly evolving history, he couldn't afford to be out of sight and out of mind. He made it to Nacogdoches on June 26. Exhausted by the journey, he had no choice but to rest a few days before moving on to San Augustine, arriving there on July 5.

He corresponded constantly with friends, worrying about the state of the army and the continuing Mexican threat. General Rusk kept him apprised of political events and, in particular, of interim president Burnet's proclamation, issued July 23, calling for a general election so Texians could choose the newly independent state's president and vice president and the first Congress. The ballot also contained two crucial referenda: One sought approval of the new constitution; the other was a vote on whether the republic's citizens desired annexation by the United States. Six weeks later the people would cast their ballots.

Given his fame, he seemed a logical candidate for president, but Houston played hard to get. He insisted he could not run against the two announced candidates, his respected colleagues Stephen Austin and former governor Henry Smith. Only after repeated popular outcries—among them a mass meeting in San Augustine and a petition with six hundred signatures from Columbia—did Houston agree to run. "You will learn that I have yielded to the wishes of my friends in allowing my name to be run for President," he announced in a letter published in the *Telegraph and Texas Register.* "The crisis requires it or I would not have yielded."[3]

A week later, on September 5, Texians spoke with one voice. The voters approved the proposed state constitution by an overwhelming margin. Virtually every voter favored annexation. And Sam Houston won in a landslide, elected the republic's president by a margin of almost nine to one (5,119 for Houston, 743 for Smith, and 587 for Austin). Gracious in victory, he named Austin secretary of state and Smith secretary of the treasury. Mirabeau Buonaparte Lamar, the man Houston promoted to colonel on the San Jacinto battlefield, was seated as vice president.

After his swearing in, on October 22, Houston faced many challenges, but one of the most immediate was the matter of His Excellency. Despite having been promised his freedom after the Treaty of Velasco, Santa Anna remained a prisoner of the Republic of Texas.

SANTA ANNA MEETS ANDREW JACKSON

His Excellency lived in limbo. On May 14, he had signed the two treaties with the Republic of Texas. The documents stipulated that he was free to return home, and on June 1, he boarded the armed schooner *Invincible*, ordered to carry him to the Mexican city of Vera Cruz. Suddenly, however, the rules changed and Santa Anna embarked instead on a bizarre, nine-month odyssey.

Before the *Invincible* could put to sea, a mob of Texian volunteers interceded. Against his will, His Excellency was escorted back to shore, where, "in accordance with the overwhelming public will of the citizens of the country, he should . . . await the public will to determine his fate."[4] In spite of what their government had agreed, many citizens wanted this man to face court-martial for war crimes. In one widely distributed pamphlet published that summer, the Mexican general's fall from grace was put in mythological terms: "Don Antonio, Icarus, in attempting to soar too high, was precipitated into the abyss below." The pamphlet condemned him as a "monster."[5] There were rumors of a plan to take him to Goliad for execution.

In July, Stephen Austin attempted to resolve the dispute. Having recently returned from the United States, Austin visited the Mexican general, whom he knew from his own time of incarceration in Mexico City two years before. Austin suggested that perhaps the American government might mediate. Impatient and nervous at his fate, Santa Anna promptly wrote directly to Andrew Jackson, complaining of his "close confinement."[6] The recuperating Sam Houston added his voice to the conversation, writing on Santa Anna's behalf to President Jackson.

Jackson took no action; he had carefully maintained his country's neutrality throughout the conflict. But he did register his opinion with his friend Sam Houston. A trial and execution of the foreign leader would be contrary to the rules of civilized warfare. "Nothing could tarnish the character of Texas more," Jackson argued. "Let not his blood be shed . . . both wisdom and humanity enjoin this course."[7]

Santa Anna had spent six weeks with a ball and chain on his leg after a suspected escape plot. Little changed until Houston was sworn in as the first duly elected president of Texas, when he took immediate charge of the matter. First, he visited the prisoner and came away persuaded that Santa Anna was the best advocate for the new nation's quest for formal recognition by Mexico. Santa Anna had already signed a treaty in which he acknowledged "in his official character as the chief of the Mexican nations . . . the full, entire, and perfect Independence of the republic of Texas."[8]

Santa Anna agreed to undertake a mission to Washington, D.C. "Convinced as I am that Texas will never be reunited with Mexico," he promised to negotiate for peace and a final resolution of boundaries.[9] After another hot debate with the Texas government about Santa Anna's fate—the Texas Congress passed a resolution to further detain Santa Anna—Houston, claiming executive privilege, authorized the departure of his old nemesis. Santa Anna quietly headed for the American capital via an overland route, accompanied by his aides and a military escort led by Colonel Hockley.

Unlikely as it seemed, the defeated dictator had become an emissary for Sam Houston and the Republic of Texas. The United States had yet to recognize Texas and thus would not meet officially with its representatives. But in an oddity of diplomatic formalities, Santa Anna could sit down with Old Hickory—a man whose interest in Texas had never waned—and speak on Texas's behalf.

The route took His Excellency to the Sabine River, then across Louisiana. "We traveled in the *Tennessee* up the Mississippi for twenty days, then continued up the Ohio river, landing close to Louisville."[10] On the stage journey that followed, Santa Anna fell ill and spent a few days with a severe cold. But he managed to charm many of the Americans he met, impressing them as a man "pleasant of countenance and speech . . . very polite, and using stately compliments."[11] Finally, on January 17, 1837, Santa Anna's entourage arrived in Washington.

President Jackson had closely followed the progress of the Texas war; during Houston's retreat, one visitor to the president's house had found him tracing the movements of both armies on a map spread before him. And he knew the score in Mexico, since the Mexican ambassador had told him officially that, as a prisoner, Santa Anna no longer spoke for his country. Nevertheless, Jackson treated him like a head of state.

"General Jackson greeted me warmly," Santa Anna reported, "and honored me at a dinner attended by notables of all countries."[12] The formal dinner with the cabinet and foreign diplomats wasn't the end of it; over the coming days, the two leaders talked privately at least twice.

At the first private meeting, Santa Anna spoke freely in favor of Texan independence. Jackson listened, dressed casually in an old calico robe and smoking a long-stemmed pipe. The Mexican reminded Jackson that, not so many years earlier, the American ambassador had offered to purchase Texas. The circumstances were different now, he admitted, but perhaps $3.5 million might be a reasonable amount. Both men knew the Texians would oppose any such deal—wasn't Texas already independent?—and the conversation carried on.

Santa Anna managed to ingratiate himself with Jackson, who commissioned his "court painter," Ralph E. W. Earl, to take the Mexican's portrait. Santa Anna went daily to the president's house to sit for Earl, who, as an intimate friend of Jackson, maintained his studio there. After six days, Jackson authorized a U.S. Navy vessel, the *Pioneer*, to carry Santa Anna to Vera Cruz, the very destination designated many months before in the Velasco treaty. His Excellency sailed from Norfolk, Virginia, on January 26.

Their conversations left President Jackson with much to think about. Perhaps Santa Anna would persuade the new Mexican administration to recognize the treaties of Velasco or the independence of Texas; maybe he wouldn't. But Jackson did know the voters of Texas wanted to join the United States, a desire shared for many years by Houston and Jackson, who now served as presidents of their respective countries. Yet, for the moment, at least, the political realities in Washington made that impossible.

The nation was grappling with a growing and angry debate about slavery. Powerful people in the North—among them Jackson's old nemesis John Quincy Adams, now an outspoken congressman—zealously guarded a delicate balance in Congress, and the admission of Texas as a slaveholding state would topple that house of cards. Jackson couldn't simply order annexation; the powers of the president did not extend that far. But he did have a hand he could play.

In the waning days of his second term, he reached out to his allies in Congress and a resolution passed; it wasn't annexation but the next best thing: recognition of the Republic of Texas as an independent nation. In Jackson's last official act before leaving office, he named a chargé d'affaires to Texas. When the appointment was confirmed by Congress near midnight on Friday, March 4, Jackson invited two Texas officials to join him in a glass of wine. They toasted: *To Texas!*[13] Officially, in the view of the United States of America, the Republic of Texas became an independent country.

EPILOGUE

The Founding and the Founders of Texas

> Our success in the action is conclusive proof of such daring intrepidity and courage; every officer and man proved himself worthy of the cause in which he battled, while the triumph received a lustre from the humanity which characterized their conduct after victory.
>
> —Sam Houston, April 25, 1836

The men who fought for Texas in 1835–36 would fill the ranks of its first generation of leaders. Some held important political offices; others continued to serve in its army. They became a permanent part of Texas history.

Not a few of those who fought—and some who died in the cause—became half-remembered names that appear on the map of today's Texas. There are counties named for Bowie, Fannin, Karnes, Milam, Burnet, and Deaf Smith, along with uncounted cities and towns whose names commemorate soldiers and officers in the Texian army. These names—and a shared commitment by the state and its educators—help keep the Texas Revolution alive in the minds of the state's citizens.

When STEPHEN F. AUSTIN died on December 27, 1836, President Houston proclaimed, "The Father of Texas is no more! The first pioneer of the wilderness has departed." He ordered a twenty-three-gun salute (one for each county in the republic), to be fired at all posts, garrisons, and detachments "as soon as information is received of this melancholy event."[1] The empresario was destined to be remembered as the William Bradford of Texas; his "Three Hundred" as the Texas pilgrims. When the Texas capital was relocated to a place called Waterloo on the Colorado River, the name was changed to Austin in his honor.

ERASTUS (DEAF) SMITH played an incalculably large role in the Texas Revolution. His intelligence gathering looms large in the narrative that led to the Battle of San Jacinto. His destruction of the bridge at Vince's Bayou meant a great deal after the battle; its destruction prevented Santa Anna's escape on the afternoon of April 21. If he had gotten away, His Excellency might have rejoined the rest of his army and engaged in further fights with the Texians. In the long list of historical what-ifs, one can only wonder.

After the war, Deaf Smith returned to San Antonio and his Tejana wife, Guadalupe. He remained in the army of the Texas republic, and after Sam Houston became president, the new chief executive commissioned a portrait of Smith from the same artist, T. Jefferson Wright, who would paint two of Houston. But Smith would die, at age fifty, just nine months after the Battle of San Jacinto. The cause of death was a lung ailment, quite likely consumption (tuberculosis), a condition no doubt worsened by his months of service to the Texian cause.

MIRABEAU BUONAPARTE LAMAR succeeded Houston, becoming the second president of Texas and Houston's chief political rival; DAVID G. BURNET served as Lamar's vice president. JAMES SYLVESTER returned to his first career and found work as a printer at the *New Orleans Picayune.* MOSELEY BAKER became a Methodist minister. JAMES COLLINSWORTH served as the republic's first chief justice (in 1836) before committing suicide (in 1838).

Although Jim Bowie and David Crockett died at the Alamo, both men gained the status of legend in Texas and beyond. Disputed mythologies emerged, with contradictory accounts of their actions and where and how each man died. Whatever the actual facts of their deaths, they did the opposite of slide into obscurity. Crockett became the ultimate symbol of the plain-speaking frontiersman—a man-versus-nature character uniquely equipped to confront the unknown, a man willing to fight for what he believed regardless of personal cost. Bowie stands as the ultimate fighter, a man as tough as he was resourceful, his fame only enhanced by the weapon that bore his name.

In military annals, the heroic lines of wordsmith William Barret Travis—*"I am determined to sustain myself as long as possible & die like a soldier who never forgets what is due to his own honor & that of his country"*—still ring as raw and powerful as any prayer.

Many survivors of the Texas War of Independence went on to record their recollections in books, essays, and interviews. To name just a few . . . after his adventures with the New Orleans Greys—which involved escaping alive from Goliad—Herman Ehrenberg returned to his native Germany and wrote a book, *Texas und seine Revolution* (1843). It didn't appear in an English translation until 1935, when it was released bearing the title *With Milam and Fannin: Adventures of a German Boy in Texas' Revolution.* Noah Smithwick, by then old and blind, dictated his memoirs to his daughter; though he died in 1899, she oversaw publication the following year. Drs. Barnard and Labadie wrote invaluable narratives of what happened at Goliad and San Jacinto, respectively. Perhaps the last of the survivors to die was Enrique Esparza, just twelve years old when the Alamo fell. As an old man, the Tejano was still telling the story into the early years of the twentieth century.

On the Mexican side, a number of officers also recorded their version of events, including Vicente Filisola, Pedro Delgado, and José Enrique de la Peña.

SUSANNA DICKINSON's life grew no less complicated. She would marry a total of five times; one soon-to-be ex-husband accused her of taking up residence in a "house of ill fame." But she lived until 1883, having spent the last quarter century married to a prosperous businessman and undertaker. Almeron and Susanna's daughter, Angelina, died less happily, of a hemorrhaging uterus, at age thirty-four, after a checkered life involving three abandoned children, three marriages, and years of working as a prostitute during the Civil War.

THE ALAMO itself assumed a place in the history and the mythology of Texas. The narrative is irresistible: Brave men fighting for freedom and democracy are crushed by a brutal autocrat and then avenged. It is a tale of good and evil, with the democratic future taking on a dictatorial regime that had robbed the people of their rights. The men at the Alamo lost both the battle and their lives, but they gained immortality in the epic of Texas.

On his return to Mexico, in February 1837, ANTONIO LÓPEZ DE SANTA ANNA, his reputation tarnished by the defeat at San Jacinto, went into retirement. A year later, however, he resumed military service and helped repel a French assault on Vera Cruz. After losing a leg in the engagement, his reputation rose to nearly its previous heights—the leg was given a state funeral—and, for a time in the early 1840s, he resumed power as president. He served as Mexico's provisional president during the war with the United States (1846–48), during which his army was defeated twice on the field of battle by American troops. He lived a long life, in and out of power, exiled for periods to Jamaica, Venezuela, Cuba, and even, in 1867, the United States. He completed his memoirs in 1874 and died two years later, lame, bitter, and senile, in Mexico City, aged eighty.

Santa Anna's role in the Texas Revolution would be debated over the decades. Even some of his own officers judged him a butcher, and within months of the events of early 1836, a Mexican officer wrote a memoir describing the "infamies that have occurred in this campaign, infamies that must have horrified the civility world." But his superiors suppressed the book; it would not be published until late in the twentieth century.[2] Military historians on all sides agree that the great Texian victory at San Jacinto was made possible in part by Santa Anna's tactical errors: He permitted too great a distance to separate him from reinforcements and his sources of supply and, even more important, he made his San Jacinto camp in a vulnerable location, with bodies of water on three sides and nearby piney woods and oak groves that provided cover for Houston and undercut the advantages of the Mexican cavalry.

THE STATE OF TEXAS

In 1838, forbidden by the Texas Constitution to serve consecutive terms, President SAM HOUSTON left office. He spent much of the following summer in Nashville, visiting Andrew Jackson at the Hermitage. In 1840, he remarried; his new wife, Margaret Lea, had first laid her violet eyes on him in New Orleans when the wounded General Houston could barely stand.

His wife was twenty-six years his junior but convinced the man once known as "the Big Drunk" to stop drinking. (Several years later at a public event he made a "Big Speech" before a barbecue that one in attendance described as "a cold water doins. The Old Chief did not touch or taste or handle the smallest drop of the ardent."[3]) Margaret would bear eight children, among them a son, Andrew Jackson Houston, who wrote a fine book about the Texas Revolution, published a century after the Battle of San Jacinto.

In 1841, Houston won reelection as president of a prosperous Texas (its population had more than doubled). As his three-year term grew to a close, he once again enlisted Andrew Jackson in a campaign to fulfill their shared wish for Texas, the immediate annexation into the Union.

By then the great Jackson suffered from many ailments; a hard life had taken a toll and he surely neared the end. But he immediately rose to Houston's challenge. The task proved sustaining for Jackson. He and his old Washington operatives made the case to congressional cohorts. It was Jackson's last great cause, and he fought for it against the determined opposition of two other great men of the time, John Quincy Adams and Henry Clay.

Houston and Jackson—and the Texans, as they soon became generally known—were rewarded with the passage of the annexation resolution. The great, unruly Texas would become the twenty-eighth American state, although Mexico, having never formally recognized the Republic of Texas, would not abandon its claims on Texas until after the Mexican-American War, with the signing of the Treaty of Guadalupe Hidalgo in 1848.

Although Jackson died within a few months, Sam Houston would, along with THOMAS JEFFERSON RUSK, represent Texas in the U.S. Senate. (Rusk would, however, take his own life in 1857, in his grief at the death of his wife.) Houston regularly found himself in the crossfire of controversy both during his two terms in the Senate and, after 1859, when, as Texas's aging elder statesman, he was reelected to yet another term as governor of Texas. His last public role ended prematurely when he was forced to resign, having taken an unpopular stance against secession. He would die on July 26, 1863, but among the last words Sam Houston spoke, according to his fifteen-year-old daughter Maggie, were "*Texas! Texas!*"[4]

The debates that seemed always to swirl around him did not end with his death. No two biographers or military historians agreed about

Houston's war, his politics, his character, or his life. In no instance is that more true than his role as Texas's commander in chief in early 1836.

As early as July 1837 a pamphlet appeared attacking his conduct of the war, asserting that the men in his command forced him to fight.[5] The debate endures to the present day concerning his willingness (or lack of willingness) to fight Santa Anna's army. The long retreat (the "Runaway Scrape"—the origins of the name remain obscure, but not its unflattering meaning); the turn south at the "Which-Way Tree"; and the final decision to attack on April 21 are all subject to disagreement. On the one hand, his detractors regarded him as a coward; among them were officers who had served him, including Moseley Baker, who in 1837 attempted to impeach Houston, who was then serving as president of Texas.

Houston defended himself, sometimes in the second person. Houston wasn't bashful about defending his "glorious victory" at San Jacinto. "Here was born, in the throes of revolution and amid the strike on contending legions, the infant of Texas independence!" he once said. "Here that latest scourge of mankind, the arrogantly self-styled 'Napoleon of the West,' met his fate."[6] Sam Houston, through some mix of luck, instinct, fortuitous timing, and the good counsel—and bravery—of the men around him, did something remarkable. He and his army of farmers and shopkeepers, men distracted by the plight of their families and friends, who had become homeless wanderers fleeing for their lives, faced off with a large professional army, one amply supplied with guns, artillery, and munitions. And won a stunning, one-sided victory.

In the days after that battle, he quickly emerged as a Texas icon, indispensable, the man most often credited with winning Texas her independence. And the flood of American citizens that poured into Texas thought of him as the founder.

Often he let other people speak to his character; for one, he gave Henderson King Yoakum, a lawyer friend, access to his closely held papers to write a history of early Texas, in which Houston was cast in favorable light (Yoakum's two-volume history of Texas's early days was published in 1846). Houston himself produced a remarkable memoir, *The Life of Sam Houston*, with the memorable subtitle *The Only Authentic Memoir of Him Ever Published.*

Sam Houston, a lover of books since childhood, recognized the power of the printed word.

In the end, this isn't a story of politics, local or geopolitical. The brief war of independence is a story of redemption: The slaughter at the Alamo was avenged with the stunning victory at San Jacinto. An unlikely hero emerged in the process and, schooled by Andrew Jackson, Sam Houston performed the role of Texas's George Washington.

In a larger context, the devastating losses and the remarkable outcome of the war helped shape the character of a new nation, one destined to flower only briefly before binding its destiny to that of the United States. Taken together, the events of spring 1836 were a defining moment in the formation of the larger American character.

In the American memory the Alamo defenders became martyrs to liberty. That's why we remember them and the place where they fell.

A wise man once observed, "Quarter hours decide the destinies of nations." The words have been credited to Napoléon, but whether he said them or not, he would undoubtedly have agreed that San Jacinto's eighteen minutes amounts to a textbook example. The fight at the Alamo remains the best-remembered event of the war, but in military and even political terms, the battle on April 21, 1836, at San Jacinto stands higher. Sam Houston's greatest day not only secured independence for what would be the Republic of Texas, but it also made possible the fulfillment of his and Jackon's dream. Thanks to Houston, Texas could now one day become part of the great American story. And thanks to Texas, America could one day spread from sea to shining sea.

AFTERWORD

Old Sam and Honest Abe

I am making my last effort to save Texas from the yawning gulf of ruin.

—Sam Houston to Ed Burleson, November 9, 1860

During the winter of 1860–61, Sam Houston looked his age. At sixty-seven, Governor Houston was a father figure to the 600,000 men, women, and children of Texas. Only it looked like the Texans weren't going to listen to their elder this time.

Beyond Texas's borders, the nation was coming apart. In response to Abraham Lincoln's election to the presidency, Southerners had called for secession in November 1860. South Carolina had, in December, withdrawn from the Union, followed the next month by Mississippi, Florida, Alabama, Georgia, and Louisiana. Now there was talk that Texas might follow them.

In 1859, Houston had run for the governorship on a pro-Union platform. At his inauguration in December he had preached unity, saying that "When Texas united her destiny with that of the government of the United States, she . . . entered into not the North, nor into the South, but into the Union; her connection was not sectional but national."[1] He wasn't about to let the state to which he had devoted his life leave the union without pushing back.

The odds were not in Houston's favor—no question, the fight for slavery and state rights was important to many, many Texans—but Houston was beloved by many Texans and used his influence. He wasn't afraid to pluck the heartstrings of those who revered him as a Texan founding father. "I cannot be long among you," he'd told a crowd the previous fall. "My sands of life are fast running out. As the glass becomes exhausted, if I can feel that I leave my country prosperous and united, I shall die content."[2]

As admired as he was, Houston's emotional appeal did not stop the secessionist tide, and Houston turned to his political wiles. First, he tried to outmaneuver the secessionists, refusing their demand that he call a special session of the Texas legislature. Then, when his opponents convened a special Texas Secession Convention anyway and promptly voted to secede, Houston declared a statewide ballot was required to make their vote legitimate. Finally, when the majority of the state voted to leave the Union, Houston insisted that Texas could withdraw from the Union only to return to independence. The reborn Republic of Texas, he argued, could not legitimately join the Confederacy.

The very last thing the old warrior wanted was for Texas to go to war—and he was sure that joining the Confederacy would make that inevitable. "I know what war is," he told a committee of Texas secessionists, opening his shirt to reveal to them fresh bandages on wounds he sustained in 1814 at the Battle of Horseshoe Bend, which had never fully healed. "War is no plaything and this war will be a bloody war. There will be thousands and thousands who march away from our homes never to come back."[3]

Houston's stratagems and arguments were ultimately in vain. On March 15, 1861, the delegates to the Texas Secession Convention swore a unanimous oath of allegiance to the Confederacy while he was not present. At eight o'clock that evening Houston heard a knock at the door of the governor's mansion. A convention delegate presented a demand, an order for Houston to appear at noon the following day to take the same vow.

With no way of pushing off the decision, the aged Houston now had to decide. Would he be loyal to Texas or the Union? Would he sign the oath presented by the representatives of the people? He had only hours to make up his mind.

After reading a Bible chapter aloud to his household, he bade his family good night. His gait uneven, he made his way upstairs to his bedroom, where he removed his coat, vest, and shoes. He then began to pace the length of the mansion's cavernous upper hall. As his eldest daughter Nancy described the long night, Houston "wrestl[ed] with his spirit as Jacob wrestled with the angel until the purple dawn of another day shone over the eastern hills."[4]

By morning, he had made a decision. His wife, who had listened to the nighttime creaking of the pine floorboards above, heard the news first when Old Sam descended.

"Margaret," he told her, "I will never do it."

As ordered, Houston did go to the capitol. In his office, he sat quietly in his chair, his eyes fixed on a small piece of wood, whittling as he so often did when deep in thought. He had prepared a speech, which read, in part, "In the name of the Constitution of Texas, which has been trampled upon, I refuse to take this oath." At noon he heard the summons.

"*Sam Houston! Sam Houston! Sam Houston,*" rang out from the chamber above.

Houston heard the summons. He exited his office. But instead of heading upstairs and delivering his speech, he simply walked out the door.

He knew he was beaten, that to give another of his powerful speeches would only inflame things. The speech could be published later, he decided. For now, he would return to the governor's mansion and allow the conventioneers to conclude what they would.

When he failed to appear, the conventioneers promptly declared the office of governor vacant. Houston, once the hero of Texas, had been kicked out.

Back at the governor's mansion, he began to pack up his papers and his books. He and Margaret and their children would be moving, bound for political exile. At last, after devoting most of the previous half century to public service, his long history of leadership was coming to an end.

Or was it?

MR. LINCOLN'S LETTERS

That same week, a messenger arrived from Washington, D.C. Leaping from his exhausted horse, the rider handed Sam Houston a letter, its official wax seal intact. The letter had traveled more than fifteen hundred miles. The sender? Abraham Lincoln.

Houston's Union sympathies were well known in Washington. One of Lincoln's most trusted advisors, Francis P. Blair, Sr., described him as "a true union man." The rumor mill suggested he might even be Lincoln's choice for secretary of war.

In the letter, Lincoln made no such offer. Instead, he asked for Houston's help. Since his inauguration, Lincoln had focused his energy on retaining any southern states that had yet to secede. He thought it particularly important to keep Virginia, the state he could see from his upstairs office at the White House. He might well lose Tennessee and Arkansas, but could the Union hold the border states of Maryland, Kentucky, and Missouri? And then there was the vast territory of Texas: If the Union could retain Houston's state, could that be a bulwark?

Desperate to keep the largest state in the Union, Lincoln had a proposition for the man Texans most respected: he would provide federal support if Houston would help keep Texas in the Union.

With Lincoln's double request, Houston found himself in a quandary. On the one hand, the president wanted Houston to join the Union cause and promised him the support of the U.S. Army and Navy. On the other, the secessionists had already outflanked Houston, dismissing him from office; he was literally packing his bags, facing an unwanted retirement and unlikely to prevail through persuasion.

Should he accept the offer? He didn't fear being an outcast; he'd been one before. He had a chance to be back in military command: Lincoln had offered him the rank of major general and there were still federal troops in Texas that would be under his command. He could undoubtedly raise Texas volunteers, perhaps tens of thousands of men. But could such an army make a difference? Would Houston somehow turn the tide? Could he tip Texas back from the brink of the kind of bloodshed he so wanted to avoid? And did he want to take up arms against his beloved state?

Rarely a man to seek the counsel of others, Houston nonetheless summoned four valued friends in the wee hours after reading the letter. In a secret meeting in the upstairs library of the governor's mansion, he told the four of Lincoln's offer. He laid out the situation. He shared with them his dilemma.

Texas legislator Ben Epperson responded first. The youngest of the party, he spoke passionately in favor of accepting the offer, of taking up arms and fighting the secessionists. David Culberson, a transplanted Georgian, thought differently. He argued that Texas, given its great distance from the likely battlefields east of the Mississippi, would escape many of the war's horrors. If, however, they were to fight the secessionists, "the State would necessarily become the theatre of active and widespread hostilities, and the land be overrun and devastated with fire and sword."[5] The other two sided with Culberson, speaking against Lincoln's proposal.

After hearing his friends out, Houston sat silently, deep in thought. Then, moving abruptly to the mantel, he crumpled the correspondence from Lincoln and tossed it into the fire on the hearth. As the men watched, Lincoln's invitation burned to ashes, along with Houston's hopes for Texas.

He turned to his friends. "Gentlemen, I have asked your advice and will take it, but if I was twenty years younger I would not."[6] He knew he was too old to fight. His family was too young, with children ranging in age from seven months to seventeen years. The offer was too late. And Sam Houston could not bring himself to start a civil war between Texans.

TWO OLD SOLDIERS

On March 31, Houston would leave Austin, headed for his home near Galveston. But before he left, Noah Smithwick, one of his Alamo Avengers, came to call.

Secession, Smithwick said, filled him with "a feeling of inexpressible sadness." He had decided to leave Texas, to head for California, "fleeing the wrath to come." But before going, he wished to offer his services to Sam Houston one last time.

"General," he told Houston, "if you will again unfurl the Lone Star from the capitol, I will bring you a hundred men to help maintain it there."

Though honored by the man's willingness to fight for him, Houston remained firm. "My friend," he told Smithwick, "I have seen Texas pass through one long, bloody war. I do not wish to involve her in civil strife. I have done all I could to keep her from seceding, and now if she won't go with me I'll have to turn and go with her."[7]

Houston's biggest fear was the outcome of the imminent war, and, in April, he warned his fellow Texans they might well be the losers. "[T]he North is determined to preserve this Union. They are not a fiery, impulsive people as you are, for they live in colder climates. But when they begin to move in a given direction . . . they move with the steady momentum and perseverance of a mighty avalanche; and what I fear is, they will overwhelm the South."[8]

A few days later, after word of the bombardment at Fort Sumter reached Texas, he tried and failed to dissuade Sam Houston Jr. from enlisting in the Confederate Army. The teenaged Sam ignored his father's pleas; though wounded at Shiloh, he would survive the war, having gained a lieutenant's rank.

Sam Sr., however, would not live to see the end of the war, dying two years before Lincoln saw the country reunited in April 1865. Had he lived, he would have rejoiced to see the Union restored and mourned to see the death of Honest Abe. Unlikely brothers, their differences outnumbering their similarities, they shared a dread of civil war and a deep love for the Constitution. They were constitutionalists to the core who put their faith in the governing document, courageous men unafraid to take hard positions. They suffered for their country, and without them we would not have the great nation we've been privileged to inherit.

—Brian Kilmeade, May 2020

ACKNOWLEDGMENTS

This book would not have been possible without John Finley, who oversaw the launch of Fox Nation in 2018 and allowed me to host a series called "What Made America Great." Finley's passion and knowledge of history rivals anyone I have met, and his faith in me to pull off this series was truly gratifying. After American viewers received our first topic, the Alamo, enthusiastically, I knew it had to be the subject of my next book.

After I had decided to write about the Alamo, legendary documentarian Ken Burns prompted me to expand the story of the Alamo into a book about American victory, ending with the Battle of San Jacinto. I'm grateful to him for his guidance and inspiration.

Thanks for getting the book made goes to the team at Sentinel, led by its president and publisher, Adrian Zackheim. He once again spearheaded a tight-knit, visionary group, including first and foremost my editor, Bria Sandford, who guided me through the writing of this book fearlessly; her talent, intelligence, and expertise is indispensable on every project. Sentinel's publicity team, led by Tara Gilbride, is the best in the business, and publicist Marisol Salaman never leaves the smallest detail unaddressed. Thank you also to Madeline Montgomery and Helen Healey, who were crucial to the marketing and editorial efforts. Special thanks to Bob Barnett for making this relationship possible.

My producer, Alyson Mansfield, is the glue who brings all of these books and book tours together, along with lining up radio and TV; her leadership is formidable. Thank you to *Brian Kilmeade Radio Show* superstars Pete Catrina and Eric Albein, who offer each book tremendous support on our airwaves—from coming up with creative ways to spread the word to bringing on special guests to discuss the book. The special and on-air support would not be possible without the backing of John Sylvester and Doug Murphy.

The special media promotion was pioneered and produced by the husband-and-wife team of Paul and Amanda Guest, who might just be the best in the business.

Lauren Petterson, Gavin Hadden, and the entire *Fox and Friends* staff are without a doubt the engine behind this book. They make every book launch feel like a holiday, getting our audience excited about another great slice of American history is coming their way. Special thanks to anchors Ainsley Earhardt and Steve Doocy for their patriotism and support, along with weather machine Janis Dean and news anchor Jillian Mele.

I'd also like to thank UTA super-agents Adam Leibner, Jerry Silbowitz, Byrd Leavell, and powerhouse president Jay Sures for their vision and loyalty.

Extraordinary thanks goes to Rupert and Lachlan Murdoch, Suzanne Scott, and Jay Wallace. Through the turmoil of last few years, they have offered me tremendous support, while allowing me to grow the history side of my career. I know full well without Fox viewers and listeners I would not have my passionate, dedicated, patriotic readers.

Thank you to Bruce Winders, curator of the Alamo museum, for his impeccable research efforts. He was invaluable to us, as were Lisa Struthers of San Jacinto Library and Museum, historian Douglas Brinkley, and Scott McMahon, who helped bring the Battle of Goliad to life in my mind.

FOR FURTHER READING

Reconstructing history is always a difficult business. In the case of the Texas Revolution—and, in particular, the Battle of the Alamo—the uncertainties, paradoxes, and even outright contradictions are many among the primary sources.

Writing history is about judgments. Whose word do you take? We have testimony from Texians and Mexicans and, when their versions coincide, recounting the story is not difficult. But Santa Anna's version, for example, is self-serving and political and often at odds with not only Texian takes but even the recollections of his own officers. Historians largely discount some versions—Félix Nuñez's version of the fall of the Alamo, for example—but largely trust others, such as José Enrique de la Peña's. In truth, each version has its own imperfections; thus, my approach has been to examine all of them, to compare and contrast, and then make my best judgment as to what most likely happened.

This book could not exist were it not for many earlier students of this war who assembled the secondary sources I've also consulted. The literature of Texas independence is vast: The Alamo alone has been the subject of more than a hundred books; dozens more have examined the battles at San Jacinto and Goliad. Sam Houston himself has engaged many biographers.

All of which leads me to a few words of appreciation: One of the joys of writing a book like this is the opportunity to make the acquaintance of the many books and articles by authors living and dead who've tread this territory before. Again, though, there is the challenge of figuring out whose version is the closest to the truth—and, yes, as you would expect, the disagreements among the storytellers are many, ranging from trivial to huge. Troop estimates always seem to vary; often dates and times do, too, along with the spelling of names (of people and places) and many other "facts." Some writers seem somehow to know what seems unknowable, which can make it difficult to distinguish between fresh but reasonable assumptions and out-there guesswork. One triangulates, makes considered judgments, consults experts where possible, and, in the end, as with any book that looks with care at the historic past, then refers back to the original documents.

Of those there are many. The papers of Sam Houston, Stephen F. Austin, and Andrew Jackson have been essential sources, along with the compendious *Papers of the Texas Revolution* (10 vols., 1973) and *Official Correspondence of the Texan Revolution* (2 vols., 1936).

In these pages you'll also find the words of many minor figures. Largely forgotten fighters like Noah Smithwick, W. C. Swearingen, Herman Ehrenberg, Abel Morgan, Pedro Delgado, Jack Shackelford, John Sowers Brooks, José Enrique de la Peña, Dr. John Sutherland, Charles Mason, Sergeant Francisco Becerra, David Macomb—and dozens of others—left us reports, letters, and memoirs. Not a few of those are found at the valuable online resource sonsofdewittcolony.org. Some of the recollections are more reliable than others, upon occasion contradicting one another and even taking sides to praise or to damn such commanders as James Fannin, William Travis, and, in particular, Sam Houston.

My thanks, then, to the writers, living and dead, and their books, listed below, for providing the facts and circumstances that enabled me to tell this tale.

Austin, Stephen F. *The Austin Papers: October 1834–January 1837.* Vol. 3. Eugene C. Barker, ed. Austin: University of Texas, 1924.

———. "General Austin's Order Book for the Campaign of 1835." *Quarterly of the Texas State Historical Association.* Vol. 11, no. 1 (July 1907), pp. 1–55.

Austin, William T. "Siege and Battle of Bexar," 1844. https://sonsofdewittcolony.org.

Barker, Eugene Campbell. "The San Jacinto Campaign." *Quarterly of the Texas State Historical Association.* Vol. 4 (April 1901), pp. 237–345.

_______. "Stephen F. Austin and the Independence of Texas." *Quarterly of the Texas State Historical Association.* Vol. 1, no. 4 (April 1910), pp. 257–84.

Barnard, Joseph Henry. "Dr. J. H. Barnard's Journal." *The Goliad Advance.* June 1912.

Barr, Alwyn. *Texans in Revolt: The Battle for San Antonio, 1835.* Austin: University of Texas Press, 1990.

Becerra, Francisco. *A Mexican Sergeant's Recollections of the Alamo and San Jacinto.* Austin, TX: Jenkins, 1980.

Belohlavek, John M. *Let the Eagle Soar!* Lincoln: University of Nebraska Press, 1985.

Bennet, Miles A. "The Battle of Gonzales, the 'Lexington' of the Texas Revolution." *Quarterly of the Texas State Historical Association.* Vol. 2, no. 4 (April 1899), pp. 313–16.

Binkley, William C., ed. *Official Correspondence of the Texan Revolution, 1835–1836.* 2 vols. New York: D. Appleton-Century, 1936.

Bowie, John. "Early Life in the Southwest—The Bowies." *De Bow's Southern and Western Review,* October 1852, pp. 378–83.

Brack, Gene M. *Mexico Views Manifest Destiny.* Albuquerque: University of New Mexico Press, 1975.

Brands, H. W. *Lone Star Nation.* New York: Doubleday, 2004.

Brogan, Evelyn. *"James Bowie," A Hero of the Alamo.* San Antonio: T. Kunzman, 1922.

Brown, Gary. *Hesitant Martyr in the Texas Revolution: James Walker Fannin.* Plano, TX: Republic of Texas Press, 2000.

Brown, John Henry. *History of Texas, 1685 to 1892.* St. Louis: L. E. Daniell, 1892.

Bruce, Henry. *Life of General Houston, 1793–1863.* New York: Dodd, Mead, 1891.

Bryan, Moses Austin. "Reminiscences of M. A. Bryan." Typescript, Moses Austin Bryan Papers. Albert and Ethel Herzstein Library, San Jacinto Museum of History, n.d.

Buell, Augustus C. *History of Andrew Jackson: Pioneer, Patriot, Soldier, Politician, President.* 2 vols. New York: Charles Scribner's Sons, 1904.

Burleson, Rufus C. *The Life and Writings of Rufus C. Burleson.* [Waco, TX], 1901.

Calder, R. J. "Recollections of the Campaign of 1836." *The Texas Almanac, 1857–1873.* Waco, TX: Texian Press, 1967, pp. 444–56.

Callcott, Wilfrid Hardy. *Santa Anna.* Norman: University of Oklahoma Press, 1936.

Cantrell, Gregg. *Stephen F. Austin, Empresario of Texas.* New Haven, CT: Yale University Press, 1999.

Castañeda, Carlos, et al. *Mexican Side of the Texan Revolution, by the Mexican Participants.* Dallas: P. L. Turner, 1928.

Chariton, Wallace O. *100 Days in Texas: The Alamo Letters.* Plano, TX: Wordware, 1990.

Clarke, Mary Whatley. *Thomas J. Rusk: Soldier, Statesman, Jurist.* Austin: Jenkins, 1971.

Cole, Donald B. *The Presidency of Andrew Jackson.* Lawrence: University Press of Kansas, 1993.

Coleman, Robert Morris. *Houston Displayed, or Who Won the Battle of San Jacinto? By a Farmer in the Army.* Austin: Brick Row Book Shop, 1964.

Crimmins, M. L. "American Powder's Part in Winning Texas Independence." *Southwestern Historical Quarterly.* Vol. 52, no. 1 (July 1948), pp. 109–11.

Crisp, James E. *Sleuthing the Alamo: Davy Crockett's Last Stand and Other Mysteries of the Texas Revolution.* New York: Oxford University Press, 2005.

Crisp, James E., and Dan Kilgore. *How Did Davy Die? And Why Do We Care So Much?* College Station: Texas A&M University Press, 2010.

Crockett, Davy. *The Autobiography of David Crockett.* New York: Charles Scribner's Sons, 1923. (Note: This volume contains several Crockett works, including *A Narrative of the Life of David Crockett, of the State of Tennessee, Written by Himself,* 1834.)

_______. *A Narrative of the Life of David Crockett by Himself.* Lincoln, NE: Bison, 1987.

Cummins, Light Townsend, and Mary L. Scheer. *Texan Identities: Moving beyond Myth, Memory, and Fallacy in Texas History.* Denton: University of North Texas Press, 2016.

Davenport, Harbert. "The Men of Goliad: Dedicatory Address and the Unveiling of the Monument Erected by the Texas Centennial Commission at the Grave of Fannin's Men." *Southwestern Historical Quarterly.* Vol. 43, no. 1 (July 1939), pp. 1–41.

Davis, William C. *Lone Star Rising: The Revolutionary Birth of the Texas Republic.* New York: Free Press, 2004.

_______. *Three Roads to the Alamo: The Lives and Fortunes of David Crockett, James Bowie, and William Barret Travis.* New York: HarperCollins, 1998.

Day, James M. *The Texas Almanac, 1857–1873.* Waco, TX: Texian Press, 1967.

De Bruhl, Marshall. *Sword of San Jacinto: A Life of Sam Houston.* New York: Random House, 1993.

Delgado, Pedro. "Delgado's Account of the Battle." Reprinted in Barker, "The San Jacinto Campaign." *Quarterly of the Texas State Historical Association.* Vol. 4 (April 1901), pp. 287–91.

Dixon, Sam Houston, and Louis Wiltz Kemp. *Heroes of San Jacinto.* Houston: Anson Jones Press, 1932.

Dobie, J. Frank. "James Bowie, Big Dealer." *Southwestern Historical Quarterly.* Vol. 60, no. 1 (January 1957), pp. 337–57.

Ehrenberg, Herman. "A Campaign in Texas." *Blackwood's Magazine.* Vol. 59, no. 363 (January 1846), pp. 37–53.

_______. *With Milam and Fannin: Adventures of a German Boy in Texas' Revolution.* Translated by Charlotte Churchill. Dallas: Tardy, 1935.

Featherstonehaugh, George William. *Excursion Through the Slave States, from Washington on the Potomac to the Frontier of Mexico; with Sketches of Popular Manners and Geological Notices.* New York: Harper & Brothers, 1844.

Field, Joseph E. *Three Years in Texas.* Greenfield, MA: Justin Jones, 1836.

Filisola, Vicente. *Memoirs for the History of the War in Texas.* Translated by Wallace Woolsey. 2 vols. Austin: Eakin Press, 1985. Originally published in 1848.

Flores, Richard R. *Remembering the Alamo: Memory, Modernity, and the Master Symbol.* Austin: University of Texas Press, 2002.

Folsom, Bradley. *Arrendondo: Last Spanish Ruler of Texas and Northeastern New Spain.* Norman: University of Oklahoma Press, 2017.

Foote, Henry Stuart. *Texas and the Texians.* Vol. 2. Philadelphia: Thomas, Cowperthwait, 1841.

Forbes, John. "Memorandum for Col. E. Yoakum," December 25, 1858. Personal Papers of Sam Houston, box 29, folder 36. Albert and Ethel Herzstein Library, San Jacinto Museum of History.

Fowler, Will. *Santa Anna of Mexico.* Lincoln: University of Nebraska Press, 2007.

Friend, Llerena. *Sam Houston: The Great Designer.* Austin: University of Texas Press, 1954.

Garrison, George Pierce, ed. Diplomatic Correspondence of the Republic of Texas. Washington, DC: Government Printing Office, 1908.

Garver, Lois. "Benjamin Rush Milam, Chapter III (continued)." *Southwestern Historical Quarterly.* Vol. 38, no. 3 (January 1935), pp. 177–222.

Gray, William Fairfax. *From Virginia to Texas, 1835. Diary of Col. Wm. F. Gray.* Houston: Gray, Dillaye, 1909.

Green, Rena Maverick, ed. *Samuel Maverick, Texan: 1803–1870.* San Antonio: privately printed, 1952.

Gregory, Jack, and Rennard Strickland. *Sam Houston with the Cherokees, 1829–1833.* Norman: University of Oklahoma Press, 1996.

Haley, James L. *Sam Houston.* Norman: University of Oklahoma Press, 2002.

Hardin, Stephen L. "The Félix Nuñez Account and the Siege of the Alamo: A Critical Appraisal." *Southwestern Historical Quarterly.* Vol. 4, no. 1 (July 1990), pp. 65–84.

———. "Line in the Sand; Lines on the Soul." In Cummins and Scheer, *Texan Identities* (2016).

———. *Texian Iliad—A Military History of the Texas Revolution, 1835–1836.* Austin: University of Texas Press, 1994.

Harris, Dilue. "The Reminiscences of Mrs. Dilue Harris." *Quarterly of the Texas State Historical Association.* Vol. 4, no. 3 (January 1901), pp. 155–89.

Hatch, Thom. *Encyclopedia of the Alamo and the Texas Revolution.* Jefferson, NC: McFarland, 1999.

Hatcher, Mattie Austin, trans. "Joaquin de Arrendondo's Report of the Battle of the Medina, August 18, 1813." *Quarterly of the Texas State Historical Association.* Vol. 11, no. 3 (January 1908), pp. 220–36.

Hatcher, Mattie Austin, ed. *Letters of an American Traveller: Mary Austin Holley, Her Life and Works, 1784–1846.* Dallas: Southwest Press, 1933.

Haythornthwaite, Philip. *The Alamo and the War of Texan Independence, 1835–1836.* London, UK: Osprey, 1986.

Hollen, W. Eugene, and Ruth Lapham, eds. *William Bolleart's Texas.* Norman: University of Oklahoma Press, 1956.

Holley, Mary Austin. *Texas.* Lexington, KY: J. Clarke, 1836.

Houston, Andrew Jackson. *Texas Independence.* Houston: Anson Jones Press, 1938.

Houston, Sam. *The Autobiography of Sam Houston.* Donald Day and Harry Herbert Ullom, eds. Norman: University of Oklahoma Press, 1954.

_______. *The Writings of Sam Houston, 1813–1863.* Amelia W. Williams and Eugene C. Barker, eds. 8 vols. Austin: University of Texas Press, 1938–43.

Hunter, Robert Hancock. *The Narrative of Robert Hancock Hunter.* Austin: Encino Press, 1966.

Huson, Hobart. *Refugio: A Comprehensive History of Refugio County from Aboriginal Times.* Woodsboro, TX: Rooke Foundation, 1953–55. Excerpted online at www.sonsofdewittcolony.org/goliadmorgan.htm.

Huston, Cleburne. *Deaf Smith, Incredible Texas Spy.* Waco, TX: Texian Press, 1973.

Jackson, Andrew. *Correspondence of Andrew Jackson.* John Spencer Bassett, ed. Vol. 1. Washington, DC: Carnegie Institution of Washington, 1931.

Jackson, Ron, Jr., and Lee Spencer White. *Joe, the Slave Who Became an Alamo Legend.* Norman: University of Oklahoma Press, 2015.

James, Marquis. *The Raven: A Biography of Sam Houston.* Indianapolis: Bobbs-Merrill, 1929.

Jenkins, John H., ed. *The Papers of the Texas Revolution, 1835–1836.* 10 vols. Austin: Presidial Press, 1973.

Johnson, Frank W. *A History of Texas and Texans.* Vol. 1. Chicago and New York: American Historical Society, 1916.

Jones, Oakah L. *Santa Anna.* New York: Twayne, 1968.

King, C. Richard. *Susanna Dickinson: Messenger of the Alamo.* Austin: Shoal Creek, 1976.

Kuykendall, Jonathan Hampton. "Reminiscences of Early Texans: A Collection from the Austin Papers." *Quarterly of the Texas State Historical Association.* Vol. 6, no. 3 (January 1903), pp. 236–53.

Labadie, Nicholas Descomps. "San Jacinto Campaign." *The Texas Almanac, 1857–1873.* Waco, TX: Texian Press, 1967, pp. 142–77.

Lack, Paul D. *The Texas Revolutionary Experience: A Political and Social History, 1835–1836.* College Station: Texas A&M University Press, 1992.

Lane, Walter P. *The Adventures and Recollections of General Walter P. Lane, A San Jacinto Veteran, Containing Sketches of the Texan, Mexican and Later Wars.* Dallas: DeGolyer Library, 2000.

Lester, Charles Edwards, ed. *The Life of Sam Houston, the Only Authentic Memoir of Him Ever Published.* New York: J. C. Derby, 1855.

Linn, John J. *Reminiscences of Fifty Years in Texas.* New York: D. & J. Sadlier, 1883.

Lord, Walter. *A Time to Stand.* New York: Harper & Brothers, 1961.

Maverick, Samuel Augustus. *Notes on the Storming of Bexar in the Close of 1835.* San Antonio: Frederick C. Chabot, 1942.

McDonald, Archie P. *William Barret Travis: A Biography.* Woodway, TX: Eakin Press, 1989.

Meacham, Jon. *American Lion: Andrew Jackson in the White House.* New York: Random House, 2008.

Moore, Stephen L. *Eighteen Minutes: The Battle of San Jacinto and the Texas Campaign.* Dallas: Republic of Texas Press, 2004.

Morgan, Abel. "Massacre at Goliad: Abel Morgan's Account." Available online at https://sonsofdewittcolony.org.

Morphis, J. M. *History of Texas, from Its Discovery and Settlement.* New York: United States Publishing Company, 1875.

Nackman, Mark E. "The Making of the Texas Citizen Soldier." *Southwestern Historical Quarterly.* Vol. 78 (January 1975), pp. 231–53.

"Notes on the Life of Benjamin Rush Milam, 1788–1835." *Register of the Kentucky Historical Society.* Vol. 71, no. 1 (January 1973), pp. 87–105.

Peña, José Enrique de la. *With Santa Anna in Texas: A Personal Narrative of the Revolution.* College Station: Texas A&M University Press, 1975.

Pierson, William H., Jr. *American Buildings and Their Architects: The Colonial and Neoclassical Styles.* New York: Oxford University Press, 1970.

Pohl, James W., and Stephen L. Hardin. "The Military History of the Texas Revolution: An Overview." *Southwestern Historical Quarterly.* Vol. 89, no. 3 (January 1986), pp. 269–308.

Potter, Reuben Marmaduke. "The Fall of the Alamo." *Magazine of American History.* Vol. 2, no. 1 (January 1878). Available online at https://sonsofdewittcolony.org.

Pruett, Jakie L., and Everett B. Cole. *Goliad Massacre: A Tragedy of the Texas Revolution.* Austin: Eakin Press, 1985.

Ramsdell, Charles. *San Antonio: A Historical and Pictorial Guide.* Austin: University of Texas Press, 1959.

Rather, Ethel Zivley. "De Witt's Colony." *Quarterly of the Texas State Historical Association.* Vol. 8, no. 2 (1904), pp. 95–192.

_______. "Recognition of the Republic of Texas by the United States." *Quarterly of the Texas State Historical Association.* Vol. 13, no. 3 (January 1910), pp. 155–256.

Reid, Stuart. *The Secret War for Texas.* College Station: Texas A&M University Press, 2007.

Remini, Robert V. *Andrew Jackson and the Course of American Democracy, 1833–1845.* New York: Harper & Row, 1984.

Rives, George Lockhart. *The United States and Mexico, 1821–1848.* Vol. 1. New York: Charles Scribner's Sons, 1913.

Santa Anna, Antonio López de. *The Eagle: The Autobiography of Santa Anna.* Ann Fears Crawford, ed. Austin: Pemberton Press, 1967.

Santos, Richard G. *Santa Anna's Campaign Against Texas, 1835–1836.* Waco, TX: Texian Press, 1996.

Scheina, Robert L. *Santa Anna: A Curse Upon Mexico.* Washington, DC: Brassey's, 2002.

Schwarz, Ted. *Forgotten Battlefield of the First Texas Revolution: The Battle of Medina, August 18, 1813.* Austin: Eakin Press, 1985.

Sellers, Charles. *James K. Polk, Jacksonian, 1795–1843.* Princeton, NJ: Princeton University Press, 1957.

Shackford, James Atkins. *David Crockett: The Man and the Legend.* Chapel Hill: University of North Carolina Press, 1956.

Smith, Ruby Cumby. "James W. Fannin, Jr., in the Texas Revolution." *Southwestern Historical Quarterly.* Vol. 23, no. 2 (January 1919), pp. 79–90.

_______. "James W. Fannin, Jr., in the Texas Revolution." *Southwestern Historical Quarterly.* Vol. 23, no. 3 (January 1920), pp. 171–203.

Smithwick, Noah. *The Evolution of a State; or Recollections of Old Texas Days.* Austin: Gammel, 1900.

Sparks, S. F. "Recollections of S. F. Sparks." *Quarterly of the Texas State Historical Association.* Vol. 12, no. 1 (July 1908), pp. 61–67.

Stenberg, Richard R. "The Texas Schemes of Jackson and Houston, 1929–1936." *Southwestern Social Science Quarterly.* Originally published in vol. 15 (December 1934); reprinted in fiftieth anniversary issue, vol. 50, no. 4 (March 1970), pp. 944–65.

Stephens, Rachel. *Selling Andrew Jackson: Ralph E. W. Earl and the Politics of Portraiture.* Columbia: University of South Carolina Press, 2018.

Sutherland, John. *The Fall of the Alamo.* San Antonio: Naylor, 1936. Available online at https://sonsofdewittcolony.org.

Swisher, John M[ilton]. *The Swisher Memoirs.* Rena Maverick Green, ed. San Antonio: Sigmund Press, 1932.

Taylor, Creed. "The Battle of San Jacinto," 1935. Available online at https://sonsofdewittcolony.org.

______. "The March, the Siege and the Battle for Bexar," 1900. Available online at https://sonsofdewittcolony.org.

Thompson, Frank. *The Alamo: A Cultural History.* Dallas: Taylor Trade, 2001.

Tolbert, Frank X. *The Day of San Jacinto.* New York: McGraw Hill, 1959.

Tucker, Phillip Thomas. *Exodus from the Alamo: The Anatomy of the Last Stand Myth.* Philadelphia: Casemate, 2010.

Wharton, Clarence R. *San Jacinto: The Sixteenth Decisive Battle.* Houston: Lamar Book Store, 1930.

White, Amelia. "Who Was the Yellow Rose of Texas?" *Alamo Messenger.* April 2015. Available online at https://medium.com/@OfficialAlamo/who-was-the-yellow-rose-of-texas-750c95617241.

Williams, Amelia Worthington. *Following General Sam Houston, from 1793 to 1863.* Austin: Steck, 1935.

Williams, Charlean Moss. *The Old Town Speaks: Reflections of Washington, Hempstead County Arkansas, Gateway to Texas, 1835, Confederate Capital, 1863.* Houston: Anson Jones Press, 1951.

Williams, John Hoyt. *Sam Houston: A Biography of the Father of Texas.* New York: Simon & Schuster, 1993.

Winders, Richard Bruce. *Crisis in the Southwest: The United States, Mexico, and the Struggle over Texas.* Wilmington, DE: Scholarly Resources, 2002.

______. *Sacrificed at the Alamo: Tragedy and Triumph in the Texas Revolution.* Abilene, TX: State House Press, 2004.

Winters, James Washington. "An Account of the Battle of San Jacinto." *Quarterly of the Texas State Historical Association.* Vol. 6, no. 2 (October 1902), pp. 139–44.

Wisehart, Marion Karl. *Sam Houston, American Giant.* Washington, DC: Robert B. Luce, 1962.

Wooten, Dudley Goodall. *A Complete History of Texas.* Dallas: Texas History Company, 1899.

Yoakum, Henderson King. *History of Texas from Its First Settlement in 1685 to Its Annexation to the United States in 1846.* 2 vols. Austin: Steck, 1935.

NOTES

Prologue: The Lessons of Battle

1. Thomas Hart Benton, Eulogy to Houston, reprinted in Lester, *The Life of Sam Houston (The Only Authentic Memoir of Him Ever Published)* (1855), p. 303.
2. Houston, *The Autobiography of Sam Houston* (1954), p. 12.
3. Lester, *The Life of Sam Houston* (1855), p. 35.
4. Houston, *The Autobiography of Sam Houston* (1954), p. 15.

Chapter 1: General Jackson's Protégé

1. Lester, *The Life of Sam Houston* (1855), p. 22.
2. William Carroll, quoted in Williams, *Sam Houston* (1993), p. 71.
3. William Carroll, quoted in Williams, *Sam Houston* (1993), p. 260.
4. James, *The Raven* (1929), p. 157.
5. Thomas Jefferson to James Monroe, May 14, 1820.
6. Sam Houston to John H. Houston, January 11, 1830.
7. Gregory and Strickland, *Sam Houston with the Cherokees* (1967), p. 44.
8. De Bruhl, *Sword of San Jacinto* (1993), p. 130. As with many Houston anecdotes, details vary from biography to biography; other sources differ as to the origin of Houston's cane.
9. William Stanbery, quoted in *Niles Weekly Register*, April 14, 1832.

10. James, *The Raven* (1929), p. 162ff.
11. Ibid., p. 172.
12. Sam Houston to James Prentiss, August 18, 1832.
13. As he told Jefferson Davis; see Williams, *Sam Houston* (1993), p. 113.
14. See Stenberg, "The Texas Schemes of Jackson and Houston" (1970), p. 945.
15. Andrew Jackson to Sam Houston, June 21, 1829.
16. Andrew Jackson to Anthony Butler, February 25, 1832.
17. Sam Houston to John H. Houston, December 2, 1832.

Chapter 2: Gone to Texas

1. Mary Brown Austin to Stephen Austin, August 25, 1821.
2. Bowie, "Early Life in the Southwest—The Bowies" (1852), p. 380.
3. Ibid.
4. Dobie, "James Bowie, Big Dealer" (1957), p. 343.
5. The town known circa 1835 as San Antonio de Béxar was, in the documents of its time, variously referred to as San Antonio de Béxar, San Antonio, Béxar, and Bejar. For the sake of clarity, this book will reference the place as simply San Antonio, except within quotations where the original authors' words will be retained.
6. Santa Anna, quoted in Brands, *Lone Star Nation* (2004), p. 227.
7. Sam Houston to Andrew Jackson, February 13, 1833.

Chapter 3: "Come and Take It"

1. Stephen F. Austin to the Illustrious Ayuntamiento of Béjar, October 2, 1833.
2. Stephen Austin to Mary Austin Holley, August 31, 1835.
3. Ibid.
4. Anthony Butler to Andrew Jackson, December 19, 1835.
5. *Texas Republican*, September 26, 1835.
6. Andrew Ponton to Political Chief, September 29, 1835.
7. Smithwick, *The Evolution of a State* (1900), pp. 102, 104–5. Accounts of the story vary, and some students of the battle believe the flag was made after the battle.
8. Joseph D. Clements to Lieutenant Castañeda, September 30, 1835.
9. Bennet, "Battle of Gonzales" (1899), p. 316.

10. David B. Macomb, "Letter from Gonzales," in Foote, *Texas and the Texians* (1841), p. 99.
11. Charles Mason, "Account," in Johnson, *A History of Texas and Texans* (1916), p. 270.
12. Macomb, in Foote, *Texas and the Texians* (1841), p. 101.
13. Smithwick, *The Evolution of a State* (1900), p. 101.
14. Hardin, *Texian Iliad—A Military History of the Texas Revolution, 1835–1836* (1994), p. 12.
15. Garver, "Benjamin Rush Milam" (1935), p. 186.
16. Ben Milam to Henry Smith, March 28, 1835.
17. S——— to ———, October 22, 1835. See Jenkins, *The Papers of the Texas Revolution, 1835–1836*, vol. 2 (1973), pp. 193–94.
18. Ira Ingram to S. F. Austin, *Austin Papers*, vol. 3 (1924), p. 181.
19. George Collinsworth to Mrs. Margard C. Linn, October 10, 1835.
20. *New York Star*, quoted in Nackman, "The Making of the Texas Citizen Soldier" (1975), p. 241.
21. Smithwick, *The Evolution of a State* (1900), p. 106.
22. Moses Austin Bryan, quoted in Barr, *Texans in Revolt* (1990), p. 6.
23. Stephen Austin to David G. Burnet, October 5, 1835.
24. General Martín Perfecto de Cos to Henry Rueg, quoted in Hardin, *Texian Iliad* (1994), p. 14.
25. Order No. 1, October 11, 1835.
26. Sam Houston to Isaac Parker, October 5, 1835.

CHAPTER 4: CONCEPCIÓN

1. Houston, *The Writings of Sam Houston*, vol. 1 (1838), p. 304.
2. Smithwick, *The Evolution of a State* (1900), p. 112.
3. Ibid., p. 138.
4. Stephen Austin to San Felipe Committee of Safety, October 11, 1835.
5. Stephen Austin to Captain Philip Dimmit, October 22, 1835.
6. James Bowie and James Fannin to Stephen Austin, October 22, 1835.
7. Ibid.
8. Smithwick, *The Evolution of a State* (1900), p. 111.
9. "San Felipe Circular," October 18, 1835.
10. Moses Austin Bryan to James F. Perry, October 26, 1835.

11. Stephen F. Austin to Council of Texas, October 26, 1836.
12. "The Most Eligible Situation" quote taken from James Bowie and J. W. Fannin, "Official Account of the Action of the 28thl ult., at the Mission of Conception, near Bejar," in Foote, *Texas and the Texians* (1841), p. 122.
13. Stephen Austin to James Bowie, October 27, 1835.
14. Ibid.
15. James Bowie and J. W. Fannin, "Official Account of the Action of the 28thl ult., at the Mission of Conception, near Bejar," in Foote, *Texas and the Texians* (1841), p. 122.
16. E. L. McIlhenny, quoted in Dobie, "James Bowie, Big Dealer" (1957), p. 399n4.
17. Davis, *Three Roads to the Alamo* (1998), pp. 440–41.
18. Bowie and Fannin, "Official Account" (1836), p. 123.
19. Smithwick, *The Evolution of a State* (1900), p. 114.
20. Ibid.
21. Bowie and Fannin, "Official Account" (1836), p. 123.
22. Smithwick, *The Evolution of a State* (1900), p. 115.
23. Austin, "Siege and Battle of Bexar" (1844).
24. Crimmins, "American Powder's Part in Winning Texas Independence" (1948), p. 109.
25. Stephen Austin to President of the Consultation of Texas, October 28, 1835.

Chapter 5: A Slow Siege at the Alamo

1. List of stores in Jenkins, *The Papers of the Texas Revolution, 1835–1836*, vol. 2 (1973), p. 251.
2. Stephen Austin to James Bowie and James Fannin, November 1, 1835.
3. William Travis to Stephen Austin, November 16, 1835.
4. Stephen Austin to William Travis, November 11, 1835.
5. Stephen Austin to President of Consultation of Texas, November 5, 1835.
6. Huston, *Deaf Smith, Incredible Texas Spy* (1973), pp. 1–5; Barr, *Texans in Revolt* (1990), p. 17.
7. Stephen Austin to President of the Consultation, November 3, 1835.
8. Anson Jones, quoted in Cantrell, *Stephen F. Austin* (1999), p. 326.
9. Austin, "Siege and Battle of Bexar" (1844).
10. Moses Austin Bryan, quoted in Cantrell, *Stephen F. Austin* (1999), p. 328.

11. Ehrenberg, "A Campaign in Texas" (1846), p. 39.
12. Moses Austin Bryan, quoted in Cantrell, *Stephen F. Austin* (1999), p. 328.
13. Two reports written the day after recount the events of the "Grass Fight." See Edward Burleson to the Provisional Government, November 27, 1835; and William H. Jack to Burlison [Burleson], same date. The latter contains the imaginative spelling of *mesquite.*
14. Barr, *Texans in Revolt* (1990), p. 40.
15. Bowie was probably closer to the mark. In his memoirs, Mexican general Vicente Filisola reported "fifty brave men . . . lying on the ground either dead or wounded." Filisola, *Memoirs for the History of the War in Texas*, vol. 2 (1848; 1985), p. 68.
16. Creed Taylor, quoted in Reid, *The Secret War for Texas* (2007), p. 52.
17. Sam Houston to James Fannin, November 13, 1835.
18. William Carey to Brother & Sister, January 12, 1836.
19. Samuel Maverick, December 4, 1835, in Green, *Samuel Maverick, Texan* (1952), p. 44.
20. Huston, *Deaf Smith, Incredible Texas Spy* (1973), p. 34. See also Foote, *Texas and the Texians* (1841), p. 165.
21. Taylor, "The March, the Siege and the Battle for Bexar" (1900).
22. Herman Ehrenberg, quoted in Huston, *Deaf Smith, Incredible Texas Spy* (1973), p. 36.
23. Ibid.
24. Taylor, "The March, the Siege and the Battle for Bexar" (1900).
25. Frank Sparks, quoted in Hardin, *Texian Iliad* (1994), p. 81.
26. Taylor, "The March, the Siege and the Battle for Bexar" (1900).
27. F. W. Johnson to General Burleson, December 11, 1835.
28. Edward Burleson and B. R. Milam to Provisional Government, December 6, 1835.
29. Field, *Three Years in Texas* (1836), p. 20.
30. Edward Burleson and B. R. Milam to Provisional Government, December 6, 1835.
31. Taylor, "The March, the Siege and the Battle for Bexar" (1900); Yoakum, *History of Texas*, vol. 1 (1935), p. 28.
32. Of the several retellings, Creed Taylor's is the most vivid. See "The March, the Siege and the Battle for Bexar" (1900).
33. William Carey to Brother & Sister, January 12, 1836.

34. Moseley Baker to Council at San Felipe, December 10, 1835.
35. Sherwood Y. Reams, quoted in Williams, *Sam Houston* (1993), p. 127.
36. Sion R. Bostick, quoted in Rives, *The United States and Mexico* (1913), pp. 300–301.
37. Barr, *Texans in Revolt* (1990), p. 52.
38. Filisola, *Memoirs for the History of the War in Texas*, vol. 2 (1848; 1985), p. 94.
39. Articles of Capitulation, Clause the First.
40. William Carey to Brother & Sister, January 12, 1836.
41. Texas General Council to Citizen Volunteers, December 15, 1835.

Chapter 6: The Defenders

1. *Telegraph and Texas Register*, January 2, 1836.
2. Sam Houston to Don Carlos Barrett, January 2, 1836.
3. Goliad Declaration, December 22, 1835.
4. Henry Smith to the President and Members of the Council, January 9, 1836; General Council to the People of Texas, January 11, 1836.
5. Sam Houston to Henry Smith, January 30, 1836.
6. J. C. Neill to Governor and Council, January 6, 1836.
7. Sam Houston to Henry Smith, January 6, 1836.
8. Lester, *The Life of Sam Houston*, p. 83.
9. Sam Houston to Henry Smith, January 30, 1836.
10. Ehrenberg, *With Milam and Fannin* (1935), pp. 124–25.
11. The principal source for Houston's speech was a volunteer named Herman Ehrenberg; in Leipzig in the 1840s he published the text as he remembered it, but in his native German. A number of scholars have expressed serious doubts as to its accuracy. See especially Crisp, *Sleuthing the Alamo* (2005), p. 27ff.
12. Sam Houston to Henry Smith, January 30, 1836.
13. Lester, *The Life of Sam Houston*, p. 85.
14. Ibid.
15. Dobie, "James Bowie, Big Dealer" (1957), p. 350.
16. J. C. Neill to Sam Houston, January 14, 1836.
17. James Bowie to Henry Smith, February 2, 1836.
18. Ibid.
19. William B. Travis, Last Will and Testament, May 25, 1835.

20. Green Jameson to Sam Houston, January 18, 1836.
21. Ibid.
22. Ibid.
23. For the most part these biographical details are drawn from the most reliable Crockett biography, James Atkins Shackford's *David Crockett: The Man and the Legend* (1956), supplemented by Crockett's own (and rather less factual) *Autobiography* (1834).
24. Shackford, *David Crockett* (1956), p. 296n11.
25. Crockett, *Autobiography* (1834), p. 40.
26. Williams, *The Old Town Speaks* (1951), p. 164.
27. Crockett, *Autobiography* (1834), p. 80.
28. *National Banner and Nashville Whig*, September 29, 1823.
29. Crockett, *Autobiography* (1834), p. 59.
30. *Niles Weekly Register*, April 9, 1836.
31. David Crockett to George Patton, November 1, 1835.
32. David Crockett to Margaret and Wiley Flowers, January [9], 1836.
33. Swisher, *The Swisher Memoirs* (1932), p. 18.
34. Ibid.
35. William B. Travis to Henry Smith, February 13, 1836.
36. Sutherland, *The Fall of the Alamo* (1936), https://sonsofdewittcolony.org. The story is also recounted in Davis, *Three Roads to the Alamo* (1998), pp. 533–35.
37. William B. Travis to Andrew Ponton, February 24, 1836.

Chapter 7: Twelve Days of Uncertainty

1. Santa Anna, "Manifesto Relative to His Operations during the Texas Campaign and His Capture 10 of May 1837," reprinted in Castañeda, *Mexican Side of the Texan Revolution* (1928), p. 13. The most essential source for Santa Anna's biographical facts is Will Fowler's *Santa Anna of Mexico* (2007).
2. Minister of War José María Tornel, quoted in Lord, *A Time to Stand* (1961), p. 61.
3. Fanny Calderone de la Barca, quoted in Brands, *Lone Star Nation* (2004), p. 41.
4. William W. Travis to Fellow Citizens and Compatriots, February 24, 1836.
5. Enrique Esparza, quoted in Ramsdell, *San Antonio* (1959), p. 76.

6. José Batres to James Bowie, February 23, 1836.
7. William Travis and James Bowie to James Fannin, February 23, 1836.
8. William Travis to Sam Houston, February 25, 1836; Potter, "The Fall of the Alamo" (1878), p. 6.
9. William Travis to the People of Texas & all Americans, February 24, 1836.
10. William Travis to Sam Houston, February 25, 1836.
11. James Fannin to James Robinson, February 25, 1836.
12. John Sowers Brooks to A. H. Brooks, February 25, 1836.
13. James Fannin to James Robinson, February 26, 1836.
14. Crockett, *A Narrative of the Life of David Crockett by Himself* (1987), p. xxxii.
15. Santa Anna to the Minister of War and Marine, February 27, 1836.
16. Potter, "The Fall of the Alamo" (1878), p. 8.
17. Lord, *A Time to Stand* (1961). In keeping with the long tradition of historical disagreements regarding the Alamo history, historian (and former New York firefighter) William Groneman has expressed doubt regarding Crockett's fiddle playing.
18. "The Unanimous Declaration of Independence made by the Delegates of the People of Texas," March 2, 1836.
19. William Travis to the President of the Convention, March 3, 1836.
20. William Travis to David Ayres, March 3, 1836.
21. "Army of Operations, General Orders of the 5th of March, 1836. 2 o'clock P.M.—Secret."
22. Quoted in the *San Antonio Daily Express*, April 28, 1881. The historic record is hazy concerning Travis's March 5 actions and words. By some accounts he spoke long and movingly; by others, his words were few and pointed. Direct testimony concerning the events of the afternoon of March 5, 1836, is limited (and variable), but include a firsthand account in a late-in-life interview with Mrs. Almeron Dickinson, conducted in 1876, and a version that appeared in *The Texas Almanac*, in 1873, purportedly based on the recollections of the soldier who chose not to step across the line.
23. See McDonald, *William Barret Travis* (1976; 1995), pp. 172–73, 194n14.

Chapter 8: The Massacre

1. Gray, *From Virginia to Texas* (1909), p. 137.
2. Peña, *With Santa Anna in Texas* (1975), p. 47.

3. Ibid.
4. Ibid., p. 46.
5. Ibid., p. 47.
6. Mexican soldier, in Chariton, *100 Days in Texas* (1990), p. 318.
7. Report of Francisco Ruiz, in Chariton, *100 Days in Texas* (1990), p. 325.
8. Wooten, *A Complete History of Texas* (1899), p. 215.
9. Peña, *With Santa Anna in Texas* (1975), pp. 42, 43.
10. Ibid., pp. 48–49.
11. Tucker, *Exodus from the Alamo* (2010), p. 235.
12. King, *Susanna Dickinson: Messenger of the Alamo* (1976), pp. 41–42. Almeron's words vary from one account to another, as do many of the details in the ensuing events of Mrs. Dickinson's life.
13. Peña, *With Santa Anna in Texas* (1975), p. 51.
14. Quoted in Houston, *Texas Independence* (1938), p. 143.
15. Letter of April 5, 1836, printed in *El Mosquito Mexicano.* Cited in Davis, *Three Roads to the Alamo* (1998), p. 734n104.
16. *Philadelphia Pennsylvanian*, July 19, 1838.
17. Letter of April 5, 1836, printed in *El Mosquito Mexicano.* Cited in Davis, *Three Roads to the Alamo* (1998), p. 734n104.
18. "Army of Operations, General Orders of the 5th of March, 1836. 2 o'clock P.M.—Secret."
19. Peña, *With Santa Anna in Texas* (1975), p. 52.

Chapter 9: Bring Out the Dead

1. Quoted in Hardin, *Texian Iliad* (1974), p. 155. Accounts vary concerning whether Santa Anna referenced the dead as "chickens" on the night before or the day of the Alamo battle. Or both.
2. Crisp and Kilgore, *How Did Davy Die? And Why Do We Care So Much?* (2010), p. 15.
3. N. D. Labadie, "San Jacinto Campaign," in Day, *Texas Almanac* (1967), p. 174. Once again, there is an ongoing argument concerning Crockett's end.
4. Peña, *With Santa Anna in Texas* (1975), p. 53.
5. Santa Anna to José María Tornel, March 6, 1836.
6. Lieutenant Colonel José Juan Sanchez Navarro, "Memoirs of a Veteran of the Two Battles of the Alamo." Online at https://sonsofdewittcolony.org.

7. King, *Susanna Dickinson: Messenger of the Alamo* (1976), p. 70.
8. Morphis, *History of Texas* (1875), pp. 176–77.
9. Enrique Esparza, cited in King, *Susanna Dickinson: Messenger of the Alamo* (1976), p. 141n36. Other reports claim the sum gifted was two pesos rather than two dollars.
10. Santa Anna to the Citizens of Texas, March 7, 1836.
11. Report of Francisco Ruiz, in Chariton, *100 Days in Texas* (1990), p. 326.

Chapter 10: Houston Hears the News

1. Wisehart, *Sam Houston, American Giant* (1962), p. 167.
2. William Travis to the President of the Convention, March 3, 1836.
3. James, *The Raven* (1929), p. 227.
4. Lester, *The Life of Sam Houston*, pp. 90–91.
5. Ibid., p. 91.
6. Sam Houston to James Fannin, March 11, 1836.
7. Sam Houston to James Collinsworth, March 13, 1836.
8. Lester, *The Life of Sam Houston*, p. 95; Huston, *Deaf Smith, Incredible Texas Spy* (1973), p. 53.
9. Jackson and White, *Joe, the Slave Who Became an Alamo Legend* (2015), p. 207.
10. R. E. Handy, quoted in *Deaf Smith, Incredible Texas Spy* (1973), p. 53.
11. Robert Morris to James Fannin, February 6, 1836.

Chapter 11: Fort Defiance

1. James Fannin to Sam Houston, November 18, 1835.
2. William Travis to James Fannin, February 23, 1836.
3. James Fannin to Joseph Mims, February 29, 1836.
4. James Fannin to James Robinson, February 22, 1836.
5. Sam Houston to James Fannin, March 11, 1836. Accounts disagree as to whether the letter was delivered late on March 13 or on the morning of March 14, 1836. See Huson, "Evacuation of Goliad," in *Refugio* (1953–55).
6. Ehrenberg, *With Milam and Fannin* (1935), pp. 169–70.
7. Ehrenberg, "A Campaign in Texas" (1846), p. 43.
8. Morgan, "Massacre at Goliad."

9. Shackelford, Jack. "Some Few Notes Upon a Part of the Texian War," in Foote, *Texas and the Texians* (1841), p. 231.
10. Ehrenberg, "A Campaign in Texas" (1846), p. 44.
11. Barnard, "Dr. J. H. Barnard's Journal" (1912), p. 16.
12. Shackelford, Jack. "Some Few Notes Upon a Part of the Texian War," in Foote, *Texas and the Texians* (1841), p. 233.
13. Ibid., p. 234.
14. Morgan, "Massacre at Goliad."
15. Barnard, "Dr. J. H. Barnard's Journal" (1912), p. 17.
16. Ehrenberg, "A Campaign in Texas" (1846), p. 45.
17. Barnard, "Dr. J. H. Barnard's Journal" (1912), p. 19. Accounts differ regarding the terms of the surrender and, very likely, Fannin got no explicit promises beyond Urrea's offer to use his influence with Santa Anna (see Urrea, "Diary of the Military Operations," in Castañeda, *Mexican Side of the Texan Revolution*, 1928, pp. 228–29). That said, Fannin, seeing no alternative, likely took Urrea's word and permitted his men to think their fate would differ from that of the defenders at the Alamo.
18. Urrea, "Diary of the Military Operations" (1838), in Castañeda, *Mexican Side of the Texan Revolution* (1928), p. 235.
19. Barnard, "Dr. J. H. Barnard's Journal" (1912), p. 22.
20. Account of Joseph Spohn, published in the *New York Evening Star*, as quoted in Brown, *Hesitant Martyr in the Texas Revolution* (2000), pp. 220–23.
21. The tale of the "Angel of Goliad," based on various references in the accounts of survivors, is a mix of confused names and details, many of which are summarized in "Angel of Goliad" at sonsofdewittcolony.org.
22. Dr. J. H. Barnard, quoted in De Bruhl, *Sword of San Jacinto* (1993), p. 195.

Chapter 12: The Texian Exodus

1. Sam Houston to James Collinsworth, March 15, 1836.
2. "Kuykendall's Recollections of the Campaign," in Barker, "The San Jacinto Campaign" (1901), p. 295.
3. Lester, *The Life of Sam Houston*, p. 99.
4. Sam Houston to James Collinsworth, March 15, 1836.
5. Swisher, *The Swisher Memoirs* (1932), p. 33.

6. Sam Houston to Thomas Rusk, March 23, 1836.
7. Labadie, "San Jacinto Campaign" (1967), pp. 144–45.

Chapter 13: An Army Assembles

1. Sam Houston to Thomas Rusk, March 23, 1836.
2. Sam Houston to Thomas Rusk, March 23, 1836.
3. With only minor differences, two Texian soldiers later told the story. See "Kuykendall's Recollections of the Campaign," in Barker, "The San Jacinto Campaign" (1901), p. 297; and Sparks, "Recollections of S. F. Sparks" (1908), p. 67.
4. Santa Anna, "Manifesto" (1928), p. 20.
5. Smithwick, *The Evolution of a State* (1900), p. 128.
6. Harris, "The Reminiscences of Mrs. Dilue Harris" (1901), pp. 155–89.
7. Moseley Baker, February 19, 1836, quoted in Moore, *Eighteen Minutes* (2004), p. 18.
8. Barker, "The San Jacinto Campaign" (1901), pp. 273–74.
9. Sam Houston to Thomas Rusk, March 29, 1836.
10. "Kuykendall's Recollections of the Campaign," in Barker, "The San Jacinto Campaign" (1901), p. 301.
11. Peña, *With Santa Anna in Texas* (1975), p. 102.
12. Tolbert, *The Day of San Jacinto* (1959), pp. 66–67; Santa Anna, "Report of the San Jacinto Campaign to the Minister of War and Marine," March 11, 1837, reprinted in Barker, "The San Jacinto Campaign" (1901), pp. 265–66.
13. Sam Houston to the Citizens of Texas, April 13, 1836.
14. Sam Houston to Thomas Rusk, March 31, 1836.
15. Labadie, "San Jacinto Campaign" (1967), p. 148.
16. David G. Burnet to Sam Houston, April 1, 1836.
17. Labadie, "San Jacinto Campaign" (1967), pp. 150–51; James, *The Raven* (1929), p. 241.
18. Sparks, "Recollections of S. F. Sparks" (1908), pp. 66–67; James, *The Raven* (1929), p. 242.
19. Santa Anna, "Manifesto" (1928), pp. 20–21.
20. Ibid., p. 22.

21. Sam Houston to John E. Ross, April 2, 1836.
22. Houston himself would acknowledge such thinking years later. See Davis, *Lone Star Rising* (2004), p. 252.
23. "Kuykendall's Recollections of the Campaign," in Barker, "The San Jacinto Campaign" (1901), p. 302.
24. King, *Susanna Dickinson: Messenger of the Alamo* (1976), p. 60.
25. Numerous versions of this story exist, the first written a month later; see W. B. Dewees to Clare Cardello, May 15, 1836. Subsequent accounts appear in Labadie, "San Jacinto Campaign" (1967), pp. 150–51; and in Hunter, *The Narrative of Robert Hancock Hunter* (1966), p. 13. The wagon master's name is variously spelled Rover and Rohrer.

Chapter 14: The Battle at San Jacinto

1. Delgado, "Delgado's Account of the Battle," in Barker, "The San Jacinto Campaign" (1901), p. 288; see also Tolbert, *The Day of San Jacinto* (1959), pp. 69–70.
2. Santa Anna to Vicente Filisola, April 14 [?], 1836.
3. "Kuykendall's Recollections of the Campaign," in Barker, "The San Jacinto Campaign" (1901), p. 303.
4. Coleman, *Houston Displayed* (1836; 1974), p. 18.
5. Bryan, "Reminiscences of M. A. Bryan," p. 20.
6. Sam Houston to David Burnet, April 25, 1836.
7. Lester, *The Life of Sam Houston*, p. 111.
8. Santa Anna, "Manifesto" (1928), p. 75.
9. "Kuykendall's Recollections of the Campaign," in Barker, "The San Jacinto Campaign" (1901), pp. 303–4.
10. Labadie, "San Jacinto Campaign" (1967), p. 155.
11. Lester, *The Life of Sam Houston*, p. 114.
12. Colonel Alexander Somervell, quoted in Labadie, "San Jacinto Campaign" (1967), p. 155.
13. Patrick Usher, quoted in James, *The Raven*, p. 203.
14. Sam Houston to Henry Raguet, April 19, 1836.
15. Lester, *The Life of Sam Houston*, p. 113.
16. Sam Houston to David Burnet, April 25, 1836.

17. Delgado, "Delgado's Account of the Battle," in Barker, "The San Jacinto Campaign" (1901), p. 290.
18. Labadie, "San Jacinto Campaign" (1967), p. 158.

Chapter 15: "Remember the Alamo!"

1. Lester, *The Life of Sam Houston*, pp. 122, 124.
2. Calder, "Recollections of the Campaign of 1836" (1861), p. 449.
3. Labadie, "San Jacinto Campaign" (1967), p. 161.
4. Later scholarship suggests that the actual number in Houston's command was more likely in the range of 925 men.
5. Labadie, "San Jacinto Campaign" (1967), p. 162. See also Lester, *The Life of Sam Houston*, pp. 125–26.
6. Winters, "An Account of the Battle of San Jacinto" (1902), pp. 141–42.
7. Fowler, *Santa Anna of Mexico* (2007), p. 172.
8. Sam Houston to David Burnet, April 25, 1836.
9. Benjamin Franklin, quoted in Moore, *Eighteen Minutes* (2004), p. 269.
10. James, *The Raven* (1929), p. 251.
11. Foote, *Texas and the Texians* (1841), p. 311. See also Tolbert, *The Day of San Jacinto* (1959), pp. 111–12.
12. John Menifee, quoted in Tolbert, *The Day of San Jacinto* (1959), p. 141.
13. Labadie, "San Jacinto Campaign" (1967), p. 163.
14. Thomas Rusk, quoted in Foote, *Texas and the Texians* (1841), p. 309.
15. Taylor, "The Battle of San Jacinto" (1935).
16. Foote, *Texas and the Texians* (1841), pp. 310–11.
17. "A Bewildered and Panic Stricken Herd" from Delgado, "Delgado's Account of the Battle" in Barker, "The San Jacinto Campaign" (1901), p. 291.
18. Ibid.
19. Filisola, *Memoirs for the History of the War in Texas*, vol. 2 (1848; 1985), p. 225.
20. Thomas Rusk to David Burnet, April 22, 1836.
21. Houston, *Texas Independence* (1938), p. 228.
22. Hunter, *The Narrative of Robert Hancock Hunter* (1966), p. 16.
23. W. C. Swearingen to his brother, April 22, 1836.
24. Bryan, "Reminiscences of M. A. Bryan," p. 24.

25. Lester, *The Life of Sam Houston*, p. 133.
26. Pedro Delgado, quoted in Tolbert, *The Day of San Jacinto* (1959), p. 170.
27. Sam Houston to David Burnet, April 25, 1836.

Chapter 16: Old San Jacinto

1. Among the various renderings of Santa Anna's capture—no two identical—are those of Dr. Labadie, Joel Robinson, and Sion Bostick, as well as James Sylvester's, of December 7, 1872, at https://sonsofdewittcolony.org.
2. As with Santa Anna's capture, numerous tellings of the tale survive. The primary sources here are Houston himself (Lester, *The Life of Sam Houston*, pp. 146–51) and Moses Austin Bryan ("Reminiscences of M. A. Bryan," p. 25ff), but other useful versions appear in James, *The Raven* (1929), p. 254ff; Labadie, "San Jacinto Campaign" (1967), p. 167ff; and Major John Forbes (see Haley, *Sam Houston* [2002], p. 153ff); and Santa Anna himself (*The Eagle: The Autobiography of Santa Anna* [1967]). Stephen Moore's *Eighteen Minutes* (2004) offers a quite complete compilation of the miscellaneous firsthand accounts. See also Brown, *History of Texas, 1685 to 1892* (1892), pp. 42–43.
3. Taylor, "The March, the Siege and the Battle for Bexar" (1900).
4. H. P. Brewster in Foote, *Texas and the Texians* (1841), pp. 314–15.
5. Santa Anna to Vicente Filisola, April 22, 1836.

Chapter 17: President Sam Houston

1. "Address to the Army of the Republic of Texas," May 5, 1836.
2. Tolbert, *The Day of San Jacinto* (1959), p. 222.
3. *Telegraph and Texas Register*, August 30, 1836.
4. Thomas Green, quoted in Yoakum, *History of Texas*, vol. 2 (1935), p. 171.
5. "The Trial of Santa Anna," quoted in Yoakum, *History of Texas*, vol. 2 (1935), p. 179.
6. Santa Anna to Andrew Jackson, July 4, 1836.
7. Andrew Jackson to Sam Houston, September 4, 1836.
8. Foote, *Texas and the Texians* (1841), p. 318.
9. Santa Anna to Sam Houston, November 5, 1836.
10. Santa Anna, *The Eagle* (1967), p. 57.

11. Callcott, *Santa Anna* (1936), pp. 146–47.
12. Santa Anna, *The Eagle* (1967), p. 57.
13. William Wharton to J. Pinckney Henderson, March 15, 1837.

Epilogue: The Founding and the Founders of Texas

1. Houston, Directive of December 27, 1836.
2. That officer was José Enrique de la Peña; the book, *With Santa Anna in Texas* (1975).
3. E. H. Winfield, quoted in James, *The Raven* (1929), p. 331.
4. Bruce, *Life of General Houston* (1891), p. 217.
5. Coleman, *Houston Displayed* (1837).
6. Sam Houston quoted in Haley, *Sam Houston* (2002), p. 154.

Afterword: Old Sam and Honest Abe

1. Sam Houston, "Inaugural Address," December 21, 1859.
2. Sam Houston, "Address at Union Mass Meeting, Austin, Texas," September 22, 1860.
3. Jeff Hamilton, *My Master* (1940), pp. 72–73.
4. Temple Houston Morrow, quoted in Friend, *Sam Houston: The Great Designer* (1954), p. 338.
5. "General Sam Houston and Secession," *Scribner's Magazine*, vol. 29 (May 1906), p. 587.
6. Howard C. Westwood, "President Lincoln's Overture to Sam Houston," *The Southwestern Historical Quarterly,* vol. 88, no. 2 (October 1984), p. 140.
7. Smithwick, *The Evolution of a State; or Recollections of Old Texas Days* (1900), pp. 331–34.
8. Houston speech of April 19, 1861.

IMAGE CREDITS

1. Prints and Photographs Collection, Archives and Information Services Division, Texas State Library and Archives Commission, 102–280
2. FineArt / Alamy Stock Photo
3. GL Archive / Alamy Stock Photo
4. World History Archive / Alamy Stock Photo
5. Science History Images / Alamy Stock Photo
6. Bettemann / Contributor
7. By William Howard, James Perry Bryan Papers, di_04428, The Dolph Briscoe Center for American History, The University of Texas at Austin
8. Everett Collection Historical / Alamy Stock Photo
9. FLHC / Alamy Stock Photo
10. Public domain
11. Prints and Photographs Collection, di_11688, The Dolph Briscoe Center for American History, The University of Texas at Austin
12. The Picture Art Collection / Alamy Stock Photo
13. Public domain
14. Prints and Photographs Collection, di_02195, The Dolph Briscoe Center for American History, The University of Texas at Austin
15. The Picture Art Collection / Alamy Stock Photo
16. Chronicle / Alamy Stock Photo
17. World History Archive / Alamy Stock Photo
18. Public domain
19. Science History Images / Alamy Stock Photo
20. North Wind Picture Archives / Alamy Stock Photo
21. Public domain
22. Painting, *March to the Massacre* by Andrew Jackson Houston. Courtesy of the San Jacinto Museum of History
23. Niday Picture Library / Alamy Stock Photo
24. World History Archive / Alamy Stock Photo
25. Science History Images / Alamy Stock Photo
26. The Picture Art Collection / Alamy Stock Photo
27. The History Collection / Alamy Stock Photo
28. Bygone Collection / Alamy Stock Photo
29. Historical / Contributor
30. Public domain

INDEX

Note: Page numbers in *italics* refer to maps or illustrations.

INDEX

AUTHOR BIO

Brian Kilmeade cohosts Fox News Channel's morning show *Fox & Friends* and hosts the national radio program *The Brian Kilmeade Show*. He is the author of six books, and he lives on Long Island.

Don't miss the other bestselling history books by Brian Kilmeade!

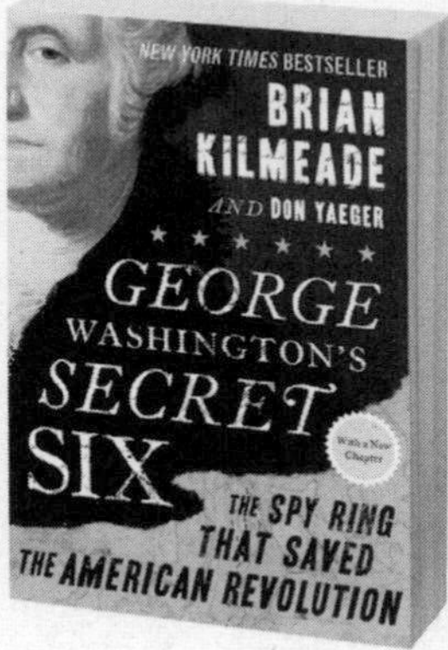

For more information, please visit BrianKilmeade.com.

Now with a new afterword: How America showed the world that we follow through for complete victory when faced with Islamic terror.

"No one captures the danger, intrigue, and drama of the American Revolution and its aftermath like Brian Kilmeade and Don Yaeger."
—**BRAD THOR,** bestselling author of *Code of Conduct*

"A riveting book of history that reads as though it were ripped from today's headlines, and a must read for anyone seeking an understanding of the roots of U.S. foreign policy."
—***ADMIRAL JAMES STAVRIDIS (Ret.),*** former Supreme Allied Commander at NATO; dean of The Fletcher School of Law and Diplomacy at Tufts University

"A colorful, exciting, and historic account of an overlooked portion of American military history, and a wonderful tribute to the brave sailors and Marines who set a high standard for U.S. maritime operations."
—***GENERAL JACK KEANE (Ret.),*** chairman of the Institute for the Study of War

"As a Navy SEAL you witness great acts of courage every day, but it's easy to forget that the Navy and Marines have been kicking ass right from their inception more than two hundred years ago. Count on Kilmeade and Yaeger to remind us of it with this swashbuckling adventure." —***MARCUS LUTTRELL,*** former Navy SEAL; author of *Lone Survivor* and *Service*

#1 NEW YORK TIMES BESTSELLER

SENTINEL

THOMAS JEFFERSON AND THE TRIPOLI PIRATES

Brian Kilmeade cohosts Fox News Channel's morning show *Fox & Friends* and also hosts the nationally syndicated radio show *The Brian Kilmeade Show*. He is the author of five books, and he lives on Long Island.

Don Yaeger has written or cowritten twenty-five books, including nine *New York Times* bestsellers. He lives in Tallahassee, Florida.

They are the coauthors of the *New York Times* bestseller *George Washington's Secret Six*.

ALSO BY BRIAN KILMEADE AND DON YAEGER

George Washington's Secret Six

BRIAN KILMEADE

AND DON YAEGER

THOMAS JEFFERSON

★ ★ ★ ★ ★ AND THE ★ ★ ★ ★ ★

TRIPOLI PIRATES

THE FORGOTTEN WAR THAT CHANGED AMERICAN HISTORY

SENTINEL

SENTINEL
An imprint of Penguin Random House LLC
375 Hudson Street
New York, New York 10014
penguin.com

First published in the United States of America by Sentinel 2015
This paperback edition with a new afterword published 2016.

Photo insert page 3 (top left): Stephen Decatur (1779–1820), by Rembrandt Peale, ca. 1815–1820; oil on canvas; overall: 29 x 23 5/8 in (73.7 x 60 cm); 1867.309, New-York Historical Society

Photo insert page 5 (bottom left): The attack made on Tripoli on the 3rd August 1804…; from PR100 (Maritime File), FF 56—Barbary War; neg #3516, New-York Historical Society

Photo insert page 6 (middle): Blowing up the fire ship *Intrepid*; from PR100 (Maritime File), FF 56, FF E, Drawer; Med Naval Battles: Barbary War; neg #90696d, New-York Historical Society

Photo insert page 7 (middle): General William Eaton and Hamet Qaramanli, *On the Desert of Barca, Approaching Derne*; from "Memories of a Hundred Years," p. 60, E173, H16 v. 1; neg #90916d, New-York Historical Society

Photo insert page 8 (bottom): The U.S. Squadron, under Command of Com. Decatur, At Anchor off the City of Algiers, June 30, 1815; from PR100 (Maritime File), box 11, folder 8; neg #90695d, New-York Historical Society

Additional credits appear adjacent to the respective images.

ISBN 978-1-59184-806-6 (hc.)
ISBN 978-0-14-312943-1 (pbk.)

Printed in the United States of America
18th Printing

Set in Bulmer MT Std
Design and Map Illustrations by Daniel Lagin

To my dad, who died way too young, and my mom, who worked way too hard. They taught me from day one that being born in America was like winning the lottery. This story is yet more proof that they were 100 percent right.

—**BK**

To Jeanette: I adore you. Thanks for encouraging this relationship, making this book happen.

—**DY**

CONTENTS

CAST OF CHARACTERS

Sidi Haji Abdrahaman: Tripolitan Envoy to Great Britain

John Adams: Minister to the Court of St. James's, later President of the United States

William Bainbridge: Captain, U.S. Navy

Joel Barlow: Consul General to the Barbary States

Samuel Barron: Captain, U.S. Navy, commander of the USS *President*

Salvador Catalano: Pilot, USS *Intrepid*

James Leander Cathcart: U.S. Consul to Tripoli

Richard Dale: Captain, U.S. Navy

James Decatur: Lieutenant, U.S. Navy, Gunboat No. 2

Stephen Decatur Jr.: Lieutenant, U.S. Navy

William Eaton: U.S. Consul General to Tunis

Daniel Frazier: Ordinary Seaman, U.S. Navy, Gunboat No. 5

Albert Gallatin: Secretary of the Treasury

Hassan: Dey of Algiers*

Isaac Hull: Captain, U.S. Navy, USS *Argus*

Martha and Mary (Polly) Jefferson: Daughters of Thomas Jefferson

Thomas Jefferson: Minister to France, later President of the United States

Ahmed Khorshid: Viceroy of Egypt

Tobias Lear: U.S. Consul General to the Barbary States

James Madison: Secretary of State, later President of the United States

Richard Valentine Morris: Captain, U.S. Navy, commander of the USS *Chesapeake*

Alexander Murray: Captain, U.S. Navy, commander of the USS *Constellation*

Bobba Mustapha: Dey of Algiers

Nicholas Nissen: Danish Consul General

Presley Neville O'Bannon: Lieutenant, U.S. Marines

Richard O'Brien: Captain of the *Dauphin*

---

* Though sometimes used interchangeably in diplomatic correspondence ca. 1800, the titles *Dey, Bey*, and *Bashaw* (sometimes rendered *Pasha*) will in the pages that follow distinguish the regency rulers dey of Algiers, bey of Tunis, and bashaw of Tripoli.

Edward Preble: Captain, U.S. Navy, commander of the USS *Constitution*

Hamet Qaramanli: Brother of Yusuf and rightful heir as Bashaw of Tripoli

Yusuf Qaramanli: Bashaw of Tripoli

Murat Rais: High Admiral, Navy of Tripoli (formerly Peter Lisle)

Mahomet Rous: Admiral, Navy of Tripoli, commander of the *Tripoli*

Richard Somers: Master Commandant, U.S. Navy, USS *Intrepid*

Andrew Sterett: Lieutenant, U.S. Navy, commander of the USS *Enterprise*

Maulay Sulaiman: Sultan of Morocco

George Washington: President of the United States

AUTHOR'S NOTE

It is my observation that American history has been for the most part focused on the genius of our founding fathers and not enough on those who fought and died for their ideals. We have written *Thomas Jefferson and the Tripoli Pirates* for those men and women who have been forgotten by most, though they were saluted in their day.

This is the story of how a new nation, saddled with war debt and desperate to establish credibility, was challenged by four Muslim powers. Our merchant ships were captured and the crews enslaved. Despite its youth, America would do what established western powers chose not to do: stand up to intimidation and lawlessness.

Tired of Americans being captured and held for ransom, our third president decided to take on the Barbary powers in a war that is barely remembered today but is one that, in many ways, we are still fighting.

In the following pages you will read how Jefferson, the so-called pacifist president, changed George Washington's and John Adams's policies to take on this collection of Muslim nations. You will travel alongside the fearless William Eaton as he treks five hundred miles across the desert. You will learn about the leadership of Stephen Decatur and Edward Preble, and about the fighting prowess of Marine lieutenant Presley O'Bannon, just to name a few. You will discover how the Marine Corps emerged as the essential military force it is today. Most important, you will see the challenges Presidents Washington, Adams, Jefferson, and Madison faced with the Barbary nations. And you will learn how military strength and the courage of our first generation of Americans led to victory, and ultimately respect in a world of nations that believed—and even hoped—that the American experiment would fail. Because of these brave men, the world would learn that in America failure is not an option.

I love this story and the brave men who secured our freedom. If this book does anything to restore them to America's memory, it will have succeeded.

—Brian Kilmeade

THOMAS
JEFFERSON
AND THE
TRIPOLI PIRATES

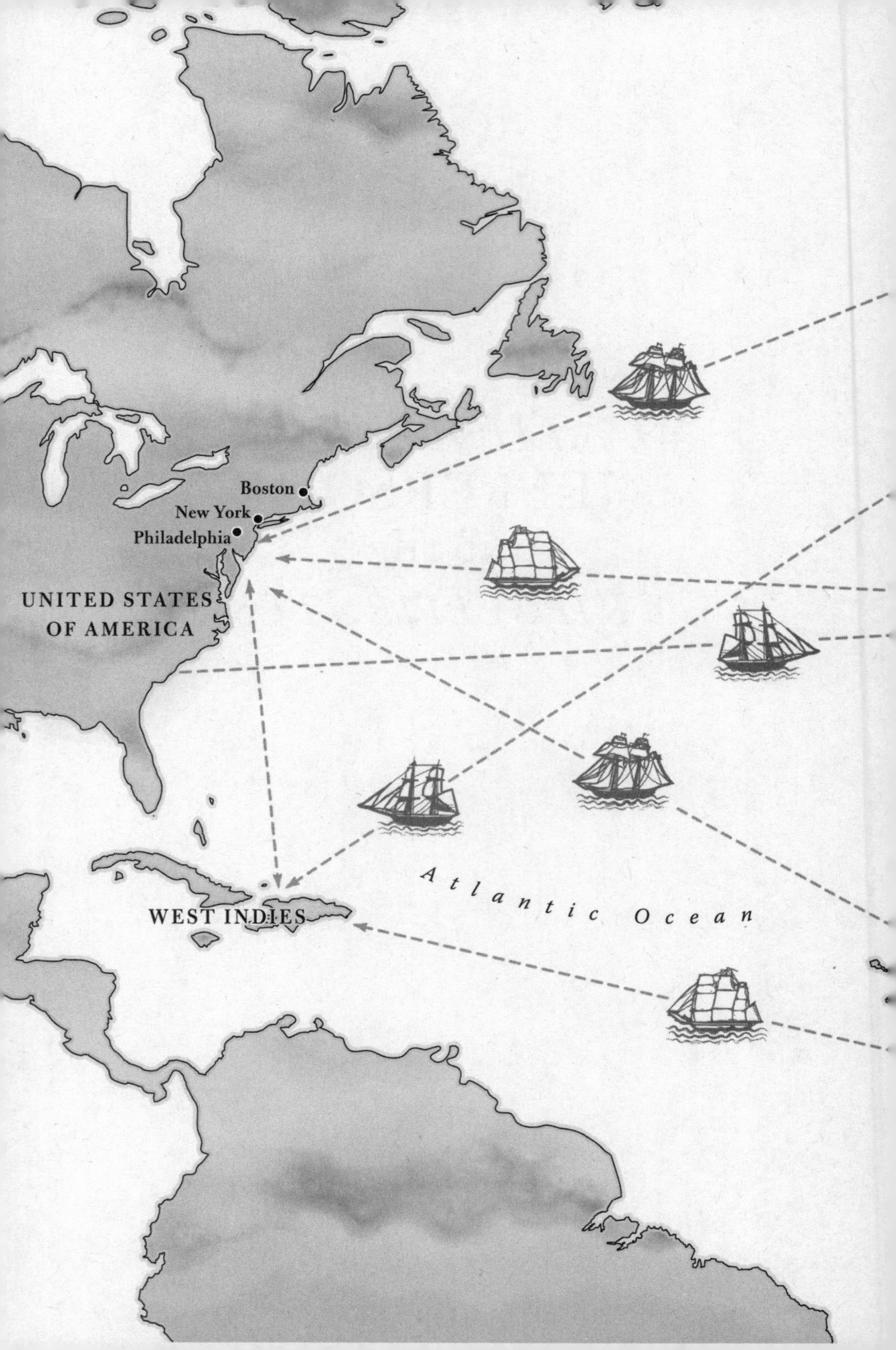

Boston
New York
Philadelphia
UNITED STATES
OF AMERICA
WEST INDIES
Atlantic Ocean

Glasgow
GREAT
BRITAIN
Bristol
FRANCE
PORTUGAL
SPAIN
Lisbon
Cádiz
Gibraltar
Tangier
PIRATE
WATERS
MOROCCO
Algiers
Tunis
Malta
Mediterranean Sea
Black Sea
Constantinople
TUNIS
Tripoli
Benghazi
Derne
Alexandria
ALGIERS
TRIPOLI
EGYPT
James Fort
Sierra Leone

PROLOGUE

Unprepared and Unprotected

Picture to yourself your Brother Citizens or Unfortunate Countrymen in the Algerian State Prisons or Damned Castile, and starved 2/3rd's and Naked. . . . Once a Citizen of the United States of America, but at present the Most Miserable Slave in Algiers.

—**Richard O'Brien, *Diary*, February 19, 1790**

As a fast-moving ship approached the *Dauphin* off the coast of Portugal, Captain Richard O'Brien saw no cause for alarm. On this warm July day in 1785, America was at peace, and there were many innocent reasons for a friendly ship to come alongside. Perhaps it was a fellow merchant ship needing information or supplies. Perhaps the ship's captain wanted to warn him of nearby pirates.

By the time O'Brien realized that the ship did not approach in peace, it was too late. The American ship was no match for the Algerian vessel armed with fourteen cannons. A raiding party with daggers gripped between their teeth swarmed over the sides of the

Dauphin. The Algerians vastly outnumbered the American crew and quickly claimed the ship and all its goods in the name of their nation's leader, the dey of Algiers.

Mercilessly, the pirates stripped O'Brien and his men of shoes, hats, and handkerchiefs, leaving them unprotected from the burning sun during the twelve-day voyage back to the North African coast. On arrival in Algiers, the American captives were paraded through the streets as spectators jeered.

The seamen were issued rough sets of native clothing and two blankets each that were to last for the entire period of captivity, whether it was a few weeks or fifty years. Kept in a slave pen, they slept on a stone floor, gazing into the night sky where the hot stars burned above them like lidless eyes, never blinking. Each night there was a roll call, and any man who failed to respond promptly would be chained to a column and whipped soundly in the morning.

Together with men of another captured ship, the *Maria*, O'Brien's *Dauphin* crew broke rocks in the mountains while wearing iron chains Saturday through Thursday. On Friday, the Muslim holy day, the Christian slaves dragged massive sleds loaded with rubble and dirt nearly two miles to the harbor to be unloaded into the sea to form a breakwater. Their workdays began before the sun rose and, for a few blissfully cool hours, they worked in darkness.

Their diet consisted of stale bread, vinegar from a shared bowl at breakfast and lunch, and, on good days, some ground olives. Water was the one necessity provided with any liberality. As a ship captain, O'Brien was treated somewhat better, but he feared that his men would starve to death.

"Our sufferings are beyond our expression or your conception," O'Brien wrote to America's minister to France, Thomas Jefferson, two weeks after his arrival in Algiers.[1] Those sufferings would only get worse. Several of the captives from the *Maria* and the *Dauphin* would die in captivity of yellow fever, overwork, and exposure—and in some ways, they were the lucky ones. The ways out of prison for the remaining prisoners were few: convert to Islam, attempt to escape, or wait for their country to negotiate their release. A few of the captives would be ransomed but, for most, their thin blankets wore out as year after year passed and freedom remained out of reach. Richard O'Brien would be ten years a slave.

America had not yet elected its first president, but it already had its first enemy.

CHAPTER 1

Americans Abroad

It is not probable the American States will have a very free trade in the Mediterranean . . . the Americans cannot protect themselves [as] they cannot pretend to [have] a Navy.

—John Baker-Holroyd, Lord Sheffield, *Observations of the Commerce of the American States,* 1783

In 1785, the same year Richard O'Brien was captured by pirates, Thomas Jefferson learned that all politics, even transatlantic politics, are personal.

He was a widower. The passing of his wife in September 1782 had left him almost beyond consolation, and what little comfort he found was in the company of his daughter Martha, then age ten. The two would take "melancholy rambles" around the large plantation, seeking to evade the grief that haunted them. When Jefferson was offered the appointment as American minister to France, he accepted because he saw an opportunity to escape the sadness that still shadowed him.

Thomas Jefferson had sailed for Europe in the summer of 1784 with Martha at his side; once they reached Paris, he enrolled his daughter in a convent school with many other well-born English-speaking students. There he would be able to see her regularly, but he had been forced to make a more difficult decision regarding Martha's two sisters. Mary, not yet six, and toddler Lucy Elizabeth, both too young to travel with him across the sea, had been left behind with their "Aunt Eppes," his late wife's half sister. The separation was painful, but it was nothing compared with the new heartbreak he experienced just months into his Paris stay when Mrs. Eppes wrote sadly to say that "hooping cough" had taken the life of two-year-old Lucy.[1]

As a fresh wave of sorrow rolled over him, Jefferson longed for "Polly the Parrot," as he affectionately called his bright and talkative Mary, to join his household again. The father wrote to his little girl that he and her sister "cannot live without you" and asked her if she would like to join them across the ocean. He promised that joining them in France meant she would learn "to play on the harpsichord, to draw, to dance, to read and talk French."[2]

"I long to see you, and hope that you . . . are well," the now seven-year-old replied. But she added that she had no desire to make the trip, harpsichord or no harpsichord. "I don't want to go to France," she stated plainly. "I had rather stay with Aunt Eppes."[3]

Jefferson was undaunted and began to plan for her safe travel. Having already lost two dear family members, he did not want to risk losing Polly and looked for ways to reduce the dangers of the journey. He instructed her uncle, Francis Eppes, to select a proven ship for Polly's crossing. "The vessel should have performed one [transatlantic] voyage at least," Jefferson ordered, "and must not be more than four or five years old."[4] He worried about the weather and insisted that his daughter travel in the warm months to avoid winter storms. As for supervision, Polly could make the journey, Jefferson advised, "with some good lady passing from America to France, or even England [or] . . . a careful gentleman."[5]

Yet an even more intimidating concern worried Jefferson: more frightening than weather or leaky ships was the threat of pirates off North Africa, a region known as the Barbary Coast. The fate of the *Dauphin* and the *Maria* was a common one for ships venturing near the area, where the Sahara's arid coast was divided into four nation-states. Running west to east were the Barbary nations Morocco, Algiers, Tunis, and Tripoli, which all fell under the ultimate authority of the Ottoman Empire, seated in present-day Turkey.

The Islamic nations of the Barbary Coast had preyed upon foreign shipping for centuries, attacking ships in international waters

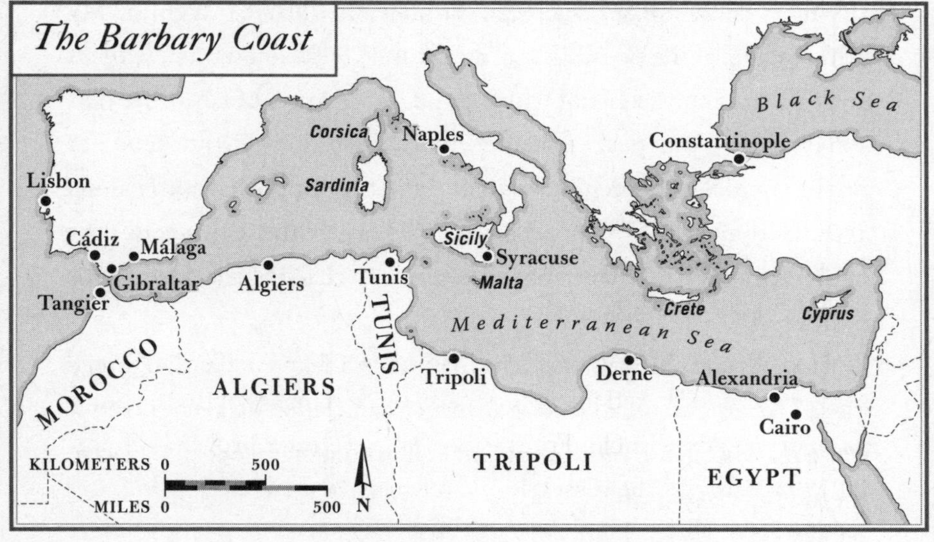

both in the Mediterranean and along the northwest coast of Africa and the Iberian peninsula. Even such naval powers as France and Great Britain were not immune, though they chose to deal with the problem by paying annual tributes of "gifts" to Barbary leaders—bribes paid to the Barbary states to persuade the pirates to leave merchant ships from the paying countries alone. But the prices were always changing, and the ships of those nations that did not meet the extortionate demands were not safe from greedy pirates.

To the deeply rational Jefferson, the lawless pirates posed perhaps the greatest danger to his sadly diminished family. He knew what had happened to O'Brien and could not risk a similar fate for his child. As he confided in a letter to brother-in-law Francis Eppes, "My anxieties on this subject could induce me to endless details. . . . The Algerines this fall took two vessels from us and now have twenty-two of our citizens in slavery." The plight of the men aboard the *Maria* and the *Dauphin* haunted him—if their hellish incarceration was terrifying to contemplate, "who can estimate . . . the fate of a child? My mind revolts at the possibility of a capture," Jefferson wrote. "Unless you hear from myself—not trusting the information of any other person on earth—that peace is made with the Algerines, do not send her but in a vessel of French or English property; for these vessels alone are safe from prize by the barbarians."[6] He knew those two countries paid a very high annual tribute, thereby purchasing safe passage for their vessels.

As a father, he could feel in his bones a fear for his daughter's safety. As an ambassador and an American, Jefferson recognized it was a fear no citizen of a free nation embarking on an oceanic voyage should have to endure.

A MEETING OF MINISTERS

A few months later, in March 1786, Jefferson would make his way to London to meet with his good friend John Adams. Together they hoped to figure out how to deal with the emerging threat to American interests.

His waistline thickening, his chin growing jowly, fifty-year-old John Adams welcomed Jefferson into his London home. Overlooking the tree-lined Grosvenor Square from the town house Adams had rented, the two men sat down to talk in the spacious drawing room.

Adams was the United States' first ambassador to Great Britain. Just arrived from Paris after a cold and blustery six-day journey, Jefferson was minister to the French government of Louis XVI. To Adams and his wife, Abigail, their old friend looked different, as Jefferson had begun powdering his ginger hair white. The stout New Englander and the tall, lean, forty-two-year-old Virginian might have been of different breeds—but then, in the years to come, they would often be of two minds in their political thinking as well.

Unlike most of the European diplomats they encountered, neither Adams nor Jefferson had been born into a tradition of diplomatic decorum. Adams was a rough-and-tumble lawyer, the son of a yeoman farmer from south of Boston, known for a damn-all attitude of speaking his mind. A man of quiet natural grace, Jefferson was learning the cosmopolitan ways of Paris but, at heart, he was a well-born country boy, heir to large farms outside Charlottesville, a tiny courthouse town in central Virginia. Both men were novices in the game of international negotiation, a game their country needed them to learn quickly.

When the Americans and British signed the Treaty of Paris in 1783, bringing to an end the Revolution, the United States' legal status changed in the view of every nation and world leader. No longer under British protection, the fledgling nation found that its status was lowly indeed. Adams's letters to the British government tended to go unanswered, and Jefferson's attempts to negotiate trade treaties with France and Spain were going nowhere. Now a more hostile international threat was rearing its head, and Adams had summoned Jefferson from Paris to discuss the danger posed by the "piratical nations" of North Africa.

In earlier days, the colonies' ships had enjoyed the protection offered by the Union Jack; but because U.S. ships no longer carried British passports, the British navy provided no protection against pirates. The French, America's wartime allies against the British, did not protect them now that there was peace. Americans abroad were very much on their own, especially in international waters. And because America had no navy to protect its interests, insurance for American ships skyrocketed to twenty times the rate of that of European ships.[7]

The expense of insurance was insupportable, but America's economy could not afford to end trade on the high seas; the Revolution had been fought with borrowed money, and repayment of those debts depended upon ongoing international commerce. One key piece of the nation's economic health was trade with southern Europe, accessible only by sailing into the Mediterranean—and within range of the Barbary pirates. According to Jefferson's calculations, a quarter of New England's most important export, dried salt cod, went to markets there, as did one sixth of the country's grain exports. Rice and lumber were also important exports, and the merchant ships provided employment for more than a thousand seamen. The trade and employment were essential to the growing American economy, and John Adams thought the numbers could easily double if a diplomatic solution in the Barbary region could be reached.

The American government had initially approved payment to the North African nations. But the bribes demanded were impossibly high, many hundreds of thousands of dollars when the American treasury could afford only token offerings of a few tens of thousands. In an era when not a single American was worth a million dollars, and Mr. Jefferson's great house, Monticello, was assessed at seventy-five hundred dollars, paying such exorbitant bribes seemed almost incomprehensible. Unable to pay enough to buy the goodwill of the Barbary countries, America was forced to let its ships sail at their own risk. Sailors like those on the *Maria* and the *Dauphin* had become pawns in a very dangerous game.

On this day, Adams and Jefferson worried over the fate of the *Dauphin* and the *Maria*. It had been nearly a year since the pirates from Algiers had taken the ships and cargoes the previous July, and now the regent of Algiers had made known his demand: until he was paid an exorbitant and, it seemed, ever-escalating ransom, the American captives were to be his slaves.

Despite their pity for the captives, Jefferson and Adams knew the new nation couldn't afford a new war or a new source of debt. They understood that the cost of keeping American ships away from the Barbary Coast would be greater than the cost of addressing the problem. That left the two American ministers, as Jefferson confided to a friend, feeling "absolutely suspended between indignation and impotence."[8]

Yet neither Jefferson nor Adams could afford to remain paralyzed in the face of the danger. Not only had American families and the economy been endangered, but rumor had it that the pirates had also captured a ship carrying the venerable Benjamin Franklin, Jefferson's predecessor as minister to France. (As one of his correspondents wrote to Franklin, "We are waiting with the greatest patience to hear from you. The newspapers have given us anxiety on your account; for some of them insist that you have been taken by the Algerines, while others pretend that you are at Morocco, enduring your slavery with all the patience of a philosopher."[9]) To everyone's relief, the reports proved false, but the scare brought the very real dangers posed by the Barbary pirates too close for comfort.

Sitting in the London house, John Adams and Thomas Jefferson discussed the idea of a negotiation that might break the impasse. Adams had a new reason to hope that the Barbary rulers could be reasoned with, and the two ministers set about deciding upon the right approach.

"MONEY IS THEIR GOD AND MAHOMET THEIR PROPHET"

A few weeks earlier, Adams had made an unannounced visit to the Barbary state of Tripoli's ambassador, freshly arrived in London. To Adams's surprise, the bearded Sidi Haji Abdrahaman had welcomed him warmly. Seated in front of a roaring fire, with two servants in attendance, they smoked tobacco from great pipes with six-foot-long stems "fit for a Walking Cane." Adams had promptly written to Jefferson. "It is long since I took a pipe, but [we] smoked in awful pomp, reciprocating whiff for whiff . . . until coffee was brought in."[10]

Adams made a strong impression on the Tripolitans. Observing his expertise with the Turkish smoking device, an attendant praised his technique, saying, *"Monsieur, vous êtes un Turk!"* ("Sir, you are a Turk!")[11] It was a high compliment.

Abdrahaman returned Adams's visit two days later, and Adams decided his new diplomatic acquaintance was "a benevolent and wise man" with whom the United States could do business.[12] He believed Abdrahaman might help broker an arrangement between the United States and the other Barbary nations, bringing an end to the capture of American merchantmen. Now reunited with his friend and fellow American, he shared his plan with Jefferson and invited him to join the conversation.

On a blustery March day, Adams, Jefferson, and Abdrahaman convened at the house of the Tripolitan envoy. The conversation began in an improvised mix of broken French and Italian, as the Tripolitan envoy spoke little English. The discussion was cordial, and Adams and Jefferson began to believe that a solution was in sight. When the talk turned to money, however, the bubble of optimism soon exploded.

Jefferson had researched the sums paid as tribute by European countries, including Denmark, Sweden, and Portugal, so he knew the going rate. But the gold Abdrahaman demanded that day was beyond the reach of the United States: a perpetual peace with Tripoli would cost some 30,000 English guineas, the equivalent of roughly $120,000, not counting the 10 percent gratuity Abdrahaman demanded for himself. And that amount bought peace with only one of the Barbary states. To buy peace in Tunis would cost another 30,000 guineas, to say nothing of what would be required to pay Morocco or even Algiers, the largest and most powerful of the four.

The $80,000 that Congress had been hard-pressed to authorize for an across-the-board understanding was no more than a down payment on what would be needed to meet the Barbary demands.[13]

Although he now despaired of an easy solution, Adams wasn't ready to stop talking. He could understand financial concerns, and he was already beginning to realize what O'Brien would later say of the pirates: "Money is their God and Mahomet their Prophet."[14] Yet greed alone couldn't explain the madness and cruelty of the demands. Unsatisfied, the famously blunt Adams wanted a better answer. While maintaining the best diplomatic reserve he could muster—whatever their frustration, the American ministers could hardly leap to their feet and walk out of the negotiations—Adams asked how the Barbary states could justify "[making] war upon nations who had done them no injury."

The response was nothing less than chilling.

According to his holy book, the Qur'an, Abdrahaman explained, "all nations which had not acknowledged the Prophet were sinners, whom it was the right and duty of the faithful to plunder and enslave."

Christian sailors were, plain and simple, fair game.

Jefferson tried to make sense of what he was hearing. He was familiar with the Muslim holy book. He had purchased a copy of the Qur'an during his days of reading law in Williamsburg twenty years before but found its values so foreign that he shelved the volume with books devoted to the mythology of the Greeks and Romans. This conversation left him even more perplexed. The man who had written that all people were "endowed by their Creator with certain inalienable rights" was horrified at Abdrahaman's religious justification for greed and cruelty.

Dashing Adams's high hopes, Abdrahaman refused to play the role of "benevolent and wise man." Despite the Americans' horror, he wasn't apologizing in any way. He showed no remorse or regret. He believed the actions of his fellow Muslims fully justified.

"Every mussulman," he explained, "who was slain in this warfare was sure to go to paradise."

To Abdrahaman, this was not complicated. In his culture, the takers of ships, the enslavers of men, the Barbarians who extorted bribes for safe passage, were all justified by the teaching of the prophet Muhammad. "It was written in our Qur'an," he said simply.[15]

When the meeting ended, the two American ministers, disheartened and outraged, left empty-handed. They had found no solution, no peaceful answer to protecting American shipping or freeing their countrymen enslaved in North Africa.

THE PRICE OF PEACE

Their initial attempt at making peace foiled, Adams and Jefferson began to plan their next approach. They agreed that the status quo was not workable, but that's where their agreement ended.

In the coming months, the two old friends would find they disagreed about how to deal with the Barbary pirates. Adams remained determined to continue the negotiations. The Americans should be willing to pay for peace, he believed, even if they had to borrow money to pay the tributes. "If it is not done," he wrote to Jefferson from London that summer, "you and I . . . ought to go home."[16]

In Paris, Jefferson expressed another view. He did not wish to "buy a peace," as he put it. He did not trust the Barbary powers to keep their word. At the same time, he did not think America could afford to stop trading with the Mediterranean. He believed in freedom on the seas, and he proposed a tougher position.

"I should prefer the obtaining of it by war," he wrote to Adams from France.[17] Jefferson argued that America needed a navy to deal with the pirates of the Barbary coast, to confront and destroy them.

He told Adams that justice, honor, and the respect of Europe for the United States would be served by establishing a fleet in "constant cruise" in Barbary waters, policing and confronting ships of the outlaw states as necessary. He argued that an armed naval presence made budgetary sense. According to his calculations, establishing a small navy would be less costly than the sum of the ransoms, bribes, and maritime losses.

Adams disagreed. He believed that a war against the Islamic nations would be costly and possibly unwinnable. It would certainly require too large a military force for America's budget. Opposing Jefferson's belief that a small navy could solve the problem, he told Jefferson, "We ought not to fight them at all unless We determine to fight them forever."[18]

Despite their differences, the two men worked tirelessly to gain the freedom of the enslaved sailors. They sent American agents to conduct negotiations with the Barbary governments. Jefferson contacted the Mathurins, also called Trinitarians, a Catholic religious order that had worked to free Christian captives since 1199. All efforts failed. O'Brien and his men remained in captivity, and eventually diplomacy between the United States and Algiers went quiet. More than five years would pass before American negotiators would return to Algiers to resume talks. During those years, several hundred more Christian men, women, and children would join the ranks of the imprisoned, as the pirates collected more ships, booty, and slaves.

But the situation continued to trouble Jefferson deeply. Remembering his fear for Polly's safety, he sympathized with the terrible worry and sleepless nights that American families endured on behalf of loved ones who made a living on the sea. In a world where the Barbary pirates roamed the eastern Atlantic and the Mediterranean, who would they capture and enslave next? Would the next captives ever make it home again, or would they die of disease or under the lash in a foreign land?

The Barbary powers, with their mixture of greed, religious fanaticism, and self-interest, would not listen to reason. They might listen to force, but with no navy, the Americans could not bring power to bear on the pirates. Both Adams and Jefferson were stymied and returned to America without solutions, but they did not give up entirely. Soon enough, Jefferson would confront the issue from a fresh vantage.

CHAPTER 2

Secretary Jefferson

> It rests with Congress to decide between war, tribute, and ransom, as the means of re-establishing our Mediterranean commerce.
>
> **—Secretary of State Thomas Jefferson, December 30, 1790**

When Thomas Jefferson stepped ashore in Norfolk, Virginia, in November 1789, he was shocked when the mayor and aldermen of the town greeted him with words of congratulation on his new appointment as George Washington's secretary of state.

During Jefferson's five years abroad, the political landscape in the United States had changed. The U.S. Constitution had been drafted and ratified, and General George Washington had taken office as the first president on April 30, 1789. Though Jefferson had still been in Europe, the president had chosen him to serve in the newly created post of secretary of state and Congress had confirmed the appointment during Jefferson's crossing.

As he absorbed the news, Jefferson was both humbled and honored that George Washington had appointed him for the daunting task. Except for matters of finance and war, the secretary of state would administer the entire government. Jefferson asked for time to consider, but back at home that winter in central Virginia, he decided to accept the appointment. He remained at his mountaintop home, Monticello, to witness the February marriage of daughter Martha, now seventeen, then he traveled to New York, temporarily the nation's capital, to join the government.

At their very first meeting, on March 22, 1790, the president and his new secretary of state discussed an issue that had been weighing on Jefferson for years—the plight of Richard O'Brien and his men.

Washington and Jefferson weren't the only Americans worrying about their captive countrymen. On May 14, 1790, a petition was read on the floor of Congress. The captured men had sent a letter to Congress asking it to intervene on their behalf as their situation grew more desperate and the outlook even bleaker as the years passed.

Congress's interest in the problem went beyond the enslaved men, because the continuing threat to ships had meant that American trade in the Mediterranean was dwindling—at a great cost to the otherwise healthy American economy. Congress and the president wasted no time, immediately referring the matter to the new secretary of state; with Washington's mandate, Jefferson set about examining the issue in detail.

A bookish man by nature, Jefferson began by looking into the history of the Barbary pirates. He planned to spend months researching the pirates' centuries-long practice of enslaving innocent sailors before making definitive suggestions for action. As he compiled an exhaustive report on the problem, he also corresponded with Richard O'Brien, who remained a prisoner of the Algerians.

Because O'Brien had the rank of sea captain, his experience in captivity was far better than that of most other prisoners, and he had been assigned relatively comfortable work at the British consulate, tilling soil, planting trees, and feeding the pigs before eventually rising to become a liaison to the dey. That privileged position allowed him to travel to Portugal, England, and Germany to beg for ransom gold from governments, private parties, and Christian aid groups. He was heavily guarded on such journeys, unable to make his escape; he also knew that if he did not return, things would be much worse for the men he left behind—men who were already subjected to hard labor and harsh treatment.

O'Brien did what he could to answer the questions Jefferson posed to him in his letters, and on December 30, 1790, President Washington laid before both houses of Congress the results of Jefferson's meticulous research. There were two reports, titled "Prisoners at Algiers" and "Mediterranean Trade."

Although his papers seemed to support the ransom strategy, Jefferson had his doubts. He maintained his long-standing skepticism about a purchased peace. For years, even before the capture of the *Dauphin* and the *Maria* and his subsequent disagreement with Adams, Jefferson had called for America to use the navy to solve the problem of the Barbary pirates. Seven years before, he had written of his objections to paying tribute. If negotiations broke down (as indeed they had, repeatedly, in the years since), what then?

> If they refuse a [fair treaty], why not go to war with them? We ought to begin a naval power if we mean to carry on our

> own commerce. Can we begin it on a more honorable occasion, or with a weaker foe? I am of opinion [that] with half a dozen frigates [we could] totally destroy their commerce.[1]

In his 1790 reports to Congress, the ever-thorough Jefferson presented detailed intelligence he had collected on the size of the naval force at Algiers and its tactics. He wasn't impressed with the Algerians' poorly equipped ships, pointing out that their battle strategies depended on boarding their target ships, rather than on their cannons.[2] He hinted that the Americans would need only a small navy to beat the pirates, but, perhaps caving to political pressure, he stopped short of calling for direct military action. "It rests with Congress to decide between war, tribute, and ransom," he concluded, "as the means of re-establishing our Mediterranean commerce."[3]

Some senators considered instituting a navy, but the nation's empty treasury ended the conversation about warships even before it got started. Ransom seemed cheaper, but the process for funding it was excruciatingly slow; it wasn't until more than a year later, in 1792, that the sum of $40,000 was authorized for a treaty with Algiers. Then distance and death increased the delay—the two men appointed to negotiate with Algiers both died of natural causes before talks could begin—so it wasn't until 1794 that any negotiations started.

O'Brien and his men, enslaved for nine years, still waited for freedom.

BUILDING A NAVY

When Jefferson became secretary of state, his nation had no navy. The last of the ships in the Continental Navy, made legendary by John Paul Jones, had been sold off after the Revolution. There had been no money to maintain them, and no threat close enough to home to justify raising funds.

The dismantling of the navy had suited President Washington perfectly. Over and over again he said he favored a policy of strict neutrality in international affairs, a position he made explicit in his "Neutrality Proclamation" of 1793. Recalling the terrible toll of the Revolution on the nation's people and resources, Washington wished to fight no more wars. He desired neither a standing army nor a navy.

That Washington and Jefferson did not see eye-to-eye on many issues was one of the worst-kept secrets in Washington. Jefferson took issue with what he perceived to be Washington's poor judgment of character, as he mentioned in an ill-advised letter that ended up being published widely. Based on his earlier years in Europe, Jefferson also believed sound judgment of the Barbary situation called for military action. He would submit to his president but push where he could.

His influence seems to have worked. A matter of months after Jefferson joined the cabinet, the political tide turned. In October 1793, the secretary of state received a desperate letter from the U.S. consul in Lisbon. A new attack fleet of Algerian ships roamed the Atlantic near Gibraltar. The flotilla consisted of eight ships, including four frigates and a twenty-gun brig. Their objective? "To cruise against the American flag."[4] The growing wealth of the United States had caught the pirates' attention. No longer would they attack just the

American vessels unlucky enough to cross their paths, but they were now actively seeking out American ships. "I have not slept since Receipt of the news of this hellish plot," the consul wrote Jefferson. "Another corsair in the Atlantic—God preserve us—."[5]

Soon a new dispatch from Gibraltar reported that ten American vessels had been captured in late October. Not only had the Algerians taken more ships, but they had also added 110 captives to their slave pens. The pirate problem could be ignored no longer, nor simply be debated. Action was required.

In Congress, a House committee was appointed to study the sort of ships needed. It soon reported back, and House debate, beginning on February 16, 1794, lasted a month. Jefferson's own Republican party, led by his dear friend and confidant Congressman James Madison, took a stance different from Jefferson's, believing that a navy would unnecessarily expand the federal government. The Federalists, using Jefferson's old argument, reasoned that the cost of establishing a navy would be less than the cost of *not* having one. Maritime insurance rates continued to skyrocket, and the cost of imported goods grew by the day. A navy, they argued, had become economically necessary.

Despite the bitter division between parties and regions—New England delegations tended to want a navy to protect their merchants while Southerners generally opposed such federal expansion—the House reached a compromise, agreeing to halt ship construction if peace was achieved. Both houses of Congress passed the Act to Provide a Naval Armament by narrow margins. Signed into law by President Washington on March 27, 1794, the act authorized the purchase or construction of six frigates, four rated for forty-four guns, two for thirty-six guns. The immense sum of $688,888 was appropriated.

Thus it had been decided: the United States would have a navy. George Washington ordered the shipbuilding contracts spread out between northern and southern ports, and construction began. Three years would pass before the first frigate was launched, and during that time, the chess match that was Barbary diplomacy would see the rules of the game shift again and again. With every failed negotiation, it would become increasingly clear that only one solution remained: those frigates would have to cross the ocean and try a different kind of diplomacy, one that came from the mouths of their cannons.

BLEEDING US DRY

As 1793 ended, Jefferson resigned, retiring to Monticello to consider his future. In the year after his departure, the United States managed to reach a peace agreement with the dey of Algiers—a deal that meant that, against Jefferson's advice, Americans would pay for peace. Though there was no longer any immediate need for more naval ships, President Washington did persuade Congress that stopping the shipbuilding would be unwise.

Washington's instincts proved sound. Because the Americans were perennially slow in making their transatlantic payments of tribute, the dey threatened war and refused to release the prisoners. The Americans were relieved that they had kept the shipbuilding going, and the USS *United States*, USS *Constellation*, and USS *Constitution* launched in 1797.

By 1797, Joel Barlow was on duty as ambassador to the volatile leader of Algiers. The president had dispatched him the previous year to "take charge of the interests of the United States of America within the Regency of Algiers."[6] His goal was to maintain the peace—and gain the release of O'Brien and his men.

If anyone was equipped for the difficult diplomacy needed in Algiers, Barlow was. A Yale graduate who had served in the Revolution, worked as a newspaperman, and been imprisoned during the French Revolution, he had emerged after the Reign of Terror as an honorary citizen of France. Barlow seemed like the man to deal with whatever came his way. He had the brains, the courage, and the courtly manner to be an expert diplomat—but it wasn't clear that that would be enough to rescue the American slaves.

When Barlow arrived as American consul to Algiers, he was confronted with the dey's refusal to release the prisoners until the United States fulfilled its monetary promises. Barlow gave his word that payment was forthcoming but, in the meantime, plied the Algerian ruler with diamond rings, brocade robes, carpets, jeweled snuffboxes, and other goods he had brought with him from France, treasures worth more than $27,000. Some mix of personality, placating gifts, and promises of money persuaded the dey, who—at last—released the prisoners. Their ranks had been reduced by harsh prison conditions and illness, but Barlow guided eighty-five survivors aboard the ship *Fortune*, and watched them depart for friendlier shores.

After O'Brien and the other captives went free, Barlow and his fellow American consuls in the region remained behind to finish a series of impossibly complicated negotiations. Committed to purchasing a treaty, he put up with diplomatic chicanery, delays, broken promises, and shaky deals. Bowing to the Algerians' humiliating demands, the American government would agree to hand over money and goods worth close to a million dollars, a cost equal to one eighth of the federal government's annual expenditures.

Because the United States didn't have the cash on hand to pay the dey, the money had to be borrowed. Richard O'Brien, who had chosen to remain behind after his shipmates were free in order to assist the American government, was by then a well-known and well-connected presence in Algiers from his years of working at the British consulate. Traveling to several cities in Europe, including London, hoping to obtain gold and silver from London bankers he finally succeeded in securing loans in Portugal and Italy, but, before the money reached Algiers, O'Brien's bad luck resurfaced. The ship he traveled on, the brig *Sophia,* was taken by Tripolitan pirates.

Because the ship had an Algerian passport, Bashaw Yusuf Qaramanli, ruler of Tripoli, promptly ordered its release. But O'Brien's capture gave Barlow an idea: he commissioned O'Brien to act as his intermediary and to negotiate with the militant bashaw.

Ruthless and cunning, Bashaw Yusuf had murdered one brother for the throne and exiled another brother, Hamet, the rightful bashaw, holding Hamet's family hostage to guarantee that he would not return to fight for his birthright. Whether the Americans would be able to successfully negotiate with such a man was unclear, but Barlow deemed it worth an attempt and the Treaty of Peace and Friendship Between the United States and Tripoli was signed in November 1796. It included the usual provisions, one for payment of tribute, another for the delivery of maritime and military stores, in return for free passage of American ships and mutual cooperation.

The treaty was ratified by the United States Congress in June 1797 and Barlow returned to France, having spent only two years in

North Africa, but leaving two new treaties in place. Two more—with the remaining Barbary states, Morocco and Tunis—would shortly be signed. Between the treaties and the freeing of the long-imprisoned sailors, Barlow's brief tenure had been a success.

Jefferson seemed to have been wrong about the necessity of force. For the moment, the United States of America and the Barbary Coast states enjoyed a purchased peace—but the Americans' new warships waited in the wings, just in case.

ENTER EATON

After Barlow's departure, a team of highly qualified men was commissioned to represent the United States in the Barbary region. At its head was Richard O'Brien, named in December 1797 to succeed Barlow as consul general to all the Barbary states.

In December 1798, another former captive, James Leander Cathcart, joined O'Brien in North Africa, assuming the post of American consul to Tripoli. Cathcart had been aboard the *Maria* when it was captured in 1785 and had also endured a decade of captivity alongside O'Brien. No stranger to harsh conditions, having spent time on a British prison ship during the Revolution prior to his Algerian enslavement, Cathcart had known how to promote himself when he found himself a prisoner once again. During his years in Algiers, he had risen slowly in the estimation of his captors, becoming a clerk and overseer before his appointment as secretary to the dey in 1792. From that post he had been able to hobnob with men of considerable power, including the Swedish consul, who eventually loaned him $5,000 to gain his freedom. But he wasn't a man who wore the hardships of his Algerian years easily.

Cathcart crossed the Atlantic in the company of the new American consul to Tunis, William Eaton, whose prematurely white hair and cleft chin gave him the appearance of a Roman general carved out of marble. A driven man of many talents, Eaton had been chosen by Secretary of State Timothy Pickering because he thought him well suited to tackle the challenges of Tunisian diplomacy.

Eaton's life had been marked by a stubborn determination. He had studied classical languages as a boy before, at age sixteen, running away to fight the British in the Revolution. After serving with a Connecticut regiment, he enrolled at Dartmouth College in 1785, but his scholarship was interrupted by winters spent teaching in country schools in order to earn his tuition money. At the end of one such break, he gathered his books, a change of clothes, and his tuition money into a small bundle he slung over his shoulder. He then set off on foot from the rural Connecticut town where he had been teaching, heading for Hanover, New Hampshire, nearly 150 miles north.

The summer of 1787 was unusually hot, and what Eaton had hoped would be a pleasant, if lengthy, journey on rustic trails through scenic countryside became a daunting slog along dusty roads overlooking fields choked by drought. Barely halfway to his destination, he found himself out of money, hungry, and still short of the New Hampshire border. But demonstrating the resourcefulness and adaptability he would display over and over in his life, he hit upon a solution. The only possessions he carried with him of any value were the pins and needles in his sewing kit. By selling the pins one at a time, he scraped together just enough to continue on the last miles to Hanover.

After graduation, Eaton returned to the army, gaining a captain's commission in 1792. Throughout his service—he would remain in the U.S. Army for five years—Captain Eaton would wrestle with his fiery temper and a tendency to take grievances personally. He narrowly avoided a duel with a fellow officer who accused him of disobeying an order. Only the intercession of other officers prevented an exchange of deadly fire, persuading the men to accept that both were culpable. "[After] Capt. B. conceded, and offered me his hand," Eaton noted in his journal, "[I] accepted it."[7] Honor—both personal and national—was a matter worth fighting for.

Eaton's reputation was for toughness; a skilled marksman, he could ride a horse all day and survive on his own wits when he had to. He spent time stationed at Fort Recovery, where he gained the respect of the legendary General Anthony Wayne. Known as "Mad Anthony" for his distinguished and fiercely committed service in General Washington's army, Wayne observed that "Eaton is firm in constitution as in resolution;—industrious, indefatigable, determined and persevering. . . . When in danger, he is in his element; and never shows to so good advantage, as when leading a charge."[8] A few years later, while stationed in swamps along the Georgia border with Spanish Florida, Eaton befriended the native tribes he had been sent to Georgia to fight. "I have frequently invited both Indians and traders to my quarters and entertained them," he wrote to an army official.[9] His unorthodox approach to frontier diplomacy aroused suspicions and irritated merchants in the region while his blunt appraisals of the campaign did not always sit well with his superiors. But Secretary of State Pickering liked what he saw. He valued Eaton's keen eye for reporting details, prompt correspondence, and gift for learning languages.

In January 1799, the new consuls made their first stop in North Africa at Algiers, where O'Brien was serving as consul to the dey, in addition to his duty as consul general. O'Brien greeted them warmly. With Cathcart's intimate knowledge of the region and Eaton's negotiating experience, O'Brien was optimistic that the new treaties could be preserved.

Eager to welcome them, O'Brien showed Cathcart and Eaton the city of Algiers. The densely packed streetscapes rose from a fortress at sea level into the hills that overlooked the Mediterranean, a place of bright sun but cooling sea breezes. After introducing his colleagues to the new dey of Algiers, hoping that the troubles would blow over, O'Brien wished them well as they sailed for their new postings.

O'Brien and Eaton initiated a lively correspondence from their cities some five hundred miles apart, discussing matters of diplomatic delicacy. O'Brien warned the new consul that the American Department of State took months to respond and had very little understanding of Barbary culture; instead, O'Brien urged Eaton to ignore irrelevant American instructions and instead to trust his instincts. Unfortunately, he would soon discover that America's purchased peace was more fragile than he'd realized. Despite having signed treaties with the United States of America, not all of the Barbary rulers would remain satisfied with the new status quo.

Jefferson's grave doubts about purchasing peace on the Barbary Coast were about to resurface. The United States' first war as a sovereign nation loomed. George Washington's decision to continue building warships even while paying for peace would prove wise when it became clear that the Barbary powers could not be trusted to keep their word.

CHAPTER 3

The Humiliation of the USS George Washington

I hope I shall never again be sent to Algiers with tribute, unless I am authorized to deliver it from the mouth of our cannon.

—Captain William Bainbridge, USS *George Washington*

William Bainbridge shaded his eyes against the September sun glinting off the Mediterranean Sea. Standing on the deck of the USS *George Washington*, the six-foot-tall Bainbridge felt honored to command one of the first ships in America's navy—even if he was carrying tribute to a foreign power.

The new century had opened with treaties in place that mandated peace. But Bainbridge remained very much on the lookout. The secretary of the navy himself had ordered his young captain to be alert for any signs of "hostilities against the Vessels of the U: States" that might be committed by "the Barbary powers." Thus captain and crew stood ready, as instructed, to offer a fight in case O'Brien, Cathcart, and Eaton's peace was broken.

His broad features framed by his thick sideburns, the twenty-six-year-old Bainbridge understood his voyage was a historic one. No other American military vessel had ever passed through the Strait of Gibraltar flying the Stars and Stripes. Now, in 1800, he had the honor of advancing the reach of the young United States. Dwarfed by massive, rocky outcroppings jutting up from the sea, the *George Washington* had made history only days before by sailing through the famous strait. A stretch of sea less than nine miles wide between Europe and North Africa, the strait had figured in maritime lore since ancient times—the boundary between the Mediterranean and the wild, mysterious open ocean of the Atlantic to the west.

On approaching the North African coast, Bainbridge saw a blazing, burning desert that appeared to extend for days and weeks, reaching far into the largely unmapped African continent. This region, the Maghreb, as the natives called it, was ruled by the Barbary nations. Despite the proximity to the pirates' homeland, Bainbridge had seen no evidence of American shipping in trouble. So far his ship's log recorded only the sighting of two English frigates peaceably at anchor in the British port of Gibraltar and of a Danish brig on which all hands were "employed in scraping Decks."[1] The Barbary pirates seemed to be honoring the treaty that would be further secured once the *George Washington* delivered its cargo.

Captain Bainbridge was carrying a tribute payment to the Algerians, fulfilling the deal made by Barlow and O'Brien, but there was something different about this delivery. It was no accident that he commanded not a commercial vessel but an armed warship from the new U.S. Navy. As it sailed toward Algiers, the ship's presence served as a potent symbol. The USS *George Washington* was meant to convey that the United States was no longer a powerless, ragtag bunch of backwater settlements clinging to survival on the edge of the western Atlantic; they were growing, prospering states, independent in their industries, united under a central government—and possessed of a navy ready to act for the sake of the nation's interests and its self-defense.

If Bainbridge's ship wasn't intended as a direct threat, the USS *George Washington* was, at the very least, an implied promise that Americans would not bow to extortion forever.

Bainbridge was no run-of-the-mill ship's captain. He constantly found himself in the middle of controversy. After the teenaged Bainbridge signed on as an ordinary seaman aboard a merchant vessel, he helped put down a mutiny, suffering life-threatening injuries in the fight. When he recovered, the brave young man received command of his own merchant ship, from which he fired upon a much larger British vessel, causing enough damage for the enemy to surrender. At twenty-four he had joined the newly established U.S. Navy in 1798, rising rapidly from lieutenant to master commandant, despite a misadventure in which he was forced to surrender the schooner he commanded, having mistaken a powerful forty-gun French ship for a British frigate.

Now, Bainbridge's primary mission was to deliver tribute to Algiers—an uncomfortable task for a proud young sailor. He and his crew had watched carefully for pirate activity, but all was calm on the afternoon of September 17 as Algiers came into view. Bainbridge relaxed his guard, as the dey of Algiers was reportedly still friendly to the United States.

When the *George Washington* approached the harbor, the captain of the port of Algiers came aboard and, as was the custom,

Bainbridge entrusted him with the piloting of the ship through shoals and into the harbor. By evening, the USS *George Washington* was moored in the inner harbor, and the log noted that the crew had "got every thing Snug."[2]

Captain Bainbridge held his head high. He felt confident that he was operating from a position of strength, that he had executed his mission faithfully and unapologetically. He was prepared to salute Bobba Mustapha, dey of Algiers, and his city, and he expected that mutual respect would prevail in the soon-to-be-completed transaction.

He could hardly have been more wrong.

Boarding the ship along with the Algerian port pilot, Richard O'Brien had been the first American to greet Bainbridge and his men. As the U.S. consul general to Algiers, O'Brien had eagerly awaited the arrival of the *George Washington* for nearly four months. In a May 16 letter to the State Department, he had urgently requested that the government rush the overdue tribute to Algiers. Without the promised goods, he warned, "we cannot expect to preserve our affairs long."[3] If he was honest, he wasn't even sure that he would be able to keep the peace even if the tribute did arrive.

O'Brien's long experience in captivity gave him a deep understanding of how the Barbary bandits operated. Since at least the sixteenth century, the pirates had been turning over their booty to the nations' leaders to line their coffers. A portion of the profits were sent to Constantinople (today's Istanbul) as tribute to the Ottoman rulers, the recognized overlords of the Mohammedan world; a smaller portion went to the parties who made the capture; and the remainder became the property of the local ruler.

Captives were treated as if they, too, were goods. Men such as O'Brien and his crew were enslaved to local rulers or sold on the auction block to caravan owners, caliphs, and slave traders. Some of the more fortunate captives would be ransomed, usually for huge sums of money; a few would escape. But the only other option was to become a "renegade"—that is, to convert to Islam, because the Qur'an forbade the enslavement of Muslims by other Muslims. However, if a renegade was caught returning to his or her original faith upon emancipation, the penalty was death. Conversion was an option chosen by few—leaving most in captivity indefinitely.

European sailors were not the only slaves in the North African markets. There were women kidnapped from Russia and Syria to be bought and sold for harems or given as gifts to political leaders. There were other Africans, dark-skinned men and women from beyond the Sahara, transported across the desert by slave-trading caravans. Children as young as six, from Africa and Eastern Europe alike, were traded to work as serving boys or sexual slaves in bathhouses. Young men were forcibly converted to Islam and trained to guard the sultan.

Punishments for slaves were gruesome. Some captives reported witnessing castration, impaling, and the throwing of the offender off the city walls onto a series of hooks. Any Christian who insulted Islam could be subjected to severe punishment, including being burned alive. If a Christian man was found to be engaging in a relationship with a Muslim woman, he could be beheaded and his lover drowned. Should a Jew raise a hand against a Muslim, the hand could be cut off. The most common punishment, however, whatever the faith or national origin of the offender, was a beating.

Some of the luckier ones were elevated to the status of servants. A few served in the ruler's court; others served in the royal kitchens or worked in the dey's gardens, minding the plants and his menagerie of wild animals. No matter the assignment, however, the work remained hard and humiliating—especially for men and women from a country established upon the ideal of personal liberty.

While most of the other former American captives vowed never to return to the Barbary Coast, O'Brien had been treated relatively well during captivity, and he had been eager for the opportunity to work for peace between the governments. Yet on arriving at the docks in Algiers with Captain Bainbridge, O'Brien experienced a renewed feeling of powerlessness. The hold of the *George Washington* contained only a few of the articles that the dey expected, and delivery of the promised gold and silver had been delayed. After O'Brien explained the facts, Bainbridge too understood that he had arrived in a tinderbox—and it wasn't only a matter of hot, dry air and burning sun.

BOXED IN

The next day, the crew of the USS *George Washington* began unloading the dey's tribute, which included oak planks and pine, along with boxes of tin and casks of nails. The weather was pleasant and the winds gentle, and the men prepared to take aboard fresh stores of grapes, green figs, oranges, and almonds as well. Unaware of the diplomatic tension, the sailors aboard the *George Washington* expected that, having completed delivery as ordered, their ship would depart promptly for the return journey to their home port of Philadelphia.

But the "despotic dey," as Bainbridge soon referred to him, had other plans for them.

In keeping with custom, the American captain, accompanied by O'Brien, sought an audience with the Algerian ruler to pay his respects. As the crew discharged the cargo back in the harbor, Captain Bainbridge, Consul O'Brien, and the Algerian minister of the harbor met the dey at his palace to give account of the tribute the Americans had brought. Dressed in flowing robes, his face half obscured by his generous beard, the aging dey grew angry upon learning that the ship had failed to bring all of the promised annuities.

"You pay me tribute," Bobba Mustapha declared. "By that, you become my slaves. I have, therefore, a right to order you as I may think proper."[4]

The outraged ruler then issued an order: he decreed that the USS *George Washington* must carry his ambassador and his entourage to the other end of the Mediterranean Sea to Constantinople, the capital of the Ottoman empire, where the dey's own annual tribute was due.

Bainbridge balked. He told his host that the assignment was impossible, as he had no orders to perform such a mission. O'Brien pointed out that the existing treaty permitted merchant vessels, but not military ships, to perform such duties for the Algerian regency. But even as they resisted, both of the Americans understood that they would have to obey. As O'Brien admitted a day later in a letter intended for the eyes of the secretary of state, "I am afraid [we] shall be obliged to give way to prevent extraordinary difficulties."[5]

What he did not explain was why the *George Washington* could not simply ignore the dey, weigh anchor, and set sail for home: On arrival in what he'd believed was a safe harbor, the gullible Bainbridge had permitted the Algerian pilot to direct the ship to a berth directly beneath the guns of the fortress, a huge tactical error. Overly trusting, Bainbridge did not consider how his ship would make its exit should the talks with the dey go poorly, and now it was too late. Dwarfed by the fortification, the vessel faced two hundred cannons and a fleet of armed Algerian ships. Moored within range of the Algerian batteries, the USS *George Washington* was hopelessly outgunned and outmanned. If Bainbridge and his men attempted to escape, their ship could easily be blasted to kindling if the dey so ordered.

Bainbridge was out of options. The only way to send a message back to the Department of the Navy was by another ship, and ships from the Mediterranean, sailing against the prevailing westerly winds, often took two months to reach the United States and another month or more to return. In the event of severe weather, the turnaround time could be even longer, and the dey wasn't going to wait several months. Entrusted with both his ship and the honor of his country, Bainbridge had to make a decision on his own.

In the coming days, Bainbridge continued to argue that he could not comply with the humiliating request. But the dey's anger deepened. He demanded payment of what O'Brien calculated was "upwards of 110 thousand dollars in debt."[6] The regency's ruler escalated his threats, warning that, if Bainbridge failed to perform the mission, friendly relations between their nations would come to an end and Algerian corsairs would again harass shipping as they had done in the past. It was a threat that O'Brien, the former captain of the captured *Dauphin,* understood very well.

Bainbridge could do little but watch as other ships departed while he remained at the dey's mercy. He supervised sail repairs, and his ship's log recorded the weather and the activity of his crew. Finally, after several weeks of demands and demurrals as the

Americans and Algerians went back and forth, O'Brien received a final summons. He was told that Bainbridge must submit to the order or surrender the ship and subject his crew to captivity. A refusal, O'Brien understood, would also have a wider consequence: it would mean war with Algiers. With no alternative, the two Americans bowed to the dey's demand.

What had begun as a proud voyage was about to become a national disgrace. As Bainbridge observed sternly to O'Brien, "Sir, I cannot help observing that the event of this day makes me ponder on the words Independent United States."[7]

A FLOATING ZOO

The humiliation of the USS *George Washington* began. Only after agreeing to transport the ambassador did Bainbridge learn the extent of the diplomatic retinue. This would be no modest delegation, but the ship, configured for a maximum crew of 220 men, would be required to accommodate the ambassador, 100 attendants, plus 100 captive Africans.

The *George Washington* had become a slave ship.

The dey further required that the overloaded ship carry gifts bound for his ruler at Constantinople, including 4 horses, 25 cattle, and 150 sheep, in addition to 4 lions, 4 tigers, 4 antelopes, and 12 parrots.[8]

The warship had become a floating zoo.

Then, just before departure, adding another insult to the cramped quarters, the deafening squawking, and the stench of manure, the dey's coup de grâce fell. He ordered the American flag taken down and the Algerine flag hoisted. Seven guns were fired in salute of the new flag. Among the American crew, the ship's log recorded, "some tears fell at this Instance of national Humility."[9]

The USS *George Washington* had become a Barbary ferry service.

The journey to Constantinople took twenty-three days. Once in open water and out of range of the harbor guns, Bainbridge raised his own flag, unopposed by the Algerians on board. Yet he wasn't truly in control of his own ship, as the uninvited passengers demanded that the ship's course be adapted to their prayer schedule. The helmsman was forced to navigate so that the *George Washington,* though pushing its way through stormy seas, pointed eastward toward Mecca five times a day for the faithful to perform their required prayers. One of the Muslims was assigned to watch the compass heading to ensure the correctness of the ship's position.

While the American crew found a certain dark humor in this peculiar manner of worship, the situation was no laughing matter. The trip was uncomfortable and degrading—and it would have serious diplomatic repercussions. When the *George Washington* deposited its haul in Constantinople and turned homeward, Captain Bainbridge remarked, his resolve firm, "I hope I shall never again be sent to Algiers with tribute, unless I am authorized to deliver it from the mouth of our cannon."

When the ship finally returned to the United States, the American public was outraged by the report. As news of the events in Algiers spread, some regarded Bainbridge's submission as inexcusable. Many believed that the United States had stared evil in the face and blinked first. Others complained that it had been blinking for years and that to continue to pay tribute was to invite more abuse. Those against the navy also felt justified; the attempt to demonstrate that the

United States possessed military might in international waters had backfired. The USS *George Washington* had been unable to prevent its own hijacking.

On learning of the events at Algiers, William Eaton, stationed at Tunis, gave vent to his strong feelings in writing to his fellow diplomat Richard O'Brien.

> *History shall tell that the United States first volunteer'd a* ship of war, *equipt, a* carrier *for a pirate—It is written—Nothing but blood can blot the impression out—Frankly I own, I would have lost the piece, and been myself impaled rather than yielded this concession.*[10]

Horrified by America's inaction in the face of the humiliation, Eaton added a final question: "Will nothing rouse my country?"

CHAPTER 4

Jefferson Takes Charge

> I will wait Six months for an Answer to my letter to the President . . . if it does not arrive in that period . . . I will declare war in form against the United States.
>
> **—Yusuf Qaramanli, bashaw of Tripoli, October 1800**

While William Bainbridge and the *George Washington* suffered humiliation abroad, Americans at home were in turmoil over the election of the nation's third president. After a bitter contest that threatened the unity of the new nation, Thomas Jefferson had beaten his friend John Adams and was inaugurated on March 4, 1801. Deeply disappointed and angry at his former companion, Adams did not attend the inauguration.

An estranged friend and a divided nation were not Jefferson's only problems. He would now have to face the problem of the Barbary powers head-on. For more than a dozen years, the nation's policy under both Presidents Washington and Adams had been to avoid resorting to military force. But Jefferson would soon learn that time had run out.

WAR AND PEACE

Unaware that the ticking time bomb of the Barbary Coast was about to go off, Jefferson settled gradually into his new home. After his walk to the Capitol for his inauguration, the third president let two full weeks pass before he moved from his rented rooms into the president's quarters.

Occupying only a few rooms on the main floor, Jefferson began to plan the social life of the place. Unlike Washington and Adams, who hosted weekly presidential receptions as if at a royal court, Jefferson preferred smaller dinners where the business of the government might get done in intimate conversations. But those would come later. First he needed to gain a fuller understanding of the state in which Adams had left various matters.

President Jefferson ordered that all correspondence be submitted to him for review. As he looked over the papers Adams had left behind, his concern about the state of America's safety grew. Jefferson had known the Barbary situation was bad, but he hadn't realized how bad it truly was as he reviewed the existing treaties with Algiers, Tripoli, and Tunis. The last had been ratified in January 1800 and promised payment of $20,000 in annual tribute, as well as the bizarre payment of one barrel of gunpowder every time an American vessel received a cannon salute. After fifteen years of observation, Jefferson knew as well as anyone that this demand was not in good faith. Instead, it was a warning that the whole region was nothing less than a powder keg.

On March 13, a stack of fresh dispatches from the Mediterranean had arrived for Jefferson's review. One in particular, from James Cathcart, had about it the whiff of a burning fuse. Writing before the *George Washington* had been commandeered, Cathcart reported that the bashaw of Tripoli had increased a demand in his annual tribute, despite the provision in the treaty stating that no "periodical tribute or farther payment is ever to be made by either party."[1] That, Cathcart reported, was of no matter whatever to the regent.

As Jefferson read on, Cathcart's long and detailed letter grew more ominous. The bashaw's rising rhetoric had turned to explicit threats. "Let your government give me a sum of money & I will be content—but I will be paid one way or the other." The bashaw set a six-month deadline, after which, if his demands were not met? "I will declare war . . . against the United States." Those six months were nearly up.

Jefferson also found a letter from Tunis consul William Eaton. Sensing that the fragile peace would not last, Eaton had begged Adams's administration to make a show of strength. He proposed sending three of America's most impressive fighting ships into Tripoli. There he would invite the bashaw to dinner and impress him with the Americans' strength. After the meal, he would point at the cannon and say, "See there our *executive power* Commissioned to Keep Guarentee of Peace."[2] If the plan worked, Eaton explained, the bashaw might be too intimidated to declare war.

Unfortunately, one of Adams's last acts in office had been to sign into law a bill shrinking the American navy. Jefferson must have sympathized with Eaton, whose plan resembled Jefferson's own from years earlier, but there were few ships to send. Jefferson did not have enough military power to take America properly to war.

A few weeks later, he learned that his time to weigh options had run out. The USS *George Washington* docked at Philadelphia on April 19. After completing their humiliating journey to Constantinople, William Bainbridge and his crew had endured a punishing winter passage home. The stormy Atlantic journey took two and a half months, twice the usual transit time. Still, the long trip and cold winds had done nothing to lessen Bainbridge's red-hot fury and, back on dry land, he set off immediately to the nation's capital to give the president a full report.

The city of Washington was full of whispered criticism of Bainbridge, as some hinted that he'd capitulated too easily to the dey's demands. But the captain found a sympathetic ear in President Jefferson. Fully aware of the region's problems, Jefferson was predisposed to believe that Bainbridge's situation had been impossible. Once he'd heard the details from Bainbridge directly, the president saw to it that Bainbridge was commended for "the able and judicious manner in which he had discharged his duty under such peculiarly embarrassing circumstances."[3] He contemplated a further reward to the dedicated captain—perhaps he might return to the Barbary Coast, this time in a vessel more intimidating than a converted merchant ship.

First, though, Jefferson needed to convene his cabinet. He wanted to secure their approval of a plan that was taking shape in his mind—a plan that would fall somewhere between submitting to the Barbary indignities and launching a full-scale war.

Jefferson had hoped to gather his cabinet in Washington by the end of April, but it was mid-May before they assembled. Washington's main newspaper, the *National Intelligencer and Daily Advertiser*, had proclaimed just four days earlier that the nation was at peace, but Jefferson and his advisers knew better. The situation on the Barbary Coast demanded action, even though everyone at the table also understood that the United States was among the least qualified of nation states to take on pirates with its small navy, which was shrinking further even as they took their seats.

Jefferson put the question boldly, asking his advisers at this, his first cabinet meeting: "Shall the squadron now at Norfolk be ordered to cruise in the Mediterranean?"[4]

The gentlemen of the cabinet immediately recognized the question had broad significance: they were being asked to consider whether the president's authority extended to take military action without first gaining permission from Congress.

With the question before the cabinet, Jefferson, as he often did, noted on a sheet of paper the opinions of each official.

Secretary of the Treasury Albert Gallatin expressed the opinion that "the Executive can not put us in a state of war." But, he added, in the event of war, whether declared by Congress or initiated by another country, "the command and direction of the public force then belongs to the Executive."

Attorney General Levi Lincoln was still more measured: "Our men of war may repel an attack," he said, "but after the repulse, may not proceed to destroy the enemy's vessels."

Secretary of War Henry Dearborn took a more bullish view. "The expedition should go forward openly to protect our commerce against the threatened hostilities of Tripoli," he offered. Secretary of State Madison concurred.

After further discussion, the cabinet was unanimous: the

squadron would be dispatched to the Mediterranean but as peacemakers rather than agents of war.[5] Jefferson and his cabinet hoped against hope that the Barbary powers would be reasonable, would recognize that the United States took seriously the seizure of its goods and citizens, and would back down from the conflict.

Richard Dale, one of the original U.S. Navy captains appointed by George Washington, was named to command the squadron. He would carry with him a letter from President Jefferson, addressed to the leader of Tripoli; in its text, Jefferson offered multiple assurances of "constant friendship."

Jefferson chose his words carefully, avoiding inflammatory terms such as *warship*. He advised the bashaw that "we have found it expedient to detach a *squadron of observation* into the Mediterranean." To the careful reader, however, the words were rich with implications: the Americans did not appreciate the Barbary Coast's treatment of their ships, but they were not yet ready to go to war. With any luck, simply letting the Muslim leaders know they were being watched would be enough to dissuade them.

"We hope [our ships'] appearance will give umbrage to no Power," Jefferson's letter continued, "for, while we mean to rest the safety of our commerce on the resources of our own strength & bravery in every sea, we have yet given to this squadron in strict command to conduct themselves toward all friendly Powers with most perfect respect and good order."

President Jefferson could only hope that his words of peace, accompanied by a modest show of power, would quiet the visions of war that danced in the mind of the bashaw of Tripoli.

CHAPTER 5

A Flagpole Falls

Facts are now indubitable. The Bashaws corsaires are actually out and fitting out against Americans.

—William Eaton to the secretary of state, April 10, 1801

While Jefferson and his cabinet prepared a response to Barbary provocation, James Cathcart stood in a diplomatic no-man's-land. For almost six months he had waited impatiently for a response from Washington to his October 1800 letter outlining the war threats from Tripolitan bashaw Yusuf Qaramanli. No instructions came. He didn't even know who had won the presidential election. For all intents and purposes, Cathcart was alone.

Over the past few months, the bashaw had alternatively threatened and flattered the United States. He had told Cathcart he wanted peace with his people, but refused to discuss the existing treaty, still legally in effect. The bashaw simply wanted more and didn't pretend otherwise, whatever he had agreed to in the past. He first demanded a gift of ships—the other regencies had gotten more in their treaties, he pointed out, in particular Algiers. Now he insisted upon further considerations, too. The bashaw demanded immense amounts of money, including a down payment of $225,000, far more than Cathcart could give or the U.S. Treasury could afford. He was entirely shameless in his demands, having had the audacity to demand an additional $10,000 in tribute when George Washington died. The bashaw, in short, was living up to the prediction made by Joel Barlow years before. The Tripolitan ruler was willing to set aside "every principle of honor at defiance more than any prince in Barbary."[1] As far as the Americans could tell, he was the worst of a bad lot.

His fear rising, Cathcart had issued a circular letter to his fellow consuls on February 21, 1801. "I am convinced that the Bashaw of Tripoli," he warned, "will commence Hostilitys against the U. States of America in less than Sixty Days."[2]

He was not far off; his fears were confirmed on May 11, 1801, three months later.

At six o'clock that Monday evening, a regency emissary arrived at the American consulate in Tripoli. When the visitor was ushered in, Cathcart immediately recognized the man as one of Bashaw Yusuf's most esteemed advisers. Cathcart greeted him with all the cordiality he could muster, which had never been much. He had done his best to remain patient with the bashaw's games, but his patience with masked aggression was wearing thin.

This time, the bashaw's emissary didn't even pretend to come in peace. He delivered his message. "The Bashaw has sent me to inform you that he has declared war against the United States and will take down your flagstaff on Thursday the 14th."[3]

The bashaw had made many threats in the past, but Cathcart understood this one was real. Tripolitan ships, in a gesture of contempt, had already raised the American colors in the place where they flew the flags of nations at war with the regency. This time there was nothing Cathcart could do to defuse the situation.

His instincts told him he must leave; he knew that the bashaw would allow him to vacate the city. But Cathcart had grown accustomed to this overgrown village that rose from the sea, its long wharf extending far into the harbor. The walled city, with the minarets of its mosques reaching high above the tightly packed stone houses, had become his home. Even the labyrinths of the bashaw's palace, situated at the highest point of the city, had become dear to him in some strange way.

Though he would always remain an outsider, Carthcart understood this world. He had sat cross-legged to share a dinner with the bashaw. He knew the odors of the main squares of the city, thick with the scent of rich coffee and tobacco smoke. He recognized the sounds of camels in harness, turning the shafts of the city's flour mill. The sight of slaves fanning their masters, driving away the flies, was familiar if unwelcome. Like it or not, the city had become part of him, and now, as he had feared, it was spitting him out.

Holding both his temper and his sorrow in check, Cathcart replied politely to the bashaw's emissary, knowing that an angry reply would only jeopardize his wife and young daughter, as well as his diplomatic staff. Without instructions from the government at home, he was authorized to do nothing else. And even if he could know the new president's mind, military backup would never reach him in time. Accordingly, Cathcart acknowledged receipt of the declaration of war and said he would charter a ship and depart the city as soon as possible. In the meantime, he would remain at the consulate and witness the first official act of war.

A TRIPOLITAN TRAGICOMEDY

Three days later, the bashaw made good on his threat. On May 14, 1801, he dispatched his men to the American consulate; the party of soldiers arrived at one o'clock that Thursday afternoon.

Cathcart was ready to make one last offer to keep the peace, to avoid what had begun to seem inevitable. He approached the *seraskier*, the leader of the squad and the bashaw's minister of war, and asked that the promise of a tribute of $10,000 be conveyed to the bashaw. A messenger departed for the castle, but returned minutes later. The bashaw had rejected the offer.

Cathcart knew any further attempts at diplomacy would be futile, and stopping the bashaw's men by force was impossible. Helpless, he stood watching on that bright, hot Thursday as the Tripolitans began hacking at the flagpole.

The bashaw's men shouted encouragement to one another as they swung their axes but to their dismay, felling the pole was harder than it looked. Chips flew, but the flagpole refused to fall. As if to mock the men, the flag fluttered with each stroke of the ax, its staff staunchly in place. A gesture meant to humble the Americans was rapidly becoming a humiliation for the Tripolitans.

The bashaw had ordered that, if the men had trouble dropping the pole, they should pull on the halyard, the line anchored at the top of the pole used to hoist the flag. He thought they might be able to break the pole in half by doing so. To the dismay of the men, that strategy failed, too, and once again, the resilient flagpole refused to fall. The men who had arrived to dishonor the flag were proving singularly inept.

More than an hour passed before the Tripolitans finally caused the pole to splinter just enough to lean against the consulate house. The American diplomats looked on, darkly amused by the whole episode. Cathcart wryly recorded the events in a dispatch to Secretary of State James Madison.

"At a quarter past two they effected the grand atchievement and our Flagstaff was chop'd down six feet from the ground & left reclining on the Terrace. . . . Thus ends the first act of this Tragedy."[4]

AMERICA AT WAR

Ten days would pass before Cathcart, his wife, and his daughter sailed out of Tripoli harbor aboard a polacca, a small three-masted ship he hired in the harbor. He entrusted the consulate affairs he left behind to the good hands of the Danish consul general, Nicholas Nissen. Cathcart specifically instructed that any American sailors brought captive to Tripoli be provided for with money for subsistence and needed medical care. Nissen agreed to do whatever was in his power to meet those needs should another American ship be captured.[5]

The fleeing family landed at Malta three days later. There Cathcart gave letters for the American government to a ship that would convey them homeward. He still had no idea who was president or what the political climate was in the United States. He could only imagine what the response would be when the documents reached America.

Once state business was taken care of, the Cathcarts' vessel made sail again, headed for the Italian city of Leghorn. But now-former consul Cathcart's tribulations were not yet at an end. Off the coast of Sicily he had another unwelcome encounter with a Barbary force, this one a small Tunisian ship manned by pirates. They proved respectful of Cathcart's credentials, although he had his "trunks tumbled" and the boarders helped themselves to his wine and foodstuffs. Mrs. Cathcart and her daughter had been terrified at the appearance of a man in their cabin wielding a saber, but the Tunisian employed the weapon, Cathcart reported, "not with any intention to hurt any person but merely to cut twine & other ligatures which were round the articles he plunder'd."[6]

The pirates having helped themselves to the ship's compass, Cathcart and the captain were forced to resort to paste and sealing wax to repair "an old french Compas whose needle fortunately retain'd its magentism." It proved adequate for charting their course, and the Cathcarts managed to make Leghorn nine days after departing Tripoli. On arrival, however, one last insult was delivered: they faced a twenty-five-day quarantine to ensure they had not contracted smallpox or any other diseases in their encounter with the Tunisians.

Once they were ashore in Italy, the news finally reached Cathcart of Jefferson's election. He sent his congratulations, via a letter to Madison, who along with Jefferson would remain unaware for many more weeks that Tripoli had declared war. Jefferson would learn of Tripoli's attack too late to assist Cathcart, who was already traveling home. But thanks to Jefferson's foresight, American ships had already been ordered to head for the Barbary Coast. They were not authorized to attack the Barbary ships, but they would be able to defend American interests against further embarrassment and blockade Barbary ports, squeezing Tripoli's economy the same way the pirates had been squeezing America's. Both nations knew that a breaking point had been reached, but neither side knew that the other had taken action.

CHAPTER 6

The First Flotilla

I hope the next Opportunity that I have of writing you, that I shall have the pleasure of Informing you that some of the Squadron has made some Captures of the Tripolitan Corsairs.

—Richard Dale to the secretary of the navy, July 19, 1801

An ocean away from Cathcart's splintered flagpole, Jefferson's four warships prepared for their voyage. The flagship would be the *President*, commanded by Commodore Richard Dale. The *Philadelphia* and the *Essex*, captained by Samuel Barron and William Bainbridge, respectively, would add additional strength. A fourth vessel, the trim schooner *Enterprise*, guided by Lieutenant Andrew Sterett, completed the flotilla. Though modest in numbers, the flotilla was surprisingly powerful due to a new design. Because of innovations in American shipbuilding, the American frigates would be able to outrun much larger ships or, in heavy seas, match up with them.

Adding to the military might of the four ships were members of the relatively new United States Marine Corps, reactivated by President Adams with the birth of the U.S. Navy in 1798. Skilled combatants, the Marines were invaluable during boarding actions and landing expeditions, and they also served to protect a ship's officers in the event of a mutiny by the crew. The fighters had a reputation for being bold, fearless men—though sometimes a little brash and reckless. Their presence would be invaluable should any of Dale's ships encounter pirates or need protection on land.

Once fully provisioned, Dale's squadron finally made sail for the Strait of Gibraltar on June 2, 1801. Soon after losing sight of the American coast, they met with rough seas. Swirling squalls made the first ten days of the crossing difficult, as easterly winds and heavy rains buffeted the ships. As the newest of the four American vessels, the USS *President* had only a few months of sailing to her credit, and the storms found every flaw in her construction. Wracked by the thrashing of the sea, she soon had rain and seawater leaking through seams that opened in her deck. Life below became damp and unpleasant, and many of the crew fell seasick. But she was a fine ship, from the top of her three tall masts to her bottom. A little stormy weather would not prevent the USS *President* from reaching her Mediterranean destination.

JEFFERSON'S COMMANDERS

The *President*'s commander was no less sturdy. At forty-five years of age, Richard Dale's portly bearing, kind eyes, and crown of graying hair hinted at the maturity of long experience that he brought to his command. He had gone to sea at age twelve, and after making his first

Atlantic crossing aboard a merchant vessel owned by an uncle, he worked himself up to the rank of mate by age seventeen.

During the American Revolution, Dale served as John Paul Jones's second-in-command aboard the converted French merchant ship USS *Bon Homme Richard.* Swinging by a rope under a moonlight sky, he had been the first American sailor to land on the deck of the HMS *Serapis* during a battle with the British ship, an act of bravery that won him widespread fame. After the war he settled for a quieter life, establishing a profitable merchant business based on trade with China and India. When the U.S. Navy was reestablished, however, Dale had been quick to accept President Washington's offer to return to the sea as one of its first captains. While a sense of duty drove the men aboard the American ships, Commodore Dale understood firsthand the need to protect American ships from capture—he himself had been imprisoned by the British during the Revolution.

Aboard the USS *Essex*, Captain Bainbridge had been chosen to go back to the region where he had suffered his degrading experience aboard the *George Washington*, and revenge was on his mind. But there were younger men about the *Essex* with simpler motives, among them the lust for adventure. Lieutenant Stephen Decatur was one.

Every now and then, fate seems to smile on an individual, gifting him with an extraordinary measure of good looks, character, and opportunity. Stephen Decatur's curly dark hair, sparkling eyes, and devil-may-care attitude caught the eye of many a woman when he entered a room. But his bravery—known to verge on recklessness—and his intense sense of honor were equally distinguishing features.

Once, when a British merchant insulted Decatur and the American navy, Decatur challenged him to a duel. Knowing his pistol skills were far superior to his foe's, Decatur confessed to a friend that he planned only to shoot for the man's leg, hoping to wound him slightly and teach him a lesson. The duel went as Decatur had planned. The Englishman missed entirely and Decatur's bullet went into the man's hip, rather than his heart. Decatur sustained no injury and his pride was satisfied. He did not want to kill the man, but he could not let the slur pass unpunished. To insult the U.S. Navy was to insult Decatur, his country, and his family.

The sea had been a part of Decatur's life for as long as he could remember. His father, Stephen Decatur Sr., had served as a naval captain in the Revolution before becoming a successful merchant. When his eight-year-old son and namesake had come down with a case of whooping cough, the doctors prescribed a regimen of sea air to help clear the recovering child's lungs, so the boy joined his father on his next voyage. When he returned from the trip to Europe, the young Decatur was cured of his cough—but freshly infected with a desire for the nautical life. Despite his mother's dearest hope that he would join the clergy, he left college after one year to pursue a naval career.

Even in the face of the stormy conditions of June 1801, Lieutenant Decatur counted himself the luckiest of men to have a place on this mission. Every creak of the frigate as she rocked on the waves whispered of glory ahead. The salty air filling his lungs gave him an invigorating sense of the honor of simply being an American—a child not of old borders and ancient alliances, but of ideals and liberty. And he took pride in his ship; although the *Essex* was smaller than the *President*, Decatur felt a swelling of pride as he considered the line of cannons, more than thirty in all.

Neither he nor any of the sailors in the four-ship fleet had any way of knowing what was brewing in Tripoli. They had their suspicions, of course, and Commodore Dale had provided Bainbridge with orders in case they should encounter hostilities. If the *Essex* should get separated as they crossed the Atlantic, Dale instructed, Bainbridge and Decatur and their men should head for Gibraltar. If they learned there that the Barbary states had declared war, they were to wait five days. If the remaining ships failed to arrive within that window, Bainbridge was to leave a message for Dale with the American consul and then proceed into the Mediterranean to provide protective escort for American merchant ships. In the event that war had not been declared, the *Essex* was to wait twenty days for the other ships before departing to carry out its mission, leaving a letter at every port of call so that Dale could trace her.

Dale's detailed orders covered other matters, too. Professional decorum and propriety were stressed, and the commodore's orders for gallantry suited young Lieutenant Decatur just fine. He was confident, handsome, and brave. He was setting off on a grand voyage for the honor of his country to an exotic place he had only ever dreamed of visiting. If there was peace, let it be lasting; if there was war, then let it be swift and decisive—and let him be bold in the heat of battle and bring honor, esteem, and victory to his country. Whatever lay ahead on the Barbary Coast, Stephen Decatur was certain it would be a great adventure.

RULES OF ENGAGEMENT

When Dale's ships emerged from the gales, the commodore began running his men through cannon drills. Each man had a precise role in the exercises, and soon the air was filled with orders—"Level your guns" . . . "Take off your tompions" . . . "Load with cartridge" . . .

"Shot your guns" . . . "Fire!" With a deafening roar, cannonball shot flew hundreds of yards before disappearing into the waves.

The captains were training their men, veteran and novice alike, for a kind of warfare peculiar to the Barbary Coast. There would be no lines of battle, with opposing enemy fleets facing off. When attacking, Barbary ships closed rapidly, their first strategy to board their opponent. Thus the best defense for a ship under Barbary attack was coordinated cannon fire to keep the pirates at a distance.

To Dale's frustration, though, a good defense was all he was authorized to do. Beginning with the debate in his cabinet in Washington two and a half months before, President Jefferson hesitated to claim with certainty that he had the constitutional right to declare war. Thus, the orders transmitted down the line of command—via

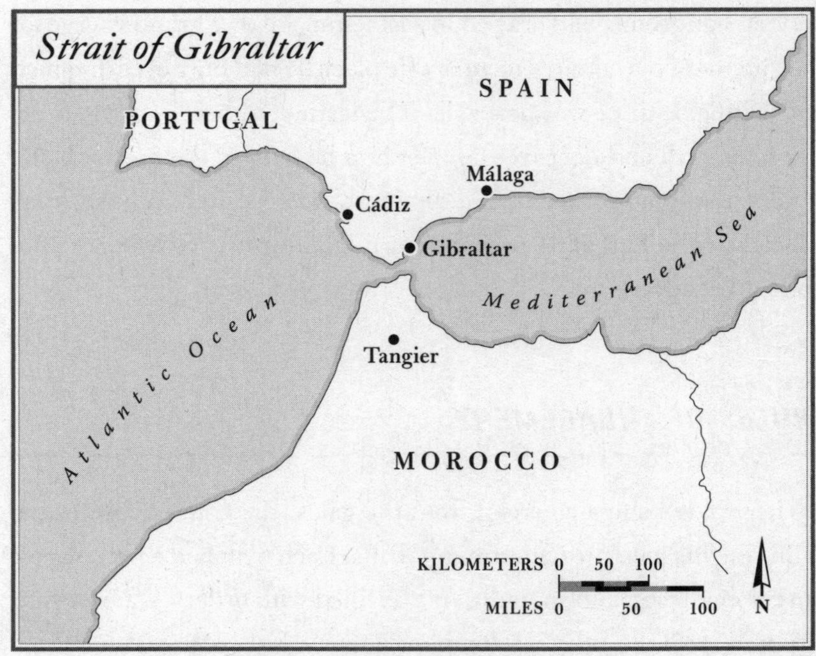

the secretary of the navy, to Commodore Dale, and on to his captains—were abundantly clear. "Should you fall in with any of the Tripolitan Corsairs . . . on your passage to Malta," Dale wrote, ". . . you will heave all his Guns Over board Cut away his Masts, & leave him In a situation, that he can Just make out to get into some Port."[1] American ships were not to capture any Barbary ships. They could hobble ships that attacked them, but they were to take no captives and to let their enemies escape.

Fortunately, American guns were fired only in practice during the journey across the Atlantic, and the USS *President* sailed into Gibraltar on July 2. The imposing frigate was followed by the smaller *Philadelphia* and the *Essex.* The fourth ship, the *Enterprise,* greeted her. The heavy seas off North America had slowed the *Enterprise* and, rather than slow the pace of his little fleet, Commodore Dale permitted the sloop to break company. Once the weather cleared, however, Lieutenant Sterett had set a speedy pace en route to Gibraltar and actually beat the other ships by five days.

The fleet may have been modest by the standards of Europe's largest navies, but the four warships of the United States made an impressive showing. Whether they would be able to secure peace was not yet known, but for the first time, a flotilla of American warships would make anchor in a Mediterranean port.

PIRATES IN PORT

On arrival at Gibraltar, Commodore Richard Dale's first duty was to find out the status of the fragile Barbary peace. But first, he wanted to settle into the harbor.

The harbor was emptier than usual. Gibraltar was home to a Royal Navy base, but all of the British ships, engaged in the war with Napoleon, a conflict that the Americans hoped to avoid, had been sent out to blockade French and Spanish forces. On spotting the USS *Enterprise* at anchor in the nearly vacant harbor, Dale made to join her, relieved that Lieutenant Sterett and his men had arrived safely, with no apparent harm to their vessel. The American squadron had been reunited.

As his ship neared the American schooner, however, Dale's attention was drawn to another vessel moored nearby. It was unlike any he had ever seen.

The ship's stern sat unusually low in the water, but it was the brightly colored hull that caught Dale's eye. As the *President* neared, Dale saw that the yellow two-masted ship, a white stripe running its length, carried many guns. A closer look with a spyglass revealed she was heavily manned, her crew much larger than normal for a ship her size.

He also noted that the ship was not alone. A second, smaller vessel accompanied her, a brig armed with fourteen guns. Both ships were elaborately painted with festoons of flowers, but the larger ship had a much more disconcerting ornament: a woman's severed head suspended above the deck.

These were pirate ships, Dale knew in an instant—most likely from Tripoli.

The presence of Barbary ships made Dale uneasy, but he didn't fear an attack. Whether a state of war existed or not, he knew neither side would open fire within the confines of a neutral harbor. Even if the two garishly painted ships were foolish enough to try, they would be no match for his firepower.

As his ship glided toward its mooring, Dale looked upon the larger of the two vessels—it bore the name *Meshuda*—and the unnamed brig. There, rocking gently in the harbor swell, lay the answer he was looking for. The Tripolitan commander of this little fleet would know whether a state of war existed between their countries.

Commodore Dale decided all he had to do was ask; whether the pirate would give him a straight answer remained to be seen.

If the *Meshuda* seemed familiar to the Americans, it was because she had once been an American ship, known as the *Betsey,* but captured by Tripolitan pirates five years earlier. Her crew had been taken captive, but all had been quickly released—except for one.

Along with the ship, a single deckhand stayed behind when his shipmates sailed for home. He did so by choice. Born in the Scots port of Perth, the fair-haired and bearded Peter Lisle had turned renegade.

Bolstered by his fluency in Arabic acquired on earlier voyages, the deckhand quickly converted to Islam and abandoned his Christian name, adopting the name Murat Rais in honor of a great sixteenth-century Ottoman admiral. Over time, Peter-Lisle-turned-Murat Rais won the trust of the bashaw, even marrying the bashaw's daughter. Abandoning loyalties to his own king and country, he became a feared and cunning pirate, and he was now the captain of the renamed *Betsey,* the flagship of the Tripolitan fleet.

When Rais and his men had arrived at Gibraltar on June 29, 1801, they paid no mind to the *Enterprise*, already three days in port, but the appearance in Gibraltar Bay of the three American frigates on July 1 represented trouble on the horizon. Rais knew that his country had declared war on America. *But did the Americans know about the war?*

Rais realized these tall ships were not a direct response to the flagpole incident; that news could not have reached American shores in time to prompt the dispatch of this fleet. Yet with rumors of war rapidly crisscrossing the streets and market stalls of Gibraltar, Rais wondered how soon the men of these great fighting ships would learn of the sawed-off staff and the defiling of the American flag. And because the American government could not yet be aware of the declaration of war from Tripoli, just what were these warships doing in Mediterranean waters?

Watching the American sailors securing their ships at anchor, High Admiral Murat Rais devised a plan. He would feign ignorance once the Americans sought him out, as they were sure to do. He would not be the one to deliver the word of war.

UNANSWERED QUESTIONS

Before approaching the pirate ship to ask about the state of the peace, Dale decided to ask friendlier powers for information first. The U.S. consul to Gibraltar came aboard to welcome the fleet, but he had no information. Dale went ashore to pay his respects to the British governor, who confirmed the *Meshuda*'s loyalties and history, but he also had no answers.[2]

Dale would have to ask the pirate commander—and his 392 men.

The *Meshuda* and the brig were in quarantine (the Gibraltar Health Office wanted to be certain they did not carry disease), but Dale approached within hailing distance. Portly but imposing, his voice amplified by a hailing trumpet, he called out to Murat Rais. "The Comodor made Enquiry of the admiral," the U.S. consul noted, describing the exchange: "were they at War or Peace with the U. States?"[3]

From the deck of the *Meshuda*, Murat Rais replied—in the King's English—that they were at peace.

A doubtful Dale tried another tack. He inquired after Consul Cathcart. On departing Tripoli, had the American seemed well?

The reply was a surprise. A fortnight before, said Rais, Cathcart had gone from Tripoli.

Why?

Rais responded that Cathcart *"was no friend to the Americans."*

After this odd piece of news, Dale was able to extract nothing further. The exchange left Dale no less perplexed than when it began.

As for Murat Rais, he was under no illusions that he had fooled Commodore Dale, but his years in the Maghreb had taught him the art of deception. His adopted home was a place where one felt bound to dicker over the price of fruit in the market. Small scenes of drama—indignation, refusal, acceptance—unfolded before the purchase of a string of figs. When it came to the elaborate rituals of diplomacy, it was essential to act as if both parties were old friends, each concerned first and foremost with the comfort and reassurance of the other. To jump straight to the point was rude and disrespectful. It was also dangerous. To have admitted at the outset in his exchange with the American that their nations were at war would have been paramount to surrender.

For Dale, what he learned in the town—if not from Murat Rais—enabled him to reach one firm resolve. Charged by Jefferson and the secretary of the navy to safeguard American ships in the Mediterranean, Dale could not take the other man's word. Instead he had to make a judgment based upon the scraps of intelligence he had gathered, as well as upon his well-honed instincts. "From every infermation that I can get here Tripoli is at war with America," he reported. That meant he had to act.

He set about issuing orders. The *Essex* was to take under convoy the merchant ship *Grand Turk*, readying to sail for Tunis, its hold full of naval stores and other goods as tribute. There were relationships with other Barbary states to be maintained.

Dale learned that more than two dozen American vessels at nearby Barcelona awaited escort, as did many other merchantmen at other ports of call along the southern European coast. He instructed Bainbridge, after completing his errand to Tunis, that the *Essex* was then to escort as many of those ships as possible out of the Strait of Gibraltar, protecting them from roving pirate cruisers. Dale hoped that the sight of the frigate, its hull lined with gun ports through which its dozens of guns could be seen, would inspire awe and deter would-be pirates of all stripes from challenging unarmed American vessels.

Dale wrote orders for Lieutenant Sterett aboard the *Enterprise.* The schooner was to accompany the *President* on its mission to deliver official correspondence from President Jefferson to Algiers and Tunis. Dale would attend to diplomatic matters there before heading to his ultimate destination, the regency of Tripoli.

For the fourth ship in the squadron, the commodore planned a special duty. Not fooled by the infamous Rais's assurances, Dale decided that the *Meshuda*'s sailing must be prevented. He ordered Captain Barron of the frigate *Philadelphia* to linger near Gibraltar. "Lay of[f] this port & watch his motions and (act in such manner as your good sense will direct) to take him when he comes out."[4] The American frigate mustn't sail too close, he warned, because the Americans could not be seen to be blockading the British-controlled territory. But if he could, when circumstances permitted, he was to free the seas of Murat Rais's murderous little convoy.

On July 4, Dale set sail for the Barbary Coast, leaving the Tripolitan's yellow flagship just where he found it. The natural protections of Gibraltar's harbor made it the perfect place to observe Rais—the watchful eye of the *Philadelphia* and the threat of her powerful cannons would keep the pirate just where Dale wanted him. In the meantime, the other American ships would do their best to restore peace in Tripoli and salvage relations with the remaining Barbary states.

CHAPTER 7

Skirmish at Sea

> I have the honor to inform you, that on the 1 of August, I fell in with a Tripolitan ship of war, called the Tripoli. An action immediately commenced within pistol shot. . . .
>
> **—Lieutenant Andrew Sterett to Commodore Richard Dale, August 6, 1801**

Even if they were not authorized for full-on war, the four American ships, Jefferson hoped, would win new respect for the United States of America. The armada's guns were impressive, and its captains brave, but whether four ships would impress the pirates remained to be seen. Whether the Barbary states would peacefully back down before a modest show of force that was not clearly backed by resolve was an even more important question.

When the *President* and *Enterprise* rode the tide into Algiers harbor on July 9, a delighted Richard O'Brien greeted his fellow Americans. He then delivered a letter to the dey on Dale's behalf—a letter designed to offer "the Profound respect which is due to your

Excellency's dignity and character." The note also explained the mission in subtle but clear terms: these ships would "superintend the safety of [American] Commerce."[1] It was lost on no one who saw U.S. Navy vessels that these guardians were armed with many guns, but Dale was careful to make no threats.

Two days later, the two ships weighed anchor and stood out for Tunis, where Commodore Dale would find, in the person of William Eaton, a kindred spirit.

MEN OF LIKE MINDS

The U.S. consul took great satisfaction in seeing Dale's warships enter the harbor. Eaton soon wrote home, "Here commences a new Era in the annals of the United States and Barbary."[2] The two men who met in those days—Consul Eaton and Commodore Dale—quickly agreed that America had to fight—it was the only way. The hostile Barbary nations needed to be confronted. Yet they were restrained by their orders.

Eaton's sense of duty and commitment to his diplomatic mission had been nurtured by a growing belief in the need for American might, but his combative nature was the result of long experience. He had been angry at the dey's tyranny since his arrival in the Mediterranean in early 1799, and his anger had not abated in the following two and a half years.

On arrival in Tunis, he had been summoned to visit the dey in his quarters. Entering the ruler's meandering palace, he had walked through a confusing maze of towers, corridors, and courtyards. Eaton, accompanied that day by consuls O'Brien and Cathcart, as well as several American ship captains, had been led into a small, cavelike room, roughly twelve by eight feet, lit only by the broken light that penetrated the iron grates on the windows. With heads uncovered and feet bare, the men shuffled into the presence of "a huge, shaggy beast," wrote Eaton, "sitting on his rump, upon a low bench, covered with a cushion of embroidered velvet, with his hind legs gathered up."[3]

This was the dey himself, who languidly "reached out his fore paw as if to receive something to eat."

Eaton had been at a loss until a servant barked, "Kiss the Dey's hand!" O'Brien obliged, and the other men followed suit. The gesture seemed to appease the dey because, as Eaton described, "The animal seemed at that moment to be in a harmless mode: he grinned several times; but made very little noise."

Later, an angry Eaton complained to his diary, "Can any man believe that this elevated brute has seven kings of Europe, two republics, and a continent, tributary to him, when his whole naval force is not equal to two lines of battle ships?"[4]

In his years of service since that first introduction, Eaton had found leisure time to observe his new home and tour the ruins at Carthage. He had come to care deeply for the landscape, a terrain utterly foreign to his native Connecticut. "The country on the sea coast of this kingdom is naturally luxuriant and beautiful beyond description," he recorded. "Well might the *Romans consider it a luxury to have a seat here*."[5] He made careful notes about the manner of dress of the Tunisian citizens, noting that they wore "Short jackets, something like those of our seamen, without sleeves, embroidered with spangles of gold, wrought in a variety of figures on the edges and sides." He admired the fine linens and the silk sashes, from which hung swords and long pistols.

The people reminded Eaton of Native Americans, though they seemed much more subdued by their harsh climate and harsh governance. "They are humbled by the double oppression of civil and religious tyranny,"[6] he wrote to his wife back in the United States. To Pickering he remarked that the Tunisian citizens "want that wild magnanimity, that air of independence, which animate those free born sons of our forests."[7]

Increased by the oppression of the Tunisians, Eaton's righteous anger with the dey only grew the longer he served at his post. Even after several years in residence, he was still horrified that the Barbary countries could demand tribute not only from his president (whom the dey called "the Prince of America") but from the rest of the world, too. That European nations would tolerate the pirates' interference in international waters of the Mediterranean was infuriating. In Eaton's mind, this submission to tyrannical force was a blemish on American honor, but his orders were still for peace.

WORDS OF WARNING

Predictably, the Tunisians responded to Dale's greetings with many demands. A few months before, the dey of Algiers had written to the president asking for forty twenty-four-pound guns and forty other pieces. He also wanted ten thousand rifles. Dale could do little but add his promises that the "regalia due to him" was on its way. Fortunately, his words soon proved true with the arrival in Tunis of the *Grand Turk* with its escort, the USS *Essex*, the following day.

Along with Eaton, Dale found his patience growing ever thinner. Dale needed more ships—and the authorization to use them in battle—if he was going to get anywhere. Frustrated by Murat Rais and the leaders of both Algiers and Tunis, Dale wrote to the secretary of the navy on July 19. "I think they must be a damned sett," he railed, "the whole tribe, Algerines Tunisians and Tripolians. [T]here is nothing that will keep there avaricious minds in any degree of order, and prevent, them from committing depredations on our commerce whenever thay May think Proper." Now that he had firsthand knowledge of the situation, he offered his advice for the future: "Keep constantly four or six Frigates in the Mediterranean, without that, there is never any security for our commerce."[8]

With little return for his diplomacy thus far, Dale headed to Tripoli, where he would encounter the most difficult leader of all. Dale hoped to resolve matters with the Tripolitans. If he could not, this time he would be authorized to use force to contain the enemy, giving them incentive to make peace.

The USS *President* and USS *Enterprise* reached Tripoli harbor on July 24, 1801. From beyond the coastal reefs and shoals, the American ships patrolled, seeking to control access to the channels leading to Tripoli's inner harbor.

Though he could not freely walk its streets, Commodore Dale knew that this port city of some thirty thousand citizens was suffering. Tripoli was already partially blockaded by ships from Sweden's Royal Navy, as the belligerent bashaw was at odds with that nation, too. If the bashaw was not hungry, most of his people were without grains and other basic foodstuffs. Dale hoped that his additional blockade, should it become necessary, would hasten the humbling of the bashaw.

On Saturday, July 25, Dale ordered a letter delivered to the town. The letter was long, couched in the best diplomatic terms that Dale could muster. He began by expressing his disappointment at the bashaw's declaration of war against the United States,[9] then followed with fair warning: "I am sorry to Inform Your Excellency—that your Conduct towards the President of the United States, In declaring war against him, has put me under the necessity of Commencing hostilities against your Excellency's Vessels and subjects, where ever I may fall in with them."

But Dale closed his note on a conciliatory word: if the bashaw had any wish to withdraw his declaration of war and make peace, he might send a delegation by boat to the *President*, where Dale would be eager to receive them.

Sunday passed with no response.

On Monday, a boat approached the *President* asking that a messenger carrying the bashaw's response be taken on board. Eager for an answer, Dale granted the request, and the Americans helped the messenger aboard.

The response was given: the bashaw declared, quite simply, that he had not declared war without provocation. No further explanation was offered.

Dale composed another letter, attempting to move the conversation, dispatching it the following day, Tuesday, July 28.

This time silence spoke for the bashaw.

If he had not been certain before, Dale knew the time for diplomatic dodges and niceties had passed, but he wanted to make sure military engagements happened on his own terms. The bashaw's navy was small and diminished by nearly a third, since the *Meshuda* and its sister ship were trapped by the *Philadelphia*. The American navy would be able to take on the Barbary forces in the open sea, but attempting to bombard the harbor was a different matter. Because

Commodore Dale and his captains lacked charts of the unfamiliar harbor, the many reefs and rocks posed a grave danger. Dale decided the wisest course was to blockade the harbor and hope for a chance to engage with enemy ships that ventured in or out.

No ships emerged from the harbor in the wearying weeks that followed. With the unforgiving July sun, the water rations aboard the *President* and *Enterprise* soon ran low. Replenishing supplies meant a trip to the nearest safe harbor, at Malta, several days' sail away. Dale didn't want to lose one of his ships for the week or more needed for the journey, but he had no choice. On July 30, Dale sent the *Enterprise* off, its orders "to take in as much water as you can possibley bring back."[10] Now on its own, the *President* would maintain its watch off the shoals of Tripoli.

BECALMED

Meanwhile, back at Gibraltar, Murat Rais was trapped. Along with almost four hundred of his best men, many of whom were the sons of the first families of Tripoli, he could do little more than listen to the lapping of the waves. He knew that the *Philadelphia* could have only one purpose in staying behind while the rest of the American fleet sailed off. If he made sail, his two ships and their small guns would be overmatched by the long guns of the American ship, and he was not going to give the Americans that satisfaction.

As summer broiled on, Murat Rais and his men faced siegelike conditions. The quarantine had been lifted, and Rais's men could come and go onshore, but they could not obtain provisions. The British merchants on the peninsula, though many had little affection for

Americans (those rebellious former colonists), seemed to revel in this opportunity to refuse the Barbary pirates. With food and water running out, the crew of the smaller Tripolitan ship threatened to mutiny. Murat Rais knew he had to act.

The men in the tops of the American frigate *Philadelphia* might watch from afar, monitoring his ships, ready to intercept them if he set sail. But from such a distance, Rais's men could scarcely be tracked in the bustling harbor. With no guards hovering over them, it was not as if they were prisoners. Could they not flee? That was a question worth pondering. He began to concoct a plan for escape.

BATTLE STATIONS

While her fellow ships blockaded Gibraltar and Tripoli, the USS *Enterprise* made sail for Malta to procure much-needed water. But Lieutenant Andrew Sterett's simple errand was about to be interrupted.

On August 1, the second day out, less than an hour into the morning watch, a lookout spied a ship at the horizon. Suspecting it was part of Bashaw Yusuf's navy, Sterett ordered his men to prepare for battle. Though his orders specified he was "not to chase out of your way particularly," young Lieutenant Sterett was itching for action and ordered his men to sail toward the ship.

Although only twenty-three, Sterett had already proved himself in battle. Two years earlier, as a lieutenant aboard the USS *Constellation*, his role in two victories over French frigates had won him promotion to first lieutenant. The son of a Revolutionary War captain, he took his duty with deadly seriousness: when a member of a *Constellation* gun crew had abandoned his post in the heat of battle,

Sterrett had pursued the seaman and run him through with his sword. Sterrett never doubted he was doing his duty. "You must not think this strange," he explained, "for we would put a man to death for even looking pale on *this* ship."[11] Cowardice aboard a U.S. Navy vessel was a capital crime.

Sterett was no coward, but he also knew when craftiness should accompany courage.

On this day, the *Enterprise* flew a British flag, as Dale's orders permitted the "use of any colours as a deception." Because Tripoli and Great Britain were at peace, the enemy ship's captain made no move to flee as a ship that appeared to be British approached.

The ships slowed, coming alongside each other at shouting distance. Sterett hailed the captain, asking the object of his cruise.

Thinking he had no quarrel with this ship, the master of the *Tripoli*, Mahomet Rous, spoke the truth. He had come out "to cruise after Americans." Before Sterett could reply, the Tripolitan captain complained that he had yet to find any Americans to fight.[12] He should have been more careful about what he wished for.

Acting instantly, Sterett ordered the British flag lowered as Dale had ordered him to engage in combat only while flying the American flag. As his colors went up the pole, Sterett in full voice issued the order to fire. The crackle of muskets filled the air.

The Tripolitans, who had at least some of their guns primed, returned scattered fire. The first shots of the war rang out over the water.

A MAN-MADE THUNDERSTORM

Within moments, the American guns produced a deafening roar. Along with the flying cannon balls, streaks of lightning seemed to emerge from the iron cannon muzzles. The crashing sound of solid shot striking the *Tripoli* followed a heartbeat later. At such close range, few shots missed their mark.

Aboard the Tripolitan ship, masts splintered, crashing to the deck. The rigging sagged, and ropes whipped back and forth as the ship rocked; holes appeared in the ship's hull above the waterline.

The first volley over, the American gunners raced to reload: swabbing, ramming, firing again. The well-drilled men hit most of their targets.

Less adept with their guns, the pirates managed to return fire only sporadically. Unaccustomed to relying entirely upon artillery, Admiral Mahomet Rous ordered his men to maneuver their vessel alongside the *Enterprise*. They would board this American adversary and swarm over her sides, knives and pistols in hand. They would fight as they preferred, hand-to-hand, man-to-man. That was the pirate way.

But the small Marine Corps detachment aboard the *Enterprise* was ready. At the order of Marine Lieutenant Enoch Lane, their deadly musket fire repulsed the approaching pirates, dropping many to the decks before they even had a chance to swing their swords.

The *Tripoli* moved off and, seeming to surrender, the Tripolitans lowered their flag. Seeing this signal of capitulation, the men of the *Enterprise* naively assembled on deck and let loose the traditional three cheers as a mark of victory. Within moments, the cheers were drowned out by the sound of gunfire. The pirates, disregarding the rules of war, had hoisted their flag again and were firing on the exposed Americans, who ran to their stations.

The battle quickly resumed and the hellish American fire brought the Tripolitans to surrender a second time—and then a *third*—only to see the enemy's flag twice lower and rise again.

Finally, seething at this treachery, Sterett ordered his gunners to fire until they were sure the *Tripoli* would sink beneath the waves. The cry of "Sink the Villains!" echoed aboard the *Enterprise.* In the long minutes that followed, the pirates' fire grew progressively weaker, but the sustained American cannonade did not cease until Admiral Mahomet Rous called for mercy. The wounded Rous, standing at his ship's gunwale, bowed deeply in genuine supplication and surrender. This time he threw his flag into the sea.

The silence that ensued was broken not by gunfire, but only by the moans of the wounded.

Rous could not be rowed to the *Enterprise* to offer his sword to Sterett, the traditional act conceding victory; the *Tripoli*'s harbor boat was no longer seaworthy, shattered by the cannon fire. Lieutenant Sterett, after receiving assurances as to their safety, dispatched a group of his officers and seamen in the *Enterprise*'s boat. When the Americans boarded the enemy's vessel, they saw a scene of terrible carnage. Thirty men had been killed, another thirty wounded. Bodies lay in pools of blood, as rivulets of red poured through the ship's hatches.

An amazed Sterett found that, in comparison with the slaughter aboard the *Tripoli*, the Americans had sustained no casualties, with no one either killed or injured. He ordered his surgeon to minister to the enemy wounded, as the Tripolitan surgeon was among the dead.

Admiral Rous's ship was in perilous condition. Her sails and rigging had been cut to pieces; one of her three masts teetered precariously before crashing over the side. Solid shot had torn eighteen holes in the hull of the *Tripoli* above the waterline.

Under other circumstances, the *Tripoli* would have been regarded as fairly won and Lieutenant Sterett would have put a prize crew of his own men aboard to sail her to port as the spoils of victory. But Sterett, a stickler for procedure, honored his orders not to take captives.

Instead of commandeering the ship, Sterett's men set about incapacitating it. Cannon, powder, cannonballs, swords, and small arms went into the sea, along with the ship's cables and anchors. After chopping down the ship's remaining masts, the victors raised a spar to which was fixed a tattered sail—just enough to move the boat along. Leaving the defeated *Tripoli* to limp home, the *Enterprise* continued on her way to Malta.

A few days later, on August 6, the crew of the frigate *President* spotted Sterett's battle-scarred victims approaching Tripoli harbor. Maintaining the blockade, Dale stopped the ship and questioned its crew. Anxious to get home, the captain of the *Tripoli* insisted that they were Tunisians headed to Malta who had been attacked by a French ship. Thinking the tale plausible, Commodore Dale lent the captain a compass "& Suffer'd him to proceed on" into Tripoli harbor.[13] The enemy ship had escaped, but only after embarrassing losses.

GOOD NEWS, AT LAST

The bashaw was as humiliated as the Americans were proud. "So strong was the sensations of shame and indignation excited [at Tripoli]," reported the *National Intelligencer* on November 18, 1801, that Bashaw Yusuf "ordered the wounded captain to be mounted on a Jack Ass, and paraded thro' the streets as an object of public scorn."[14] Wearing a necklace of sheep entrails, the admiral was bastinadoed—beaten with five hundred strokes of a switch delivered to the soles of his feet.

The news of Lieutenant Sterett's actions met with the opposite reaction in the halls of the newly completed U.S. Capitol building. With the slow transmission of news across the Atlantic, Americans did not learn what happened off Malta until two months later. But on November 11, 1801, the editors of the *National Intelligencer* declaimed proudly the stunning victory of the USS *Enterprise.* Thrilled by the American triumph, Congress voted to commission a commemorative sword for Sterett and awarded his officers and crewmen an extra month's pay.

To Jefferson, the dramatic vanquishing of the *Tripoli* in the hard-fought three-hour sea battle sounded like political leverage. On December 8, he proudly cited the bravery of Lieutenant Sterett and the men aboard the USS *Enterprise* in his annual presidential message. "After a heavy slaughter of [enemy] men," Jefferson told Congress, the U.S. Navy ship had prevailed "without the loss of a single one on our part."[15]

The encouragement brought by Sterett's victory came none too soon. America had been dealing with the Barbary pirates for years with few results. Appeasement had not worked—poor Cathcart had suffered the results of that tactic. Richard Dale's diplomacy tour had been ineffective—his blockade was letting ships through. The only effective action so far had been the use of focused military power in the face of a threat.

Jefferson was no warmonger. He had attempted to keep the peace despite his instincts. But now he felt justified in calling for America to go to war. It was about time. The Barbary states were already at war with America, and they seemed to understand only one kind of diplomacy—the kind that was accompanied by a cannon.

CHAPTER 8

Patience Wears Thin

I know that nothing will stop the eternal increase of demand from these pirates but the presence of an armed force.

—President Thomas Jefferson to Secretary of State James Madison, August 28, 1801

Boosted by the success of Sterett's military action, Jefferson wanted congressional approval to finally admit there was a war on. He had no desire to conquer the Barbary states, but he wanted the newly convened Congress to approve the use of force so that the navy could launch an effective blockade—a blockade that could attack and capture ships as needed. With the USS *President* bound for home and the *Philadelphia* passing the winter in the harbor at Syracuse, in Sicily, a new and different array of frigates and commanders would need to be deployed, and Jefferson wanted the authority to fight the pirates properly.

Just a week after Jefferson's message, an ally in Congress introduced a resolution stating "that it is expedient that the President be authorized by law . . . to protect the commerce of the United States against the Barbary powers."[1] After a brief debate, the House voted in favor and passed the bill on. As January came to a close, Jefferson waited—and hoped—for Senate action.

That waiting for the Senate would turn into two years of waiting for another victory. During those twenty-four months, the Americans would experience little but frustration as blockades failed, a ship ran aground, and a commodore proved incompetent. But the time would not be completely wasted; while America seemed to slumber and the pirates continued to thrive, Jefferson was planning his next move.

FRUSTRATION AND FUTILITY

Jefferson could not know it at the time, but even as he pushed for the House to act, Richard Dale's blockade off the North African coast was producing little but frustration. Dale was forced to abandon Tripoli on September 3. Though his ships had replenished their supply of water thanks to Sterett, the lack of fresh food on board had taken a toll, as more than 150 members of his crew were down with a "kind of Enfluenza."[2]

On his return to Gibraltar, Dale was greeted by the news that Murat Rais and his crew had escaped Gibraltar, though they'd left their ships behind. Tired of remaining in the harbor, Rais's men had threatened a mutiny until their admiral found a way for them to escape their unofficial captivity. Blending in with the crews of ships friendly to the Barbary powers, the men had sneaked past the

Americans and been ferried to Morocco. From there, they were making their way home overland to Tripoli.

With his men safely away from Gibraltar, Rais himself had chosen another route. Blending into the British population in Gibraltar, the man born Peter Lisle talked his way to freedom, and, in September, James Cathcart reported that Rais had been recognized walking the deck of a ship loaded with wine intended for the British government.[3] By the time Dale got word that the high admiral of Tripoli had slipped from his grasp, Murat Rais had long since returned to Tripoli, his bout of shadowboxing with the Americans over. He would fight another day, under better terms.

For Commodore Richard Dale, the news was just one of several disappointments. Not only had Murat Rais escaped his grasp but, in the waning days of October, sickness overcame Dale. "Not feeling easy in my mind," he admitted, he had been confined to his cot.[4] Even more frustrating were his orders to return home. Congress's designated one-year enlistment period meant his crew's term of service expired in a few months. On his sickbed, Dale regretted leaving without humbling the Barbary powers, his only consolation Lieutenant Sterett's success, but he had little choice but to ready his ship to return home.

With the ship's water supply replenished and repairs to the rigging completed, Dale gave orders from his cabin to weigh anchor and take advantage of a fresh westward breeze. The harbor pilot guided the big frigate into Gibraltar harbor's narrow channel but, as the wind in her sails brought her speed to an easy six knots, the *President* suddenly lurched. Her forward momentum slammed to a halt as if the ship had struck a brick wall.

Down in his cabin, Dale reported he felt a "shock so great as almost, to Heave me of[f] my feet."[5]

The big frigate had run aground. She rolled heavily, but as Dale hurried to the quarterdeck, the sturdy ship quickly recovered herself. Dale worried that the *President* might have structural damage and immediately ordered an inspection. The news was surprisingly good: the well-made ship had withstood the impact of striking the sea bottom, and her hull was intact. The officers decided to proceed. They would trust their vessel and continue on their journey.

But almost immediately the ship's sturdiness would again be tested when, after leaving the protected harbor, the USS *President* sailed into a violent gale. On the first day of the storm, buffeted by high winds and seas, the ship made little headway. Then, on the second day, the hold began to fill with water. After changing course to head for the French coast and emerging from the three-day storm, the ship finally made port at Toulon. There, an inspection of the ship's hull found the forward portion of the keel entirely gone, and its extension, the stem, badly damaged. The USS *President* could go nowhere until repairs were completed.

"How long it will take to Heave down & be in readiness again to sail . . . it is out of my power to say," Dale wrote to William Bainbridge from France in mid-December.[6] But he did know that a season of disappointment off the Barbary Coast was to be followed by a winter of repairs. The USS *President* would not reach home until April 14, 1802.

MR. JEFFERSON'S SECRET

While Dale chafed under his enforced rest, Jefferson also appeared to be waiting passively for Congress to act. In reality, he was hatching a clandestine plan. This one was not for the pages of the *National Intelligencer* or the ears of Congress. This plan would not just persuade Barbary states to stop harassing Americans; it would instead change the rulers of those states. So far it was little more than an idea, but that idea had begun to grow.

U.S. consul William Eaton had ventured to write to Secretary of State James Madison, hoping that a strategy that went beyond frigates might meet with sympathetic ears. Learning from Cathcart about the bashaw's bloody path to power, Eaton had a wild proposal. In a dispatch home, Eaton proposed to Madison that the Americans ally themselves with the bashaw's exiled brother.[7]

Bashaw Yusuf of Tripoli had declared war on the United States, but he really had no legal right to lead the country. Hamet Qaramanli, his brother, was the rightful heir to the throne that Yusuf had stolen when he'd murdered his oldest brother. Hamet, banished by his brother, now lived in exile, pining for his wife and four children, whom his brother kept as hostages in Tripoli.

Eaton had met Hamet briefly when Hamet had stopped in Tunis after his banishment. The two men had shared a meal of lamb and vegetables and discussed the best way to deal with the dangerous new bashaw.[8] In the plan they concocted, the American consul had seen a chance both to right Hamet's personal injustices and to solve America's problems once and for all.

Captain Eaton—for this venture he planned to abandon his

consul's garb and don his military uniform—wrote to Madison that he wanted "to attack the usurper by land, while our operations are going on by sea." It would be a military mission, with the goal of revolution in Tripoli, the overthrow of Yusuf, and nothing less than the restoration of Hamet to the throne.

If the idea seemed outlandish at first, Madison and Jefferson realized they had to take Eaton seriously. Eaton had gained intimate knowledge of the Barbary Coast. In his years in Tunis, his skill with languages had enabled him to master several Arabic dialects. He was now well acquainted with the people and their place, and reports had it that he was known to adopt Arab garb, sometimes wearing their robes, and even a scimitar.

Eaton knew the traditions of North Africa as well as any foreigner could. When he reported that "the subjects in general of the reigning Bashaw are very discontented, and ripe for revolt," he spoke from firsthand knowledge. He offered assurances that the United States would not be the only government supporting such an effort—"the Bey of Tunis, though prudence will keep him behind the curtain, I have strong reason to believe, will cheerfully promote the scheme."[9]

For years Consul Eaton had been making a persuasive case for ships in the Mediterranean. He had called for force, and he had been right. Jefferson knew he had to listen to this new idea, but there was no denying that it was a brash departure from all earlier strategies, so he was determined to act prudently and wait for the right moment.

As 1801 ended, Jefferson and Madison conducted business as usual in the nation's capital, publicly looking to get the use of force for a blockade formally authorized. The other plan, the secret plan, was still just an idea, a future option. But far away, on a Mediterranean shore, William Eaton and Hamet, the rightful bashaw, carried on their conversation.

AN ACT OF PROTECTION

On February 6, 1802, President Jefferson got his wish when the Senate approved the use of force. Brandishing his pen, he signed into law "An Act for the protection of the Commerce and Seamen of the United States, against Tripolitan Corsairs."

Though it was less than a war declaration, the legislation spoke without ambiguity. Hereafter, as set forth in the act, "it shall be lawful fully to equip, officer, man, and employ such of the armed vessels of the United States as may be judged requisite by the President of the United States, for protecting effectually the commerce and seamen thereof on the Atlantic ocean, the Mediterranean and adjoining seas." Jefferson could now send as many ships as he needed to North Africa, and they could do whatever it took to keep American ships safe. No longer would Jefferson have to worry that he overstepped his authority in ordering the U.S. Navy to the Mediterranean. Mr. Jefferson's navy could now pursue the Tripolitan pirates as he saw fit.

Although President Jefferson had been shaping a strategy for years, he depended on the opinion of his consuls at the front more than on his own judgment. More than one of his men in the Maghreb had asked for added military might, but Richard O'Brien, writing to Madison in mid-1801, put the case plainly: "I am convinced that Tripoli should have . . . [cannon] Balls without delay. We want sir 3—or 6—or more of our frigates in this sea."[10]

Now that Jefferson was free to act, he honored O'Brien's request, ordering an increase in the size of the American naval force in early 1802. The ship designated as the fleet's flagship was the USS *Chesapeake.* The frigate would join the USS *Philadelphia*, which, along with the USS *Essex,* remained in the Mediterranean convoying merchant ships. Two other frigates would sail from Norfolk that spring, the USS *Constellation* and the USS *Adams.* On returning from the Mediterranean, the master of the sloop *Enterprise*, Lieutenant Sterett, was to turn his ship around again and recross the Atlantic to rejoin the five frigates.

With the new fleet assembling, Jefferson finally had the firepower and the authorization to defend American interests. Intimidating the pirates would be easier than getting involved in their government, and if all went well, there would be no need to secretly plan a coup. Jefferson anticipated a quick and tidy ending to the years of conflict, but he had made one key mistake: he'd appointed the wrong man to lead the new force.

CHAPTER 9

The Doldrums of Summer

The advance period of the season . . . has made it so late, as to render it impossible to appear off Tripoli before January.

—Captain Richard Valentine Morris, October 15, 1802

Up until 1802, the American navy had been suffering setbacks, but these misfortunes were brought about by circumstances, not failures of leadership. Storms, disease, shipwreck, Barbary trickery, and a lack of support at home had kept Dale and his captains from full success. Now, circumstances had changed. The new navy had all of the manpower and authorization necessary to put an end to Barbary tyranny once and for all. Unfortunately, poor leadership would cause a frustrating delay.

Captain Richard Valentine Morris was the president's choice for commander of the new flotilla. A victor in several sea battles with the French in 1798, Richard Morris was a bold young officer who accepted the assignment eagerly. But the thirty-four-year-old captain's marital status had changed since his service in the Caribbean—and it was *Mrs.* Morris who submitted an unusual appeal regarding her husband's terms of deployment. Writing directly to the secretary of the navy, she asked permission to sail with her husband.

The request was not without precedent, but it was rare for a wife to travel on her husband's ship at a time of war. Nevertheless, the secretary immediately granted it, and when Captain Morris came aboard the *Chesapeake* he was accompanied by not only his wife but also their young son. It isn't precisely clear what the sailors thought of the family's presence, but their remarks about Mrs. Morris were not flattering; a midshipman observed that "her person is not beautiful, or even handsome, but she looks very well in a veil."[1] Whatever Mrs. Morris's charms, she had not won over the crew, and her presence seemed indicative of a larger problem: her husband's mind was not on his job.

The secretary of the navy wanted an American show of force off Tripoli as soon as possible, so the six ships sailed not as a convoy but as soon as their individual preparations permitted. Aboard the *Chesapeake,* Morris wanted an easy passage and chose to wait out blustery conditions at Norfolk. After departing at last on April 27, the ship's progress was slowed three days out by the appearance of a crack in the frigate's mainmast. Rot was detected in the great timber, and an inspection revealed defective spars. Making matters worse, poorly stowed cargo meant the ship rolled dramatically, further contributing to a slow and anxious crossing. "I never was at Sea in so uneasy a Ship," reported Morris after finally dropping anchor in Gibraltar on May 25.[2]

Since replacement of the mast and spars was required, the *Chesapeake* could go nowhere until the repairs were completed. But that proved no hardship for Morris and his wife, who soon settled into the busy social life of the British port, dining with the new governor of

Gibraltar and hobnobbing with British royalty. The English officers and their wives welcomed both the commodore and the "Commodoress," as Mrs. Morris came to be known. Meanwhile, disgruntled American sailors found themselves sentenced to remain in port for a period of weeks—which stretched out into months. While their captain feasted with foreign aristocrats, they were stuck swabbing the decks, sewing their sails, and waiting.

A SHOW OF FORCE

As the first of Morris's squadron to cross the Atlantic, the USS *Constellation* had dropped anchor at Gibraltar on April 28, 1802, well before Morris arrived. By Captain Alexander Murray's reckoning, the absence of Commodore Morris put him in charge, and that suited the aging Murray—he was an old salt who'd been a ship's captain since before the War of Independence. He took on provisions and promptly sailed for his post off Tripoli, where a determined blockade was to begin.

After a stop at Algiers—Consul Richard O'Brien came aboard for a briefing—Murray and the *Constellation* sailed east to Tunis and took aboard fresh vegetables and other goods. Captain Murray also unloaded an impressive array of long-promised tribute that the bey found "highly pleasing." This included diamond-studded daggers and gold-inlaid pistols from the finest London makers. Calculated to the penny, the American taxpayers had footed a bill for $27,576.96. But this fresh cache of tribute—it was the cost of doing business in a country with which the United States remained officially at peace—still did not pacify the leader in Tunis, who soon demanded of

Consul Eaton a fully armed warship. Another purchased peace was becoming too expensive.

But Murray did not want to start a new war on his own, and by June 9, he had moved on from Tunis and now patrolled the waters off Tripoli. The American captain thought his ship made a good impression. "It is not amiss," he reported to the secretary of the navy, "to shew these Folks our Ships, now, & Then, they are powerful advocates in our favor."[3] Aside from a trip to replenish the ship's water supply, Captain Murray had little else to report—until the arrival of two corsairs.

They were about to make a mockery of the powerful American frigate.

THE PIRATES' NEW PRIZE

While Morris luxuriated in Gibraltar, on June 17 three corsairs had escaped Murray's blockade of Tripoli. Once in the open sea, the pirates spotted the *Franklin*, an America merchantman bound for the Caribbean, its hold loaded with wine, oil, perfumes, soaps, and hats. When the pirates pointed their cannons at him, the captain of the American ship had little choice but to surrender. The Tripolitans boarded the *Franklin*, put its officers and crew in chains, and sailed for Algiers. There they sold their prize and its cargo before sailing for home with their captives. The story of the *Dauphin*, the *Maria*, and many other ships was being replayed.

Returning to Tripoli, the pirates boldly sailed into port within sight of the *Constellation*. The American ship's size made it difficult for Murray to follow the speedy and maneuverable pirate ships through the shallow coastal waters, so the men aboard the *Constellation* were merely humiliated spectators as the pirates flew the Stars and Stripes upside down in contempt of the American warship. Safely in the harbor, the Tripolitans celebrated with cannon fire in salute of their success.

Once on land, the *Franklin*'s captured captain and his crew were paraded through the streets while Murray and his men made no rescue attempts. Only the intercession of the Algerian dey, Bobba Mustapha, gained the Americans' freedom—but that would be nearly three months later and only after the payment by the United States of $5,000 in ransom.

When Consul William Eaton heard the story of the failure of the *Constellation* to intervene, he wrote to James Madison, "Government may as well send out *quaker meeting-houses* to float in these seas as frigates."[4]

The words were damning. This was no "close and vigorous blockade," as ordered by the secretary of the navy.[5] Although American ships could destroy them in a fight, the elusive pirate boats still interfered with American commerce.

As a Tunisian minister warned William Eaton, "Though a fly in a man's throat will not kill him, it will make him vomit."[6] Even with Captain Murray within sight of Tripoli, the national humiliation of the United States off the Barbary Coast was far from over.

A SECOND CHANCE

A few days after the failure to intervene on behalf of the crew of the *Franklin*, Captain Murray had another chance to confront a corsair.

As the sun rose to fresh breezes and pleasant weather, the *Constellation* sailed easily on July 22, 1802. The ship was a dozen miles northeast of the city of Tripoli when, at nine o'clock, the lookouts sighted ships just west of the town. Though the seas had begun to grow heavy, Murray decided that on this day he would give chase.

Within the hour, the *Constellation* had narrowed the distance enough to distinguish nine gunboats. One of the corsairs fired on the American frigate, but the range was too distant. As the pirates "plyed their Oars, & sails," the *Constellation* kept coming.[7]

At eleven o'clock, Murray returned fire with the pair of guns mounted in the bow. As the battle escalated and the cannons continued to boom, Murray's men took a precautionary depth sounding. Though they were near the shore, the depth of seventy feet seemed safe enough but sharp eyes spied a shallows in the ship's path and warned Murray. Seeing the Tripolitan's "design was to entice us on a reef, which lay between us and them," Murray ordered that the *Constellation* turn away from the wind, avoiding the trap.

Under fire from the *Constellation*, the Tripolitan gunboats scattered, some heading for the rocky cover and inlets ashore. From Murray's ship, now less than two miles away, guns could fire not only on the retreating ships but on threatened Tripolitan troops, now visible on land. Captain Murray estimated they were several thousand in number, including cavalry, which had appeared on the sand hills above the shore.

When the cannons in a nearby Tripolitan fort began to fire at the ships, the shots fell short but still uncomfortably close to the *Constellation*. With the wind shifting dangerously—Murray could not risk being driven into shallow waters—he and his men abandoned the battle and were soon well away.[8] In Murray's judgment, it had been a near thing: "Had they Been 1 mile more to leeward of the reef," he wrote in the ship's journal, "we must inevitably have destroyed them all."[9]

Murray reported on the action to the secretary of the navy, noting that the fight "had a pleasing effect upon our Young Officers, who stood their fire admirably well."[10] Reportedly at least a dozen of the enemy had been killed, among them one of the bashaw's favorite generals. In his mind, the skirmish was ultimately a victory despite his early withdrawal.

Consul Eaton took a dimmer view—he offered direct criticism of Murray and the other U.S. Navy captains and their laughable attempts at a blockade. The incident with the *Franklin* demonstrated their impotence, the Tunis consul wrote to Madison. Two years of U.S. Navy warships in the Mediterranean, Eaton wrote, had produced "nothing . . . but additional enemies and national contempt."[11]

Despite making a good initial show, thus far American naval power had impressed few on the North African coast, American or Barbarian. Only the arrival of Morris and more ships could change that. But would it?

SLOW TO SAIL

When the USS *Adams*, far behind her sister ships, arrived in Gibraltar on July 21, 1802, her captain found Morris's *Chesapeake* still at anchor, though her mast was repaired and she was fully seaworthy. The Morris family was enjoying the high life in the port city and seemed to have no desire to move on to war.

The new arrival carried orders from the secretary of the navy for the lazy commodore. Now three months old, the instructions were clear and specific. Morris was to take his entire naval force to Tripoli. The hope was that "holding out the olive Branch in one hand & displaying in the other the means of offensive operations [will] produce a peaceful disposition toward us in the mind of the Bashaw, and essentially to contribute to our obtaining an advantageous treat with him."[12] The flotilla was to make the case for peace even as it threatened military action.

On August 17, Morris finally left Gibraltar, but still chose not to do as instructed. He made no strong military show off Tripoli, but instead cruised the southern European coast, making stops at friendly ports. At one port he found Captain Murray and the USS *Constellation*, which had left Tripoli in need of both water and repairs. That meant the ineffective American blockade had officially ceased. Far from Tripoli, Morris wrote his first report in several months to the secretary of the navy. Morris would make no effort to reestablish a naval presence in enemy waters—because of the "advanced period of the season," he explained, it would be "impossible to appear off Tripoli before January."[13] The *Chesapeake* would not see the Barbary Coast until February 1803, after spending the winter among allies; more than nine months had passed since it left American shores. The Tripolitan pirates had little to fear that winter.

THE PRESIDENT PONDERS

Back in Washington, President Jefferson had many matters to occupy his mind. Worried at the presence of the French along the

Mississippi, he told Congress in a secret session his plans for negotiating the purchase of New Orleans, and the treaty to acquire the entirety of the Louisiana Territory would be signed that spring. Jefferson and Madison were also engaged in an angry wrestling match with another Virginian, Supreme Court Chief Justice John Marshall, over presidential appointments; the landmark *Marbury v. Madison* case, with its broad ramifications concerning judicial review, would soon be handed down.

Yet despite these distractions, President Jefferson, even an ocean away from Tripoli, was mindful of the lack of aggression in the Mediterranean. Now two commodores had failed him: Dale through no fault of his own, but Morris because of laziness. Morris, it was clear, was a wartime tourist more interested in convoying ships and visiting friendly harbors than sailing at Tripoli. "I have for some time believed that Commodore Morris's conduct would require investigation," Jefferson wrote to Albert Gallatin, his secretary of the treasury, in early 1803.[14] The angry president, well aware that a year had been wasted, indulged in an uncharacteristically sarcastic aside. "His progress from Gibraltar has been astonishing."

Before a change in command could be made, matters got worse.

AN AUDIENCE WITH THE BEY

In the new year, Commodore Richard Valentine Morris at last sailed south to the Barbary Coast. He stopped first at Tunis, arriving on February 22, 1803. For Consul William Eaton, the long-awaited sight of the American flotilla was deeply gratifying. Three imposing frigates in Tunis Bay—the *New York*, *John Adams*, and *Chesapeake*, accompanied by the schooner USS *Enterprise*—made a fine display of cannons and sails.

Eaton's relief at seeing the ships was both patriotic and personal. For years the former army captain had been the most outspoken of the Barbary consuls on the necessity of a show of force in the region. More recently, however, he had also occupied himself on behalf of his country in the quiet pursuit of the plan to depose Bashaw Yusuf at Tripoli. In order to carry it out, America's naval presence off the coast would need to be strong, and now the required ships had appeared.

While waiting for final approval of his plan for regime change, Eaton encouraged Hamet Qaramanli by giving him $2,000, with the promise of more. Although the reigning bashaw offered Hamet a post in the eastern city of Derne, Eaton warned him he should refuse. "Remember that your brother thirsts for your blood," he warned Hamet. "I have learned from a certain source that his project of getting you to Derne was to murder you. He . . . has intercepted some of your letters to your friends in Tripoli."[15] Hamet now waited in exile with his family still held hostage—but Eaton had a larger and more immediate problem right here in Tunis.

He had accumulated debts on behalf of both his government and himself. He now owned two small commercial ships that had made him a prosperous man. But the falling prices of goods and unexpected expenses had meant borrowing money—and his primary creditor was the Tunisian government's chief agent for trade. This debt was a personal embarrassment and, even worse, a serious liability to America's relations with Tunis. Whether out of shame or apathy, Eaton told Morris nothing about his situation. This proved a major mistake.

After a formal written exchange with the bey of Tunis, Commodore Morris, newly arrived in Tunis, was rowed ashore. The country's leader greeted Morris in his palace. After the ceremonial shaking of hands and the ritual drinking of coffee, the two leaders opened up negotiations concerning a Tunisian ship that the *Enterprise* had captured a month earlier. All problems seemed solvable and the men reached an understanding, much to Morris's satisfaction. Then Eaton's debt surfaced, and what had been a personal matter suddenly became an international issue.

As the commodore, his officers, and other American officials stood at the breakwater in the harbor, preparing to return to the fleet, the Tunisian minister suddenly demanded payment of Eaton's debts. Morris, unaware that Eaton could not pay, disregarded the demand and prepared to leave, readying himself to climb aboard a small Tunisian harbor boat hired to row him down the channel to the *Chesapeake*. But the bey's prime minister claimed that Eaton had promised that, on arrival of the American fleet, the debt of $34,000 would be paid—by the Commodore.

The prime minister wanted the money. Now.

Eaton denied making any such promise, but the Tripolitan was insistent and, to Morris's surprise, made clear that Commodore Morris was going nowhere until the debt had been cleared.

The Americans were obliged to return to their nation's consulate onshore.

The next morning, Morris met with the bey, an audience that went on for two hours. As the same ground was revisited again and again, his protests ignored, Consul Eaton lost his patience. He demanded of the bey whether the Tunisian leader had ever been deceived by him.

"You have a good heart," the bey told Eaton, "but a bad head."[16]

Eaton retorted angrily, "[If] my head is bad [t]hen I am surrounded by imposters."

The Tunisian minister, from a culture where to insult an absolute ruler was to flirt with severe punishment or even death, recoiled in amazement. The enraged bey spoke next: "'You are Mad' stuttered the [Bey] in a Phrenzy, at the same time curling his Whiskers." Eaton was courting disaster.

Speaking through an interpreter, the angry bey ordered, "I will turn you out of my kingdom."

"I thank you," Eaton replied, refusing to back down. "I long wanted to go away."

Commodore Morris agreed to take Eaton out of the leader's sight, but that would not be for five more days, during which time Morris would be held under house arrest until the debt was at last satisfied. When the U.S. Navy contingent finally returned to its ship, Consul Eaton accompanied them but, unwelcome aboard the furious Morris's *Chesapeake*, Eaton was forced to find a berth on the *Enterprise.*

Even when he tried to do his duty, Commodore Morris had encountered rough waters. Like Bainbridge before him at Algiers, Morris had blundered into a great embarrassment. As he subsequently reported to the secretary of the navy, "I should not have put myself in the power of the Bey of Tunis."[17] With his superiors in Washington growing impatient, his time to prove himself was running short.

Commodore Morris had one more chance, and it was about to blow up—in a very literal sense.

Originally printed in *Histoire de Barbarie et de Ses Corsairs* by Father Pierre Dan (1636), this etching depicts twenty-two different forms of torture by which Barbary masters punished their Christian slaves.

HULTON ARCHIVE/GETTY IMAGES

As president, Thomas Jefferson (1743–1826) dared to do what his two predecessors had not: rather than pay for peace and free passage for his ships, he confronted the Barbary powers with military force and, ultimately, earned the world's respect for doing so.

CHARLES SAINT-MÉMIN, COURTESY LIBRARY OF CONGRESS PRINTS AND PHOTOGRAPHS DIVISION

John Adams (1735–1826) and Jefferson were among the first Americans to meet with the Barbary diplomats immediately after the American Revolution, when the friends served as the U.S. ministers to Great Britain and France. Despite face-to-face encounters, the two ambassadors were never quite able to persuade Sidi Haji Abdrahaman and the other Barbary state representatives to stop attacking American ships.

GILBERT STUART, COURTESY NATIONAL GALLERY OF ART

In 1785, James Leander Cathcart (1767–1843) was enslaved by Tunisian pirates and spent more than eleven years imprisoned in Tunis. The language skills and cultural knowledge he acquired in captivity would later prove valuable in his work as a U.S. consul in the Barbary region.

FROM *THE CAPTIVES* BY JAMES LEANDER CATHCART (LA PORTE: HERALD PRINT, 1899), COURTESY NEW YORK PUBLIC LIBRARY

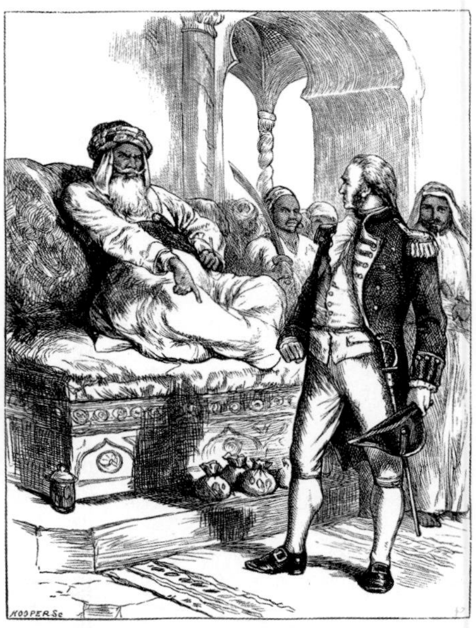

Captain William Bainbridge (1774–1833), though deeply humiliated, had little choice but to agree to the dey of Algiers's demand that, in September 1800, he lower the American flag and take aboard the USS *George Washington* animals, goods, officials, and slaves in order to ferry them to Constantinople.

HOOPER, UNIVERSAL HISTORY ARCHIVE/UIG VIA GETTY IMAGES

As a young lieutenant, Stephen Decatur (1779–1820) was part of the first U.S. Navy fleet to cross into the Mediterranean in 1801. His exploits—most famously the nighttime raid on the captured *Philadelphia*—made him a captain. He would serve honorably in the War of 1812, and, in 1815, prove a hero again in the Second Barbary War.

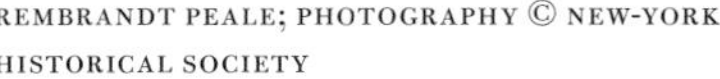

REMBRANDT PEALE; PHOTOGRAPHY © NEW-YORK HISTORICAL SOCIETY

Commodore Richard Dale (1756–1826) led the first fleet of four U.S. Navy ships to the Mediterranean. A respected leader, he found his options were limited by the terms of engagement specified in his official orders.

R. W. DOBSON, COURTESY NAVY ART COLLECTION, NAVAL HISTORY AND HERITAGE COMMAND

Lieutenant Andrew Sterett (1778–1807) was an early hero of the Barbary Wars, giving the United States its first naval victory in the region.

CHARLES SAINT-MÉMIN, COURTESY NAVY ART COLLECTION, NAVAL HISTORY AND HERITAGE COMMAND

An artist's rendering of Lieutenant Andrew Sterett's leaving the USS *Enterprise* to board the *Tripoli,* after the fourteen-gun enemy ship surrendered on August 1, 1801.

RODOLFO CLAUDU, COURTESY OF U.S. NAVAL ACADEMY MUSEUM

The transfer of command of U.S. Navy forces in the Mediterranean to Captain Edward Preble (1761–1807) marked a turning point in the First Barbary War. Though his tenure expired before a peace treaty was signed, he was responsible for increasing the American presence and launching effective offensive maneuvers in the region.

REMBRANDT PEALE, COURTESY U.S. NAVAL ACADEMY MUSEUM

The long naval career of Captain William Bainbridge was marked by great victories as well as more than one humiliating defeat. One of the U.S. Navy's most memorable setbacks occurred when the USS *Philadelphia*, with Bainbridge as its captain, ran aground in Tripoli Harbor, in 1803. Bainbridge surrendered his ship, and he and the crew were held captive for nineteen months.

GILBERT STUART, COURTESY USS *CONSTITUTION* MUSEUM; PHOTOGRAPH BY DAVID BOHL

In this dramatic rendering from the later nineteenth century, the artist conveys the fearlessness of Stephen Decatur, by then a legendary American warrior.

DENNIS MALONE CARTER, COURTESY NAVY ART COLLECTION, NAVAL HISTORY AND HERITAGE COMMAND

The battle at Tripoli Harbor, on August 3, 1804, with the American frigate USS *Constitution*, captained by Edward Preble, and his squadron preparing to bombard the Tripolitan gunboats arrayed at the mouth of the harbor.

JOHN B. GUERRAZZI; PHOTOGRAPHY © NEW-YORK HISTORICAL SOCIETY

An artist's depiction of Stephen Decatur's fighting for his life—and attempting to avenge his brother James's death—after boarding a Tripolitan gunboat on the day James died.

COURTESY THE MARINERS' MUSEUM, NEWPORT NEWS, VIRGINIA

The USS *Philadelphia* was saved from becoming a pirate ship when, after its shocking loss to the Tripolitans, a brilliant and daring band of sailors, led by Stephen Decatur, set it afire in Tripoli Harbor.

NICOLINO CALYO, COURTESY THE MARINERS' MUSEUM, NEWPORT NEWS, VIRGINIA

The Tripolitan merchant vessel *Mastico* was captured during the war with Tripoli. Converted into a warship and renamed USS *Intrepid,* it played an essential role on February 16, 1804, in the daring and dramatic raid to destroy the captured U.S. frigate *Philadelphia*. Later that year, on September 3, it embarked on one last perilous mission.

PHOTOGRAPHY © NEW-YORK HISTORICAL SOCIETY

A soldier, a diplomat, and, finally, an intrepid general, William Eaton (1764–1811) led one of the most remarkable military assaults in American military history, marching six hundred miles through desert terrain in an effort to restore Bashaw Hamet to his rightful throne in Tripoli.

REMBRANDT PEALE, COLLECTION OF THE MARYLAND STATE ARCHIVES

Hailed as the "Hero of Derne," Presley O'Bannon (1776–1850) led a contingent of seven American Marines and other foot soldiers on a charge of the city's defenses. Despite being greatly outnumbered, the victorious Marines raised the American flag for the first time on foreign soil. In honor of his brave leadership and heroism, O'Bannon was presented with a scimitar, a sword modeled after the Mameluke style, which is still part of the dress uniform of the United States Marine Corps.

COURTESY U.S. NAVAL ACADEMY MUSEUM

In this early-nineteenth-century woodcut, General Eaton and Hamet Qaramanli are pictured at the head of their diverse collection of warriors en route to the defining Battle of Derne. They took the city against great odds in under three hours.

PHOTOGRAPHY © NEW-YORK HISTORICAL SOCIETY

In this twentieth-century rendering, the U.S. Marines assault Derne on April 27, 1805. The events were also immortalized in the opening stanza of the Marines' Hymn: "From the Halls of Montezuma/To the Shores of Tripoli;/We fight our country's battles/In the air, on land, and sea."

CHARLES WATERHOUSE, ART COLLECTION, NATIONAL MUSEUM OF THE MARINE CORPS, TRIANGLE, VIRGINIA

Tobias Lear (1762–1816) served as personal secretary to President George Washington until his death. In 1803, Jefferson appointed him consul general to the Barbary States, where Lear pursued a negotiated end to the Tripoli War, undercutting Eaton's hard-won victory in Derne.

S. HOLLYER, COURTESY CLEMENTS LIBRARY, UNIVERSITY OF MICHIGAN

As Jefferson's confidant and secretary of state, James Madison (1751–1836) played a key role in conducting the First Barbary War. As the fourth president of the United States, he would order the U.S. Navy to the Mediterranean once again after the War of 1812. The U.S. Navy finally ended the hostage taking and tribute payments by the Barbary States in 1815.

JOHN VANDERLYN, COURTESY WHITE HOUSE HISTORICAL ASSOCIATION

Decatur's imposing squadron in a show of force in Algiers Harbor brought a close to the Barbary Wars, in June 1815.

G. MUNGER AND S. S. JOCELIN; PHOTOGRAPHY © NEW-YORK HISTORICAL SOCIETY

FIRE AT SEA

Due for a refitting, the *Chesapeake* had been ordered back to the United States. But Commodore Morris was to stay in the Mediterranean and transfer to a new flagship, the *New York*. On departing Gibraltar, Morris made his usual leisurely stop in Leghorn, then sailed to Malta, where his wife and children now resided (a second child had been born in a Maltese hospital), before sailing for Tripoli. Not quite eleven months into his service in the Mediterranean station, the commodore now planned to lay eyes—for the first time—on the place he had been assigned to blockade.

As the sun rose on Monday, April 25, 1803, the *New York* sailed easily just off the coast of Sardinia. At eight o'clock, the drums called the sailors to eat and, tin cups in hand, they waited their turns for their morning meal.

A loud *boom!* interrupted breakfast. The sound echoed from belowdecks and, moments later, the warning that sailors dread most was heard: "The magazine is on fire!"[18] The storeroom where the gunpowder was kept was in flames.

With the rising of the sun, a seaman had gone below to stow the signal lanterns that the ship ran at night. When the gunner's mate later went to the storeroom to check that all was in its proper place, he found a still-burning candle that had been overlooked in the cockpit storeroom. He extinguished the tallow, returned to the main deck, and reprimanded the sailor for his carelessness in leaving an open flame so close to the powder magazine. On returning to the cockpit storeroom, the gunner discovered that he, too, had missed something: the candle he extinguished had started a slow, smoldering fire in a stack of sheepskins. When he shifted the skins, a shower of red-hot coals fell into a bucket on the floor below. Its contents—a small amount of high-grade gunpowder—instantly exploded.

When the flames reached powder horns hanging nearby, another blast blew off the bulkhead door of the marine storeroom. Dozens of blank cartridges were the next to explode. With flames spreading after the series of deafening roars, the nearby powder magazine was in grave danger.

The men in or near the ship's cockpit were all badly burned. But two lieutenants on deck, David Porter and Isaac Chauncey, reacted quickly. They descended to the magazine, groping amid the wreckage in the choking smoke. Using wet blankets, they sought to protect the ship's main powder store—every man aboard knew that one spark in the magazine would cause a chain reaction, blowing the wooden ship to smithereens, killing them all.

The sailors formed two lines, passing water hand-to-hand in buckets to douse the flames. An hour and a half later, the exhausted crew—coughing, blackened by smoke—could take the measure of their losses.

The fire was out, but a toll had been taken. According to the *New York*'s log, fourteen men were "so shockingly burnt that their lives are despair'd of."[19] Lieutenants Chauncey and Porter would survive (and later gain fame in the War of 1812), but four men, including the gunner, died of their burns.

Forced to seek repairs, the USS *New York* returned to Malta. Morris's arrival to blockade Tripoli would be delayed yet again.

MORRIS ON PATROL, AT LAST

For a grand total of five weeks, commencing May 22, 1803, Morris did manage to watch over the enemy's harbor. Together with the frigates *John Adams* and *Adams* and the sloop *Enterprise*, the USS *New York* patrolled the outer harbor at Tripoli. There were several skirmishes during that time, including one where the *New York* delivered more damage by friendly fire to the rigging of the *John Adams* than to the pirate ships. Though the great American warships engaged in sporadic fire with a few smaller enemy ships in their weeks off Tripoli, the fleet accomplished little before once again sailing for Malta.

By early July, his family once again aboard, Morris headed for Gibraltar. He was about to be relieved of duty, and the end of the commodore's service was an anticlimax. William Eaton, having returned to Washington in the late spring, had duly reported on Morris's inactivity. By Eaton's count, Morris had been off the coast of Tripoli a total of only nineteen days in the course of his seventeen-month tour of duty. Perhaps motivated partly by his humiliation at Morris's angry response to his debt, Eaton told the Speaker of the House of Representatives, "It is true that during this term . . . [the Commodore] never burnt an ounce of powder; except at a royal salute fired at Gibraltar in celebration of the birth day *of his Britanic Majesty*."[20]

When Commodore Morris arrived in Málaga, Spain, he found a letter addressed to him from the secretary of the navy. The words were unambiguous: "You will upon receipt of this consider yourself Suspended in the command of the Squadron on the Mediterranean Station."[21] Morris had been relieved of duty.

Given his lackluster performance, he would be required to face a court-martial. The trial lasted for nine days. After due deliberation, the four-man panel determined that "captain Morris did not conduct himself, in his command of the Mediterranean squadron, with the diligence or activity necessary." His bravery was not questioned; his fault, the panel ruled, lay in "his indolence, and want of capacity."[22] He was forthwith dismissed from the U.S. Navy.

By then, however, the command of a still larger and more powerful Mediterranean fleet had been put in more capable hands. Jefferson wanted the United States of America to have the respect of the world; it was a matter of pride—and of financial necessity—that American trading ships be able to ply international waters safely. Yet the late efforts of his navy sent no message of intimidation. Jefferson put it plainly in a letter to a friend. Morris's tour of duty in the Mediterranean had amounted to "two years of sleep."[23]

This was not effective foreign policy. On the contrary, as former Tunisian consul Eaton had reported, "The Minister puffs a whistle in my face, and says; 'We find it is all a puff! We see how you carry on the war with Tripoli.'"[24] Jefferson could only hope that the new commodore could accomplish what Morris hadn't gotten around to attempting.

CHAPTER 10

The Omens of October

The President is extremely desirous that the United States should have peace and free commercial intercourse with all the states of Barbary . . . but is determined neither to purchase or maintain that peace and intercourse by submitting to treatment dishonorable to our country.

—Commodore Edward Preble, September 13, 1803

Appalled at how poorly Morris had performed, Jefferson took great care in appointing his next commander. He needed a man of both diplomatic tact and courage, a leader who would take initiative and press for his country's best interests. Jefferson's patience with both the pirates and incompetent American leadership had worn thin. It was time for action, so he would appoint a man of action: Edward Preble.

At age forty, Edward Preble had spent more of his years at sea than on land. At sixteen, after announcing to his father that he had hoed his last row of potatoes, he had shipped out on a privateer he spotted in the harbor. He gained a midshipman's warrant in 1779, serving aboard the Massachusetts state navy frigate *Protector* during the Revolution. Although he barely survived a bout of typhoid fever contracted aboard the prison ship *Jersey* after his capture by the Royal Navy, he gained financial success following the war as a captain and owner of a merchant ship. With the establishment of the U.S. Navy, he sought a commission and, in 1798, President John Adams made him a lieutenant. Two years later he gained his captaincy and, as master of the USS *Essex,* spent a full year sailing the frigate across the Pacific Ocean to Jakarta to escort a convoy of merchantmen home.

Preble was not an easygoing captain. When his Barbary Coast orders came through in 1803, Preble supervised the refitting of his ship. While waiting for the repairs to finish, he found time to write elaborate standing orders—107 of them, something of a record. One forbade "blasphemy, profanity, and all species of obscenity." Another instructed officers to learn the names of their men (there were four hundred aboard). But beyond the specifics, one more general message came through clearly: this was no pleasure cruise.

Preble's fair skin had been made ruddy by his years at sea, and he combed his graying hair forward in an unsuccessful effort to conceal his baldness. But his intense blue eyes and his sometimes impatient manner—he suffered from chronic ulcers—conveyed as clearly as his orders did that Preble expected his officers and crew to sail a tight, highly disciplined ship.

From Boston's Long Wharf, Edward Preble readied to sail for the Barbary Coast. With his departure imminent, he wrote to his sweetheart, Mary Deering, expressing his devout hope that "we may again meet and be long happy in each other's society."[1] Unlike Mrs.

Morris, his predecessor's spouse, the woman Preble loved would remain at home, back in Portland, Maine.

In the months to come Preble would demonstrate that he could not be more different from Morris. He would not hesitate to put himself and his just-refitted frigate, the USS *Constitution*, in the line of fire.

When the USS *Constitution* set out on August 12, 1803, she sailed with light but often unfavorable winds, which would make for a calm but long crossing. Preble may have been impatient with the speed, but the uneventful twenty-nine-day sail also meant the captain could become better acquainted with his principal passengers, Colonel and Mrs. Tobias Lear. The colonel was President Jefferson's new appointee to the post of consul general at Algiers following O'Brien's retirement.

Like Preble, Lear grew up on the New England coast, hailing from Portsmouth, New Hampshire. Though Lear bore the honorary title *Colonel*, granted him by George Washington, he could claim no experience as either soldier or sailor. He spent the closing years of the Revolution at Harvard, graduating in 1783, and it was at the recommendation of that college's president that he had been hired for a domestic position at a large Virginia plantation. The job had been the making of the somber, awkward young man with the long nose and lantern jaw.

He was to tutor two grandchildren being raised by an aging Virginia couple and to handle the voluminous correspondence of the man of the house. That tall, broad-shouldered patriarch—known to his family as "The General"—happened to be the former commander-in-chief of the Continental Army, George Washington.

Though of well-established Yankee stock, Lear became a virtual member of the Washington family after his arrival in 1786. He dined with the Washingtons. He had his socks darned and his clothes washed by Mount Vernon's house slaves. When Washington became president in 1789, Lear was charged with making the domestic arrangements in lower Manhattan, the nation's temporary capital, before Martha arrived along with her grandchildren. Lear kept the household accounts, managing the Washingtons' private purse.

President Washington trusted Lear to be his eyes and ears, to report back after "mixing with people in different walks, high and low, of different descriptions and of different political sentiments . . . have afforded you an extensive range for observation and comparison."[2] From 1786 until the general's unexpected death in 1799, Lear remained a trusted member of Washington's circle. It was Lear, standing at Washington's bedside in December, who heard Washington preparing to die. "I am just going," Washington said softly, his throat constricted by the infection that would take his life. Then he offered a last instruction to his trusted secretary regarding his burial. And it was Lear who was said to have burned angry correspondence between Washington and Jefferson.

The whispers about Lear weren't just about the rumored destruction of the letters. There were hints that Lear wasn't quite aboveboard in his dealings with Washington's tenants. And his obvious ambition and close relationships with the most powerful people in the land didn't help dispel the rumors.

If Jefferson felt he owed Lear for the rumored destruction of damning letters, he did not acknowledge it. But during his years as secretary of state, Jefferson had had regular exchanges with Lear, often in person at the president's house. Soon after Washington's death, Jefferson had named Lear to serve as consul in Santo Domingo. On his return from that post, Jefferson turned to him to lead the negotiations on the Barbary Coast.

Just days before the *Constitution* sailed, the secretary of the navy had advised Preble, "Your experience in affairs and your good sense and the tried merits of Mr. Lear all conspire to persuade me that you and he will move in the most perfect harmony."[3] The man of war and the seeker of treaties had become collaborators. It was their task to sort out the mess, militarily and diplomatically. They were to do, in short, whatever it took along the Barbary Coast. They spent the transatlantic voyage planning accordingly.

ON ARRIVAL

A surprise awaited Preble and Lear in Gibraltar Bay. William Bainbridge, whose ship, the USS *Philadelphia*, was anchored in Gibraltar, informed Preble that Tripoli wasn't their only sworn enemy. After confronting a strange ship at sea, Bainbridge had discovered that it carried a kidnapped American crew and orders from the sultan of Morocco to capture American assets. Adding insult to injury, the sultan had obtained Murat Rais's old ship, the *Meshuda*, and returned her to Tripoli. With Morocco joining Algiers and Tripoli in the hostilities, Tunis was the only Barbary state not at war with the Americans, and even that peace looked shaky.

Fortunately for Preble, his squadron was also growing by the day. In addition to the *Constitution* and the *Philadelphia*, three more frigates arrived in port: the *Adams*, the *John Adams*, and the *New York*. Preble also had new options that neither Dale nor Morris had had. Congress had enacted new legislation empowering President

Jefferson to add to the U.S. Navy four warships, smaller and quicker than the older ones, which had been too large to get close to shore and too slow to catch up with the pirates. Construction on the *Vixen*, the *Syren*, the *Argus*, and the *Nautilus* began immediately, and the *Vixen* was ready in time to join Preble's convoy.

Preble saw his challenges escalating, but his orders—direct from the secretary of the navy—gave him leeway to do what he thought right. "We therefore leave you unrestrained in your movements," the secretary had written, "and at liberty to pursue the dictates of your own judgment."[4] He had a freedom Dale had lacked—and the courage that Morris had refused to exercise.

After deliberations with Lear, Preble decided to proceed on two fronts. First, Preble and most of his squadron would present a great show of force at Morocco. He didn't want to expand the war—he could hardly attack Tripoli if his forces were badly divided—but he couldn't afford to ignore this new antagonist, either. He wanted his Moroccan challengers to think he was spoiling for a fight; that might lead to a quick settlement that would then free him up to focus his energies on the threats posed elsewhere in the region. Like President Jefferson, he was convinced that "nothing will keep the [Villains] so quiet as a respectable naval force near them."[5] If a show of power was required, he was there to provide it.

While he took care of Morocco, Preble issued orders to Bainbridge and the *Philadelphia* to sail to Tripoli. They were to aid American vessels along the way, and all pirate ships encountered were to be attacked and captured. Then, together with the *Vixen*, the *Philadelphia* was to proceed to Tripoli to blockade that port and to attack the enemy by whatever means.

CRISIS CONTAINED

When the sultan of Morocco finally returned from a journey two weeks later, the full force of the U.S. Navy was on display in Tangier Harbor. Before the sultan's eyes was an intimidating vista of raw naval power—the American guns, numbering well over 150 cannons, could likely pound the city's crumbling stone castle and sink every vessel in the harbor.

Preble had avoided falling into a trap as Bainbridge had done with the USS *George Washington.* From his commanding position looking in on Tangier, he could choose a tactic that was both direct and deferential.

From his position well outside the range of the sultan's cannons, Preble exchanged letters with that ruler. The two men agreed upon a meeting, and two days before the date the sultan sent gifts from shore: ten bulls, twenty sheep, and four dozen fowl arrived for distribution to the U.S. Navy ships. Moroccan troops and horses were paraded on the shore in an impressive show. The sultan himself made his way to the end of the stone breakwater to view the American ships through a telescope mounted on a tripod. Already he was much more deferential than Barbary leaders had been earlier in the face of smaller displays of power.

When the day of reckoning came—October 10—the American ships had for almost a week been kept in readiness for battle; as Preble noted in his diary, "All hands Slept at quarters."[6] As agreed, Preble himself would go ashore, but he would not arrive in the company of a large delegation. Instead, his party would consist of only himself, Consul Tobias Lear, and two midshipmen serving as aides.

At eleven o'clock, the four men prepared to go ashore, but before they did, Preble issued clear instructions. "If the least injury is offered to my person," he ordered those who remained aboard the ships, "immediately attack the batteries, the castle, the city and the troops, regardless of my personal safety."[7]

At one o'clock, the American delegation was summoned to the castle. The walk through the town did not impress Lear, and he noted the "very narrow and dirty streets [and] the wretched appearance of the inhabitants. . . . There appear to be no shops, no trade—nothing to please the eye or amuse the fancy."[8] On reaching the castle, the Americans were ushered through a double file of guards, but Preble found that the sultan sat not on a throne but on the stone steps in a castle courtyard. One of the midshipmen reported his disappointment at the sight. "I had connected with the idea of Emperor of Morocco, something grand," he wrote to his mother back in South Carolina, "but what was my disappointment at seeing a small man, wrapped up in a woolen *heik* or cloak."[9]

Faced with Preble's overwhelming navy, the sultan seemed almost apologetic. He regretted the hostilities, he said through an interpreter. His country was at peace with the United States, and he would honor the treaty his father had made in 1786. He promised to punish Alcady Hashash, the Tangier governor who had ordered the attacks on the American ships. He would see to it that the captains of the pirate vessels paid dearly, too.

Then the sultan listened as Preble "endeavored to impress on his mind the advantages of a free commercial intercourse . . . and that the revenues of the Emperor arising from that source, would be much greater than any thing they could expect if at war with us."[10] It was an

American argument, a case made for free trade. And the sultan, confronted with America's newfound strength, was paying attention.

The following day, the sultan produced a letter for Jefferson. "Know Ye that all the Treaties entered into between the two nations, remain as they were," the sultan wrote.[11] Several more days were required to exchange and translate the documents that made the understanding official, but the pressure was off.

Commodore Edward Preble had achieved a significant victory without firing a shot. Just as remarkable, tribute had neither been paid nor promised. Preble put it simply in writing home to Mary Deering in Maine once he had returned to Gibraltar: "An honorable peace is established."[12] A clear show of force, backed up by a genuine threat, had resulted in harmony between the nations.

Now, the commodore and the consul had to focus their energies on Bashaw Yusuf and the troublesome Tripolitans. Preble had promised Bainbridge that more force would follow him and the *Philadelphia* after the matter of Morocco had been resolved, and he prepared to keep his word. But neither man could know that the commodore had ordered the *Philadelphia* to embark on what would be its last voyage.

CHAPTER 11

The Philadelphia *Disaster*

After giving up the chase in pursuit of the cruiser, striking on the rocks was as unexpected to me as if it had happened in the middle of the Mediterranean sea.

—Captain William Bainbridge, November 12, 1803[1]

Cruising off Tripoli according to Preble's orders, Captain William Bainbridge met up with no pirate ships for nearly the entire month of October. The few suspicious ships sighted remained out of reach, staying within the protection of the gun batteries that lined the city walls overlooking the harbor.

At nine o'clock on the morning of October 31, some fifteen miles east of Tripoli, a suspicious sail was sighted near the coast, headed for Tripoli. The *Philadelphia* gave chase. As if to taunt the much larger warship, the unidentified vessel hoisted the Tripolitan colors; it was a Barbary ship trying to slip the blockade, and now the race was on.

The *Philadelphia* was soon at full sail. Though well offshore,

Bainbridge aimed to cut off the smaller vessel before she reached port. Increasing speed, the *Philadelphia* gained on the corsair and, as eleven o'clock neared, Bainbridge judged the little ship might be within range. He ordered the firing of the cannon mounted at the front of the ship. Wary of the unfamiliar waters off Tripoli—other American captains had reported uncharted obstacles and unpredictable winds near shore—three sailors took repeated depth soundings. They reported a depth of forty feet and more, roughly twice the draft of the *Philadelphia*. The ship was in no danger.

The American gunners kept a constant fire as they chased the ship. By eleven-thirty, the city grew closer and the fortress walls could be plainly seen. Rather than put his ship at risk of coming within range of the shore guns, Bainbridge reluctantly ordered the helmsman to change course. To his frustration, he had to accept that he could not overtake the Tripolitan pirates, and the *Philadelphia* began a long, slow turn into the wind, away from the city. The chase was over, and the pirates would go unpunished.

ON THE ROCKS

Moments later, the USS *Philadelphia* lurched with the impact. The ship's great frame shuddered as her bow rose a full six feet out of the water. One moment she was coursing through the sea at the land equivalent of roughly ten miles an hour; the next, she was fixed, immobile, a man-made wooden island halted less than two miles from shore.

The *Philadelphia* had run aground.

The captain stood stunned on the bridge. The charts indicated no reefs, and the last sounding had measured a more than sufficient thirty-five feet. But there was no time to wonder. The men aboard the *Philadelphia* needed to act to save their ship stranded so close to the enemy stronghold.

Bainbridge remained calm and deliberate. He soon learned that the ship's bow rested on rocks just twelve feet below the surface. Consulting his officers, Bainbridge determined to try to back the ship into the deeper water off her stern in order to float her free. He ordered the sails laid aback in hopes the press of sail could drive her clear. Three bow anchors were cast into the sea, their lines cut, to lighten the ship. The guns were shifted back. But as the bow began almost perceptibly to rise, a strong wind and rising waves drove the ship further aground.

Even at two miles out, the distress of the great ship was glaringly apparent. Her bow elevated, the vessel now leaned sharply to one side. To the Tripolitans, the *Philadelphia* looked like an easy target for their guns—and for capture. Nine Barbary gunboats were soon spotted making sail from the inner harbor, bound for the stranded ship.

Aboard the *Philadelphia*, the next hours were a blur. The officers concluded that most of the guns should be sunk to lighten the ship; soon, the seamen aboard sent most of the great iron cannons tumbling into the sea. Barrels of water were cast overboard, and any and all heavy articles dumped. As a last resort, the foremast was cut away. But the ship refused to float free.

A few gunners manned the remaining guns, firing as best they could at the attacking gunboats that circled the stern of the American frigate. But the angle of the ship meant that the guns on one side pointed toward the water while those on the other pointed to the sky.

The well-drilled U.S. Navy gunners could do little, and the enemy quickly recognized their advantage. Establishing positions where the Americans were unable to return fire, the enemy gunners aimed high at the masts of the *Philadelphia*, shattering spars and rigging as they attempted to disable the ship and prevent any chance of escape.

By mid-afternoon, Bainbridge and his officers recognized their situation was hopeless. As Bainbridge later put it to Tobias Lear, "a just comparison of our situation, is one man tied to a stake attacked by another with arms."[2] For the third time in his life, the hapless young captain would surrender his ship.

Bainbridge ordered the gunpowder dampened and the ship's pumps clogged with shot. He sent carpenters below with their augers to drill holes in the bottom to make the ship unsailable once she was in Tripolitan hands. Recognizing the extreme damage done to the British fleet when the Americans got hold of their naval codebook ahead of the Battle of Yorktown some twenty-two years before, Bainbridge tore his copies of the American signaling codes into shreds and ordered the sheets set afire and thrown overboard. Pistols, muskets, cutlasses, pikes, and other weapons were tossed into the sea. If he had to hand over his ship to the bashaw, Bainbridge was going to make sure it was as worthless a prize as possible.

At four o'clock, the USS *Philadelphia* struck her colors.

A SECOND HUMILIATION

The unlucky William Bainbridge almost wished he were dead. This was worse even than his humiliation as captain of the USS *George*

Washington. The day after surrendering the *Philadelphia*, he wrote to his wife, "It would have been a merciful dispensation of Providence if my head had been shot off by the enemy, while our vessel lay rolling on the rock."[3]

With the flag lowered to the deck of the *Philadelphia*, the enemy gunboats ceased their fire. Strangely, however, the Tripolitan gunboats didn't surge toward the American ship. The corsairs seemed either to disbelieve their dumb luck or else to fear an ambush if they attempted to board. Finally, in exasperation, Bainbridge dispatched an officer and one of his ship's boats to assure the enemy of his intention to hand over the ship peacefully. Only then, at six o'clock on October 31, did the Tripolitans board the frigate, clambering over the gunwales.

The Americans looked very odd to the pirates. Spooked by stories of exposed skin that blistered in the noonday sun and freezing desert nights, many sailors had put on three or four pairs of trousers and crammed their several shirts with provisions. The well-clad men made inviting targets, and the pirates tore at the layers of clothing, ripped open the sailors' pockets, and stole watches, money, rings, and any object of value. The officers' swords were snatched and their coats removed; these items were quickly donned by the pirates, who paraded around the ship in their new costumes. Bainbridge had to fight off one pirate who wanted a locket strung from his neck that held a miniature portrait of his wife.[4] The *Philadelphia*'s surgeon lost his surgical instruments. No one was safe from harm when the pillaging boarders began to fight among themselves over the Americans' belongings.

Ordered into the gunboats, the captives were forced to row toward land, their captors "standing with drawn sabres over our heads."[5] Some men were thrown from the overcrowded boats into the sea, left to swim for shore—or drown.

When they landed at the base of the bashaw's palace, the captives were marched through the streets to jeers from the elated Tripolitans. They were prodded past the bashaw's elite guards, armed with glittering sabers, muskets, pistols, and tomahawks. Some of the guards spat on the prisoners as they passed.

Once they were in the bashaw's castle, a series of darkened halls and stairs opened onto a richly decorated room with a variegated marble floor, elegant carpets, and walls decorated with elaborate enamel work. The men were arranged in a semicircle around a raised velvet-covered throne, fringed with cloth of gold and jewels. Seated on it was the bashaw himself. He wore a gold-embroidered silk robe and a large white turban decorated with ribbons. From his broad, diamond-studded belt hung two gold pistols and a saber.

His bearing impressed the Americans. A man of about thirty-five years, he was tall, his beard long and dark. He said nothing to his audience of enlisted seamen, but dismissed the prisoners after "he had satiated his pride and curiosity by gazing on us with complacent triumph."[6] He then had the officers paraded before him.

The officers were fed at the bashaw's castle, then taken to what had been the American consulate prior to Consul Cathcart's departure. There they slept on the floor on mats and blankets. At Bainbridge's request, the man Cathcart had left in charge of American affairs, the Danish consul, Nicholas C. Nissen, was summoned. He promised to do what he could to provide basic comforts and, the following day, he returned with mattresses, blankets, and baskets of fruit. In the months to come, he would be the conduit for money and goods sent to the prisoners.

The officers had the run of the abandoned house and received adequate food, but the members of the crew faced real hardships. Many had arrived dripping wet and gratefully accepted the dry clothing other slaves brought in exchange for their waterlogged uniforms, not suspecting they were never to see their uniforms again. That first night the crewmen were fed nothing and slept in an outdoor courtyard.

The following morning, the men of the *Philadelphia* were questioned by High Admiral Murat Rais, the renegade Scotsman who had commanded the *Meshuda*. Peter Lisle ridiculed Bainbridge. "Who with a frigate of forty-four guns, and three hundred men, would strike his colours to solitary gun-boats, must surely be . . . a coward, or traitor."[7] Finally, the crew was fed coarse bread and confined to a dark and dreary prison, a single large room with too little floor space for all the men to stretch out. Many were obliged to sit or even stand all night, with nothing but tattered sailcloth for covers.

Many were put to work on the city walls. Teams of forty to fifty men transported great stones, ranging from two to four tons, some sixteen feet in length, loaded on crude carts with wheels ten feet in diameter. Like yoked oxen, the men were forced to pull the awkward vehicles, guarded by soldiers with muskets and whips. "We worked bare-headed and bare-footed," reported ship's carpenter Elijah Shaw. "Our necks were burnt to a perfect blister." They were frequently whipped and "the famished condition of our bodies" spoke for the quality of the food.[8]

The officers, on the other hand, were spared such labor. From the terrace at the top of the house where they were quartered, they enjoyed a broad vista of the town, the bashaw's palace, the harbor, and the Mediterranean beyond. On arrival they also took in the melancholy sight of the *Philadelphia*, angled and astride the reef where she'd run aground. On their first day of incarceration, harbor boats shuttled back and forth, returning with plunder from the American ship. Trunks of clothes and other salvaged goods were offered to the captives but at such exorbitant prices that few of the officers could afford to buy back their own belongings.

Afforded pen and paper at the consulate, Captain Bainbridge wrote of the events, not only to his wife but also in a formal letter for dispatch to the secretary of the navy. "Misfortune necessitates me to make a communication, the most distressing of my life," he lamented. "It is with the deepest regret that I inform you of the loss of the United States Frigate *Philadelphia*."[9]

Bainbridge regarded the ship as beyond salvage, subject now to rot and ruin in the waves of the sea. Yet had he been atop the consulate a few hours later, he might have seen one of his fellow prisoners, the carpenter's mate, together with a crew of fifty men, being taken aboard the *Philadelphia*, supervised by their armed jailers. The pirates sensed that a storm was brewing and hoped that, with the wind rising, the morning would bring a storm surge that would lift the *Philadelphia* off the reef. If that happened, the carpenter was to supervise rapid repairs, and the men were to sail her in.

The pirates had read the weather correctly. A violent gale powered by westerly winds raised the *Philadelphia*. The once-stranded ship, lifted off the reef by the rising tide, floated free. Despite the holes drilled in her hull by her carpenters at Bainbridge's orders—or perhaps because of the repairs her men were forced to make by their captors—the sturdy USS *Philadelphia* remained seaworthy.

Bainbridge had bungled again. Had he held on a few hours longer, he might have been able to sail his ship off the reef. Instead, he had once again been part of an unnecessary surrender. Now in the full possession of the Tripolitans, the *Philadelphia* had become a prize of which the bashaw could be well and truly proud. The second prong of Preble's strategy—the attack on Tripoli—had gone terribly wrong.

CHAPTER 12

By the Cover of Darkness

> To strike [our flag] to any foe was mortifying, but to yield to an uncivilized, barbarous enemy, who were objects of contempt was humiliating.
>
> —**Captain William Bainbridge, USS *Philadelphia***

Commodore Preble knew nothing of the USS *Philadelphia*'s fate when, in mid-November, he delivered Tobias Lear, along with Lear's wife and their baggage, to the consul general's new post at Algiers.

On going ashore, Preble found the city a welcoming place. Richard O'Brien was still in residence, and would remain so until spring to ease Colonel Lear's adjustment to his new situation. Though the dey was absent at his country seat, O'Brien gave the new arrivals the tour.

In Algiers, Preble viewed the ruler's orchards, stables, granaries, and dockyards. The visitors took a turn through the palace gardens, which Preble thought so well tended that they had "the effect of enchantment." It was a most agreeable day, he wrote Mary back in Maine. He concluded that Algiers was "an enviable situation." Being a cautious man, he also acknowledged that "the caprice of the tyrant who governs makes it a dangerous residence."[1]

The next day the USS *Constitution* weighed anchor. Ready to resume the rigors of navy life, preparing to tend once again to his assigned task, Preble ordered the ship's course set for Tripoli to join Bainbridge.

The USS *Constitution* was nearing the Sardinian coast when, on November 24, a midsize ship flying the Union Jack was sighted. Once within hailing range, the foreign frigate identified herself as the HMS *Amazon.* Its British captain gave Preble the distressing news of the loss of the *Philadelphia.*

The commodore pushed the passing pleasures of his day in Algiers from his mind. All in a moment, the successful settlement at Morocco seemed long ago and far away. In its place loomed the knowledge that his hope to subdue Tripoli by spring had ground to a halt on that sandbar.

It pained him that Bainbridge and the 306 men in his command were captives. Preble knew, even in the absence of fresh orders from America, which could not arrive for months, that the freedom of the men aboard the *Philadelphia* must be obtained. Having nearly died during his incarceration aboard the British prison ship *Jersey*, he understood the terrors and trials of imprisonment. And he knew full well these events put the honor of the United States very much at stake.

Then the news got worse. Making straight for Malta, Preble found letters awaiting him from Captain Bainbridge. Not only had the *Philadelphia* been lost to the U.S. Navy but now it was a free-floating Tripolitan warship whose guns could be turned on the Americans. Even as Preble read the dispatches, the mighty frigate was being refitted under the watchful eye of the bashaw. Divers had recovered much of the weaponry that had been thrown overboard onto the shallow reef. Armed with her rescued weapons, the *Philadelphia* was the most powerful ship by far in any of the Barbary fleets.

The commodore promptly wrote to Washington, asking Congress for more frigates. Just a few weeks before, he held a winning hand when his four-of-a-kind frigates awed the sultan of Morocco. Since then three of them—the USS *New York*, USS *Adams*, and the USS *John Adams*—had sailed home for the States, part of the annual ebb and flow of men and ships. Confident in America's powerlessness, the Tripolitan leader would surely demand a king's ransom for the U.S. Navy mariners.

"This affair distresses me beyond description," he confided in the secretary of the navy. Preble also admitted new worries about the solo *Constitution*—"should any accident happen to this ship," he fretted, "the consequences may be dreadful to our commerce in these Seas." With his reduced fleet, he could no longer play the enforcer. At best, he could harass.

While the odds had shifted, Preble could not permit his adversaries to gain the upper hand. He recognized that the *Philadelphia* was the key piece—she must be removed from the game. Two young officers in Preble's command, the dashing young Philadelphian Lieutenant Stephen Decatur and his friend Lieutenant Charles Stewart, had already volunteered to sail into Tripoli and set her afire. But Preble told them that such a mission "was too hazardous to be effected in that way."[2] Left unspoken was that he could hardly afford to lose another ship if they were captured.

Preble did promise the eager Decatur that he might lead the mission once they had a plan. And the more Preble thought about it, the more he realized that any plan would be dangerous—but it was worth the risk. Writing to the secretary of the navy, he promised bluntly, "I shall hazard much to destroy her." He acknowledged that it might mean a loss of life. He didn't yet know how his small armada would do the job—but his mind was made up.

"It must be done," he wrote.[3]

But first they had to prepare a plan.

THE CAPTURE

On December 23, 1803, roughly two months after Bainbridge's capture, Preble's *Constitution* and the *Enterprise* sailed in tandem. The two ships made a fine team, with the *Enterprise* sailing along the Barbary Coast exchanging signals with the *Constitution*, which remained in deeper waters.

Preble was determined to maintain the Tripoli blockade even as he mourned the loss of the *Philadelphia*, but the rigors of winter weather had made keeping up the blockade difficult. During a two-week stormy span, the Americans harbored at the Sicilian port of Syracuse, a break that permitted the installation of new rigging on the *Enterprise* and new sails on the *Constitution*. During that time, the pirates at Tripoli had been free to come and go, but now the Americans were back and ready to fight.

At half past eight on the morning of December 23, nine miles east of Tripoli, the lookout at the masthead of the *Constitution* hailed the men on deck. He had spied two masts on the horizon. Preble signaled the *Enterprise* to pursue the ship they spotted. The *Constitution* would follow.

Young Stephen Decatur commanded the schooner *Enterprise.* Like many of his fellow sailors, he found parading the fleet and blockading ports to be dull work. After all, when a blockade worked properly, nothing happened because ships stayed in port. By nature, he favored more adventure. In his first two tours of duty in the Mediterranean, he had confronted no enemy in battle, and the ineffectiveness of Commodore Morris's time left Decatur itching for the chance to show his mettle. He had hopes for his chances under the determined Preble.

Now in pursuit of the unidentified ship, the *Enterprise* sailed beneath the Union Jack, hoping to keep her American identity a secret. Within the hour, the crew of Decatur's ship saw that their target flew Tripolitan colors. A shift in the wind permitted the *Enterprise* to gain on the boat, which was suddenly dead in the water. By ten o'clock, the Tripolitan captain, thinking he had nothing to fear from the Royal Navy, stood on deck with some twenty of his men, waiting to greet the approaching ship.

When the two American ships abruptly lowered the Union Jack and raised the Stars and Stripes, there was a flurry of confused activity aboard the Tripolitan vessel. However, as his ship was outgunned by the *Enterprise*, more than twice its size, the master of the little trader had no choice but to submit.

A U.S. Navy officer sent aboard the Tripolitan ship was told, through a translator, that the master was a Turk, his destination Constantinople. According to the captain, the vessel, called the *Mastico*, was only a small trading vessel of Ottoman registry, sailing the coast and making stops in Tripoli and Benghazi. The crew of eleven Greeks and Turks was in keeping with his claim. But the assortment of passengers seemed odd to the Americans. In addition to forty-two African slaves, there were two Tripolitan officers leading ten soldiers. The ship also had two cannons mounted on its deck and, doubly odd for a merchant, two more stowed below, along with a cache of muskets and pistols.

The *Mastico* carried no passport in English, and none of the Americans could read her papers, which were written in Arabic and Turkish. But one of the *Constitution*'s medical officers spotted a hole in the captain's story: A few weeks before, Preble had hired Dr. Pietro Francisco Corcillo to be his surgeon's mate, and Corcillo brought more than medical knowledge to the commodore's fleet. Having been the bashaw's personal physician, he knew Tripoli and its people well. When he got a look at the crew aboard the trader, Corcillo recognized its captain and its officers. This was no innocent trader, he told Preble. This ship had taken part in the capture of the *Philadelphia*.[4]

A thorough search of the small ship—it didn't take long, as the vessel was just sixty feet long, twelve wide—proved him right. An American sailor found a sword hidden aboard the *Mastico*, one that belonged to a lieutenant on the *Philadelphia*. It was proof enough to Preble that her men had been among those who plundered the American frigate.

That made the *Mastico* a prize of war, and Preble ordered a crew to go aboard the vessel. They were to sail her to Syracuse where, in February, an admiralty court would condemn the ship, and officially award her to the United States.

By then, however, she had already been given a new name, a new master, and orders to return to Tripoli harbor.

A SPY WITHIN

Preble had been busily gathering intelligence on the workings of Tripoli, but the best information came from William Bainbridge. Under house arrest in Tripoli, Bainbridge could see with his own eyes—and a spyglass provided by Consul Nissen—what happened in the harbor. He also had a means of communicating with the Americans; the bashaw permitted him to send letters, believing that a captive was his own best advocate for securing ransom payments. But because his captors read his letters before sending them, Bainbridge couldn't simply report on the results of his reconnaissance. At least not in the usual way.

Determined to be of service even during his imprisonment, Bainbridge found clandestine means by which to impart information that might be of military use. At first, he employed a cypher, coding his communications. When the bashaw started to suspect the code, Bainbridge resorted to "sympathetic ink," a dilute mix of lime or lemon juice. Using that method, invisible messages written between visible lines on a page emerged as a readable brown when held to a flame. Writing in letters and in books borrowed from the ever-helpful Consul Nissen, William Bainbridge helped Preble lay the groundwork for a secret scheme.[5]

Since his capture, Bainbridge had reported on the business of the harbor, including the coming and going of the cruisers. He listed the ships launched and in the works. He counted the guns in the "Marine force of this Regency (as near as I can learn)."[6] Most valuable of all, he kept his commanding officer informed of the bashaw's plans regarding the *Philadelphia*.

By early December, the ship's cannons had been restored to her decks. She remained moored in the harbor, where her presence was a painful reminder to Bainbridge of that awful October day. But her presence also got him thinking.

His notion, he wrote to Preble on December 5, was to destroy her using powder and shot. Bainbridge thought the job might be done by a "Merchant Vessel . . . [sent] into the Harbour, with the men secreted and steering directly on board the Frigate." The mission faced little danger from Tripolitan artillery, as many of the gunboats in the harbor had been hauled up onto the beach for the winter and, as far as he could tell, only four shore guns pointed at the *Philadelphia*. He was certain the Tripolitans could be taken completely by surprise.

The captain offered his plan humbly. After all, he was the one whose honor was at stake in the *Philadelphia*'s capture, not Preble. "I beg that you not consider me too officious," he wrote to Preble, "in giving my ideas on a conjectural practicability."

When he read Bainbridge's letter, Preble realized that solving the *Philadelphia* problem might not be a suicide mission after all. If he put together his best thinking, along with Decatur's daring and Bainbridge's reconnaissance, there just might be a solution. Perhaps Preble already had on hand the right ingredients: a mix of luck—he already had a "Merchant Vessel," the *Mastico*—and pluck of the sort that the eager Lieutenant Decatur seemed to possess in abundance.

THE HAMET OPTION

Preble was also developing a larger secret strategy. With Jefferson's and Madison's authorization, Consul Eaton and others had continued talking to Sidi Hamet Qaramanli, brother of Yusuf. He still wanted his rightful place on the throne as bashaw of Tripoli, but to get it he needed American help. When letters from Hamet's agents reached Preble, he arranged to meet the men in Malta.

Hamet had traveled to Alexandria, Egypt, they told Preble, and was still very much in exile. But he had a plan, too, and he also had followers. Hamet would assemble a large army of Arabs. If the Americans could help underwrite the venture and provide some naval support, this force might march overland from Egypt to Derne, a provincial capital in eastern Tripoli. With the help of American firepower from the sea, Hamet and Eaton believed, Tripoli could be taken back.

Hamet also had a promise for the Americans, one that Preble knew would please his superiors. If the Americans aided him with money and military equipment in his quest, Hamet, once restored to his rightful place as bashaw, would release all Christian slaves and captives, including the 307 men who had been aboard the *Philadelphia*. He would also agree to a permanent peace with the United States. Furthermore, he would allow the U.S. Navy to make Tripoli its permanent base and to garrison the main fort.

Though he could make no commitment without approval from Washington, Preble applauded the plan—and he immediately wrote to the secretary of the navy saying so. "Though destitute of Money, Powder, [and] Field Artillery . . . he thinks our assistance by sea would put him in possession of Tripoly; and I am very certain that it would in less than two Months."[7] He encouraged Hamet's representatives, telling them something of his thinking about an assault on Tripoli once his squadron regained the ships and firepower required.

While the two sides left their meetings with optimism about what would be done in the spring and summer, Preble's concerns were more immediate. He had told Hamet's agents nothing of the plan for the *Philadelphia*. Even a hint of that plan, if it was to be overheard in the wrong quarters, could result in a disastrous failure and many lives lost.

During Preble's January 1804 meetings in Malta, he had another conversation. The Tripolitan ambassador presented him with the bashaw's demand: $100,000 for the prisoners. There was talk of exchanging the *Philadelphia* for a schooner—the Tripolitans admitted they didn't have the skilled sailors to sail the big frigate, despite the presence of High Admiral Murat Rais, the renegade Scotsman. But Preble was in no hurry to make a deal. For one thing, he lacked the required funds; for another, he hoped the ransom would not be necessary.

A DANGEROUS MISSION

The orders made the operation sound simple. "Enter the Harbor in the night," Preble instructed. "Board the Frigate Philadelphia, burn her and make your retreat good."[8]

The recipient of those orders, Lieutenant Stephen Decatur Jr., intended to execute them to the letter, but Mother Nature refused to cooperate. As his little two-ship fleet neared Tripoli harbor on February 7, a big blow from the north drove both U.S. Navy ships many miles east of their destination. Only after the three-day gale finally quieted did a five-day sail bring Decatur's little *Intrepid*, along with the USS *Syren*, back within striking distance of Tripoli harbor.

Crowded conditions prevailed aboard the *Intrepid*. She was the former *Mastico,* rechristened and reconfigured as a warship. Designed for a crew of two dozen, the little ship was now manned by seventy-five men. With berths for fewer than a third of those aboard, Decatur shared his small cabin with three other officers and the ship's surgeon while many men bedded down among the casks in the rat-infested hold. Spoiled food, heavy seas, and the fear that their little ship might founder did nothing for morale. But at last, late in the morning on February 16, the *Intrepid* was almost at its destination.

The plan called for the *Intrepid* to run ahead, as it had been rerigged with short masts and triangular sails, mimicking the look of local ships; its appearance should raise no alarms. The USS *Syren* would trail five miles behind. The planners of the mission—Preble and Decatur (with guidance from Bainbridge)—had ordered that the look of the military brig be altered, too, so the *Syren* had a fresh coat of paint. Her topgallant masts had been removed and her gun ports closed.

As dark approached, the *Intrepid* was to anchor at the mouth of the harbor, east of the town. Then, after the arrival of the *Syren*, the *Intrepid* and the boats from the *Syren* would make for the *Philadelphia* under the cover of night. The lieutenants and midshipmen would then lead teams of sailors aboard the frigate to set her afire. They would destroy the ship, boosting American morale and snatching the advantage from their enemies. It would be a master stroke—if it worked.

Almost immediately, the plan went awry. Decatur realized that the easy sail into Tripoli was too easy: the *Intrepid*, normally a slow sailer, was making good speed and ran the risk of arriving in daylight. Not daring to shorten the sails—a wary sentinel might be suspicious of a merchant slowing his progress—Decatur ordered his men to toss overboard a drag line rigged with ladders, spars, buckets, and lumber in hopes that the resistance of all of the debris would slow the ship down.

After a scramble of activity to get the drag line overboard, there were a few tense minutes of waiting. Then the sailors breathed a sigh of relief as the ship slowed while still appearing to be sailing full speed ahead. Their plan had worked, and they could count on the darkness to help avoid discovery.

Decatur ordered most of his crew to remain below. Just six men at a time could walk the deck, and those who did wore the uniform of Maltese merchant sailors, with showy gold braid. The British flag they flew also seemed to fool those onshore. As they came within sight of the English fort at Tripoli, the English colors that waved over the *Intrepid* were answered by the raising of the Union Jack at the British consulate.

For Decatur, this slow sail into Tripoli was bittersweet. He had asked to head this dangerous expedition and desperately wanted to prove his bravery in battle. His reward for success, he hoped, would be a captaincy in the small U.S. Navy, where only a few gained such a promotion. But his assignment was to destroy a ship built with money raised by the citizens of and handmade by the shipwrights of his home city, for which the frigate was named. And her first captain had been his own father, Stephen Decatur Sr.

At dusk, the wind dropped. As the *Intrepid* negotiated the narrows at the harbor entrance at seven o'clock, Decatur could see that the *Syren* had fallen well behind in the diminishing breeze, despite the *Intrepid*'s intentional slowdown. It was a moment for naval calculus: the plan called for an attack at ten o'clock, and it would take much of the time remaining for Decatur to work his ship over to the

Philadelphia. The *Syren* was well back, and it would not be able to make up the distance in time.

For Decatur, failure was not an option. He remembered Preble's orders: "I rely with confidence on your Intrepedity & Enterprize."[9] Decatur saw his choice as between aborting the mission and taking the *Intrepid* in alone.

In the twilight, he had little time to decide. Emboldened by the frustrations of serving under Morris, proud of the trust Preble put in him, Decatur made the call. He told his men they would sail on, despite the absence of the *Syren.*

One of his midshipmen recorded Decatur's quiet words: "The fewer the number the greater the honor."[10]

As darkness fell, the light of a crescent moon revealed the *Philadelphia* in silhouette. She was a heartrending sight to Decatur and his men. Her foremast remained a stump, and her upper yards were laid out on the deck. Stripped of sails, she could go nowhere under her own power. Yet her sheer scale seemed awesome in a harbor where little local boats skimmed the waves. To see the frigate's guns remounted and to imagine them manned by Tripoli pirates? That was too horrible even to contemplate.

The *Intrepid* made her way slowly down the channel, an almost imperceptible wind puffing her sails. The castle and shore fortifications seemed to grow taller as the crew covered the distance. Decatur's little ship was dwarfed as it floated closer to the white walls of the city—and the gun batteries on her ramparts. Any lookout from the city could see them, but he would have no reason to be alarmed by the little ship's appearance.

As the ten o'clock hour approached, the *Intrepid* came within hailing distance of the *Philadelphia*. Decatur's seventy-man crew, obeying his order of wordless silence, heard the exchange.

A Tripolitan spoke from the tall frigate. In a foreign tongue, he ordered the smaller vessel to keep away.

Though he stood by the helm, Decatur remained silent. In his stead, Salvador Catalano answered. A Sicilian hired by Preble for his knowledge of Barbary harbors, Catalano was fluent in the common tongue of sailors in the southern Mediterranean, a mix of Berber, Arabic, Italian, Spanish, Portuguese, and Maltese.

Catalano called back that his merchant vessel had been stripped of its anchors during the violent storm the preceding week; they sought only a safe place to tether their little ship for the night. He explained that they didn't want to risk fouling the lines of other ships in the harbor and, in the morning, would secure new anchors ashore.

Another voice from above asked the name of the ship observed offshore in the direction from which the *Intrepid* had come. Catalano offered a well-rehearsed reply, one he knew the men aboard the *Philadelphia* wanted to hear. He told his inquisitor the ship they spied was the *Transfer*. That vessel was a former British warship, recently purchased in Malta by the bashaw, and much awaited in Tripoli to reinforce his navy.

Catalano's answers satisfied the men aboard the *Philadelphia*, and the two ships—the little *Intrepid* and the looming frigate—dispatched boats carrying lines to fasten them to each other. With the cables bound fast, the ships were soon being drawn together.

As the *Intrepid* neared, a sharp-eyed Tripolitan spotted something amiss. Perhaps the anchors aboard the *Intrepid* had been seen. Maybe it was the glint of sword worn by one of the dozens of sailors lying in the shadows cast by the bulwarks. Whatever the tell, the game was nearly up.

"Americanos!" came the cry.

Once again Catalano spoke, his manner unruffled. He offered assurances that only Maltese and Englishmen were aboard. With the men aboard the *Intrepid* continuing to haul the hawsers, the ships were soon alongside.

This time, when the shout *"Americanos! Americanos!"* rang out again, the warning came too late. As the ships touched, Stephen Decatur issued a simple order, uttered as he himself leapt for the main chains of the *Philadelphia* to climb the dozen feet to the deck of the taller ship.

The one-word order—"*Board!*" Decatur yelled—initiated a blur of action.

"The effect was truly electric," Surgeon's Mate Lewis Heermann would later write. "Not a man had been seen or heard to breathe a moment before; at the next, the boarders hung on the ship's side like cluster bees; and, in another instant, every man was on board the frigate."[11]

No gunshots echoed. Decatur had decreed that only blades were to be used, because the invaders wanted to attract as little attention as possible to the fight for the *Philadelphia*, which was moored just a few hundred yards from the fortress guns. Of the thirty or so Tripolitans aboard the ship, roughly a dozen ran for a boat and rowed for safety. Of those who fought the boarding party, one midshipman remembered, "[They] were dreadfully alarmed when they found who we were. Poor fellows! About 20 of them were cut to pieces & the rest jumped overboard."[12]

In less than ten minutes, the savage fight was over without having attracted the notice of sentries onshore, and the carefully planned torching of the ship could begin. A team of ten men went below to set fire to the berth deck and forward storeroom. A dozen men went deeper into the ship to the wardroom and steerage, a third squad to the cockpit and storeroom. A fourth team manned the *Intrepid*'s cutter, patrolling the area in the harbor boat used to ferry passengers and goods, while eight men remained aboard the little ketch.

The fire crews carried three-inch-long candles, with wicks that had been immersed in turpentine to enhance their flammability, and each team had a pair of lanterns. With the Tripolitan defenders subdued, combustibles were swiftly handed up from the *Intrepid* and taken below. The disciplined operation proceeded at speed and, in a matter of minutes, the men waited at their stations for Decatur's next command.

Walking the deck from forward to aft, he called his simple order down each hatchway—*Fire!*—and the men, their candles lit from the lanterns, ignited dozens of conflagrations in every part of the ship.

As the men raced to return to the deck, columns of suffocating smoke rose in columns from the hatches. Flames soon followed as the sailors and officers alike leapt back aboard the *Intrepid.* Decatur watched as the last of his men climbed down to the deck of the ketch—only one sailor had been wounded, none killed. Decatur himself would be the last man to step off the deck of the *Philadelphia*—and he did so in dramatic style, leaping into the rigging of the *Intrepid.*

Back aboard their little ship, the crew attempted to escape the harbor but were momentarily trapped. The flames roaring forth from every gun port on the *Philadelphia* threatened the cotton sail fluttering from the foremast of the getaway boat. They used swords to cut the rope connecting the two boats, but the smaller ship still refused

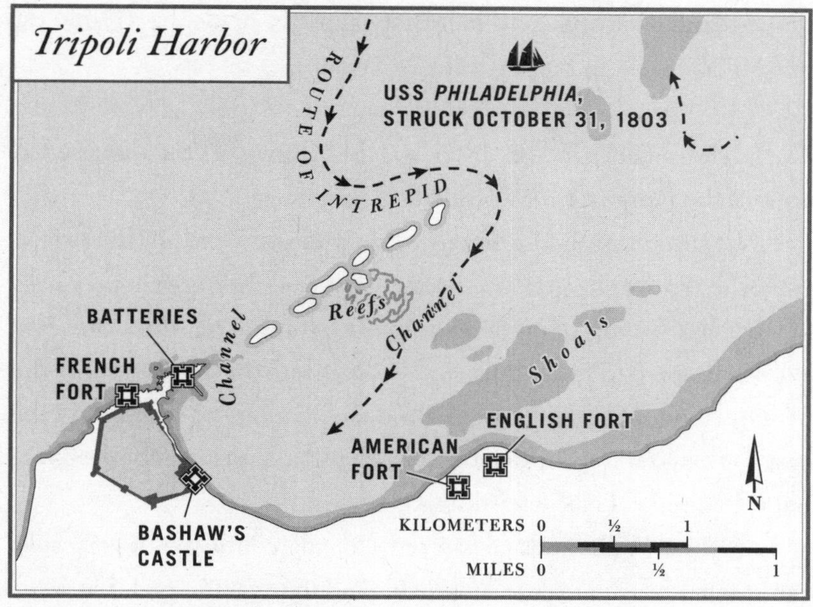

to sail free. The hungry fire, which seemed to be inhaling every breath of air, drew the *Intrepid* back. Only after Decatur ordered a crew to man a boat to tow the bow around did the sails fill. Men took hold of the great oars, eight to a side, and stroked until they were in open water.

As the *Intrepid* made her retreat, harassing fire from Tripolitan cannons and muskets threatened Decatur's vessel, but the poorly aimed gunfire struck only her upper sails. Much more dangerous than the volleys from shore were the cannons aboard the *Philadelphia*, which discharged as the fire consumed the gun deck. But even the report of the frigate's long guns could not drown out the three hearty cheers issuing from the American sailors as they headed out to sea. By then flames had licked up the mastheads and begun consuming the rigging at the tops. The sight of the columns of flame, topped with what appeared to be fiery capitals, made a terrifying yet magnificent sight in the night sky of Tripoli.

The night of February 16, 1804, would be one that the imprisoned crew of the *Philadelphia* would never forget.

The tumult in the harbor awakened the city and, in the prison yard, the captives heard the screams of women; the harsh, loud voices of men; and the report of the guns in the harbor. The Americans had expected something as they had recognized the *Intrepid* and the *Syren* just out of reach of the harbor the previous afternoon. As the castle guns fired on the departing *Intrepid*, the prison floors shook, but the sounds of battle represented hope.

As sailor William Ray reported, "In the confusion of voices we could often hear the word American, and therefore hoped that some of our countrymen were landing, to liberate us."[13] Their hope for rescue was not realized, they found the next morning, when they learned of the demise of the *Philadelphia*. The once proud ship now lay on the rocks, free of her anchors after her cables burned. She was a smoking hulk, reduced to a long row of ribs barely visible at the waterline. The frigate would never put to sea as a pirate ship.

The burning of the American ship was a victory for the American navy but a blow for the captives. Just the day before the bashaw, anticipating that his terms of a prisoner exchange would be accepted, had sent two barrels of pork and beef to the men in the bagnio. Now, with the burning of the *Philadelphia*, all goodwill evaporated just as quickly as it had appeared. The jail keepers, Ray reported, "like so many fiends from the infernal regions, rushed in among us and began to beat everyone they could see, spitting in our faces, and hissing like the serpents of hell. . . . [E]very boy we met in the streets, would spit on us and pelt us with stones; our tasks doubled, our bread withheld, and every driver exercised cruelties tenfold more rigid and intolerable than before."[14]

Unaware of the suffering of their compatriots, Decatur and his men were well on their way to safety, and a two-day sail brought them within range of Syracuse harbor. The sight of the *Intrepid* and the *Syren* was a great relief to Commodore Preble; he had wondered at the seaworthiness of the little ship a week before when the violent storm had buffeted his ships at anchor. Both ships could have gone down, yet here they were.

Signal flags were quickly hoisted. The USS *Constitution* signaled: *"Business or Enterprize, have you completed, that you were sent on?"*

On the quarterdeck of the frigate, anxious minutes ticked by. Then the answering flags could be read slowly. For Preble, it was most gratifying to read the message: *"Business, I have completed, that I was sent on."*

CHAPTER 13

The Battle of Tripoli

I find hand to hand is not child's play, 'tis kill or be killed.

—Lieutenant Stephen Decatur[1]

More than four months passed before anyone in Washington knew anything of the fate of the USS *Philadelphia.* Since the previous autumn of 1803, mail had accumulated in Malta; letters home from sailors, dispatches from Preble, and consular correspondence remained unsent. Only when Commodore Preble stumbled upon a cache of mail in the charge of a former consul to the bashaw who spoke no English did four great stacks of long-delayed correspondence begin their transatlantic journey in early February.[2]

That meant President Jefferson learned of the grounding of the USS *Philadelphia*—but not of its sacrificial fire—on March 19, 1804. It also meant that, for the third winter in a row, despite Preble's good efforts, only ill tidings reached Washington from the Barbary Coast.

Jefferson's political enemies used the news of the frigate's capture like a club. By the end of March, Alexander Hamilton's *New York Evening Post* termed it "a practical lesson in Jefferson's economy"—if there'd been more ships in the Mediterranean, the argument went, the loss could have been averted.[3] Rather than disagree, Jefferson went to Congress and made the argument that the bad news meant even more firepower was needed. Within a week, he had authorization to spend a million dollars to supplement the fleet with leased gunboats and two new ships. In addition, a bill was introduced to raise customs duties by 2.5 percent to establish a "Mediterranean Fund" to pay for the war. The House unanimously approved the measure and, the same day, the Senate passed it by a vote of 20 to 5.

Orders went out for four more frigates to sail for the Mediterranean. With almost the entire U.S. Navy in or on its way to service off the North African coast, Jefferson intended "to leave no doubt of our compelling the existing Enemy to submit to our own terms, and of effectually checking any hostile dispositions that might be entertained towards us by any of the other Barbary Powers."[4] The *President*, *Congress*, *Essex*, and *Constellation* would require time to be refitted and provisioned, so the latest fleet—all veteran ships at this point—would not return to the region until summer, but the full force of the United States Navy had finally been mustered.

Behind the scenes, Secretary of State Madison quietly tried to allay the concerns of the families of the 307 *Philadelphia* men in captivity, offering the "sympathy of the Executive." But he made no promises. The U.S. government wouldn't be offering to buy the freedom of Captain Bainbridge and his men anytime soon because "of the encouragement it might hold out to the other Barbary States, and even to Tripoli, to repeat their aggressions."[5]

Then, like a lightning bolt, the news of Decatur's successful raid electrified Washington. Word of the burning of the *Philadelphia* had already shocked Europe. No less a military man than Lord Nelson called Decatur's exploit "the most bold and daring act of the age."[6] On hearing the news, Jefferson promptly awarded his brave lieutenant a captaincy (though Decatur would not learn of his promotion until September), and Congress voted to award Decatur a ceremonial sword and his men two months' bonus pay. The entire country celebrated. By early June, New Yorkers saw the opening of a silent play, a pantomime entitled *Preparations for the Recapture of the Frigate Philadelphia*.

Stephen Decatur and his seventy-five-man crew had transformed a humiliation into an act of heroism. For Jefferson, this shift in tides also had a practical meaning. As one Barbary consul told James Madison, "The burning of the *Philadelphia*, under the Bashaw's forts . . . is the only occurrence, which has forced them to view the *American character* with proper respect."[7] This was progress, a long-awaited sign that American forces could make a significant difference in the region.

IF NOT PEACE, THEN BOMBARDMENT

Meanwhile, on the other side of the Atlantic, Commodore Preble decided he would give peace one more chance—and he hoped to gain freedom for the men of the *Philadelphia*. An array of American ships bore up on Tripoli harbor on a June day in 1804. Captain Preble stationed the USS *Argus* and the USS *Enterprise* as lookouts to the west. He sent the USS *Vixen* to the east, along with his newest ship, the *Scourge*, recently captured from the Tripolitan navy.

Flying a white flag of truce, he ordered his flagship, the USS *Constitution*, to set sail for the city. At noon on June 13, 1804, anchored where the water was a safe depth of twenty-four fathoms, Preble dispatched a barge carrying Richard O'Brien to present American terms of peace to Bashaw Yusuf Qaramanli. Chief Consul Tobias Lear, unable to leave his post in Algiers, had deputized O'Brien to act as his representative.

As the little vessel neared shore, O'Brien could see some of the Philadelphia's officers waving their hats at him. He would have liked nothing better than to secure their freedom before the day was over.

Preble's charge to O'Brien sounded simple: "to endeavor to ransom our unfortunate Countrymen, and if the bashaw should desire it, to establish Peace."[8] Lear had authorized a larger payment, but Preble specified what he thought were reasonable terms. O'Brien was instructed to offer $40,000 in ransom, along with a $10,000 "present" (that is, bribe) for the prime minister and others. A treaty of peace might be entered into, but, Preble told O'Brien, "I cannot pay one cent for Peace."[9] Payment for ransom was a stretch as it was.

The bashaw's representatives kept O'Brien waiting for an hour on the beach. "The Tyrant," as Preble called the Tripolitan ruler, still beside himself at the burning of the *Philadelphia* within sight of his own castle, refused to see O'Brien and rejected the offer relayed to him out of hand. He was insulted by the offer; it was so much less than he had imagined, *and* he suspected the Americans' real motive was espionage. Thinking O'Brien might be gathering intelligence about the city and its armaments, he refused permission for the American consul to enter the town and forbade him to meet with Captain Bainbridge or visit the other prisoners. He did not allow clothing to be sent ashore for the captives, and his men dropped the white flag of truce as soon as O'Brien returned to the *Constitution*.

The conclusion was clear. Once again, as Preble confided to his diary, we "must endeavor to beat & distress his savage highness into a disposition more favourable to our views than what he at present possesses."[10] Persuasion and pacifism had not worked. The Americans would have to speak to the bashaw in a way that would force him to respond reasonably. That, Preble believed, was something a bombardment could certainly do.

WILLIAM EATON, SECRET AGENT

Meanwhile, at home, the news of the *Philadelphia* had been good for William Eaton's pet cause. After his expulsion by the bey of Tunis in early March 1803, Eaton had returned to the United States. On arrival at Boston in May, he visited his wife in the central Massachusetts town of Brimfield; they had been separated by an ocean for four and a half years. By June, however, he was striding the streets of the nation's capital, "urg[ing] the administration to the adoption of more vigorous measures against Tripoli."[11]

More than anything, Eaton wanted to persuade the powers that be to support his plan to replace Bashaw Yusuf on Tripoli's throne with the exiled Hamet Qaramanli. He also wanted to be the leader of the expedition that would land in Alexandria, join Hamet, and march to Derne, as Preble schemed. Eaton was the driving force on the American side, writing to the Speaker of the House of Representatives, detailing his case and meeting with Secretary of State Madison.

In a meeting with the president's cabinet, Eaton thought Jefferson *"civil"* and his attorney general *"grave"* as he "endeavored to enforce conviction . . . of the necessity of meeting the aggressions of Barbary by retaliation."[12] The secretary of war was skeptical, but the secretary of the navy, Robert Smith, was won over. Growing cautiously optimistic, Eaton commissioned a custom scimitar to be fashioned for himself of the finest Spanish steel. He also ordered tents, saddles, and cooking equipment. He wanted to be ready.[13]

Eaton had at least one ally in Preble, but for a time nothing had happened. With the congressional session at an end, Eaton traveled north. He spent much of the summer and fall tending to his hardscrabble New England farm. During the next congressional session, however, he returned to Washington. If at first he again found many of those he met indifferent to him, the news of the loss of the USS *Philadelphia* shifted the balance. Suddenly, there were ears in Washington more attuned to his ideas. On March 30, 1804, eleven days after the shocking news of the frigate's grounding but not her destruction had reached American shores, Eaton was "engaged to take the management of an Enterprize on the coast of Barbary."[14]

The long, sticky summer that followed proved eventful for the young nation. The exploration team led by Meriwether Lewis and William Clark began its journey up the Missouri River. In July, Alexander Hamilton was shot and killed in a duel by Vice President Aaron Burr, and the further conflict in Europe provoked by Napoleon had America's foreign affairs in a state of uncertainty.

As for President Jefferson, he was dealing with his own personal tragedy. His beloved Mary, whom he had nicknamed "Polly" so long ago and whose safety upon the seas had made the matter of Barbary piracy personal, died in childbirth in April. Her father and her husband were both at her deathbed, and she was buried beside her mother on the grounds of Monticello. Jefferson was deeply affected by Polly's passing. "My loss is great indeed," he wrote to a friend in June. "Others may lose of their abundance, but I, of my want, have lost even the half of all I had. . . . The hope with which I had looked forward to the moment when, resigning public cares to younger hands, I was to retire to that domestic comfort from which the last great step is to be taken, is fearfully blighted."[15]

Jefferson was nearing the end of his first term as president and eyeing a second one, but his passion for life and zeal for leadership had been extinguished with Polly's death. Former first lady Abigail Adams, wife of Jefferson's friend and rival John Adams, broke the years-long silence between the two families by sending her deepest condolences. The gesture proved to be the first step in mending the friendship that had been so deeply—and some thought irreconcilably—damaged during the contentious election of 1800.

But world events would not stop for Jefferson's mourning. Eaton's quest moved forward, with Eaton ordered to act as a liaison with Hamet. Madison wrote to the Barbary chief consul Tobias Lear authorizing the plan, though he did so in his usual cautious fashion. "Of the co-operation of the Elder brother of the Bashaw of Tripoli we are . . . willing to avail ourselves."[16] Madison also instructed Lear to make available to Eaton $20,000 to carry out the plan.

There were other changes to the American strategy as well. The time had come for another changing of the guard and, after serving honorably and with distinction, Preble was to return home and Commodore Samuel Barron, who had been with the first fleet as the captain of the *Philadelphia* two years before her fateful wreck, was to take his place. In his orders to the new squadron commander, the secretary of the navy authorized a plan involving the ex-bashaw—one in which, the secretary advised, "you will, it is believed, find Mr Eaton extremely useful to you."[17]

When, after multiple delays, Commodore Barron's squadron sailed from Norfolk on July 5, 1804, one of those aboard his flagship was William Eaton, U.S. Navy agent for the Barbary regencies. Eaton's salary was a modest $1,200 a year and his immediate task was to win Barron's enthusiastic support before he could throw himself into planning the ground offensive.

He knew he was embarking on the adventure of a lifetime, but he had no idea the extent of the warfare into which he was sailing.

A SMALL VICTORY

In the Mediterranean, on August 3, 1804, the long-suppressed tension in the bashaw's harbor broke out into battle.

Commodore Preble had spent much of the previous week dealing with heavy seas off the Tripoli coast where he tried to maintain his blockade. A strong gale brought the month of July to a close, and Preble, with a new assortment of ships at his command, had new worries as well. He knew the schooners accompanying him, the *Vixen* and *Nautilus*, were seaworthy, as were the two brigs *Argus* and *Syren*, which had been blockading the harbor for many weeks. But he couldn't be so sure about the six gunboats and the two mortar boats on loan from Sicily, which was now also at war with the bashaw. Preble had reached an understanding to borrow these boats, along with some men to sail them, but he worried whether the flat-bottomed harbor craft could withstand the weather of the open sea.

Somehow, though, they had, and now he would put them to the test in battle.

With the weather clear at last, Preble surveyed his enemy from the deck of the *Constitution*. Through his spyglass he counted 115 guns mounted on the city's fortifications. These cannons were supplemented by nineteen gunboats and several small corsairs, all sheltered behind the long line of rocks that, like an immense, submerged stone wall, stood between the American armada in the open sea and the protected harbor. The combined firepower of the American and allied ships—132 guns and 2 mortars—was more or less equal to the Tripolitan guns, but the range of most of Preble's short-barreled cannonades was limited. Still, Preble felt confident that he and his men could make "[the bashaw's] old walls rattle about his ears."[18] All he needed was the opportunity.

Then, at noon on August 3, Preble finally saw his chance to engage the enemy. He observed from his station two miles out to sea that enemy gunboats were coming out from behind the stony barrier reef, leaving them exposed in the open water. He ordered the signal hoisted: *Prepare for battle.*

With his entire flotilla within hearing distance of his hailing trumpet, the commodore issued his final orders. The brigs and schooners, with the gunboats in tow, were to sail halfway to the stone barrier. From there the gunboats would head for the shore while the four larger ships remained in deeper waters. The bombing ships would take a position west of the town. The *Constitution* would follow the smaller boats toward the harbor and, on Preble's signal, the firing would begin.

By two o'clock, the gunboats were under their own power, advancing on the harbor with sails and oars. At two-thirty, the flagship raised a blue flag, followed by a yellow and blue one, and the third and last, red and blue. This was the signal for the battle to begin, and the *Constitution*, followed by the brigs and schooners, sailed for the harbor.

Fifteen minutes later, the first mortars boomed. Rather than cannonballs, the ships' guns launched hollow projectiles, packed with charges of gunpowder. Flying in a high arc into the city, some exploded in midair, scattering deadly shrapnel in all directions.

The Tripolitans fired back and the American gunboats responded in kind. The *Constitution*, now within a mile of Tripoli's batteries, opened fire with its long guns. The fortress batteries were silenced as the gunners took shelter from the Constitution's broadsides, though, as the big ship sailed past, the Tripolitans resumed firing. "I most sensibly felt the want of another frigate," Preble observed later.[19]

The USS *Constitution* served well, despite taking a cannonball to her mainmast. With Preble standing nearby, another blasted one of the ship's guns; shrapnel shattered a sailor's arm, but Preble escaped with just torn garments.[20] The big frigate and the other larger ships provided covering fire, but the heart of the battle unfolded nearer the waterline. There it was gunboat-to-gunboat and man-to-man.

Within the fortress walls, the American captives could hear little beyond the rumble of guns. On the streets of Tripoli, the townspeople ran for their guns in a scene of excited disorder. At last, the bashaw was getting the full-fledged war he had seemed so keen on provoking for the last three years.

The American gunboats, although outnumbered nineteen to six, bore down on the enemy's boats. Stephen Decatur, captaining one gunboat and accompanied by four other gunboats—the sixth lagged behind—fired at two Tripolitan boats at point-blank range until they retreated behind the line of rocks that protected the inner harbor. Sailing off to find other prey, Decatur's boat, followed by the gunboat commanded by his younger brother James and two other gunboats, headed for a line of five Tripolitan boats moored at the mouth of the harbor's western passage. After a round of American canister shot and musketry, those boats also pulled back into the harbor.

The little American squadron advanced next on a division of nine enemy vessels to the east. None of these fled as Decatur and his men sailed straight at them, looking to get close enough to board. The Americans wished to turn the Tripolitan tactic back upon them, leaping aboard the enemy vessels and fighting hand-to-hand with pistol, saber, pike, and tomahawk. This tactic did not favor the Americans, as a typical two-dozen-man U.S. Navy crew would be met by up to fifty men aboard a Tripolitan ship. But the numbers didn't daunt Decatur: "I always thought we could lick them their own way and give them two to one."[21]

Not long after three o'clock, he had a chance to prove his confidence.

The gunboats closed on the enemy, firing barrage after barrage of round shot. As the Americans neared the westernmost Tripolitan vessel, the enemy fired their pistols but, before they could reload, the Americans clambered from gunwale to gunwale and leapt onto their decks.

Within ten bloody minutes, Decatur's nineteen men had killed sixteen Tripolitans, wounded fifteen others, and taken the remaining five prisoner. Decatur personally lowered the Tripolitan flag.

Meanwhile, Lieutenant James Decatur, Stephen's brother, aimed for the largest of the Tripolitan gunboats and softened up the enemy with intense fire. As his gunboat closed and James Decatur and his men were poised to board, the Tripolitan captain, with a large portion of his crew already dead or wounded by musket and canister fire, ordered his colors struck in surrender.

For a moment, each Decatur brother possessed a prize.

Putting himself at the front of the boarding party, James stepped aboard the captured Tripolitan vessel. As he did so, the treacherous Tripolitan captain shot him at point-blank range.[22] The young lieutenant, struck in the forehead, tumbled into the sea between the two craft. As the American crew pulled their commander from the water, the master of the Tripolitan gunboat ordered his crew to pull for their harbor.

A dishonorable act left a brave officer, his life in the balance, bleeding on the deck.

When Stephen Decatur's boat, towing a captured ship of its own, happened upon James's boat, a short time later, the crew informed Stephen that his younger brother was hovering between life and death.

Suddenly, the thrill of battle was gone from Decatur's eyes, replaced by the cold fury of a man set on revenge. Taking a small crew of eleven men, he set out to chase down the enemy ship that had acted so deceitfully and swore that the murderous captain would find no mercy at his hand. Decatur's crew, some of whom had been part of the *Philadelphia* mission, were determined to follow their leader to hell and back, and proved it in the ensuing fight.

Racing through the water, they managed to spot the very ship they sought and swarmed upon it with a shout.

Decatur went for the captain of the enemy ship, a muscular man of imposing height. The American wielded a pike, a wooden pole with an iron spearhead, long a favorite infantry weapon for close combat. His powerful opponent, avoiding the thrust of Decatur's pike, managed to get one hand, then two, on its wooden shaft. The two men struggled briefly before the stronger Tripolitan wrenched the pike from Decatur's grasp.

As his adversary turned his own weapon against him, Decatur drew his saber to counter the coming blow. Though he deflected the pike, Decatur's blade broke at the hilt.

An instant later, his opponent thrust again, aiming for Decatur's heart. Decatur leapt aside, but the tip of the blade penetrated the flesh of his upper chest. He grappled for the weapon and, as the two men tumbled to the deck, Decatur managed to wrest the weapon from his opponent's grip and pull the blade from his wound.

The pike clattered out of reach.

Their hands now empty of weapons, the two men rolled and wrestled. The Tripolitan reached for a slim dagger that hung at his waist and a Tripolitan sailor, seeing his commander in a life-and-death embrace on the deck, raised his sword to strike Decatur.

The American was as good as dead, but as the Tripolitan's scimitar arced toward Decatur's exposed skull, a sailor named Daniel Frazier, already wounded in the fight, launched himself into the path of the blade, taking the blow for his captain. Frazier sustained a deep head wound, but the captains fought on.

Though weakened by the wound in his bloodied shoulder, Decatur held his opponent's blade away from his throat. With his other hand, he felt for his own pocket—and his pistol. Grasping the gun, he cocked it and, twisting the barrel away from himself, pulled the trigger.

When the ball ripped into his abdomen, the Tripolitan's body went slack.

Decatur had won this contest. But the victory—the Tripolitan gunboat was his—was soon diminished by word of his brother's condition.

By four-thirty Preble, noting a change in the wind, signaled his ships to retire from the action. Within fifteen minutes, all his vessels were out of range of the Tripolitan guns.

As evening fell, the fates of both Daniel Frazier and James Decatur hung in the balance. Despite his own wounds, Stephen Decatur stayed all night at his brother's side. When dawn broke, Frazier was still clinging to life but James's body was committed to the sea. According to his brother's first biographer, Stephen said upon the expiration of his brother, "I would rather see him thus than living with an cloud upon his conduct."[23]

Though another lieutenant suffered severe saber wounds, James Decatur was the only American killed. Just eleven men were wounded, and the man who had sacrificed himself for Decatur, Daniel Frazier, recovered from his wounds. An exact enemy casualty count was unknown, but the dead numbered at least fifty, the wounded perhaps double that.

In two and a half hours of fighting and bombardment, the Tripolitans lost six gunboats. The shore batteries sustained some damage, but the fifty mortar shells thrown into the town had inflicted little damage. Though a good day for Preble, this had been far from an absolute victory. More than exploding mortar shells and a few dead pirates would be required to persuade the bashaw to consider peace.

For weeks, Preble did his considerable best to annoy the Tripolitans from the sea. His fleet bombarded the city from the west on August 7, but the results were disappointing. Most of the bombs landed well away from the bashaw's castle. Preble's forces sustained a painful loss when one of the captured gunboats exploded and killed ten American crewmen.

August 7 was also the day that Preble learned he was being replaced by Commodore Barron. Preble was mortified, though it made sense that the senior officer would take command, and he decided to return to America once the new commodore arrived. But until then he would continue his duty. On the night of August 24, Preble dispatched the gunboats to pound the city. He inflicted little damage on the bashaw's defenses, although, unknown to Preble, a cannonball crashed through one wall of Captain Bainbridge's room. He had been asleep in his bed but the ball ricocheted off another wall before pulling off the prisoner's bedclothes. Cut and bruised by falling masonry, Bainbridge sustained no serious injury, though a deep ankle wound left him limping for some weeks.

Another nighttime bombardment on August 28 sank another gunboat, but with the supply of ammunition running low and Barron expected any day, the fleet needed a new strategy. Preble decided that the USS *Intrepid* would once again take center stage in what was likely his closing scene in the war with Tripoli. If he could not end the war, he might at least shock the bashaw into negotiation.

Since conveying Decatur and his men on their February mission to the captured *Philadelphia*, the *Intrepid* had been a transport, ferrying water and provisions from Syracuse. Now, however, Preble decided to dispatch the former *Mastico* again into the dangers of Tripoli harbor. But this time, the *Intrepid* would not return.

Preble personally supervised the conversion of the little ship into an "infernal machine." Using wooden planks, the squadron's men stowed five tons of powder below her deck. Stacked above on the ship's deck were one hundred thirteen-inch and fifty nine-inch shells, together with iron scraps and pig iron ballast. The ship had become a floating bomb.

The gunners calculated that, after being lit, fuses would give the crew eleven minutes to make their getaway. A small room in the stern of the ship was filled with kindling and other combustibles. It was to be set afire to discourage Tripolitan boarders as the Americans made their escape in the two fastest rowing boats in the squadron, pulling for the harbor entrance and the *Nautilus* just beyond.

The fleet continued an on-again, off-again bombardment of Tripoli into early September, waiting for perfect conditions. Then, on September 3, at eight o'clock in the evening, the *Intrepid* slipped her cable and sailed for Tripoli.

No moon lit her way and, powered by a moderate breeze, she glided swiftly toward the harbor. The *Nautilus* accompanied her to a distance of some seven hundred yards from the western mouth of the harbor, then stopped to wait at a distance.

The *Intrepid*'s Captain Richard Somers and his crew were on their own in the starry night. Their mission was dangerous—their ship was a tinderbox, after all—but they carried another burden. The blockaded Tripolitans were probably running low on gunpowder. If, by some misfortune, the *Intrepid* were to fall into their hands, its large stores of ammunition could prolong the war. Knowing this must not happen, Somers had asked that no volunteer accompany him who would not be willing, in the event the enemy should board the *Intrepid*, to "put a match to the magazine, and blow themselves and their enemies up together."[24]

The men aboard the *Nautilus* watched as the *Intrepid* made way toward Tripoli. As the minutes passed, the smaller ship, barely discernible in the dim light, seemed to be entering the harbor passage. Then two gunshots were heard. Were they alarm guns fired from the Tripolitan batteries? Silence followed, and the crew of the *Nautilus* waited anxiously.

For ten minutes, the only sound to be heard was the lapping of the waves.

Then, at 9:47 p.m. according to the *Constitution*'s log, a blaze of light suddenly illuminated the sky and the towers, minarets, and castellated walls of Tripoli. An instant later, a deafening explosion of sound struck the American ships, its concussion shaking even the *Constitution* six miles out to sea.

A different, more profound silence fell.

The lookouts on the *Nautilus* strained their eyes, hoping to see Somers and his men stroking for safety in their two boats. From his more distant anchorage, Preble studied the sky anxiously, praying to spot a rocket, the agreed-upon signal that Somers and his men had escaped the harbor. The sky remained an unbroken black.

With the sunrise, the three ships Preble sent to stand offshore reported that the fort appeared undamaged, the Tripolitan navy intact.

Finally the remains of her hull were spotted, the keel and ribs of the *Intrepid* grounded just outside the rocky barrier. The ship had exploded well short of the bashaw's castle, for reasons that could not be known (a sniper's bullet? an accidental spark? the powder touched off by Somers when a Tripolitan boarding party neared?). Even before the bashaw permitted Captain Bainbridge to view the remains of "six persons in a most mangled and burnt condition lying on the shore,"[25] it became clear there could be no survivors.

Preble's final attempt to persuade the bashaw to surrender had failed.

THE NEW COMMODORE

On September 9, the USS *President* and USS *Constellation* were sighted as Preble's flagship cruised off the Tripoli coast. Preble ordered his pennant struck. With the arrival of Commodore Samuel Barron, Preble officially ceased being squadron commander, and his thoughts turned to home.

"Commodore Barron's arrival to supersede me in the command of the fleet has determined me to return," a dispirited Preble wrote to Mary.[26] Yet before departing, he would spend many hours in conference with Barron. And in attendance at some of those briefings would be William Eaton, who had sailed with Barron. A favored topic of conversation between the three men was Eaton's proposal to aid Hamet Qaramanli.

Eaton helped assure Preble that, although he was being displaced by Barron, he could go home with his head held high. Although Edward Preble would not remain in the Mediterranean to see the war through to its close, in his time of service in the Maghreb he had established a negotiated peace with Morocco. During his service as commodore, his men had demonstrated a new and remarkable fighting prowess. Even if he had not achieved the larger victory he hoped for, Preble's service in the region was another honorable chapter in his distinguished career.

When Preble did finally arrive in Washington on March 4, 1805, he received a well-deserved hero's welcome. Despite his disappointment with his own performance, there was no way to term his Barbary tour anything but a success. He'd taken the fight to Tripoli, destroyed pirate vessels, and made sure the *Philadelphia* wasn't used against the United States. Recognizing his achievements, the president welcomed him as an honored guest, and he was celebrated at the home of the secretary of state, as well as at dinners in Philadelphia, Trenton, and Boston. Congress ordered a medal struck with his likeness. For his valiant efforts and sound strategies off the Barbary Coast, he had become an American legend.

The Americans were still riding high on Preble's and Decatur's successes, but there was one fact they couldn't ignore: though America's sea victories had won respect and concessions from some of the Barbary states, Tripoli was still unrepentantly hostile. In the months that followed Preble's return, the president and his advisers began to turn their hopes toward Eaton's plan. Perhaps a land war and accompanying coup could finally solve the Tripoli problem.

CHAPTER 14

Opening a New Front

> It grates me mortally when I see a lazy Turk reclining at his ease upon an embroidered sofa, with one Christian slave to hold his pipe, another to hold his coffee, and a third to fan away the flies.
>
> —**William Eaton**[1]

Jefferson's government left the decision of whether to help Hamet in the hands of their men in the Mediterranean. The chief diplomat and the commodore, Lear and Barron, would have to approve Eaton's efforts if he was to move forward. Accordingly, on their transatlantic crossing, William Eaton had presented Commodore Samuel Barron with impassioned arguments for his scheme.

Eaton's lawyerly arguments were strong. He maintained that only a ground campaign would force Yusuf into accepting a peace on American terms. He pointed out that the Americans most familiar with the politics of the region, Richard O'Brien and James Leander Cathcart, had endorsed the idea of restoring Hamet as bashaw. On arrival in the Mediterranean, they found that Captain Preble had, too.

Even if Barron remained vague about how it was to be done, he could hardly reject the collective advice of these experienced Barbary men. With some reluctance, he agreed to provide Eaton transport to go in search of the deposed bashaw.

But not all the American officials stationed in the Mediterranean and involved in Barbary affairs thought the mission a good one. Chief Consul Tobias Lear, the region's most important representative of the Department of State, complained that Hamet lacked the force or influence needed to make him helpful to the Americans. But it is difficult to know whether Lear's objections were based more on his doubts about Hamet's strength or on fears that the plan would diminish his own power. During Commodore Preble's time, Lear's role in America's foreign relations had been minor. Preble thought military strength, not negotiations, were the means to peace, relegating Lear's work to the background. With the arrival of Barron, especially now that the commodore had suddenly been confined to his cabin, sick with liver disease, Lear saw the door might be open for him to wield more influence. Eaton's plan, also based on military strength instead of negotiations, might close that door again.

MARINES

Despite Colonel Lear's doubts, Eaton's plan received approval. He was authorized to find Hamet, negotiate with him, and raise an Arab army to help restore the rightful bashaw to power. These orders in hand, in November 1804, Eaton sailed for Egypt aboard the USS *Argus*. Built to hold 142 men, the snug ship easily took aboard

Eaton's tiny army, which, at that moment, consisted solely of Eaton, 2 U.S. Navy midshipmen, and 8 U.S. Marines.

If Eaton's band fell far short of the army he hoped to build, he still maintained high hopes—and one reason was the presence of the Marines and their leader, Lieutenant Presley O'Bannon. Eaton needed such men, skilled fighters on land and sea.

Lithe and lean with red hair, O'Bannon was popular as a lively violin player who could dance as well as he could fiddle a tune. He was also a born fighter. A young man from the heart of Virginia's Piedmont region, he was eager to defend American interests in an exotic climate. The Marines' reputation for toughness and tenacity, along with the promise of adventure coupled with patriotic duty, had attracted the naturally spirited young man, and he had enthusiastically embraced Eaton's plan.

Eaton's ten men amounted to a small start, of course, but these committed young fighters, Eaton believed, would soon be supplemented by Hamet's larger army in Egypt. Hamet's loyal followers could also be reinforced by hiring mercenaries and, thanks to his years in North Africa, Eaton understood the value of local soldiers, men acclimated to the unique demands of desert living. He also felt confident that disaffected Tripolitans would flock to Hamet's side once he marched back into his country. A fine team was in the making.

FINDING THE TRAIL

Before Eaton and his Marines could help Hamet, though, they had to find him—and in 1804 no one seemed to know where Sidi Hamet

Qaramanli was hiding. When the rumor had circulated, in July 1803, that Bashaw Yusuf had dispatched assassins to kill him in the eastern Tripolitan city of Derne, Hamet had run for his life, fleeing to Egypt. Reports indicated that the thin, soft-spoken former bashaw remained there. But where, exactly? Forced to be on the move out of fear of his brother's agents, he seemed to have disappeared into the sands of the Sahara.

Eaton's first port of call in November 1804 was the ancient city of Alexandria, Egypt. On arrival, the Americans found a country divided. Albanian Turks held power on behalf of the Ottoman Empire, but their rule extended only to Cairo. Farther upriver were the rebellious Mamelukes, heirs to an Egyptian dynasty that dated to medieval times. Meanwhile both French and British colonial forces had, in recent years, been stationed in the country. As if the competing political interests were not enough, Egypt was in the midst of a famine, a result of a scant harvest. "Egypt has no master," Eaton noted a few days into his visit. "Pale Wretchedness and dumb melancholy stalk here!"[2]

Eaton recognized that he needed Egyptian help if he was to find Hamet. Accordingly, he befriended the natives and, over candies and coffee, he learned that the man he sought was upriver. However, Eaton's blood ran cold on being told that Hamet had joined forces with the Mamelukes, the sworn enemies of the Ottoman Empire and, more immediately, the powers that controlled the mouth of the river. Supposing he found Hamet, how was Eaton to extract him and his supporters, as they would have to travel through Ottoman territory? That would require a miraculous act of diplomacy, but even so, the intrepid William Eaton, having persuaded a president, a government, and the U.S. Navy to support his scheme, gamely headed up the Nile to Cairo. There he would next make his case to the viceroy of Egypt.

MAKING FRIENDS WITH EGYPT

Eaton's expedition sailed south, the waters of the Nile guiding them farther into Egypt. Evidence of political instability was everywhere. One village had been raided by a roving band of deserters from the Turkish army just days before who had destroyed anything valuable or growing. At one town, the Americans were mistaken for British soldiers, and the locals "flocked around with demonstrations of joy," offering to help any army that would protect them from the marauding forces.[3]

Letters from the British consul gained Eaton an audience with the Egyptian viceroy in Cairo. Because it was Ramadan, the holy month of fasting when no refreshments could be served during the day, Viceroy Ahmed Khorshid invited Eaton to call upon him at nine o'clock in the evening. Eaton was conducted from the British consulate to the viceroy's citadel in a torch-lit procession, escorted by servants and dignitaries and six lavishly decorated Arabian horses. He looked upon the spectators lining the streets of the mile-and-a-half route, an enormous crowd "curious to see *the men who had come from the new world*."[4] His welcome was worthy of a great visitor.

The viceroy himself seemed most interested to learn about the United States, and asked Eaton many question about America, the "situation and extent of our territory; date of our independence; nations with whom we were at peace or war; productions and commerce of the country? &c &c." The two men sat in a large hall, Eaton reported, which "surpassed in magnificence everything I have ever seen of its kind." Seated side by side, they shared an embroidered purple couch with damask cushions and sat drinking coffee, smoking pipes, and eating sherbet.

Then the viceroy dismissed everyone from his presence except Eaton and an interpreter. The pleasantries ended as the ruler observed, "[Y]our visit to this country at so critical a moment must have something more for its object than mere gratification of curiosity."

Eaton went straight to the heart of the matter. Replying in French, which the Turkish interpreter understood better than English, Eaton described "our intercourse and relation with Tripoli." He explained that the current bashaw of Tripoli had declared the war, which the Americans wanted to end. Although often criticized for being blunt, Eaton demonstrated great subtlety in winning the viceroy over to his plan. He flattered the Egyptian, contrasting his magnanimity with the tyranny of the Barbary princes.

He argued that Islam and Christianity had many commonalities, hinting that the Egyptian could ally with him as a matter of faith. "I touched upon the affinity of principle between the Islam and Americans religion. Both taught the existence and supremacy of *one* God . . . both enjoyed the universal exercise of humanity, and both forbade unnecessary bloodshed."

The viceroy had to agree: indeed, these were maxims of his faith. Eaton pressed on.

He told the viceroy that he was seeking Hamet: "I declared that we sought in his province a legitimate sovereign of Tripoli: who had been treacherously driven from his government and country; in whose good faith we could place reliance, and whom we intended to restore to his throne." And he explained that America had no interest in occupying Tripoli: "we do not unsheathe the sword for conquest nor for spoil, but to vindicate our rights." The United States sought only to defend its own citizens and interests from unwarranted attack.

The viceroy recognized the American as a worthy brother and, "by an inclination of his head, [the viceroy] signified assent and promised to send couriers in search of Hamet Bashaw."

Eaton's persuasive words had won him an ally in the search for Hamet. Now, however, he must wait for the man to be found.

The viceroy was true to his word, and he dispatched messengers upriver to find Hamet. Eaton, too, sent a mercenary to discover the whereabouts of the missing man. Several nervous weeks passed before the messengers located the former bashaw, but they delivered Eaton's message to him on January 3. Five days later, Eaton received Hamet's eager reply.

The former bashaw was ready for the expedition, confident "that God will aid us in establishing peace and tranquility."[5] On February 5, 1805, Eaton and Hamet, who had met years earlier in Tunis, were reunited outside Cairo.

On first sight, Hamet struck no one as a powerful prince. His cheeks were pockmarked, his chin and lips obscured by a long beard. On meeting him, one American captain had pronounced Hamet a "mild, amiable man [who] would be perfectly friendly and Peaceable toward us."[6] Though a sympathetic figure, he possessed no great personal magnetism, and no one described him as a warrior. When his brother had taken the throne in 1795, Hamet had seemed incapable of fighting back, and almost a decade later he still lived in exile, separated from his wife and four children, who remained under house arrest in Tripoli.

If Hamet was indecisive and uninspiring, Eaton also recognized him as someone he could mold, someone he could persuade. But before they could embark on the great mission Eaton envisioned, one more delicate negotiation needed to be completed.

Taking it upon himself to represent the United States of America, Eaton negotiated with the former bashaw concerning their respective promises. Hamet needed to be sure the Americans would support him. Eaton needed assurances that Hamet would treat Americans well once he was in power. Their conversations yielded a formal agreement.

The treaty opened with one line—"GOD IS INFINITE"—followed by an oath of friendship between the government of the United States and the one to be reestablished by Hamet. Per the contract, the United States would provide the force, funds, and supplies to restore the throne to Hamet. In return, the once and future bashaw would ask no ransom for the release of the men of the *Philadelphia*. Hamet also promised to deliver Yusuf and Admiral Murat Rais to the Americans. Signed by Eaton and Hamet, the document was witnessed by Presley O'Bannon and the British consul.

With the treaty in place, the plan that William Eaton had been shaping for more than three years was about to unfold. America, pounding Tripoli from the sea, would soon be continuing the attack on land. Together, Eaton and Hamet would raise a mercenary army that would join the Marines for a historic land march across more than five hundred miles of rocky desert to Derne, Tripoli's second-largest city. Once Derne had fallen, they would march west to Benghazi. They would capture that city, and then U.S. warships would carry them the last four hundred miles to take Tripoli. It was a bold plan—but despite the doubts of Lear and others, Eaton felt confident that it could work.

CHAPTER 15

Win in the Desert or Die in the Desert

’Tis done, the hornéd crescent falls!
The Star-flag flouts the broken walls!

—**John Greenleaf Whittier, “Derne,” 1850**

On March 6, 1805, the trek began. Four hundred men set out from Alexandria, their goal—to change the history of the Barbary Coast. Among their number were just ten Americans, including Lieutenant O’Bannon, a midshipman, a Marine sergeant, and six Marine privates. Hamet brought along ninety Tripolitans. The rest were hired mercenaries, mostly Greek and Arab cavalrymen and foot soldiers. It was a long caravan, led from the front with martial efficiency but diminishing to pack animals with supplies well to the rear.

Newly self-declared “General, and Commander in Chief of the land forces,” William Eaton marched proudly in uniform, epaulets on his shoulders, his hat decorated with lace, his buttons and spurs polished brass. One of the oddest—and yet most effective—military campaigns in American history had begun, with General Eaton leading the charge.

UPS AND DOWNS

The march to Derne had barely started before a mutiny jeopardized the whole trip. After just three days of marching along the coast, the camel wranglers hired to guide the pack animals demanded to be paid in advance. When an irresolute Hamet did nothing, Eaton threatened to abandon the expedition. The mutineers quieted, and the little revolutionary army marched on, averaging roughly twenty miles a day.

As they marched, Eaton marveled over the beautiful but hostile desert. The men passed incredible scenes, both man-made and natural. "Passed some vestiges of ancient fortifications," Eaton noted on March 14 as they camped on the high ridge that marked the boundary between Egypt and Tripoli. The sights were inspiring, but the weather was less so. The long column soon encountered incessant rain blowing in from the coast that soaked the men and their supplies. Temperatures rose to almost 100 degrees Fahrenheit by day and plunged to near freezing at night. The Sahara was not making Eaton's task easy.

At intervals, the Arabs who owned the camels made new demands. They looted the food supplies, and the caravan grew shorter as some of the Arabs deserted. During the day, O'Bannon and his Marines, imposing in their blue uniforms with scarlet collars and trimmings, and distinguished by their firm and decided conduct, helped prevent further mutinies. After sundown, O'Bannon gained popularity among the Americans, Turks, Arabs, and Greeks alike. He had brought his violin along, and he would play for the camp—for perhaps the first time, the strains of Irish and Appalachian fiddle tunes echoed across the North African desert's rocky terrain.

After almost a month of marching, Eaton's army encountered a large camp of several thousand Bedouins. "We were the first Christians ever seen by these wild people," Eaton observed. Just as he had hoped, the ranks of his little army began to swell. Eighty mounted warriors joined from the Bedouins and, by early April, Eaton counted "between six and seven hundred fighting men on the ground, exclusive of followers of the camp and Bedouin families, who inclusively make a body of about twelve hundred people."[1] As it marched across the plateau that overlooked the seas, Eaton's army was becoming more formidable, ready to take on the official Tripolitan forces.

REBELLION

Good fortune was not to last. By mid-April, the company's food supply had dwindled to just six days' rations of rice, the bread and meat exhausted. The marchers had already slaughtered a camel for meat, and the Marines sold their brass buttons to local Bedouins for a few dates. Wild fennel and sorrel were harvested when they could be found, but everyone remained hungry. The procession came to a standstill when the sheiks commanding the Arabs in the force refused to march until a messenger sent to Bomba returned with assurances that Isaac Hull, in command of the USS *Argus*, awaited them with fresh supplies.

Eaton refused to halt. He saw the choice as between famine and fatigue. Bomba was ninety miles away and, he believed, to remain in place in the heat of the desert would amount to suicide. They needed to push on—and he ordered all rations stopped until they did.

The bashaw walked out of camp, refusing to take sides in the dispute, but the Arab mercenaries prepared to raid the provisions tent. Reading their intentions, Eaton ordered O'Bannon and the Marines to form a line. The armed, uniformed men stood their ground, immobile as a "body of about two hundred advanced in full charge"[2] in a frenzied panic driven by hunger, desperation, and distrust. Amazed by O'Bannon's men's resolute refusal to so much as blink in light of the approaching mob, the Arabs stopped, then withdrew. The sheiks were about to order their men to shoot the American officers, but just as the cry went up to draw their weapons, a few of Hamet's officers called out in Arabic, "For God's sake, do not fire! The Christians are our friends!" O'Bannon and company again stood firm, unmoving.

Hamet's officers then rushed forward, their sabers drawn, and drove the mutineers back. A crisis averted, at least for the night, Eaton vented his frustrations in his journal. Despite apparent gains in mutual understanding with their Arab comrades, Eaton noted, "We find it almost impossible to inspire these wild bigots with confidence in us, or to persuade them that, being Christians, we can be otherwise than enemies to Mussulmen. We have a difficult undertaking!"[3]

Things got no easier when, a week later, the caravan stumbled

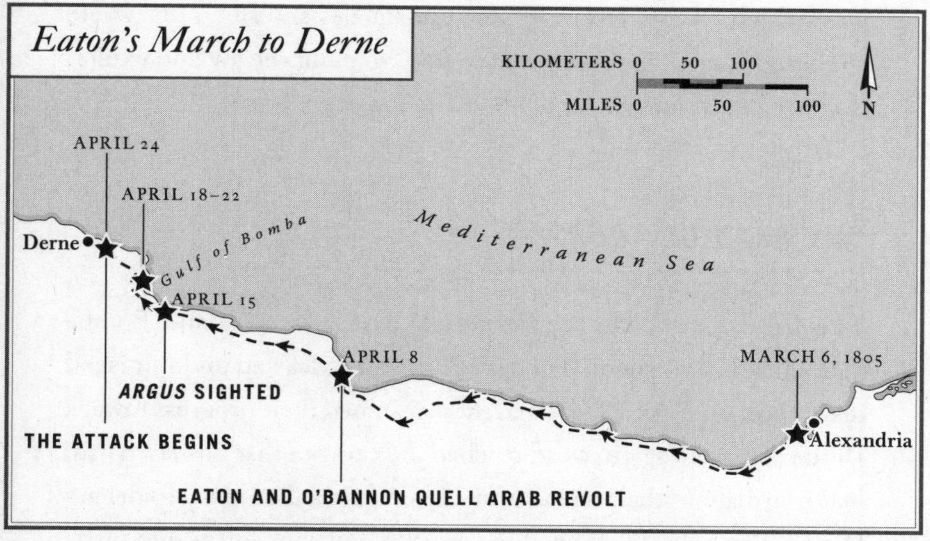

into Bomba, wild with hunger and thirst, and eager to rest with full bellies and no fear of starvation. They found Eaton's often-repeated promise—that American ships awaited the army at Bomba—proved untrue: there were no American ships in the harbor. The Arabs and Bedouins alike immediately declared their intentions to leave in the morning, to countermarch home. The Americans could go forth toward whatever folly they desired, but they would do so alone.

"All began now to think of the means of individual safety," Eaton wrote. "I went off with my Christians, and kept up fires upon a high mountain in our rear all night." He desperately hoped that huge hilltop fire would not only provide security for their camp but also signal any American ships in the area, because native scouts had sworn to their presence just a few days earlier.

The plan worked. At eight o'clock the following morning a sail was sighted. "Capt. Hull had seen our smokes and stood in," wrote a relieved Eaton. "Language is too poor to paint the joy and exultation which this messenger of life excited in every breast."[4]

"MY HEAD OR YOURS"

The *Argus*, followed by the *Hornet* two days later, sailed into Bomba and unloaded its goods. For a week the army feasted and refreshed itself until, on April 23, the marchers resumed their progress toward Derne. En route again, word reached the caravan that Bashaw Yusuf had heard about their march and had dispatched an army to defend Derne. The news dampened the recently buoyant spirits and made poor Hamet fear for himself and his family. "I thought the Bashaw [Hamet] wished himself back in Egypt,"[5] Eaton observed. Still, Hamet rallied. The little army pressed on and, on April 25, made camp on a ridge overlooking its destination.

The next morning, Eaton sent a letter to the governor of Derne. "I want no territory," his message read. "With me is advancing the legitimate Sovereign of your country—give us a passage through your city, and for the supplies of which we shall have need, you will receive fair compensation. . . . I shall see you tomorrow in a way of your choice."[6]

By early afternoon, Eaton had his reply. "The flag of truce was sent back to me with this laconic answer, 'My head or yours!'"[7]

As the sun rose over the Sahara on April 27, Bashaw Hamet, William Eaton, Presley O'Bannon, and their unlikely army of mercenaries, midshipmen, Marines, Greeks, Arabs, and Bedouins—a brave band of misfits—prepared to storm the city gates.

CAPTURING THE CASTLE

Looking down upon the town of Derne on April 27, 1805, General William Eaton concocted the plan of attack.

Derne was nestled into a crook of the Mediterranean coast. The governor's palace sat upon an easterly spit of land that jutted into the blue waters of the bay. A ten-inch howitzer had been mounted on its terrace. Word having reached the provincial capital that an invading force approached, the town had been armed with a battery of eight guns aimed out to sea. To the landward, loopholes had been opened in houses along the city walls to form a line of defense.

Eaton's plan called for an attack on Derne on three fronts. First, from the sea, the guns aboard the three American ships would bombard the city. Second, using field guns sent by Barron, Eaton and his men would fire upon the walls of the city from the southeast. Finally, a wave of men led by Hamet Qaramanli would descend on the rear of the town from the west.

On the morning of April 27, the *Nautilus* brought Eaton's guns to shore. There a narrow beach immediately gave way to a steep climb, but the task of hauling a heavy carronade up the slope with block and tackle proved time-consuming. Eager to get to the coming fight, Eaton decided to settle for just one artillery piece.

Finally, at one-thirty on the afternoon of April 27, the assault began. From a distance of half a mile out to sea, the *Argus* and the *Nautilus* began firing into the town. From their vantage on the hillside, O'Bannon and his men maintained a steady musket fire, accompanied by round shot from the carronade. With the *Hornet* positioned

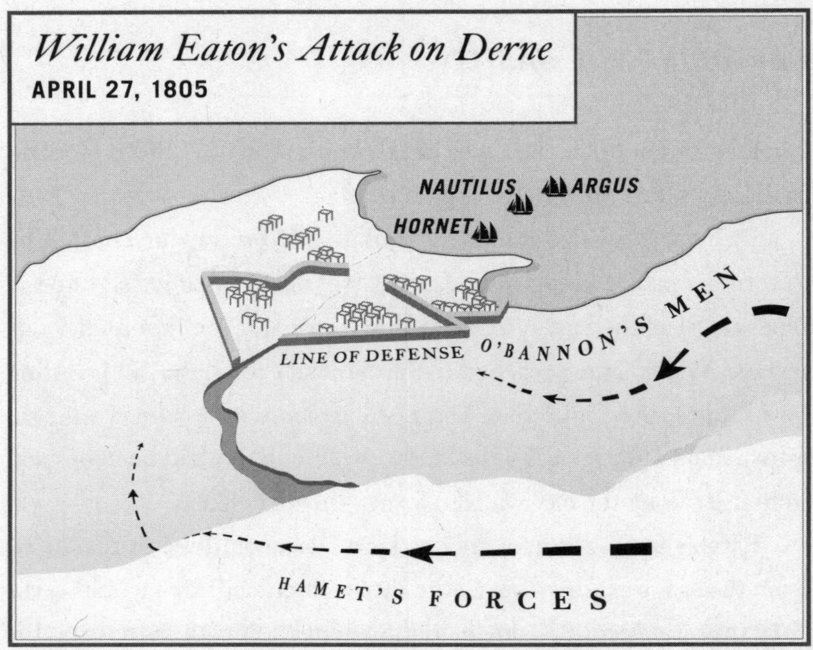

in the bay to fire on the city from a distance of just one hundred yards, Derne was taking heavy bombardment.

At first, the attack seemed to go well. Within forty-five minutes, Derne's harbor guns fell silent. Under heavy fire from the U.S. Navy ships, the Tripolitans operating the harbor guns had withdrawn and moved to reinforce the defenders of the more vulnerable south wall.

Eaton's cannoneers kept up their fire until a cannonball shattered their rammer, the long wooden tool used to drive the shot and powder wad down the bore of the large gun. No longer able to load and fire the gun, the men around O'Bannon and Eaton were thrown into confusion.

Thinking fast, Eaton saw but one alternative: he ordered a charge down the hill, directly into the teeth of the enemy's defense. The odds were not in his favor but he remained undaunted.

"We rushed forward against a host of savages more than ten to our one."[8] On horseback, Eaton led the charge at a gallop, an intimidating sight as he swung his custom-made scimitar over his head. By some miracle, he was not injured by the enemy's gunfire, though he would find five bullet holes in his robes.[9]

On the other side of town, Hamet and his troops occupied an old castle and awaited their signal. Eaton had instructed the Tripolitan to lead his force of more than seven hundred men, some on foot, others on horseback, and attack the city via a deep ravine southwest of Derne. Sheiks sympathetic to the former bashaw had advised that he could expect support from most of the population in that part of the city. Other horsemen in Hamet's force were to take positions in the surrounding hills to the rear, ready to cut off any Tripolitan forces attempting to retreat from the city.

As a dense cloud of blue smoke rose from the harbor, a delighted Eaton had seen Hamet's horsemen swooping down to the city. Knowing that Hamet's army was fighting fiercely on the other side of the city emboldened him for the daring charge of the city walls. Cannon fire from the ships offered cover as Eaton, O'Bannon, and their men crossed the beach, but the men still faced volleys of musket balls from the ramparts.

One of O'Bannon's seven Marines fell, seriously wounded. Another took a bullet to the chest, dying immediately. Then Eaton himself took a musket ball to the left wrist. Yet the wave of men and their flashing bayonets continued their charge.

To the surprise of the small brigade of invaders, the city's defenders began to retreat into the city as the Americans approached. The frontal assault produced a growing panic. The ragged fire from behind the walls ceased, and the Tripolitan defenders melted into the dizzying maze of the city's twisting streets and stacked houses. The retreating army managed only sporadic fire as they retreated.

With Eaton wounded, O'Bannon took full command. Breaching the city's walls, he led the charge directly to the oceanfront guns. There, after lowering the bashaw's ensign, O'Bannon planted the American flag on the ramparts. He then turned the enemy's own guns on them—abandoned in a rush during the naval bombardment, many were still loaded, powdered, and ready to fire. In a matter of minutes, the Americans held the high ground and the artillery.

Meanwhile, at the other end of town, Hamet's flag could now be seen flying from the governor's palace. After years of planning, months of preparations, and a fifty-two-day march that covered more than five hundred miles, the city had fallen in the short span of two and a half hours.

All told, there were fourteen dead and wounded among the contingent of Americans and Greeks led by Eaton and O'Bannon. Two of the dead were O'Bannon's Marines. The number of casualties among Hamet's party and the Tripolitan forces was not recorded but totaled in the hundreds.

Eaton was elated. His plan had worked thus far, and an army of fewer than a thousand men had overrun a fighting force of four thousand. The governor of Derne was still at large—he found refuge in a mosque—but Eaton felt certain the victory would win many Tripolitans to Hamet's side—and it would demonstrate to the world that the Americans were not to be trifled with. Eaton had proved that distance was no barrier to the Americans and put the world on notice that Hamet, the rightful ruler of their country, had his sights set on regaining his throne and his family. Rejoicing at the prospect of victory, Hamet is said to have offered his sword to O'Bannon as a token of his thanks.

Word of the fall of Derne was bound to anger and panic the bashaw. Hamet and the Americans were coming for him, and Bashaw Yusuf knew it. But Eaton's victory would be stymied by a surprising source.

CHAPTER 16

Endgame

Our captive countrymen have been restored to the bosom of their country, peace has been made on honorable terms. . . . We have got all we wanted.

—***National Intelligencer,*** **October 25, 1805**

With Eaton's resounding victory in Derne, a military victory in Tripoli seemed within reach. But Tobias Lear had other plans. He wanted a diplomatic deal, and a deal is what he made.

Lear had opposed launching the assault on Derne from the first, and he fully expected the mission to fail. In his mind, Eaton was a failed consul, a man playing at being soldier, even a "madman."[1] His presence in the region undercut Lear's diplomatic authority, and Lear feared that a military victory would ruin his chances for brokering a diplomatic peace.

Now Lear received news of Eaton's success. Lear's prediction had been wrong, but he was determined not to let the news go to waste. With a little quick thinking, Eaton's victory could be leveraged, not for an absolute victory, but for a brokered peace.

A few weeks before the attack on Derne, Bashaw Yusuf had showed signs of wanting to make peace—but only on his terms. In return for $200,000, he promised to release Captain Bainbridge and the men of the USS *Philadelphia*. Though desperate for a deal, Lear recognized the offer for the extortion it was and rejected it.

Then the news of the capture of Derne arrived—and Lear saw his great chance. He felt certain that the news of Hamet's victory would strike fear into Bashaw Yusuf—and he was right.

Although Lear did not know it, when the Tripolitan leader heard of the fall of Derne on May 21, he was terrified. "The Bashaw was so much agitated at the news of the approach of his brother, that he . . . declared, that if it was in his power now to make peace and give up the American prisoners, he would gladly do it, without the consideration of money. . . ," one Philadelphia captive reported. "He heartily repented for not accepting the terms of peace last offered."[2] Had Lear acted with strength, he might have been granted all of his demands without having to pay.

Instead, Lear underestimated the effect of Eaton's victory on the Barbary powers. Aboard the USS *Constitution*, Lear took what he thought was a hard position: he offered $60,000 in payment for the freedom of the *Philadelphia*'s captives and refused to go ashore until the bashaw agreed to his terms.

The relieved bashaw saw a chance to save his throne. He accepted the deal, and by June 3, the terms were agreed upon. Two days later, Colonel Lear went into the city and was welcomed into the palace. Peace was declared and the prisoners freed—but the achievement was tainted. Lear had paid for the release of American prisoners, and even worse, he had betrayed Eaton and Hamet. As part of the deal, Lear had promised that all American forces would evacuate Derne.

THE END OF THE ROAD

Unaware of Lear's negotiation, General Eaton, Hamet, and their men stood firm as their enemies counterattacked. The governor of Derne had fled, taking with him intelligence about the invading forces, and he was using the information as he struck back at the Americans. As the attacks continued, Eaton feared that either his supplies or the nerves of his men would give out. He noted in his journal that the apprehensive Hamet tended to become "deeply agitated."[3] The brave liberators of Derne held the city securely, but they could not hold out indefinitely without supplies and reinforcements.

Yet Eaton could do little but wait for the American response to his call for support. When the response came, it was not the men, munitions, and other aid he had requested. Instead, he got a letter advising him that the peace process had begun and no further advancement of his army would be necessary or supported.

Eaton was stunned.

Even more stunning was the accompanying order for him to abandon Derne and come home. The flabbergasted Eaton, who had fully expected to carry his fight to Benghazi and even Tripoli, was told to give up the ground purchased with his men's blood and to renege on his promises to Hamet.

Outraged, Eaton immediately wrote a long letter to Commodore Barron. He argued that a withdrawal would be a dangerous sign of weakness in a region that respected only strength. "Certainly they, and perhaps the world, will place an unjust construction on this retreat: at any rate it is a retreat—and a retreat of Americans!"[4]

Rather than withdraw from Derne as he waited for a reply to his letter to Barron, Eaton remained in place. He refused to accept that he would be forced to return hard-won ground to the pirates. Then, on June 11, another ship sailed into Derne harbor bringing a new message.

This time, it was the USS *Constellation*, and the dispatches that came ashore included one from Tobias Lear, dated five days earlier. Lear credited "the heroic bravery of our few countrymen at Derne . . . [that] made a deep impression on the Bashaw." The result had been a formal end to the war, but word of Lear's treaty was a blow to Eaton from which he would never recover. He was again told to abandon his prize and even his hopes of helping Hamet. This time Eaton saw that with the treaty in place, there was no getting around orders.

Even as the victor at Derne accepted that he had little choice but to leave, Eaton realized that withdrawal would be a delicate matter. If word leaked that the American forces were preparing to depart, enemy forces might be emboldened to attack. That meant the Americans must leave in secrecy.

Behaving as if nothing had changed, Eaton spent the next day inspecting the garrison and issuing orders as usual. Then, at eight o'clock in the evening, he posted the Marines in a conspicuous place, hoping they would serve as a decoy. Over the next several hours, the rest of the small American force was ferried to the *Constellation* as unobtrusively as possible. Eaton then summoned the outraged and brokenhearted Hamet, who reluctantly joined the retreat because he had no choice but to accept that pursuing the battle without

American help was impossible. The Marines, the officers, and Eaton went last. There could be no farewells, no ceremony. Just a quiet exit, a retreat that felt shameful.

When Hamet's Arab allies discovered that the Americans had left, they panicked. Once the bashaw's men learned the news, they would visit their fury on those left behind. Humiliated and betrayed, the sympathetic Arabs ran for the mountains, abandoning the town. In Tripoli there might be peace, but the citizens of Derne who had embraced Hamet would pay a heavy price for their support.

The resourceful William Eaton had won—against all odds—a stunning victory in Derne. And yet as Eaton sailed away, he saw his chance for greater glory—and for an even greater victory for his country—wash away with the tides that brought word of the treaty. Now he simply wished to go home. Listless and defeated, he wrote to Commodore John Rodgers, "I have no reasons for remaining any longer in this sea."[5]

A Senate committee would later investigate what had unfolded in Tripoli that June. Eaton's old friend Senator Timothy Pickering would offer a blistering condemnation of Lear, describing his conduct as "nothing but the basest treachery on the basest principles."[6] The committee strongly criticized the treaty as an "inglorious deed."[7] Yet the Senate still mustered the required two-thirds majority to ratify the Treaty of Peace and Amity between the United States and Tripoli. Whatever the disagreements about the way in which it had come to pass, the peace, at that moment, became an established fact.

CHAPTER 17

Fair Winds and Following Seas

Peace has been made on honorable terms.

—***National Intelligencer*, November 6, 1805**

The new Barbary peace truly was a victory, though an incomplete one. For President Jefferson, who got wind of Lear's treaty on September 6, 1805, the end of the conflict with Tripoli was a great relief. The war that had dogged his administration for more than four years was finally at an end—and it had ended Jefferson's way.

The *National Intelligencer* proclaimed victory. "Our captive countrymen have been restored to the bosom of their country. . . . We have got what we wanted."[1] Indeed, the terms of the treaty stipulated that in the future, captives would not be made slaves but would, in effect, be given the status of prisoners of war. American shipping could flow freely again. The two most essential goals in declaring war had been accomplished.

The country cheered the heroes as they returned to the United

States. In mid-September William Bainbridge arrived, already cleared of blame for the loss of the USS *Philadelphia*. He stepped off the ship along with 117 of his officers and crewmen and they were feted with awards, honors, and a warm welcome. Other returning captains and captives were paraded down main streets and toasted as heroes, too. The Virginia General Assembly honored U.S. Marine Lieutenant Presley O'Bannon, presenting him with a curved sword modeled after the Mameluke scimitar.

A complete victory over the Barbary pirates would come under another president, but for now America had much to be grateful for. The murky ending of the Barbary War didn't take away from the fact that America had stood up to the pirates, something that most of the more established European nations hadn't been willing to do. America had held firm and fought, and now the young nation's navy had the experience it would need to take on Britain in the War of 1812. Like the Barbary War, that war would begin with devastating losses but end with a huge leap in respect from the world.

In prevailing off the Barbary Coast, the United States proved that it would not only go to war for its own interests but would do what it could for oppressed citizens of other nations. Despite Lear's betrayal of Hamet, the American government did not let him down completely. Bringing a little pressure to bear, the Americans were able to free his wife and four children and reunite the family. Granted a $200-a-month payment by Congress, Hamet would end his life in exile in Egypt, dying in 1811. His brother, Yusuf Qaramanli, ruled as bashaw until 1832, when he stepped down to make way for his son Ali II; Yusuf died in 1838.

Tobias Lear kept his job. He would remain consul general to the Barbary states despite the disapproval of his treaty by many back in

Washington. Yet he was not a happy man. He left no note when he took his own life with a pistol shot in 1816.

Richard O'Brien and his wife Elizabeth lived a quiet life after returning to the United States. The O'Briens had five children, including a son named George Africanus, in honor of the continent where Richard had spent ten years in captivity and almost as many again in service to his country. O'Brien died in Washington, D.C., in 1824.

James Leander Cathcart would be appointed to diplomatic posts in Madeira, an island chain off the western coast of Portugal, and in Cádiz, Spain, before returning to the United States. He died in Washington, D.C., in 1843, but his journals and other writings were later collected in *The Captives: Eleven Years a Prisoner in Algiers* (1899).

William Eaton returned to America a national war hero for his role in winning America's first battle on foreign soil. In recognition of his service, the Commonwealth of Massachusetts awarded him ten thousand acres of land in the Maine Territory. In 1807, claims he put before Congress for expenses incurred in the Barbary campaign eventually brought him a windfall of $12,636, but by then his body had begun to betray him. He suffered from gout, and too many tankards bought by admirers took a toll. As his health declined, he penned his life story and collected his journals, knowing they would be published posthumously. By the time the volume appeared as *The Life of the Late Gen. William Eaton,* in 1813, the forty-seven-year-old Eaton had been dead two years.

The names *Philadelphia*, *Intrepid*, and *Constitution* had become well known to readers of American newspapers during the Barbary War. The commodore most closely associated with their

Barbary exploits, Edward Preble, lived until just 1807, succumbing, at age forty-six, to consumption. But his reputation would survive him. Pope Pius VII reportedly said Preble had done more for the cause of Christianity in an hour than the nations of Christendom ever had. And his name gained further luster in the next decade when several of the officers who fought for him—"Preble's Boys," as they would later come to be known—served with distinction in the War of 1812.

William Bainbridge won a measure of redemption for his twin failures with the *George Washington* and the *Philadelphia* off the Barbary Coast. Though later wounded in both legs in a battle with a British ship, Bainbridge managed to remain upright, commanding the USS *Constitution* to victory in a memorable sea battle with the HMS *Java*. Surviving his injuries, he would live to age fifty-nine, dying peacefully in his bed in 1833.

President Thomas Jefferson spent his retirement at his beloved home in Monticello, where both his wife and daughter Polly were buried. With his health declining, he was bedridden in the late spring and early summer of 1826. Seized by a severe fever on July 3, Jefferson realized that his death was imminent but was determined to hold on until the following day—the fiftieth anniversary of the adoption of the Declaration of Independence. With his family gathered around, he prepared for the end. Later that night, Jefferson awoke and asked his doctor, "Is it the fourth yet?" They were among his final words.

The following day, Jefferson died in his sleep at 1:10 p.m. Five hours later and nearly six hundred miles away, at 6:20 p.m. at Braintree Farm, Massachusetts, President John Adams also breathed his last. Adams, noting the significance of the date, remarked, "It is a great day. It is a *good* day." Unaware of Jefferson's passing, Adams's final words were "Jefferson still lives." The two men, longtime friends and rivals, passed from life within hours of each other on the 50th birthday of the country to whose service they had dedicated their lives, their fortunes, and their sacred honor. Not only did they see America through her tumultuous infancy, but also nurtured her growth into a respected global presence to carry her into the future.

When it unfolded, the Barbary War was no more than a ripple in the much larger waters of world politics. Bashaw Yusuf had declared war on America by the absurd act of chopping down an American flagstaff. Thomas Jefferson, as president of the first democracy of the modern era, responded in a manner that he, as one of the great political philosophers of his or any time, thought right. Today, the war's military legacy cannot be ignored. It saw the emergence of the U.S. Navy as a force to be reckoned with in foreign seas. It saw the American flag planted for the first time in victory on terrain outside the Western Hemisphere. It saw the first fight in which U.S. Navy gunfire worked in concert with United States land forces. So great was the war's significance for the Marines that their hymn refers to "the shores of Tripoli," and the Corps adopted the Mameluke sword as part of its officers' uniforms in 1825. Most important, here in the twenty-first century, the broader story—the great confrontation between the United States and militant Islamic states—has a new significance.

To Jefferson's way of thinking, the captivity of American seamen and the interference with American commerce demanded a strong military response. The subject was one he had been considering for many years. It had been the subject of many discussions between him and his friend John Adams, back in their ministerial days, in 1780s Europe. In fact, they had set the terms of the debate very clearly.

Adams had told his solemn friend he thought it possible to buy a peace.

Jefferson had countered, "I should prefer the obtaining of it by war."

In response to events on the Barbary Coast, Jefferson, in 1801, had dispatched a small U.S. Navy squadron to the Mediterranean. For the next four years, he responded to circumstances, expanding the fleet to a much larger naval presence. In the end, thanks to the bold leadership of men like Preble and Decatur and Eaton and O'Bannon, military force had helped regain national honor. Even the Federalists, who liked little that Jefferson did, came to accept that the United States needed to play a military role in overseas affairs.

In the end, it was Mr. Jefferson, not Mr. Adams, who won the argument.

EPILOGUE

Captain Stephen Decatur must have smiled as he sailed the Barbary Coast in 1815. This time he did not sneak in under cover of night, bravely risking his life to destroy a captured American ship. This time he was not leading outnumbered Americans into a battle. And this time he would not leave without getting what he came for.

Perhaps Decatur's smile saddened as he sailed through the waters where his brother had been slain, but the sharpest pangs of grief had dulled in the eleven years since James's death. During the first few years after the Treaty of Tripoli, America had enjoyed the partial peace purchased by the blood of brave men like James Decatur, and now Stephen had the honor of making the peace complete.

William Eaton's instinct that not going for absolute victory was a mistake had been proven correct. During the War of 1812, at the urging of the British, the Barbary pirates had begun taking Americans prisoner again. After the Treaty of Ghent had ended the second war with Great Britain in 1815, the United States Congress authorized an American military presence to return to the Maghreb. The dey of

Algiers had declared war on the United States, and Decatur was commissioned to put an end to the Barbary threat once and for all.

His fleet included his flagship, the USS *Guerriere,* and nine other warships; it was the largest naval force the United States had ever sent to sea. Once in Mediterranean waters, Decatur made short work of dispatching the Algerian leader's navy. He first captured the old enemy ship the *Meshuda.* Two days later, the fleet intercepted the *Estedio* and made it his prize. Both battles were concluded in less than half an hour each. Decatur took nearly five hundred prisoners.

When Decatur reached Algiers harbor on June 28, with the captured sailors and the pride of the Algerian navy under his command, the dey realized that he had made a grave mistake in provoking the Americans into another fight. Backed by his impressive naval force, Decatur obtained a peace treaty within forty-eight hours. This time the treaty called for no payment of tribute. Instead, the terms called for the immediate release of all remaining American hostages (at that point, only ten), $10,000 paid in restitution for merchandise stolen from American ships, full shipping rights guaranteed to all American ships, and no further demands for any future tributes.

Setting out from Algiers, Decatur sailed to Tunis. There he also reached a peace agreement with similar terms and once again insisted that the Barbary state pay reparations. In return for two American ships the Tunisians had captured, they paid Decatur a tribute of $60,000.

Finally, Decatur moved on to Tripoli, the Barbary city where his greatest adventures—and greatest loss—had occurred. Here he demanded that Bashaw Yusuf pay the Americans $30,000 in compensation for Tripolitan interference with American ships during the War of 1812. Decatur insisted upon the release of prisoners from other nations, besides just the United States. He even secured the freedom of British sailors, despite the fact that their nation had so recently been at war with his own. It was a bold, unprecedented move that was celebrated across Europe. America's newfound prestige was not blinded by its own power; might and mercy could work in harmony.

On learning of the outcome of Decatur's mission, the American minister to the Court of St. James's, John Quincy Adams, who now occupied the same post his father had a generation earlier, wrote to Decatur. "I most ardently pray that the example, which you have given, of rescuing our country from the disgrace of a tributary treaty, may become our irrevocable law for all future times."[1] Along the Barbary Coast, the centuries-old practice of building economies around kidnappings, theft, and terror was at last brought to a close. The war that had begun on Jefferson's watch was at last resolved on Madison's.

AFTERWORD

The flush of victory still upon him, Commodore Stephen Decatur was still not satisfied. Not content with having secured America's safety on the high seas, he hoped that America's success securing peace through strength would be an inspiration to the rest of the world.

"I trust that the successful result of our expedition, so honorable to our country, will induce other nations to follow the example; in which case the Barbary states will be compelled to abandon their piratical system," he wrote to the Secretary of the Navy on August 31, 1815.

His words proved prophetic. The Barbary pirates, though they stopped harassing American ships, continued attacking European ships. But Europe had taken a lesson from America, and its nations were no longer content to accept raids as part of life. In 1816, a combined British and Dutch force of nearly two dozen warships bombarded Algiers and forced the humiliated dey to release three thousand Christian captives and sign a treaty agreeing to cease enslaving Europeans. When the Algerians reneged on the deal, the French followed up with stronger military action. In 1830, they occupied Algiers and sent the dey into exile. Only then was piracy along the North African coast eradicated.

When so many years before Thomas Jefferson had written to his friend James Madison wondering "why not go to war with them?" he had foreseen the need for military intervention. Following through with it had been a controversial act in young America, especially since George Washington had famously declared that his countrymen ought to mind their own business when it came to world affairs. But in Jefferson's time and after, Jefferson's tough-minded approach to securing the safety of Americans abroad prevailed—and changed the course of history. The British, Dutch, and French, who all possessed vastly larger navies and had greater resources than the young United States, had flinched when faced with the Islamic threat, but they now followed the lead of the new nation.

These events amounted to the first signs of a significant shift in the world's balance of power.

Part of the reason Jefferson was motivated to shock the world by sending warships to the North African coast was that he understood in human terms the cost of piracy.

The Barbary enslavement of Americans was not new when Jefferson became president. He was probably familiar with the story of Abraham Browne, who, in 1655, was enslaved when the Dutch ship that he was working on was captured off the North African coast. A dozen more captivity narratives followed Browne's over the course of the next century, and it's likely Jefferson was aware of the stories.

The publication of William Ray's journals in 1808 increased the pressure on Americans to stop the pirate slave trade once and for all. Ray had been aboard the *Philadelphia* when it ran aground in

Tripoli harbor, and his account of how brutal and bizarre the bashaw's tyranny had been shocked the world.

Ray detailed the terror that American captives had experienced. Their living conditions were dismal. When first captured, the large crew was marched to an old weapons warehouse, about fifty feet long and twenty feet wide, and ordered to move a large pile of rubbish contained within it to a neighboring building. The cleared space would be their living quarters.

The jailers entered the warehouse at sundown and counted the men, demanding that each one doff his hat as his superiors passed. The prisoners were given a piece of sailcloth and ordered to sleep on the rocky dirt floor of their cell, staring up at the ceiling of clouds and stars winking down at them beyond the twenty-five-foot-tall walls that closed them in.

A number of the sailors were British by birth, having immigrated to America as children or young men. Several sent word to the British consul, hoping their place of birth might warrant their freedom. It was a desperate and highly unpopular move, as William Ray noted "a large majority of our patriotic tars" resolved "that they would not be released by a government which they detested . . . swearing that they would sooner remain under the Bashaw than George the third."[1]

Though most of the prisoners did not attempt to change loyalties, it's hard to blame those who did, considering the brutality the men experienced. In just one instance of abuse, on December 22, 1803, the *Philadelphia* captives were forced to march to the sea to dredge sand from the base of a merchant ship abandoned in the harbor. The men worked for hours, chest-deep in cold water, hauling their loads in baskets to the shore. "We were kept in the water from sunrise until about two o'clock, before we had a mouthful to eat, or were permitted to sun ourselves," Ray recalled. After bread and drink and a brief afternoon respite, the men were ordered back to their tedious, bone-chilling work until sundown, then returned to their prison with no dry clothes, extra blankets, or even a fire to warm them. The harsh exercise affected the men's health terribly, giving "many of us severe colds, and caused one man to lose the use of his limbs upwards of a year afterwards." The American sailors and Marines, whom Ray had praised for showing high spirits just weeks earlier, had reached a breaking point. Ray wrote, "Every night when I laid my head upon the earth to sleep, I most sincerely prayed that I might never experience the horrors of another morning."[2] The ill treatment continued for months.

When the news reached Tripoli of Eaton's victory at Derne, Ray reported that the bashaw panicked and "called a council of his chiefs, and proposed to put all American prisoners to death, but it was agreed to postpone this measure for that time."[3]

Finally, on June 2, 1805, more than a year and a half after their capture, the men received a letter in their prison informing them that freedom was at hand. Ray noted in his journal, "I immediately read this letter to our crew, who were so overjoyed that many of them shed tears." The celebration was short-lived, since the overseers were determined to work their slaves to the last: "They were still drove hard to work, and many of them flogged."[4] When their captain, William Bainbridge, visited—he had been living under house arrest at the quarters of the American consul with the other officers—he confirmed the long-awaited news. But he also warned that until the final treaties were signed, care should be taken not to cause any disruptions that might throw the agreement into jeopardy.

All told, 296 of the 307 officers and crew of the *Philadelphia* would leave Tripoli to return to the United States; many were in ill health and at least two died during the voyage home. Five others had died during their captivity, and five more had "turned renegade," converting to Islam to avoid slavery. Another captive stayed voluntarily in a diplomatic role as a temporary consul to Tripoli until a permanent one was appointed.

The five converts were called before the bashaw and asked their intentions. One, a sailor named John Wilson, had served as an overseer of the prisoners and expressed his wish to remain in Tripoli. Although the other four declared their determination to return with their shipmates and rebuild their lives in America, they would get no such chance. "Wilson was honored and caressed by the Bashaw and his Divan for his singular fidelity—while the other four were sent into the country with a formidable guard."

Once back in the United States, Ray compiled his recollections and published *Horrors of Slavery; or, The American Tars in Tripoli*, in 1808. The stories of Ray and the other captives who recorded their experiences changed America's future, helping to steel determination to stop piracy—and to inspire others to do the same—once and for all. And they continue to remind readers today that the fight for freedom is central to the American story and to the nation's success.

In the decades after the Barbary wars, America's standing in the world shot up while the Barbary States' standing went down. The four "piratical states" became colonial dependents of either Spain or France. In the same span of time, the United States became a power to be reckoned with in the Atlantic world.

In part, this emergence was economic. The rapid renewal of commerce following the War of 1812 led to a sevenfold increase in trade with Great Britain alone in the years leading up to the Civil War. But the emerging nation's power was based on more than trade.

During the Second War of Independence, as many chose to call the War of 1812, the American Navy outperformed all expectations, with American warships victorious in five of the first six ship-to-ship confrontations with the vaunted Royal Navy. Later, the navy's dramatic success in 1815 off the Barbary Coast boosted patriotism and made Americans more willing to invest in national defense than they had been. In the months after Decatur and Bainbridge and their flotillas returned victorious to the United States, James Madison asked Congress to pass the Act for the Gradual Increase of the Navy. Enacted in April 1816, the law authorized the spending of a whopping $1 million a year over eight years to build nine battleships and twelve frigates.

Americans knew what it was to stand up to enemies both at home and abroad now, and they did not want to be caught unprepared ever again. As Madison himself put it at the time, "A certain degree of preparation for war is not only indispensable to avert disasters in the onset, but affords also security for the continuance of the peace." The conclusion was based on experience, since the exploits of the U.S. Navy and Marines had gained American merchant sailors freedom of the seas. No more American ships were being taken by Barbary pirates as prizes, and the captivity of sailors had ceased.

The growing confidence in the nation's military strength fueled national policy. The United States had successfully rejected the Old World's model of complying with the pirates off the coast of Europe and Africa, and it was now bold enough to reject European interference with life on its own side of the Atlantic. Military strength made possible an unprecedented assertion by President Monroe in his annual message of 1823. The Monroe Doctrine, as the principle he introduced came to be called, warned the European powers not to trespass on North or South American shores. Monroe vowed that any attempt to interfere with the destiny of nations in the American hemisphere would be regarded "as the manifestation of an unfriendly disposition toward the United States."

The idea wasn't new. Continental Army forces a half-century earlier had fought under a flag that warned DON'T TREAD ON ME. What was new was that, with the nation's world-class navy, Monroe and his Secretary of State, John Adams (who played a crucial part in drafting the Monroe Doctrine), felt confident their country had the capability to back up such strong words.

Individually and collectively, presidents Jefferson, Madison, and Monroe (and future president John Quincy Adams) had come to recognize that, at times, military force was necessary to ensure national dignity and to protect the nation's interests. They had learned that in some quarters and at certain times, diplomacy alone was simply not sufficient to maintain peace. And they had learned that it was worth spending money on a military, since American lives were at stake.

Many men and women suffered in captivity before America's intervention rid the world of North African piracy, but their suffering was not in vain. After centuries of piracy along the Barbary Coast, only the exercise of military strength had succeeded in ending the state-sanctioned practice of terror on the high seas. The lesson was not lost on America. The young nation gained from this chapter the courage to exercise its strength in the world, and it would remember that lesson in the future when other innocent lives were at stake.

—B.K.
August 2016

ACKNOWLEDGMENTS

I know that readers often skip the acknowledgments when they breeze through a book, but I urge you to make an exception here because this project was a true team effort. Unlike our last book, *George Washington's Secret Six*, which was on a subject I had been studying since 1988, this book had a shorter runway, but the passion and intensity of the research were even greater.

First, I have to credit my role models for this project and for *GWSS*, beginning with the most vital: Roger Ailes. I always sectioned off my love of history from my passion for news, but talking with and observing Roger Ailes shape Fox News, it became clear to me that the only way to truly appreciate how special this nation is is to understand our past and the hurdles we had to clear to even exist. There are two other people I have to credit for inspiring me from afar: Bill O'Reilly and Glenn Beck. They were the first news hosts I saw soar to success while always providing a sense of history and relevance. Glenn often did it as an element of his show and Bill has completed a series of American history books that have sold tens of millions of copies. This helped me realize that there is a need for books like this and that so many of our viewers are passionate readers as well!

Now in terms of this project, it's always a thrill working with Don Yaeger, one of this nation's finest authors, and his incredible cohort Tiffany Yecke Brooks. Tiffany has an unmatched work ethic; she is smarter and more humble than anyone I know and was indispensable in this book's completion (and—dare I say?—success). I must mention that Tiffany had the wisdom to marry a Marine, so maybe that explains the passion she had for telling this great story.

Special thanks to Adrian Zackheim, president and publisher of Sentinel, for believing in us to tell the story and for editing and encouraging us over the last three years. Of course, nothing happens without our amazing agent, Bob Barnett. Without the respect Bob has earned in this business we would not have had the good fortune to work with Sentinel on our first project, let alone come back for this one. He works hard, is available almost anytime you need him, and always sports a smile. Thanks, Bob!

If you can keep a secret let me also tell you about one of the stars of the book business, Bria Sandford. She defines the word "indispensable." You rarely get to work with someone who is so deadline oriented but never shows stress or sacrifices creativity. Bria has all those skills. Her ability to help us find our voice in this project and put it on the page was almost magical. Her assistant, Kaushik Viswanath, was also a big help in the process.

As for research, the first person I called when we were considering doing this book was University of Virginia's director of politics, Dr. Larry Sabato. His blessing was vitally important, as was the introduction and meeting with Jim Sofka. Jim might just be the most respected scholar on the Barbary War period and UVA must be thrilled to have him; his kindness and insight were truly needed and appreciated. Hugh Howard was also a huge ally for this book and his encyclopedic knowledge of American history is mind-boggling.

I can't overstate how moving it was to see the great lengths the Marine Corps History Division took to make this book complete. The department is led by Dr. Charles P. Neimeyer, a great leader and just a great all-around person. He's surrounded by an incredible can-do team that includes Ms. Annette D. Amerman (Historian, Marine Corps History Division), Mr. Gregory L. Cina (Archivist, Marine Corps Archives), Ms. Beth L. Crumley (Historian, Marine Corps History Division), and Colonel Peter J. Ferraro, USMC, Retired (Historian, Marine Corps History Division).

It is with great admiration that I would like to thank Congresswoman Marsha Blackburn. She helped clear my path in Washington, opening doors and guiding me through the National Archives/Jefferson Collection.

The best place to research Thomas Jefferson will always be his estate in Monticello and that's where Anna Berkes stepped up big for us. When you research our third president, you are dealing with a man who accomplished enough for ten lifetimes and it can be overwhelming, to say the least. As a research librarian at the Jefferson Library, Anna has knowledge of the president's work that was invaluable, along with her patience! Special thanks, too, for the great tour of the grounds.

Of course, this project wouldn't get off the ground without the support of the Fox News family and no acknowledgments section would be complete without saluting their loyalty. VP Bill Shine has to keep two networks rolling, but still finds time to advise and guide me on my books and I love that he has a special affinity for great

American stories. Suzanne Scott and Shari Berg have been sensational supporters, despite their wide swath of work responsibilities.

Since 1997, I have had the chance to cohost *Fox and Friends*, which is the foundation of my eighteen-year stay at the channel, and knowing the morning show team was behind me was extremely humbling. Despite being in charge of twenty-eight hours of LIVE TV a week and having families of their own, Executive Producers Lauren Petterson and Jennifer Rauchet constantly expressed great enthusiasm for a book and topic they knew little about, but showed boundless curiosity to support. Senior Producers Gavin Hadden, Sean Groman, and Megan Albano have been vital to my completing this project and their skill in weaving the book into our show is noted and appreciated.

I also have to salute my *Fox and Friends* cohosts, Steve Doocy and Elisabeth Hasselback. Their preparation, performance, and patriotism have been inspiring to me through the construction of this story and I look forward to introducing America to this slice of American history with both of these pros by my side. As viewers know, I am always privileged to appear alongside superstar *Friends* anchors Heather Nauert, Ainsley Earhardt, and Heather Childers, and weathercaster Maria Molina. And, of course, the *Fox and Friends* franchise would not be complete without the weekend ratings champs Tucker Carlson, Clayton Morris, and Anna Kooiman.

I look forward to bringing the story to my radio family and fans on *Kilmeade and Friends* as well. First, I have to thank Alyson Mansfield. As senior producer she goes above and beyond on a daily basis, and when the book launches it gets four times as hard—yet she somehow always makes it work. She has heard the play-by-play of this book from concept to completion and her feedback along the way has been invaluable. Harry Kapsalis and Eric Albeen, you have also heard me talk about and work through this book and watched me sign thirty thousand copies. I appreciate all your support and hard work every day.

On the planning and promotion front, Will Weisser and Tara Gilbride at Sentinel showed leadership and enthusiasm that set a great tone for the rollout. Taylor Fleming is a true pro and innovator who seems to never rest when it comes to working on our behalf. Preparation for this promotion began six months ago and George Uribe, founder of Guest Booker, has been endlessly creative and innovative; in fact, I think he likes the book even more than I do (which is a great feeling)! His secret weapons, Molly Polcari and Victoria Delgado, have made it their mission to spread the word on this project and are often the most spirited on our weekly conference calls. As you know, so much of today's sales are done over the Internet and heading up that operation are Paul Guest and Lindsay Wallace, two talented and vital cogs in the wheel of success. I cannot thank them enough.

Last and most important, thanks to the world's best family. My wife, Dawn, and children Bryan, Kirstyn, and Kaitlyn—this is why I have been working late and spending hours reading, writing, and reviewing instead of playing or spending more time with you. Thanks for understanding or at least pretending to. I hope when you read this you will decide that it was worth it!

In conclusion, this book (like *George Washington's Secret Six*) features historic figures of huge importance playing supporting roles to relatively unknown, unsung patriots. This book is dedicated to all those who fight our wars and never seek or receive the credit they deserve. It's up to the next generation to tell their stories, because without the Americans fighting in the trenches and on the seas, we would not be able to enjoy life as citizens of the world's greatest economic and military superpower.

NOTES

PROLOGUE: UNPREPARED AND UNPROTECTED

1. Richard O'Brien to Thomas Jefferson, August 24, 1785.

CHAPTER 1: AMERICANS ABROAD

1. Elizabeth Wayles Eppes to Thomas Jefferson, October 13, 1784.
2. Thomas Jefferson to Mary Jefferson, September 20, 1785.
3. Mary Jefferson to Thomas Jefferson, ca. May 1786.
4. Thomas Jefferson to Francis Eppes, August 30, 1785.
5. Ibid.
6. Thomas Jefferson to Francis Eppes, December 11, 1785.
7. Lambert, *The Barbary Wars*, p. 16.
8. Thomas Jefferson to Nathaniel Greene, January 12, 1785.
9. M. Le Veillard to Dr. Franklin, October 9, 1785.
10. John Adams to Thomas Jefferson, February 17, 1786.
11. Ibid.
12. John Adams to John Jay, February 20, 1786.
13. Thomas Jefferson to William Carmichael, May 5, 1786.
14. George Washington address to Congress, December 30, 1790.

15. "American Commissioners to John Jay," March 28, 1786.
16. John Adams to Thomas Jefferson, July 3, 1786.
17. Thomas Jefferson to John Adams, July 11, 1786.
18. John Adams to Thomas Jefferson, July 31, 1786.

CHAPTER 2: SECRETARY JEFFERSON

1. Thomas Jefferson to James Monroe, November 11, 1784.
2. "Mediterranean Trade," December 30, 1790.
3. Ibid.
4. David Humphreys to Michael Murphy, October 6, 1793.
5. Edward Church to Thomas Jefferson, October 12, 1793.
6. "Appointment of Joel Barlow as U.S. Agent, Algiers," February 10, 1796.
7. Eaton, *The Life of the Late Gen. William Eaton*, p. 17.
8. Ibid., pp. 19–20.
9. Ibid., p. 26.

CHAPTER 3: THE HUMILIATION OF THE USS *GEORGE WASHINGTON*

1. Log of the USS *George Washington*.
2. Ibid.
3. Richard O'Brien to the secretary of state, May 16, 1800.
4. London, *Victory in Tripoli*, p. 4.
5. Richard O'Brien to the secretary of state, September 20, 1800.
6. Ibid.
7. William Bainbridge to Richard O'Brien, October 9, 1800.
8. Richard O'Brien to William Eaton, October 19, 1800.
9. Log of the USS *George Washington*.
10. William Eaton, personal note on letter to Richard O'Brien, October 19, 1800.

CHAPTER 4: JEFFERSON TAKES CHARGE

1. "Treaty of Peace and Friendship Between the United States of America and the Bey and Subjects of Tripoli of Barbary."
2. William Eaton to Timothy Pickering, June 24, 1800.
3. Dearborn, *The Life of William Bainbridge*, p. 40.
4. Jefferson, notes, May 15, 1801–April 8, 1803.
5. Ibid.

CHAPTER 5: A FLAGPOLE FALLS

1. Joel Barlow to the secretary of state, August 18, 1797.
2. James L. Cathcart, "Circular Letter," February 21, 1801.
3. James L. Cathcart to Secretary of State James Madison, May 11, 1801.
4. Ibid., May 16, 1801.
5. James L. Cathcart to Nicholas C. Nissen, May 15, 1801.
6. James L. Cathcart to Secretary of State James Madison, June 4, 1801.

CHAPTER 6: THE FIRST FLOTILLA

1. Richard Dale to Andrew Sterett, July 30, 1801.
2. Captain Richard Dale to the secretary of the navy, July 2, 1801.
3. Ibid.
4. Captain Richard Dale to Samuel Barron, July 4, 1801.

CHAPTER 7: SKIRMISH AT SEA

1. Richard Dale to the dey of Algiers and the bey of Tunis, July 10, 1801.
2. William Eaton to James Madison, July 10, 1801.
3. Eaton, *The Life of the Late Gen. William Eaton,* p. 59.
4. William Eaton, "Journal," February 22, 1799.
5. William Eaton to Secretary of State Timothy Pickering, June 15, 1799.
6. William Eaton to Eliza Eaton, April 6, 1799.

7. William Eaton to Secretary of State Timothy Pickering, June 15, 1799.
8. Richard Dale to the secretary of the navy, July 19, 1801.
9. Richard Dale to the bashaw of Tripoli, July 25, 1801.
10. Richard Dale to Andrew Sterett, July 30, 1801.
11. Extract of a letter from Andrew Sterett.
12. "Capture of the Ship of War *Tripoli* by U.S. Schooner *Enterprize*," *National Intelligencer and Washington Advertiser*, November 18, 1801.
13. Newton Keene to William W. Burrows, August 10, 1801.
14. "Capture of the Ship of War *Tripoli* by U.S. Schooner *Enterprize*," *National Intelligencer and Washington Advertiser*, November 18, 1801.
15. Thomas Jefferson, "Presidential Message," December 8, 1801.

CHAPTER 8: PATIENCE WEARS THIN

1. Annals of Congress, Seventh Congress, First Session, pp. 325–26.
2. Newton Keene to William W. Burrows, September 28, 1801.
3. James Brown to James Leander Cathcart, September 16, 1801.
4. Richard Dale to the secretary of the navy, December 13, 1801.
5. Ibid.
6. Richard Dale to William Bainbridge, December 15, 1801.
7. William Eaton to Secretary of State James Madison, September 5, 1801.
8. Edwards, *Barbary General*, p. 95.
9. William Eaton to James Madison, September 5, 1801.
10. Richard O'Brien to James Madison, July 22, 1801.

CHAPTER 9: THE DOLDRUMS OF SUMMER

1. Henry Wadsworth, from his personal journal, September 13, 1802, reprinted in *Naval Documents*.
2. Richard V. Morris to the secretary of the navy, May 31, 1802.
3. Alexander Murray to the secretary of the navy, June 1, 1802.
4. William Eaton to James Madison, August 9, 1802.
5. Secretary of the navy to Richard V. Morris, April 20, 1802.

6. William Eaton to James L. Cathcart, April 26, 1802.
7. Alexander Murray, "Journal of the U.S. Frigate *Constellation,*" July 22, 1802.
8. Cooper, *History of the Navy of the United States of America*, pp. 157–58.
9. Alexander Murray, "Journal of the U.S. Frigate *Constellation,*" July 22, 1802.
10. Alexander Murray to the secretary of the navy, July 30, 1802.
11. William Eaton to James Madison, August 23, 1802.
12. Secretary of the navy to Richard V. Morris, April 20, 1802.
13. Richard V. Morris to the secretary of the navy, October 15, 1802.
14. Thomas Jefferson to Albert Gallatin, March 28, 1803.
15. William Eaton to Hamet Qaramanli, August 6, 1802.
16. James L. Cathcart, journal notes for James Madison, March 14, 1803.
17. Richard V. Morris to the secretary of the navy, March 30, 1803.
18. Abbot, *The Naval History of the United States*, p. 189.
19. "Journal of Midshipman Henry Wadsworth," April 2, 1803.
20. Eaton, *The Life of the Late Gen. William Eaton*, p. 244.
21. Secretary of the navy to Richard V. Morris, June 21, 1803.
22. "Concerning Commodore Morris' Squadron in the Mediterranean."
23. Thomas Jefferson to Phillip Mazzei, July 18, 1804.
24. William Eaton to James Madison, August 23, 1802.

CHAPTER 10: THE OMENS OF OCTOBER

1. Edward Preble to Mary Deering, August 13, 1803.
2. Quoted in Flexner, *George Washington and the New Nation,* vol. 3, pp. 321–22, 377.
3. Secretary of the navy to Edward Preble, August 2, 1803.
4. Ibid., July 13, 1803.
5. Edward Preble to the secretary of the navy, September 23, 1803.
6. Edward Preble, *Diary*, October 6, 1803.
7. Edward Preble, quoted in Tucker, *Dawn Like Thunder*, p. 205.
8. Tobias Lear to Mrs. Lear, October 13, 1803.
9. Ralph Izard Jr. to Mrs. Ralph Izard Sr., October 11, 1803.

10. Edward Preble to the secretary of the navy, October 10, 1803.
11. Emperor of Morocco to Thomas Jefferson, October 11, 1803.
12. Edward Preble to Mary Deering, ca. October 1803.

CHAPTER 11: THE *PHILADELPHIA* DISASTER

1. William Bainbridge to Edward Preble, November 12, 1803.
2. William Bainbridge to Tobias Lear, February 8, 1804.
3. William Bainbridge to Susan Bainbridge, November 1, 1803.
4. Whipple, *To the Shores of Tripoli*, p. 118.
5. Cowdery, in Baepler, *White Slaves, African Masters*, p. 162.
6. Ibid., p. 190.
7. Ibid., p. 191.
8. Shaw, *A Short Sketch*, p. 23, reprinted in Baepler, *White Slaves, African Masters*, p. 19.
9. William Bainbridge to the Secretary of the Navy, November 1, 1803.

CHAPTER 12: BY THE COVER OF DARKNESS

1. Edward Preble to Mary Deering, November 20, 1803.
2. Charles Stewart to Susan Decatur, December 12, 1826.
3. Edward Preble to the secretary of the navy, December 10, 1803.
4. Tucker, *Stephen Decatur*, pp. 42–43.
5. Dearborn, *The Life of William Bainbridge*, p. 60.
6. William Bainbridge to Edward Preble, December 5, 1803.
7. Edward Preble to the secretary of the navy, January 17, 1804.
8. Edward Preble to Stephen Decatur, January 31, 1804.
9. Ibid.
10. Morris, *The Autobiography of Commodore Charles Morris, U.S. Navy*, p. 27.
11. Lewis Heermann, quoted in McKee, *Edward Preble: A Naval Biography, 1761–1807*, p. 197.
12. Ralph Izard Jr. to Mrs. Ralph Izard Sr., February 20, 1804.

13. Ray, *Horrors of Slavery*, p. 76.
14. Ibid.

CHAPTER 13: THE BATTLE OF TRIPOLI

1. Stephen Decatur to Keith Spence, January 9, 1805.
2. Edward Preble to the secretary of the navy, February 3, 1804.
3. *New York Evening Post,* March 28, 1804.
4. Secretary of the navy to Edward Preble, May 22, 1804.
5. James Madison to Thomas FitzSimons, April 13, 1804.
6. The oft-quoted words might or might not have been Nelson's but have long been attributed to him, though by a biographer some forty years after the burning of the USS *Philadelphia*. Allen, *Our Navy and the Barbary Corsairs*, p. 173.
7. George Davis to the secretary of state, March 26, 1804.
8. Edward Preble to the secretary of the navy, June 14, 1804.
9. Edward Preble to Richard O'Brien, June 13, 1804.
10. Preble, *Diary*, June 14, 1804.
11. Eaton, *The Life of the Late Gen. William Eaton*, p. 242.
12. Ibid., p. 262.
13. Edwards, *Barbary General*, p. 131.
14. Eaton, *The Life of the Late Gen. William Eaton*, p. 265.
15. Thomas Jefferson to John Page, June 25, 1804.
16. James Madison to Tobias Lear, June 6, 1804.
17. Secretary of the navy to Samuel Barron, June 6, 1804.
18. Edward Preble to James L. Cathcart, May 28, 1804.
19. Edward Preble to the secretary of the navy, September 18, 1804.
20. Ibid.; McKee, *Edward Preble: A Naval Biography, 1761–1807*, p. 262.
21. Stephen Decatur to Keith Spence, January 9, 1805.
22. Edward Preble to the secretary of the navy, September 18, 1804.
23. Mackenzie, *Life of Stephen Decatur*, p. 97.
24. Edward Preble to the secretary of the navy, September 18, 1804.

25. Dearborn, *The Life of William Bainbridge, Esq.*, pp. 74–75.
26. Edward Preble to Mary Deering, quoted in McKee, *Edward Preble: A Naval Biography, 1761–1807*, p. 307.

CHAPTER 14: OPENING A NEW FRONT

1. William Eaton to Congressman Samuel Lyman, October 12, 1801.
2. William Eaton to Alexander Ball, December 13, 1804.
3. William Eaton, "Journal," December 7, 1804.
4. William Eaton to the secretary of the navy, December 13, 1804.
5. Hamet Qaramanli to William Eaton, January 3, 1805.
6. Alexander Murray to Richard V. Morris, August 22, 1802.

CHAPTER 15: WIN IN THE DESERT OR DIE IN THE DESERT

1. William Eaton, "Journal," April 2, 1805; *The Life of the Late Gen. William Eaton*, p. 317.
2. Eaton, *The Life of the Late Gen. William Eaton*, p. 323.
3. William Eaton, "Journal," April 2, 1805; *The Life of the Late Gen. William Eaton*, p. 323.
4. Eaton, ibid., April 16, 1805; ibid., p. 329.
5. Eaton, ibid.," April 25, 1805; ibid., p. 330.
6. William Eaton to the Governor of Derne, April 26, 1805; ibid., p. 337.
7. William Eaton to Samuel Barron, April 29, 1805; ibid., p. 337.
8. Ibid.
9. Edwards, *Barbary General*, p. 214.

CHAPTER 16: ENDGAME

1. Tobias Lear to John Rodgers, May 1, 1805.
2. Jonathan Cowdery, "Journal," May 24, 1805.
3. William Eaton, "Journal," May 12, 1805; *The Life of the Late Gen. William Eaton*, p. 340.

4. William Eaton to Samuel Barron, May 29, 1805.
5. William Eaton to John Rodgers, June 13, 1805.
6. Timothy Pickering to unknown, March 21, 1806.
7. "Report of the Committee," March 17, 1806.

CHAPTER 17: FAIR WINDS AND FOLLOWING SEAS

1. *National Intelligencer,* November 6, 1805.

EPILOGUE

1. John Quincy Adams to Stephen Decatur, quoted in Mackenzie, *Decatur*, p. 27.

AFTERWORD

1. Riley, *Sufferings in Africa*, p. 64.
2. Ibid, p. 72.
3. Ray *Horrors of Slavery*, May 22.
4. Ibid, p. 106.

A NOTE ON SOURCES

A book like this could not exist if not for the documents—the letters, the journals, the ships' logs, and the rest—left by the participants. A compilation of the most essential of those is to be found in *Naval Documents Related to the United States Wars with the Barbary Powers* (1939–1944). The encyclopedic contents of this six-volume set must form the basis of any book written on this subject.

Another essential primary source is the collection called *American State Papers.* In effect, it is Congress's diary, and contains reports, letters, and other materials, as well as congressional motions and minutes. It is available online at http://memory.loc.gov/ammem/amlaw/lwsp.html.

As the page-by-page source notes suggest, the personal papers of the participants have also been invaluable: the collected papers of Thomas Jefferson, John Adams, and George Washington have all been published in richly annotated editions that are generally available. Less accessible are the papers of Tobias Lear (not published but in the archives of the Clements Library at the University of Michigan) and Edward Preble (Library of Congress). Numerous other players in this drama left memoirs and correspondence. Many of those documents have been published and are listed in the bibliography below, including writings from James Leander Cathcart, many of the Barbary captives (among them William Ray and Elijah Shaw), and, in particular, the remarkable William Eaton.

Numerous other writers have written on this subject over the last two centuries, and below you'll find a selected list of the best of the primary and secondary works.

Abbot, Willis J. *The Naval History of the United States.* New York: Dodd, Mead and Company, 1896.

Adams, Henry. *History of the United States During the Administration of Thomas Jefferson.* New York: Library of America, 1986.

Allen, Gardner W. *Our Navy and the Barbary Corsairs.* Boston: Houghton Mifflin Company, 1905.

Allison, Robert J. *The Crescent Obscured.* New York: Oxford University Press, 1995.

Baepler, Paul. *White Slaves, African Masters: An Anthology of American Barbary Captivity Narratives.* Chicago: University of Chicago Press, 1999.

Cathcart, James Leander. *Tripoli: First War with the United States.* La Porte, IN: Herald Print, 1901.

Cogliano, Francis D. *Emperor of Liberty: Thomas Jefferson's Foreign Policy.* New Haven, CT: Yale University Press, 2014.

Cooper, J. Fenimore. *History of the Navy of the United States of America.* New York: Stringer and Townsend, 1856.

Cunningham, Noble E., Jr. *The Process of Government Under Jefferson.* Princeton, NJ: Princeton University Press, 1978.

Dearborn, H. A. S. *The Life of William Bainbridge, Esq., of the United States Navy.* Princeton, NJ: Princeton University Press, 1931.

Eaton, William. *The Life of the Late Gen. William Eaton.* Brookfield, MA: E. Merriam & Co., 1813.

Edwards, Samuel. *Barbary General: The Life of William H. Eaton*. Englewood Cliffs, NJ: Prentice-Hall, Inc., 1968.

Ellis, Joseph J. *American Sphinx: The Character of Thomas Jefferson*. New York: Alfred A. Knopf, 1996.

Ferguson, Eugene S. *Truxtun of the Constellation: The Life of Commodore Thomas Truxtun, U.S. Navy, 1755–1822*. Baltimore, MD: Johns Hopkins University Press, 1959.

Flexner, James Thomas. *George Washington*. 4 vols. Boston: Little, Brown & Co., 1965–1972.

Irwin, Ray D. *Diplomatic Relations of the United States with the Barbary Powers: 1776–1816*. Chapel Hill: University of North Carolina Press, 1931.

Kimball, Marie. *Jefferson: The Scene of Europe*. New York: Coward-McCann, Inc., 1950.

Kitzen, Michael L. S. *Tripoli and the United States at War: A History of American Relations with the Barbary States, 1785–1805*. Jefferson, NC: McFarland & Co., Inc., 1992.

Lambert, Frank. *The Barbary Wars*. New York: Hill and Wang, 2005.

Lane-Poole, Stanley. *The Story of the Barbary Corsairs*. New York: G. P. Putnam's Sons, 1890.

London, Joshua E. *Victory in Tripoli: How America's War with the Barbary Pirates Established the U.S. Navy and Built a Nation*. New York: John Wiley & Sons, Inc., 2005.

McCullough, David. *John Adams*. New York: Simon & Schuster, 2001.

McKee, Christopher. *Edward Preble: A Naval Biography, 1761–1807*. Annapolis, MD: Naval Institute Press, 1972.

Mackenzie, Alexander Slidell. *Life of Stephen Decatur, Commodore in the U.S. Navy*. Boston: Charles C. Little and James Brown, 1846.

Magoun, F. Alexander. *The Frigate Constitution and Other Historic Ships*. New York: Dover Publications, 1987.

Malone, Dumas. *Jefferson and His Time*. 6 vols. Boston: Little, Brown & Company, 1948–1981.

Morris, Charles. *The Autobiography of Commodore Charles Morris, U.S. Navy*. Boston: A. Williams, 1880.

Nash, Howard P. Jr. *The Forgotten Wars: The Role of the U.S. Navy in the Quasi War with France and the Barbary Wars, 1798–1805.* South Brunswick, NJ: A. S. Barnes & Co., 1968.

Naval Documents Related to the United States Wars with the Barbary Powers. 6 vols. Washington, DC: Government Printing Office, 1939–1944.

Parker, Richard B. *Uncle Sam in Barbary: A Diplomatic History.* Gainesville: University Press of Florida, 2004.

Quincy, Josiah. *Figures of the Past from the Leaves of Old Journals.* Boston: Roberts Brothers, 1883.

Ray, William. *Horrors of Slavery; or, The American Tars in Tripoli.* New Brunswick, NJ: Rutgers University Press, 2008.

Riley, James, *Sufferings in Africa.* New York: T. & W. Mercein, 1817.

Shaw, Elijah. *A Short Sketch of the Life of Elijah Shaw.* Rochester, NY: Strong & Dawson, 1843.

Sumner, Charles. *White Slavery in the Barbary States.* Boston: P. J. Jewett and Company, 1853.

Toll, Ian W. *Six Frigates: The Epic History of the Founding of the U.S. Navy.* New York: W. W. Norton and Company, 2006.

Tucker, Glenn. *Dawn Like Thunder: The Barbary Wars and the Birth of the U.S. Navy.* Indianapolis: Bobbs-Merrill Company, 1963.

Tucker, Spencer. *Stephen Decatur: A Life Most Bold and Daring.* Annapolis, MD: Naval Institute Press, 2005.

Whipple, A. B. C. *To the Shores of Tripoli: The Birth of the U.S. Navy and Marines.* William Morrow and Company, Inc., 1991.

Wright, Louis B., and Julia H. Macleod. *The First Americans in North Africa: William Eaton's Struggle for a Vigorous Policy Against the Barbary Pirates, 1799–1805.* Princeton, NJ: Princeton University Press, 1945.

Zacks, Richard. *The Pirate Coast: Thomas Jefferson, the First Marines, and the Secret Mission of 1805.* New York: Hyperion, 2005.

INDEX

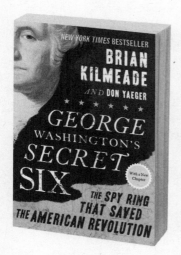

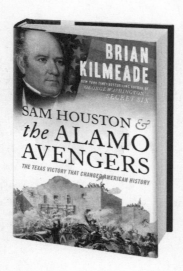

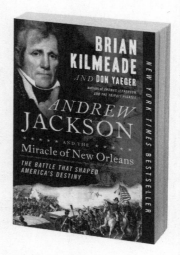

"A tale as improbable as it is spellbinding, told with a deft touch and insightful clarity. Brian Kilmeade has done it again."

—**GENERAL STANLEY McCHRYSTAL** (U.S. Army, Retired), author of *Team of Teams*

"The reader gets an inkling of the grit that made America great."

—**ERIK PRINCE**, author of *Civilian Warriors*

"A wild, page-turning history of one of America's most fascinating battles." —**BRAD MELTZER**, author of *The President's Shadow*

"A riveting introduction to one of the seminal battles in U.S. history. The War of 1812 folk legend of Old Hickory rides high on his horse again in this engrossing overview for readers of all ages. Highly recommended!" —**DOUGLAS BRINKLEY**, professor of history, Rice University, and author of *Rightful Heritage*

"The scholarship is impeccable, the topic immensely important, the story masterfully crafted. This little gem of a book belongs on the bookshelf of every history buff. What a triumph!" —**JAY WINIK**, author of *April 1865* and *1944*

"Kilmeade shows how the patriotism of Jackson and his generation made America great in the first place. A terrific read."

—**JANE HAMPTON COOK**, presidential historian and author of *The Burning of the White House*

ANDREW JACKSON

★ ★ ★ ★ ★ AND THE ★ ★ ★ ★ ★

MIRACLE OF NEW ORLEANS

ALSO BY BRIAN KILMEADE AND DON YAEGER

Thomas Jefferson and the Tripoli Pirates
George Washington's Secret Six

BRIAN KILMEADE

AND DON YAEGER

ANDREW JACKSON

AND THE

MIRACLE of NEW ORLEANS

THE BATTLE THAT SHAPED AMERICA'S DESTINY

SENTINEL

An imprint of Penguin Random House LLC
375 Hudson Street
New York, New York 10014

THE LIBRARY OF CONGRESS HAS CATALOGUED THE HARDCOVER EDITION AS FOLLOWS:
Names: Kilmeade, Brian, author. | Yaeger, Don, author.
Title: Andrew Jackson and the miracle of New Orleans : the battle that shaped America's destiny / Brian Kilmeade and Don Yaeger.
Description: New York, New York : Sentinel, an imprint of Penguin Random House, 2017. | Includes bibliographical references and index.
Identifiers: LCCN 2017027754 | ISBN 9780735213234 (hardcover) | ISBN 9780735213258 (epub)
Subjects: LCSH: New Orleans, Battle of, New Orleans, La., 1815. | Jackson, Andrew, 1767–1845—Military leadership. | Generals—United States—Biography. | United States—History—War of 1812—Campaigns.
Classification: LCC E356.N5 K55 2017 | DDC 973.5/239—dc23 LC record available at https://lccn.loc.gov/2017027754

First Sentinel hardcover edition: October 2017
First Sentinel trade paperback edition: October 2018
Sentinel trade paperback ISBN: 9780735213241

Printed in the United States of America

Book design by George Towne
Map illustrations by Daniel Lagin

5th Printing

To the unsung men and women whose faithful military service has kept us free and made generals like Jackson famous. Your names and faces may not be known by the world, but you'll never be forgotten by me.

—BK

Our situation seemed desperate. In case of an attack, we could hope to be saved only by a miracle, or by the wisdom and genius of a commander-in-chief. Accordingly, on his arrival, [Jackson] was immediately invested with the confidence of the public, and all hope centered in him. We shall, hereafter, see how amply he merited the confidence which he inspired.

—Major Arsène Lacarrière Latour

Historical Memoir of the War in West Florida and Louisiana in 1814–15: With an Atlas (1816)

CONTENTS

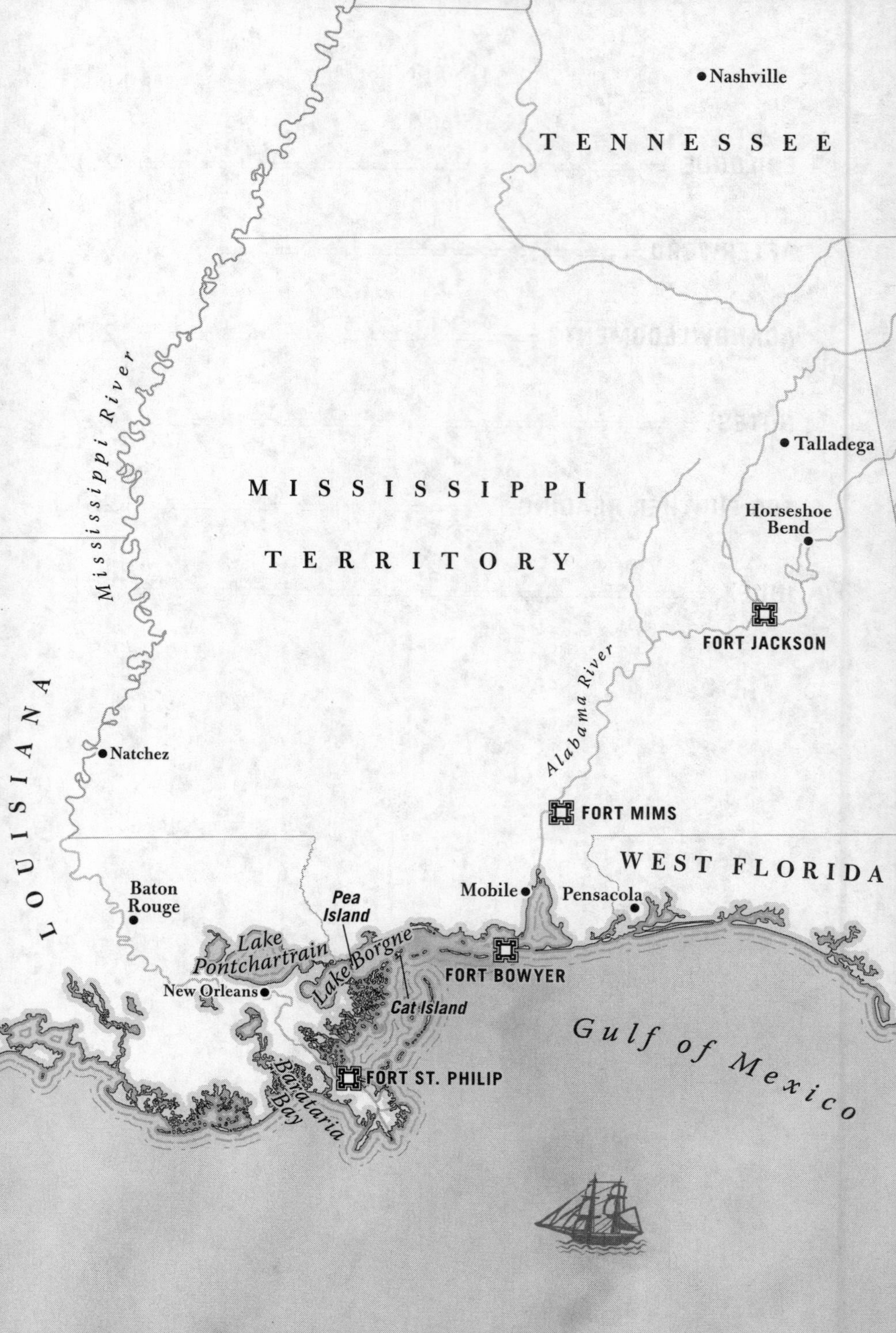

Nashville
TENNESSEE
Mississippi River
MISSISSIPPI
TERRITORY
Talladega
Horseshoe Bend
FORT JACKSON
Alabama River
LOUISIANA
Natchez
FORT MIMS
WEST FLORIDA
Baton Rouge
Pea Island
Mobile
Pensacola
Lake Pontchartrain
Lake Borgne
FORT BOWYER
New Orleans
Cat Island
Gulf of Mexico
Barataria Bay
FORT ST. PHILIP

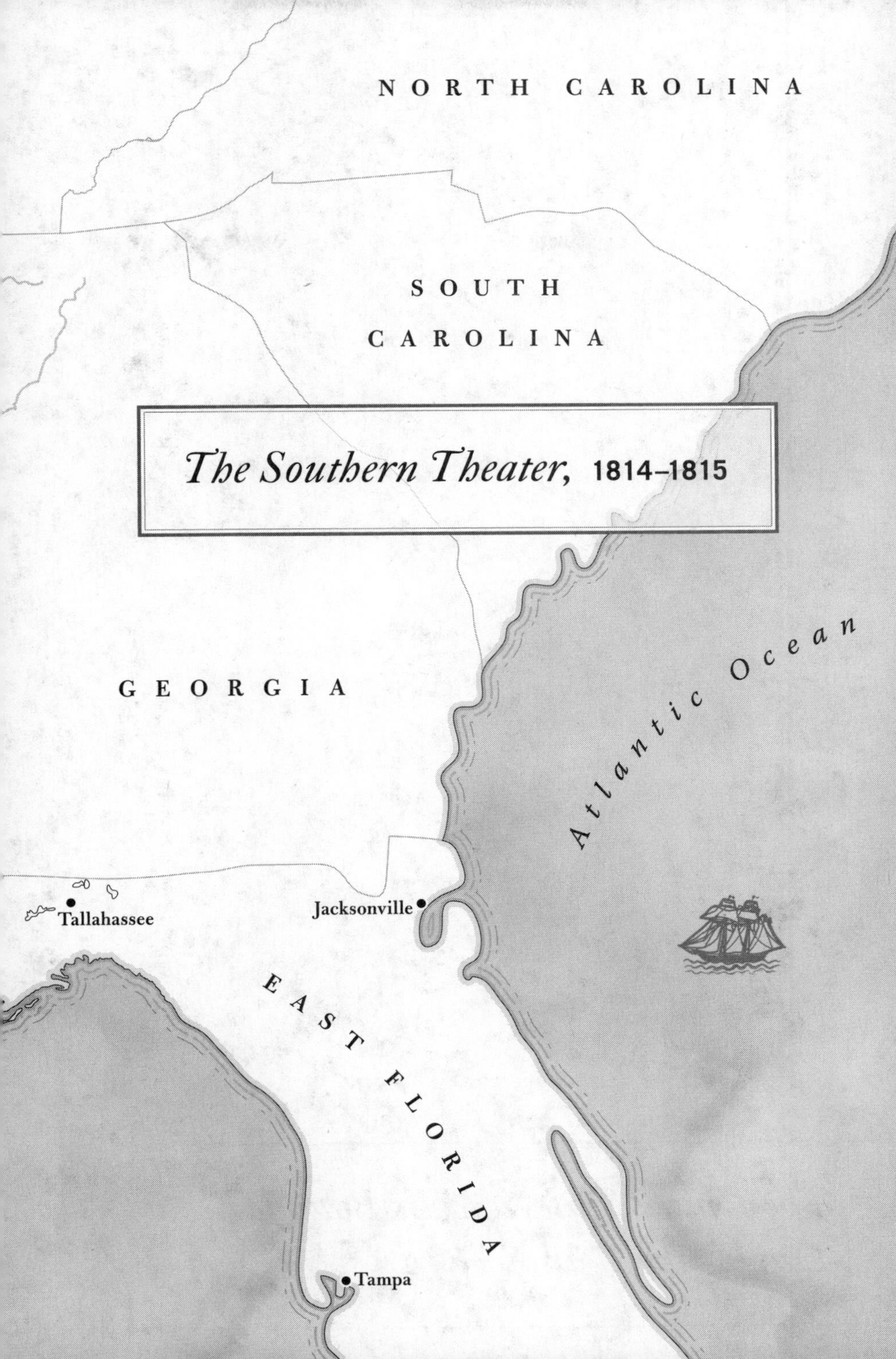
NORTH CAROLINA
SOUTH
CAROLINA
The Southern Theater, 1814–1815
GEORGIA
Atlantic Ocean
Tallahassee
Jacksonville
EAST FLORIDA
Tampa

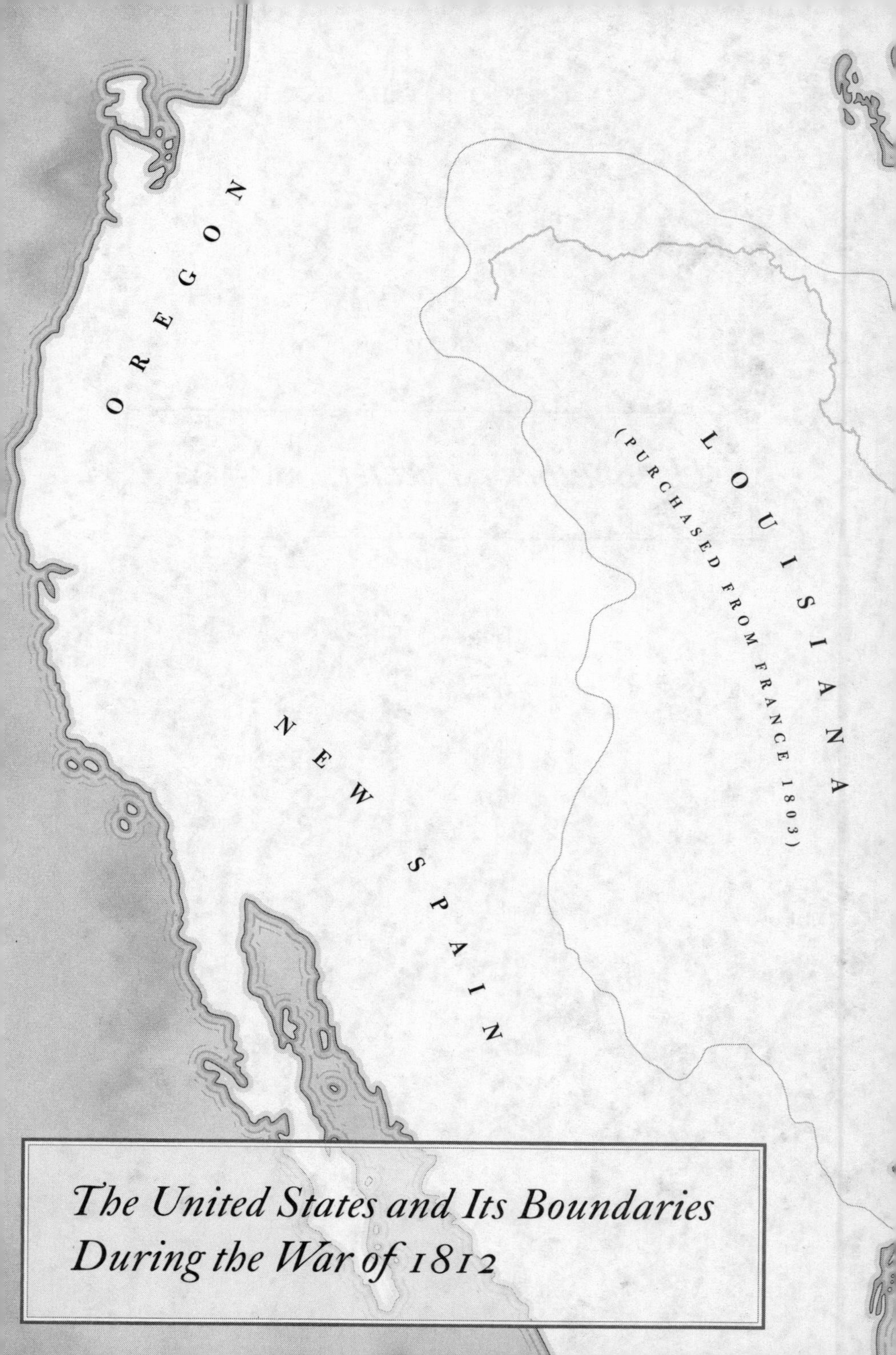

The United States and Its Boundaries During the War of 1812

INDIANA TERRITORY
Missouri River
ILLINOIS
INDIANA
MICHIGAN
OHIO
Ohio River
Mississippi River
NEW YORK
VERMONT
NEW HAMPSHIRE
MAINE
Boston
MASS.
RHODE ISLAND
CONNECTICUT
New York
PENNSYLVANIA
Philadelphia
NEW JERSEY
Baltimore
MARYLAND
DELAWARE
Washington, DC
VIRGINIA
KENTUCKY
Nashville
TENNESSEE
NORTH CAROLINA
SOUTH CAROLINA
MISSISSIPPI TERRITORY
GEORGIA
Natchez
Mobile
New Orleans
SPANISH FLORIDA

ANDREW JACKSON

* * * * * AND THE * * * * *

MIRACLE OF NEW ORLEANS

PROLOGUE

In the spring of 1781, the redcoats arrived in upland Carolina, and they brought terror with them. As they searched the countryside for the rebels, they turned the region the Jackson family called home into an armed camp. Elizabeth Jackson's youngest son, Andrew, though barely fourteen years of age, hated their presence—and quickly learned just how costly the fight for liberty could be.

On April 9, Andy and his brother, Robert, two years older, earned the wrath of the invading force by joining a battle to defend the local meetinghouse against a band of Tories reinforced by British dragoons. The fight went badly for the Americans, but the brothers, unlike a cousin who was severely wounded and captured, were lucky. They escaped and, after spending a night hiding in the brush, the two Jackson boys managed to reach their cousin's home to deliver the news of his fate. Once there, however, their luck ran out: a Tory spy spotted their horses and informed the British of their whereabouts.

A lesson in the cruelties of war was soon delivered. As the Jackson brothers stood helplessly at the point of British swords, the enemy set about destroying their aunt and uncle's home. Determined to make an example of these rebels, the redcoats shattered dishes. They ripped clothing to rags. They smashed furniture. Then, with the house in ruins, the commanding officer decided upon one more humiliation. He chose Andy Jackson as his target.

He ordered tall and gangly Andy Jackson to kneel before him and clean the mud from his boots. The boy refused.

"Sir, I am a prisoner of war, and claim to be treated as such."[1]

Enraged by the young American's defiance, the British officer raised his sword and brought it down on Jackson's head. Had Andy not raised his arm to deflect the blow, his skull might have been split open. As it was, the blade gashed his forehead and sliced his hand to the bone. Not satisfied at drawing blood from Andy, the soldier turned and slashed at his brother, tearing into his scalp, leaving him dazed and bleeding.

No one dressed their wounds. Instead, the Jackson brothers were marched forty miles, with neither food nor water, to join more than two hundred other rebellious colonists in a prison camp in Camden. There they were fed stale bread and exposed to the smallpox that raged among the prisoners kept in tightly packed conditions.

Their mother, Elizabeth Jackson, had already lost too much. Her husband, Andrew Jackson Sr., had worked himself to death shortly before Andrew was born, leaving the pregnant Elizabeth with two, soon to be three, young sons in the rugged wilderness of upland South Carolina. She had raised the baby and his brothers as best she could and tried to protect them from the dangers of the war, but the boys had joined the fight despite her pleas. Hugh, the oldest, had died at age sixteen of heat exhaustion after a battle the year before. Elizabeth was not about to lose her remaining sons now.

Traveling the long distance to their prison, she managed to persuade their jailers to include them in a prisoner exchange. But freedom didn't mean safety. Robert had fallen dangerously ill, his wound infected, and the family of three had many miles to travel—on just two horses. Robert, delirious, rode one, and the exhausted Elizabeth the other.

Andrew walked. He made the journey barefoot, since the British had taken his shoes. Although all three made it home through driving rains, Robert died two days later. Elizabeth had no time to nurse her grief—or her remaining son. As Andrew recovered from a fever, she set off for Charleston, where two of the nephews she helped raise were prisoners. She would never return. After completing a 160-mile journey, much of it through enemy territory, she became ill with cholera and died. Andrew would learn he was an orphan when a small bundle of her clothes was returned to his home.

Andrew Jackson would never forget the pain and humiliation of that summer. His father, mother, and brothers were dead. He himself bore the memory of British brutality, his forehead and hand forever marked by the British officer's sword, a reminder of the callous cruelty that had destroyed his family.

His mother may have left him alone, but she had not left him without words to live by. Years later, he would report that she had told him, "Make friends by being honest and keep them by being steadfast. Never tell a lie, nor take what is not your own, nor sue for slander—settle them cases yourself!"[2]

Andy wouldn't forget her advice, and he would take care to settle more than just slander. Great Britain had left him an orphan, and one day he would settle that score.

CHAPTER 1

Freedoms at Risk

These are the times which distinguish the real friend of his country from the town-meeting brawler and the sunshine patriot. . . . The former steps forth, and proclaims his readiness to march.

—Major General Andrew Jackson

On June 1, 1812, America declared war. After a hot debate, James Madison's war resolution was passed by a vote of 19–13 in the Senate and 79–49 in the House of Representatives, and, once again, the new nation would be taking on the world's premier military and economic power: Great Britain.

Twenty-nine years had passed since the colonists' improbable victory in the Revolutionary War, and for twenty-nine years the British had failed to respect American sovereignty. Now, the nation James Madison led had reached the limit of its tolerance. Great Britain's kidnapping of American sailors and stirring up of Indian tribes to attack settlers on the western frontier had made life intolerably difficult for many of America's second generation, including those hardscrabble men and women pushing the boundaries westward.

Though reluctant to risk the new nation's liberty, Madison was now ready to send a message to England and the world that America would stand up to the bully that chose to do her harm. The unanswered question was: Could America win? Less than thirty years removed from the last war, and with virtually no national army, were Americans prepared to take on Britain and defend themselves, this time without the help of France? The world was about to find out.

In fact, so many Americans opposed the war that the declaration posed a real risk to the country's national unity. The Federalist Party, mainly representing northerners whose economy relied on British trade, had unanimously opposed the war declaration. Many New Englanders wanted peace with Britain, and it was likely that some would even be willing to leave the Union in order to avoid a fight.

Yet peaceful attempts at resolving the conflict with Britain had already been tried—and hadn't helped the economy much. Five years earlier, when a British ship attacked the U.S. Navy's *Chesapeake,* killing three sailors and taking four others from the ship to impress them into service to the Crown, then-president Thomas Jefferson had attempted to retaliate. To protest this blatant hostility, Congress passed the Embargo Act, prohibiting overseas trade with Great Britain. Unfortunately, the act hurt Americans more than the British. In just fifteen months, the embargo produced a depression that cruelly punished merchants and farmers while doing little to deter the Royal Navy's interference and hardening New England's resistance to conflict. Further attempts at legislative pressure in the early years of James Madison's presidency had little effect, and British impressment had continued. By the time of the war declaration in June 1812, the number of sailors seized off the decks of American ships had risen to more than five thousand men.

To many, including Andrew Jackson, then forty years old, the attack on the *Chesapeake* alone had been an insult to American pride that demanded a military response. As Jackson wrote to a Virginia friend after learning of the *Chesapeake*'s fate, "The degradation offered to our government . . . has roused every feeling of the American heart, and war with that nation is inevitable."[1]

Yet America had waited, and the losses at sea mounted. At the same time, attempts to pacify the British had only resulted in further losses in America's new territory, "the West," which ran south to north from the Gulf of Mexico to Canada, bounded on the west by the Mississippi. There British agents were said to be agitating the Indians. For many years, the Five Civilized Tribes in the region (Cherokee, Chickasaw, Choctaw, Creek, and Seminole) had maintained peaceful relations with the European arrivals. But as more and more white settlers moved into native territories, tensions had risen and open conflict had broken out. In some places, travelers could no longer be certain whether the Native Americans they encountered were friendly; for inhabitants of the frontier, that meant the events of daily life were accompanied by fear. Stories circulated of fathers who returned from a day of hunting to find their children butchered, and of wives who stumbled upon their husbands scalped in the fields.

A major Shawnee uprising in the Indiana Territory in 1811 escalated the fear. And as the bloodshed increased, there were reports that the British were providing the Indians with weapons and promising them land if they carried out violent raids against American settlers. For Andrew Jackson, the threat had become too close for comfort when, in the spring of 1812, just a hundred miles from his home, a marauding band of Creeks killed six settlers and took a woman hostage. Jackson was certain the British were behind the attack on the little settlement at the mouth of the Duck River.

Westerners like Jackson fumed at the government's inability to resolve the country's problems, but their clout in Washington was limited. The decision makers from Virginia and New England had little sympathy for their inland countrymen. Eastern newspapers poked fun at the hill folks' backward ways, and much of the territory west of the Appalachian Mountains remained mysterious and wild, with few good roads and even fewer maps. The dangers faced by westerners were not felt by easterners, and their anguished demands for retaliation were scorned and dismissed by those whose wallets would be hurt by the war.

But eventually, despite many politicians' disdain for their hick neighbors to the west, Washington politics had begun to shift along with the nation's growing population. The West had gained new influence in the elections of 1810 and 1811, when the region sent a spirited band of new representatives to the Capitol. These men saw British attitudes toward the United States as a threat to American liberty and independence; they also saw the need for westward expansion, a move that the British were trying to thwart. Led by a young Kentuckian named Henry Clay, they quickly gained the nickname War Hawks, because, despite the risks, they knew it was time to fight.

Clay became Speaker of the House and he, along with the War Hawks and like-minded Republicans from the coastal states, put pressure on the Madison administration. Now, after years of resistance, Madison listened, and with Congress's vote, the War of 1812 began. America decided to stand up for its sovereignty on the sea and its security in the West.

The War Hawks in Washington were ecstatic about the declaration of war, and so was Jackson in Tennessee. At last he would have the chance to defend the nation he loved, to protect his family and friends—and, personally, to take revenge on the nation that had left him alone and scarred so many years before.

The Boy Becomes a Man

A quarter century before, Jackson had swallowed his grudge. When the Treaty of Paris made U.S. independence official in 1783, the orphaned sixteen-year-old adopted America as his family.

Relatives had taken him in after his mother's death. He became a saddler's apprentice, then, his ambitions rising, he clerked for a North Carolina attorney. Andrew Jackson's cobbled-together upbringing would serve him well, though he also gained a reputation as a young man who loved drinking, playing cards, and horse racing.

Admitted to the bar to practice law at age twenty, a year later he accepted an appointment as a public prosecutor in North Carolina's western district. That took him beyond the boundaries of the state, to the other side of the Appalachians. Jackson arrived in a region that, a few years after his arrival, became the state of Tennessee.

The red-haired, blue-eyed, and rangy six-foot-one young man made an immediate impression in Nashville, a frontier outpost established just eight years earlier. As Jackson put down roots, he became one of its chief citizens as his and his city's reputations grew. His rise gained momentum after he met Rachel Donelson, the youngest daughter of one of Nashville's founding families. Dark-eyed Rachel was the prettiest of the Donelson sisters and full of life. It was said she was "the best story-teller, the best dancer, . . . [and] the most dashing horsewoman in the western country."[2] Jackson was smitten, and after she extricated herself from a marriage already gone bad, he took her as his wife.

As a lawyer, a trader, and a merchant, Jackson bought and sold land. By the time Tennessee joined the Union, in 1796, he had won the respect of his neighbors, who chose him as their delegate to the state's constitutional convention. Jackson then served as Tennessee's first congressman for one session before becoming a U.S. senator. But he found life in the political realm of the Federal City frustrating—too little got done for the decisive young Jackson—and he accepted an appointment to Tennessee's Supreme Court. In the early years of the nineteenth century, he divided his energies between administering the law and establishing himself at his growing plantation, the Hermitage, ten miles outside Nashville. "His house was the seat of hospitality," wrote a young officer friend, "the resort of friends and acquaintances, and of all strangers visiting the state."[3]

His next venture into public service would suit him better: thanks to his strong relationships and sound political instincts, he was elected major general of the Tennessee militia, in February 1802. Maintained by the state, not the federal government, the militia was provisioned by local men who supplied their own weapons and uniforms and served short contracts of a few months' duration. Leading the militia was a good fit for Jackson's style, because it gave him the chance to serve the people he loved with the freedom he needed and the challenge he craved.

General Jackson repeatedly won reelection as well as the deep loyalty of his men. They liked what he said. He was often outspoken, and many shared his uncompromising views on defending settlers' rights. With rumors of war, he was ready to defend his people and was just the man to rally westerners to the cause of American liberty.

"Citizens!" he wrote in a broadside. "Your government has at last yielded to the impulse of a nation. . . . Are we the titled slaves of George the Third? The military conscripts of Napoleon the great? Or the frozen peasants of the Russian czar? No—we are the free-born sons of America; the citizens of the only republic now existing in the world."[4]

Jackson understood the stakes of the war, and he recognized the strategy as only a westerner could. Of critical importance to victory in the West was a port city near the Gulf Coast. As Jackson would soon say to his troops, in the autumn of 1812, "Every man of the western country turns his eyes intuitively upon the mouth of the Mississippi." Together, he observed, "[we are] committed by nature herself [to] the defense of the lower Mississippi and the city of New Orleans."[5]

The City of New Orleans

New Orleans was important—so important, in fact, that upon becoming president a dozen years earlier, Thomas Jefferson had made acquiring it a key objective. Recognizing the city's singular strategic importance to his young nation, he wrote, "There is on the globe one single spot, the possessor of which is our natural and habitual enemy. It is New Orleans."[6]

Knowing that Napoleon's plan for extending his American empire had suffered a major setback in the Caribbean, where his expeditionary force had been decimated by yellow fever, Jefferson sensed an opportunity. He dispatched his friend James Monroe to Paris, instructing him to try to purchase New Orleans.

Monroe had succeeded in his assignment beyond Jefferson's wildest dreams. Recognizing his resources were already overextended in his quest to dominate Europe, Napoleon agreed to sell all of Louisiana. That conveyed an immense wilderness to the United States, effectively doubling the size of the new country. The Louisiana Purchase had been completed in 1803 and, at a purchase price of $15 million for more than eight hundred thousand square miles of territory, the land had been a staggering bargain (the cost to America's treasury worked out to less than three cents an acre).

The Louisiana city of New Orleans was the great gateway to and from the heart of the country. America's inland waterways—the Ohio,

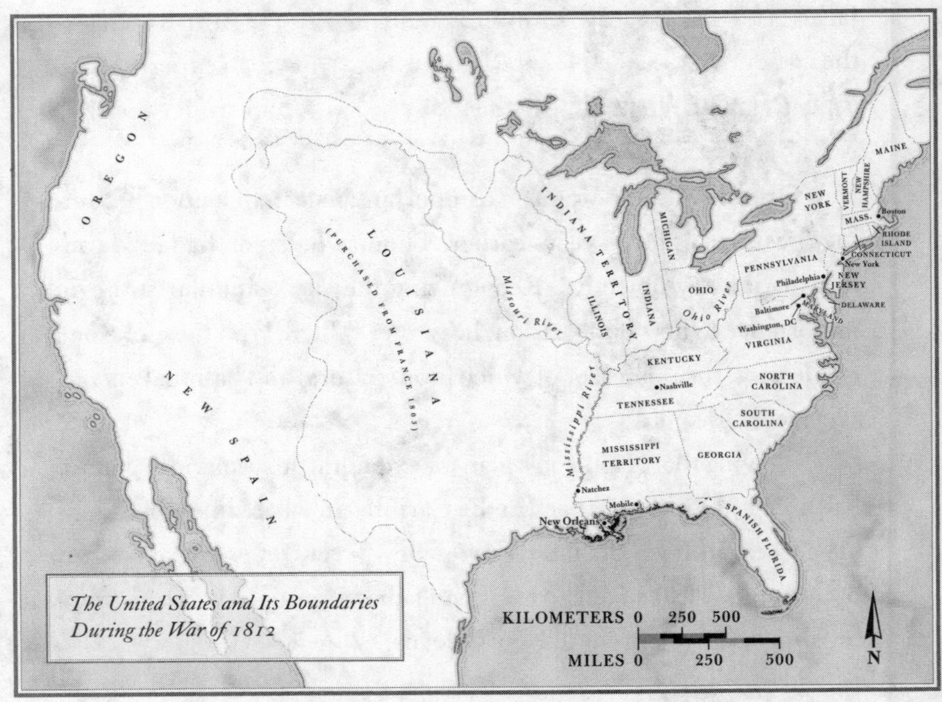

The United States and Its Boundaries During the War of 1812

the Missouri, and the numerous other rivers that emptied into the Mississippi—amounted to an economic lifeline for farmers, trappers, and lumbermen upstream. On these waters flatboats and keelboats were a common sight, carrying manufactured goods from Pennsylvania, as well as crops, pelts, and logs from the burgeoning farms and lush forests across the Ohio Valley, Cumberland Gap, and Great Smoky Mountains. On reaching the wharves, warehouses, and quays of New Orleans, the goods went aboard waiting ships to be transported all over the world.

Although Louisiana became a state in April 1812, the British still questioned the legitimacy of America's ownership of the Louisiana Territory—Napoleon had taken Louisiana from Spain and, to some Europeans, it remained rightfully a possession of the Spanish Crown. Jackson feared that sort of thinking could provide the British with just the pretext they needed to interfere with the American experiment—capturing New Orleans would be the perfect way to disrupt America's western expansion.

Now that America had finally gone to war, many nagging practical questions hung in the air in Washington. Who would determine America's military strategy? Who would lead the nation to war? The generals of the revolutionary generation were aging or dead. The passing of George Washington had sent the nation into mourning thirteen years before, and no military leader had the stature to take the general's place. Although the country had prevailed in the previous decade in a war on the Barbary Coast of North Africa, defeating pirate states that had attacked its shipping and held its men hostage, this was a bigger fight for even bigger stakes.

Although neither Mr. Madison nor the members of Congress could know it in June 1812, the burden of protecting the West would eventually settle onto the narrow but resilient shoulders of General Andrew Jackson, a man little known and less liked outside his region. But first Jackson had to convince the men in Washington that a general from the backwoods was the one to lead the fight. That would be anything but easy.

CHAPTER 2

How to Lose a War

> Resolved, that we consider the war commenced against Great Britain under existing circumstances unnecessary, impolitic and ruinous.
>
> **—Citizens of Lincoln County, Maine, August 3, 1812**

The *Boston Evening Post* soon dubbed the conflict "Mr. Madison's War." With no template to follow—he was the first American president ever to sign a formal declaration of war—James Madison was largely on his own.

There was nothing battle-hardened about Madison. Soft-spoken as well as short, he weighed perhaps 120 pounds. Genteel in manner, he was sickly and bookish, with a face that bore the age lines of a man of sixty-one years. He was a far cry from the strategist George Washington had been and had little choice when it came to military matters but to rely on the advice of his counselors. Many of them also lacked war experience.

Much of their guidance turned out to be less than sound. His advisers agreed that attacking Canada, which remained part of the British Empire, would be the perfect way to launch a war with Great

Britain and to gain a key bargaining chip in future treaty negotiations. Henry Clay, for one, believed a land war with the United States' neighbor to the north would end with "Canada at your feet."[1]

Madison's usually reliable friend Thomas Jefferson added his voice from Monticello. He thought the capture of Canada a sure thing. "The acquisition of Canada this year," he wrote, "will be a mere matter of marching."[2] All these words reflected the strong sense among American politicians that Canada, too, would like to be free of British rule and would welcome a liberating army from the United States. On the other hand, no one seemed to wonder what would happen if sending American troops north to invade Canada left the country's long coast unprotected, and few seemed to be considering the bigger danger to the South—if the British took New Orleans, they could hamstring its economy and prepare to squeeze the young nation.

If America was to fight in Canada, it might as well bring enough troops to win. Accordingly, several westerners, most notably Andrew Jackson, wrote to Madison to volunteer their military assistance. Jackson suggested moving 2,500 of his men to Canada within three months. But Washington never issued orders for Jackson's men to move, and Jackson became increasingly certain that the East Coast men Madison had running the war effort were incompetent.

Guiding the charge toward Canada was Madison's secretary of war, William Eustis, who had served as a regimental surgeon during the American Revolution. Neither a strategist nor a soldier, Eustis lacked battle experience, and it soon showed. Within six months, everyone in Washington knew that Dr. Eustis was no better prepared than Madison to direct the nation's military affairs.

Eustis's strategy had called for attacking Canada on three fronts. The first assault, which was to be launched from Fort Detroit, was directed by another veteran of the Revolution, General William Hull, who hadn't been in uniform for thirty years and looked like the grandfather he was with a shock of white hair. Though ordered to move on the British at a nearby Canadian fort, he folded when his men, along with a community of women and children, were bombarded by British guns. Hull surrendered Fort Detroit and the entire North-Western Army of the United States to a British and Indian force half its size.

The second assault, opened near Niagara in October 1812, also went badly wrong, this time because of division and lack of discipline within the American forces. When New York militiamen refused to cross the Niagara River into Canada to reinforce Ohio troops fighting the British, 950 Ohio militiamen were taken prisoner.

Desperate for a victory, Secretary of War Eustis placed all of his hope in the third assault. In a letter to Major General Henry Dearborn, another elderly warhorse who hadn't seen combat in three decades, Eustis warned him that he needed good news in time for Washington's January session: "Congress must not meet without a victory to announce to them."[3] Fighting in the vicinity of Lake Champlain, Dearborn and his men also failed. Some of the militia under his command refused to cross the border. Those who did march on Canada skirmished briefly with the enemy, only to find themselves, with the coming of darkness, shooting at one another. They retreated—from the British and their own friendly fire—ending the year's Canadian assault.

So much for what John Randolph of Virginia had told his fellow congressmen would be a "holiday campaign."[4] With the arrival of the year 1813, James Madison knew his war strategy needed to change.

The president felt embattled. Congress and the nation were deeply divided. During the congressional debates concerning the declaration of war, Madison's party had called the conflict a necessity, "a second war of independence." On the other side of the aisle, the Federalists regarded going to war as foolhardy and unnecessary, and they had unanimously voted against the president's war declaration. Though the War Hawks had prevailed, with bad news from the front, opposition voices had only grown louder.

There were too few troops to protect American cities, especially those on the coast, including Washington. The U.S. Navy had performed relatively well at sea, sinking a few British ships, but those victories meant little. The two dozen warships of the American fleet were outnumbered at least thirty to one by the Royal Navy, and already more enemy ships were arriving to blockade American ports.

Yet the divided Congress was often unwilling to provide funding for the military. The North, as demonstrated by the refusal of the New England militiamen to fight in Canada, was far from committed to the war. (From afar, Jackson offered a solution to the problem of soldiers refusing to fight: "I would hang them all."[5]) Even if Madison had the money and unity he needed, his military leaders were not what they should be: his generals were old, his secretary of war was incompetent, and his secretary of the navy was usually intoxicated. As the year 1812 ended, Madison faced a painful truth: those who wrote the military histories would surely wonder at the misguided way the United States had launched its Second War of Independence.

A Sense of Betrayal

Both Tennessee governor Willie Blount and his confidant General Andrew Jackson saw the immediate danger in the West of the British-supported Indians, and Jackson told Blount, on July 3, 1812, that he was ready and willing "to penetrate the Creek towns . . . [to] obtain a surrender of the captive and the captors."[6] But Jackson's offer to Washington, volunteering the services of his 2,500 Tennessee militiamen to serve the cause, produced no orders to march.

For months, Jackson awaited word from the War Department. He could do nothing but bide his time at the Hermitage and complain angrily about the "old grannies" in Washington.[7] Only in November did he get word from Governor Blount, writing on behalf of President Madison, ordering Jackson to protect the territory of the Mississippi Valley. Finally, the men in Washington were recognizing the needs of the West! Jackson was to assemble a force and proceed to New Orleans immediately to defend it from a likely British invasion.

Jackson issued a call to arms, and a flood of farmers, planters, and businessmen, many of them descendants of Revolutionary War veterans, poured into Nashville. These Volunteers, as their ranks would be called, were eager to fight for their country, to protect their homes, and to serve General Jackson.

Jackson had little time to organize and train his new recruits before they started for New Orleans in January 1813. Loaded into thirty boats, Jackson and more than two thousand men floated down the Cumberland River only to run into trouble. A cold snap blocked the river with ice, delaying the troops for four days. The unusually severe weather also brought frequent rain, hail, and snow, making the troops miserable. Jackson himself fell ill "with a severe pain in the neck and head," but he recovered.[8] When the ice melted, the boats continued on but not without accident. The difficult passage took five weeks and cost one boat and three lives.

On reaching Natchez, Mississippi, eight hundred miles downriver from Nashville, Jackson and his officers made camp, drilled their

Volunteers, and, with each passing day, grew more impatient. As instructed, they awaited orders regarding their final push toward New Orleans.

While encamped outside Natchez, Jackson took the opportunity to strengthen his relationships with his officer corps. Chief among them was John Coffee, Jackson's old friend and sometime business partner. Coffee was an imposing figure, with shoulders as broad as Jackson's were narrow, an ideal commander for Jackson's cavalry. There were other good men in Jackson's inner circle, including his chief aide-de-camp, Thomas Hart Benton, a young Nashville lawyer who had impressed Jackson with his diligence, and John Reid, Virginia-born and -educated, whose writing skills earned him the role of Jackson's secretary. Jackson also named William Carroll, a Nashville shop owner originally from Pennsylvania, to be brigade inspector.

The pause also allowed Jackson to begin the process of turning inexperienced volunteers into a fighting force. He and his officers watched as their troops cleaned and tested their weapons. The men practiced packing and unpacking their kits in order to be ready to march at a moment's notice. To a man, they were eager to take on the British forces said to be bearing down on New Orleans.

Finally, on March 15, 1813, a much-anticipated letter from the War Department arrived—only to humiliate and infuriate Jackson and his men, who had sacrificed their time, their money, and, in some cases, their lives to travel to defend New Orleans. As a result of America's many failures early in the war, General John Armstrong had replaced William Eustis as secretary of war in January, and Armstrong had decided to upend all of Eustis's strategy. "On receipt of this Letter," General Armstrong had written, "consider [your corps] as dismissed from public service."[9] Armstrong's focus would not be on the South but on the East Coast, where he thought the greatest jeopardy lay.

At first Jackson was confused about the missive's meaning. Could Armstrong really be telling him to disband his army and turn back? But the brief and pointed orders from the new secretary of war left no room for interpretation. The Volunteers were to abandon their plans to defend New Orleans and return home. Jackson's confusion gave way to shock and then anger. Eustis had been bad, but this move from Armstrong scarcely seemed an improvement.

Not that Jackson wouldn't be happy to go home. Deeply devoted to Rachel, his wife of almost twenty years, he carried a miniature portrait of her with him. They doted on four-year-old Andrew Jr., the boy the aging and childless couple had adopted as their own when one of Rachel's sisters-in-law birthed twins in 1808. The general would like nothing better than to be reunited with his family.

But what of New Orleans? As James Madison himself had put it years earlier, New Orleans held the key to "the country on the West side of the Mississippi."[10] Who would protect that essential port if Jackson turned back?

And what of the other military objectives on the Gulf Coast? For months, Jackson had argued that to defeat Great Britain, America needed to keep Florida's deep-water harbors out of British hands. Many of these small cities along the Gulf remained under Spanish rule, and the British were forming alliances with the Spanish in order to control the coast. Whoever held those forts was a threat to the likes of Mobile, as well as to the ultimate prize, New Orleans.

Yet in the face of what Jackson saw as the urgent need to protect the Gulf Coast and the mouth of the Mississippi, Secretary of War

Armstrong had not issued battle orders; he had told the general and his men to go home. Not only that, but Armstrong's letter specified that Jackson was to confiscate his men's weapons and to "take measures to have [them] delivered" to James Wilkinson, the overall commander of the American forces in the West.[11] Essentially, Armstrong was asking Jackson to disband his army, disarm his men, and leave them to find their way home as best they could. They would not be paid, nor would they be issued supplies.

Jackson faced a dilemma: he must follow orders—but to do so would put his men in grave danger.

Like Jackson, many of the men were sick; unlike Jackson, many of them were young and inexperienced. Together, when commanded by a seasoned leader, they could defend themselves from the British and Indians, but alone and scattered, they would be easy prey. *Abandon them?* Jackson was a tough man, but he wasn't cruel. Yes, he would obey the order to march home but he must do it his way.

He set about composing a reply.

"Must our band of citizen soldiers wander and fall a sacrifice to the tomahawk and scalping knife of the wilderness; our sick left naked in the open field and remain without supplies, without nourishment, or an earthly comfort?"[12] To do that, Jackson wrote, would be to choose their destruction.

That he simply would not do. If he had his choice, he would have led his men on defend New Orleans, since he was eager to "meet the invader and drive him back into the sea,"[13] as he had promised his recruits they would do together. But his more immediate concern was the well-being of the men in his charge.

As ridiculous as it seemed, he would have to turn his men around and lead them back to Nashville.

The Long Trek Home

The forty-mile march Jackson had made as a fourteen-year-old prisoner would not be the longest walk of his life. With no steamboat service to carry his army upstream against the current, Jackson and his Tennessee Volunteers faced a long march, one that would take them across five hundred miles of rugged ground, much of it in Indian country.

On March 25, 1813, they began the trek—but not before Jackson wrote to his congressman: "As long as I have funds or credit, I will stick by [my Volunteers]. I shall march them to Nashville or bury them with the honors of war—Should I die I know they will bury me."[14]

He wrote defiant letters to both Secretary of War Armstrong and General Wilkinson. He would not, could not, abandon his troops. "These brave men, at the call of their country, . . . followed me to the field—I shall carefully march them back to their homes."[15] He even wrote to the president: "I cannot believe [that] after inviting us to rally round the standard of country in its defense . . . you would dismiss us from service eight hundred miles from our homes, without money, without supplies." It has to be a "mistake," wrote Jackson.[16]

As the dispirited men, let down by their government but not by their general, marched north, illness spread through the ranks. Jackson soon had 150 men on the sick list, 56 of them so ill they could not sit unassisted. Jackson managed to commandeer wagons to carry some of them, but the eleven he found were not enough. He ordered his officers to surrender their horses to the sick. He asked no less of himself, turning over his three horses and walking so that ill Volunteers would travel easier.

"It is . . . my duty," he wrote to Rachel, "to act as a father to the sick and to the well and stay with them until I march them into Nashville."[17] He walked alongside his men; they covered an average of eighteen miles a day. He insisted upon order and discipline, but he led by example. He revealed no fatigue; he urged the troops homeward, and they understood his concern for their safety and comfort. As he moved along the column, this man, though well known for his violent and hasty temper, appeared to his men benevolent, humane, and fatherly. "There is not a man belonging to the detachment but what loves him," one reported.[18]

At forty-six, he was older than most of his troops—his face lined, his hair mostly gray—but Jackson made no complaint as he marched. Despite his slight build he was an imposing presence, with his erect posture. He did not need the gold epaulets and other adornments of a general's uniform to convey his authority. His intense blue eyes, people said, blazed when he was angry. But here Jackson was also the sympathetic man who urged his Volunteers toward home and safety. Admiration for him soared; among the ranks it was whispered that he was defying orders to shepherd them home, that he had reached into his own pockets to provide supplies. The men revered their general, who shared their hardships as they marched together toward Nashville.

Along the way, one soldier remarked upon Jackson's toughness.

Then another observed that he was as "tough as hickory." Said aloud, the comparison rang true and, soon enough, his men took to calling their commander "Hickory" and eventually "Old Hickory."[19]

The nickname would last a lifetime, long enough for a truly great New Orleans adventure. Madison's administration had judged the fear for the city's safety to be a false alarm this time. But the threat would surface again in 1814, when this natural leader and his men would prove their military merit by fighting the hated British.

In the meantime, another danger to the people of the West was brewing. As Jackson had feared, the Indian trouble in the region was growing more serious by the day. A warring faction of Creeks called the Red Sticks (the tomahawk-like war clubs they carried were painted red) had allied themselves with the British. Soon enough, Andrew Jackson would have to face them down.

CHAPTER 3

The Making of a General

> They must be punished—and our frontier protected . . . as I have no doubt but they are urged on by British agents.
>
> —**Andrew Jackson**

After marching his troops back to Nashville, Andrew Jackson once again waited for Washington. His Volunteers' enlistments had yet to expire (most joined up for a year) but, with no dispatch from the War Department ordering them into battle, the general released his militiamen from duty in the spring of 1813, sending them home to tend to their families and their fields. Then he did the same.

Life at the Hermitage had many obligations. A well-known horse breeder, Jackson also raised cows and mules. He owned a sawmill and a cotton gin; over the years, he had operated a store and a distillery, and had even invested in a boatyard. Hundreds of his acres were dedicated to growing the all-important cash crop, cotton.

As Jackson turned to his own interests during the spring of 1813, Mr. Madison's War was concentrated more than a thousand miles north of New Orleans. For once, good news arrived from Canada: the U.S.

Army had captured York, Ontario, in May, although drunken American soldiers had plundered the place, violating the rules of war by burning most of York's public buildings in celebration. But the rest of the news was bad for the Americans. The British continued to ravage the coast, burning the city of Havre de Grace, Maryland, in May. Reports circulated of women and children running for their lives as the attackers looted the town's church. A month later the ill-fated *Chesapeake* was captured once again by the Royal Navy. And then the president fell ill with "bilious fever." At Montpelier, their home in central Virginia, with Mr. Madison in a delirium, Mrs. Madison worried he might die.

In Tennessee, however, the summer passed peacefully until, with August giving way to September, life in Andrew Jackson's West took a sudden turn. In a matter of days, two events would alter the course of Jackson's life. One almost killed him, and the other accelerated his rise to the status of genuine American hero.

Caught in the Cross Fire

Years earlier, Jackson, known for his fiery temper, had fought several duels. As an angry twenty-two-year-old, he had issued a challenge over a minor courtroom disagreement, but both duelists had fired harmlessly in the air, realizing their argument was not worth dying for.[1] The more serious matter of a slander to Rachel Jackson's honor had led Jackson to an armed face-to-face with the sitting governor of Tennessee, John Sevier, in 1803. Once more, however, no blood was let, and the confrontation ended in a cascade of insults. In an 1806 duel, he killed a man who had called him a "worthless scoundrel" and a "coward."[2] Jackson had sustained a chest wound when a lead ball broke two ribs and lodged deep in his left lung (the injury would never entirely heal, causing periodic lung hemorrhages later in life). In 1813, however, Andrew Jackson most wanted to fight America's enemies, not argumentative opponents.

Then in June one of his officers, William Carroll, asked the general to be his second. Carroll was to duel Jesse Benton, the younger brother of another of Jackson's officers, Thomas Hart Benton; an exchange of insults between the two men had escalated until Benton, believing his honor as a gentleman had been questioned, demanded satisfaction. Jackson tried to talk his way out of participating, knowing he had nothing to prove and much to lose. "I am not the man for such an affair," he told Carroll. "I am too old."[3] But his attempt to negotiate a peaceful solution failed, and the duel was fought with the general standing by.

Unfortunately for Jackson, that was not the end of the matter.

In the June 14 duel, Jesse Benton sustained a wound to his buttocks, which some saw as a sign of cowardice, since it meant he had turned his back. Soon both Bentons were blaming Jackson, who had been charged with making sure the duel was fairly fought. The brothers publicly accused him of overseeing a duel "conducted . . . in a savage, unequal, unfair, and base manner."[4] The general, deeply offended, let it be known that he would horsewhip Lieutenant Colonel Thomas Hart Benton the next time they met.

On September 4, hearing the Bentons were in town, Jackson went to confront them, horsewhip in hand, at Nashville's City Hotel. The action quickly escalated. Gunshots were exchanged, and Jackson was left bleeding profusely after lead from Jesse Benton's pistol smashed the general's left shoulder and lodged in his upper arm. Jackson's blood soaked through not one mattress but two, and doctors saw no alternative to amputation. But Jackson refused.

"I'll keep my arm," he managed to say as he blacked out, and the respect and fear in which he was held meant no doctor would go against his order.[5]

Rachel arrived from the Hermitage to attend to her husband and, for many days, Old Hickory seemed suspended between life and death. But he refused to die. More than two weeks would pass before he could rise from his bed.

Then a courier brought news of an Indian massacre of settlers at Fort Mims, more than four hundred miles away. Red Stick Creeks were responsible, led by Chief Red Eagle, also known as William Weatherford, the son of a Native American mother and a Scots trader. Red Eagle and his band of Creeks had surprised the inhabitants of a small village inside a crude stockade near the Alabama River. The news was shocking: although protected by militiamen, on August 30, 1813, all but a handful of the roughly three hundred inhabitants—including many women and children—had been slaughtered. As a U.S. Army major reported from the scene some days later, the devastation was terrible, with the remains of "Indians, Negroes, white men, women and children . . . in one promiscuous ruin. . . . The main building was burned to ashes, which were filled with bones. The plains and the woods around were covered with dead bodies."[6]

Emerging from his fever-induced delirium, Jackson absorbed the news and saw the call to action: Fort Mims must be avenged and, soon enough, Governor Blount and President Madison so ordered. (It wasn't lost on Jackson that Fort Mims, located within range of the Gulf Coast, would bring him much closer to New Orleans, once again raising concern about a possible British invasion.) Though he still lay on what might have been his deathbed, Major General Andrew Jackson issued his own orders, on September 24, 1813, for his "brave Tennesseans" to assemble. The two thousand men of his division were to gather at Fayetteville, Tennessee, in two weeks' time.

Jackson's left arm and shoulder were unusable, thanks to his injuries, but he made his men a promise. "The health of your General is restored," he told them. "He will command in person."[7]

Not even a near-fatal gun brawl could keep Andrew Jackson from doing his duty.

Marching to Battle

A month to the day after the City Hotel gunfight, the first of the Tennessee Volunteers headed south. John Coffee, now a brigadier general, sat on his horse at the head of the army since Andrew Jackson, though gaining strength, was still recovering. But Old Hickory sent a message that was read to the men. "The blood of our women and children, recently spilled at Fort Mims, calls for our vengeance," he exhorted. "It must not call in vain."[8]

Jackson would not be far behind Coffee, mounting his horse three days later. Pale and drawn, he pushed himself hard, even though his left arm was in a sling, Jesse Benton's bullet still lodged in the bone. As November approached, he caught up with his Volunteers, and they made their way into Creek country. Supplies would be a continuing problem so far from civilization, but Jackson would not be deterred.

Impatient though he was, Jackson considered with care information on the enemy provided by friendly Creeks, Choctaws, and

Cherokees. Setting aside his deep distrust of Indians, he urged his commanders to make allies of Native Americans who had chosen not to join the Red Sticks' uprising. Out of instinct rather than military training—of which he had little—Jackson understood that intelligence concerning his enemies' forces would be invaluable.

When his spies reported a large enemy force a dozen miles south of his encampment on the Coosa River, Jackson ordered General John Coffee and his brigade of nine hundred horsemen to attack the Red Sticks at the island community known as Tallushatchee.

Jackson was not there, but a young enlistee named David Crockett witnessed the battle. "I saw some warriors run into a house," he remembered years later. "We pursued them until we got near the house, when we saw a squaw sitting in the door, and she placed her feet against the bow she had in her hand, and then took an arrow, and, raising her feet, she drew with all her might, and let fly at us, and she killed a man. . . . His death so enraged us all, that she was fired on, and had at least twenty balls blown through her. This was the first man I ever saw killed with a bow and arrow."[9]

The American force, outnumbering the Tallushatchee defenders five to one, decimated the Red Sticks, just as Jackson had ordered. After counting 186 dead warriors, Coffee reported, "Not one . . . escaped to carry the news."[10]

Jackson arrived to inspect the smoking ruins of Tallushatchee. No wholesale slaughter of families had occurred, and Coffee's forces held eighty-four prisoners, all women and children. Jackson's interpreter, an Indian trader fluent in Creek, brought a Native American infant to the general. The boy had been found in the embrace of his dead mother. When urged to give the child nourishment, the surviving Creek women had refused. "All his relations are dead," they reportedly said, "[so] kill him too."[11]

Having lost his own mother in wartime, Jackson was moved by the orphaned boy. Only hours after ordering the assault on the Indian camp, the general mixed a few grains of brown sugar with water and coaxed the tiny child to drink.

"Charity and Christianity says he ought to be taken care of," he wrote to Rachel.[12] The boy, named Lyncoya, would be adopted as a member of their family, to be raised and educated at the Hermitage as if he were the couple's blood child.

As he had been ordered to do, Jackson avenged the Fort Mims massacre. Yet, while the warrior Jackson could be ruthless, the aftermath at Tallushatchee revealed his strong instincts as a father not only to his men but to the meek and the vanquished.

Jackson Takes Talladega

Six days later, Jackson faced a test of his personal toughness.

Not all the Creeks had taken up arms against the Americans, and Jackson promised to protect the friendly Indians, who also included Cherokees and Choctaws. As he assured one Native American ally, "If one hair of your head is hurt, . . . I will sacrifice a hundred lives to pay for it."[13]

He got his chance with the arrival, at sunset, on November 7, 1813, of an express rider. Having grunted and rooted his way through Red Stick lines, disguised beneath the skin of a hog with head and hooves still attached, the messenger brought word that an estimated one thousand warriors had besieged the settlement of friendly Creeks at Talladega. William Weatherford—Red Eagle—and his Red Sticks stood poised to do to their brothers, who were allied with the enemy, what they had done to the settlers at Fort Mims.

Andrew Jackson was in no condition to field this call to action. As if the wounds to his useless left arm were not enough—he needed help mounting his horse, and simply unfolding a map posed a challenge—a case of dysentery racked him. For years, he had suffered almost constantly from intestinal problems, ranging from bouts of diarrhea to constipation, but now the discomfort was so intense that he had trouble sitting up straight. Still, pain could not be allowed to stand in the way, and slouched against a tree, he rapidly conceived a plan. Jackson and his men were on the march by midnight.

As he rode to the endangered Indian settlement at Talladega, he leaned forward in the saddle, almost hugging the neck of his horse, attempting to ease his abdominal pain. The ride was more than twenty-five miles long, but by sunset the following day, Jackson's army, consisting of twelve hundred foot soldiers and eight hundred men on horseback, made camp within range of their destination. Again Jackson did not sleep, but questioned his scouts about the terrain as he formulated a battle plan. At 4:00 a.m., he ordered his sleeping men awakened. His battle orders, as Jackson himself described them in a letter to Governor Blount, called for the advance of the infantry "in three lines—the militia on the left, and the volunteers on the right. The cavalry formed the two extreme wings, and were ordered to advance in a curve."[14]

With the bulk of his forces fixed in position, he ordered three mounted companies of men armed with rifles and muskets to advance. Jackson expected the hostile Indians to attack this American vanguard, which could then fall back as if in retreat. The Indians in pursuit would come into the range of his larger force, where his cavalry could trap them in a deadly crossfire.

The fight began with a roar of Indian guns as Weatherford's Red Sticks, naked but for their red war paint, burst from a dense thicket. They were "like a cloud of Egyptian locusts," Davy Crockett wrote, "screaming like all the young devils had been turned loose, with the old devil of all at their head."[15]

The plan unfolded as designed, and the Red Sticks ran directly into Jackson's trap. A hail of American bullets began to take a terrible toll, though the Indians, some with guns, many armed only with bows and arrows, fought back. There should have been no escape—but Weatherford and a large contingent of Creeks swarmed through a gap in the line. Though some of Jackson's men pursued them, seven hundred warriors escaped into the hills.

When the dead were counted, Weatherford had lost 299, Jackson 15. And Jackson gained a new nickname: to the Red Sticks, he became Sharp Knife.

The inexperienced general, despite a useless left arm, his body more than a little wasted by dysentery, had masterminded his first big battle and led his men to victory. Although Jackson, as ever, was ready to carry on the honorable fight, the result at Talladega would be the last good news for many weeks to come.

CHAPTER 4

A River Dyed Red

The power of the Creeks is I think forever broken.

—Andrew Jackson

Andrew Jackson faced new challenges as the winter of 1813–14 approached. In the back of his mind was the worry about a British advance on New Orleans (in fact, a British admiral had quietly proposed such a move a full year earlier[1]), but much more immediate concerns occupied Jackson's attention.

His Volunteers had little food and no feed for their horses. With expected supply shipments delayed, Jackson saw that his starving troops were growing more restless by the day. He realized that, despite the victory at Talladega less than a month before, his army was about to come apart at the seams—and if his Volunteers deserted, he would be able to fight neither Indians nor the British. After weeks of cajoling, Jackson finally had to threaten his men to restore order.

When one brigade of frustrated Volunteers prepared to head for home in early December, Jackson showed his resolve. Facing the desertion of troops, he planted his mount in their path. Because his left arm was still in a sling, he rested his musket on the horse's neck.

Looking down the barrel at the mutinous men, he warned, "You say you will march. I say by the Eternal God you shall not march while a cartridge can sound fire!"[2]

General Coffee and Major John Reid took up positions on either side of Jackson. No one moved for long minutes—until several loyal companies broke ranks and assembled behind the trio. Out of fear and respect for General Jackson, a few of the rebels moved in the direction of the camp. Others followed, and no one headed back to Tennessee that day.

Jackson also faced a deadline. The first Volunteers had enlisted for one year and expected to be discharged from service on December 10. Many lacked the clothing necessary for a winter campaign, and their farms and families awaited their return. "If they do not get home soon," one officer told Jackson, "there are many of them who will be literally ruined."[3]

Their commander sympathized with their plight, but he saw the enlistment period differently. Because they had been dismissed for the summer, these soldiers, Jackson reasoned, had yet to serve twelve months. And their task remained unfinished, with the dangerous Red Stick Creeks still at large.

Jackson was again forced to face down his own men. He told them they could depart only "by passing over [my] body."[4] He tried to shame them into remaining, saying they were about to become "the tarnishers of their own fame" as they went into "inglorious retirement."[5] He said he expected reinforcements would soon arrive—and some did. But several of those regiments were also nearing the end of their enlistments, on January 1 and January 14, 1814. Finally, realizing there was little he could do to salvage the campaign, Jackson released the majority of his men without extending their obligations.

Meanwhile, Jackson's health deteriorated. Year's end found him still unable to maneuver his left arm into the sleeve of his coat unassisted. His army was dwindling by the day. About all he could do was write home to Tennessee.

At "1/2 past 11 o'clock at night," on December 29, 1813, he opened his heart to his wife, Rachel. He bemoaned "the shameful desertion from their posts of the Volunteer infantry . . . and the apathy displayed in the interior of the state by the fireside patriots." But his letter offered his wife assurances. "Be not uneasy . . . if I have trials, and perils, [God] has fortified me with fortitude to do my duty under every circumstance."[6] In the next hour, he wrote harder words to his old friend Governor Willie Blount, reminding him that the fight had to be carried on to protect the people from the Creeks. The Indians needed to be "exterminated or conquered," said Jackson, and he challenged the governor to act. "Are you, my dear friend, sitting with your arms folded?"

Jackson's letter was an insistent demand for help. "Arouse from your lethargy," he wrote. "Give me a force for 6 months in whose term of service there is no doubt . . . and all may be safe. Withhold it, and all is lost."[7]

Before Blount could react, still more enlistments ended and the army encamped with Jackson amounted to just 130 able-bodied soldiers. And the dangers had grown: Jackson's spies brought word that British troops had landed at Pensacola. This could mean only one thing: as long expected, the enemy had to be preparing to assault the Gulf Coast—and, in particular, its most important city, New Orleans. Jackson knew he must, somehow, keep his army together. He must prevail against this first foe—and be ready for the next.

Meanwhile, Red Eagle's fame continued to grow. On December 23, with Jackson struggling to keep his army together, Weatherford confronted a force of Mississippi militiamen. Again outnumbered, the Red Sticks fled and Red Eagle, riding his prized gray, Arrow, took the only avenue of escape he saw. Racing along a high bluff overlooking the Alabama River, he pointed the horse toward the precipice and drove his spurs into Arrow's flanks.

From a height of roughly fifteen feet, both rider and horse took flight. They seemed to float in midair before plunging into the water. The astonished Mississippi militiamen watched: neither man nor animal was visible, entirely submerged. Then Weatherford surfaced, still astride his mount. With one hand, he grasped the horse's mane; with the other, he held his gun aloft.

The troops unleashed musket volleys as Arrow swam for the opposite bank but, despite the hail of lead, man and beast reached the shore. Safely out of range, Red Eagle dismounted and inspected his steed for wounds. Finding none, he rode off.[8]

The Creek chief survived to fight another day. As for Andrew Jackson, he could only hope that when that day came, the two of them would finally look each other in the eye across the line of battle.

Battle Preparations

Early in the new year, fresh recruits finally arrived from Nashville. Although the 850 men had little or no military experience, Jackson wasted no time. He ordered a march deep into enemy territory.

The new force met the enemy, fighting skirmishes with Red Eagle's braves at two Red Stick villages late in January 1814. Though he and his men managed to prevail, the battles were hard fought, and Jackson himself was nearly killed when he rode directly into the fighting. "In the midst of showers of balls, of which he seemed unmindful," one officer recalled, "he . . . [rallied] the alarmed, halting them in their flight, forming his columns, and inspiriting them by his example."[9]

After that near-debacle, Jackson pulled back to drill his inexperienced men. His army continued to grow, and not just with fresh recruits from Tennessee. Jackson's reputation was beginning to travel farther afield, and, for the first time, U.S. Army regulars were put under his command in addition to the Volunteers, raising the total troops in Jackson's army to more than 3,500 men.

The Battle of Horseshoe Bend

Before long, spies reported that William Weatherford and a thousand warriors waited almost a hundred miles away in a village overlooking the Tallapoosa River. Jackson was determined to make this the Creeks' last stand. This enemy posed a dual danger: they were a threat to frontier life, and they had chosen to ally themselves with the nation's larger enemy, Great Britain. The British were known to be providing the Creeks with supplies—a few months before, American militiamen had intercepted the Creeks with wagonloads of supplies offloaded from the British at Pensacola.

Jackson's scouts—among them, Davy Crockett—informed him that the Indians were camped at a place called Horseshoe Bend. The enemy used a great U-shaped curve in the river as a moat to protect them on three sides. The Creek warriors, together with several hundred women and children, inhabited a cluster of huts at the southern end of the hundred-acre peninsula. A narrow neck to the north provided the only land entry, across which the Red Sticks had constructed a breastwork. Built of large timbers and earth, this fortress wall was 8 feet tall and 350 yards wide. It was lined with portholes through which the Indians could shoot at attackers.

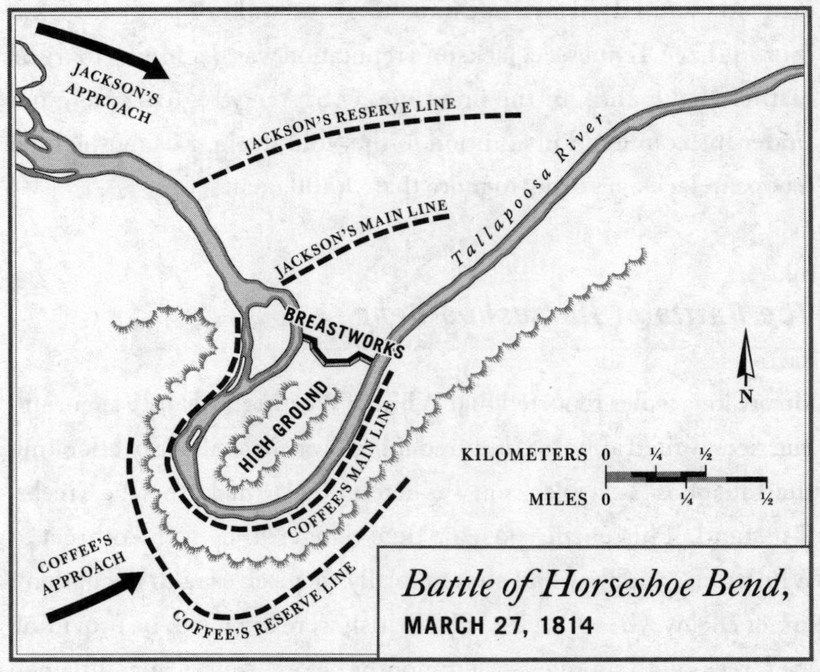

Battle of Horseshoe Bend,
MARCH 27, 1814

General Jackson was impressed. "Nature furnishes few situations as eligible for defense," he reported to Governor Blount, "and barbarians have never rendered one more secure by art."[10] Even though his men outnumbered the Creeks, conquering this fort would be no easy task.

Despite Jackson's inexperience with military strategy, he was undaunted. After all, he had attributes that couldn't be taught: unrivaled courage, natural leadership, and—he would soon discover—uncanny battlefield instincts. Working with his advisers, he devised a plan.

At first light on March 27, 1814, General John Coffee's cavalry headed out with a band of Cherokees and friendly Creeks. Per Jackson's orders, they were to take positions south of the enemy village along the bend of the Tallapoosa on the opposite bank. From there they could shoot any Red Sticks attempting to escape Jackson and his men.

Meanwhile Jackson marched the rest of his army directly toward the breastwork. They halted, remaining at the ready while artillerymen set their two cannons. At 10:30 a.m., with word that Coffee and his men were in place, the cannoneers fired.

The cannonballs did little damage, bouncing away or thudding harmlessly into the sturdy breastwork. Any Red Stick who showed himself was quickly the target of heavy musket fire from Jackson's line, but, remaining behind their earthworks, the Creeks mocked their attackers with war whoops.

At the other end of the peninsula, a different attack had begun. When Jackson's gunners started firing on the fort, some of the Indians in Coffee's command charged the river. Under fire, they plunged into the water, swam across the river, and seized their enemies' canoes on the opposite bank.[11] After paddling back in stolen vessels, they ferried two hundred Indians and thirty Tennessee militiamen to the Creek side and began to fight their way toward the Red Stick village, about half a mile away from where Jackson's men were fighting. They soon set the huts aflame and marched on to join Jackson in attacking the Indian fort.

When Jackson saw the billowing smoke rising from the village, he ordered his men to charge. He'd prepared his troops for this moment: "In the hour of battle," Jackson's general orders from three days earlier read, "you must be cool and collected. When your officer orders you to fire, you must execute the command with deliberateness and aim. *Let every shot tell*."[12]

His men did as ordered and, despite a storm of enemy bullets and arrows, the first attackers soon reached the ramparts. There they fought muzzle to muzzle, the Tennesseans and Indians shooting point-blank at one another through the portholes.

The first man to scale the wall and go over the top, Major Lemuel Montgomery, collapsed onto the breastwork, lifeless, shot through the head. A platoon leader named Sam Houston next led the charge, brandishing his sword. A Red Stick arrow penetrated his upper thigh, but Houston didn't fall. He leapt to the ground inside the fort, his uniformed men close behind.

Overwhelmed by this breach of their trusted wall, Red Stick defenders retreated into nearby brush and woods. They fired on the invaders, but the attackers had every advantage—more men, more guns, the momentum of the battle. Even so, the Indians continued to fight.

So did Sam Houston. At his order, another officer withdrew the barbed arrow from Houston's left thigh, opening a gaping wound. When Jackson called to men to attack the Creeks holding a nearby redoubt, Houston picked up a musket and led the charge. This time he took two musket balls, one entering his right arm, the other his right shoulder.

The battle raged on, with Jackson's men clearly winning the day. Even so, the outnumbered Indians refused his offer of surrender in the early afternoon, firing upon Jackson's messenger and his interpreter, wounding one of them. The Creeks preferred a fight to surrender, and the battle went on. "The *carnage* was *dreadful*," Jackson would write to his wife.[13]

A few Red Sticks would escape in the night, but the morning body count totaled 557 Indian corpses. Many more Creeks had died trying to escape; the Tallapoosa River, dyed red with human blood, had carried away an estimated 300 braves. On Jackson's side, just 43 soldiers lost their lives, while his Indian allies lost 23.

Red Eagle no longer commanded a viable fighting force and, by mid-April, most of the other Creek chiefs had presented themselves at Jackson's camp under flags of truce. They accepted that they were not in a position to dictate peace terms. But General Jackson was, and, before negotiations could begin, he made one simple demand: He wanted the man behind the Fort Mims massacre. Only when William Weatherford was in his hands could the Creek War be ended.

A few days later, a lone Indian arrived in Jackson's camp. The stranger had a freshly shot deer tied across the rump of his horse; he was directed to the general's tent and rode up just as Jackson was emerging.

"General Jackson?"

Jackson looked up in surprise at the man riding the handsome gray horse. Bare to the waist, the light-skinned Indian wore buckskin breeches and moccasins.

His next statement was still more surprising. "I am Bill Weatherford."

More than anything else, his desire to avenge Fort Mims had driven Jackson over the preceding months. Now the man responsible for the massacre stood unarmed before him.

His first response was anger at Weatherford's nerve. "How dare you show yourself at my tent after having murdered the women and children at Fort Mims!" he exclaimed.

His second response was puzzlement. Had Jackson's men captured the Indian leader, the general would no doubt have ordered his speedy execution. It had never occurred to him that Weatherford might surrender. Now Jackson had to decide what to do with him.

"I had directed that you should be brought to me confined; had you appeared in this way, I should have known how to treat you," he told Weatherford.

"I am in your power," the man replied. "Do with me as you please. I am a soldier. I have done to the white people all the harm I could; I have fought them, and fought them bravely: if I had an army, I would yet fight, and contend to the last: but I have none; my people are all gone. I can now do no more than weep over the misfortune of my nation."[14]

To the surprise of his men, Old Hickory did not order Weatherford's imprisonment or execution. Instead, Jackson offered Red Eagle a deal: He would grant him his life and liberty if he would serve as a peacemaker to the Creeks who were still fighting. If he chose to fight again, "his life should pay the forfeit of his crimes." If he chose peace? "[You will] be protected."[15]

Weatherford took the deal, telling Jackson that "those who would still hold out can be influenced only by a mean spirit of revenge; and to this they must not, and shall not sacrifice the last remnant of their country. You have told us where we might go, and be safe. This is a good talk, and my nation ought to listen to it."[16]

The man's manner and words left a deep impression on Major Reid. Weatherford, he wrote, "possessed all the manliness of sentiment—all the heroism of soul, all the comprehension of intellect calculated to make an able commander. . . . His looks and gestures—the modesty and yet the firmness that were in them."[17]

Unlikely as it might seem, Andrew Jackson recognized a kindred spirit "as high-toned and fearless as any man he had met with."[18] Here was a man who understood the rules of war, a man who knew the time had passed for bloodshed between the Creeks and the settlers. And he could help assure the peace.

With the U.S. victory at Horseshoe Bend, the Creek War was effectively over. The Creeks recognized that their only choice was to bargain, and, with the help of Red Eagle, Jackson negotiated the Treaty of Fort Jackson. On August 9, 1814, the Creek chiefs signed it, agreeing to give the United States—and the man they called Sharp Knife—more than twenty-two million acres of land. American settlers were now safe and had room to expand.

Red Eagle had helped make the case for peace, having retired from making war. As for Jackson, even with an Indian treaty in hand, he had no such luxury. He was already hearing the sound of British footsteps moving toward New Orleans.

Major General Jackson

Word of Jackson's battlefield success reached the War Department.

This man Jackson, whom they had mistrusted as a stubborn and crude westerner, was outperforming Washington's military strategists and its aging generals.

His troops both loved and feared him. To everyone's surprise, he had made an effective fighting force out of volunteer militiamen. He knew when to be tough, and he knew when to temper that toughness with kindness. He was fearless in battle, but not reckless. In fact, he balanced his courage with great caution and surprising patience for gathering intelligence and listening to the advice of others. He knew when to stand firm on his convictions but wasn't blind to the possibility of compromise. Finally, and most important, he possessed a natural instinct for military strategy that made up for his lack of formal training.

Even Secretary of War John Armstrong, whose orders Jackson had quarreled with in Natchez, recognized Jackson's potential. "Something ought to be done for General Jackson," he wrote to President Madison after news of the triumph at Horseshoe Bend elated the nation's capital, where politicians were weary of a war that was draining the treasury, brought too few victories to cheer, and had gone on far longer than expected.[19] Something would be done for Jackson and, on June 18, 1814, militia general Jackson was promoted to the rank of major general of the regular U.S. Army, a larger and more powerful command.

Jackson's rise to national prominence could not have come at a better time. After two decades spent fighting France, the British had forced Napoleon to abdicate in April. That meant the Royal Navy and the immense army of the victorious Duke of Wellington could be sent to engage in the fight in North America. An invading force was already cruising the Mid-Atlantic coast, worrying President Madison and his cabinet. What would unfold elsewhere wasn't clear—but, with Jackson in command of the Seventh Military District, which encompassed Louisiana, Tennessee, and all of the Mississippi Territory, it became Jackson's job to ponder what might happen in his region.

This was also a responsibility he had long wished for. As he wrote

Rachel from his quarters in Creek country, near the Coosa River, "I owe Britain a debt of . . . vengeance."[20]

In Jackson's view, the enemy's ultimate objective was clear enough: the British wanted New Orleans. Anyone who could read a map knew that by capturing the city, His Majesty's forces would consolidate control of the North American continent from the Gulf Coast to Canada—and that could end the United States' westward expansion. For Jackson, that prospect was unacceptable.

In August 1814, his army was small. His Tennessee Volunteers had returned to their farms and shops after defeating the Indians, and he had just 531 enlisted soldiers. But Jackson's knowledge of what the British might do was even smaller. He knew neither when the British warships might land nor how many troops they carried. What he was certain of was that he and his army had to move south immediately. With the Creeks disposed of, he could focus on protecting the coast from his European enemy.

Two days after the Creek treaty was signed, Jackson and his little army set off toward the Gulf of Mexico, marching as quickly as they could. The new reality of a British threat fed an existing fear: those who read the papers already knew the British could be ruthless. The previous summer the Crown's men, rampaging through the Virginia countryside, committed terrible atrocities. One woman seeking to escape was said to have been "pursued up to her waist in the water, and dragged on shore by ten or twelve of these ruffians, who satiated their desires upon her, after pulling off her clothes, stockings, shoes, etc."[21] Another report claimed a sick man was murdered in his bed. According to one congressman, "The town of Hampton, and the surrounding country were given up to the indiscriminate plunder of a licentious soldiery."[22] Such stories, linked with rumors of the impending British approach, prompted General Jackson, sitting in his saddle for four hundred miles, to think very hard about possible strategies for preventing the same from happening to the people of the Gulf Coast.

Yet even for the most powerful military in the world, an attack on New Orleans would be no simple matter. The Royal Navy might lead the siege, but to get to New Orleans its ships would have to sail a hundred miles up the Mississippi. Along the way, they would face American guns, changing tides, and several sharp turns in the river, making for a slow and dangerous approach to their objective. Though he had no naval experience, Jackson understood these obstacles and guessed that the British would avoid a river assault.

Assuming the British would launch an overland attack against the city, Jackson considered his possibilities. The Mississippi delta south of New Orleans, a swampy morass of bayous, would be practically impossible to march across. And the British had no easy land access from the north. Thus, Jackson and his advisers concluded that their enemy would come from the east.

If the British were to send a land force from the east, where would they land? Jackson believed that the most likely site was Mobile, a city 150 miles to the east, with its own protected bay. When, on August 22, he rode into Mobile with his army, he was already thinking one move ahead. Although he had never visited New Orleans, he would, somehow, find a way to protect this city unlike any other.

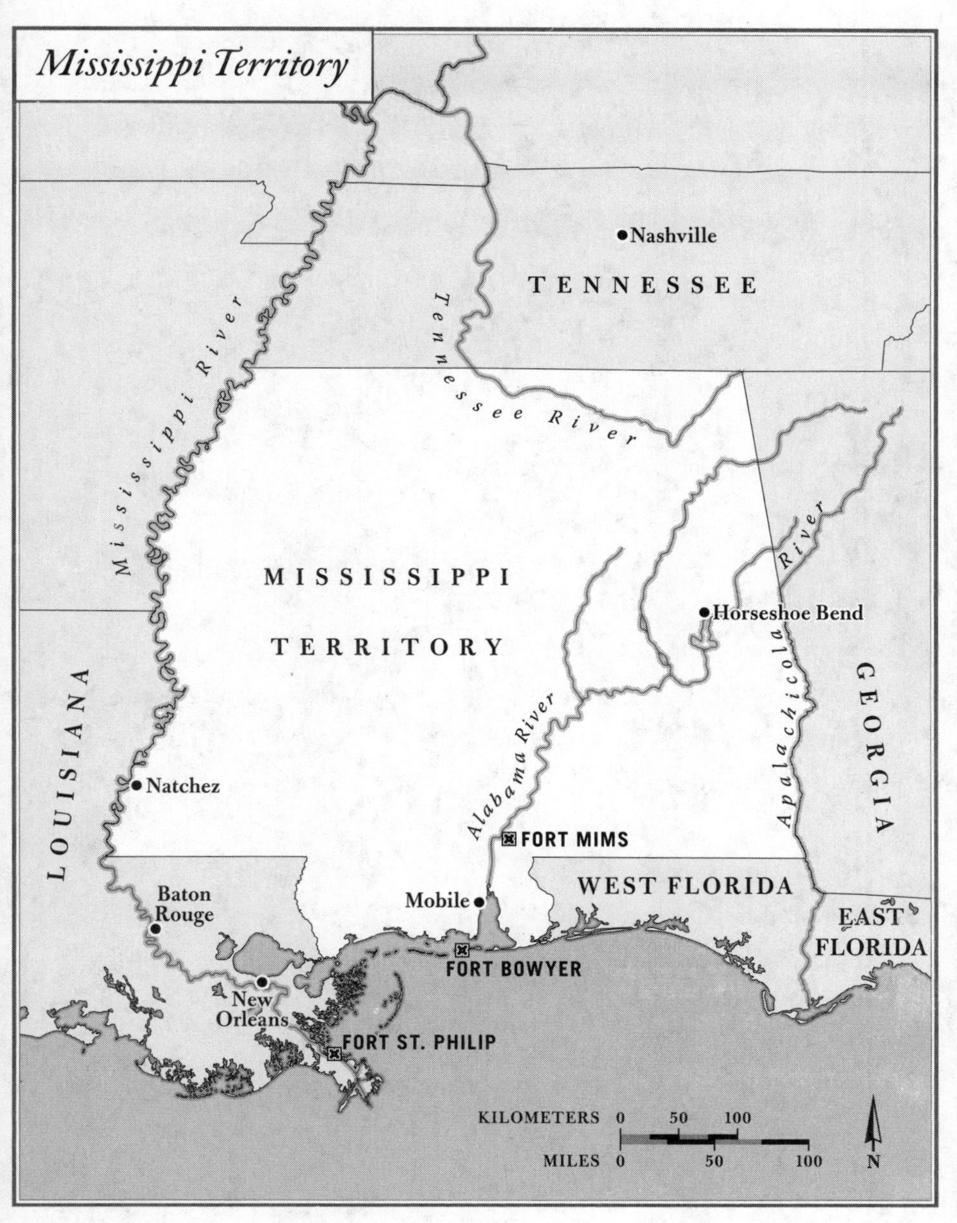

Mississippi Territory
Nashville
TENNESSEE
Tennessee River
Mississippi River
MISSISSIPPI
TERRITORY
Horseshoe Bend
Apalachicola River
GEORGIA
LOUISIANA
Alabama River
Natchez
FORT MIMS
WEST FLORIDA
Mobile
Baton Rouge
EAST FLORIDA
FORT BOWYER
New Orleans
FORT ST. PHILIP
KILOMETERS 0 50 100
MILES 0 50 100
N

CHAPTER 5

The British on Offense

I have it much at heart to give [the Americans] a complete drubbing before peace is made, when I trust their . . . command of the Mississippi [will be] wrested from them.

—Admiral Alexander Cochrane to Earl Bathurst, July 14, 1814

Would New Orleans welcome America's protection? The answer to that question was far from certain. The most important city in Jefferson's Louisiana Purchase was in transition. An American possession since 1803, Louisiana had been a state for only two years, and its loyalty to the Union was not yet proven.

The young and precariously American city was also a place of contradictions. Though isolated amid low-lying mudflats, in a climate where withering tropical heat and violent hurricanes were normal, New Orleans had nevertheless become a center of European refinement and culture. An outpost of law and order in the wilderness, it was still home to more than a few outlaws. The most important city in the newest American state, it was French in spirit, but had also been a possession of both the British and the Spanish; many of its inhabitants didn't even speak the language of their new government. In the event of invasion, Jackson would have to shape an unprecedented unity among a motley population of French colonials, Native Americans, freed slaves, American woodsmen, and even pirates.

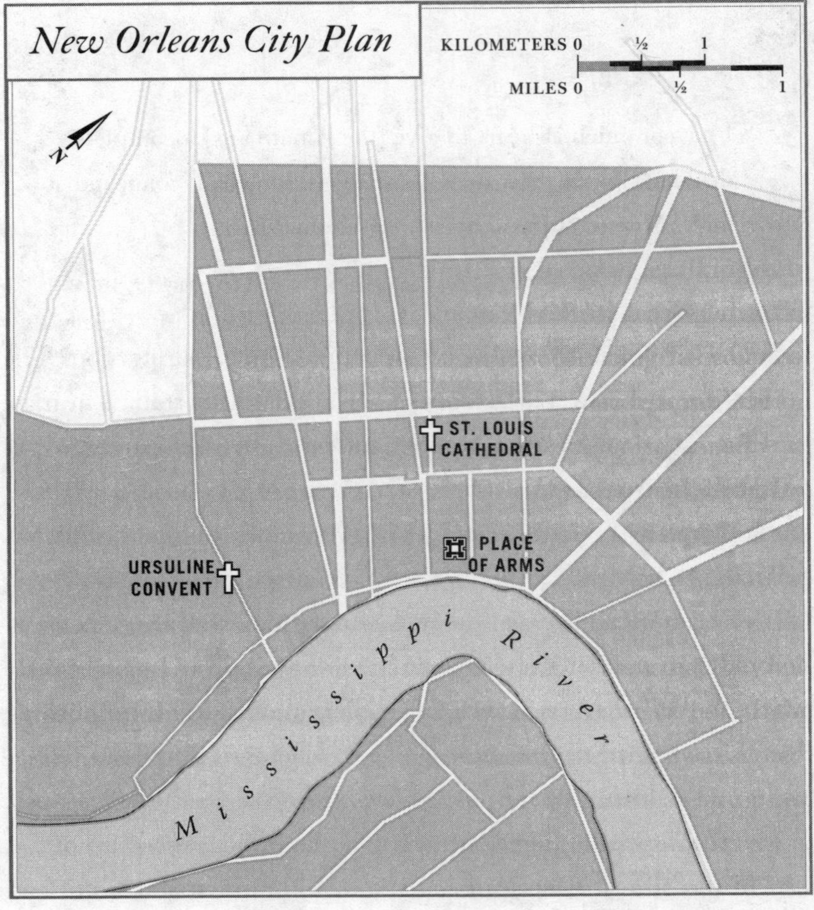

New Orleans had been a place of constant change simply because of its geography. A natural bank, or levee, had risen along a crescent-shaped turn in the meandering Mississippi and, over the centuries, Native Americans had found the spot, located about a hundred miles upstream from the Gulf of Mexico, a convenient place to travel farther inland. Their overland route took them to a slow-moving stream at a water level different from the river's (Andrew Jackson would soon come to know it as Bayou St. John), which, in turn, drained into a shallow body of water called Lake Pontchartrain. That enormous lake emptied into Lake Borgne and, eventually, the Gulf, north and east of what had become New Orleans.

In 1718, an early European arrival in the region, Jean-Baptiste Le Moyne, sieur de Bienville, founded a community at the watery crossroads and called it La Nouvelle-Orléans, in honor of France's ruler, Philippe II, duc d'Orléans. The settlement began as little more than an array of shacks, and most of those were obliterated by a massive flood in 1719. Bienville supervised a rebuilding, with taller and sturdier levees constructed to protect his settlement, which, behind the wall of earth, sat several feet below the Mississippi at high tide. The growing town became the capital of French Louisiana in 1722, but later that same year a hurricane destroyed most of New Orleans's buildings.

Slaves brought from Senegal dug drainage canals and built higher levees, and as they pushed the water back, Bienville's village grew into a good-size town. As settlers poured in, New Orleans gained its first cathedral and a convent for Ursuline nuns. The Ursuline sisters established a school for girls and a hospital where soldiers and slaves alike were treated for ailments common to the region, like malaria and yellow fever. When the Seven Years' War in Europe shifted the political landscape (the 1756–63 conflict was known to Americans as the French and Indian War), Louisiana was ceded to Spain. But the Spaniards' luck during their decades in charge proved no better than that of the French. Three major hurricanes hurtled through; a great flood swamped most of lower Louisiana in 1782; and two great fires nearly flattened the city of New Orleans in 1788 and 1794.

Nevertheless, by the time of Mr. Jefferson's Louisiana Purchase, New Orleans had become a European-style city with an aura such that a contemporary visitor described the place as a "French Ville de Province."[1] The oldest quarter was a central checkerboard of streets, the Vieux Carré, which retained a grid planned long before by French royal engineers. In the next decade, the population more than doubled to eighteen thousand inhabitants.

In the heat and humidity of its bayou country, lower Louisiana proved a perfect melting pot for blending cultures. There were slaves and free persons of color and many Native Americans (the area had once been Choctaw territory). During and after the French and Indian War, French-speaking Acadians from Canada's maritime provinces had been expelled by the British, and thousands of them took refuge in Louisiana. These "Cajuns" established their own unique culture in nearby bayous. A German community had been established upstream. On New Orleans's streets and wharves, Spanish, Dutch, Swedish, and French were spoken. River trade had lured many frontiersmen from Kentucky, Tennessee, and Ohio, adding English speakers to a city where once they had been few.

When war was declared in 1812, Louisiana had no long-term allegiance to the United States, but the British increasingly interfered with trade, and goods quickly accumulated at the city's docks, generating profits for no one. Louisiana's governor, William Charles Cole Claiborne, had been dispatched from Washington—first appointed to the post by President Jefferson and then elected after statehood—but the city's powerful Creoles, as white New Orleanians of Spanish or French heritage were called, had little respect for him. In truth, no one in New Orleans controlled the levers of power, and the city's competing interests coexisted but didn't necessarily cooperate.

This was amply demonstrated by the fact that a brash band of privateers—some called them pirates—sold their contraband openly in New Orleans, flouting the law. They paid no customs duties on the coffee, linens, silks, iron, mahogany, spices, and wine they smuggled into the city using hollowed-out cypress canoes and other flat-bottomed boats adapted to the marshy waterscape of the delta. Although they operated outside the law, these men were essential to the local economy and publicly advertised their wares. Few among New Orleans high society showed a willingness to crack down on the purveyors of much-desired bootlegged goods.

Persuading the city's population of sturdily independent peoples to support one another and fight together would be Jackson's first challenge: corralling a throng of rich and poor, blacks and whites, speakers of many tongues, Americans and men of mixed allegiance wouldn't be easy.

Yet there was still a chance that cooler heads would prevail, and a diplomatic end to the war might be reached before any confrontation with the British took place at or near New Orleans. On the other side of the Atlantic, in fact, there were a number of Americans vitally concerned with avoiding what loomed as a potential military disaster in Louisiana.

The Negotiations: Ghent, Belgium

Many months before, President Madison had sent his diplomats to discuss an end to the conflict with representatives of the British Crown. After many delays, the ministers from both countries finally sat down together in August 1814 to talk treaty. If the Americans had hoped the end of the French wars would lead the British to tender peace offerings, they were very much mistaken. Even on day one of the talks, the U.S. envoys understood—perhaps more than anyone in Washington—the very real British threat to the Gulf of Mexico.

One of them, Albert Gallatin, had kept his ears and eyes open on his way to Ghent, in Flanders, the site of the peace talks. He was an old friend of President Madison's, having previously served as secretary of the treasury. During a stopover in London in the spring, Gallatin had heard things.

Some of what he picked up was common street knowledge. The London *Times* stated in its pages the position that many Britons held: "Mr. Madison's dirty swindling maneuvers in respect to Louisiana and the Floridas remain to be punished."[2] A few members of Parliament even called for New Orleans to be handed over to Great Britain. The dutiful Gallatin took notes of the chatter and wrote home, relaying it to Secretary of State James Monroe.

"To use their own language," he warned, "[the British] mean to inflict on America a chastisement that will teach her that war is not to be declared against Great Britain with impunity."[3] Gallatin added ominously that he had heard whispers that a force of between fifteen and twenty thousand men was on its way across the Atlantic Ocean.

Their aim was clearly to deliver punishment, not peace, to the colonies they'd lost thirty-one years before.

After writing from London, Gallatin had made his way across the English Channel where he joined forces with the rest of the American negotiating team, including the sharp-spoken Kentucky politician Henry Clay and John Quincy Adams, son of founding father John Adams, the most experienced of the American envoys.

As Speaker of the House of Representatives, Henry Clay had helped persuade his colleagues in Congress to declare war, asserting that capturing Canada would be a simple matter. Two years later, humbled by American military failures in Canada and elsewhere, Clay resigned as Speaker to accept the posting to Europe. There he hoped his considerable negotiating abilities would help salvage an honorable peace.

But Clay, like Gallatin, was deeply worried as the August meetings with the British representatives got under way. Although Madison had agreed to the proposal for peace talks back in January, Lord Castlereagh, the British foreign secretary, and the men around him had dragged their feet ever since. Clay had to ask himself: *Why are there so many delays in sending a team to talk peace?*

Tall and congenial, Henry Clay was a hail-fellow-well-met sort of man who liked his liquor. He could walk into a roomful of strangers and depart with new friends, even if, as a demon cardplayer, he had managed to take some of their money. Now, in Ghent, those same gambling instincts put Minister Clay on edge. He could smell risk when he encountered it, and he had come to think the British were slow to open the treaty talks for a reason: *With a large force from Great Britain attacking the United States, mustn't the odds favor the superior British troops?* he thought. Clay believed the Crown's representatives were awaiting news of battlefield successes in North America. In the meantime, the king's statesmen had little incentive to negotiate.

This all made painful sense to Clay. He was a man who understood better than most the advantage of having bargaining chips on one's own side of the table. And British victories on the battlefield could provide just that to his enemy.

When, at last, the Britons did sit down to present their terms of peace on the afternoon of August 8, 1814, at one o'clock, the aura of doom darkened for Madison's diplomats. The demands made on behalf of Foreign Secretary Lord Castlereagh were harsh, involving unacceptable limitations on fishing rights in the Atlantic as well as a large buffer zone for the Indians in the center of the North American continent.

The American envoys recognized that the British demands were those of a conqueror—and that the United States had by no means been conquered. At least not yet.

In the days that followed, the British and American negotiators continued to meet and exchange notes about possible treaty terms. But they made little progress. As Clay wrote home to Secretary of State Monroe ten days into the talks, "I am inclined to think . . . that their policy is to consume as much time as possible . . . [in] the hope that they will strike some signal blow, during the present campaign."[4]

Both sides in the Ghent negotiations awaited news from the front.

"Bloody Noses"

As the peace negotiators talked across the Atlantic, an express messenger arrived in Mobile, bringing Jackson bad news. His hunch had been correct: the British were indeed planning to land along the Gulf

Coast east of New Orleans. The dispatch Jackson received at five o'clock on the evening of August 27, 1814, reported that three warships, the HMS *Hermes, Carron,* and *Sophie* from the Royal Navy station at Bermuda, had already landed a small force of men and armaments at Pensacola in Spanish Florida.

With British boots on the ground just fifty miles east of his station, Jackson wondered what might happen next. A large invasion seemed likely; another source, this one writing from Havana, reported that a loose-lipped British officer had bragged about a plan to capture Pensacola, to move on to Mobile, then to march overland to New Orleans.[5] London had already sent thirteen additional warships with ten thousand troops aboard, the officer claimed, with still more soon to follow.[6]

When Jackson looked at his own forces, they seemed laughably small. He had arrived with his five-hundred-man Third Infantry force and found that Mobile was manned by just the Thirty-Ninth Tennessee Regiment. Scattered over his large southwestern command—from Tennessee to the Gulf Coast—were fewer than two thousand more troops. Only the Third and the Thirty-Ninth had ever seen combat.

That night Jackson put pen to paper, writing home to Tennessee, asking to be reinforced with the entire state militia. In particular, he wanted General Coffee and his cavalry. He wanted Cherokees and artillerymen, and he needed transport and supplies.

Action was required; the threat was real. "Before one month," he warned, "the British . . . expect to be in possession of Mobile and all the surrounding country." If he did not get the support he needed, he was not sure he could stop the British from taking this key port and then moving on to New Orleans.

But Jackson couldn't afford to sit around waiting for reinforcements: his first task would be to get Fort Bowyer into fighting shape.

Because of its location thirty miles south, at the opening of Mobile Bay, Fort Bowyer would be the first line of defense if British ships moved on Mobile. Enemy vessels would have to pass within range of the fort's guns as they sailed through the narrow channel at the entrance to the bay. But from Jackson's position, that was both good and bad: its location was certainly a strategic advantage, but, having been abandoned due to a lack of men a few months earlier, Fort Bowyer was far from ready to repel a sustained attack.

Jackson needed a man he could trust to get the fort back in line. He chose Lieutenant Colonel William Lawrence for the task. A career U.S. Army officer from Maryland, Lawrence set out immediately from Mobile for the seaside battery. A tall, stern man with a full head of curly brown hair, he loaded his 160 infantrymen into boats along with supplies and all the munitions he could muster.

On reaching Fort Bowyer, Lawrence saw the challenge before him. The semicircular battery was really just a wall of sand and earth. With its low walls lined on the inside with resinous pine boards, the fort could be set afire by one well-placed shell. No hardened shelter protected the fort's ammunition and, worst of all, more than half of its twenty guns were mounted on outmoded Spanish carriages, making them difficult to aim and operate.

Lawrence and his men threw themselves into the task and, with the British expected to arrive at any moment from their new base at Pensacola, worked night and day, reinforcing the little bastion on the spit of sand with wood, stone, sand, and whatever else came to hand. Even after sunset, the Americans remained ready for action, always expecting to see British sails on the horizon. They didn't know how many days they had to prepare.

Back in Mobile, Jackson continued his writing campaign. One of his correspondents was Governor William Claiborne. Jackson was looking beyond Fort Bowyer and Pensacola, worrying about New Orleans.

Though born and educated in Virginia, the ambitious young Claiborne had, by the age of twenty-five, already earned a law degree, moved west, and served as a congressman (he won Andrew Jackson's vacated seat in 1797). After a decade as governor of New Orleans, he carried himself with what some saw as a haughty confidence; he relished his power and influence in Louisiana. The governor was respected for his administrative abilities but not loved by those he governed, with whom he, as a Virginian, had little in common.

Jackson's letter to him was a warning: "The present intention of Britain," he told his former Washington colleague "is to make an attack on [Mobile], and New Orleans. Part of the British force for this purpose, has landed at Pensacola, and the balance, hourly expected."

The letter was also an urgent call to arms: "You must summon up all your energy, your quota of militia must be in the field without delay. . . . The country must and shall be defended."[7] From Mobile, the best Jackson could do was to urge Claiborne to raise the alarm. Somehow, Jackson hoped, the governor would begin pulling Creoles and Anglos, Indians and freemen, and the rest to fight together.

The British clearly expected to win Mobile and to move on to New Orleans. The odds that Jackson's small army could repel them seemed slim. But the pugnacious General Jackson, channeling his long-simmering anger, was as always ready to fight. Writing home to Tennessee, he reported on the prospect of the British taking Mobile, resolving solemnly, "Th[ere] will be bloody noses before this happens."[8]

The Burning of Washington

When Jackson wrote to the secretary of war in Washington, he did not know that, days earlier, partly due to John Armstrong's incompetence, the nation's capital had sustained a terrible attack.

Back on August 16, a British fleet of some fifty warships had been sighted in Chesapeake Bay. Though its presence was clearly a sign of nothing good, the Americans were unsure what to expect. In an eerie parallel to Jackson's situation near New Orleans, Madison and his men in Washington received only fractured reports concerning the enemy force; British strategy and even their ultimate objective were uncertain. One option was to attack Annapolis, Maryland's capital. General Armstrong didn't think that likely; he was certain the enemy would attack Baltimore, a busy commercial city. Armstrong assured Madison that Washington was safe—he thought it had little strategic value—but others worried that if the armada veered into the nearby Patuxent River, the British could land troops and move on the capital.

On August 20, Secretary of State James Monroe took it upon himself to find out and rode to a nearby hilltop from which he could see the enemy fleet. And there, before him on the shore of Benedict, Maryland, he saw the British had established a base camp and soldiers were coming ashore. Their exact target still wasn't certain, but there was no doubt an invasion had begun.

On August 24, the British played their hand: At the little town of Bladensburg, eight miles from Washington, the British attacked. The town's American defenders—a mix of militiamen from Washington, Baltimore, and Annapolis, almost none of whom were in uniform—were no match for the men in bright red coats. Dragoons on horseback led the charge across the bridge that defined the sleepy village on the East Branch of the Potomac River. A flood of British infantryman followed, bearing polished bayonets that glinted in the sun. To the intimidating sound of exploding rockets overhead, the king's veteran troops drove into the American line. General Armstrong had expected his troops to hold off the outnumbered British—there were some four thousand British troops facing perhaps seven thousand American defenders—but he was wrong. Led by the British general Robert Ross and Sir George Cockburn, a hot-tempered admiral in the Royal Navy, the enemy sliced through the line of intimidated militiamen, captured Bladensburg, and headed straight for Washington.

Madison and the other government officials had been watching the battle from an overlook and had to rush back to Washington, making it there just in time to join a larger retreat. Before fleeing, the First Lady and others had sought to save a few precious relics—a portrait of Washington, a copy of the Declaration of Independence in the Library of Congress—but a few hours later, after stopping for an afternoon dinner, the British marched into a nearly empty Washington. Then shots rang out, as hidden snipers fired into the ranks of the 150-man British force. The angry British commander regarded the snipers' behavior as "dastardly and provoking." He promptly ordered the house from which the muskets fired set afire.

That would be the first of a series of conflagrations. Next it was off to the president's house. When the British arrived there, they found Mr. and Mrs. Madison's dinner table still set, the aroma of cooking food still wafting up from the recently abandoned kitchen. They drank the president's wine and ate a generous meal before building bonfires in the rooms and retreating to the street to watch the mansion burn. By nine o'clock, great billows of flame reached into the sky; the

Capitol had also become an inferno and by morning it was a roofless, smoking ruin, and the light gray stone of the president's house had been burned black.

The British made a point of sacking the offices of the Washington newspaper the *National Intelligencer,* building a bonfire to burn its type and presses. The *Intelligencer* was known for printing stories critical of Cockburn, and he was determined to teach its editor and readers a lesson. "Be sure all the c's are destroyed," he is said to have told his men, "so that they can't abuse my name anymore."

In the end, it wasn't the brave efforts of the American people that put out the fires or stopped the destruction. Only the arrival, with miraculous timing, of a powerful storm prevented more of the city from being damaged by the flames. Rain poured down and strong winds blew, lifting British cannons off the ground, according to some reports. Others claimed that the storm formed a tornado, a rare phenomenon in Washington. Whatever the case, the British were discouraged and the fires quenched thanks not to the work of men, but to an act of God.

Although the British returned to their ships several days later, President James Madison and the U.S. Congress were left homeless. The attack tore the fabric of the nation, too, with hopes of a peace deal growing dim. Many of the northern states had refused to go to war; the Eastern Seaboard was ill equipped to fight off its attackers, and when it came to protecting the new nation's capital, no one had fought. Perhaps more than ever before America needed something—or someone—to knit the country back together.

The events of August 24 also meant that when Jackson's dispatch arrived in Washington, it didn't land on John Armstrong's desk. That desk was gone—the building the War and Treasury Departments shared had also been torched—and John Armstrong had been dismissed. At Madison's request, James Monroe took on a second job in the cabinet, becoming secretary of war as well as secretary of state. Yet even Monroe, despite his good intentions, would not be able to provide much help to his Tennessee general, given that the national government was struggling to survive and reestablish itself.

Meanwhile, one of the first British ships to arrive in the Gulf of Mexico was about to make its presence felt. But the British success did something they never expected. It galvanized more ambivalent Americans, who now found themselves motivated to support the war as they realized that America was facing not only the possibility of defeat, but of complete destruction.

A Message from the British

On the morning of September 2, 1814, the British *Sophie* sailed into view, sailing directly for the shallow channel that led to Barataria Bay, south of the city of New Orleans. The two-masted warship, armed with eighteen guns, dropped anchor several miles from shore. British gunners fired a cannon, but the men on shore recognized that it was a greeting, not an act of war.

Since 1805, the island of Grand Terre had been home to the men who thought of themselves as coastal privateers. They had fled the Caribbean island of Santo Domingo following the slave rebellion that led to the founding of the independent nation of Haiti. Their adopted home in Barataria Bay offered access to New Orleans via the muddy waters of shallow streams, bayous, and channels camouflaged by reeds and grasses. In turn, the city provided a ready market for captured goods. Led by a pair of brothers, Jean and Pierre Lafitte, the pirates had constructed dozens of warehouses deep in the bayous on Grand Terre Island, all the while maintaining businesses in the city, including a store on Royal Street (where Jean could often be found) and a blacksmith shop, operated by Pierre, on St. Philip Street. The store offered a wide range of hard-to-find goods to the well-to-do of New Orleans, and the shop doubled as an in-town warehouse.

The British had arrived in Barataria Bay to seek a parley. Like Jackson, the British understood that they would need local knowledge of the New Orleans landscape in order to take the city. They expected to conquer Mobile first but were confident enough of their success that they were looking ahead, and the HMS *Sophie* approached Grand Terre hoping to find the guidance they needed.

Who better to provide it? With their fleet of perhaps thirty vessels, the pirates routinely attacked shipping in the Gulf, taking as prizes passing merchant ships flying the British and especially the Spanish flag. After capturing their prey—their artillery was considerable, their daring greater—the pirates would disappear into the sanctuary of the bayous, beneath the canopy of live oaks laden with Spanish moss. These backwater buccaneers knew the terrain around New Orleans as no one else did.

From the deck of the *Sophie,* British sailors lowered a longboat, flying a flag of truce, into the waters. Two uniformed officers were aboard—one was the *Sophie*'s commander, Captain Nicholas Lockyer—along with a handful of sailors who rowed for shore.

Soon a second boat launched from the beach, rowing toward the small British vessel. One Baratarian stood in its bow, and four pirates manned the oars.

When the two bobbing vessels were within hailing distance, a British voice called out, in French, "We are looking for Jean Lafitte."[9]

"Follow me," called the tall, thin man with the long mustache standing in the bow.

With the two boats now headed for the beach, more and more Baratarians assembled on the shore to greet them. Some in boots, some barefoot, the pirates in their brightly colored pantaloons and blouses stood in contrast to the uniformed men of the Royal Navy. Knives, cutlasses, and pistols hung from their belts, and bandannas covered their heads. These men deserved the name that Andrew Jackson soon coined for them: they were "piratical banditti."

When the boats were drawn onto the sand, the pirates crowded toward the handful of British visitors. With no more than a movement of his head, the tall man stepping from the pirate boat made it plain that the men on the shore should keep their distance. He then turned to the leader of the English, Captain Lockyer.

To the visitor's surprise, the elegant man identified himself, speaking in his native French.

"Monsieur," he said, "I am Lafitte."

He beckoned them to follow.

The British Proposition

Jean Lafitte's comfortable house had a broad covered gallery, a deep porch in the Caribbean style, which looked out on the Gulf. There Lafitte served his British guests fish and game, Spanish wine, and the fruits of the Indies. He offered Cuban cigars.[10] Only then did he examine a packet of letters handed him by the visitors. They contained the terms of a British proposal.

"I call on you, with your brave followers, to enter into the service of Great Britain, in which you shall have the rank of a captain," Lafitte read. "Your ships and vessels [will] be placed under the orders of the commanding officer on this station."[11] Lafitte and his men were being invited—or were they being forced?—into British service.

Lafitte looked upon his guests and they, in turn, studied this unusual man. At thirty-four, he was something of a mystery. Some said he was born in Bordeaux. Or was his birthplace Haiti? He was dark-haired and sunburned. Rumor had it he had served in both the British and the French navies and had been incarcerated for a time in a Spanish prison, but no one seemed certain. Clearly he was not a man to be easily intimidated, and he had a shrewd and adventuresome look. Renowned for his skills both as a fencer in battle and as a dancer in society, he carried himself with a gentleman's grace.

Through his translator, Lockyer assured Lafitte the offer was a generous one. For his cooperation in fighting the United States, Lafitte would be paid $30,000 in cash. There would be grants of land for him and his men, pardons for former British subjects, and other guarantees.

Next Lafitte gained confirmation of the rumor he had already heard: yes, New Orleans was to be attacked by the British.

But along with the carrot came the stick: Should Lafitte and the Baratarians choose not to side with the British, a great armada of ships would make Grand Terre their target. The refusal of the offer to join forces would result in the obliteration of the village at Barataria, along with every pirate sailing vessel.

The message was clear: *Join us or we will destroy you.*

When Lafitte spoke, his words to the British officers were measured and diplomatic.

He needed to consider the proposal before him, he said. His habit of closing one eye when he spoke suited his words; he could not, he explained, give an immediate answer. They were his guests, but as they had seen on the beach, he reminded them, they were among violent men, many of whom were hostile to the British. He needed to discuss any proposed alliance with his fellow privateers. But he promised his English visitors safe passage back to their ship in the morning. With their little boat now under pirate guard, the men of the Royal Navy had no choice but to agree.

Good to his word, Jean Lafitte saw his visitors off the following morning and, after their departure, he drafted a formal response.

He opened his letter with an apology for being unable to give an immediate answer, but the pirate leader stood firm: He needed time to decide. After taking two weeks to put his affairs in order, he would meet the British again with an answer. When he finished writing, he ordered his letter be delivered to the HMS *Sophie* and, later in the day, he watched the warship as her unfurled sails caught the breeze. The *Sophie* headed out to sea, making for the deep Gulf waters and a return to Pensacola.

The Baratarians and the British would indeed meet again—but on terms yet to be determined.

Lafitte wrote a second letter, this one addressed to a trusted friend in New Orleans. Writing as a "true American," Lafitte confided that he wished to be of service to his adopted country. "I make you the depository of the secret on which perhaps depends the tranquillity of our country,"[12] he wrote, before recounting the story of the arrival of the British ship at Grand Terre.

Lafitte had decided to play the double agent, offering the Americans fair warning of the British plan.

His third letter of the morning was addressed to Governor William Claiborne. "I tender my services to defend [Louisiana]," he told Claiborne. "I am the stray sheep, wishing to return to the sheepfold."[13]

Whether General Jackson wanted the help of the piratical banditti or not, Lafitte had just declared himself at his service in the fight to save New Orleans.

CHAPTER 6

Jackson Unleashed

I was born for a storm, and a calm does not suit me.

—**Andrew Jackson**

More than a week would pass before Andrew Jackson learned of the British visit to Barataria. He was 150 miles away in Mobile—and worrying about the security of that port. For him the stakes were clear: if he didn't hold Mobile, the British would have a clear road to New Orleans.

Knowing Fort Bowyer was Mobile's first line of defense, Jackson wanted to be sure he could keep the town safe and secured. On the evening of September 13, 1814, the general, together with a small guard of infantrymen, climbed aboard a schooner. Sailing south that evening toward Fort Bowyer, the little craft was well short of its destination when, at about eleven o'clock, another schooner hailed Jackson's vessel. She brought bad news: It was too late for Jackson to inspect Mobile's defenses. "A number of British armed ships . . . lay off the bar, and from their maneuvering and sounding, etc., showed a design of attacking that fort, or passing it for Mobile."[1]

Jackson, with no wish to be captured by a vastly superior force, ordered the crew to reverse course and return to Mobile. There was no way for him to consult with Colonel Lawrence. At this point, all he could do was pray that the little fort withstood the attack and prepare Mobile to face the British if it didn't.

Unknown to Jackson, a small force of 72 Royal Marines and 130 Indian recruits had landed nine miles east of Fort Bowyer three days earlier. Armed with a cannon and a howitzer, they planned to attack the fort from behind, while four warships, mounted with seventy-eight guns, would attack from the sea. Even now, the *Hermes,* the *Carron,* and the sloops *Sophie* and *Anaconda* were sailing around Mobile Point, getting into position.

By the afternoon of September 15, all was ready. The British announced their presence with the roar of cannons, firing their guns in unison at four o'clock in the afternoon. Fortunately for the Americans,

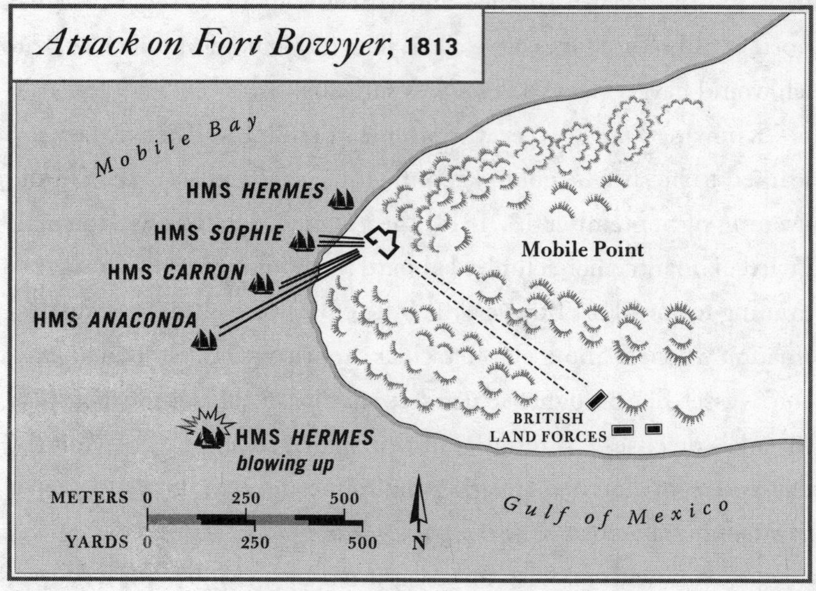

the wind wasn't cooperating, which meant just two of the British warships, the HMS *Sophie* and the flotilla's flagship, the HMS *Hermes,* had managed to maneuver into firing range.

With enemy shots and shells bombarding their fortification, Colonel Lawrence and his men returned fire. They had little time to answer that attack from the sea before the attack from the land began.

At the center of the approaching British land force were Creeks and Choctaws the British had recruited as their allies. Wearing British red coats over their bare legs, the Indians were flanked by confident—and more completely clad—Royal Marines. The British veterans expected Fort Bowyer to fall as easily as Washington had three weeks earlier. But as the combined force marched boldly toward Fort Bowyer, Lawrence's men dampened their hopes. A barrage of cannon shot pinned the British down, halting their advance. As the ground force took cover and attempted to regroup, Lawrence concentrated on the seaside battle.

Along the seawall, the American gunners had found the range and were making the cannonballs count, shooting away the bowsprit of the *Hermes*. Yet as great clouds of gun smoke enveloped both the fort and the ships, neither side seemed to be gaining the upper hand. The Americans were holding their own, but there was no reason to believe that the British, attacking from both sides, would not be able to wear them down and prevail once the Americans ran out of ammunition.

Then, with a lucky shot, an American cannonball tore through the anchor cable that was holding the *Hermes* in firing position. Suddenly cut loose, the ship drifted helplessly toward the fort, carried by the incoming current. While sailors frantically tried to get the sails to catch the falling wind and carry the *Hermes* out of range of American guns, shots thudded into her hull and shredded the ship's sails and rigging.

Just as the crew managed to turn the ship, her keel scraped the sandy bottom. The *Hermes* had run aground. Trapped just six hundred yards from Fort Bowyer's guns, the ship was now an easy—and stationary—target.

With American artillery fire raining down, the British commander had no choice but to abandon ship. By seven o'clock that evening, the departing sailors set fire to the crippled vessel before fleeing to the British ships waiting safely out of range. As night fell, the great flames aboard the *Hermes* rose into the sky. For three hours, the ship burned slowly but steadily, a brilliant light show against the dark sea. Then the flames reached the gunpowder in the ship's hold. In a moment, the *Hermes* exploded, blasted into fragments that rained down on the sea and shore.

Waiting and Wondering

Thirty miles away, the earth trembled. Feeling the ground shake in Mobile, Andrew Jackson looked south toward Fort Bowyer and there, at the horizon line, he saw the *Hermes* light the sky.

From his faraway vantage he couldn't be sure what had happened at Mobile Point. What he did know was that the reinforcements he had sent the day before had been turned back, their ship prevented from reaching the fort by the much larger HMS *Hermes*. If Lawrence and his men were to hold Fort Bowyer against the British, they would do so on their own. There was nothing else he could do.

As he watched the sun rise the following morning, General Jackson still didn't know whether Fort Bowyer was safe. More anxious hours would pass before a dispatch from Colonel Lawrence finally arrived, reporting the destruction of the *Hermes* and the flight of the three other British ships. The British had sustained significant casualties (thirty-two killed, thirty-seven wounded). The fort's defenders reported just four dead and five wounded.

Although the men defending Fort Bowyer had been outnumbered by roughly ten to one, Jackson's strategy and Lawrence's hard labors produced a victory. Lawrence's band of 158 soldiers had prevented the British from winning a beachhead and, more important, gaining access to a harbor from which they might march overland to invade New Orleans. Washington may have fallen, but little Fort Bowyer still stood. The Americans had finally held.

"Success has crowned the gallant efforts of our brave soldiers," Jackson wrote, passing the good news to Secretary of War James Monroe in Washington.[2] He intended to keep that success going.

"Defence of Fort McHenry"

Far away, a full one thousand miles to the north and east, another fort had just been bombarded by the British, and a major American victory had been won. The fight for the nation's third-largest city would help launch a turnaround of U.S. military fortunes—and national morale would rise as Francis Scott Key's poem about the events in Baltimore Harbor reverberated around the country.

Before dawn, on September 12, 1814, British troops had gone

ashore east of Baltimore for a land assault on the city. The British ground forces had been stunned when, only minutes into the first skirmish, an officer on horseback returned at speed from the vanguard, calling for a surgeon. The infantrymen recognized the riderless horse that followed: it belonged to the commanding general, Robert Ross, the man responsible for the burning of Washington. He had fallen from his steed, mortally wounded with a musket ball to his chest. The old gentlemen's agreement not to target officers had been breached during the Revolution—to the outrage of the British—and targeting officers had since become an accepted strategy.

Despite Ross's loss, the British were undeterred. At first light the next day, the people of Baltimore were awakened by the sound of mortars exploding overhead. A convoy of British frigates and a half-dozen bomb vessels were firing on Fort McHenry, which guarded the entrance to Baltimore's harbor. The Americans had sunk ships in the channel to prevent the British from sailing in, hoping to keep them out of range of the town. A relentless barrage of mortar shells continued all day and into the night; the hollow projectiles, some of which weighed up to two hundred pounds, flew in a high arc, remaining in flight up to thirty seconds. Many exploded in midair, scattering deadly shrapnel in all directions, accompanied by exploding rockets that brightened the sky like fireworks. The artillery attack ceased briefly at one o'clock on the morning of September 14 when an attempt by British barges to land troops west of Fort McHenry was rebuffed, but the pounding soon resumed. Finally, shortly before dawn, the gunners ceased their fire.

Five miles downstream from the port of Baltimore and in British custody, Francis Scott Key had watched the great fight unfold. Commissioned by President Madison to negotiate the freedom of a Maryland doctor detained by the British after the burning of Washington,

Key was aboard a British ship awaiting the outcome of the battle. From the ship's deck he watched the fireworks of the bombardment, then waited in the darkness, watching and wondering. He did not know what the silence meant, but he worried: *Had Baltimore fallen?* He paced the deck of the ship, periodically peering through a spyglass at Fort McHenry, fearing he would see, instead of the Stars and Stripes, the Union Jack or a white flag of surrender.

A feeling of pride swelled his breast as the morning mist cleared, revealing an American flag still flying over the fort. The British attack had failed.

Finding an envelope in his pocket, Key began to compose a poem on the back of a letter, seeking to express the relief he felt. He had a tune in his head—once before, he'd written a celebratory

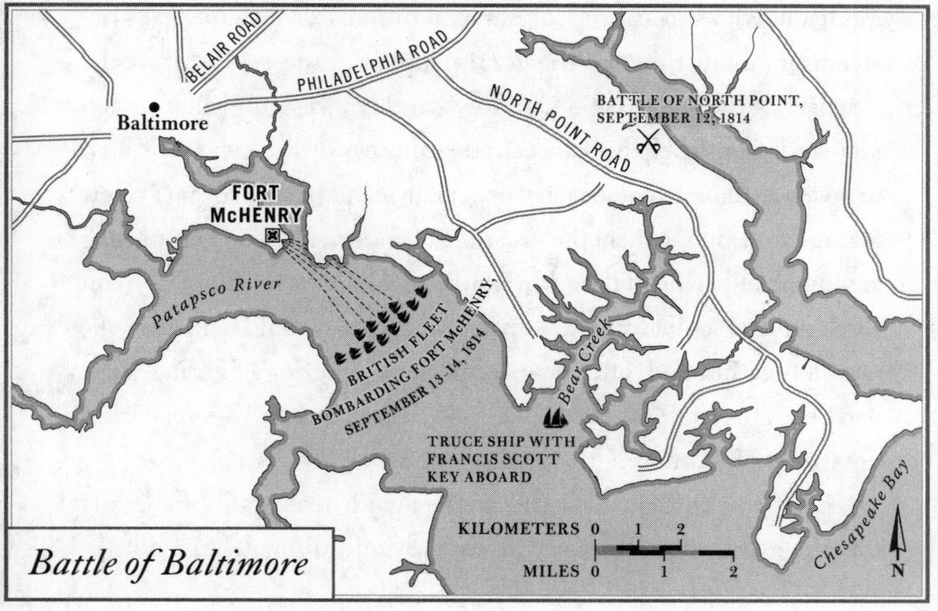

Battle of Baltimore

poem to fit the melody—and he jotted down his thoughts and sentiments, as well as a couplet that would ring familiar in the ears of his countrymen for generations to come. "'Tis the star spangled banner, O! long may it wave / O'er the land of the free and the home of the brave."[3]

That morning the Royal Navy withdrew, retreating to the Chesapeake. No longer held captive, Key landed in Baltimore and completed his ballad. A friend arranged for freshly printed broadside copies of the poem bearing the title "The Defence of Fort McHenry" to be distributed on the streets of the city, on September 17. Three days later, when the *Baltimore Patriot and Evening Advertiser* resumed publication, the newspaper published the poem in its pages.

Earlier in the war, Francis Scott Key, a Federalist by affiliation, had opposed the decision to go to war. But recent events—the burning of Washington, the fight for Baltimore—had allied him with President Madison, who was calling for national unity after Washington's destruction, exhorting "all the good people . . . in providing for the defense" of the nation.[4] Though Key's anthem was published anonymously, it would help the cause. In the coming weeks, it was reprinted in no fewer than seventeen newspapers, in states from Georgia to New Hampshire, among them the *Federal Republican* of Georgetown, long an outspoken critic of both Mr. Madison and his war.[5] Francis Scott Key's four verses had sparked a patriotic fire that would help draw the nation together and, after years of defeats, America's fighting spirit had been stirred. Washington may have fallen, but the Union Jack did not fly over Baltimore.

Even so the British would strike again, reasonably believing that the greatest naval power on earth would ultimately be able to conquer New Orleans. The only thing standing in their way was Andrew Jackson.

On to Pensacola

After the Fort Bowyer victory, Jackson's sense of elation was short-lived. He knew it was only a matter of time before the next attack. Without sufficient land forces to defend the entire coast, his job, above all, was to outguess his enemy. For the moment, Jackson himself would remain at Mobile. He would work his network of spies, monitoring British military moves from Florida to Louisiana and in the Caribbean.

Where would the British strike next? His first guess had been a good one: the British attack on Fort Bowyer confirmed that the enemy had hoped to use Mobile as a base for their move on Louisiana. But even after Lawrence and his guns had repelled them, who was to say the enemy wouldn't return another day to the mouth of Mobile Bay with a much larger flotilla of ships, perhaps accompanied by Royal Marines and infantry?

Jackson would take no chances. "We will be better prepared to receive them on the next visit," he wrote to an old Tennessee friend serving in Congress.[6] As he waited for reinforcements, he set about further improving the defenses at Fort Bowyer. He ordered Colonel Lawrence to salvage the cannons from the blasted wreck of the *Hermes*. If the British returned, they would find the fort even harder to take than before.

Meanwhile, Jackson also plotted his next move: once Fort Bowyer was reinforced with the new guns, the best course, Jackson decided, would be to eject the British force from Pensacola, the next large port town some fifty miles east of Mobile.[7] That seemed the obvious next step. As his aide-de-camp John Reid observed, unless Pensacola could be taken from British hands, "it was vain to think of defending the country."[8]

Pensacola was in Spanish territory, and the Spaniards were not proving friendly to the Americans. The Spanish governor, Don Mateo González Manrique, had granted the British Royal Navy safe harbor in Pensacola two months earlier, which meant that the British were free to land troops there for an overland assault on New Orleans—and the young country would be in danger as long as the British held the harbor. Taking it might not be easy, though; the British ships could repel a water attack, and any force attempting a land attack would meet up with unfriendly Red Sticks living in the swamps surrounding Pensacola.

Knowing these dangers, Jackson decided he would attack nonetheless—only he would need reinforcements. As October tilted toward November, the task of refortification at Fort Bowyer neared completion and, leaving the place in Colonel Lawrence's good hands, General Jackson led a column of five hundred army regulars headed for Pensacola. He and his troops took a circular route, looping north in order to meet up with General Coffee and, on October 25, the old friends joined forces. Coffee brought eighteen hundred men, each on horseback, all with their own rifles.

The generals and their combined force crossed the Alabama River at the Fort Mims ferry. In the coming days, more Tennessee troops joined them—rangers from West Tennessee, militiamen from East Tennessee—and the ranks of the army swelled with 750 Choctaws and Chickasaws.

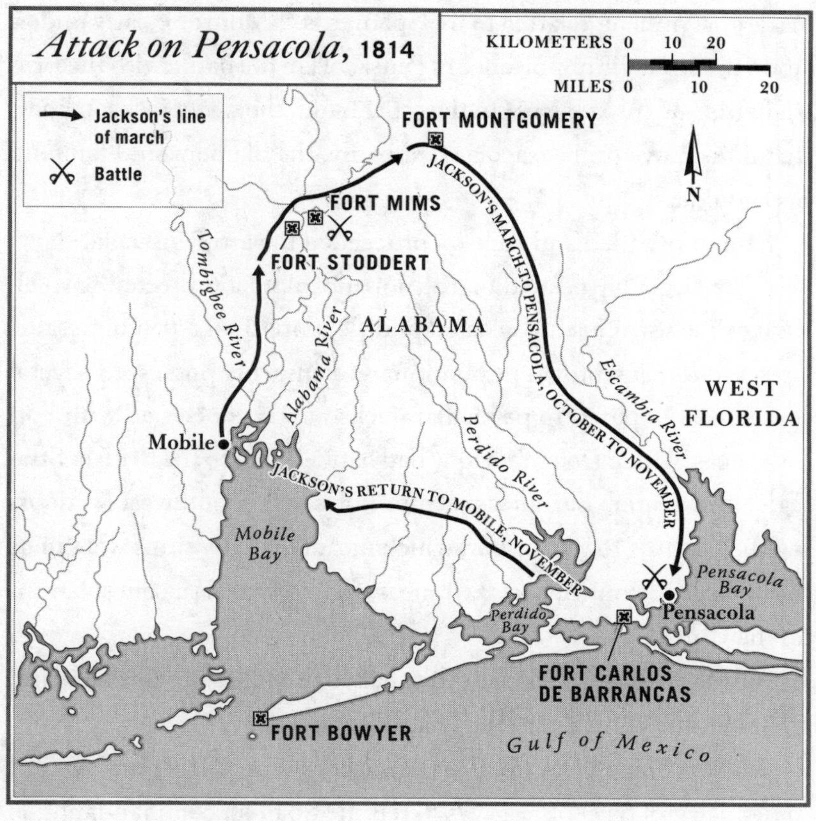

Although his army now numbered more than four thousand troops, Jackson was politically very much on his own. In official correspondence, Secretary of State James Monroe warned Jackson away from Pensacola. President James Madison's government was afraid that the United States, already at war with one powerful European foe, risked a war with Spain, too, if they threatened Pensacola. Yet Monroe had also made it known to Jackson in "*strong* terms" via back channels that the general "would receive all the support in the power of the government, relating to the Spaniards."[9] Monroe clearly understood the strategic importance of Pensacola in the battle with the British in the Gulf of Mexico. On the other hand, the savvy Jackson knew that if his move on Pensacola went badly, the blame would fall onto his shoulders.

But duty called and Jackson proceeded toward Pensacola.

The target lay nestled on the north bank of a protected bay. Although the town itself consisted of little more than a trio of parallel streets and a downtown public square, Pensacola possessed several protective ramparts. In particular, Jackson was concerned with Fort Barrancas, which Don Manrique had handed over to the British. Strategically essential, Barrancas sat nine miles to the southwest overlooking the opening to the harbor, which meant arriving ships were in its line of fire. To control Fort Barrancas was to control the finest harbor on the Gulf Coast.

On November 6, Jackson's army halted two miles west of Pensacola.

First, the general tried approaching in peace.

He sent Major Henry B. Piere of the Forty-Fourth Infantry forward under a flag of truce. Piere was to tell the Spanish commandant that he did not come with demands of war but with suggestions for preserving neutrality. Then he would present Jackson's written demands: the United States wanted control of the fortifications around Pensacola, in particular Fort Barrancas, with its strategic overlook at the entrance to Pensacola Bay.

But before he could arrive in the town to present the American case, Piere and a small escort took artillery fire from one of the city's fortifications. They retreated to consult with Jackson.

Jackson was a man with a hair-trigger disposition, but he could also be a man of calm in chaos when necessary. In this case, he held his temper and tried a second peaceable approach, this time sending as his emissary a Spanish prisoner captured the previous day. Through the messenger, Jackson demanded an explanation for the firing on his men. Governor Manrique hedged, blaming the British. They had fired on Piere without the governor's authorization, he claimed, and he assured Jackson that he would, of course, talk with Jackson's representative.

That evening, Major Piere, now welcomed by the governor, went to Pensacola to deliver Jackson's demands. The governor read Jackson's note: "I come not as the enemy of Spain; not to make war but to ask for peace." But though Jackson used words of peace, his demands hinted at the consequence of war should his request be ignored. The governor should give him Barrancas, he insisted—and he gave the Spaniard one hour to respond. Governor Manrique deemed the terms unacceptable, insisting that his duty did not permit him to do as Jackson asked. Piere brought the news back to the American camp.[10]

Done negotiating, Jackson grimly laid out his plan for storming the town. Manrique left him no alternative: they would have to do this the hard way.

Meanwhile, in Ghent . . .

The American diplomats in Europe didn't have it much easier, as the peace negotiations proceeded at a snail's pace. The British commissioners had to write home to London whenever the Americans made a proposal, forcing the U.S. delegation to spend weeks waiting in the three-story house they shared on the Rue des Champs.

The American team had little in common. John Quincy Adams,

Henry Clay, and Albert Gallatin disagreed over the style and tone of their responses to the British demands and differed in style of life, too. As the days and weeks passed, Adams couldn't help but notice when, rising to read his Bible before dawn, he heard Henry Clay retiring to his room after a long night of cigars, port, and cards. About the only thing the envoys agreed upon was what they told their betters in Washington: "We need hardly say . . . that there is not at present, any hope of peace."[11]

When the news had arrived, on October 1, of the August burning of Washington, John Quincy Adams spent a sleepless night worrying about the fortunes of his country. A habitual diarist, he found, on the morning after hearing of his capital's capture, that his sense of shock remained so great that "it was almost impossible to write."[12]

The American team had little choice but to continue talking until a subtle British move shocked them anew. The British asked that the treaty include two Latin words: *uti possidetis*. Meaning "as you possess," the term specified that the land held by each side at ratification of the treaty would remain with its possessor.

The precise purpose of the simple little phrase wasn't clear, but Gallatin thought he knew. He had suspected for some time that the British were attempting to capture the mouth of the Mississippi, writing to Monroe six weeks earlier, "It appears to me most likely that their true and immediate object is New Orleans."[13] Now that they had introduced this term into the treaty, he was even more certain. If the British were able to conquer New Orleans before the treaty was signed, America's westward expansion would be cut off, and the future shape of the United States would be determined by the British.

From a distance of five thousand miles from New Orleans, the diplomats could do little. They could issue warnings that Jackson and his men were in grave danger; they could wring their hands at the worrisome prospect that their independent nation was in danger. (As Gallatin wrote to the U.S. ambassador to France, "A belief is said to be entertained that a continuance of the war would produce a separation of the Union, and perhaps a return of the New England states to the mother country.")[14]

Gallatin was right to be worried. Late in 1814, delegates of the New England states met secretly in what became known as the Hartford Convention to discuss their complaints about Madison and his war. Several delegates pushed for secession even as the British moved toward New Orleans.

For now, the thought of secession was only one of the looming difficulties. The diplomats considered all the obstacles and could offer no optimism at the likelihood their negotiations would succeed. As Clay bluntly put it to Monroe, "The safest opinion to adopt is . . . that our mission will terminate unsuccessfully."[15]

Jackson and his American soldiers would get no help from Ghent—and, in the coming weeks, the predictions of Ministers Gallatin and Clay would prove all too correct.

Back to New Orleans

Unaware of the dark turn in British negotiations, General Jackson nonetheless continued to move to the defense of New Orleans. He waited for no man—in Europe or in Washington—and under the cover of night, on November 7, 1814, he marched all but five hundred of his men into the woods on the outskirts of Pensacola. The town's Spanish defenders, believing the Americans were still in their original camp, kept their guns pointed toward the nearly empty tents, while their British allies repositioned their warships to bear on the westward approach to Pensacola.

At daylight, the token force Jackson left behind made a feint toward Pensacola from the west, while the much larger army, which Jackson had led around the town in darkness, attacked along the narrow beach from the northeast.

Taking both the Spanish and the British by surprise, the combined force of Choctaws, Jackson's infantrymen, and General Coffee's brigade quickly overwhelmed the first band of startled defenders. As the Americans entered the town, Spanish musket fire raked the attackers from gardens and houses along the center street, but the Royal Navy was no help. Unprepared, their supporting fire came too late.

The fight lasted only minutes, as the Spanish corps, numbering fewer than five hundred men, was no match for the attacking Americans. A U.S. Army lieutenant lowered the Spanish flag and Governor Manrique, looking old and ill, brandishing a white flag, appeared in the street looking for an American officer. General Jackson was summoned and rode into town with an escort of dragoons for the formal surrender.

The Spanish agreed to relinquish control of Fort Barrancas, and Jackson sent men off to take charge of it, but before they could get there, the retreating British lit a fuse that ignited three hundred barrels of powder stored in its magazine. The explosion left the fort unusable, and the enemy fleet was seen heading out to sea.

The British had relinquished the fort and, though Jackson had not won quite the victory he expected—he had come to capture Fort Barrancas, only to see it destroyed—Pensacola had been rendered defenseless. The British would not be able to use it as a base of attack, and Jackson needed to waste no men garrisoning the town or the blasted hulk that had been Fort Barrancas.

General Jackson had repulsed the British at Pensacola. His men had sent one British warship to the bottom of the sea at Fort Bowyer, and twice the Royal Navy flotilla had been forced to abandon good harbors on the Gulf Coast. The British had hoped to enlist the rebellious Creeks into their ranks, but Jackson had vanquished his Indian foes, too.

The preceding months had seen Andrew Jackson emerge as the best general in service to the American cause. President Madison knew it. So did James Monroe, who scurried around the ruins of Washington to find money for Jackson to pay his army's bills. Despite the nation's empty coffers, Monroe somehow came up with $100,000. And the secretary of war promised more troops would be sent to his winning general.

But Jackson could feel the pressure rising. His health was far from perfect, with his left shoulder still nearly useless and his gut a constant discomfort. He saw the line he had to walk, taking care not to overcommit his inexperienced force while aggressively challenging the British. He would have to balance rage and reason as he took on his new task: by disrupting the larger British strategy—enemy ground troops wouldn't be landing any time soon at either Pensacola or Mobile—he had put New Orleans directly into the line of fire.

Suspecting the increased danger to New Orleans, Jackson pushed his men hard, hurrying back whence they had come. A mere three and a half days later, on November 11, 1814, they were back in Mobile.

The general found a stack of letters waiting for him. Some had been mailed from Washington, where James Monroe sounded almost panicked. Word from his ministers in Ghent persuaded the secretary of state of the certainty of an imminent assault on New Orleans. The worried Monroe wrote to his Tennessee general he had "strong reason" to think that the British would soon attempt "to take possession of that city [on which] the whole of the states westward of the Allegany mountains so essentially depend."[16] Other letters had come from New Orleans, where Governor Claiborne feared an attack was imminent.

For more than three months, Jackson's secret informants—a merchant in Havana, a spy in Pensacola, well-connected Indian chiefs, and others—warned of British invasion plans. Now, however, the arrival of the flood of ever-more-anxious letters from Washington and New Orleans meant that reports of a British attack no longer seemed exaggerated.

On Tuesday, November 22, 1814, Andrew Jackson and his army began a new trek, this time to Louisiana to defend America's heartland from a looming enemy.

CHAPTER 7

Target: New Orleans

> I expect at this moment that most of the large seaport towns of America are . . . laid to ashes; that we are in possession of New Orleans, and have command of all the rivers of the Mississippi valley and the lakes, and that the Americans are now little better than prisoners in their own country.
>
> **—Lord Castlereagh, British foreign secretary**

The armada in Jamaica's Negril Bay was stunning to see. Along a four-mile stretch of pristine white beach, a forest of tall masts swayed in the gentle tropical breezes. No one on the west coast of Jamaica or anywhere else in the Caribbean had seen anything like it before. The fifty large vessels, each flying the Union Jack, amounted to the largest naval force ever assembled in the hemisphere.

On November 26, 1814, the hardened old Scotsman in command surveyed his flotilla, proud of its power. He watched with care as his captains carried out his orders to set sail. After months of planning, this was an exhilarating moment.

High on the poop deck of the eighty-gun HMS *Tonnant,*

fifty-six-year-old Vice Admiral Sir Alexander Forrester Inglis Cochrane, his hair turned white, looked older than his years. His courtly manner revealed his pedigree: he was a younger son of an earl. Though softened by age—round through his middle, jowls overhanging his high collar—Cochrane revealed a steelier side. As one of the admirals in his command remarked, Cochrane was "a rough, brutal, and overbearing officer."[1]

From his flagship, he looked upon five other ships of the line, each armed with seventy-four guns; his enemy, the U.S. Navy, had no ships that were their equal. There were eight three-masted frigates with thirty-eight or more cannons, along with smaller two-masted brigs and schooners with a single mast. Lower in the water sat the sloops of war and barges, along with uncounted transports and other smaller craft. As one observer remarked, the vessels were "so closely wedged together that to walk across the decks from one to the other seemed, when at a little distance, to be far from impracticable."[2]

Cochrane had risen in the ranks during the war with Napoleon. After commanding the HMS *Ajax* in Egypt, he served in Martinique, Santo Domingo, and then in Guadeloupe, where he won a knighthood and earned the assignment to take on the United States. Sir Alexander had bided his time since the Americans had declared war on Great Britain two years before, but his charge now was to bring home victory, a task he accepted with grim determination.

He had sworn to "give to Great Britain the command of . . . New Orleans." He had promised to hand the Americans "a complete drubbing before peace is made." He would deliver to the king complete "command of the Mississippi."[3] And now he had the force to do it: the more than ten thousand Royal Navy sailors and officers that manned the formidable show of sail around him constituted just half of the

British force Cochrane would soon send into battle. Belowdecks, an army of foot soldiers waited as British tars hoisted the sails of the fleet.

Since his arrival in Jamaica nine days earlier, Cochrane had watched a parade of vessels sail in from Ireland and France and, like the *Tonnant,* from the Chesapeake Bay. After dropping anchor in Negril Bay, the warships disgorged thousands of troops dressed in red and green and even tartan uniforms. There were detachments of engineers, artillerymen, and rocketeers. The ground troops under the command of Major General John Keane included two black regiments from the West Indies.

Only a few men among this amphibious force had been certain of their destination. But this day the word got around and reached the ear of Lieutenant George Gleig, of the Eighty-Fifth Light Infantry. Gleig, who would help write the story of Cochrane and the invading force, noted in his journal, "It was soon known throughout the fleet that the conquest of New Orleans was the object in view."[4]

So far in 1814, the Americans had done little to persuade Cochrane they were worthy opponents. He and his ships had delivered the army to Maryland that had so effortlessly overrun Washington. True, the siege at Baltimore in September had failed after a sharp-eyed sniper killed Robert Ross, Cochrane's commanding general, and Fort McHenry at the mouth of Baltimore Harbor proved more resilient than expected. But that only upped Cochrane's desire to vanquish the Americans once and for all.

Cochrane's interest in beating the Americans was personal. Many years before, he had fought in the American Revolution, but it had been an older brother, Charles, who died at the hands of the rebellious colonists. At the deciding battle of that war, in Yorktown, Virginia, in 1781, a cannonball parted Charles Cochrane's head from his body.

That painful loss, it was said, led to Sir Alexander's hatred of Americans. He had nothing but contempt for the "American character." He dismissed the former colonists as no better than dogs: "Like spaniels," he said, "they must be treated with great severity."[5]

Cochrane had another motive, too. Back in Scotland, Sir Alexander would inherit neither property nor title. That meant New Orleans, an immensely valuable prize, represented exactly the change in fortune he needed (among the crew, there was talk of the "beauty and booty" to be had in the Louisiana city). For hundreds of years, the law of the seas had permitted officers and crew to share in the spoils of war and, with exports at a standstill because of the war, New Orleans's warehouses were packed with sugar, tobacco, hemp, and, in particular, bales of cotton. The goods were worth a great deal of money, perhaps £4 million. As the commander, Cochrane's portion of the plunder would be the largest of all.

British confidence ran high. Among the many ships departing Negril Bay were cargo vessels for carrying off the spoils, together with civilian administrators and barristers, an admiralty judge, customs officials, and tax collectors. It was a battalion of bureaucrats, complete with wives and daughters, a British team ready to take control of the city they planned to capture. And Cochrane had promised his naval superiors at the Admiralty in London he would deliver a resounding triumph. It was inconceivable that these American upstarts could hold out against the most powerful military force in the world.

Though not all Cochrane's forces had arrived, the fleet would delay no longer. More British soldiers were expected any day, along with General Sir Edward Pakenham, who was to take command of the invading army. But the British force was about to be on its way to New Orleans without him.

There, Cochrane vowed to his men, he would have his Christmas dinner.

Arriving in New Orleans

What Admiral Cochrane could not know was that, a thousand miles north on the Gulf Coast, another man with a personal stake in the war was headed to New Orleans to stop him. Andrew Jackson, born in a log cabin, was very different indeed from the high and mighty Cochrane, whose family roots lay in a great castle in Scotland. Jackson wasn't looking to win fame or enhance his wealth but, like Cochrane, he had a personal grudge against the country that had killed his brother. And both men knew the stakes.

Jackson didn't know for sure that Cochrane's force was on its way from Jamaica, but he suspected the British navy would be coming—and soon. Accordingly, he had chosen an overland route from Mobile. He wished to gather intelligence on the way; as he wrote to Monroe, he wanted "to have a view of the points at which the enemy might effect a landing."[6]

Before leaving Pensacola, Jackson had written to Rachel, confiding how ill he felt. "There [were] eight days," he wrote to his wife of the preceding month, "that I never broke bread." He had consulted an army doctor, who administered an herbal concoction containing mercury. Jackson reported the purgative cleansed his system but—no surprise, given how thin he already was—it left him "very weak."[7]

Though Jackson was a man whose sense of duty seemed to empower him to press on no matter his physical condition, he could lower his guard with Rachel. When they first met a quarter century before, he had arrived seeking only a bed at the boardinghouse that Rachel's widowed mother ran. Instead, the long-orphaned Jackson found a family to replace the one he had lost. In particular, the strapping young man had been drawn to the handsome young woman who had recently escaped a violent first marriage. In each other the two found solace.

In two decades of marriage, he and Rachel had shared public embarrassment when the shadowy status of her divorce from her first husband became public. She had matured into a short and plump woman, he ever more gangly, wasted by his battle with dysentery and other intestinal problems. But Andrew and Rachel developed an intimate bond. Despite a shared dislike of being separated, over the preceding thirteen months they had spent no more than thirty days together. As the British approached, he realized he needed to be with her.

In a perfect world, he wrote to Rachel, he might travel home to the Hermitage and "return to your arms on the wings of love and affection, to spend with you the rest of my days in peaceful domestic retirement."[8] But knowing that he had to travel to New Orleans for the biggest battle of his life, he instead asked for her to travel to him. "It is my wish," he had written from Mobile, "that you join me at . . . New Orleans." He would arrange for her to travel by riverboat in early December. In the meantime, he traveled toward the city on horseback.

Jackson's plan had allowed twelve days for the trek. Against the odds, his army reached its destination in ten, covering some three hundred miles, slogging through forests and fields. Where they could, Jackson's army followed the Federal Road but often had to blaze its own trail. His soldiers cut down many trees to support the horses and wagons as they crossed flooded streambeds.

On nearing New Orleans Jackson and his officers had been ferried across Lake Pontchartrain, landing after dark on the last day of November. When the morning haze burned off the large lake, they headed south for the last half-dozen miles, paralleling the meandering waters of Bayou St. John.

According to witnesses who saw them, Jackson stood out as the oldest of the riders, "a tall, gaunt man, of very erect carriage, with a countenance full of stern decision and fearless energy, but furrowed with care and anxiety." His iron gray hair peeked out from beneath the leather cap he wore to keep off the morning chill. Tall dragoon boots, much in need of polish, protected his legs, but even the loose blue cloak that hung from his shoulders couldn't hide how emaciated the man was. His complexion looked "sallow and unhealthy," but "the fierce glare of his bright and hawk-like gray eye betrayed a soul and spirit which triumphed over all the infirmities of the body."[9]

One lady of the neighborhood who saw Jackson on the morning of December 1, 1814, as he rode along the Bayou St. John road, said he looked like "an ugly, old Kaintuck-flat-boatman."[10] She was a native of New Orleans, a Creole. She would not be the last Creole to look askance, at least at first, at the general charged with saving their city.

Meeting the General

As Jackson neared the city limits, carriages were sent to greet him, and the general and his aides gratefully accepted the offered ride. Seated in unaccustomed luxury, they looked with curiosity at the city they were to defend.

The cobbled streets of New Orleans were abuzz with expectation at meeting the man some already called the "Savior of New Orleans."

As Jackson's carriage arrived at 106 Rue Royale, the handsome house chosen for his headquarters, he was greeted by the men of the town decked out in ties, gloves, and hats for the occasion. Everyone expected the British, but first they would welcome this tall Tennessean.

Climbing down from his carriage, Jackson was greeted by Governor Claiborne and the city's mayor, an affable Creole named Nicholas Giroud. As gray skies gave way to rain, the assembled crowd listened to Claiborne and Giroud give speeches in preparation to handing off responsibility for the city's defense to General Jackson. But mostly those in attendance wanted to hear from this gaunt American. What would the rough soldier from upriver have to say to a city of French and English speakers, merchants and pirates, freemen and slaves, woodsmen and Indians, a city that wasn't even sure it wanted to be American?

Unfortunately for Jackson, he spoke no French at all, but he was saved by his old congressional colleague Edward Livingston, who spoke it fluently. From the second-floor gallery, Jackson spoke to the crowd and Livingston translated for his friends and neighbors. Jackson assured them of his determination, promising to "drive their enemies into the sea, or perish in the effort."[11]

Jackson's words were met with cheers, but Livingston knew New Orleans high society well enough to understand that his neighbors were still unsure what to make of this weathered general. A transplant from New York, Livingston understood what it took to win the approval of the Creole upper class. He had worked hard to be accepted, but it was only when he married Louise Davezac, a well-born young widow from French Santo Domingo, that he had felt secure. With Louise on his arm, his entrée to the French culture of New Orleans was assured and, from their home on Royal Street, the Livingstons had become central figures in the city's society.[12]

Livingston decided to invite New Orleans's finest and Jackson to dinner to help the general secure the confidence of the city's elite. His wife's reaction to the idea demonstrated just how badly the introduction was needed. When Livingston told Louise that he had invited the Tennessean to take a seat at her table of fashionable friends, she expressed some annoyance. The man's fame had preceded him, of course, but wasn't he supposed to be a "wild man of the woods—an Indian almost"?

Jackson may have been a man of the woods, but he could hold his own with the haughty. When he entered the Livingston drawing room that afternoon, the other guests saw a man "erect, composed, perfectly self-possessed, with martial bearing." In place of his worn and dirty traveling clothes he wore a full dress uniform, and "the soldier who stood before them [was] one whom nature had stamped a gentleman." When dinner was announced, he exhibited perfect manners, offering his hostess his arm and, during dinner, he proved agreeable company. Mr. Livingston—soon to be Jackson's aide-de-camp—and the general departed early. But one guest who remained, both surprised and favorably impressed, remarked, "Is this your backwoodsman? He is a prince!"[13]

In a matter of hours, Jackson had left a strong impression on the inhabitants. In the same span, Edward Livingston had demonstrated he could be invaluable to the general. Livingston possessed skills as an orator and a translator, as well as a deep knowledge of Creole society. He was also an attorney, and his opinions on martial law might soon be put to use. In recognition of the man's usefulness, Jackson made him a colonel. In the coming weeks, Livingston would function as Jackson's military secretary and confidant. His inside knowledge of the peculiar circumstances of New Orleans society would prove invaluable.

Surveying the Surroundings

A wise general imprints on his mind the local topography as he prepares to do battle. So Andrew Jackson began with the maps, even as he wondered whether the fight would commence in two days or twenty-two.

New Orleans was the nation's seventh-largest city. The dense streetscapes at its center were packed together in the Vieux Carré and a few surrounding suburbs that stretched along the Mississippi riverbank and atop curving ridges just inland.

The swampy land surrounding New Orleans looked nothing like the rugged rolling hills that encircled Jackson's Nashville. The city resembled an island amid a marsh, with little dry land in any direction. Jackson was in the midst of a vast wetland, with millions of acres of waterlogged swamps dominated by towering cypress trees. A breeding ground for mosquitoes, the swamplands provided a better habitat for water snakes and alligators than for man.

Thanks to trade from upriver, New Orleans had become a place where people got rich. To his surprise, however, Jackson found that the city's people knew little of their larger surroundings. "The numerous bayous and canals," he noted, "appear to be almost as little understood by the inhabitants as by the citizens of Tennessee."[14]

Clearly, this was a precarious place, one subject to fires and hurricanes and floods. But Jackson's job was to cut through all the paradoxes and mysteries to figure out how to keep it out of British hands. As one of the engineers on Jackson's staff, Major Howell Tatum, noted in his log, "The first days of the General's arrival at New Orleans [were] devoted to the acquisition of such information, upon various points, as were deemed necessary, in order to enable him to adopt the most efficacious plan for the defense of Louisiana."[15]

First, that meant identifying—and then obstructing—any and all routes the British might take to attack the city. To help with that process, Edward Livingston brought the architect Arsène Lacarrière Latour to Jackson's headquarters on Royal Street. Jackson was impressed, both with the man and with the maps of New Orleans and its vicinity. Because Latour displayed the kind of knowledge the general needed, Jackson promptly named him principal engineer of the U.S. Army's Seventh Military District.

From afar, Jackson's pet theory had been that the British would put their troops ashore well east of the city—namely, landing at Mobile—then march in a great arc north of their objective. When they reached the Mississippi River upstream from New Orleans, Jackson reasoned, they could commandeer boats and barges; then, carried by the current, they would attack from the river. That thinking had led Jackson to secure both Mobile and Pensacola.

Even now, after moving his army to New Orleans, Jackson understood the British might still return to Mobile Bay and overpower Fort Bowyer, making an overland attack route possible. In order to prevent that, Jackson had dispatched General Coffee; he and his Volunteer cavalry had parted with Jackson on the march from Mobile, going on to Baton Rouge. Coffee's job would be to halt any such assault from upstream or, on Jackson's orders, to come at double time to New

Orleans, when and if intelligence reports determined the British were approaching via another route.

That left half a dozen other distinct paths for a possible British invasion. Jackson had no way of knowing which the enemy would choose but, again, he would have to take steps to obstruct their progress, whatever the angle of approach.

Three of the possibilities involved rivers, the most obvious being

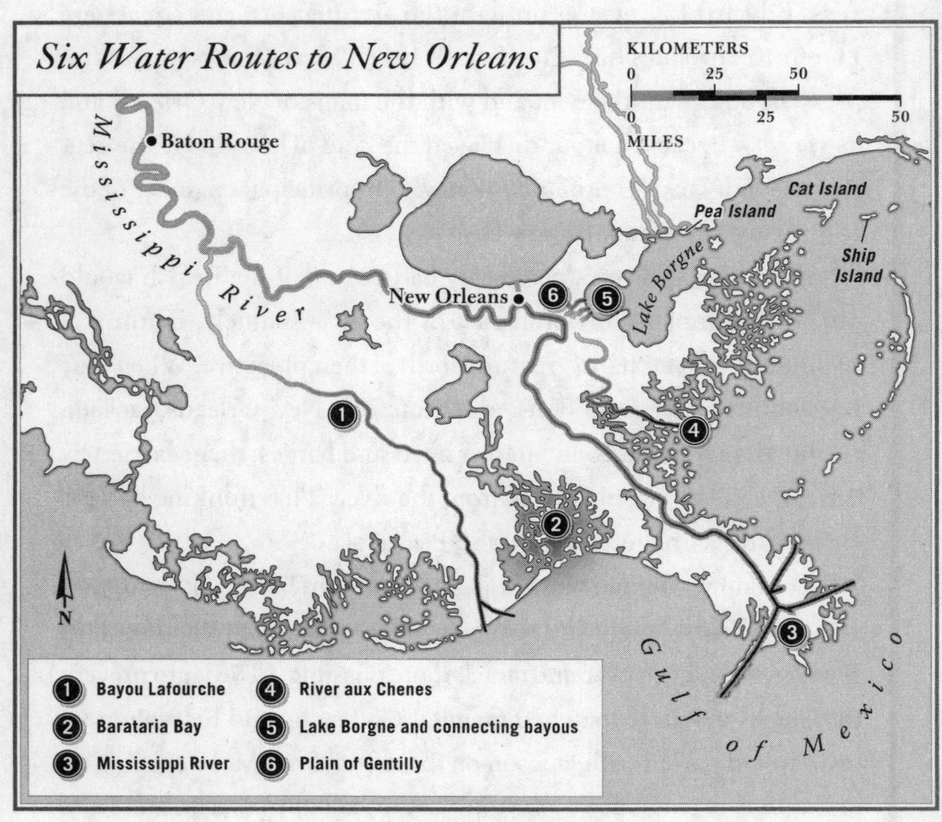

the Mississippi itself. That approach was guarded by fortifications well downstream; but those he needed to inspect personally. In a day or two, he'd go there.

Bayou Lafourche, which lay to the west, was another option for the British. A narrow but deep stream that veered south off the Mississippi between Baton Rouge and New Orleans, it emptied into the Gulf. If the British could sail up Bayou Lafourche and reach the parent river, they could then attack New Orleans from upstream. However, the breadth of the river and its ever-changing currents would make attacking from the opposite bank difficult. This seemed to Jackson and his advisers an unlikely—though still possible—British strategy.

To the east of the city was the River aux Chenes, which connected to Bayou Terre aux Boeufs. Both of these watercourses were sluggish but navigable for small boats. Again, Jackson was doubtful that the British attack would approach via these waters.

The other three angles of attack were via larger bodies of water.

Barataria Bay, south of the city, was linked to a maze of smaller waterways. Even though the pirates routinely used this network of streams to bring their goods to New Orleans, landing an army was another matter, especially without skilled pilots—and, it seemed, the Lafittes and the corsairs of Barataria had rejected the British offer. Again, the likelihood was low.

East of the city, Lake Borgne offered two plausible lines of attack: If the British could take possession of this large inlet, they might move on New Orleans via Bayou Chef Menteur, which led to a mile-wide strip of dry land called the Plain of Gentilly. Or they could carry the boats some five miles from the lake toward the Mississippi. On reaching the far side, however, the army could then march along the dry land that bordered the river through a series of plantations directly to the city. These two attack routes seemed to pose the greatest risk.

After absorbing the larger picture using the maps provided to him by Latour, Jackson and Governor Claiborne issued orders on December 2. Jackson sent guards to the least likely lines of attack, where they would watch and report if he had gambled wrong and the British were coming that way. Commanded by General Jacques Villere, detachments of the Louisiana militia marched out to the bayous and toward Barataria Bay armed not only with guns but also with axes. Their job was to clog the waterways with enough logs and other debris to slow the progress of boats carrying an oncoming army. Guards were then to be posted to speed the word if the enemy did approach. Jackson wasn't going to commit many soldiers to these low-probability lines of attack, but the sentries would become part of the intelligence network he needed to monitor enemy movements.

Because there was one route that might allow Royal Navy warships to get within firing range of the city, Jackson himself headed downriver the next day. As the engineer Latour reported, Jackson, "adhering to his constant practice of seeing everything himself," and his command, with Latour as their guide, went to inspect the fortifications on the banks of the Mississippi.[16]

Fort St. Philip was about sixty-five miles downstream; it was manned by regular troops and armed with two dozen cannons. This was enough to make it a formidable obstacle to a British onslaught, but Jackson knew that an attacking armada would have vastly greater firepower that would probably overcome the American defenders. He ordered the construction of new batteries before moving on to the next fort.

Closer to the city, he visited Fort St. Leon, which overlooked one of the Mississippi's many great bends. The abrupt curve was known as English Turn, having gained its name in 1699, when the future founder of New Orleans, the sieur de Bienville, persuaded a band of English explorers to turn back because, he said, France had already claimed the territory. Jackson hoped to convince the British to turn back there, too, and planned to take advantage of the difficulties the British navy would have navigating the arching bend. Sailing ships needed a change of wind in order to make the curve, which meant a naval force coming up the river might have to linger for hours exposed to Fort St. Leon's guns. To increase chances of holding the British there, Jackson again ordered the construction of added artillery batteries.

The scouting trip down the Mississippi left Jackson and his officers feeling confident. "It is almost impossible for an invading enemy to gain possession of New Orleans," noted his aide, the engineer Tatum, "by ascending the Mississippi. . . . At the *English Turn* . . . heavy cannon . . . would destroy every armed vessel that dared to attempt the ascent."[17]

After his six-day tour of the Mississippi, Jackson returned to New Orleans on December 9 and informed Claiborne that, given the added batteries, the river could be well defended.

But Jackson still needed to evaluate the last and perhaps the most likely approach for the British, via Lake Borgne. Repelling an attack there would be a challenge, but the general was ready and willing. He had already, almost single-handedly, lifted the morale of New Orleanians. As the engineer Latour reported, "The citizens were preparing for battle as cheerfully as if it had been a party of pleasure, each in his vernacular tongue singing songs of victory. The streets resounded with 'Yankee Doodle,' the 'Marseilles Hymn,' the 'Chat du Depart,' and other martial airs."[18] In a matter of less than a fortnight, Jackson had brought a new sense of unity to the city's factions, turning them into a patriotic force eager to fight off the British no matter which approach Cochrane and his invading army chose.

CHAPTER 8

Losing Lake Borgne

The courage and skill which was displayed in the defense of the gun vessels . . . against such an overwhelming force as they had to contend with, reflects additional splendor on our naval glory.

—Master Commander Daniel T. Patterson to the secretary of the navy

The weather was fair—the thermometer read a tropical eighty-four degrees—when Admiral Cochrane and his fleet left Jamaica. But, as Andrew Jackson took his tour of the Mississippi's fortifications, the British encountered a severe storm in the Gulf of Mexico. During the last few days of the passage swells rocked the warships violently enough that the soldiers on board stayed below. "So great was the motion," Lieutenant George Gleig noted, "that all walking was prevented."[1]

After the storm exhausted itself, on December 9, 1814, blue skies appeared and, with sight distances increased, the sailors spied the Chandeleurs, a string of barrier islands with few signs of habitation. Just thirty miles beyond lay the mouth of Lake Borgne. There, the

British intended to land the ground troops who would march through to New Orleans.

There was a distinct chill in the air as the fleet's flagship, the HMS *Tonnant,* along with the other tall ships, dropped anchor in the deep water off the Chandeleurs. Smaller warships sailed deeper into the sound, reefing their sails as they found anchorage between Cat and Ship Islands.

When one of the smaller ships, the HMS *Sophie,* approached the

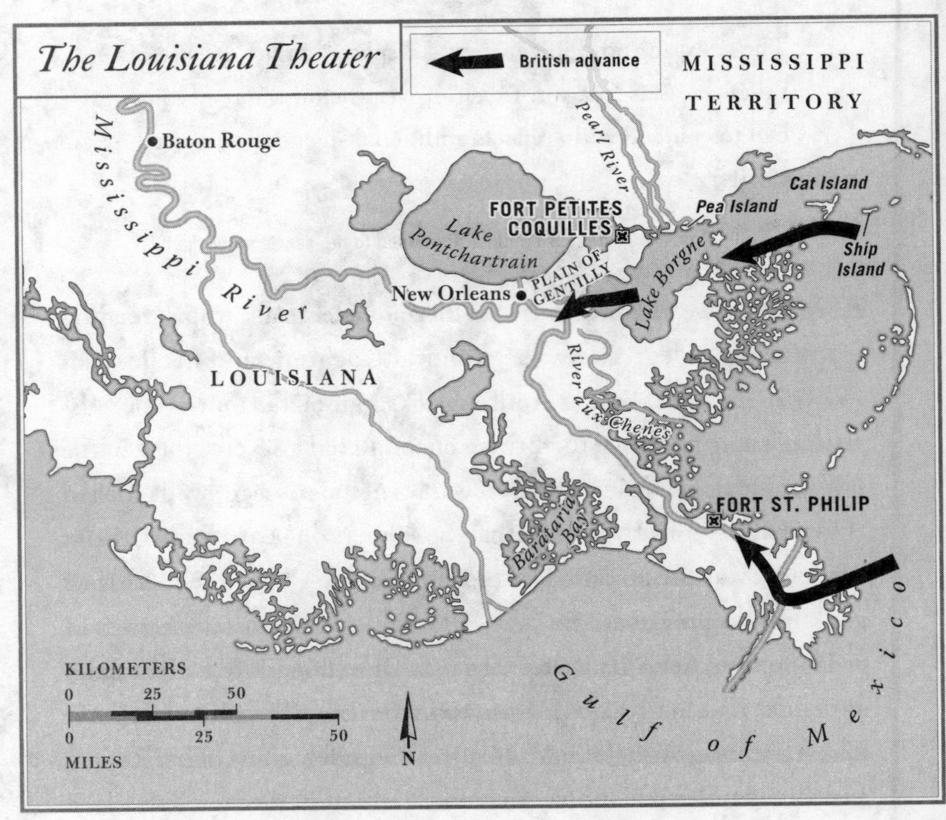

nearby coast, it came upon two small American gunboats, which sailed quickly away, presumably to warn their army of the coming attack. The captain of the *Sophie,* Nicholas Lockyer, may have wished to follow, but the coastal waters were tricky. A sandbar lay dead ahead, guarding the mouth of Lake Borgne, and the lake's shoals were known to pose a danger to all boats with more than the shallowest draft. The Americans, knowing the waters, escaped unscathed as the British watched, unable to stop them from ruining Cochrane's surprise. Within a day or two, Andrew Jackson would know that his fears were confirmed and that a huge British invasion force was heading toward Lake Borgne.

Patterson and Jones, USN

Lacking experience with warships, Andrew Jackson had no choice but to rely on the men of the U.S. Navy. But he didn't know quite what to think of Daniel Todd Patterson.

Although Patterson was just twenty-eight, his career in the navy had already spanned more than fifteen years. He had served two years in the West Indies before shipping out as a midshipman aboard the USS *Philadelphia* during the war with the Barbary pirates. In the Mediterranean, after the big frigate's grounding in the harbor at Tripoli, he had been a prisoner for eighteen months. Yet even that experience had added to his store of naval knowledge, because the *Philadelphia*'s captain had used the time wisely, running an informal academy to tutor his young officers while in captivity.

Patterson had served on the Mississippi River, rising to the rank of lieutenant while commanding a dozen gunboats operating at

Natchez in the Mississippi Territory. Having been elevated to the rank of master commander in 1813, he now ran the New Orleans station. Married to a daughter of New Orleans and with a growing family, Patterson called the city home.

A stout, compact man, Patterson carried himself with confidence, but that very boldness gave Andrew Jackson pause. Writing from Mobile on his arrival there in August, the general had summoned Patterson to help defend Mobile Point—only to have Patterson flat out refuse to come. In the most respectful terms (he wrote that it was his "most ardent wish" to cooperate with the U.S. Army), Patterson had told Jackson that he thought coming to Mobile was a fool's errand. In his judgment, if he went to Jackson's aid, the more powerful Royal Navy would inevitably blockade his vessels in Mobile Bay, rendering his gunboats useless for the more important job of protecting New Orleans.

Whatever the merits of Patterson's argument, this smacked of insubordination even if, strictly speaking, the chain of command called for Patterson to report to the secretary of the navy rather than to Jackson.

On the general's arrival in New Orleans, the two men had been thrown into a collaboration. Patterson, as the city's naval commander, had joined Jackson and his engineers on their reconnaissance trip down the Mississippi. He proved useful, his counsel valuable in improving the fortifications along the river. Jackson began to appreciate that, after almost five years in New Orleans, Patterson knew the city and, in particular, the big river, the many lakes, and the seascapes that surrounded it.

Furthermore, Jackson had to admit, Patterson was no yes-man; he was willing to stand up to his superiors. Having himself seen the need from time to time to disobey orders, Jackson had a grudging respect for the fact that Master Commander Patterson was clearly his own man.

Patterson had also thought long and hard about protecting New Orleans. Some of his thinking appeared suddenly prescient, because he had been pleading with the secretary of the navy for twelve months to send him more men, matériel, and warships. New Orleans was in danger: "The great depot of the western country," he warned, was "left open to the enemy."[2] Jackson recognized that he and Patterson had shared the same fears for many months.

Back at headquarters on 106 Royal Street, the two men considered how to protect the city from a northeastern attack via the lakes. Having never seen a gunboat, Jackson looked to Patterson; as a former gunboat commander, Patterson knew the vessels intimately. They were small by the standards of naval ships, typically fifty to sixty feet in length and eighteen feet wide, with a shallow draft and rigged with mast and sails. Armed with a large-bore cannon each and several smaller guns, the little vessels were notoriously top-heavy, making them unstable in heavy seas. Still, Patterson advised, they were well adapted to the shallow waters of the Gulf Coast.

Five U.S. Navy gunboats already actively patrolled the waters near the mouth of Lake Borgne. The gunboats were served by a schooner, the *Sea Horse,* to carry dispatches, and the *Alligator,* a converted fishing boat used for transporting men and supplies from shore to ship. Armed with a total of twenty-three guns, the little flotilla was manned by 182 officers and seamen.

Its commander was Lieutenant Thomas ap Catesby Jones. He and his sailors were to be General Jackson's eyes and ears, watching and reporting to Patterson frequently concerning the enemy's movements. If challenged by the British, Jones was under instructions to retire to the Rigolets, the narrow strait that was the passage from Lake Borgne to Lake Pontchartrain. There he was to "wait for the enemy, and sink him or be sunk."[3]

Jackson agreed that Patterson's plan seemed sound. The mouth of the big lake offered defensive advantages, and the two men believed that Jones and his well-armed boats could hold off any small craft Admiral Cochrane might send his way. Patterson also assured Jackson that no deep-draft warship could possibly sail into Lake Borgne.

Jackson wrote to James Monroe. "The gun boats on the lakes," he told the secretary of war confidently, on December 10, "will prevent the British from approaching in that quarter."[4]

Neither man knew that Lieutenant Jones and his men, on that very morning, awakened to the sight of a flotilla of enemy vessels at anchor and, with the chiming of every hour, even more ships were sailing into view. All Jones could do was watch and wait from a safe distance.

Gunning for the Gunboats

As the fog lifted on the morning of December 10, British sailors and officers alike looked curiously at the tall grasses that lined an unfamiliar shoreline. As one artilleryman noted, the landscape resembled "trembling prairies," with no beaches in sight, and only matted reeds and soggy ground where the water and land merged.[5] One thing was obvious: moving troops and hauling big guns on this terrain would not be easy.

But Admiral Cochrane had a strategy.

Though the new army commander, General Pakenham, would arrive any day from England—replacing the previous expedition leader, Robert Ross, who had been killed in September in the Battle of Baltimore—Cochrane couldn't wait for Pakenham to arrive to begin getting the troops off the ships and into fighting position. He favored ferrying the troops across Lake Borgne to a landing site. On the advice of two former Spanish residents of New Orleans, Cochrane thought the beachhead on the far side might be Bayou Bienvenue, a waterway said to be navigable by good-size barges.[6] From there a short march of a few miles would take the invading army to the outskirts of New Orleans.

Before any of this could happen, however, Lake Borgne would have to be cleared of enemy ships. Though there were only five small American gunboats in the lake, their cannons were a grave danger to the open boats the British would use to ferry soldiers ashore. Cochrane would not expose his men to that kind of danger and gave an order: "[No] movement of the troops could take place till this formidable flotilla was either captured or destroyed."[7]

From his anchorage outside the waters of Lake Borgne, Cochrane gave the reliable Nicholas Lockyer, captain of the *Sophie,* command of the venture to exterminate the gunboats. Having visited the pirate Lafitte in Barataria Bay, patrolled the Gulf, and commanded the attack on Lake Bowyer, he was the Briton most experienced in the ways and waters of the Gulf Coast.

On the night of Monday, December 12, a mix of seamen in blue coats and marines in red jackets boarded forty-two barges. Three unarmed ship's boats accompanied the barges and, taken together, the vessels carried 1,200 men.

Lockyer's assignment: *Dispose of the gunboats.* Capture them, if possible, Cochrane ordered; the shallow-draft boats might well be useful in the operation to come. But, most of all, the admiral wanted them out of the path of his amphibious assault.

On Guard

Aboard one of the American gunboats in Lake Borgne, Lieutenant Thomas ap Catesby Jones watched and waited for the British attack. For the past three days, the twenty-four-year-old commander had played a cautious game of cat and mouse with the enemy. He had ventured near to the channel near Ship Island where many of the Royal Navy ships rocked with the tides, close enough to confirm how many ships were there, and had then retreated, dispatching one of his boats with a report to Patterson. As the number of British ships increased, Jones had decided it was "no longer safe or prudent for me to continue on that part of the lakes."[8] He retreated to the mouth of Lake Borgne just north of Malheureux Island.

From there, on December 13, he spotted the British barges at 10:00 a.m. As he watched the flotilla proceed westward, he knew that the assault on New Orleans had begun. Cochrane would be taking the route Jackson had thought most likely, crossing the lakes to land his men and march on the city.

Seeing how much larger the British force was than his own, Jones quickly took action. Reasoning that the British were likely to reach vital supplies waiting on the nearby shore, he dispatched the schooner *Sea Horse* to blow up the goods, wanting to prevent them from falling into enemy hands. There was little else he could do; though he might be able to inflict some damage on the barges, his little fleet of gunboats was much too small to stop the enemy completely.

Lieutenant Jones watched as the British convoy made steady though laborious progress across the lake. The front of the imposing flotilla was half a mile wide and moved relentlessly westward despite strong headwinds. As noon came and went, Jones waited for the enemy force to make a move south toward shore—and to New Orleans—to unload the troops. But the flotilla did not change course.

At last, as the hour struck two, a terrible intuition struck Lieutenant Jones: *The British intended to attack his gunboats.* They weren't yet looking to land an army. He and his men were their objective. Jones's reaction was immediate. If the British wanted to destroy his little fleet—and they clearly had the manpower to do it—the time had come to retreat deeper into Lake Borgne. Per Patterson's orders, Jones prepared to sail his badly outnumbered force to the narrow strait, the Rigolets, where he might make a stand. If that failed, he could retreat into Lake Pontchartrain.

Ordered to weigh anchor and set sail, his men soon discovered that days of sustained winds and low tide had made the marshy waters off Malheureux Island uncommonly shallow: three of the gunboats ran aground on the sandy bottom. In a frantic effort to lighten the craft, Jones's men threw all dispensable heavy items overboard, but the boats still refused to budge. They sat helplessly, watching the British approach, until 3:30 when, finally, the rising tide floated the boats free.

Just a few minutes later, Jones noticed that, while most of the British boats were still heading for him and his recently freed flotilla, three of the British barges were veering northward toward shore. Their unmistakable target was the schooner *Sea Horse,* still visible on its mission to keep the supplies on land from falling into British hands. With darkness falling, the *Sea Horse* attempted to fight off its attackers, firing a deadly discharge of grapeshot at the British boats. The rain of iron balls brought the British attack to a temporary halt and gave the *Sea Horse* time to make for the shore, but the reprieve was short-lived. As Jones watched, four more launches broke from the flotilla's ranks to join the attack on the *Sea Horse*.

By the time the combined British force of seven boats closed in on the schooner, the *Sea Horse* was moored at the shoreline, and some of its crewmen were on dry land, readying their cannons, two six-pounders, to fire on their attackers. The sun was setting, and from a distance Jones could only watch and wonder in the growing darkness as gunfire echoed across the lake. Would the outnumbered Americans be able to hold out?

Jones didn't have long to wonder. Within half an hour, the British discovered that the single American ship put up a better fight than they'd expected. Despite their advantage in numbers, the British lost one boat and sustained many casualties before pulling back.

But the British retreat was no victory for Jones's men. Although the Americans on the *Sea Horse* had fought off this first attack, they remained trapped—and they understood they would not be able to hold off a second assault. Unwilling to let the ship fall into enemy hands, they made a painful decision. At 7:30 p.m., a tremendous explosion rent the air, sending flames high into the sky. The Americans had blown up the *Sea Horse* and the supplies. Neither would be of any use to the British.

As the *Sea Horse* burned, Jones and the men aboard the five gunboats continued north, attempting to avoid a fight with the many barges. For a few hours, they made progress but, as midnight approached, the wind failed them. They were well short of the shallow passage north of Malheureux Island that would lead them to safety when it became clear their sails would carry them no farther. But the British boats, powered by oarsmen, would be unaffected by the stillness. Though the enemy had stopped for the night nearly ten miles back, they would easily catch Jones and his men when they resumed their pursuit at daybreak. At one o'clock in the morning, Jones decided he and his becalmed force had only one option: they must turn and fight.

Summoning the commanders of the five gunboats, he laid out the plan. They would form a line across the mile-wide strip of shallow water where they were becalmed, anchoring the boats at the stern. The tide retreating from Lake Borgne would keep their bows—and thus their cannons—pointing at the oncoming British. His intent, Jones explained, was to put them "in the most advantageous position, to give the enemy as warm a reception as possible."[9]

Laboriously moving their craft into place, the gunboat commanders did as ordered before dropping anchor and attempting to get some much-needed rest. In the morning, they would face the fight of their lives.

Morning, December 14

The day started early. British sailors had begun rowing at 4:00 a.m. With the first light of day, Captain Nicholas Lockyer spied the American flotilla. Less than ten miles ahead, the gunboats, five abreast, were obviously looking to hold the line against the British onslaught.

Lockyer's orders were to capture or destroy any American ship he saw, whatever the cost. The previous evening the *Sea Horse,* trapped and alone, had been the first victim. Now Lockyer spotted a second quarry. The *Alligator,* sailing back toward the gunboats after delivering Jones's letters for Commodore Patterson, attempted to make a run past the British barges despite the light winds. Lockyer ordered the small boat's capture, and his barges moved on the *Alligator* too quickly for her to escape. Though the Americans attempted to ward off the British with their cannons, the shot splashed harmlessly into the lake. Recognizing they would soon be overpowered by a force that numbered in the hundreds, the eight-man crew of the American vessel surrendered. Lockyer could now note in his log that the *Alligator* no longer flew the Stars and Stripes but henceforth would sail with Cochrane's convoy.

With the *Alligator* captured, Lockyer's barges resumed their progress toward Jones's gunboats, now anchored in place. The outgoing tide meant that Lockyer's tired oarsmen worked against the current. But the veteran captain knew the ripples coming his way meant something

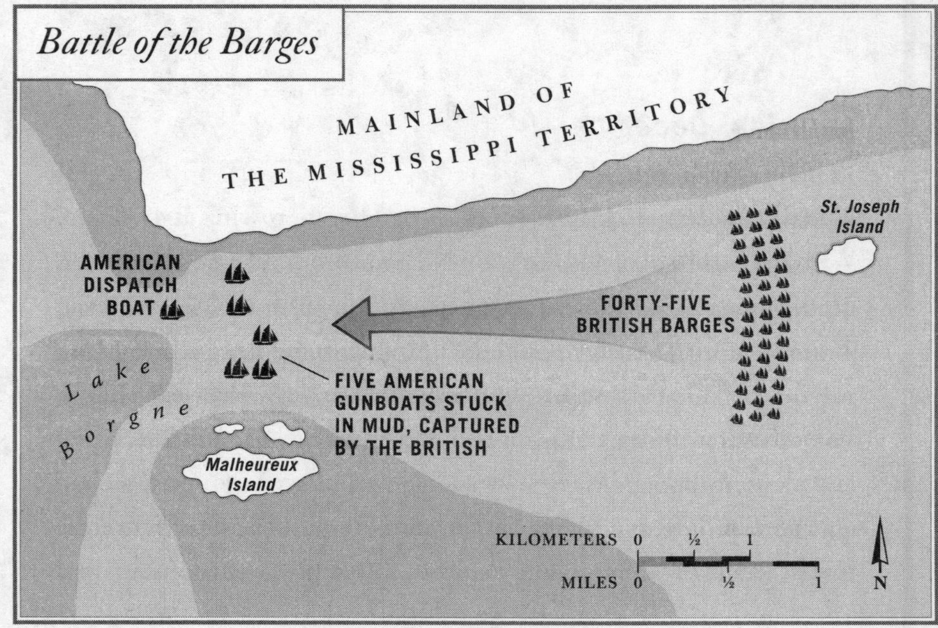

else, too. His opponent would not be retreating this morning. With the push of the tide and no wind to fill his sails, Jones had no choice but to wait and fight.

The more than forty British boats continued to close in on the Americans. As they neared the five gunboats, they saw unmistakable signs of the American determination to fight: Jones's men had hung their boarding nets on the sides of the vessels. These webs of thick rope, like coarse spiderwebs, would hamper British marines seeking to board once the close fighting began.

Now nearly within striking distance, Lockyer ordered a pause just outside the range of American guns. It was 10:00 a.m., and his men had been rowing for six hours. As the Americans watched and waited anxiously, the British commander gave his men thirty minutes to breakfast and rest. Confident of victory, the British were in no rush, and they would defeat their unhappy prey much more easily if they were refreshed.

The Fight

The American boats waited in an uneven row, despite the best efforts of Jones's men. In the night strong currents from Lake Borgne had carried two gunboats a hundred yards forward of the planned line of defense. One of them, at the center, was Jones's, and his position meant he would be the first target of the cannons in the prows of the British barges.

When the British had finished their meal and began their progress toward Jones's men, the U.S. Navy guns sounded first. The Americans' long-barreled cannons possessed greater range than the shorter

British guns, but at a distance of more than a mile, the barges made small targets. Undamaged and undeterred, the British flotilla drew closer with every stroke of the oars.

Soon, with the American boats within the range of his guns, Lockyer issued the order for his gunners to fire. With an ear-shattering roar, the British carronades boomed as one. Jones's men returned fire and, as the British boats grew nearer and nearer, the British marines aimed their muskets at the little flotilla.

The maneuverable British boats held an advantage over Jones's gunboats, which remained fixed at anchor. Three British barges led by Lockyer's closed rapidly on Jones's boat, their first target. This would be a battle of commanders.

Jones's gunners landed shot in two of the attacking barges, and with water rising through holes in their hulls, the British boats began to sink. But the undamaged third barge soon pulled alongside Jones's boat, and Royal Marines attempted to board the American ship. Fighting with pistols and swords, the U.S. Navy crew of forty-one men repulsed the attack, wounding or killing most of the British officers. Lockyer himself sustained a wound, but he continued to rally his men as four more barges from his column joined the fight.

The Americans fought valiantly, but just as it appeared they might again repulse a wave of attackers, a musket ball smashed into Lieutenant Jones's left shoulder, and he fell to the deck. As his men carried their commander below, he ordered, "Keep up the fight! Keep up the fight!"[10] His second in command took charge of the defense, but the attackers had shot away the gunboat's defensive netting and British marines soon managed to clamber over the gunwales of the American ship. After a few minutes of bloody hand-to-hand action, the British gained possession of the gunboat's deck.

Lockyer himself sustained another wound in the fight, but, lying on the deck, he ordered the cannons aboard Jones's gunboat turned on the other American craft. Because Jones's boat had drifted well in front of the others, they were easily within its line of fire. Jones's vessel sent shot cascading at the other U.S. Navy ships even before its flag came down.

The end of the battle neared. According to Jones's report, "The action continued with unabating severity until 40 minutes past 12 o'clock, when it terminated."[11] By then, all the gunboats belonged to the British.

In a fight that lasted just less than two hours, the British prevailed. But the Americans had fought hard, despite being outnumbered almost seven to one. The British casualties numbered at least 17 killed, 77 wounded. On the American side, 10 men died and 35 were reported wounded.

British surgeons set about treating the injured, including Captain Lockyer and the American commander, Lieutenant Jones, now held captive by the British. Neither officer would see further action in the battle for New Orleans. But Captain Lockyer had handed his admiral the signal advantage of clear sailing on the lakes.

Despite his losses—his men, his gunboats, he himself a prisoner—the American lieutenant had, in turn, done Andrew Jackson a significant service: the brave action of Jones and his men bought the general vital time. The first British warship had been sighted off the Gulf Coast almost a week earlier; at the moment of their victory at Lake Borgne, not so much as a platoon of the British army had stepped ashore. True, the handful of American gunboats had been captured (Jones's was promptly renamed the HMS *Destruction*). But Jones and many of his men, despite being held prisoner, continued to serve their country, telling their interrogators tall tales about the size of Jackson's army. Now Admiral Cochrane might have unfettered access to land his army for the march to New Orleans, but he did not know with any accuracy what the troops aboard his ships were about to march into.

CHAPTER 9

The Armies Assemble

> Our lakes are open to the approach of the enemy, and I am with my feeble force prepared to meet him and die in the last ditch before he shall reach the city.
>
> **—Andrew Jackson, December 16, 1814**

When, hours later, the news of Lieutenant Jones's defeat reached New Orleans, its citizens were terrified. But General Jackson was not in the city to hear the news. A full day would pass before Jackson learned that the American defense on the lakes had been shredded like the sails on the U.S. Navy gunboats.

While Jones was being taken captive, Jackson had been north of town, scouting the terrain, believing the lake waters were well protected. If the British did attack from the north—and even without knowing about Jones's loss, the location of Cochrane's armada in Mississippi Sound suggested to Jackson that they would come from that quarter—then the general must have a clear picture in his mind of the lay of the land.

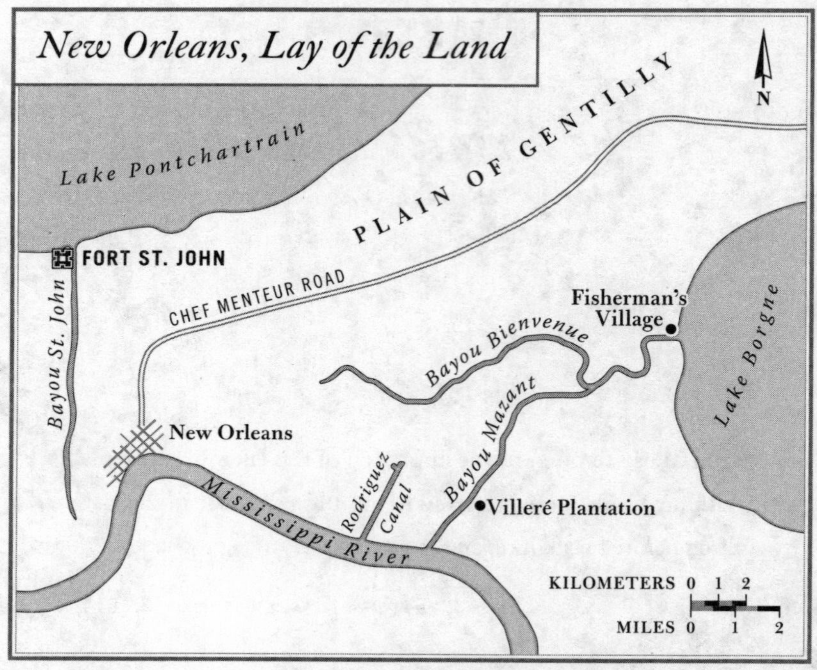

Despite a recurrence of his dysentery, which made riding a horse intensely painful, Jackson ventured to the head of Lake Borgne. There he inspected the end of the large lake opposite from where Jones confronted Lockyer. Next Jackson went west to look at the expanse of Lake Pontchartrain, then traveled along the Chef Menteur Road, which seemed to him the best and most likely route for a British attack on the city. He issued many orders. Streams he saw were to be blocked, defenses enhanced, guards stationed, and a chain of sentinels organized to bring him word of any British appearance.

Then, on December 15, he received the bad news of Jones's defeat. Having assured now secretary of war James Monroe just days before that the lakes were still secure, he learned that, quite to the contrary, they were not. Jones's flotilla now belonged to the British and the American lieutenant was their prisoner.

Jackson galloped back to his headquarters in New Orleans, knowing that, almost overnight, he had to pull together his army to protect the city. His journey had taken a toll on his worn body and, too ill to stand, he lay upon a sofa, dictating orders to his aides and reinforcing himself with sips of brandy.

With barely a thousand regular troops in his command, he wrote to General Coffee, the man he called his "right arm."[1] His order sounded like a plea: "You must not sleep until you reach me, or arrive within striking distance."[2] He sent a letter to Natchez, where he hoped it would reach William Carroll, another Tennessee militia general. Carroll was on his way downriver with some 1,400 men with arms and ammunition.

Jackson also anticipated the arrival of General John Thomas's Kentucky militia, an estimated 2,500 troops. And he worried about a shipment of guns and munitions, en route from Pittsburgh since November 3.[3] Would it arrive on time?

Even as General Jackson fretted, he received some spiritual assurance. From their convent overlooking Ursuline and Chartres Streets, four nuns wrote him a letter. They wanted to do their bit, volunteering to take in wounded men. Since word of the British arrival in the region had reached them, they had already taken the precaution of sending the boarding students and orphans in their care out of New Orleans and had plenty of space.[4] But most of all, they offered their prayer for Jackson and his men and for the safety of the city they had come to love.

The people of New Orleans needed prayers desperately—and not just prayers for ammunition and troops to stand up to the fighting force that had defeated Napoleon. Most immediately, it looked like it might take a miracle to pull the city's factions together. The townsfolk had been comforted by Jackson's return, but one of his attempts to unite the city's population against the British almost destroyed the fragile unity he had achieved in his weeks in New Orleans. Against the advice of some Louisianans, Jackson accepted into his army two battalions of freemen of color. Though he required that officers of the two corps be white men, he also ordered that black soldiers be treated the same way as white volunteers, a shocking attitude in a society that doubted the humanity and trustworthiness of nonwhites. When one paymaster objected, Jackson made his position clear. He needed every man he could get and was determined not to worry about the prejudices of the white men: "Be pleased to keep to yourself your opinions . . . without inquiring whether the troops are white, black or tea."[5]

The people of New Orleans, no matter their skin color, whether French or American, male or female, young or old, devout or not, would have to rally behind General Andrew Jackson if the city was to fight off its attackers. Outnumbered and outgunned, they were unlikely to defeat the British even if they did unite. Divided, they had no chance.

The Grand Parade

Jackson turned his attention to calming a panicked populace and persuading everyone to pull together.

New Orleans was a city that loved a parade, and Jackson decided there was no better way to cheer and inspire the anxious townspeople. He announced there would be a procession into the city's central downtown square, the Place d'Armes, on Sunday, December 18.

On the day of the parade, the people of New Orleans crowded together in the doors and windows lining the square. Even more townspeople lined the balconies and roofs, and the surrounding streets were packed with sailors and laborers and freemen.

With the towering old Spanish Cathedral of St. Louis as the backdrop, and accompanied by the roll of drums and the cheers of the crowd, two regiments of Louisiana state militia marched in, most dressed in civilian clothes. Not all carried guns, and those who did brought what they had, shouldering a mix of rifles, muskets, and fowling pieces. The militia was followed by uniformed companies resplendent in full parade dress. Major Jean Baptiste Plauché, a cotton broker who had volunteered when he felt the call of duty, led one battalion of 287 men, which consisted of two generations of local businessmen, planters, and lawyers. Stirred to patriotic fervor, women of the town waved scarves and handkerchiefs as their husbands and sons marched by.

But would they cheer for the next wave of marchers? As martial music was played, the troops of Frenchmen were followed by a well-drilled battalion of 210 freemen, most of them Haitians, commanded by a bakery owner, Major Jean Daquin. Choctaws marched, too, commanded by Pierre Jugeat, a trader who had married into the tribe. Here was a test of the unity that Jackson hoped the parade would create. The townspeople had celebrated their own; now would they celebrate these protectors who didn't look like them and whom they sometimes regarded with suspicion?

It's possible there was a break in the cheering, but if there was, it was not long enough to record. Whatever the motive—fear of the

British, a change of heart, or the frenzy of the moment—the people of New Orleans together honored even these troops that they had so recently questioned.

Proudly following the Haitians and Choctaws were representatives of the city's high society. Thomas Beale, a gentleman from Virginia, had just days before persuaded several dozen of his friends—a range of merchants and New Orleans professionals—to don blue hunting shirts and wide-brimmed black hats and to shoulder their long Kentucky rifles.[6] These sharpshooters called themselves Beale's Rifles and many of them wore miniature bouquets of flowers pinned to their shoulders, good luck tokens from wives and mothers.

The force that filled the square, some 1,500 men, seemed suddenly formidable and impressive. Together with the militiamen en route, the number of troops defending New Orleans had doubled in the sixteen days since Jackson arrived. This army had come together in a matter of weeks. Even more remarkably, the patchwork force of the high- and low-born seemed prepared to work together to save their city, perhaps in answer to the nuns' prayers, perhaps because of Jackson's leadership genius.

Although the total number of soldiers was not large, Jackson made a point of giving each group representation on his staff. In addition to Livingston and Claiborne, a mix of merchants, French nationals, and other locals held freshly issued officer ranks. Now, because of Jackson's careful delegation and savvy reading of the city's mood, a once-divided New Orleans was caught up in the fervor of the moment, and morale soared as they saw the clear proof that they would not go unprotected. The parade had been a stroke of genius, galvanizing the fighting force of freed slaves, Indians, pirates, woodsmen, militiamen, and French colonials.

But the general wasn't there only to display the growing power of his army. He wished to deliver a message himself. Riding his favorite horse, Duke, Jackson cut an imposing figure as he rode to the center of the square. Again, he entrusted Edward Livingston to deliver his message in French and, as the cheers quieted, Livingston began his translation.

First, he complimented the people of New Orleans on their bravery even as he exhorted them to further heroism: "The American nation shall applaud your valour, as your general now praises your ardour." Jackson's promise, he told them, was of victory: "Continue with the energy you have began, and he promises you not only safety, but victory."[7] Then he addressed the various factions, with specific words for the militia, for the Creoles, and for the blacks.

But Jackson's action to unify the city went one step further. He left his appreciative audience reassured and inspired—but he had also, just the day before, issued a declaration of martial law. Henceforth, anyone entering the city would have to report to the office of the general; those wishing to leave needed written permission from Jackson or a member of his staff. The streets would go dark at 9:00 p.m. Every able-bodied man was expected to fight, while the old or infirm would police the streets. The legality of the declaration wasn't clear, but Jackson would stop at nothing to beat back the British.

The declaration of martial law also meant that men, whatever their color or nationality, could be conscripted forthwith to become sailors—and Commodore Patterson chose to put this new authority to immediate use. With the loss of the flotilla on Lake Borgne, Patterson's force had shrunk to one warship on the Mississippi, the schooner USS *Carolina,* and a converted merchantman, the USS *Louisiana.* Reportedly a speedy ship before she was armed with sixteen guns, the

Louisiana had no crew, but now, under Jackson's authority, Patterson and his officers could draft the sturdiest sailors they could find to man the ninety-nine-foot sloop. In a matter of hours, the new tars of the *Louisiana* were drilling on its decks.

Jackson's words in the Place d'Armes calmed the city; panic had ebbed as the citizens witnessed his preparations and leadership, and little grumbling was heard. Applause had rippled across the crowd as Livingston brought the speech to a close, and when the troops in the Place d'Armes were dismissed, they melted into the crowd of well-wishers. Everyone knew this might be his last chance to visit with family before the call to fight.

The urgency of their need to defend family and friends was one of the few advantages the Americans had. Jackson and his men might be less experienced than the British, but they had the added motivation of fighting for their homes and their loved ones. If they lost, they had nowhere to go, unlike Gleig and his men, who could return to their families in England.

The stakes of the battle weighing on him, Jackson, ailing and anxious, returned to his quarters more determined than ever to hold off the British. Little did he know that the invaders were already well on their way.

Men on the Move

On the morning before Jackson's parade, the British had begun their advance. Because deep-draft warships could not penetrate Lake Borgne, the British embarked once again in barges. Stroke by wearying stroke, oarsmen propelled the first loads of British soldiers westward from the navy's anchorage in Mississippi Sound into the lake.

The danger of the American gunboats had been eliminated, but the trip across the lake was still not an easy one for the British. The men sat so tightly packed that shifting position was almost impossible, and storms that blew across the lake soon made the ten-hour, thirty-mile journey truly miserable. As the infantry officer Lieutenant Gleig noted, he and his men were pummeled by "heavy rains, such as an inhabitant of England cannot dream of, and against which no cloak will furnish protection."[8] The open boats posed a particular hardship to African-Caribbeans, dressed in light clothing and unused to chilly temperatures, and many of them died later after becoming ill in the cold.[9]

Many hours into the journey across the lake, the invaders' first destination came into view. Known to the Creoles as Isle aux Pois, but called Pea Island by the British, this swampy mound of land, little more than a sandbar, would serve as a staging point in the attack. The soldiers disembarked and then the empty boats reversed course back to the fleet. At least three round-trips would be needed to move the full invading force to Pea Island, meaning the sailors would have to row the thirty-mile distance five times before returning to the ships once again for stores and artillery.

Even then, however, the job of ferrying Cochrane's force was only half complete: Pea Island with its wild ducks and alligators sat at the northern end of Lake Borgne, halfway to the beachhead from which the troops could march on the city. Another hard row of some thirty miles was necessary before the march to New Orleans could commence.

Pea Island offered neither buildings nor trees for shelter. The soldiers, stiff and wet from the crossing, carried no tents and suffered as bad weather continued. After the rain slowed to a stop, the conditions improved little. The temperature dropped rapidly at night and, with a sharp wind off the water, the soldiers' uniforms stiffened with frost. The dinner fare wasn't very appetizing, consisting of "salt meat and ship biscuit . . . moistened by a small allowance of rum . . . not such as to reconcile us to the cold and wet under which we suffered," as one officer noted.[10] Even Admiral Cochrane and the commanding army general, John Keane, far from the comforts aboard the HMS *Tonnant,* had to adapt, their island quarters makeshift shelters of thatched grasses.

Five full days were required to move the first several thousand troops to Pea Island but morale remained high. "From the General, down to the youngest drum-boy, a confident anticipation of success seemed to pervade all ranks; and in the hope of an ample reward in store for them, the toils and grievances of the moment were forgotten."[11] As the troops assembled, there was heady talk of a "speedy and bloodless conquest," as well as of rich booty, because even the lowliest of cabin boys could expect a share of the spoils when the wealth of New Orleans was divided up.

On its way into battle, despite the hardships of the trip, the finest army in the world had little doubt that New Orleans would soon be theirs.

The British Make Landfall

While the British shuttled their troops to shore, Jackson waited blindly. He knew the enemy now controlled Lake Borgne, but what route would they take from the lake?

One clue arrived compliments of a schooner captain named Brown. Sailing on Lake Borgne, together with his pilot, a black man named Michaud, he had seen a daunting sight, "count[ing] three hundred and forty-eight barges, carrying each forty or fifty men, infantry, cavalry, and two regiments of Negroes." Brown was brought to Jackson.

Where, the general asked, did they observe this flotilla?

"They disembarked at Ile-aux-Poix," Brown replied.[12] Jackson wished to know more, but the schooner captain could offer no further details.

Jackson was left to ponder—as he advised the secretary of war—where the enemy would "choose his point of attack."[13] He knew from his own reconnoitering that the best approach from Pea Island could be along the Plain of Gentilly, so Jackson dispatched defenders, including a regiment of Louisiana militia and a battalion of free blacks. Because it was also possible that His Majesty's soldiers would take a route south of the plain, Jackson ordered another Louisiana regiment downriver to be posted at Jumonville. At the Villeré plantation just downstream, a picket was posted to watch for danger from that approach, while another division of the militia marched toward English Turn, in case the British came that way. Every fort in the vicinity was manned and everyone was on watch and alert.

The most direct routes were now covered, but Jackson still had two problems. First, he did not have enough ammunition for his men. Second, he had insufficient knowledge of the bayous to truly plan to repel every possible attack. He had examined the local topography to the best of his ability, but it wasn't enough. To ensure the safety of the city, he would need to add one more group to his motley coalition of troops.

Partnering with the Pirates

For months, Jackson resisted making a deal with the devil. When Governor Claiborne had forwarded Jean Lafitte's warning back in September concerning the British attempt to recruit the pirates of Barataria Bay, Jackson had written back, angrily dismissing the Lafitte brothers and their fellow privateers as "hellish banditti." Claiborne concurred: Louisiana's governor was a sworn enemy of the privateers and, in September, had even ordered a raid of Barataria Bay, driving the outlaws into hiding elsewhere in the marshes south of the city.

Yet the Lafittes still had powerful friends in New Orleans and, with the danger of invasion on everyone's mind, attitudes softened toward Jean who, at great risk to himself, had relayed word of the British approach. The motives of the pirates were hard to decipher—were they really pro-American or was Lafitte just looking for pardons for past offenses?—but many in the Creole community wanted to enlist their help under these desperate circumstances. Indeed, on December 14, the Louisiana legislature passed a resolution promising amnesty for their piratical transgressions if the Lafittes and their men helped fight the British.

With the British now so near at hand, Jackson consulted Edward Livingston. For three years, Livingston had been Jean Lafitte's legal adviser. Until now, Jackson had followed William Claiborne's lead and regarded the Baratarians as infamous bandits. But Jackson's army was low on matériel—and he had gotten wind of Lafitte's boast that he could outfit an army of thirty thousand.

The time had come for Monsieur Lafitte and General Jackson to meet.

After obtaining a pass into the city from a federal judge—there remained a warrant out for his arrest—Jean Lafitte arrived at the three-story brick house on Royal Street. Major Latour, now a trusted member of Jackson's brain trust, offered to bring his friend Lafitte in. He did the introductions and helped bridge the language gap.

Jackson listened to Monsieur Lafitte's proposal, as he "solicited for himself and for all the Baratarians, the honor of serving under our banners . . . to defend the country and combat its enemies."[14] Jackson had his doubts—more than once he had dismissed Lafitte and his men as "pirates and robbers." Still, this proposal was beginning to make sense.

Lafitte explained he could offer more than his allegiance. He claimed to have one thousand men, all willing to fight. Just as important to Jackson, however, was the cache of powder, shot, and essential flints—some seven thousand of them, he said—which were needed to provide the spark used to fire muzzle-loaded flintlock muskets and pistols.

The general and the pirate regarded each other. The two shared little in life experience, yet both had a native gift for leadership; they were men around whom other men rallied. They had differing moral codes but shared a respect for what they regarded as fairness and natural law. Just as Jackson had recognized the Red Stick chief Weatherford as a man who, at great risk to himself, had confronted Jackson seeking common cause, he began to see Lafitte in the same light. The pirate just might prove to be a key ally.

Lafitte knew the backwaters of this region intimately.

The man who stood before Jackson promised him men and munitions.

The artillerists in his band were famously skilled.

His stores of gunpowder would be invaluable.

A deal was struck, and Jackson dictated a note saying, "Jean Lafitte has offered me his services to go down and give every information in his power. You will therefore please to afford him the necessary protection from insult and injury and when you have derived the information you wish, furnish him with a passport for his return, dismissing him as soon as possible as I shall want him here."[15]

Lafitte's intelligence would be critical, and some of his privateers would be assigned to help protect Bayou St. John north of the city and to reinforce Fort St. Philip downstream on the Mississippi. Others would be organized into two artillery companies. The stores of munitions the pirates had accumulated would be removed to Jackson's magazine. Lafitte himself would then join Jackson's officer corps.

Together, they would seek to save New Orleans.

Across the Sea, in Ghent

Across the Atlantic, a quieter confrontation brewed. The American and British negotiators in Ghent grew closer to a meeting of the minds and, as November became December, the Americans had begun to think a treaty was within reach. The differences between the parties seemed to have been whittled down to talk of fishing rights off the New England coast and navigation of the Mississippi.

These discussions had revealed a regional rift between the American negotiators. John Quincy Adams saw no great harm in trading away access to the Mississippi and, to him, the right to fish off his native coast was an essential and absolute right. He felt bound to protect it, partly because his father had negotiated similar terms in the

Treaty of Paris when the American Revolution ended. For the Kentuckian Henry Clay, however, the importance of the fisheries was dwarfed by the matter of navigating the great river that defined the westernmost boundary of his state. For him, the Mississippi was central to the development of his nation's middle, and he could never agree to compromise those American rights.

In the midst of these distractions, the American ministers briefly furrowed their brows at a new wrinkle the British introduced to the discussion.

In early December, the English diplomats returned once more to the language concerning territory captured by either party in the war. At first, the renewed discussion seemed a simple continuation of the earlier negotiations concerning the Latin phrase *uti possidetis* ("as you possess") and the restoration of territory with a peace. But the wrangling over language puzzled the ever-thoughtful John Quincy Adams. He pondered the British insistence on splitting linguistic hairs concerning who owned what and when—and what it might mean in practical terms.

In Louisiana, he knew, a battle for New Orleans might just be unfolding. If so, the city would be successfully defended or it would fall. Neither he nor anyone else—in Europe or in North America—knew what the outcome would be.

Yet a great deal might hinge on that result: half hidden in the diplomatic and legal language of the document lay a grave danger—one that, despite Adams's suspicions, remained undetected by Adams and the American negotiators.

What would happen if the British captured New Orleans?

In the new draft of the document, all "territories, places, and possessions" captured by one side were to be returned. Regardless of the outcome when Admiral Cochrane's forces met up with General Jackson's, the Treaty of Ghent would assure that Louisiana remained the property of the United States of America. Right?

However, to a legalistic eye, wasn't that subject to interpretation? What if there was a deeper subtext to the British insistence upon the insertion of the word *possessions*? Given that the British had never accepted Louisiana as a legitimate American *possession*—the Crown regarded the territory as the rightful property of the king of Spain, taken wrongly by Napoleon and therefore illegally transferred to the United States of America—might this open-ended treaty invite dispute?

And in the event the British captured New Orleans, did they intend to keep it?

What none of the Americans knew was that Edward Pakenham, the new general sent to defeat the Americans in the great battle for New Orleans, had very specific instructions. The British secretary of state for war, Earl Bathurst, had instructed Pakenham precisely. Even if he heard a treaty had been signed, Earl Bathurst ordered, "hostilities should not be suspended *until you shall have official information*" that the treaty had been ratified. The British commander was, quite specifically, to fight on to gain "Possession of the Country."[16]

If Adams didn't recognize them, how could Pakenham's opponent, Andrew Jackson, have known of the perils posed by a treaty being negotiated five thousand miles away? He could no more have anticipated the peace terms than he could have sensed an earthquake in the days before it struck. But Jackson's own remarkable instincts did tell him that holding New Orleans—keeping it out of the hands of the British—meant everything to his beloved country.

The British Approach

Admiral Cochrane had begun the process of landing his attack force, but he still had serious reason to be cautious. Some days earlier two men had arrived under a flag of truce, and the admiral received them aboard the HMS *Tonnant*. One of them, a physician named Dr. Robert Morrell, explained they came on behalf of Commodore Patterson. Morrell wanted to attend to the wounded American sailors, while his companion, Thomas Shields, a purser, wanted to negotiate the release of Lieutenant Jones and the other prisoners.

Cochrane suspected they were spies.

The admiral questioned the Americans closely. They were quick to assure him that Jackson's was an enormous and powerful force, that "myriads of Western riflemen . . . were flocking to his standard."[17]

Cochrane remained skeptical of American battle skills after the pathetic failure of the militia outside Washington on August 24, when thousands of ill-trained farmers and shopkeepers had scattered in the face of a British charge and beneath a sky alight with exploding rockets.

But Cochrane asked himself: Was he sending his men to face an army that might be two thousand strong—or did it number twenty thousand, as these men told him? As much as the possibility worried him, he doubted so large a force existed. In any case, he certainly couldn't permit these men to leave the fleet to report to Jackson what they had seen of his ships and soldiers.

"Until the battle was over," Cochrane had told them, "and the fate of the town determined," they were going nowhere.[18] They would be guests of the Royal Navy, waiting out the battle aboard the frigate HMS *Gordon*.

From Pea Island, Cochrane decided to send two of his own men on a spying mission.

He consulted with General John Keane, commander of the army forces, and, on December 20, Captain Robert Spencer of the Royal Navy and Quartermaster Lieutenant John Peddie of His Majesty's army set out for Bayou Bienvenue, a watercourse that led from Lake Borgne to the outskirts of New Orleans. Their task was to determine whether Cochrane's plan was indeed the best route for landing the army.

The men returned the next day from reconnoitering Bayou Bienvenue bearing good news. After spotting Fisherman's Village, a small settlement of a dozen cabins a short distance upstream on the bayou, the two Englishmen had gone ashore. Spencer and Peddie hired as their guides two Spanish fishermen who sold their catch upstream in New Orleans and knew the area well. Having disguised themselves in the blue shirts and the oilskin hats the locals wore, Spencer and Peddie studied the landscape as the fishermen stroked them miles inland. Amazingly, they saw no sentinels, and Spencer and Peddie went ashore and walked to the high road that led into the city. They took in a view of the Mississippi. Within a mere six miles of New Orleans, the two British spies tasted the water of the big river.

Back on Pea Island, they told Cochrane that the plan to land at Bayou Bienvenue was "perfectly practicable," because the bayou was both unobstructed and—this was almost laughable—unguarded ("the enemy had no look-out in that quarter").[19] The bayou was roughly a hundred yards wide and more than six feet deep. Not only could the army go ashore at Bayou Bienvenue, but the advance men had done their job doubly well, returning with more than a dozen fishermen, all with intimate knowledge of Lake Borgne. They would act as pilots for the British barges.

A definite plan was in place.

Bayou Bienvenue

Cochrane gave the order to move. The first of General Keane's force embarked on December 22. The advance guard would be a light brigade consisting of the Fourth Regiment, Eighty-Fifth Light Infantry, and the green-uniformed Ninety-Fifth Rifles. Its commander would be Colonel William Thornton, who had distinguished himself in August at the big victory in Washington.

In addition to regular troops, Thornton took rocketeers armed with rockets. A squad of artillerymen went along, too, with two portable three-pound guns, as did a company of sappers, engineers charged with repairing roads and building bridges. Two other brigades accompanied by heavier armaments would follow.

The first barges shoved off by ten o'clock: the lead expeditionary force of more than 1,600 men was on its way, and after a long row, they entered Bayou Bienvenue in the darkness.

Spotting U.S. pickets on guard a half mile ahead near Fisherman's Village, a party of British infantrymen, stealthy under the cover of night, surprised and quickly overcame the Americans. None of them were able to run back to New Orleans to warn Jackson that the British were on the way.

In the morning, when they resumed their advance after some hours of sleep, a vanguard of troops commanded by Thornton led the string of barges upstream on Bayou Bienvenue and its extension, Bayou Mazant. When they reached the head of the waterway, they found the water shallower than expected, and the soldiers had to walk from one boat to the next, as over an unsteady bridge, to reach land. The sappers went on ahead to clear a path and, where necessary, improvised bridges over streams. The British force-marched toward their destination, camouflaged by reeds that stood seven feet tall.

At first, progress was slow, but, after almost a mile, the boggy swampland gave way to firmer ground and a cover of cypress trees. A mile beyond, open fields came into view.

Over the decades, farmers had reclaimed fertile soil along the Mississippi. Levees and canals made cultivation possible, and plantations now lined the river, where well-irrigated acreage produced valuable crops. One such property now lay directly in the British path—but little did Thornton realize that it was a station for Jackson's sentinels.

Under orders from Colonel Thornton, a company of soldiers fanned out, surrounding the main house of the Villeré plantation. Its owner, General Jacques Villeré, guarded the coastline elsewhere with his Louisiana militia; his son Gabriel remained at home, charged by Jackson with watching Bayou Bienvenue. As the British crept closer, Villeré stood on the house's gallery, smoking a cigar. Deep in conversation with a younger brother, Major Gabriel Villeré failed to see the first redcoats as they approached through an orange grove near the house.

When he did, it was too late. He attempted to flee, but the British quickly took possession of the house, capturing him and easily overcoming the entire company of thirty militiamen he commanded.

New Orleans was now just seven miles away, an easy two-hour march along what General Keane regarded as a "tolerably good" road.[20] Despite Colonel Thornton's argument that they should take the fight immediately to the Americans, the British made camp. After long nights on the barges, they hoped for a full night's rest. The invasion, months in the making, could wait until tomorrow. This would be their first critical mistake.

A Daring Escape

Though a captive in his own house, Major Villeré refused to resign himself to his fate. Despite being closely guarded, he saw an opportunity and made his move. Managing to get to a window, he leapt out, knocking several surprised British soldiers outside to the ground. He ran for the fence at the edge of a field; to the pop of gunfire and musket balls whistling past his head, he hurdled over the barrier. Before the riflemen could get him in their sights, he disappeared into the dense cypress wood.

The fleeing prisoner understood he was one man pursued by many, but he knew his home terrain well. He raced deeper into the woods, headed for one of the enormous trees he had known since boyhood. He would climb high, he thought, and obscure himself in its dense vegetation. But when he halted at the foot of a great live oak with its netting of Spanish moss, he heard a familiar whimper. There, at his feet, crouched his bird dog, who had dutifully followed her master.

Gabriel Villeré had only moments—he could hear the approaching voices of the British searchers calling to one another—but knew immediately that his dog would betray him. With a heavy heart, he struck the animal with a large stick, killing his friendly traitor. After concealing her body, he ascended into the canopy, and the British proceeded without finding him.

Later that morning, after concluding he had eluded them, the British returned to the plantation. Villeré made his escape. As the Scotsman George Gleig ruefully observed, "The rumour of our landing would, we knew, spread faster than we could march."[21]

"The British Are Below"

At 1:30 p.m. on December 23, 1814, Jackson, at work in his parlor, heard hoofbeats. Three men galloped up to the stoop at 106 Rue Royale and announced that they had important intelligence for the general.

Jackson ordered them admitted.

"What news do you bring, gentlemen?" Jackson asked from his seat.

The breathless Gabriel Villeré, who just hours earlier had escaped the British, had borrowed a horse and hurried to Jackson's headquarters along with two of his neighbors. Though Villeré spoke French, he had Jackson's complete attention as one of the other men translated.

"The British . . . nine miles below the city . . . Villeré"—indicating Gabriel—"captured . . . escaped."

At last Jackson had the information he needed. The long waiting game was over. The world's most powerful army had at last invaded the shores of Louisiana, and after weeks of wondering where and when they would strike, Jackson finally had clarity. He hammered his fist on the table before him as he rose to his full height.

"By the Eternal," he exclaimed, "they shall not sleep on our soil!"

Summoning his staff officers, Jackson ordered that wine be served and, with glass in hand, thanked Villeré for his news. Then he turned to his officers and aides-de-camp.

"Gentlemen," he said simply, "the British are below, we must fight them tonight."[22]

His voice was even, his manner calm, but no one missed the man's absolute determination. Orders were soon flying in every direction. Drumbeats sounded in the streets, and the firing of three cannons signaled to the city a call to arms.

General Carroll and his men were dispatched in the direction of upper Bayou Bienvenue. North of town, under the command of Governor Claiborne, Louisiana militiamen would stand guard over the wide road through the Plain of Gentilly—because Jackson fully expected a British assault on more than one front, he didn't want to leave his back door open. Meanwhile, Edward Livingston relayed to Master Commander Patterson aboard the USS *Carolina* orders to weigh anchor and sail downstream.

Jackson would lead the attack force, which would include the Seventh and Forty-Fourth U.S. Infantry, the Creole battalions, the Choctaws, and a corps of freemen. Together with the marines and the artillery company, Jackson would march south with more than 1,600 men. This assembled army would proceed six miles to the Rodriguez Canal and meet up with Coffee's mounted brigade and the Mississippi dragoons.

With the first stage of his plan prepared, General Jackson could respond to a message received from a lady of New Orleans who wrote on behalf of the women of the city. Alarmed at the rumored British approach, she asked what were they to do if the city was attacked.

"Say to the ladies," Jackson instructed an aide, "not to be uneasy.

No British soldier shall enter the city as an enemy, unless over my dead body."[23]

With that, he ate a small helping of boiled rice, then stretched his lanky frame upon the sofa and closed his eyes for an afternoon nap.[24] With a long and uncertain evening before him, the weary general could use a few minutes' rest. By sunset, the city would be empty of troops—and Jackson would be at the head of his army, marching toward a nighttime fight. The British at their bivouac, just nine miles away, were going to get some unexpected visitors.

CHAPTER 10

The First Battle of New Orleans

> Wellington's heroes discovered that they were ill-qualified to contend with us in woods where they must fight knee-deep in water.
>
> **—Major Arsène Lacarrière Latour**

As Villeré had rushed to Jackson's headquarters, the British took stock of their position in preparation for their attack. Admiral Cochrane remained at the mouth of Bayou Bienvenue at Fisherman's Village, while Keane made the Villeré dwelling house his army's headquarters. The advance guard marched past the house and, bearing right, reached a larger road a short distance on. There the troops halted, taking in a view of more large plantations beyond. These great farms lined the flat, dry ribbon of land all the way to New Orleans.

Though the landscape was dotted with fruit trees, sugarcane was the main crop grown there. Ditches that fed into bayous and swamps to the north drained the fields that, now brown and scruffy, had yielded the year's harvest to machete-wielding slaves and overseers. Bounded as it was on one side by the marshes and, to the south, by the

Mississippi, the site seemed defensible, as good a place to pause before the attack as any. Stacking their guns within reach, Keane's men formed a bivouac in the open fields. Here they would lay out their bedrolls for the night.

The levee—"a lofty and strong embankment, resembling the dykes in Holland, and meant to serve a similar purpose," as George Gleig described it—protected the encampment, since the ground on which they camped was below the level of the water on the other side.[1] Exhausted from their journey through this strange terrain, the British posted a watch, positioning pickets at the periphery of their mile-long camp. Scouting parties dispersed to reconnoiter; some returned having helped themselves at the abandoned cabins and poultry yards they found, carrying hams, cheeses, wines, and other goods. Meanwhile, other soldiers dismantled nearby rail fences made of resinous cypress to build large fires. With smoke swirling into the sky, water was brought from the river.

"Fatigued," General Keane noted, after their "long confinement in the boats," the soldiers set about making an afternoon dinner.[2]

With two brigades of reinforcements soon to land to his rear at Bayou Bienvenue, General Keane planned to wait until the full force from Pea Island caught up. Some of the soldiers took advantage of the warm afternoon, washing up in the river. The relaxed air was broken briefly when, shortly after three o'clock, a bugle warning sent the troops scrambling for their guns. Within minutes, however, the all clear was sounded. A few American cavalrymen had been sighted but they quickly scampered—one of them wounded, the pickets claimed—when fired on by the British advance guard.

A calm set in once again in the camp. Tomorrow they would move on but, as the crisp December night fell, the men warmed themselves around their campfires, more comfortable and better fed than they had been in a week.

British confidence ran so high that Admiral Cochrane and General Keane had ordered the posting of handbills on plantation fences that announced their coming. "LOUISIANIANS! REMAIN QUIET IN YOUR HOUSES," the flyers read. "YOUR SLAVES SHALL BE PRESERVED TO YOU, AND YOUR PROPERTY RESPECTED. WE MAKE WAR ONLY AGAINST AMERICANS!"[3]

The British, confident that the people of New Orleans were too newly American to have any sense of patriotism, were sure they would divide and conquer.

Firefight!

Shortly after seven o'clock, one of Keane's lookouts atop the levee spotted a ship in the Mississippi just out of musket range. The British had been relaxed, unworried, laughter ringing out from time to time, but now the easy mood of the evening tensed.

Though silhouetted against the opposite bank, the large vessel defied identification. Might it be a Royal Navy cruiser coming to render assistance?

Or could it be the enemy?

With her sails furled, she wasn't going anywhere. The British on the shore hailed the vessel but got no answer. They tried firing into the air but, once more, all remained quiet on the water. No response.

When the soldiers standing on the levee heard a loud splash, the noise remained a mystery. But aboard the USS *Carolina,* every sailor among the hundred-man crew knew the cause. They had cast a great weight into the sea—that sound had been the bow anchor striking the surface of the Mississippi.

When the anchor struck bottom, Commodore Patterson's men pulled its cable taut. Slowly the eighty-nine-foot vessel came about, her bow pointing into the current flowing toward the sea. She stood steady and ready, her starboard side aligned with the shoreline a few hundred yards away.

In the quiet of the night, the American schooner had just become a floating battery. Armed with three long nine-pound cannons and a dozen twelve-pound carronades, she was perfectly positioned to unleash a broadside. The gunners carefully set their sights on "the [British] fires, like so many landmarks or beacons, enabl[ing] the Americans to point their guns accordingly."[4]

At 7:30 p.m., the onlookers on the shore heard a deep, loud voice, speaking in English. The man's exclamation echoed over the water.

"Now, damn their eyes, give it 'em!"[5]

In the next moment, brilliant muzzle flashes revealed the full outline of the ship. The accompanying thunder of cannons preceded by barely a heartbeat the crash of grapeshot. Well-aimed shot struck the British fires, scattering burning wood and blazing embers; kettles crashed to ground. The cannon fire landed "like so many thunderbolts amongst the astounded troops."[6] Men were knocked to the ground; others were wounded and killed in their sleep.

The calm of the evening, all in a minute, gave way to complete havoc. The British soldiers raced for their arms, looking at the sky and out to sea as the enemy warship continued to pound the camp with regular and accurate fire.

Ground Attack

The king's troops found shelter behind the levee, but their answering muskets did little harm, and the guns of the USS *Carolina* continued to lob deadly iron into the camp. Some soldiers worked to extinguish the fires and to drag wounded men, unable to seek cover on their own, to safety. British artillerists managed to discharge a few rockets in the direction of the ship, but the skyrockets, too, failed to do damage.

After ten minutes the bombardment from the *Carolina* slackened—but Andrew Jackson's second surprise was about to be delivered.

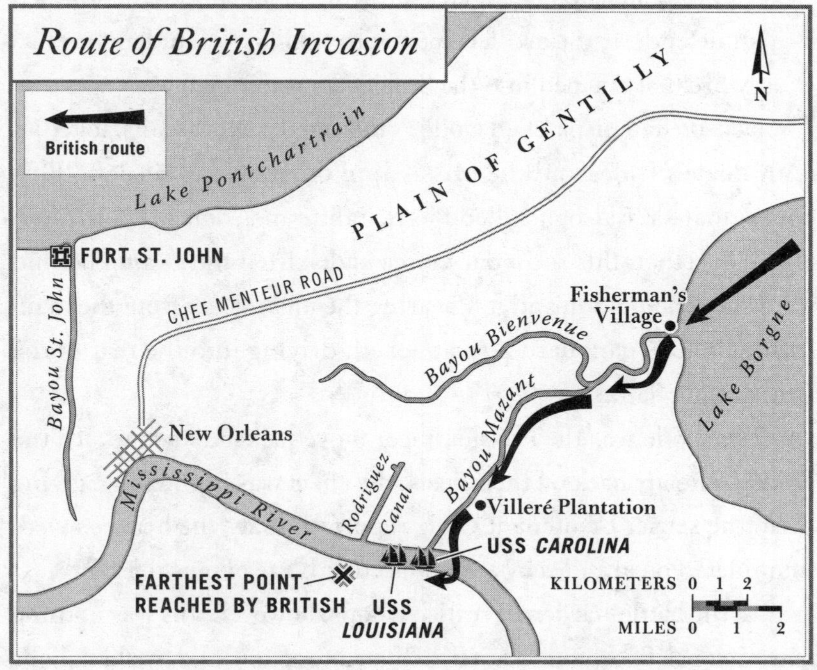

Lying prostrate behind the levee, British soldiers heard the report of muskets from the vicinity of their sentinels; there, with no moon to illuminate their attackers, the advance guard "mistook every tree for an American."[7] As the sporadic gunshots gave way to rapid volleys, a new sense of alarm swept through the British ranks. The realization dawned that the Americans were launching another assault—and this one was coming not from the water but from the land.

Jackson's main force had marched along the river to the Rodriguez Canal; once there, at Jackson's orders, they had moved in near silence to within five hundred yards of the British sentinels and formed a line perpendicular to the river. Two brass fieldpieces were readied, and the troops had waited for the *Carolina* to begin her bombardment.

Now they attacked. With Jackson's line advancing on the stunned British defenders, the artillerymen with their six-pounders began a deadly fire that crashed into the besieged encampment.

Jackson had dispatched Coffee's mounted Tennesseans, together with Beale's Rifles and the Mississippi dragoons, to his left. This substantial force also included Pierre Lafitte and some of his Baratarians.[8] Together, this secondary force had skirted the swamp behind the Villeré plantation and, on hearing the musket fire from the main front, Coffee's vanguard also attacked, driving into the rear of the British right flank.

The tactic was the classic pincer move Jackson favored. To the British, already back on their heels, the effect was frightening, giving them the sense, Lieutenant Gleig reported, that "the heavens were illuminated on all sides by a semi-circular blaze of musketry."[9]

To the battle-hardened British troops, however, this was nothing new. Colonel Thornton ordered his men into action, and two battalions charged the main line of oncoming Americans. Many men fell but the

British penetrated the American line. Catching sight of the American artillery position, they made a bold push for the guns, managing to wound some of the draft horses and upset one of the cannons. But the marines charged with protecting them took to heart General Jackson's words.

"Save the guns, my boys," he called to them, "at every sacrifice!"[10]

Seeing what was unfolding before him, Jackson then spurred his horse and charged into the fray. He was "within pistol shot, in the midst of a shower of bullets, . . . urging on the marines." The fighting was so hot that one of Jackson's officers questioned whether the general wasn't "expos[ing] himself rather too much."[11] But they held the guns and moved forward.

Meanwhile, General Coffee, who had ordered his men to dismount in order "to give them a freer and more certain use of the rifle," attacked the right flank of the British.[12] The fresh fire from these superior marksmen was murderous, made more terrifying by the blackness of the night. Beale's Rifles joined Coffee's men, adding to the pressure on the British.

Having softened up the redcoat ranks with their gunfire, the Americans advanced into the darkness and into their camp. Muzzle fire flashed in the gloom but, even at close range, the darkness and clouds of gun smoke made it nearly impossible to distinguish friend from foe. Shouts of "Don't fire, we are your friends!"[13] rang out as both Americans and British encountered friendly fire in the confusion.

Wary of shooting their own, infantrymen fought hand to hand, bayonet to bayonet, and sword to sword. The British used their guns as clubs, and the Tennesseans who carried tomahawks and hunting knives didn't hesitate to use them. In the darkness, officers lost control of their men, and soon it was each man fighting his own duel in the dark. "No man could tell what was going forward in any quarter," reported Gleig, "except where he himself chanced immediately to stand; no one part of the line could bring assistance to another, because, in truth, no line existed. It was in one word a perfect tumult."[14] The entire assault was a shock to the invaders: as Colonel Thornton observed, "This bold attacking us in our camp is a new feature in American warfare."[15]

As the fighting entered its second hour, the clouds began to break and a quarter moon cast its ghostly light on the field of battle. At first, the direction of the light better illuminated the faces of the American attackers, giving the British a decided advantage. But soon a ground fog rolled in off the river, decreasing visibility again. Finally, with conditions worsening near nine o'clock, Jackson ordered his men to withdraw from the field. They had accomplished enough for one night. Though localized skirmishing continued for some time, most of the Americans marched back upriver, halting at a canal on a nearby plantation. The British retired to their camp.

Counting the Dead

On the morning after, surgeons on both sides worked to save what lives they could. Jackson's surprise attack inflicted serious damage: 24 Americans were dead, 115 wounded, and 74 missing and presumed captured. But enemy casualties were much greater: according to one British source, the toll was more than 500 men. Roughly a square mile in area, the battlefield was tragic to behold, and even a veteran of the French wars like George Gleig was stunned by the carnage. "Not only were the wounds themselves exceedingly frightful, but the very countenances of the dead exhibited the most savage and ghastly expressions. . . . Such had been the deadly closeness of the strife that . . . an English and American soldier might be seen with the bayonet of each fastened in the other's body."[16]

Most of the wounded Americans were carried back to New Orleans, while the injured British were treated at the Villeré plantation, where a makeshift field hospital was established. Doctors amputated limbs and bandaged wounds, while soldiers buried the dead. The wounded British healthy enough to travel were loaded aboard the barges and taken to the fleet. Their beds on land would be needed soon enough; more casualties would surely follow.

General Keane was stunned at the outcome of this first real battle with General Jackson's makeshift army. The Americans had penetrated deeply into the British camp; the British had yielded ground. They had won it back, but what would have happened had Jackson not withdrawn his men? Unable or unwilling to believe that fewer than two thousand Americans could have done such damage to his force of roughly the same size, Keane exaggerated the size of the American force in his report of the battle, more than doubling the actual count.

The intimidation factor of the great Royal Army was beginning to fade; the Americans had held their own. The fight had temporarily halted the advance of the British, and the Americans had demonstrated to their enemy that they could fight the best military in the world. In the hours before the battle, those British who had faced the American militia outside Washington hadn't felt "the smallest sensation of alarm" at seeing American troops nearby. "We held them in too much contempt to fear their attack."[17] A dozen hours later, however, they had been shocked into acknowledging that these American forces, under the command of Andrew Jackson, were a high-caliber opponent.

Most of Jackson's troops were inexperienced; the fresh mix of militiamen and regulars and volunteers had never fought together until that day. Yet the American officers and their men seemed to possess a dangerous mix of military skills that caught the British off guard—initiative, strategic thinking, determination, and fighting techniques. Many of them were superb marksmen, their guns deadly accurate, and even in hand-to-hand combat the American soldier had held his own.

Above all, Andrew Jackson demonstrated he was a man to be reckoned with. In just five hours he had formulated a combined land-and-sea assault plan, assembled a dispersed and diverse force, marched it undetected to the enemy camp, and reduced the king's attackers to near total confusion. Then he and his men had slipped away just as they had come.

Newly aware of how potent their opponents could be, the British recognized the need to exercise caution—meaning that, once again, the Americans had bought themselves time, precious hours and even days to dig in, to establish a solid line of defense at their new camp.

Less than two miles away from the British, Jackson was determined to hold the line, to halt a British march on New Orleans.

December 24, 1814

Under very different circumstances, the British and American peace commissioners met that same day, an ocean away, in Ghent, Belgium. Assembling at a former monastery on the Rue des Chartreux, the teams of negotiators arrived on Christmas Eve afternoon to sign an agreed-upon treaty of peace.

The document actually decided little; it was essentially an agreement to halt hostilities. The first article stated, "There shall be a firm and universal Peace between His Britannic Majesty and the United States," but, amazingly, key issues such as impressment and harassment of trade, the very matters that had led to the American war declaration, were not mentioned.

Henry Clay thought it was a "damn bad treaty," but, like everyone else, he wanted the war to be over.

The American copies of the treaty would cross the Atlantic in a small leather document box; with delays due to stormy weather, it would take thirty-eight days to reach New York. The treaty wouldn't reach President Madison's study in Washington until February 14, 1815. As for New Orleans, the news of the peace would come far too late to avoid the casualties sustained by both sides in the interim. Just as important, the treaty's terms would not be in full force and effect until the governments in both capitals ratified the document.

Thus, the future of the city of New Orleans and the territory of Louisiana—as well as the lives of many men—hung in the balance. The pressure stayed on General Jackson. Now that he knew the route the British assault would take, his job would be to establish a solid defensive line.

CHAPTER 11

The Defensive Line

> It is true the enemy is on our coast and threatens an invasion of our territory, but it is equally true, with union, energy, and the approbation of Heaven, we will beat him at every point.
>
> **—Andrew Jackson**

"I expect the enemy is pretty sore today," General Jackson observed on the morning after the firefight.[1] Even so, with British reinforcements continuing to step ashore at Bayous Bienvenue and Mazant, a counterattack seemed inevitable.

But when?

Spies reported that, at least for the moment, the British looked to be stationary. But Jackson couldn't just wait—not a minute could be wasted—and he made sure the men around him were anything but idle.

When falling back from the field of battle the night before, the army had marched across several plantation properties toward New Orleans. At 4:00 a.m., Jackson ordered a halt at the Rodriguez Canal, two miles upstream from the British front at the Villeré plantation and six miles short of New Orleans.

This was to be his line in the silty Louisiana soil, and he would make it a breastwork he could defend. The *Carolina* could provide supporting artillery fire from the river and, in the course of the morning, she would be reinforced by the arrival of her sister ship, the *Louisiana*. Commodore Patterson's crew was a motley one—there were Yankees, Portuguese, Norwegians, Spanish, Greeks, Italians, Germans, Arabs, Hindus, and Swedes aboard. As Patterson advised the secretary of the navy, "the crew of the Louisiana is composed of men of all nations, (English excepted) taken from the streets of New Orleans."[2] In other words, this force was diverse enough to be pure American.

General Jackson took Augustin Macarty's mansion for his headquarters. The large house stood on piers, with the main living quarters raised a full story above the Mississippi floodplain. The porch that

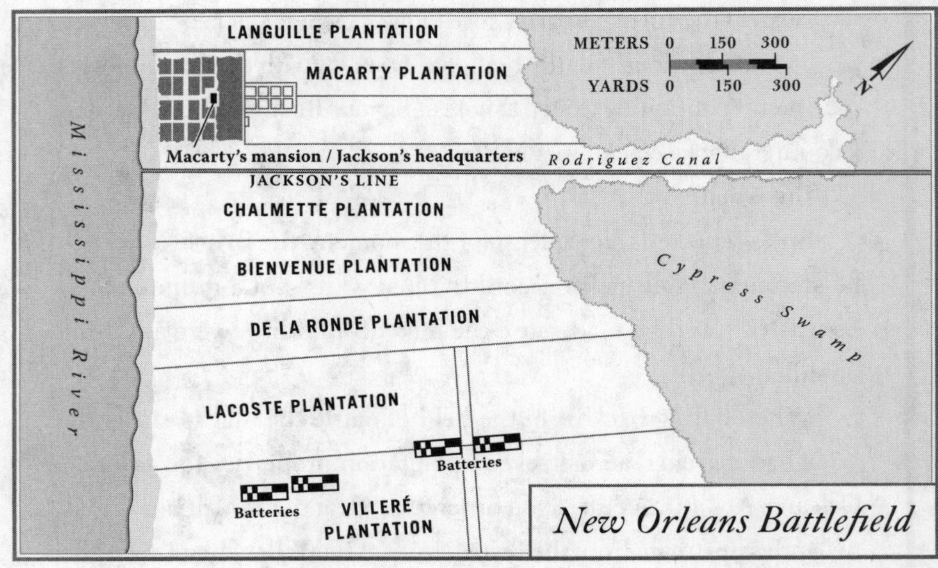

New Orleans Battlefield

swept around the perimeter overlooked the Rodriguez Canal to the east, just a hundred yards away. On the other side of the canal lay another plantation, the property of the Creole family Chalmette, its roughly two hundred acres of open fields mostly given over to the cultivation of sugarcane. From the dormers that peered out of the steep roof of the Macarty house, Jackson, using a telescope, took in a broad view of the more distant British encampment located on two other properties, the Bienvenue and De La Ronde plantations.

Jackson ordered platoons of Mississippi mounted rifles and Louisiana dragoons to patrol the no-man's-land in between the two armies. But the rest of his men were about to become ditchdiggers.

A nearby disused millstream (it had once powered a sawmill), the so-called Rodriguez Canal held no water. Four feet deep and twenty wide, the ditch extended north-south at the boundary of the Macarty plantation. Its strategic value lay in the fact that it ran at a right angle all the way from the levee at the river's edge to a nearly impenetrable wooded swamp at the far edge of the field.

Jackson consulted his chief engineer, Major Arsène Lacarrière Latour, who knew the soils and topography of the region intimately. Latour agreed with Jackson's assessment: Once cleared of weeds and silt, the Rodriguez Canal could be flooded with water from the river to serve as a moat, an obstacle to an oncoming army. And parapets could be raised on the New Orleans side of the canal, ramparts behind which American soldiers and artillery could take cover.

Jackson issued an order to have every shovel in the area commandeered. By the time the morning fog had burned off, Jackson's men were at work, spades in hand, together with slaves from nearby plantations. They moved earth forward from behind the line to form an embankment and used posts taken from nearby fences to prevent the rising mound of soil from falling into the ditch. Other men worked at cutting a sluiceway to permit the flow of water into the canal, and Jackson ordered more channels dug in the levee to flood open land between the armies. Having to march through mud and standing water, Jackson thought, would slow any British attack.[3]

Working in shifts, the army labored through Christmas Day and into the night. The job would be a long one, requiring more than a day or even two or three. But no one knew how much time they had.

Jackson himself supervised. On his horse, he was a constant presence, vigilant and refusing to sleep. One of Rachel's nephews, a captain in the Tennessee militia, soon observed the toll the intense days were taking on the general. "Uncle Jackson," he wrote home, "looks very badly at present, and has broken very much."[4]

His body suffering, Jackson's spirit was strong. When one British prisoner reported to him that Admiral Cochrane had sworn he would take his Christmas dinner in New Orleans, Jackson had a sharp answer.

"Perhaps so," he snapped, "but I shall have the honor of presiding at that dinner."[5]

London's Christmas Gift

On the other side of the line, the British needed some bucking up. The cold, damp weather sat heavily on the exposed soldiers, another hardship after the bitter journey in the barges.

The regular boom of the guns aboard the *Carolina* and now the *Louisiana* continued to endanger life and limb. Even on Christmas Day the British troops had to remain ever-wary of incoming rounds and shrapnel. As one group of officers shared a Christmas dinner made from their dwindling stock of provisions, they heard a loud scream. The men raced outside the little building where they had been eating and found a soldier mortally wounded by a cannonball. "Though fairly cut in two at the lower part of the belly," George Gleig reported, "the poor wretch lived for nearly an hour, gasping for breath."[6]

The risks were constant. Anyone who ventured into the no-man's-land between the two encampments was a target for sharp-eyed American snipers and, once night fell, any exposed Britishers were in danger of periodic hit-and-run volleys from American cavalry and stealthy visits from the Choctaws. Some five dozen Indians armed with tomahawks and bands of Tennesseans with long rifles made deadly work of sneaking up on—and killing—British sentries. The British thought this behavior uncivilized but it had its effect. As one British quartermaster reported, the invaders were robbed of "much time for comfortable rest."[7]

Then, at two o'clock on Christmas afternoon, the British got a gift that lifted their spirits. The Americans were still digging on their side of the battlefield-to-be, but their pickets, stationed forward of the line, heard loud cheering from the British position. When pistol shots rang out and an artillery salvo was fired, everyone snapped to attention.

Were the British attacking?

They were celebrating. In the enemy camp, a name ricocheted from unit to unit: the Honorable Sir Edward Pakenham, major general, had arrived. And the happy news lifted morale instantly.

To the British fighters, "Ned" Pakenham was one of them. He had proved himself on battlefields across Spain and France. Though born to the nobility as the son of an earl, he wasn't afraid to put himself at risk. In helping defeat Napoleon, he repeatedly demonstrated his valor, charging headlong into enemy ranks; his rout of one French force had earned him the nickname Hero of Salamanca. He had been injured in battle many times, including two musket wounds to the neck. The first, it was said, left the legendary fighter with a pronounced tilt to his head; the second, sustained years later, left him with his military posture restored.[8]

A survivor on his own terms, Pakenham was also brother-in-law to the formidable Duke of Wellington, who admired his leadership. "My partiality for him does not lead me astray when I tell you he is one of the best we have," Wellington said of Pakenham. (The Iron Duke himself would not go to America; he was both dubious at the likely outcome—"I don't promise myself much success there," he mused—and otherwise engaged in Paris, where he was wrapping up affairs after being named British ambassador to France.) But on the outskirts of New Orleans, Sir Edward had something new to prove: this campaign was his first independent command and, if he succeeded in taking the city, he carried with him a paper commissioning him as the governor of the captured territory.[9]

Shortly after his arrival, General Pakenham set off for an inspection of the front to see for himself the nature of the landscape and the position of his enemy. Almost immediately, he began to question the decisions made by General Keane and Admiral Cochrane; soon he was furious, recognizing the dangerous position he had been handed.

He and his new command were in a box, with a narrow path of attack that was confined by the river on one side and the swamp on the other. Dead ahead there was an American force busily digging itself in. Behind lay a narrow path of retreat. The source of supply was the fleet, moored sixty miles away, with only small open boats to deliver food, men, and munitions. Communications were poor.

In short, as Pakenham saw it, the first fight with the Americans had left the British with an "ominous result," a position of real "jeopardy."[10] One of his officers reported that Pakenham was so angry that his cursing was overheard by men of all ranks.

Still, he had a job to do: he would have to extricate his force; he had to devise and execute a plan that he thought would work. He convened a meeting of the advisers he'd brought with him, together with Keane and Cochrane and their officers.

Sitting in the parlor of the Villeré house—the owner was with his Louisiana militiamen, awaiting the battle on other side of the line—Pakenham didn't mince words. "Our troops should have advanced to New Orleans immediately [on December 23]," he told them. That failure, he said, was an "error."[11] If they had marched straight on, rather than pausing for the night, the city might already be theirs.

Keane and Cochrane shifted the subject to the fight of December 23, attempting to portray the battle as a British victory. Keane claimed that he and his men had held their ground and "repulsed" the attacking Americans who, after attacking, had "thought it prudent to retire [from the field of battle]."

Pakenham disagreed. He saw the night battle quite simply as a "defeat."[12]

That brought the discussion around to their present position.

Pakenham told the officers around him that he was considering a full withdrawal. A better plan could be made, he believed. The entire operation could begin afresh. This fine British force could be deployed elsewhere and odds of a big victory increased.

At this, Admiral Cochrane exploded.

The seasoned navy veteran would have none of it. Cochrane rejected Pakenham's argument: he didn't see defeat—far from it. And the very suggestion that he, his men, and his plan had failed made him immensely angry.

The now-furious Cochrane challenged Pakenham: if the general's army couldn't do the job of taking New Orleans, he threatened, Cochrane's sailors and marines of the Royal Navy would storm the American lines and move on New Orleans.

"The soldiers could then," he taunted Pakenham caustically, "bring up the baggage."[13]

For a moment, the men were at an impasse.

Pakenham was taken aback by Cochrane's outrage, but he knew he needed the admiral's willing cooperation. Under these circumstances, there could be no wholesale rethinking of the strategy, and he realized he had no choice but to relent. As the guns of the *Carolina* and the *Louisiana* continued to send cannonballs into the British encampment, Pakenham resigned himself to trying to make the best of what he recognized was a wretched situation.

He would begin by destroying the *Carolina*.

A Shattering Surprise

On December 27, Andrew Jackson awakened from his first sustained sleep in three days. Following a quiet day of supervising the digging on the American side, the general, to his dismay, found that the British had decided to begin this new day with a barrage of artillery fire shortly after seven o'clock.

Jackson hurried to the dormer windows on the top floor of the Macarty mansion. He saw that the British objective was neither his army nor the line at the Rodriguez Canal. Instead, the enemy cannons bombarded the USS *Carolina,* which had annoyed them with its guns for several days.

Billowing smoke revealed the position of the British guns, dug in downstream on the levee. Standing near them was General Edward Pakenham himself, commanding an artillery battery that, as far as Jackson knew, hadn't even existed just the day before. And the guns were new to the battle, too, longer and with greater range than the ones his men had faced four days before.

A corps of officers had arrived with Pakenham, one of whom was artillery commander Colonel Alexander Dickson. Regarded as one of the ablest gunners in the Royal Army, he had been Wellington's artillery commander and fought with Pakenham at Salamanca, Spain. He had immediately taken charge of the guns that, after arriving on the bayous in boats and barges, had been dragged along the path toward the river by horses. Cochrane promised larger guns would follow but, as of Christmas Day, the Royal Artillery had on hand a pair of nine-pounders, four six-pounders, four three-pounders, and two five-and-a-half-inch howitzers.

Dickson and his men had positioned them to destroy the *Carolina.* Wishing to keep their strategy secret—as well as to avoid drawing fire from the *Carolina*—the guns had been brought to the levee after dark on Christmas night. Colonel Dickson ordered that the guns be spaced out over a distance of several hundred yards, and trenches were dug into the rear of the levee to protect the guns from returning fire. The barrels were set just above grade, and the carriages rested on lengths of wood repurposed from nearby fencing to prevent the heavy iron weapons from sinking into the soft ground. With their work nearly completed before dawn on December 26, the redcoats camouflaged the guns with bundles of sugarcane stalks left on the fields after the harvest. The British withdrew before daylight; they would wait a day before firing, since needed artillery rounds were still arriving on the bayous.

After sunset, the British had gone back to work. They made their final preparations and, at 2:00 a.m., the gunners lit fires to heat the nine-pound balls. The artillerymen had their orders: General Pakenham wished them to commence fire at daylight.

On the morning of December 27, with the firing under way and the booms of the British guns filling his ears, Jackson issued an order that the *Louisiana,* presently moored less than a mile upstream from the *Carolina,* sail out of range. The *Carolina* returned the British fire with her twelve-pounder, the only gun aboard with the range to hit the British position from the ship's mooring on the far side of the Mississippi.

Jackson watched helplessly as deadly accurate British gunnery began to take its toll. Within a half hour, a cannonball baked in a fire as hot as a blacksmith's furnace crashed through the deck of the *Carolina.* It came to rest deep in the ship's main hold, beneath the control cables, a spot difficult for the crew to reach. The hot shot soon ignited a fire whose flames spread rapidly and, within minutes, the uncontrollable blaze was consuming the schooner from within.

More hot shot struck the ship. With several fires threatening to envelop the vessel, the crew had no alternative but to abandon ship. As nine o'clock approached, with flames licking closer and closer to the powder magazine belowdecks, the crew, some of them Lafitte's pirates, managed to roll two of the ship's cannons overboard before they clambered into the *Carolina*'s boats, pushed off, and rowed madly for shore.

When the powder in the hold exploded, windows rattled miles away in New Orleans. Shattered and flaming remnants of the schooner, sent skyward by the blast, hissed into the water and fell to earth as far away as the opposite side of the Mississippi. In the momentary quiet that followed, ash and debris continued to rain down—and the soldiers on the American line heard shouts and cheers from the British side.

Then the enemy fire resumed and, with knowing dread, Andrew Jackson observed that the British had shifted the trajectory of their cannon fire toward the last of the American warships. The USS *Louisiana,* though more than a mile upstream, had just become the target.

Her crew had unfurled her sails, but the *Louisiana,* aided by no more than a whisper of wind and fighting the Mississippi current, could make no headway upstream; that was her only escape route. To the men across the river, British and American alike, the outcome seemed inevitable—but one option remained to save her from the British fire that was now breaking over her quarterdeck. If the wind could not deliver the ship to safety, then manpower would have to do the job.

The *Louisiana*'s boats went over the side, followed by her sailors as they clambered into position at their oars. As if to emphasize the importance of their errand, a shell smashed into the deck of the immobilized ship.

With great ropes tethered to the ninety-nine-foot sloop, the sailors strained at their oars. Other men standing in the shallow water near the shore pulled on ropes, too, but once the cables were taut, the scene seemed frozen, with the little boats, like children tugging on their mother's apron strings, striving to pull the immobilized *Louisiana* to safety.

At first: nothing. Then, slowly, almost imperceptibly, the mother ship began to move. Despite continued fire, fortune was with the Americans and the oarsmen managed to pull the *Louisiana* the half mile needed to get out of the range of the British ordnance.

This time the Americans cheered and, with the cessation of British artillery fire, the day's hostilities came to an end.

A British Assault

The assault on Patterson's little flotilla had blown up one ship and driven the other out of range. Although that action made a direct attack on Jackson's line more feasible, General Pakenham still lacked clear knowledge of his opponent's power and position. The persistent American snipers and militia cavalry patrolling the area between the armies had limited British reconnaissance, a problem that, Pakenham knew, he must correct.

From their position, all the British could see of the American force were the unimpressive cavalry patrols, which, Dickson reported, consisted of men wearing "a kind of blanket dress." The volunteer soldiers had been issued no uniforms, but were dressed in woolen shirts, homemade trousers, and hats of wool or raccoon skin. With long hair and scruffy, unkempt beards, these woodsmen carried "long muskets or rifles."[14]

On December 28, Pakenham organized his force to advance for the purpose of "reconnoit[ering] the enemy's position, or to attack if . . . practicable."[15] He wanted to get closer, to get a better sense of how large Jackson's force was, to try softening up the defenses. The Americans still had to prove themselves to the war-hardened Pakenham.

A frosty morning mist had burned off when four British regiments,

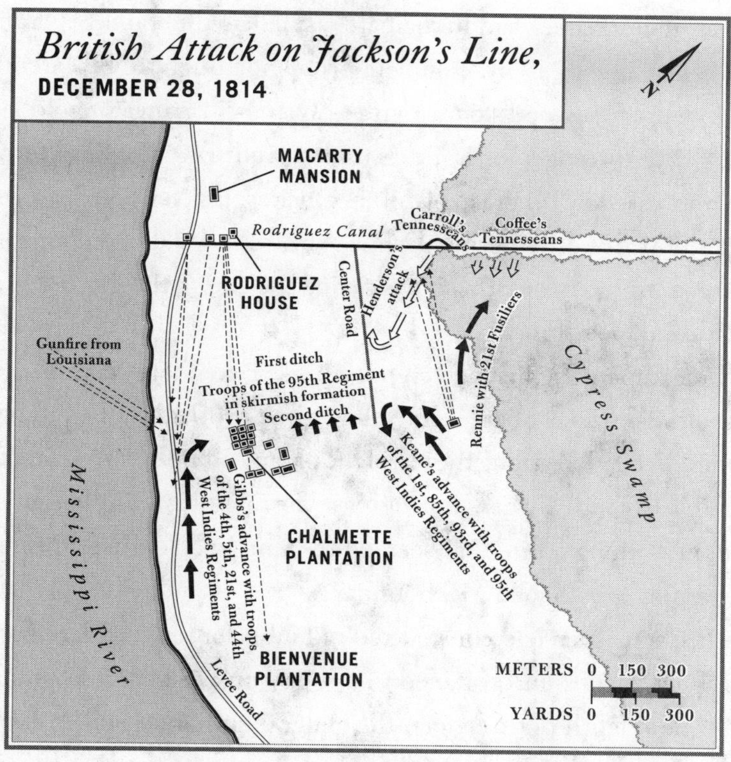

commanded by General Keane, advanced along the edge of the swamp. Four other regiments stepped off along the levee road, led by General Samuel Gibbs, who had arrived with Pakenham as his second in command. Artillerists supported both columns, prepared to bombard the Americans with mortars and rockets.

As the redcoats moved closer to the American line, the rising sun in a clear sky revealed a breastwork before them that, in some places, had reached five feet in height. The American line spanned the terrain from the riverbank to the cypress swamp. When Edward Livingston had brought Jean Lafitte to inspect the line of defense a few days earlier, the privateer had immediately spied a vulnerability. "Lafitte thinks our line to afford complete protection ought to be extended *through* the first wood, to the cypress swamp," Livingston told Jackson.[16] Out of respect for Lafitte's understanding of the local terrain and impressed by his grasp of military tactics, Jackson acted upon the suggestion at once, ordering the line to be extended deep enough into the swampy perimeter that any skirting the end of the defense was a practical impossibility.

Accompanying his men on horseback, Pakenham was surprised to see the muzzles of at least five big guns protruding through the crude crenellations along the top of the parapet. The built-up ramparts were clearly still a work in progress, varying greatly in height and thickness along a line that seemed to bend back on itself near the cypress swamp to follow its boundary.

Jackson's men had constructed redoubts for four artillery batteries. Since the ground softened to a soggy mix of mud and groundwater at a depth of three feet, the general had once again adopted someone else's idea, one that may have been suggested by a ditch-digging slave. The suggestion was to bring bales of unshipped cotton, warehoused in the city, to fill and stiffen the muddy hollows. Jackson ordered it done, and girdled by iron rings, the bales were buried beneath a layer of dirt, with wooden platforms for the guns mounted on top. Two of the cannons were good-size twenty-four-pounders. Two of the gunnery crews were Baratarians, who had arrived that very morning, "red-shirted, bewhiskered, rough and desperate-looking men, all begrimed with smoke and mud."[17]

As the British approached, the outnumbered American pickets in the fields fired volleys but quickly retreated. Pakenham's columns marched forward and soon came within half a mile of the Rodriguez

Canal. The oncoming British troops made an impressive sight in their colorful uniforms of red, gray, green, and tartan, marching to the beat of drums and the call of bugles. To the novice soldiers on the American side this was their first real look at the mighty British war machine on the march. Even as rockets began exploding overhead and British artillery lobbed shells and deadly iron toward the American line, the disciplined British "veterans moved as steadily and closely together as if marching in review."[18]

When the American gunners began returning fire, however, their aim proved deadly: "Scarce a bullet passed over, or fell short of its mark," Gleig recorded, "but all striking full into the midst of our ranks, occasioned terrible havoc."[19] Master Commander Daniel Patterson and the men aboard the *Louisiana,* moored on the opposite bank of the Mississippi, fired a broadside that swept the line of redcoats along the levee. Over the next several hours, the ship's guns would maintain a constant fire, bombarding the British with eight hundred shots, now that the enemy was back in their range.

Hearing the screams of their wounded, the British column hesitated and then stopped. At the order of their officers, the men by the levee sought shelter in ditches, behind tall reeds, finding whatever cover they could.

The British column advancing along the swampland on the other side of the field fared better. They had to deal with fire from the Americans' left flank, manned by Tennesseans under the command of Generals Coffee and Carroll, but they were out of range of the *Louisiana.*

Seeking to get a better understanding of the situation, Pakenham dismounted and moved forward on foot for a better look at the American batteries and battlement. One thing was clear immediately: his limited artillery was inadequate in the face of such fire. He sent back word that work should begin immediately on an earthwork to bring forward his own guns.

Meanwhile, the *Louisiana* continued to bombard the troops closer to the levee, and the land guns mounted on the ramparts maintained a steady fire, aiming in particular at the small British artillery installations.

As the fight unfolded, Jackson received an uninvited visitor, one bringing news from Governor Claiborne.

In the city, he was told, there was talk of surrender: The residents knew about the British approach and their recent attacks, and had heard rumors of the enemy's sheer numbers and military power. Jackson, eager to return to his spyglass and the fight before him, listened with growing impatience to talk of the state legislature and the concern that he might not prevail in the battle now raging outside.

Finally, he had had enough.

"Return to . . . your honorable body," he said firmly, "and say to them from me, that if I was so unfortunate to be beaten . . . and compelled to retreat through New Orleans, they would have a *warm session.*"[20]

"Warm session"?

Jackson later elaborated on his meaning. If he could not defend it, he would burn the city, take up a position up the river, and cut off supplies to the British, thereby forcing them to leave the country. Quite simply, the British were not going to march victorious into any city that he was defending. Nor were any treasonous legislators with a doubtful allegiance to the United States of America going to raise the white flag.

With that, he went back to fighting his battle.

On the British side, Pakenham learned that his handful of artillery pieces were out of action, their carriages shot away. The American cannoneers got high marks for their marksmanship, and Pakenham, seeing that the attack on his left was going nowhere beneath the shower of iron from the *Louisiana,* decided to order a withdrawal.

The British soldiers, accustomed to prevailing in their battles, admitted to shame and indignation as they fell back. Their morale wasn't aided by the fact that the American gunfire required a stealthy withdrawal, one that could not be completed until after dark, leaving many redcoats lying in the field waiting for sunset. A humiliating retreat had followed a proud march into battle, and Pakenham's force slowly countermarched two miles back from the American line, making camp just beyond range of all but the largest of the enemy's cannons.

Whatever the attack's failures—surely Ned Pakenham hadn't led them to the easy victory they expected—the general had managed to get a good look at the enemy position. The deadly American guns, Pakenham resolved, would be his next objective. If he was to succeed in overrunning the American line, the enemy artillery would have to be silenced first and, with only four-, six-, and nine-pound guns at hand, Pakenham ordered that the two eighteen-pounders already dragged to Villeré's plantation be brought forward. And he ordered another eight guns to be brought from the fleet.

As Pakenham made his plans, Jackson supervised the installation of another gun at the center of his ramparts, this one a thirty-two-pounder. He knew the British would be back and better prepared, and he was going to be ready.

The New Year's Day Artillery Fight

Aside from a few minor skirmishes, the opposing armies maintained their distance for three days. Jackson waited for the enemy to make the next big move, since his force, still smaller than Pakenham's, was better protected behind the earthworks. But Jackson tolerated no idleness.

His aide-de-camp Major Latour observed that despite Jackson's evident fatigue, "the energy manifested by General Jackson spread, as it were, . . . and communicated itself to the whole army. . . . If he ordered it to be done . . . immediately a crowd of volunteers offered themselves to carry his views into execution."[21]

Jackson's directives continued to radiate in all directions. At his orders, the city of New Orleans was scoured for needed guns and ammunition, since many freshly recruited militiamen had arrived without weapons. At the front, the commanding general hadn't lessened the pressure to reinforce the earthworks, and the excavation continued without letup. From the British line, one soldier reported, "We could plainly perceive great numbers of men continually at work upon [the American ramparts], mostly blacks . . . but their white people also (the army, we conclude) were constantly employed upon it."[22] After noting that troops at the far end of the defensive line, closest to the swamp, had been badly outnumbered by the force Pakenham led several days earlier, Jackson sent more men to strengthen that flank, including more Tennesseans and Choctaws.

Aware that there was a chance his major line of defense could be overrun by Pakenham's superior force, Jackson ordered his engineers to design and construct two secondary lines to the rear; one was a mile and a half west of the Rodriguez Canal, the other almost two miles closer to New Orleans. Jackson added more artillery batteries to the main front so a baker's dozen guns protruded through the defensive wall, ranging from a small brass carronade near the swamp to the big thirty-two-pounder near the center.

Nor had Jackson neglected the opposite bank of the river. A team of 150 slaves worked to complete a parapet lining a canal there. From the *Louisiana,* Commodore Patterson's men brought more cannons ashore—a twenty-four-pounder and two twelve-pounders—and dug them in at the right bank post. They were reinforced there by Brigadier General David Morgan and 450 Louisiana militiamen laboring at the earthworks.

But the British had been busy, too, readying to put in place a new strategy for a new year.

Silent Marching

At nightfall on New Year's Eve, half the British army advanced in near silence. They passed the position of their pickets, stopping just six hundred yards from the Rodriguez Canal. With two regiments on guard duty, the rest of the soldiers stacked their arms and went to work with the spades, picks, and sledges they carried.

Speed was of the essence: Pakenham's men were constructing new gun emplacements and had only a few hours before the sun would rise, exposing them to the guns of the watching Americans. As the men mounded up earth, sculpting a small version of the American embankment behind which their gunners could take cover, Admiral Cochrane's sailors dragged ten eighteen- and four twenty-four-pound carronades forward. They had rowed their heavy loads (the bigger guns weighed more than two tons) from the fleet at Ship Island and dragged them to the camp, using country carts designed for moving sugar barrels. Now they used the last of their strength to position the iron guns and their heavy carriages behind the new earthworks. They aimed them at the American camp.

As the sky brightened in the early hours, the American lookouts watched nervously. General Jackson and his men had heard the British at work in the darkness, and were anxious to see what the enemy had been up to. But the arrival of morning brought no clarity; a dense fog rolled in, completely concealing the field of battle.

Dread mounted as the fog lingered, leaving the Americans in uncomfortable anticipation of an attack. Interrogations of British deserters had revealed that Pakenham had called for major troop reinforcements. Once they arrived, everyone assumed he would attack, and it was possible that the sound in the night had been that of the fresh troops preparing. Then, just as the blanket of thick morning mist burned off around eight o'clock, the ominous calm gave way to the deafening din of artillery. The British were firing their newly advanced cannons at the American line. In particular, the British artillery aimed for the Macarty house, where they knew General Jackson made his headquarters.

The guns hit their mark, and the shrill scream of rockets overhead accompanied the sounds of the house's destruction. "Bricks, splinters of wood and furniture, rockets and balls," Major Latour reported, "were flying in all directions."[23] In the minutes that followed, more than a hundred cannonballs, rockets, and shells crashed into the plantation house. Its porches were "beaten down, and the building made a complete wreck." Miraculously, no one was hurt, and Jackson, as was his habit, had quickly departed—not to flee, but to fight. According to his adjutant Major Reid, it was Jackson's practice, "on the first appearance of danger . . . instantly to proceed to the line."[24]

From the front, Jackson could look upon the result of the enemy's overnight labors as the British bombardment continued: There were three new gun emplacements, crescent-shaped batteries that offered the gunnery crews protection both from the American line and from guns fired across the Mississippi. Including three mortars and two howitzers, twenty-two guns had been positioned by the English on crude wooden platforms. In the interests of speedy installation, the British had brought forward barrels of sugar found at plantations they'd ransacked as a substitute for sandbags. Rolled into place upright, the hogsheads became a protective parapet atop the batteries.

Jackson also took in another ominous sight: Some two hundred yards to the rear of the British guns stood the brightly uniformed infantry. Again, two columns had been formed into battle array, one on either side of the field, ready to attack. Less obvious was a third, smaller party, hidden in the dense cover at the edge of the swamp.[25]

There was little Jackson's men could do but hope their guns would hold off the invasion. And at the order of Jackson's chief artillerist—"*Let her off!*"—the American guns were soon returning fire.[26]

The British had more guns than the Americans, but from their lower elevation on the plain, their aim was skewed, often shooting high above their marks, sending their loads soaring over the American line. Other shots thudded harmlessly into the soft earth of the embankment, though one arching round hit an American powder carriage; the explosion was so loud, the gunnery paused briefly and a distant cheer was heard from the British line. Another almost hit its mark when it grazed the Baratarian Dominique You, a gun commander and half brother of Jean Lafitte. Furious, he swore an oath even before binding up his wound: "I will pay them for that!"[27]

Meanwhile, General Jackson rode back and forth along the line encouraging his men. "Don't mind these rockets, they are mere toys to amuse children," he told them, calming the inexperienced soldiers and rallying the seasoned.[28] His encouragement worked and the earthworks held; a few of the American guns were eventually silenced, but the parapet was little damaged by the English artillery. The Americans' fire proved better directed and, within an hour, several of the enemy guns had been put out of commission.

On the other side of the line, General Pakenham watched as his options faded. The hogsheads of sugar were ineffective; cannonballs penetrated them as if the barrels were empty. The supply of ammunition was dwindling, and his artillery fire began to slow, then became irregular; finally, by midafternoon, the British had retired from the field. "When the batteries have silenced the enemy's fire and opened his works, the position will be carried as follows . . ." read Pakenham's written orders from the night before.[29] But that had not happened. It was British artillery that had been silenced; no hole had been torn in the American line. No attack had been possible.

"We retired, therefore, not only baffled and disappointed, but in some degree disheartened and discontented," Gleig observed. "All our plans had as yet proved abortive."[30] The British fighters still had nothing to show for the hardships they had suffered over the course of the preceding days—not to mention weeks.

A New Plan

The redcoats' morale was at low ebb. To retreat was not in the nature of the Royal Army; however, as the year 1815 began, Wellington's veterans had been forced to retrace their own steps for the second time in a week. Having to laboriously drag their ordnance back to their own lines after dark on New Year's Day only added to the sense of insult. British casualty counts were at least twice the American losses.

Dysentery was taking hold in the camp, and rations were poor, the army having exhausted the resources of the surrounding plantations. The men subsisted on "maggoty pork and weevily biscuit."[31] The coffee supply had been depleted. The round-the-clock harassment by American snipers and artillery continued, and the rate of desertion was rising. The siege was lasting far longer than the invaders had expected, and the easy and glorious victory they anticipated had not come to pass.

Andrew Jackson and the Americans had proved formidable foes, but Sir Edward Pakenham was undeterred. He had faced the finest armies in Europe. He had delivered the decisive blow in victories that won Great Britain, Wellington, and himself great honor. And here, on the American Gulf Coast, his enemy was little more than a ragtag array of volunteers. They ranged from dandily dressed New Orleans gentlemen to the "dirty shirts," men armed with "duck guns." This band was led by a broken-down country lawyer whose only claim to military fame was the defeat of some underequipped Indians.

Certain he could still defeat the Americans, Pakenham summoned his officers to a brief meeting: Ned had a plan. To capture New Orleans, his army had to accomplish one simple thing: blast through Jackson's fortification. To do that, he explained, they must hurl the army, with even greater force than before, at their opponents—but this time they would do it after pummeling the enemy into near submission *with its own guns*.

The key was a direct attack on the American line on the west bank. Once the guns across the river had been captured, they could turn Patterson's cannons back on Jackson's army, catching the Americans in a cross fire between the west bank artillery and Pakenham's Chalmette batteries. Then the main force of the ever-enlarging British army would drive through the American earthworks in the biggest attack yet.

To do so, however, boats from the bayous and Lake Borgne would have to be taken overland to the Mississippi since there was no waterway linking the bayou to the river. Pakenham proposed rolling the boats on timbers, but Admiral Cochrane suggested an alternative: his men could extend the waterway from the Villeré canal to the levee. Initially, Pakenham had his doubts, but Cochrane got the nod.

The excavation of the waterway would take days, so crews of soldiers and sailors went to work on January 2, in four six-hour shifts. By Friday, January 6, it was done. And, on the American side, the ramparts had grown taller, thanks to the continued exertions of men with shovels.

That same day, Pakenham's spirits got a real lift. More reinforcements arrived, adding two full regiments to an army that now exceeded eight thousand men. And these men were superb soldiers. One of Pakenham's generals sang their praises: "Two such corps would turn the tide of a general action. We were rejoiced!"[32] Ammunition for the guns was brought forward, some of it in the knapsacks of the arriving infantry. The work of preparing cartridges was undertaken; more than four hundred men spent their days packing powder and shot. The notion of an imminent victory, of shared spoils after the capture of the city, began once again to take hold among the invaders.

On Saturday, January 7, Pakenham confidently issued his orders. William Thornton was to lead the west bank attack force. Using vessels floated into the Mississippi via the newly dug canal, his two regiments, together with 200 sailors and 400 marines, would embark at midnight. He and his 1,300 men were to land at daylight and capture the American force on the right bank.

On firing a rocket to signal their success, the main attack on the works overlooking the Rodriguez Canal could begin. Pakenham had reason to feel optimistic. After all, he had the finest fighting force in the world and, if his scouts had it right, a considerable advantage in both men and artillery. What didn't he have? Andrew Jackson and the American commitment to victory.

The Quiet Before the Tumult

On the night of January 7, General Jackson retired early. The intelligence of the preceding hours, gained from prisoners captured on the river, led him to one conclusion: the British attack was imminent; almost certainly it would come with dawn the following day.

He had seen for himself through his spyglass that the British camp was a den of activity. Major Latour told him that the British were bundling sugarcane stalks and making scaling ladders, to be used, they supposed, to bridge the moat and climb the American earthworks.

The overextended general understood very well that a few hours' rest could only help him do his duty: the past week had been enervating, as changeable as the weather.

After the fight on the first, there was good news on January 2: some three thousand new militiamen, most from Kentucky, would soon arrive to join Jackson's melting-pot army. Every man mattered in this tough fight and, as Jackson watched for the Kentuckians on the third, he wrote to Secretary of War James Monroe: "I do not know what may be [the Britishers'] further design—Whether [they will] redouble their efforts, or . . . apply them elsewhere."[33]

On the fourth, the Kentuckians did arrive, but they were poorly armed (fewer than one in ten carried a rifle) and so badly clothed the men visibly shivered as they walked through New Orleans. A frustrated General Jackson observed, "I have never in my life seen a Kentuckian without a gun, a pack of cards, and jug of whiskey."[34]

His anticipation of another British attack elevated his impatience with everyone around him. When he discovered that promised shipments of ammunition had not arrived from the city, he summoned Governor Claiborne, the man charged with providing munitions. Jackson warned the intimidated Claiborne, "By the Almighty God, if you do not send me balls and powder instantly, I shall chop off your head, and have it rammed into one of those fieldpieces."[35]

On the sixth, he had the Kentuckians with guns take positions at the Rodriguez Canal; the others would reinforce the secondary lines of defense.

All week long, Jackson configured his troops with care. He chose the 430 men of the Seventh Regular Infantry to anchor his right, shoulder to shoulder with 740 Louisiana militiamen. Next came the Forty-Fourth Regiment, numbering 240 men, with the Kentuckians (500 in number) and the largest corps of all, 1,600 of his fellow Tennesseans, at the far left. The 230 Mississippi dragoons remained to the rear, with a mix of others completing the left bank army. The total came to almost 5,000 men. Across the river were roughly 1,000 troops, including some Kentuckians and more Louisiana militia.[36] What Andrew Jackson had was a collection of Americans of all colors, creeds, and ethnic groups, melted into one fighting force, coming together to make military history.

All but two of his cannons were embedded in the earthworks; only a new, not-yet-finished redoubt, with two 6-pounders, sat forward of the main line, giving it a commanding view of both the levee road and the front of the earthworks. The other eleven guns—a mix of 6-, 12-, 18-, and 24-pounders—plus the big 32-pounder, were arranged in batteries at intervals along the main line. They were manned by a mix of navy gunners, Louisiana militiamen, and Baratarians.

The ramparts themselves, the work of a fortnight and more of tedious, backbreaking labor, remained as varied as the men charged with defending them. At the base, the earthen wall ranged from fourteen to twenty feet in thickness; its height, too, depended upon where on the line a man stood. In some places, the ramparts reached just five feet, in others perhaps twice that, but the elevation was enhanced by the four-foot depth of the muddy canal at the foot.

Jackson ordered the ramparts constantly manned and, as night fell on January 7, he rode the line. He and the men could hear hammering and digging sounds in the near distance but Jackson offered encouraging words, talking to gunners and soldiers, officers and infantry, the volunteers and the regulars. By order and by example, in every way he knew how, Jackson had readied his army, in mind and body, to defend New Orleans. The array of troops he had managed to assemble was truly remarkable: Tennesseans and Kentuckians on the left, battalions of Indians and Africans in the middle, dragoons from Mississippi in reserve, and a blending of regulars and militias from a mix of places distributed such that the length of earthworks was lined with American guns.

After dining lightly, Jackson took to his sofa to try to sleep. Several of his aides lay on the floor, still in uniform, their guns and sword belts at their sides. On previous evenings, the night watch in the camp had been entrusted to alternating companies of soldiers, but on this Saturday night the entire army had been instructed to bed down with their weapons within reach.

A few hours later, Jackson awoke in the darkness. The time was one o'clock, and he heard footsteps in the hall.

"Who's there?" he called.

The sentry admitted a courier with a message from Commodore Patterson. Late the previous day, standing on the shore opposite the Villeré plantation, he had seen enemy forces loading cannons in the barges. He assumed that he and his west bank position would be their target. The navy man asked Jackson to send reinforcements to the opposite side of the river in case the British attacked there.

Anxious and impatient, the general required only a moment to consider the matter before turning Patterson down. Time was too short for more men to reach Patterson—Jackson had already dispatched four hundred Kentuckians to reinforce Patterson and Brigadier General Morgan, the Louisiana militiaman posted with him. And nothing Patterson said persuaded Jackson that the major attack would be anywhere but on his own side of the Mississippi.

"I have no men to spare," he told the messenger.[37] Patterson and Morgan were on their own. Jackson had no idea of the misstep he had just made, but he was uninterested in going back to sleep. Turning, he addressed the aides around him.

"Gentlemen, we have slept enough. Rise. The enemy will be upon us in a few minutes."[38]

They would indeed, and not only in the way Jackson expected.

The Ursuline Nuns

Jackson enjoyed one advantage over Pakenham. As he and his officers dressed for battle, many of the devout women of New Orleans knelt just five miles away, praying that he and his soldiers would save the city.

The word of imminent battle had reached the households of New Orleans. Many women—wives and sisters and mothers of soldiers—feared not just for the men they loved as they prepared to fight the enemy. Rumors spreading dread of what a mob of conquering British soldiers might do to the women and to New Orleans if the city fell had been circulating, too. Determined to lend their voices and entreaties, female residents had made their way on the night of January 7 to the Ursuline convent.

The women joined the sisters in a vigil at the Chapel of Our Lady of Consolation. There the nuns had moved their most honored icon to a prominent place over the altar. It was a wooden sculpture of Our Lady of Prompt Succor. Five years earlier the large carved statue had arrived from France: dressed in a sweeping golden robe, her head adorned with a great crown, Mary held the child Jesus in her arms. Another statue of Our Lady of Prompt Succor was said to have miraculously defended the nuns in the past; in one of the great fires that had swept New Orleans, the flames had approached the convent but had been turned away by a sudden change in the wind's direction when a nun placed a statue of Our Lady in the window. The convent was one of the few buildings in the city that survived the fire.

Now, the people of New Orleans were hoping for more divine intervention. With the great statue of a wordless Blessed Virgin looming over the nuns and the women of the city, the nearly inaudible whispers of petitioners sent skyward pleas, "implor[ing] the God of battles to nerve the arm of their protectors, and turn the tide of combat against the invaders of their country."[39]

During the night, more and more women thronged to the chapel.

Within its walls, some wept, while others called out for divine intervention. Vows were made, including one by the Mother Superior, Sainte Marie Olivier de Vézin, who had previously offered General Jackson the services of the Ursuline sisters in caring for the wounded.

In the early hours of January 8, she made a fresh promise, this time to God. If the Americans prevailed in the day's battle—and that remained a mighty *if*—a solemn mass of Thanksgiving would be held in celebration and remembrance every year into the distant future.

In not so many hours, the outcome would be known.

CHAPTER 12

Day of Destiny

These d——d Yankee riflemen can pick a squirrel's eye out as far as they can see it.

—**Anonymous British prisoner of war**

A flagstaff stood at the center of the American line, defiantly flying the American colors. On January 8, 1815, the question of the day was, *Would it still wave at sunset?*

General Edward Pakenham, like Jackson, had also retired to his bed the night before, but he'd risen a little later, at five o'clock. In the predawn darkness he and his army, once again, had advanced toward the Americans; now, with the sky in the east just gaining the vague reddish tinge of dawn, he listened. From his position near the middle of the Chalmette Plain, the British commander wanted nothing more than to hear the sounds of William Thornton's guns echoing across the Mississippi.

The new waterway at the Villeré plantation had broken through to the river two days before, making possible the planned launch of Thornton and his men the previous night. But, to his acute regret, Pakenham would learn soon after waking that the wished-for gunfire would be delayed. Nor would he see a rocket fired from the opposite shore, the agreed-upon signal for success in breaching Patterson's works.

Colonel William Thornton and his entire mission were running late, very late indeed.

Thanks to the failure of Admiral Cochrane's design for a temporary lock between the river and the bayou, most of the British ships had grounded in the canal. The hastily constructed dam at the near end of the canal extension had given way, permitting the water in the lock to run off toward Lake Borgne. That meant only a few of the craft in the planned forty-seven-boat flotilla reached the river's shallows before the larger barges grounded in the mud of the canal. Royal Navy sailors had set to work to drag more boats to open water, but less than two-thirds of the boats, many of them small, had made it through. When Thornton's amphibious force finally departed, it had shrunk to fewer than five hundred men.

Worse yet, given all the delays in maneuvering the boats through the makeshift canal, they sailed eight hours late.

Standing poised to order the main attack, his men in readiness, Pakenham, an experienced military tactician, understood exactly what the delay at the watercourse meant for the battle. "Thornton's people," a resigned General Pakenham said to a trusted officer beside him, "will be of no use whatever to the general attack."[1] With the night move across the water badly delayed, the general faced a momentous decision. Attack head on, or wait for Thornton's men to breach the flank?

Observing Pakenham's agitation—and knowing how crucial Patterson's guns might be to the success or failure of the day's fighting—one of his adjutants, Captain Harry Smith, suggested a rapid retreat in the last moments before sunrise. "We [will be] under the enemy's fire so soon as discovered," he warned. There might be time to reset the plan and return another day.

After almost a fortnight of delays and setbacks, Pakenham rejected the idea.

"I have twice deferred the attack," he replied. "We are strong in numbers now comparatively. It will cost more men, [but] the assault must be made."

Smith tried once more, again urging delay, but Pakenham's mind was made up.

"Smith, order the rocket to be fired."[2]

With a whistling message skittering across the sky, the British marched forward.

"That is their signal for advance, I believe," said General Andrew Jackson, hearing the hiss and bang of the first rocket. It shot skyward from the edge of the swamp, followed by a second, this one from the other side of the field.[3]

Since 4:00 a.m., Jackson's men had been awake, armed, and ready behind their earthworks. Suddenly alert, as after the crack of the pistol shot signaling the start of a horse race, the American artillerists stood by, their loggerheads red-hot and ready to fire their guns. The soldiers peered over the ramparts. The rifles and muskets had been loaded. In that moment, every heart began to beat more rapidly.

But to the Americans' surprise, the enemy remained unseen. A thick morning fog hugged the ground, obscuring the oncoming army.

The British Ranks

Pakenham's orders, written and issued the night before, divided his forces on the Chalmette Plain into three brigades.

Under the command of General Samuel Gibbs, the main attack was to come from the British right. At the vanguard would be the Forty-Fourth Infantry, an Irish regiment ordered to collect the three hundred bundles of sugarcane and sixteen ladders from an earthen redoubt partway to the American line. On reaching the canal, they were to throw the cane stalks into the ditch and then raise the scaling ladders. Two regiments of infantry, along with three companies of rifles, were charged with protecting the column's right from any counterattack and to provide cover as the Forty-Fourth approached the ditch. If all went well, the larger body of Gibbs's brigade would follow the Forty-Fourth. Crossing the ditch on the canes and scaling the ladders over the earthworks, they would penetrate the previously unbreakable American line and be face-to-face with American forces.

But this plan would fall apart, when whether intentionally or unintentionally, the Forty-Fourth would leave the canes and ladders behind, realizing perhaps that running full speed into the teeth of lethal American fire would amount to a suicide mission. Carrying ladders instead of pointing guns, they would be easy targets for Jackson's skilled marksmen.

Barely a half hour before dawn, a dismayed General Gibbs discovered the blunder. Without the ladders, Gibbs's men had no way to scale Jackson's wall. Knowing this, Gibbs instantly ordered the regiment to retreat some five hundred yards and bring the ladders forward, but, when first rocket's report echoed, the men with the heavy ones were still well behind the van and moving "in a most irregular and unsoldier-like manner."[4]

The outraged General Gibbs bellowed at Thomas Mullins, the leader of the Forty-Fourth, threatening to hang him from the "highest tree in that swamp."[5] But, the error made, it could not be undone, and Mullins's crucial failure would become the subject of debate for generations of historians.[6] (Mullins himself faced a court-martial back in England; though convicted of having neglected orders, he was cleared of the charge of having done so willfully.)

Whatever the cause of the mistake, the British plan to scale the earthworks had been foiled and, for Mullins's men, the consequences

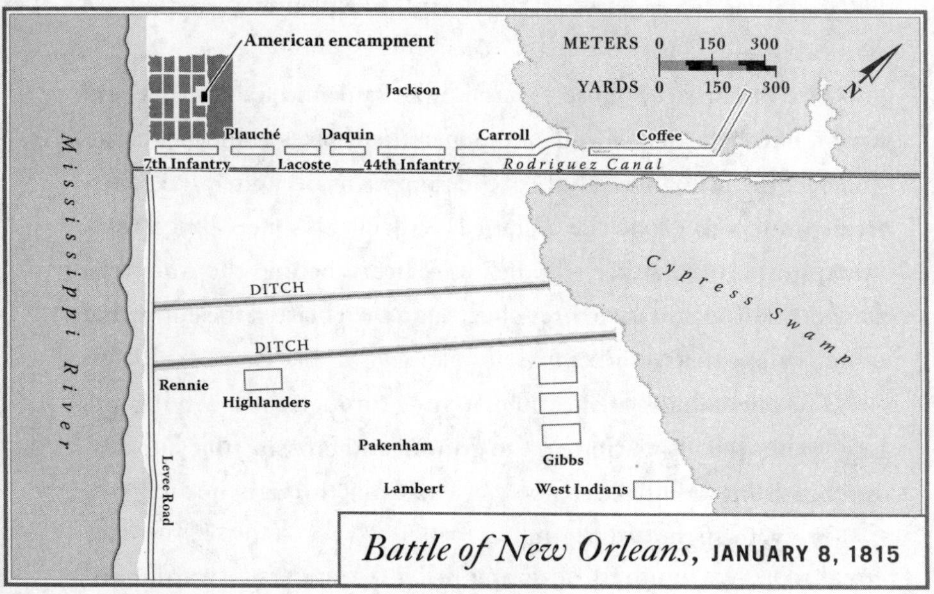

Battle of New Orleans, JANUARY 8, 1815

on January 8 were awful. "In less time than one can write it, the 44th Foot was literary swept from the face of the earth," recorded Quartermaster E. N. Burroughs. "No such execution by small arms has ever been or heard of."[7]

On the opposite flank, a smaller force of companies commanded by Lieutenant Colonel Robert Rennie was to advance along the riverbank. Their objective was to overrun Jackson's new forward redoubt—at any cost. Pakenham needed its two guns, with their line of sight across the field, to be silenced, thereby preventing a slaughter of British troops as they reached the Rodriguez Canal and clambered up the earthworks.

A third force—consisting of General Keane, in command, and the Ninety-Third Highlanders and Ninety-Fifth Rifles—was to move on the center of the earthworks. Pakenham left in reserve the latest arrivals, the Seventh Fusiliers and the Forty-Third, led by General John Lambert.

The British drew closer, marching in rank and file to bugle and drum, but, before the forms of the men themselves could be distinguished, the brilliant red hues of their uniforms permitted the American gunners to gauge the distance. As Jackson's men aimed their guns, strains of "Yankee Doodle" were heard behind the American ranks. The Yankees gave three cheers and then blasted the entire line of redcoats with a round of fire.

The oncoming British, still marching through the low-lying fog, saw "cannon-balls tearing up the ground and crossing one another, and bounding along like so many cricket-balls through the air."[8]

Truly, the fight had begun.

The Bloodiest Parade

From the ramparts, the entire field of battle was visible to General Jackson. To his left, a British column, some sixty men across and marching in close ranks, walked out of the mist near the swamp. The sky was suddenly alight with a shower of rockets and, on the opposite side of the field, an even larger British force emerged, advancing en masse. For the American officers watching from behind the earthwork, two-thirds of the Chalmette Plain appeared suddenly to be occupied by a very determined enemy. It was a relentless red wall of British soldiers marching toward them.

As they charged the American gun emplacements, the Twenty-First Regiment looked down the huge barrel of the biggest American cannon, the thirty-two-pounder. Charging forward, advancing in double-quick time, George Gleig and his men failed to reach the gun position before the weapon discharged. Packed with musket balls, the load "served to sweep the center of the attacking force into eternity."[9]

Although the Twenty-First fell into disarray, the troops behind continued to push forward.

On the left, Colonel Rennie's force advanced rapidly, making for the crescent-shaped battery. Despite intense rifle and artillery fire, some of which came from across the river where Patterson's guns were now in action, the British closed rapidly on their objective. Rennie led the British attackers. He took a shrapnel wound in the calf, but that didn't stop him. He managed to leap through a gun embrasure a moment after its cannon fired, calling to his men, "Hurra, boys, the day is ours!"[10]

An instant later, on the exposed rear of the unfinished gun emplacement, Rennie fell. A musket ball entered his skull just above the eyebrows, lodging in his brain. He'd become an easy target for the marksmen in Captain Beale's Rifles, and the same volley that killed him took the lives of several men around him. Seeing the danger, the others in his company turned and fled.

When the main British force approached the center of the American line at a distance of two hundred yards, rifle fire erupted: the enemy walked into "a sparkling sheet of fire."[11] Farther along the line, the charging British soldiers met with the same shower of musket balls. Jackson's forces, crowded behind the parapets, took turns: One man in front fired, then fell back to reload, making way for the next soldier to empty his gun into the mass of oncoming humanity. Some riflemen fired as quickly as they could reload; others sighted carefully from the top of the breastwork, took deliberate aim, then shot.[12]

Standing high on the parapet with a panoramic view of the field, Jackson surveyed the battle unfolding beneath him. He offered repeated exhortations.

"Stand to your guns, don't waste your ammunition," he cried.

"See that every shot tells!"

"Give it to them, boys; let us finish the business today!"[13]

He was the backbone.

As the battle continued, supplies were running low, and tempers were running high. Jackson moved along the line but stopped at gun battery number three, under the command of the Baratarian Dominique You. A short, barrel-chested man, the pirate had impressed the general. ("If I were ordered to storm the gates of hell, with Captain Dominique as my lieutenant," Jackson said, "I would have no misgivings of the result.")[14]

Now, however, with eyes swollen from the smoke in the air, You stood by a silent twenty-four-pounder.

"What! What! By the Eternal, what is the matter?" Jackson demanded. "You have ceased firing!"

You looked up at Jackson. "Of course, general, of course!" he explained. "The powder is good for nothing—fit only to shoot blackbirds with, and not redcoats!"

Jackson turned to an aide. Before galloping off, he ordered, "Tell the ordnance officer that I will have him shot in five minutes as a traitor, if Dominique complains any more of his powder."[15]

Just minutes into the battle, according to one Kentucky rifleman, "the smoke was so thick that everything seemed to be covered up in it."[16] But the woodsmen, armed with .38-caliber long rifles (the barrels were forty-two inches long), kept firing with deadly accuracy. Half-hidden in the dense cypress vegetation, they loaded their guns with balls and buckshot. Their fire was nearly constant and, according to one Louisiana merchant watching down the line, "the whole right of the British column was mowed down by these invisible riflemen."[17]

General Keane's column had also fallen under intense fire, and Keane himself, with wounds in the neck and thigh, had been carried from the field. With him gone, the resolution of his men wavered and they began to fall back even as General Lambert's forces advanced to reinforce the charge.[18]

Some British troops had reached the Rodriguez Canal and tried to scale the earthen parapet. But firm footholds proved hard to find in the slippery mud and, without ladders, those who began the climb found the soft earth gave way, sending them sliding back down. From above, "a murderous discharge of musketry [caused] . . . a dreadful loss of men and officers."[19]

The immense battle was being fought across the breadth of the plain but, to the veteran British fighters, their enemy seemed close to invisible. From below, it appeared to the attackers as if the Americans, "without so much as lifting their faces above the rampart, swung their firelocks by one arm over the wall, and discharged them directly upon [our] heads."[20]

Even to a seasoned infantry officer who earned honors fighting Napoleon, this field of battle was overwhelming: "The echo from the cannonade and musketry was so tremendous . . . [that it] seemed as if the earth was cracking and tumbling to pieces, or as if the heavens were rent asunder by the most terrific peals of thunder that ever rumbled; it was the most awful and the grandest mixture of sounds."[21]

"And the flashes of fire looked as if coming out of the bowels of the earth."[22]

On the British right, General Gibbs went down. As Gibbs was carried from the field, Pakenham, together with his staff, galloped forward from his post well back from the front line. After removing his hat, the commanding general rode into midst of the battle.

The men around him were "falling and staggering like drunken men from the effects of the fire."[23] Some were advancing, others retreating, but they responded to Pakenham's desperate urging. "For shame," he called to them, "recollect that you are British soldiers!"[24] The troops had begun to re-form when a musket ball slammed into the general's knee. When another rifleman shot his horse dead, Pakenham fell to the ground but, despite an arm that hung limp from still another wound, he demanded the mount of a junior officer. The general needed the help of an aide-de-camp to mount the animal and, just as he was attempting to settle into the saddle, an artillery round whistled in.

A deadly iron ball ripped into Pakenham's groin. This time, his spine mangled by the grapeshot, the general collapsed into the arms of his aide-de-camp.

He, too, was carried to the rear, and the bearers laid their commanding general down beneath a great live oak tree in the center of the field, just out of firing range. The surgeon summoned to his side could do nothing, but the dying Pakenham was able to utter one last command. For the ear of John Lambert, the only British major general left standing, Pakenham whispered, "Tell him . . . to send forward the reserves."

Pakenham had fallen, well short of New Orleans, and would die quietly on the battlefield within the hour. General Gibbs, though in evident agony, survived into the next day, before joining Pakenham in death.[25]

Barely two hundred yards away, Jackson's men suffered miraculously few casualties behind their protective parapet. And in the convent, the nuns prayed on.

On the West Bank

The attack across the river—Pakenham's best hope, his only hope—occurred altogether too late. Pakenham himself was beyond hearing, but more than an hour into the attack, the sound of gunfire could finally be distinguished across the water.

The *pop, pop, pop* of a musketry volley was followed by the boom of artillery. Colonel Thornton's force was attacking the forward line of Captain Morgan's Louisiana militia.

Far behind schedule at launch, Thornton's mission had been

further delayed by the boatmen's complete failure to anticipate the strong Mississippi currents. Once the British boats were well launched into the river, the driving waters carried them far downstream from the intended landing place. By the time they reached the opposite shore, the redcoats had a four-mile march north toward their objective—and it would be a trek accompanied by the sounds of the battle already begun across the river at the Chalmette Plain. To their chagrin, Thornton and his men could also see Patterson's guns just ahead, firing freely at the wave of attacking redcoats across the river.

More determined than ever, however, Thornton's band of soldiers, sailors, and marines attacked the breastwork manned by the advance guard of Louisiana militia. Unlike the great berm that loomed over the Chalmette battlefield, the west bank ramparts proved to be no great obstacle to the British. At first, artillery fire slowed their advance, but, noting the Americans' right flank was poorly protected, Thornton ordered his troops to sweep left and attack there. Seeing that they would soon be overrun, many of the militia troops simply fled.

Patterson, watching from his redoubt a few hundred yards away, recognized that the tide ran against him. Before the British force could reach him, he ordered his men to spike the guns. A length of iron rod was hammered into the vent, or touchhole, at the rear of each gun. The guns would not fire again until the spikes were removed, a time-consuming and laborious process. Then the Americans retreated.

The west bank battle was over; the British now controlled the position. Yet there were no true winners: Thornton was wounded in the fight and Patterson had walked away unscathed. The British had the guns but the artillery had been rendered entirely useless—Jackson's men at the Rodriguez Canal would not be fired upon by Patterson's guns, this day or any other. The fight would become a postscript to the terrible tragedy that had befallen General Pakenham's force on the opposite bank.

There, as the only British major general still standing, Lambert by default had become the ranking officer of the New Orleans mission. He had watched as the regiments Pakenham had sent into battle were shredded by Jackson's firepower. His two regiments remained largely intact; they had been held in reserve that morning. But he had no doubt he was left to shoulder a great defeat, that his job now was to begin to plan his exit. In the coming hours, he would order Thornton—against the recommendations of Admiral Cochrane—to abandon the hard-won west bank and rejoin the main British force.

A Flag of Truce

The guns had quieted across the field by the time a flag of truce reached Jackson at midday. With the outcome of the battle no longer in doubt, he had retired to his quarters at the Macarty house. Before doing so, he walked the entire length of the American line and, in the company of his staff, he stopped at each command. He addressed the men and their officers, offering "words of praise and grateful commendation." To his troops, he seemed the most erect, warm, and relaxed version of himself, the proud victor.[26]

The enemy's courier brought him a request for a cease-fire so the British could bury their dead. The signer was General Lambert—a name unknown to Jackson—but the two men soon agreed to terms.

Though it was the official end of the battle, a more poignant surrender had occurred earlier when, on the left of the American earthworks, some Kentucky riflemen noticed a white flag waving. The

Kentuckians held their fire and, as word moved up the line, the din of gunshots ceased. In the quiet, a fresh gust of wind cleared the dense gun smoke, and the Americans could see the bearer of the white handkerchief. A British officer, he held the makeshift pennant high on a sword or a stick. Some said he was a major, and epaulets decorated his shoulders.

He stepped over the breastwork and was quickly surrounded by Americans. One of the Tennesseans, "a private all over begrimed with dust and powder," demanded his sword. The enemy officer hesitated until an American officer ordered, "Give it up!"

In the next moment, holding the weapon in both hands, the man who represented the Crown handed his sword to a humble American soldier, executing a polite bow as he did so.[27]

No one on the Chalmette Plain remained in doubt as to the victor in the Battle of New Orleans.

The Bloodied Field

With the roar of artillery in the distance, the women gathered at the Cathedral of St. Louis had continued to pray. The doors were open as usual to the people of the town, but this morning's High Mass was said to "a congregation of shuddering women."[28] Their fears were fed by the sounds of war.

"The cannon [fire] . . . seemed like one continued peal of tremendous thunder," wrote one lady of the city. She and her neighbors listened in horror. "We were prepared to run . . . knowing that if [the British] got the upper hand . . . our lives would be destroyed."[29] Instead, many sought spiritual solace in the pews beneath the cathedral's twin towers. The service was conducted by the Very Reverend William Dubourg, the vicar apostolic. He offered up the holy sacrifice of the Mass to the accompaniment of collective prayers of the citizenry at the cathedral and the pious sisters of the Ursuline convent, all seeking the success of General Jackson and the troops on the Chalmette Plain. According to one later account, a courier entered the chapel in the middle of the Mass, crying, "Victory is ours!"[30] Were the community's supplications being answered?

On the Chalmette Plain, the firing had stopped. Long before any official word arrived from the front, rumors of a big victory traveled up the riverbank, neighbor to neighbor. The people of New Orleans ran into the streets; in place of distant gunfire, cheers of joy echoed. When a messenger from the battlefield arrived, riding a worn-out-looking horse, he hurried about, asking surgeons, apothecaries, and anyone with a cart to come to the field of battle. There were wounded to be tended, too many to count—most of them British.[31]

Back at the Rodriguez Canal, said one soldier, the scene was "a sea of blood." The illusion resulted from hundreds of red uniforms obscuring the stubble of last year's sugarcane crop. The letting of blood had indeed been great, leaving an unfathomable number of dead and dying soldiers prostrate on the Chalmette Plain. In some places the bodies were so numerous that it seemed possible to walk without ever touching the ground for a distance of perhaps two hundred yards.[32]

The lines of attack could easily be read in the array of dead. The terrible carnage was at its worst near the center of the field, but other broad bands of slain soldiers commemorated the British assaults near the levee and by the swamp.

There were rows and stacks of bodies even before the field

surgeons began their work. Some corpses had no heads, while others were missing arms or legs. The lifeless faces were a distillation of fear and pain; the dying men's expressions had been frozen as they screamed or cried. Oddly, some looked to have been laughing.

There were stirrings amid the corpses. Wounded men moaned and screamed and called out for help but, as the astonished Americans watched from the ramparts, hundreds of the British got to their feet, men who had "fallen at our first fire upon them, without having received so much as a scratch."[33] Some of the cowards ran for the British line; others surrendered. Said Jackson later, "I never had so grand and awful an idea of the resurrection as on that day."[34]

No two accounts of the battle, whether written that week, that month, that century, or in the many decades since, would agree on the exact casualty count, but all agreed it was stunningly high. According to one British infantry captain, "three generals, seven colonels, seventy-five officers, . . . a total of seventeen hundred and eighty-one officers and soldiers, had fallen in a few minutes."[35] Some writers elevated the number—General Keane reported 2,030, other sources have said 3,000. Jackson initially gave Monroe an estimate of 1,500, a number he later revised to 2,600.

The American losses on the Chalmette Plain on January 8 amounted to no more than a dozen dead. More would be killed on the west bank and in skirmishes in the days following, but the battle, indisputably, was a far greater disaster for the British. General Jackson's earthworks and his unlikely melding of men had held. The city of New Orleans no longer feared a British invasion.

For the nation, the meaning was larger, too. Against all odds, General Jackson had preserved the mouth of the Mississippi for America. At the center of the muddy earthworks, atop its staff, untouched by British hands and overlooking the Chalmette Plain, the Stars and Stripes still waved.

General Jackson and his multiethnic, multigenerational army made up of people from every American social class and occupation had come together to do what Napoleon had failed to do: destroy the finest fighting force in the world. Thanks to Jackson's military instincts, his impeccable planning, and his ferocious leadership, America had prevailed in the most important fight of its young life.

The boy becomes a man: a brutish British officer is about to strike young Andy Jackson. The boy survived, scarred and angry, to resist another British attack, this one at the Battle of New Orleans thirty-five years later.

CURRIER & IVES, LIBRARY OF CONGRESS

Hoping to expand America westward, President Thomas Jefferson sent James Monroe to Paris to negotiate the Louisiana Purchase in 1803. Pictured here, Monroe (left) and Robert R. Livingston (center) complete negotiations with French foreign minister Comte Talleyrand. Monroe would later go on to be involved in the territory's defense in his positions as secretary of war and secretary of state during the War of 1812.

MPI/GETTY IMAGES

Captain James Barron of the USS *Chesapeake* formally surrenders, offering his sword to the captain of the victorious HMS *Leopard* in June 1807. The unprovoked attack by the British warship on the American frigate helped set the stage for the War of 1812.

UNIVERSAL HISTORY ARCHIVE/UIG VIA GETTY IMAGES

After the War of 1812, Jackson became known for his military demeanor, as captured in this image of him with his hand gripping his sword, his eyes fixed on his adversary. Major General Andrew Jackson was a confident and natural leader of men in battle.

JOHN VANDERLYN, THE HISTORIC NEW ORLEANS COLLECTION

Jackson's beloved wife, Rachel Donelson Jackson (1767–1828), was the only person to whom Jackson could confide his innermost fears and doubts. Born into a well-established Nashville family, Rachel was a partner to the roughhewn Jackson in his rise to prominence.

JOHN CHESTER BUTTRE/ THE HISTORIC NEW ORLEANS COLLECTION

In 1812, James Madison (1751–1836) was an unpopular president; in 1817, after Jackson's big victory in New Orleans, Madison left office riding a wave of popular acclaim. In the face of daunting odds, he had led his country into its second war of independence.

THE WHITE HOUSE HISTORICAL ASSOCIATION/WHITE HOUSE COLLECTION

Known as Chief Red Eagle to his fellow Creeks, William Weatherford (ca. 1781–1824) was born of mixed parentage, with a Scots father and a Native American mother. A courageous and resourceful opponent, Red Eagle had, by the time of the surrender (pictured here), won Andrew Jackson's grudging respect.

J. R. CHAPIN, W. RIDGWAY, LIBRARY OF CONGRESS

The signing of the Treaty of Ghent on Christmas Eve 1814 appeared to bring the War of 1812 to a close. John Quincy Adams shakes hands with a uniformed British minister as Albert Gallatin (to the right of Adams) and Henry Clay (seated) look on.

SIR AMÉDÉE FORESTIER, SMITHSONIAN AMERICAN ART MUSEUM, WASHINGTON, DC/ART RESOURCE, NY

With the powerful Royal Navy patrolling the coast, American goods accumulated on the docks. At the port of New Orleans, that meant millions of dollars in bales of cotton.

E. H. NEWTON, JR., THE HISTORIC NEW ORLEANS COLLECTION

Dashing and dangerous, Jean Lafitte (1780–1823) was a privateer, smuggler, and entrepreneur. Along with his brothers and the other Baratarian pirates, many of them superb cannoneers, Lafitte lent his deep knowledge of the waters around New Orleans to the cause of saving New Orleans from the British.

UNIVERSAL HISTORY ARCHIVE/UIG VIA GETTY IMAGES

The wellborn Louise d'Avezac (1785–1860) married a prominent New Orleans lawyer, Edward Livingston (1764–1836). As Mrs. Livingston, she offered the transplanted New Yorker entrée into New Orleans society—and, in turn, Livingston, appointed an adjutant to General Jackson in 1814, helped Jackson win the support of the city's powerful Creole class in the defense of the city.

BARD COLLEGE

A trusted aide to Jackson during the early days of the war, Thomas Hart Benton (1782–1858) played a role in the gunfight that almost killed the general in Nashville in 1813. Much later, as a powerful senator from Missouri, Benton proved to be a congressional ally of then president Andrew Jackson.

THE PRINT COLLECTOR/PRINT COLLECTOR/GETTY IMAGES

A stalwart friend and sometime business partner of Jackson's, General John Coffee (1772–1833) proved his military skills again and again, leading his cavalry brigade of fellow Tennesseans against the Creeks and the British alike.

LITHOGRAPH © GETTY IMAGES

JOHN COFFEE.

Perhaps the lowest point in the nation's history, August 24, 1814, was the day the British set fire to the public buildings in Washington, DC, leaving both the President's House and the Capitol smoking ruins. The humiliation of that moment proved to be a great motivation for Jackson and his men.

LITHOGRAPH © LIBRARY OF CONGRESS

The bombs bursting over Baltimore on the night of September 13, 1814, signaled a change in America's fortunes. The British failure to take the city in Maryland, together with other losses at Plattsburgh, New York, and New Orleans, assured that the United States would remain independent.

J. BOWER, GETTY IMAGES

The five American gunboats on Lake Borgne were besieged by a flotilla of British barges. In less than two hours, on December 14, 1814, the vastly larger British forces captured the outgunned American ships under the command of Lieutenant Thomas ap Catesby Jones.

THOMAS L. HORNBROOK, THE HISTORIC NEW ORLEANS COLLECTION

A veteran of the fight with the Tripoli pirates, Master Commander Daniel Todd Patterson (1786–1839) was the senior officer of the U.S. Navy at the New Orleans station. He and Jackson would collaborate by putting the limited naval resources in Patterson's command to very good use to defend the city.

JOHN WESLEY JARVIS, CHRYSLER MUSEUM OF ART

Long before Jackson set foot in New Orleans, Governor William C. C. Claiborne (1775–1817) sought the general's help. Appointed by President Jefferson as the first Louisiana territorial governor, Claiborne had been duly elected to that office with Louisiana's statehood in 1812.

JAMES BARTON LONGACRE, THE HISTORIC NEW ORLEANS COLLECTION

Young Samuel Houston (1793–1863) fought with his fellow Tennesseans against the Creeks; despite sustaining wounds at the Battle of Horseshoe Bend, he rose to fight again. A longtime ally of Jackson's, he later became governor of Tennessee and the first president of the Republic of Texas.

PHOTOGRAPH © LIBRARY OF CONGRESS

VILLERÉ'S MANSION.

When the British arrived to attack New Orleans, their officers established headquarters at the mansion on the Villeré plantation, just downriver from the encampment of Jackson's army.

VIEW OF THE RODRIGUEZ CANAL—JACKSON'S LINES.

Jackson set thousands of his men to hard labor to transform the Rodriguez Canal into a tall embankment lined with gun emplacements. Before that, the canal was little more than a drainage ditch.

A much-honored soldier who had fought bravely in Europe under the command of his brother-in-law the Duke of Wellington, General Edward "Ned" Pakenham (1778–1815) was dispatched by London to lead the enormous British force to victory in New Orleans. After capturing Louisiana, he was to become the territory's British governor—but General Jackson had different ideas.

GOUPIL & CO., THE HISTORIC NEW ORLEANS COLLECTION

Also a veteran of the French wars, Vice Admiral Sir Alexander Forrester Inglis Cochrane (1758–1832) commanded the British expeditionary force in the Gulf of Mexico. The greedy Cochrane looked both to improve his fortunes and to avenge the death of a brother killed in the American Revolution.

LIBRARY OF CONGRESS

In what is today's Alabama, Jackson prepares to fight on Indian turf. Whether his opponent was Indian or British, Jackson was unafraid to ride into the heat of battle.

JOHN VANDERLYN, LIBRARY OF CONGRESS

Painted by Jean Hyacinthe de Laclotte, a Louisiana militiaman who fought in the January 8, 1815, battle, this vivid view of the events of the day was based on sketches Laclotte made as the battle unfolded.

JEAN HYACINTHE DE LACLOTTE, *BATTLE OF NEW ORLEANS*, NEW ORLEANS MUSEUM OF ART: GIFT OF EDGAR WILLIAM AND BERNICE CHRYSLER GARBISH, 65.7

The flag still waves—with Jean Lafitte and three freemen of color celebrating in the foreground while a dead General Pakenham, left, falls from his horse.

EUGENE LOUIS-LAMI, LOUISIANA STATE MUSEUM

In a historical exaggeration, this image portrays Jackson conferring with an aide near battlements consisting almost entirely of cotton bales.

DENNIS MALONE CARTER, THE HISTORIC NEW ORLEANS COLLECTION

This commemorative print, made ca. 1820, puts a lot of the battle's elements together in one composition. Along with General Jackson, it is thought to portray General William Carroll and Edward Livingston in the foreground, the redcoats and the U.S. infantry, and navy ships in the river at the horizon line.

SAMUEL SEYMOUR, THE HISTORIC NEW ORLEANS COLLECTION

For Major General Sir Edward Pakenham, the Battle of New Orleans ended in death. He sustained several wounds in the first hour before a musket ball severed his spine. His men laid him at the base of a massive live oak tree, where he quietly bled to death as both sides fought on.

FELIX OCTAVIUS CARR DARLEY, THE HISTORIC NEW ORLEANS COLLECTION

The Ursuline nuns of New Orleans prayed for victory, asking Our Lady of Prompt Succor—an honorific title the sisters used for the Blessed Virgin—to save their city from the invaders. In this late-nineteenth-century composite, an image (lower right) commemorates the Battle of New Orleans.

F. CHAMPENOIS, THE HISTORIC NEW ORLEANS COLLECTION

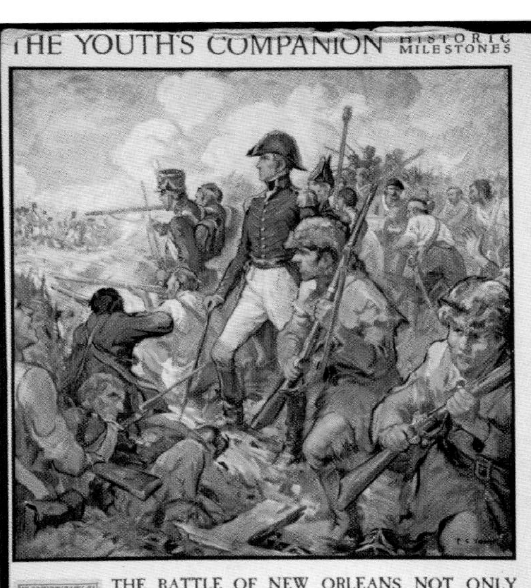

Jackson stood tall in the memories of American schoolboys for generations, as suggested by this 1922 illustration for a children's magazine, *The Youth's Companion*.

LIBRARY OF CONGRESS

The victorious general waves to the crowd from his open carriage in a mid-nineteenth-century image bearing the title *Jackson's Triumph at New Orleans* from an illustrated magazine.

LOSSING & BARRITT, THE HISTORIC NEW ORLEANS COLLECTION

A photograph of Andrew Jackson just before his death. When he saw it, a furious Jackson dismissed the likeness; he said it made him "look like a monkey."

LIBRARY OF CONGRESS

CHAPTER 13

The British Withdraw

> We, who only seven weeks ago had set out in the surest confidence of glory, and, I may add, of emolument, were brought back dispirited and dejected.
>
> —**George Gleig,** *A Narrative of the Campaigns of the British Army at Washington and New Orleans*

General Jackson took nothing for granted. He watched the British camp like a hawk from the top of the Macarty house and, on his orders, American artillerymen kept up a constant barrage of round shot and mortar shells. He wanted the British to know their American enemy was both vigilant and determined.

Jackson considered ordering a ground attack on his wounded foe, but to come out from behind his ramparts to fight the British—they were still a far larger and better-trained force—and to do so in an open plain? He and his counselors decided that such a battle need not be fought and that to undertake it might even provoke the enemy to renew their attack.[1]

Such worries seemed all the more real when Jackson got word from Fort St. Philip, sixty miles downstream on the Mississippi, that five of Admiral Cochrane's gunships were firing on the fortification. American gunners managed to keep the British vessels out of cannon range, but the British still bombarded the fort with long-range mortar shells. That the British still had designs on New Orleans seemed hard to deny, but after nine days of indecisive artillery exchanges (the British fired more than a thousand rounds, killing just one American and wounding seven) Cochrane's ships sailed away on the night of January 17. Fort St. Philip was pockmarked but intact.[2]

Jackson might have prepared a trap for the enemy's land force. If General Lambert's army wasn't going to advance, the troops would have to retreat from the Chalmette Plain. The American woodsmen with their long rifles could have made the wounded enemy run a hellish gauntlet as they retraced the narrow path through swampland to the shore before embarking, one barge at a time, to be relayed across Lake Borgne. But as Jackson wrote to James Monroe, that also seemed an unnecessary "risque."[3]

Finally, Jackson's patience paid off. On January 19, he awoke to find "the enemy [had] precipitately decamped."[4] The British had stoked their nighttime campfires to lull the American pickets into thinking all was as usual. Then, at midnight, the army wordlessly began an all-night march through the mud, back along the Bayou Bienvenue to the Fisherman's Village. Nine days had been required to improvise a roadbed along the creek, stiffening the muddy morass with reeds and tree limbs.

Finally, the British were truly gone. Even the late General Pakenham had departed. Disemboweled and submerged in a hogshead of rum, the remains of the British commander had begun the journey home to Ireland, there to be interred in the family vault in County Meath, a few miles from Dublin.

Contrary to widespread expectations—his own, Parliament's, Admiral Cochrane's, and others'—General Pakenham would never be the governor of Louisiana.

A Celebration in New Orleans

Jackson made his way back to the city he had saved. On January 20, returning for the first time in nearly a month, he marched his army into the heart of New Orleans.

The streets were lined with "the aged, the infirm, the matrons, daughters and children," recorded one adjutant. "Every countenance was expressive of gratitude—joy sparkled in every feature, on beholding fathers, brothers, husbands, sons, who had so recently . . . repell[ed] an enemy [who came] to conquer and subjugate the country."[5]

The men of New Orleans and the other defenders were welcomed home, as Jackson's aide Major Reid saw it, in "a scene well calculated to excite the tenderest emotions."[6] The sense of relief in the city was enhanced by the disparity in casualty totals on the battlefield: British dead and wounded exceeded a thousand, but there were remarkably few American widows and orphans.

A man of simple religious faith, Jackson wished to give thanks to the "Ruler of all events," as he put it. He wrote to the Abbé Dubourg at New Orleans's cathedral, requesting that Dubourg organize a "service of public thanksgiving" for "the signal interposition of Heaven in giving success to our arms against the enemy."[7]

On January 23, the people of the city gathered once again at the Place d'Armes, the city's main square. A triumphal arch had been erected and festooned with evergreens and flowers. A dense throng of people packed the streets and the nearby levee. A battalion of New Orleans militiamen lined the path to the entrance of the cathedral. Spectators filled the balconies and windows overlooking the square. Eighteen young women lined the approach from the arch to the church, one for each of the eighteen states. Wearing white dresses and blue veils, the girls held flags and baskets. Everyone awaited the arrival of the victorious general.

An artillery salvo announced his coming, and his appearance on horseback produced a deafening cheer from the crowd.

Jackson dismounted, stepping onto the raised floor of the arch. Two girls placed a laurel crown on his head. On a path strewn with flowers, Jackson progressed to the cathedral's entrance, where he was met by the abbé and his college of priests, all dressed in sacramental vestments. They entered the church, accompanied by the reading of an ode composed for the occasion. Its last couplet proclaimed, "Remembrance, long, shall keep alive thy fame / And future infants learn to lisp thy name."[8]

The Abbé Dubourg welcomed Jackson, thanking the man he called the city's "deliverer." He compared him to George Washington; he was among the first to do so but very far from the last. The cathedral could not accommodate the crowd of more than ten thousand people, but those admitted saw Jackson take a seat near the altar to the accompaniment of organ music. After the chanting of the hymn "Te Deum," the Mass, lit by a thousand candles, came to a close as Jackson accepted the honors and his crown humbly. He told the hushed crowd, "I receive it in the name of the brave men who . . . well deserve the laurels which their country will bestow."[9]

With the ceremonies concluded, the crowd escorted Jackson to his quarters, but only after the general, hearing reports of the sisters' all-night vigil on the eve of the battle, visited the Ursuline convent to thank them for their prayers.[10] "By the blessing of heaven, directing the valor of the troops under my command, one of the most brilliant victories in the annals of war was obtained," he said.[11] That night, Jackson suspended the curfew, and the city of New Orleans would celebrate until dawn.

Unfinished Business

Despite the aura of victory, Andrew Jackson remained watchful. As his aide Major Reid observed, "[The enemy] had now retired; yet, from their convenient situation, and having command of the surrounding waters, it was in their power at a short notice, to reappear."[12] Just in case, Jackson left infantry regulars at the Rodriguez Canal, and he stationed Tennessee militiamen and Kentucky rifles near the landing place at the Villeré plantation.

The British might find another target. "I have no idea that [the] enemy will attempt Fort Bowyer," Jackson noted in a letter. "Still you cannot be too well prepared or too vigilant—[Admiral] Cochrane is sore, and [General] Lambert crazy; they may in this situation attempt some act of madness."[13]

Jackson's hunch proved dead right: Fort Bowyer was in the British sights.

As far as Admiral Cochrane was concerned, the American war wasn't over, since no messenger from Ghent had yet reached American shores. And there was Fort Bowyer, just up the coast. A smaller navy force had failed to capture the fortification back in September, but now the admiral had sixty ships at his disposal and many thousands of troops. So, with what was now General Lambert's army back aboard, the fleet set sail on January 27.

Destination: Mobile Bay.

Though the fort was surely a lesser target than New Orleans, this opportunity to regain lost prestige could hardly be passed by. And General Lambert wanted to dispel "the sullen carelessness [and] indifference" evident in his men after the beating they had taken at the Chalmette Plain.[14]

On Wednesday, February 8, Cochrane's armada landed three regiments of some five thousand men several miles from Fort Bowyer. Although the American commander, Colonel William Lawrence, ordered his guns to fire on the British, they would not be deterred: by Saturday, the muzzles of four eighteen-pounders, two six-pounders, a pair of howitzers, and eight mortars were pointed at the fort. The British were ready.

Before opening fire, however, Captain Harry Smith, under a flag of truce, carried a demand from his commanding officer, General Lambert, to Colonel Lawrence.

His message in short: *Surrender your fort.*

Looking out at his powerful enemy from the confines of the highly flammable wooden fort, Lawrence asked for time. He wanted two hours to consider the offer, which included a promise that, if he declined to accept Lambert's terms, he could evacuate the women and children inside Fort Bowyer. He had watched helplessly for the preceding three days. With only 360 men in his command, he faced overwhelming odds.

Lawrence saw no alternative but to surrender. To fight would be to waste lives in an unwinnable battle, and his officers seconded his decision. At noon, on February 12, 1815, Lawrence and his men marched out of Fort Bowyer, accompanied by twenty women and sixteen children. They laid down their arms and yielded the fort to the British.

When he heard what happened, Jackson expressed to Monroe his mortification at the handover. It had occurred without a shot being fired but, worse yet, the capitulation of Fort Bowyer cleared the way for the British to enter Mobile Bay and besiege Mobile.

The news took Jackson back in time: Months before, he had foreseen a British strategy that began with Mobile. Now, it seemed, the sequence of events he feared most was about to unfold. Could this signal a new offensive cycle?

In a matter of hours, however, the momentum shifted for good when, the next day, the British frigate HMS *Brazen* sailed into view. Fresh from an Atlantic crossing, she brought word of the Treaty of Ghent. Cochrane and his generals were ordered to end hostilities and prepare to sail home.

Yet for Andrew Jackson, the war would be over only when he knew for certain it was over; he could never take Admiral Cochrane's word for that.

The Slow Pace of Peace

On the evening of February 14, 1815, a messenger carrying a leather document box arrived at the borrowed home in Washington occupied by James Madison. Eager hands opened the cast brass lockset to reveal a thick sheaf of papers.

A cover letter from Henry Clay explained the contents. Accompanied by many position papers prepared in the negotiation process, there was the all-important Treaty of Ghent, sealed and signed and very official. The treaty was brief (just eleven articles) and to the point, beginning with its most basic assertion: "There shall be a firm and universal Peace between His Britannic Majesty and the United States."

Mr. Madison submitted the document to the Senate without delay. It was read aloud three times to the assembled body, and some senators wondered at the absence of any reference to impressment and the harassment of neutral trade, two of the main reasons for declaring war two and a half years earlier. Nor was there mention of navigation of the Mississippi. Nevertheless, when the key question was asked in proper parliamentary fashion—"Will the Senate advise and consent to the ratification of this treaty?"—the resulting vote was for ratification, thirty-five yeas, no one opposed. On February 17, a second copy arrived in Washington from London, this one bearing the signature of the prince regent.

The men of the government could finally relax: Mr. Madison's War was over.

A thousand miles away, however, in his headquarters on Rue Royale in New Orleans, General Jackson still awaited the news. Not that rumors hadn't reached him—on February 19, a clipping from a London newspaper appeared that reported the war had ended—but Jackson continued to refuse to lower his guard until he got the official word from Washington. Even after Edward Livingston returned from a further negotiation with Admiral Cochrane over prisoner exchanges with news that the HMS *Brazen* had brought word of a peace treaty, Jackson suspected the reports of a peace deal were merely a "stratagem."[15]

To many in the city, the hero of New Orleans began to seem like their jailer with his insistence that the draconian restraints of martial law remain in place. With the war over to their satisfaction, merchants resented the general's tight rein on commerce. Militiamen wanted to be released from duty to return to their civilian lives but, despite their pleas, Jackson continued stubbornly to insist that he needed formal notification from the secretary of war.

A woman's touch, however, eased some of the tension.

Nine months had elapsed since the surrender of the Creek chief William Weatherford, an event that had prompted Andrew Jackson's last visit home. Rachel had, in turn, postponed her December trip to New Orleans after the British arrived on the city's doorstep. When news of the January 8 victory reached Rachel, she decided the couple had been separated long enough. Though winter travel posed worrisome dangers, Mrs. Jackson set out, along with other Tennessee officers' wives, for New Orleans.

Several weeks later, the general welcomed his wife; throughout their long marriage, he would always mourn their separations. She arrived with their adoptive son Andrew Jr. on whom the general doted. The moment was one of pure delight for Jackson.

As for Rachel, her arrival amounted to more than a reunion with the man she loved: having never visited a city larger than provincial Nashville, New Orleans was a grand revelation to her. The Jacksons were the guests of Edward Livingston and his stylish wife. Louise Livingston took a liking to the unaffected Mrs. Jackson, despite her visitor's dowdy clothes and an unfashionably sunned complexion, the result of managing their plantation in her husband's absence.

The Jacksons became the guests of choice around town at "balls, concerts, plays, theaters, [etc.]," even though, Rachel allowed, "we don't attend the half of them."[16] But one they did go to was a great ball to celebrate George Washington's birthday.

The site of the February 22 gala was the French Exchange where, for three days, preparations had been under way for the grand evening.

Flowers abounded, as did colored lamps that, from the rear, illuminated transparencies painted on varnished glass. One read, "Jackson and Victory: they are but one." Jackson, taking an advance look at the decorations, took note of it. He inquired lightly, "Why did you not write 'Hickory and Victory: they are but one'?"[17]

Supper was served and dancing followed. When the hero took the floor with Rachel in his arms, the crowd was transfixed. To some observers, the savior of the city and his lady looked mismatched. The slim and girlish divorcée that Jackson had married twenty-one years before had aged into a rather stout, round woman; the poorly nourished Jackson looked more haggard and angular than ever.

To one Creole gentleman still smarting over Jackson's refusal to lift his martial law decree, the sight invited a snide remark. "To see these two figures, the general a long, haggard man, with limbs like a skeleton, and Madame la Generale, a short, fat dumpling, bobbing opposite each other like half-drunken Indians, to the wild melody of *Possum up de Gum Tree,* and endeavoring to make a spring into the air, was very remarkable."[18] Though some made fun, the ladies of the city raised a subscription to purchase jewels for presentation to the well-liked Mrs. Jackson.

At last, on March 8, 1815, having received "persuasive evidence" of ratification of the treaty, Jackson released the reins. He dismissed the Louisiana militia and, after official word arrived, on March 13, he issued orders for Generals Carroll and Coffee to march their commands without delay back home. He expressed his thanks and admiration.

"Farewell, fellow soldiers. The expression of your general's thanks is feeble," he said in his closing address, "but the gratitude of a country of freemen is yours—yours the applause of an admiring world."[19]

Finally, the Hero of New Orleans could go home. In early April, accompanied by a small band of devoted officers and men, he and Rachel began a slow progress northward. They were feted in Natchez and other towns on the way and, as they neared Nashville, an ever-larger throng of Volunteers escorted the victor and his wife. The state's politicians, wishing to share in Jackson's newfound radiance and renown, would give yet another banquet, but his desired stopping place was the Hermitage.

When his adoring public delivered him to his home, Andrew Jackson addressed his friends and neighbors, both in welcome and in farewell. For most of the last eighteen months, Jackson had been a stranger, a warrior and traveler away from home, and the time had taken a toll. He looked more sinewy than ever, carrying perhaps 145 pounds on his six-foot-one-inch frame.[20] But his blue eyes remained as penetrating as ever, his posture still ramrod straight, despite the hardships of the war.

During his months away he had become accustomed to addressing crowds; his Tennessee apprenticeship as a regional politician and judge may have prepared him for greater things, but it had been the trial that was the Battle of New Orleans that made him not merely a public man but a national figure, a man whose name and accomplishments had been celebrated in newspapers and taverns across the country.

But his homecoming in Nashville meant a great deal to him. "Your friendship and regard," he told the crowd, "is a rich compensation for many sacrifices and many labors."

Jackson's rhetorical style, once wooden and strident, had become the voice of a wise elder. In that manner, and cherishing the warm welcome, he explained what the events just ended signified.

"The sons of America," he went on, "have given a new proof how impossible it is to conquer freemen fighting in defense of all that is dear to them. Henceforward we shall be respected by nations who, mistaking our character, had treated us with the utmost contumely and outrage. Years will continue to develop our inherent qualities, until, from being the youngest and the weakest, we shall become the most powerful nation in the universe."[21]

Andrew Jackson, once and for all, had evened an old score. This time it had been the British who left the battle bloodied and defeated. The Union was intact. He had proved himself to the powers in Washington. A war that could have ended in partition instead closed with the rise of an army of new American heroes with Andrew Jackson at its head. Thanks to the scarred orphan, never again would America be invaded by a foreign power, and the enemy it defeated would one day become an ally.

General Jackson's War

Back in the summer of 1812, a Federalist pamphleteer had dismissively nicknamed the conflict "Mr. Madison's War."[22] Madison's political opposition didn't want to go to war and, once it was declared, they wanted to tar him with it. But in 1815, with the return of peace and Jackson's big triumph, the stain rapidly faded. The press coverage helped: the *Niles' Weekly Register* spoke for many Americans that February and March: "The last six months is the proudest period in the history of the republic," its columns asserted. "[We] demonstrated to mankind a capacity to acquire a skill in arms to conquer 'the conquerors of the conquerors of all' as Wellington's invincibles were modestly styled," Furthermore, the *Register*'s editors concluded, "Who would not be an American? Long live the republic! . . . Last asylum of oppressed humanity! Peace is signed in the arms of victory!"[23]

The brilliance of the victory in New Orleans overshadowed the dark humiliation of the burning of the public buildings in Washington; in time, with the blurring of memory, the nation's recollections of the war would center on Andrew Jackson. Mr. Madison's War would become General Jackson's War. He was remembered as having restored America's honor.

The end of the war and its best moments—a handful of sea battles won by U.S. warships, the rocket's red glare that illuminated a giant flag in Baltimore (memorialized by the barrister Francis Scott Key), and, most of all, the Battle of New Orleans—provided Americans with a new sense of nationhood. In Europe, particularly among the inhabitants of Great Britain, a new recognition emerged that their American cousins couldn't be regarded merely as poor relations; one had to respect a people who stood up and defended themselves against the British Empire. Once dismissed by George Gleig as "an enemy unworthy of serious regard,"[24] the American military—whether regular or militia, army or navy or marines—had become a force to be reckoned with.

General Andrew Jackson had melded a largely amateur force into an army, one that had vanquished a sophisticated force perhaps twice its size. His attack on December 23 had been a masterstroke, one that stunned the British and bought Jackson and the defenders of New Orleans essential time. The general had marshaled his limited naval resources to harry the British from the Mississippi. He had improvised a brilliant defensive strategy. He had exercised restraint and discipline.

He deployed his men in a way that took advantage of their strengths as riflemen and minimized their weaknesses. His tactics forced General Pakenham's well-drilled force to confront American strengths on U.S. terms.

Despite a lack of formal military training, Jackson proved himself to be the ablest general in the war. Significantly, he was also a man capable of inspiring other men to do their duty. That mix of confidence and resolution boded well for a future foray into the realm of politics. As both a general and a politician, he pursued fixed goals because he had a vision for his country.

He wasn't a complicated man, but he possessed—and was possessed by—an extraordinary certainty. He was a man who could be fired by anger. Jackson hadn't been much of a student; his mother's forlorn wish for him to join the ministry died even before she did. His intelligence was not book-learned; he operated on instinct and experience. His orientations were the essential verities: duty to country (at first that meant region but, with the life-changing events in Louisiana, it became nation); duty to God; and duty to family, not only, in the narrow sense, to his relations but also to his neighbors, whom he regarded as his brothers and his sisters, and to his men and those who voted for him, whom he regarded as children given unto his care.

Jackson's unyielding belief in the Republic and his instinct for democratic values help explain why later historians would refer to his time as the Age of Jackson.

Epilogue

The Hero's Return: January 1840

> The instrument chosen by the Lord to get His will done, as Gideon was chosen in Biblical times, was General Andrew Jackson.
>
> —**Wilburt S. Brown,** *The Amphibious Campaign for West Florida and Louisiana,* 1969

As the year 1839 drew to a close, Andrew Jackson faced a decision. He held an invitation in his hand: with the twenty-fifth anniversary of the big battle just weeks away—the "silver jubilee" the organizers called it—the city he had saved invited him to return to celebrate his greatest military triumph.

The old man was honored, of course; he acknowledged that he had "sacrificed both property and health in the salvation of New Orleans."[1] He believed January 8 meant as much to American history as July 4, and his role in the victory was perhaps his greatest pride, despite having gone on to serve two terms as the nation's seventh chief executive (1829–37) and to dominate his era, a common man, as Jackson saw himself, captaining the ship of state through enormous changes.

But traveling all the way to New Orleans? That looked like a problem.

For one thing, his health was poor. He had spent the last five months of his presidency confined to his bed after almost dying following another of the periodic lung hemorrhages that plagued him (the lead ball from his 1806 duel remained embedded in his lung). In contemplating a long trip, he feared the physical challenges of a jarring ride in winter weather.

Another problem was that, despite his fame and considerable landholdings, he had little cash to spare. "I am out of funds," he confided to his namesake nephew, Andrew Jackson Donelson. Some years hadn't been good on Jackson's plantation, and Andrew Jr. had grown into a spendthrift, a constant drag on his famous father's finances. But the general, whatever his health and circumstances, remained a proud man. "I cannot bear to borrow or travel as a pauper," he admitted.[2]

At seventy-two, Jackson was no longer young—but the opportunity to return to the Crescent City did bring back powerful memories. The tall earthworks at the Battle of New Orleans had truly elevated him; that was one reason he insisted on being called *general* rather than *president*.

His defeat of the British had gained him respect in Washington, where, in February 1815, Congress had ordered a medal be struck—featuring his profile, dressed in his high-collared uniform—to honor his "splendid achievement." Almost overnight, he had unexpectedly become a national figure, his fame exploding far beyond the bounds of New Orleans and the Southwest. In the nation's cultural center, Philadelphia, a printmaker had produced a commemorative engraving; Jackson's likeness, with his arched brows, the crest of hair atop his tall forehead, and his imperious expression, became recognizable across the land. Jackson entrusted Major John Reid with his correspondence and other papers in order that his aide might write an account of the battle. Although Reid died before completing *The Life of Andrew Jackson, Major-General in the Service of the United States,* the book, bearing the bylines of both Reid and John Henry Eaton, appeared in 1817. It would be the closest thing to an account of his part in the War of 1812 by Jackson himself.

In the twenty-five years since the Battle of New Orleans, Jackson had seen vast changes. The once-unpopular President James Madison had emerged from the Second War of Independence a much-honored man. His successor, James Monroe, rode a wave of new prosperity and goodwill into an "era of good feelings," as one Boston newspaper put it after Monroe's inauguration in 1817.[3] The westward boom that Jackson had foreseen brought soaring land values, rapid population growth, and the appearance of new and substantial towns. New states joined the Union, including Indiana, Mississippi, Illinois, Alabama, and Missouri. Foreign trade and shipping blossomed.

Jackson continued to do his bit—and then some—after the war. His defeat of the Creeks had already cleared a great swath of territory for settlement, but in 1818, pursuing the Seminoles at President Monroe's orders, he wrested Florida from Spain, and then served as its territorial governor. Jackson had emerged as the most important leader of his region. In 1823, as a U.S. senator from Tennessee, he had been positioned to run for the presidency. Though he won the most electoral votes in the four-man race of 1824, his lack of a plurality meant the contest was decided in the House of Representatives, where John Quincy Adams prevailed. The vote left a sour taste in Jackson's mouth: another of the candidates, the former Ghent negotiator Henry Clay, had thrown his support to Adams and soon thereafter been named secretary of state. To Jackson, the deal was a dirty one—and he labeled Clay the "Judas of the West."

The 1828 election ended differently when changes in voter eligibility (property requirements for suffrage were eliminated in most states, quadrupling the electorate) helped Jackson prevail. He had a gift for intuiting what the common man wanted, but his victory also seemed preordained: His friend Edward Livingston had spoken for many when he told Jackson, back in 1815, "General, you are the man. You must be President of the United States."[4] Barely a dozen years later, Livingston's prognostication came true.

Andrew Jackson was far from the only person whose prospects had been changed by the battle. Edward Livingston, for one, had prospered. He had become a Louisiana congressman (1823–29) and a U.S. senator (1829–31). His friendship with the general proved lasting, and during Jackson's presidency, Livingston had been a key confidant as secretary of state (1831–33) and minister to France (1833–35).

Thomas Hart Benton, Jackson's former subordinate in the Tennessee militia and an opponent in the 1813 gunfight that left Jackson gravely wounded, had resurfaced as a powerful U.S. senator from Missouri (and a valuable Jackson ally) during Jackson's presidency.

In contrast, Governor William Claiborne continued to have an uneasy relationship with his varied Louisiana constituency; he died young, at just forty-two years of age, in 1817.

Some of the military men who served with Jackson had risen in the ranks, but others floundered. Daniel Todd Patterson's service in New Orleans gained him a captaincy and, for a time, the ship he commanded was the legendary USS *Constitution* (the frigate had gained its nickname, "Old Ironsides," during Mr. Madison's War). At the time of his death, in 1839, Patterson was commander of the Washington Navy Yard.

Thomas ap Catesby Jones remained in the U.S. Navy, gaining a minor place in American literature after he crossed paths with a navy deserter named Herman Melville, who would memorialize him as Commodore J—— in *Moby-Dick; or, The Whale* (1851).

The militia general William Carroll returned to civilian life and was twice elected governor of Tennessee. John Coffee returned to real estate speculation, often in partnership with his friend Andrew Jackson.

The least likely of Jackson's men, the Baratarian pirates, had won his respect and appreciation for their artillery skills and, in his general orders after the Battle of New Orleans, he acknowledged as much: "The general cannot avoid giving his warm approbation of the manner in which [the privateers] have uniformly conducted themselves while under his command. . . . The brothers Lafitte have exhibited the same courage and fidelity, and the general promises that the government shall be duly apprised of their conduct."[5] In February 1815, they received their pardons but the life of the straight and narrow proved difficult. Jean Lafitte resumed privateering, eventually from a new base of operations at the port of Galveston in Spanish Texas. Lafitte died in 1823 of wounds sustained in a ship-to-ship battle but his legend lived on: the swashbuckler would fire the imaginations of novelists and scriptwriters. His brother Pierre, once more a pirate, operated out of an island base between Cuba and Mexico. He died of fever in 1821 and was buried in a convent churchyard in northeastern Yucatán.

Some of Jackson's fellow fighters in the Indian wars had gone on to fame and fortune. Sam Houston's enduring popularity won him the governorship of Tennessee before he went west to Texas. There he would serve as both president of the short-lived Republic of Texas and as governor of the state of Texas after it joined the Union.

Davy Crockett became a U.S. congressman and later died at the Alamo, but not before writing his colorful, if rather folkloric, *A Narrative of the Life of David Crockett, of the State of Tennessee* (1834). At the time of his death a decade after the Battle of Horseshoe Bend, William Weatherford—Jackson's worthy Red Stick opponent, once known as Red Eagle—had become a planter, horse breeder, and owner of three hundred black slaves, residing on a farm near the site of Fort Mims.[6]

On the other side of the line, Sir John Lambert and John Keane—unlike the deceased generals Pakenham and Gibbs—made it back to Europe alive. Both joined the Duke of Wellington in defeating Napoleon once more, this time at the Battle of Waterloo, on June 18, 1815. Both Lambert and Keane went on to serve in Jamaica, administering the civil government of the colony. Lambert died a general, in 1847, but Keane, raised to a peerage after service in India, died a baron, in 1844.

When Alexander Forrester Inglis Cochrane retired from the Royal Navy, in 1824, he was commander of the Plymouth navy headquarters; he died in Paris, in 1832.

Colonel William Thornton became a lieutenant general and received a knighthood in 1836. Subject to delusions—perhaps a consequence of head wounds sustained years earlier—he shot himself in 1840. Captain Nicholas Lockyer recovered from the several wounds he sustained on Lake Borgne and served a long career in the Royal Navy, dying aboard the ship he captained, the HMS *Albion,* at age sixty-five in 1847.

The Ursuline nuns who had prayed for victory on January 8, 1815, rose from their knees after the firing stopped and, hospital cots at the ready, welcomed the wounded to their school. They nursed men from Kentucky and Tennessee, and even British soldiers. One novice, Sister Sainte Angèle Johnston, was fondly remembered by her patients. Most of the nuns spoke only French; Sister Angèle, a native of Baltimore, was one of the few who spoke English. "Wait until the little sister . . . comes," one wounded soldier said to another. "She will understand you and give you what you want."[7]

In the years after the war, the Ursuline nuns remained true to the promise that Mother Superior Olivier de Vézin had made to the Almighty. To this day, on January 8, the Ursuline nuns conduct an annual Mass of Thanksgiving in honor of Our Lady of Prompt Succor and the Battle of New Orleans.

Remembering the Battle of New Orleans

In the months and years after the battle, there was much hand-wringing in Great Britain concerning the great defeat at New Orleans. Cochrane and Keane got the blame—Wellington himself thought an attack via Lake Borgne foolhardy, a violation of his cherished principle that an army must always be in contact with its base. Wellington also believed Cochrane's greed for plunder distorted his military judgment and preparations.

On the American side, military historians have argued over how Bayou Bienvenue could have been left open to the British (a court-martial convened on the matter in 1815 exonerated young Gabriel Villeré). A case has been made repeatedly that Jackson's force was vulnerable and that, had Admiral Cochrane and General Keane listened to the pleading of Colonel Thornton on December 23, 1814—he is said to have argued for immediately marching on New Orleans as the British had at Washington—then Jackson might have lost the Battle of New Orleans. As with all such hypotheticals, however, no firm conclusion can ever be reached.

Jackson's failure to properly defend the west bank raises another what-if. Many military historians believe that, given only slightly altered circumstances, the capture of Patterson's position could have been catastrophic to the American cause.

Some analysts blame the failure of the British campaign on the lack of secrecy; their attack on the Americans was not a surprise. The explanation for that has been alternately assigned to loose British lips and to Jackson for his cultivation and use of intelligence sources. In the same way, the debate continues to swirl about troop numbers: Did the British have five thousand effectives? Six thousand? Nine thousand? Or many more? The Americans certainly had fewer, but there is no agreement as to how many on that side, either.

In the end, though, everyone understood—then and now—that Jackson was the man of the hour, the man who met his moment standing atop his earthworks. He was ready to fight to the last man, to give his own life, and to burn the city of New Orleans before surrendering it to the British.

He made a series of decisions that have come to be seen as wise, even profound, in the eyes of most commentators: his double-time march on Pensacola; his flexible approach to defending the city of New Orleans; his surprise attack on December 23; his choice to shift from offense to defense; his decision before the big day to make his stand at the Rodriguez Canal and then to remain safely behind his ramparts after January 8, 1815.

On the other hand, his stubbornness alienated the populace of New Orleans after the victory at the Chalmette Plain. And he failed to designate a second in command: he might have died, for example, in the cross fire on December 23; if he had, could anyone else have held his army together? Yet his single-mindedness in leadership won the allegiance of his troops through a mix of intimidation and fatherly affection. They would fight heroically, despite the rockets zooming crazily overhead, rather than risk the wrath of Old Hickory.

On reading the accounts in most textbooks, the student comes away with the sense that the War of 1812 ended in a draw. Furthermore, if weights were assigned to the gives and the takes as specified in the Treaty of Ghent, Lady Justice's scale would likely find they balance, more or less, as the two sides come out about even. No territory changed hands; Great Britain made no promises regarding impressment; the world went back to the peaceable business of trade.

But General Jackson knew better: he had saved New Orleans; if he had not, the postwar history of his nation would have been different indeed.

The General's Last Stand

At the Hermitage, Andrew Jackson lived the life of a recluse, old and infirm, rarely leaving home and avoiding public appearances. He and his family worried that a simple cold—and the accompanying cough—could endanger his life. Yet the general's old determination still burned and, in December 1839, he decided that neither his fragile health nor his straitened finances could be allowed to stand in the way of a trip to New Orleans for the silver jubilee.

He saw a higher purpose: the journey, he believed, would forward the cause of democracy. As he told President Martin Van Buren, "My whole life has been employed to establish and perpetuate our republican system [and] if I should die in the effort, it cannot end better than endeavoring to open the eyes of the people to the blessings we enjoy."[8]

Jackson borrowed against the sale of his cotton crop to defray the costs; he simply had to make the journey.

On Christmas Eve, he left Nashville in a carriage, with his traveling companion, his nephew, Major Donelson. The roads were rough, snow-covered in places, and four long days were required to travel the 125 miles to the mouth of the Cumberland River. There he boarded the *Gallatin*, a steam-powered packet boat headed down the Ohio River.

If Jackson had had his way, he would have been accompanied by Rachel, but the stresses of the 1828 election a dozen years earlier had cost him dearly. So many insults were cast at both husband and wife that Rachel remarked to a friend just before ballots were cast, "I would rather be a doorkeeper in the house of God than live in that palace in Washington." Just days after the close of the hard-fought electoral battle, Rachel Jackson was indeed summoned by her Lord, stricken with an intense pain in her left arm, shoulder, and chest. Suddenly, the president-elect was in mourning for the love of his life.

As the *Gallatin* steamed south—the ship was named after Albert Gallatin, one of the men who had negotiated the Treaty of Ghent and, later, served as President John Quincy Adams's minister to the Court of St James's—Jackson observed many signs of how, in his lifetime, his nation had changed, shifting from a largely agricultural society to one increasingly based on industry. The advent of new technology meant that regularly scheduled steamboats made his march home from Natchez, back in the spring of 1813, seem like a quaint historical oddity. More than a thousand steamers now plied the Mississippi, making travel more rapid, predictable, and comfortable.

The general and his entourage arrived in New Orleans right on schedule, on the morning of Wednesday, January 8. The convoy had grown to five steamboats and, on stepping ashore at ten o'clock, Jackson, ignoring his illnesses and age, impressed the crowd of an estimated thirty thousand people.

Hatless, his hair a striking silver, and looking heartier than he felt, the general saluted the spectators as he rode in a carriage, part of a procession to the familiar confines of the Place d'Armes. For many hours, he would endure receptions, a service in the cathedral, speechifying, a reunion with officers from the army that defended the city, and fireworks.

Although the exhausted Jackson excused himself from a scheduled trip to the Chalmette Plain, even his political enemies cheered him that day. As one opposition newspaper reported, "[We] forgot the politician and thought only of the man—welcom[ing] him as the 'Hero of New Orleans' and the fearless defender of his country."[9]

If the Battle of New Orleans had made the man—and rising to the challenge as he did can certainly be said to have been Jackson's most essential rite of passage—then he did the same for his nation. He saved not only New Orleans from the British but preserved the Union.

But Andrew Jackson had stood in Pakenham's path. If he had not, the entire Gulf Coast might have been returned to Spain or remained in British hands.

With the celebrations in New Orleans concluded, Jackson returned to his stateroom aboard the *Vicksburg* and the steamship began its voyage upstream. Back at the Hermitage, Jackson would live five more years before dying quietly, on June 8, 1845. A year later the sculptor Clark Mills would be commissioned to execute an equestrian stature of Jackson and, in 1853, the twelve-foot-tall likeness of Jackson astride a rearing horse was dedicated. It stood—and stands today—at the center of Jackson Square, as the Place d'Armes was renamed in honor of the general.

His legacy was large and, like the War of 1812 and the Battle of New Orleans, subject to debate. Saving New Orleans made Andrew Jackson a national hero and, with his nation still mourning George Washington, Jackson inherited the great man's mantle. General Washington led the first fight with the British—but Andrew Jackson's success at New Orleans preserved his nation's hard-fought independence.

AFTERWORD

Presidential Memory

The more I learn about Jackson, the more I love him.

—President Franklin Delano Roosevelt, 1936

Since the release of the hardcover edition of this book last year, I have followed closely the debate raging over Andrew Jackson's legacy. I myself fall in the category of Jackson admirer, though I acknowledge that some of his decisions in life, politics, and battle were wrong. Despite his flaws, no clear-eyed evaluator can dispute Jackson's patriotic motivations and the significance of his legacy even today. In fact, in some ways Old Hickory is more relevant than ever; President Donald Trump sees enough importance in Jackson to return his portrait to the Oval Office.

Our forty-fifth president is not the only one who looked up to Jackson. Some of our finest leaders saw in him someone to emulate. While this generation of Americans feels compelled to evaluate him by the standards of today, iconic presidents of America's past saw in him primarily someone to admire.

After the Battle of New Orleans, Andrew Jackson's countrymen adored him. They knew he saved the nation and thought of him, along with George Washington, as a defining national figure. In one way, Jackson was even more their man than the founders; unlike the presidents up to that point, Jackson inherited no land or family reputation. He owed no allegiance to what he called the "aristocracy of the union," and the common people claimed him as their own. Birth registries across the county offered one sign of that status. In years to come, for every baby named, say, "George Washington Smith," another would be christened "Andrew Jackson Jones."

In 1828, his admirers elected him president in a landslide—his 178 electoral votes more than doubled incumbent John Quincy Adams's 83. On March 4, 1829, a great crowd gathered to cheer as he took the oath of office; in the view of one watcher, he was "the People's President" on "the People's Day."[1] So enthusiastic was the crowd that the celebration got a bit out of hand at the White House, ending in broken furniture, smashed crystal, and men clambering out windows. Forced to escape to a hotel, this new president was dubbed "King Mob" by one Supreme Court justice.[2]

The more refined members of the judicial branch may have disapproved, but Jackson had a mandate and acted on it. Thanks to his fiscal policies, the nation had no debt (for the only time in history) for one year of his presidency. He vetoed more legislation than all his predecessors combined. A firm believer in America's "Manifest Destiny," he pursued territorial expansion as if it were a moral duty. When a national controversy over tariffs threatened the Union (South Carolina claimed they could "nullify" the tariffs), everyone believed

President Jackson's threat to "hang the first man I can lay my hand on engaged in such treasonable conduct, upon the first tree I can reach."[3] All talk of secession faded.

Since then, Jackson's reputation has fluctuated as his politics and bluster have come in and out of favor, but he shows no signs of being forgotten. From the nineteenth century into the twenty-first, the seventh president has influenced many of America's presidents, who have turned to him for inspiration both in war and in politics.

Theodore Roosevelt

Theodore Roosevelt encountered Jackson's legacy early in life. Suffering from a case of unrequited love as a senior at Harvard, he buried his sorrows at the library. A voracious reader who would read a book a day throughout his life, he decided, in 1879, to write a book of his own. The topic? The War of 1812.

After a few months, he set the project aside—the woman he loved, Alice Lee, finally consented to be his wife—but he returned to his manuscript after his marriage. On publication, in 1882, *The Naval War of 1812* quickly sold out three printings. It became a standard reference on the war and, at twenty-three, Roosevelt gained recognition as a serious historian.

One figure stands especially tall in his book. Roosevelt wasted little ink on the U.S. Army in 1812, 1813, and 1814; as he put it, "the war on land had been for us full of humiliation."[4] But he found General Jackson mesmerizing. "The only military genius," Roosevelt concluded, "that the struggle developed was Andrew Jackson."

Yet young Roosevelt also recognized how complex a man Andrew

Jackson had been. In 1882, he wrote, "In after-years [Jackson] did to his country some good and more evil; but no true American can think of his deeds at New Orleans without profound and unmixed thankfulness." An advocate of military preparedness and, above all, strong leadership, Roosevelt could not help but admire how Jackson managed his unlikely army of frontiersmen, pirates, Creoles, and blacks. "Even their fierce natures quailed before the ungovernable fury of a spirit greater than their own; and their sullen, stubborn wills were bent at last before [Jackson's] unyielding temper and iron hand."

As president years later, Roosevelt pursued his policy of the Square Deal, which echoed Jackson's desire to fight for common people in the face of moneyed interests. He saw political equity in associating his name with the strong-willed Jackson (Roosevelt, after all, was a proponent of "speak softly and carry a big stick"). Later still, in his post-presidential autobiography, Roosevelt disparaged Jackson as "King Andrew." But he would be far from the last president to honor, even with mixed feelings, the Jackson legacy.

Harry S. Truman

At age ten, Harry Truman first chanced upon Andrew Jackson. Harry was recuperating from a bout with diphtheria; for months his legs and arms had been paralyzed and his mother had been forced to move him about in a baby carriage. But as the symptoms faded, Truman regained his strength and he devoured a four-volume set of *Great Men and Famous Women*, a gift from his mother.

The subjects ranged from Goethe to Grover Cleveland, Hannibal to Robert E. Lee. Truman quickly found favorites, one of them Andrew Jackson. For Truman, the Tennessean became a lifelong hero.[5]

Unlike Theodore Roosevelt, who was the son a wealthy New York family, Harry Truman came from rough-and-ready stock. His father (nicknamed "Peanuts") worked at different times as a mule trader, farmer, and night watchman, and, despite his father's lack of military experience, Harry saw a connection between Jackson and John Truman. "My father was a fighter," Harry Truman would say, "and if he didn't like what you did, he'd fight you. He was an Andrew Jackson descendent."[6] Though the families weren't directly related, they did share Scotch-Irish ancestry and undeniable frontier toughness.

When, at twenty-four, Truman joined the Freemasons, he reveled in knowing that Jackson, too, had been a member. In business selling men's clothing, Truman spent more time reading books about Jackson (according to his partner's recollections) than he did serving his customers.[7] That business would fail but while serving as a judge in Missouri in the thirties, Truman commissioned an equestrian statue of Jackson that still stands in front of the courthouse. The former clothier was so concerned about the correctness of the likeness that he took measurements of a surviving Jackson uniform. As president, he positioned a bronze model of that Jackson statue on a table in his office for all visitors to see.

When he posed with Franklin Roosevelt after the latter had invited him to be his running mate, in August 1944, they stood in shirtsleeves beneath a tree planted by then president Andrew Jackson on the White House's South Lawn. "Give 'em Hell" Harry could hardly have known that less than a year later he would become the nation's thirty-third president when FDR died in office.

President Truman would be a tough fiscal conservative in the vein of his favorite president. He wanted, as Jackson had done, to reawaken "the people again to the fact that they control the government."[8] He chose to stand with average men and women. "Jackson wanted sincerely to look after the little fellow who had no pull," Truman once said, "and that's what a president is supposed to do."[9]

He was a plain speaker, at least partly in honor of the tradition of backcountry politics he shared with Andrew Jackson. And the general public knew it, too. Thousands gathered in Washington for his first inaugural, in 1949; another ten million people watched what was the first inauguration broadcast on television.

To the end, Jackson was a living presence for Truman. When he chose not to run for reelection in 1952, he named Andrew Jackson (and others) as a precedent for a two-term presidency. Over a century after his death, Jackson's legacy lingered.

Continuing Influence

Other presidents also paid homage, making trips to Jackson's Hermitage, as many did to Washington's Mount Vernon. When Teddy's cousin Franklin Delano Roosevelt visited, in 1934, he was a first-term president. He and his wife, Eleanor, were heading for the Little White House in Warm Springs, Georgia, but Jackson and the Hermitage left a strong impression. To the tune of "Hail to the Chief" (played on Jackson's pianoforte), he was greeted by a descendant of Rachel Jackson's. Despite his disabilities—only steel braces, his cane, and an aide at his elbow permitted FDR to stand—he honored the general's toughness by touring the Hermitage without his wheelchair.[10]

In the next presidential campaign, Roosevelt and his New Deal programs were under siege. He saw a parallel to Jackson's battles while in office. As Roosevelt confided to his vice president, "It is absolutely true that [Jackson's] opponents represented the same social outlook and the same element of the population that ours do. The more I learn about Andy Jackson, the more I love him."[11]

Perhaps Jackson's many ailments were another connection for the usually wheelchair-bound Roosevelt, but, having won a second term, he ordered the construction of a replica of the Hermitage's facade on the White House lawn to serve as a reviewing stand for his 1937 inauguration. In March 1941, as FDR pondered war with the Axis powers, he spoke to his radio audience from the deck of the USS *Potomac* and once again invoked the memory of Jackson. He compared the approaching war—just nine months later the Japanese would attack Pearl Harbor—to the "responsibility [that] lay heavily upon the shoulders of Andrew Jackson."[12]

Although John F. Kennedy did not visit the Hermitage, he counted Jackson as a Democratic forefather, describing him rather ambiguously as "both a picture of dignity and a master of profanity."[13] Lyndon Baines Johnson did make it to Hermitage, Tennessee, arriving, in March 1967, for a celebration of Jackson's two hundredth birthday. Just a year away from what was shaping up to be a hard-fought reelection campaign, Johnson spoke in his Hermitage speech of the "Jacksonian revolution." He also mentioned Jackson had been a slaveholder as he described the goals of his own Great Society agenda. "We are still striving," Johnson told the crowd, "to involve the poor, the deprived, the forgotten American, white and Negro, in the future of their society." In closing, he cited Jackson's "rugged confidence," probably a reference to the anti-war opposition Johnson faced, a major factor in his unexpected decision not to pursue another presidential term in 1968.[14]

Perhaps it was inevitable that Ronald Reagan, a man who knew star power firsthand, chose to pair portraits of Washington and a youthful-looking Andrew Jackson in the Oval Office. He, too, would attend a Jackson birthday party, and in a Nashville speech, in 1982, he aligned Jackson's legacy with his own vision for smaller government. "Our federal government has become so bloated and fat that Jackson wouldn't recognize it," Reagan told his audience. He reminded them of the kind of leader his long-ago predecessor had been. "It was Jackson," said Reagan, "who reminded us that 'One man with courage makes a majority.'"[15]

More presidents than we have space for visited the Hermitage; in the future, more will do the same. We will also see Jackson's stock continue to rise and fall. Recently there's been discontent at celebrating a man with Jackson's history regarding Native Americans, as well as controversy over the plan, advanced during the Obama administration, to replace Jackson on the twenty-dollar bill with Harriet Tubman, a decision more recently postponed.

Although his era was very different from ours, the desire of so many presidents, Republican and Democratic, to relate to him speaks to his importance. Whatever his flaws, the general rose above humble roots to command an army and, later, to captain his country. His leadership remains inspiring. His presence in the public mind, in the writings of historians, and in the eyes of presidents demonstrates the man's immortality. In short, the Hero of New Orleans remains an indisputable, if debated, American icon long after he vanquished an unbeatable foe on the Chalmette Plain.

—Brian Kilmeade, May 2018

ACKNOWLEDGMENTS

As someone who first fell in love with American history by learning about the local history where I grew up, I have a tremendous amount of appreciation for the enthusiasm that scholars, researchers, and reenactors bring to their study of the people and events who helped shape their corner of the world and the nation at large. This project was no exception. The dedication of the men and women in Louisiana and Tennessee who assisted us with our reconstruction of the Battle of New Orleans as well as the character of Andrew Jackson is a testament to their field.

This book could not possibly have happened without our superlative team at Sentinel, headed by Adrian Zackheim. He proved once again that he is a man of tremendous vision and appreciation for the impact of dynamic, meaningful stories; it is truly an honor to be able to develop these books under his guidance and expertise. Will Weisser can best be described as a high-octane executive who fuels all the books we have produced at Sentinel, and his involvement is essential and deeply appreciated. Bria Sandford, likewise, is one of the most outstanding individuals with whom I have ever had the pleasure of working. She keeps an unimaginable number of plates spinning and does so without ever breaking her stride or her smile. She is both gracious and tenacious, a delight and a powerhouse; it was her suggestion for the title, after many long and agonizing conversations as a team, that was the breakthrough that allowed this story to find its way.

Bob Barnett, our tremendous agent, has built a reputation as one of the most respected people in the business—and for good reason. He not only represents the book but also truly cares about its development and success in a way that goes above and beyond a simple business transaction. I am continually awed by and grateful for his involvement in our work, and his support for everything it takes to make each book all it can be.

It's always great working with the award-winning writer Don Yaeger, whose humor, talent, and experience make these projects so much better and so much more fun. And with Don comes his longtime cohort Tiffany Yecke Brooks. Without her incredible contribution, this book would simply not be the same. *(Here's the big secret in my opinion, Don: Tiffany likes history more than sports.)*

The research component of this project was staggering in its magnitude—primary documents, secondary documents, tangential documents that proved essential, and in-person tours of numerous sites. Thankfully, we were blessed with historian after historian who responded to our requests for information with amazing enthusiasm and humbling brilliance. In New Orleans, world-class historian Douglas Brinkley was able to share his tremendous knowledge as well as steer us to the great people at the Historic New Orleans Collection and the Jean Lafitte National Historical Park's visitors' center. Thank you, too, to Ron Drez, who does as much as anyone in this country to keep American history alive. And a huge thanks to Ron Chapman, who gave us way too much of his personal time taking us through the Chalmette

Battlefield and giving us tours of downtown. His passion, knowledge, and book (*The Battle of New Orleans: "But for a Piece of Wood"*) helped bring this story to life.

In Tennessee, I'd like to spotlight the great help from Tom Kanon, a talented archivist with the Tennessee secretary of state's office. His guidance was essential in helping us develop a fuller picture of the character of Andrew Jackson. Additionally, the entire staff at the Hermitage, Andrew and Rachel Jackson's home, was unbelievably welcoming, helpful, and incredibly knowledgeable. I would especially like to thank Marsha Mullin, vice president of museum services and chief curator. Your dedication to preserving Jackson's legacy is humbling, and your knowledge is astounding. Thank you for giving us such valuable insight while also showing true southern hospitality.

And to Hugh Howard, whose depth of knowledge never fails to astound me, thank you for your suggestions and guidance in getting us started and keeping us on track with what felt, at times, like an overwhelming number of sources.

The key to the success of any book is the promotion and marketing, and most of that falls on the shoulders of George Uribe and his company, Guestbooker. George and the outstanding Victoria Delgado Chism have headed the promotion, working tirelessly to make *Thomas Jefferson and the Tripoli Pirates* an enormous success and a *New York Times* bestseller. Their work to ensure past successes helped lay the path for future ones.

The entire Fox News family has been outstanding in all they have done to support my work on this project as well as to help spread its important message. I would like to spotlight all those who built and sustain Fox News Channel today. Special thanks to Rupert Murdoch, Suzanne Scott, Jay Wallace, and Jack Abernathy for supporting my passion for American history and for launching the one-hour TV special in conjunction with the publication of the book. I'm grateful to John Finley for putting together an amazing team, including Brian Gaffney, Jennings Grant, and Carrie Flatley, leading up to the special's release, and I owe tremendous thanks to Paul Guest and Amanda Muehlenkamp, social media mavens who worked around the clock to get the word out about this book. And nothing gets done without the legal team, of course, so I am indebted to them for all of their behind-the-scenes help, especially Dianne Brandi, the legal eagle who keeps us on the straight and narrow.

Steve Doocy and Ainsley Earhardt were great allies in the monumental process of getting this book out, all while Ainsley had the additional challenge of writing and promoting her children's book. Their support for the project was truly appreciated.

I also am thrilled to spotlight the incredible support of the staffs of my two programs: on TV, *Fox & Friends,* and on the radio, *The Brian Kilmeade Show.* I have the pleasure of working with such great people on a daily basis, and they are consistently looking to bend their schedules so that I can develop and promote projects like this. To Vice President Lauren Petterson, how you oversee thirty hours of weekly programming and still support me in all my extra work is beyond me. Gavin Hadden, you are a positive, patriotic EP—thank you. I would also like to single out the ceaseless support from my other star TV producers: Sean Groman, Brian Tully, A. J. Hall, Andrew Murray, Lauren Peikoff, Chris White, Kelly McNally, Kelly May, Stephanie Freeman, and Lee Kushnir.

On the radio, I constantly need flexibility for interviews, specials, and appearances, and my support team is endlessly patient and professional. Led by Alyson Mansfield, who helps me beyond radio as my coordinating producer, Eric Albeen, Peter Caterina, and Aaron Spielberg round out the radio A team.

Finally, to my wife and children, I can never thank you enough. My wife, Dawn, the most patient and supportive woman in the world, I know this book took time away from our family. I am forever grateful for your willingness to shoulder more of the responsibilities while I am researching, writing, or traveling for what has become, during its production, a kind of second full-time job. To Bryan, Kirstyn, and Kaitlyn, I deeply appreciate your understanding and even your enthusiasm for this work. May you someday be as blessed as I am to have a family that encourages you to similarly pursue your interests and passions.

Andrew Jackson and the Miracle at New Orleans is a story of a highly factionalized society coming together at a time of crisis and uniting their skills, valor, and spirit for the sake of preserving this nation. I can think of no message more timely or important. Jackson led the way, but it was the willingness of the ordinary citizens—soldiers, militiamen, civilians, outlaws—who carried out his vision. Despite the vast differences in language, ethnicity, national origin, race, social class, and countless other factors, the people who defended New Orleans recognized that what united them was stronger than what divided them. This story is a testament to Americans' willingness to reach out across lines and come together to protect our beautiful liberty. Perhaps no moment in American history better encapsulates our national motto: *E pluribus unum*. Out of many, one.

NOTES

PROLOGUE

1. Parton, *Life of Andrew Jackson,* vol. 1 (1861), p. 89.
2. Quoted in Groom, *Patriotic Fire,* p. 37.

CHAPTER 1: FREEDOMS AT RISK

1. Andrew Jackson to Thomas Monteagle Bayly, June 27, 1807.
2. Parton, *Life of Andrew Jackson,* vol. 1 (1861), p. 133.
3. Benton, *Thirty Years' View* (1854), vol. 1, p. 736.
4. Andrew Jackson, Proclamation to the Tennessee Militia, March 7, 1812.
5. "Jackson's Announcement to His Soldiers," November 14, 1812.
6. Thomas Jefferson to Robert R. Livingston, April 18, 1802.

CHAPTER 2: HOW TO LOSE A WAR

1. Henry Clay, speech to Senate, February 22, 1810.
2. Thomas Jefferson to William Duane, August 4, 1812.
3. William Eustis to Henry Dearborn, July 9, 1812.
4. John Randolph, speech to Congress, December 10, 1811, in *Annals of Congress,* 12th Congress, 1st Session, p. 447.

5. Quoted in Groom, *Patriotic Fire,* p.166.
6. Andrew Jackson to Willie Blount, July 3, 1812.
7. Andrew Jackson, quoted in Remini, *Andrew Jackson and the Course of American Empire* (1977), p. 170.
8. "The Departure from Nashville, a Journal of the Trip Down the Mississippi," in Jackson, *Correspondence of Andrew Jackson,* vol. 1. (1926), pp. 256–71.
9. John Armstrong to Andrew Jackson, February 5, 1813.
10. James Madison to Robert R. Livingston and James Monroe, April 18, 1803.
11. John Armstrong to Andrew Jackson, February 5, 1813.
12. Andrew Jackson to John Armstrong, March 15, 1813.
13. "Jackson's Announcement to His Soldiers," November 14, 1812.
14. Andrew Jackson to Felix Grundy, March 15, 1813.
15. Andrew Jackson to James Wilkinson, March 22, 1813.
16. Andrew Jackson to James Madison, March 15, 1813.
17. Andrew Jackson to Rachel Jackson, March 15, 1813.
18. *Nashville Whig,* quoted in Remini, *Andrew Jackson and the Course of American Empire* (1977), p. 180.
19. Parton, *Life of Andrew Jackson,* vol. 1 (1861), p. 382.

CHAPTER 3: THE MAKING OF A GENERAL

1. Groom, *Patriotic Fire* (2006), p. 38.
2. Charles Dickinson, May 21, 1806, in *Correspondence of Andrew Jackson,* vol. 1 (1926), p. 143.
3. Parton, *Life of Andrew Jackson,* vol. 1 (1861), p. 387.
4. Thomas Hart Benton to Andrew Jackson, July 25, 1813.
5. Parton, *Life of Andrew Jackson,* vol. 1 (1861), p. 394.
6. Griffith, *McIntosh and Weatherford* (1988), p. 111.
7. Andrew Jackson to the Tennessee Volunteers, September 24, 1813.
8. Reid and Eaton, *Life* (1817), p. 33.
9. Crockett, *Narrative of the Life of David Crockett* (1834), p. 88.
10. John Coffee, Official Report, November 3, 1813, in Parton, *Life of Andrew Jackson,* vol. 1 (1861), p. 437.

11. Parton, *Life of Andrew Jackson,* vol. 1 (1861), p. 439.
12. Andrew Jackson to Rachel Jackson, November 4, 1813.
13. Quoted in Remini, *Andrew Jackson and the Course of American Empire* (1977), p. 193.
14. Andrew Jackson to Willie Blount, November 11, 1813.
15. Crockett, *Narrative of the Life of David Crockett* (1834), p. 92.

CHAPTER 4: A RIVER DYED RED

1. John Borlase Warren to Lord Melville, November 18, 1812.
2. Matthew D. Cooper, quoted in Owsley, *Struggle for the Gulf Borderland* (1981), p. 69.
3. Colonel William Martin to Andrew Jackson, December 4, 1813.
4. Reid and Eaton, *Life* (1817), p. 84.
5. Andrew Jackson to the First Brigade, Tennessee Volunteer Infantry, December 13, 1813.
6. Andrew Jackson to Rachel Jackson, December 29, 1813.
7. Andrew Jackson to Willie Blount, December 29, 1813.
8. See Pickett, *History of Alabama,* vol. 2 (1851), pp. 324–25, and Griffith, *McIntosh and Weatherford* (1988), pp. 129–31.
9. Reid and Eaton, *Life* (1817), p. 136.
10. "Report of Jackson to Governor Blount," March 31, 1814.
11. John Coffee to Andrew Jackson, April 11, 1814.
12. Andrew Jackson, "General Order," March 24[?], 1814.
13. Andrew Jackson to Rachel Jackson, April 1, 1814.
14. Reid and Eaton, *Life* (1817), p. 165. Variant versions of Jackson and Weatherford's meeting are found in Pickett, *History of Alabama,* vol. 2 (1851), pp. 348–52, and in Royall, *Letters from Alabama* (1830), pp. 17–19, as recounted by one of Jackson's subalterns in 1817 to Anne Royall, whom some consider to be the first American woman journalist.
15. Reid and Eaton, *Life* (1817), p. 166.
16. Ibid., pp. 166–67.
17. Major John Reid, quoted in James, *Life of Andrew Jackson* (1933), p. 172.

18. Attributed to Andrew Jackson in Woodward, *Woodward's Reminiscences of the Creek* (1939), p. 102.
19. John Armstrong to James Madison, May 14, 1814.
20. Andrew Jackson to Rachel Jackson, August 5, 1814.
21. *American State Papers,* Military Affairs, vol. 1, p. 379.
22. Ingersoll, *Historical Sketch of the Second War,* vol. 1 (1853), pp. 197–200.

CHAPTER 5: THE BRITISH ON OFFENSE

1. Crété, *Daily Life in Louisiana* (1978), p. 61.
2. *Times* (London), April 27, 1814.
3. Albert Gallatin to James Monroe, June 13, 1814.
4. Henry Clay to James Monroe, August 18, 1814.
5. Letter fragment of August 13, 1814, cited in James, *Life of Andrew Jackson* (1933), p. 184. See also letter of August 8, 1814, reprinted in Latour, *Historical Memoir* (1816, 1999), pp. 184–85.
6. Andrew Jackson to Robert Butler, August 27, 1814.
7. Andrew Jackson to William C. C. Claiborne, August 30, 1814.
8. Andrew Jackson to Robert Butler, August 27, 1814.
9. Although the story of the Lafitte-Lockyer encounter has been told many times in different ways (including by Lafitte himself many years later in his less-than-reliable *Journal*), perhaps the best and most authoritative version appeared shortly after the Battle of New Orleans in Latour, *Historical Memoir* (1816, 1999), pp. 24ff. See also James, *Life of Andrew Jackson* (1933) and "Napoleon, Junior" (1927).
10. Walker, *Jackson and New Orleans* (1856), p. 41.
11. Edward Nicholls to Jean Lafitte, August 31, 1814, in Latour, *Historical Memoir* (1816, 1999), appendix III, pp. 186–87.
12. Jean Lafitte to Jean Blanque, September 4, 1814, in ibid., appendix V, p. 189.
13. Jean Lafitte to William C. C. Claiborne, September 4, 1814, in ibid., p. 191.

CHAPTER 6: JACKSON UNLEASHED

1. Tatum, "Major H. Tatum's Journal" (1922), p. 55.
2. Andrew Jackson to James Monroe, September 17, 1814.
3. Kouwenhoven and Patten, "New Light on 'The Star Spangled Banner'" (1937), p. 199.
4. James Madison, "A Proclamation," September 1, 1814.
5. Latimer, *1812: War with America* (2007), p. 331.
6. Andrew Jackson to John Rhea, October 11, 1814.
7. Andrew Jackson to James Monroe, October 10, 1814.
8. Reid and Eaton, *Life* (1817), p. 221.
9. Charles Cassiday to Andrew Jackson, September 23, 1814.
10. González Manrique to Andrew Jackson, November 6, 1814.
11. "From Our Ministers at Ghent," *Niles' Weekly Register,* October 15, 1814.
12. Adams, *Memoirs of John Quincy Adams,* vol. 3 (1874), p. 45.
13. Albert Gallatin to James Monroe, August 20, 1814.
14. Albert Gallatin to William Crawford, April 21, 1814.
15. Henry Clay to James Monroe, October 26, 1814, in *Papers of Henry Clay,* vol. 1 (1959), p. 996.
16. James Monroe to Andrew Jackson, October 10, 1814.

CHAPTER 7: TARGET: NEW ORLEANS

1. Edward Codrington to his wife, November 12, December 10, 1814, quoted in Mahon, "British Command Decisions" (1965), p. 54.
2. Carter, *Blaze of Glory* (1971), pp. 87–88.
3. Alexander F. I. Cochrane to Earl Bathurst, July 14, 1814, reprinted in Crawford, ed., *Naval War of 1812* (2002), p. 131.
4. [Gleig], *Narrative of the Campaigns of the British Army* (1821), p. 240.
5. Adams, *War of 1812,* p. 223.
6. Andrew Jackson to James Monroe, November 20, 1814.
7. Andrew Jackson to Rachel Jackson, November 15, 1814. The medicament prescribed was a mix of calomel and the Mexican herbal jalap, which, like

other purgatives in a time of primitive medicines, tended to induce vomiting or diarrhea.

8. Andrew Jackson to Rachel Jackson, February 21, 1814.
9. Walker, *Jackson and New Orleans* (1856), p. 13.
10. Ibid., p. 15.
11. Reilly, *British at the Gates* (1974), p. 210.
12. Hatcher, *Edward Livingston* (1940), p. 123.
13. Hunt, *Memoir of Mrs. Edward Livingston* (1886), pp. 52–53; James, *Life of Andrew Jackson* (1933), p. 204.
14. Andrew Jackson to James Brown, February 4, 1815.
15. Tatum, "Major H. Tatum's Journal" (1922), pp. 96–97.
16. Latour, *Historical Memoir* (1816, 1999), p. 48.
17. Tatum, "Major H. Tatum's Journal" (1922), p. 99.
18. Latour, *Historical Memoir* (1816, 1999), p. 59.

CHAPTER 8: LOSING LAKE BORGNE

1. [Gleig], *Narrative of the Campaigns of the British Army* (1821), p. 247.
2. Daniel Patterson to Andrew Jackson, quoted in McClellan, "Navy at the Battle of New Orleans" (1924), p. 2044.
3. Latour, *Historical Memoir* (1816, 1999), p. 50.
4. Andrew Jackson to James Monroe, December 10, 1814.
5. B. E. Hill, quoted in Latimer, *1812: War with America* (2007), p. 376.
6. Lossing, *Pictorial Field-Book of the War of 1812* (1868), p. 1026.
7. Alexander Cochrane, quoted in Carter, *Blaze of Glory* (1971), p. 123.
8. Thomas ap Catesby Jones to Daniel T. Patterson, March 12, 1815, reprinted in Latour, *Historical Memoir* (1816, 1999), p. 213.
9. Ibid., p. 214.
10. Carter, *Blaze of Glory* (1971), p. 126.
11. Thomas ap Catesby Jones to Daniel T. Patterson, March 12, 1815, reprinted in Latour, *Historical Memoir* (1816, 1999), p. 214.

CHAPTER 9: THE ARMIES ASSEMBLE

1. Walker, *Jackson and New Orleans* (1856), p. 153.
2. Quoted in Parton, *Life of Andrew Jackson,* vol. 2 (1861), p. 56.
3. Tatum, "Major H. Tatum's Journal" (1922), p. 106.
4. Heaney, *Century of Pioneering* (1993), p. 380n16.
5. Andrew Jackson to W. Allen, quoted in Remini, *Andrew Jackson and the Course of American Empire* (1977), p. 254.
6. Tatum, "Major H. Tatum's Journal" (1922), p. 105.
7. "Jackson's Address to the Troops in New Orleans," December 18, 1814.
8. [Gleig], *Narrative of the Campaigns of the British Army* (1821), p. 260.
9. Aitchison, *British Eyewitness at the Battle of New Orleans* (2004), p. 61.
10. [Gleig], *Narrative of the Campaigns of the British Army* (1821), pp. 261–62.
11. Ibid., p. 262.
12. Walker, *Jackson and New Orleans* (1856), pp. 138–39n.
13. Andrew Jackson to James Monroe, December 27, 1814.
14. Latour, *Historical Memoir* (1816), p. 71.
15. Andrew Jackson to Major Reynolds, December 22, 1814.
16. Earl Bathurst to Edward Pakenham, October 24, 1814.
17. Walker, *Jackson and New Orleans* (1856), p. 111.
18. Thomas Shields and Robert Morrell to Daniel T. Patterson, January 14, 1815, reprinted in Latour, *Historical Memoir* (1816, 1999), p. 219.
19. Keane, "A Journal of the Operations Against New Orleans," reprinted in Wellington, *Supplementary Despatches,* vol. 10 (1863), p. 395.
20. Ibid., p. 397.
21. [Gleig], *Narrative of the Campaigns of the British Army* (1821), pp. 277–78.
22. Walker, *Jackson and New Orleans* (1856), pp. 150–51; see also James, *Life of Andrew Jackson* (1933), p. 820n55.
23. Walker, *Jackson and New Orleans* (1856), p. 161.
24. Ibid., p. 157.

CHAPTER 10: THE FIRST BATTLE OF NEW ORLEANS

1. [Gleig], *Narrative of the Campaigns of the British Army* (1821), p. 279.
2. Keane, "A Journal of Operations Against New Orleans," reprinted in Wellington, *Supplementary Despatches,* vol. 10 (1863), pp. 396–97.
3. Parton, *Life of Andrew Jackson,* vol. 2 (1861), p. 84.
4. Cooke, *Narrative of Events* (1835), pp. 190–91.
5. Ibid.
6. Ibid.
7. [Gleig], *Narrative of the Campaigns of the British Army* (1821), p. 286.
8. Davis, *Pirates Lafitte* (2005), pp. 214–15.
9. [Gleig], *Narrative of the Campaigns of the British Army* (1821), p. 286.
10. Walker, *Jackson and New Orleans* (1856), p. 171.
11. Latour, *Historical Memoir* (1816, 1999), p. 83.
12. Thomson, *Historical Sketches of the Late War Between the United States and Great Britain* (1817), p. 351.
13. Cooke, *Narrative of Events* (1835), p. 195.
14. [Gleig], *Narrative of the Campaigns of the British Army* (1821), p. 292.
15. Quoted in Groom, *Patriotic Fire* (2006), p. 141.
16. Ibid., p. 294.
17. [Gleig], *Subaltern in America* (1833), p. 219.

CHAPTER 11: THE DEFENSIVE LINE

1. Andrew Jackson to William Claiborne, December 24, 1814.
2. Daniel Patterson to the secretary of the navy, December 29, 1814, reprinted in Latour, *Historical Memoir* (1816, 1999), p. 233.
3. *Historical and Archaeological Investigations at the Chalmette Battlefield* (2009), pp. 48–49.
4. John Donelson, quoted in Parton, *Life of Andrew Jackson,* vol. 2 (1861), p. 102.
5. Walker, *Jackson and New Orleans* (1856), p. 213.

6. [Gleig], *Narrative of the Campaigns of the British Army* (1821), pp. 301–2.
7. Surtees, *Twenty-Five Years in the Rifle Brigade* (1833), p. 356.
8. Walker, *Jackson and New Orleans* (1856), p. 201.
9. Brands, *Andrew Jackson* (2005), pp. 272–73.
10. Cooke, *Narrative of Events* (1835), p. 203.
11. Remini, *Battle of New Orleans* (1999), p. 89.
12. General Keane to General Pakenham, December 26, 1814, reprinted in James, *Full and Correct Account of the Military Occurrences of the Late War,* vol. 2 (1818), p. 531.
13. Walker, *Jackson and New Orleans* (1856), p. 212.
14. Dickson, "Artillery Services in North America in 1814 and 1815" (1919), p. 98.
15. Smith, *Autobiography,* vol. 1 (1902), p. 228.
16. Edward Livingston to Andrew Jackson, December 25, 1814.
17. Walker, *Jackson and New Orleans* (1856), p. 226.
18. Ibid., p. 227.
19. [Gleig], *Narrative of the Campaigns of the British Army* (1821), p. 309.
20. Andrew Jackson to John McLean, March 22, 1824.
21. Latour, *Historical Memoir* (1816, 1999), p. 12.
22. Surtees, *Twenty-Five Years in the Rifle Brigade* (1833), p. 363.
23. Latour, *Historical Memoir* (1816, 1999), p. 95.
24. Reid and Eaton, *Life* (1817), pp. 326–27.
25. Smith, *Autobiography,* vol. 1 (1902), n.p.
26. Walker, *Jackson and New Orleans* (1856), p. 257.
27. Remini, *Battle of New Orleans* (1999), p. 109.
28. Walker, *Jackson and New Orleans* (1856), p. 257.
29. Edward Pakenham, Orders, December 31, 1814, reprinted in Wellington, *Supplementary Despatches,* vol. 10 (1863), p. 398.
30. [Gleig], *Narrative of the Campaigns of the British Army* (1821), p. 318.
31. Walker, *Jackson and New Orleans* (1856), p. 238.
32. Smith, *Autobiography,* vol. 1 (1902), p. 233.
33. Andrew Jackson to James Monroe, January 3, 1815.
34. Buell, *History of Andrew Jackson,* vol. 1 (1904), p. 423.

35. Nolte, *Fifty Years* (1854), p. 219.
36. The numbers vary greatly, depending upon the source, among them Roosevelt, *Naval War of 1812* (1889), pp. 225–26.
37. Jackson's Manuscript Narrative, Library of Congress, quoted in James, *Life of Andrew Jackson* (1933), p. 241.
38. Parton, *Life of Andrew Jackson,* vol. 2 (1861), p. 188.
39. Edward Livingston, quoted in ibid., p. 228. See also Heaney, *Century of Pioneering* (1993), pp. 237–38.

CHAPTER 12: DAY OF DESTINY

1. Smith, *Autobiography,* vol. 1 (1902), p. 235.
2. Ibid., pp. 235–36.
3. Buell, *History of Andrew Jackson,* vol. 2 (1904), p. 12; Reid and Eaton, *Life* (1817), p. 338.
4. Parton, *Life of Andrew Jackson,* vol. 2 (1861), pp. 192–94.
5. Quoted in Groom, *Patriotic Fire* (2006), p. 196.
6. Reilly, *British at the Gates* (1974), p. 296.
7. Quoted in Carter, *Blaze of Glory* (1971), p. 254.
8. Cooke, *Narrative of Events* (1835), p. 231.
9. [Gleig], *Subaltern in America* (1833), p. 262.
10. Walker, *Jackson and New Orleans* (1856), p. 335; Cooke, *Narrative of Events* (1835), p. 253.
11. Cooke, *Narrative of Events* (1835), p. 235.
12. Anonymous, "A Kentucky Soldier's Account" (1926), reprinted in Hickey, ed., *War of 1812* (2013), p. 671.
13. Walker, *Jackson and New Orleans* (1856), p. 327.
14. Quoted in Remini, *Battle of New Orleans* (1999), p. 210.
15. Gayarré, *Historical Sketch of Pierre and Jean Lafitte* (1964).
16. Anonymous, "A Kentucky Soldier's Account" (1926), reprinted in Hickey, ed., *War of 1812* (2013), p. 670.
17. Nolte, *Fifty Years* (1854), p. 221.

18. John Lambert to Earl Bathurst, January 10, 1815, reprinted in Latour, *Historical Memoir* (1816, 1999), pp. 312–13.
19. Cooper, *Rough Notes of Seven Campaigns* (1914), p. 139.
20. [Gleig], *Narrative of the Campaigns of the British Army* (1821), p. 326.
21. Cooke, *Narrative of Events* (1835), p. 234.
22. Ibid.
23. Ibid., p. 252.
24. Parton, *Life of Andrew Jackson,* vol. 2 (1861), pp. 196–97.
25. The stories of Pakenham's death vary. Among the choice versions are General Lambert's account—see John Lambert to Earl Bathurst, January 10, 1815, reprinted in Latour, *Historical Memoir* (1816, 1999), pp. 312–13; Parton, *Life of Andrew Jackson,* vol. 2 (1861), pp. 196–98; and Walker, *Jackson and New Orleans* (1856), p. 331.
26. Walker, *Jackson and New Orleans* (1856), p. 340.
27. Anonymous, "A Kentucky Soldier's Account" (1926), reprinted in Hickey, ed., *War of 1812* (2013), p. 672.
28. Arthur, *Story of the Battle of New Orleans* (1915), p. 239.
29. Mrs. Henry Clement, quoted in Clement, *Plantation Life on the Mississippi* (1952), pp. 135–36.
30. Heaney, *Century of Pioneering* (1993), p. 238.
31. Walker, *Jackson and New Orleans* (1856), pp. 346–47.
32. Anonymous, "A Kentucky Soldier's Account" (1926), reprinted in Hickey, ed., *War of 1812* (2013), p. 673.
33. Parton, *Life of Andrew Jackson,* vol. 2 (1861), pp. 208–9.
34. Ibid., p. 208.
35. Cooke, *Narrative of Events* (1835), p. 239.

CHAPTER 13: THE BRITISH WITHDRAW

1. For a fuller description of this deliberation, see Nolte, *Fifty Years* (1854), pp. 224–25, and Parton, *Life of Andrew Jackson,* vol. 2 (1861), pp. 234–36.

2. Brown, *Amphibious Campaign* (1969), p. 160, and Reid and Eaton, *Life* (1817), p. 361ff.
3. Andrew Jackson to James Monroe, January 19, 1815.
4. Ibid.
5. Latour, *Historical Memoir* (1816), p. 197.
6. Reid and Eaton, *Life* (1817), p. 367.
7. Andrew Jackson to Abbé Dubourg, January 19, 1815.
8. Arthur, *Story of the Battle of New Orleans* (1915), p. 236.
9. Andrew Jackson's reply to the Reverend W. Dubourg, in Reid and Eaton, *Life* (1817), p. 407.
10. Heaney, *Century of Pioneering* (1993), p. 239.
11. Quoted in Drez, *War of 1812* (2014), p. 347n252.
12. Reid and Eaton, *Life* (1817), p. 365.
13. Andrew Jackson to James Winchester, January 30, 1815.
14. [Gleig], *Narrative of the Campaigns of the British Army* (1821), p. 349.
15. Andrew Jackson address, February 19, 1815, reprinted in Latour, *Historical Memoir* (1816), p. xc.
16. Rachel Jackson to Robert Hays, March 5, 1815.
17. Nolte, *Fifty Years* (1854), p. 238.
18. Ibid., pp. 238–39.
19. Andrew Jackson address, March 14, 1815.
20. Reid and Eaton, *Life* (1817), p. 392.
21. Parton, *Life of Andrew Jackson*, vol. 2 (1861), pp. 330–31.
22. John Lowell, "Mr. Madison's War," in Boston *Evening Post*, July 31–August 10, 1812.
23. *Niles' Weekly Register*, February 18 and March 14, 1815.
24. [Gleig], *Narrative of the Campaigns of the British Army* (1821), p. 374.

EPILOGUE

1. Andrew Jackson to Andrew Jackson Donelson, December 10, 1839.
2. Ibid.
3. *Columbian Centinel*, July 12, 1817.

4. Hunt, *Memoir of Mrs. Edward Livingston* (1886), p. 52.
5. Andrew Jackson, "General Orders," January 21, 1815.
6. Griffith, *McIntosh and Weatherford* (1988), p. 252.
7. Heaney, *Century of Pioneering* (1993), p. 239.
8. Andrew Jackson to Martin Van Buren, December 23, 1839, quoted in Remini, *Andrew Jackson and the Course of American Democracy* (1984), p. 456.
9. *Nashville Union*, January 22, 1840.

AFTERWORD

1. Margaret Bayard Smith, *The First Forty Years of Washington Society* (1906), p. 296
2. Joseph Story to Mrs. Story, March 7, 1829.
3. Remini, *Andrew Jackson and the Course of American Democracy* (1984), pp. 233–37.
4. Here and after, quotations have been drawn from Roosevelt, *The Naval War of 1812* (1882).
5. David McCullough, *Truman* (New York: Simon & Schuster, 1992), p. 43.
6. Merle Miller, *Plain Speaking: An Oral Biography of Harry S. Truman* (New York: Berkley, 1974), p. 67.
7. Jon Meacham, *American Lion: Andrew Jackson in the White House* (New York: Random House, 2008), p. 257.
8. Ralph E. Weber, ed., *Talking with Harry: Candid Conversations with President Harry S. Truman* (Wilmington, DE: Scholarly Resources Books, 2001), p. 124.
9. Harry S. Truman, *Where the Buck Stops: The Personal and Private Writings of Harry Truman* (New York: Warner Books, 1989), p. 295.
10. Mary French Caldwell, "Another Breakfast at the Hermitage: Part II: 1934," *Tennessee Historical Quarterly*, vol. 26 (fall 1967), p. 249–50.
11. Franklin Delano Roosevelt to John Nance Garner, quoted in Elliott Roosevelt, ed., *F.D.R.: His Personal Letters*, vol. 1 (New York: Duell, Sloan, and Pearce, 1950), p. 433.

12. Franklin Delano Roosevelt, "Radio Address from the USS *Potomac* for Jackson Day Dinners," March 29, 1941.
13. John F. Kennedy, "The Heritage of Andrew Jackson" (1960), p. 1.
14. Lyndon Baines Johnson, "Remarks at the Hermitage at Ceremonies Marking the 200th Anniversary of the Birth of Andrew Jackson" (March 15, 1967).
15. Ronald Reagan, "Address Before a Joint Session of the Tennessee State Legislature in Nashville," March 15, 1982. Jackson's words regarding courage may—or may not—have been uttered by him, but an early biographer, James Parton, attributed them to him in his *Life of Andrew Jackson*.

FOR FURTHER READING

The stories recounted in this book have been told multiple times; the accounts often vary in their particulars, with higher or lower troop numbers, discrepancies of dates, and many variant details. To tell this story in the most accurate way possible, we have proceeded with great care, working from the earliest sources where possible, quoting and citing the individuals who were actually on the scene. Prominent among them, of course, was Andrew Jackson. You will see him quoted often, in quotations drawn from the two main editions of his papers unless otherwise specified.

Throughout the text, you will find the narrative enhanced by the voices of many historical figures. Although the quotations have been precisely rendered from original sources, odd spellings, capitalization, and punctuation—none of which were standardized circa 1815—have been modernized for the twenty-first-century reader.

Adams, Henry. *History of the United States of America During the Administrations of James Madison.* New York: Charles Scribner's Sons, 1890.

_______. *The War of 1812.* Edited by Major H. A. DeWeerd. Washington, DC: Infantry Journal, 1944.

Adams, John Quincy. *Memoirs of John Quincy Adams, Comprising Portions of His Diary from 1795 to 1848*. Vol. 3. Philadelphia: J. B. Lippincott, 1874.

Aitchison, Robert. *A British Eyewitness at the Battle of New Orleans: The Memoir of Royal Navy Admiral Robert Aitchison, 1808–1827*. Edited by Gene A. Smith. New Orleans: Historic New Orleans Collections, 2004.

Ambrose, Stephen. "The Battle of New Orleans." In *To America: Personal Reflections of an Historian*. New York: Simon & Schuster, 2002.

Arthur, Stanley Clisby. *The Story of the Battle of New Orleans*. New Orleans: Louisiana Historical Society, 1915.

Bassett, John Spencer. *The Life of Andrew Jackson*. Garden City, NY: Doubleday, Page, 1911.

Benton, Thomas Hart. *Thirty Years' View*. 2 vols. New York: D. Appleton, 1854.

Brands, H. W. *Andrew Jackson: His Life and Times*. New York: Doubleday, 2005.

Brooks, Charles B. *The Siege of New Orleans*. Seattle: University of Washington Press, 1961.

Brown, Wilburt S. *The Amphibious Campaign for West Florida and Louisiana, 1814–1815*. Tuscaloosa: University of Alabama Press, 1969.

Buell, Augustus C. *History of Andrew Jackson: Pioneer, Patriot, Soldier, Politician, President*. 2 vols. New York: Charles Scribner's Sons, 1904.

Carpenter, Edwin H., Jr. "Arsène Lacarrière Latour." *Hispanic American Historical Review*, vol. 18, no. 2 (May 1938), pp. 221–27.

Carter, Samuel, III. *Blaze of Glory: The Fight for New Orleans, 1814–1815*. New York: St. Martin's Press, 1971.

Channing, Edward A. *The Jeffersonian System*. New York: Harper & Brothers, 1906.

Claiborne, John F. H. *Life and Times of Gen. Sam. Dale, the Mississippi Partisan*. New York: Harper & Brothers, 1860.

Clay, Henry. *The Papers of Henry Clay*. Vol. 1. Lexington: University of Kentucky Press, 1959.

Clement, William Edwards. *Plantation Life on the Mississippi*. New Orleans: Pelican, 1952.

Cooke, John Henry. *A Narrative of Events in the South of France, and of the Attack on New Orleans, in 1814 and 1815*. London: T. & W. Boone, 1835.

Cooper, John Spencer. *Rough Notes of Seven Campaigns in Portugal, Spain, France and America During the Years 1809-10-11-12-13-14-15*. Carlisle, UK: G. & T. Coward, 1914.

Crawford, Michael J., ed. *The Naval War of 1812: A Documentary History*. Vol. 3. Washington, DC: Naval Historical Center, 2002.

Crété, Liliane. *Daily Life in Louisiana: 1815–1830*. Baton Rouge: Louisiana State University Press, 1978.

Crockett, David [Davy]. *A Narrative of the Life of David Crockett, of the State of Tennessee*. Philadelphia: E. L. Carey and A. Hart, 1834.

Davis, William. *The Pirates Lafitte: The Treacherous World of the Corsairs of the Gulf*. Orlando, FL: Harcourt, 2005.

Dickson, Alexander. "Artillery Services in North America in 1814 and 1815." *Journal for the Society of Army Historical Research*, vol. 8, no. 32 (April 1919), pp. 79–112.

Dictionary of American Biography. New York: Charles Scribner's Sons, 1928–58.

Drez, Ronald J. *The War of 1812, Conflict and Deception: The British Attempt to Seize New Orleans and Nullify the Louisiana Purchase*. Baton Rouge: Louisiana State University Press, 2014.

Eaton, John Henry. *Memoirs of Andrew Jackson, Late Major-General and Commander in Chief of the Southern Division of the Army of the United States.* Boston: C. Ewer, 1828.

Fernandez, Mark. "Edward Livingston, America, and France: Making Law." In *Empires of the Imagination: Transatlantic Histories of the Louisiana Purchase,* edited by Peter J. Kastor and François Weil. Charlottesville: University of Virginia Press, 2009.

Gallatin, Albert. *The Writings of Henry Gallatin.* Vol. 1. Philadelphia: J. B. Lippincott, 1879.

Gayarré, Charles. *Historical Sketch of Pierre and Jean Lafitte: The Famous Smugglers of Louisiana.* Austin, TX: Pemberton Press, 1964.

________. *The Story of Jean and Pierre Lafitte.* New Orleans: Press of T. J. Moran's Sons, 1938.

[Gleig, George Robert]. *A Narrative of the Campaigns of the British Army at Washington and New Orleans.* London: John Murray, 1821.

________. *A Subaltern in America; Comprising His Narrative of the Campaigns of the British Army, at Baltimore, Washington, &c. &c., During the Late War.* Philadelphia: E. L. Carey & A. Hart, 1833.

Griffith, Benjamin W., Jr. *McIntosh and Weatherford, Creek Indian Leaders.* Tuscaloosa: University of Alabama Press, 1988.

Groom, Winston. *Patriotic Fire: Andrew Jackson and Jean Laffite at the Battle of New Orleans.* New York: Alfred A. Knopf, 2006.

Hatcher, William B. *Edward Livingston: Jeffersonian Republican and Jacksonian Democrat.* Baton Rouge: Louisiana State University Press, 1940.

Heaney, Jane Frances. *A Century of Pioneering: A History of the Ursuline Nuns in New Orleans, 1727–1827.* Edited by Mary Ethel Booker Siefken. New Orleans: Ursuline Sisters of New Orleans, Louisiana, 1993.

Hickey, Donald. *Glorious Victory: Andrew Jackson and the Battle of New Orleans.* Baltimore: Johns Hopkins University Press, 2015.

_______. *The War of 1812: A Forgotten Conflict.* Urbana: University of Illinois Press, 1989.

_______, ed. *The War of 1812: Writing from America's Second War of Independence.* New York: Library of America, 2013.

Historical and Archaeological Investigations at the Chalmette Battlefield. New Orleans: U.S. Army Corps of Engineers, 2009.

Hume, Edgar Erskine, ed. "Letters Written During the War of 1812 by the British Naval Commander in American Waters." *William and Mary Quarterly,* vol. 10, no. 4 (October 1930), pp. 279–301.

Hunt, Charles Havens. *Life of Edward Livingston.* New York: D. Appleton, 1864.

Hunt, Louise Livingston. *Memoir of Mrs. Edward Livingston: With Letters Hitherto Unpublished.* New York: Harper & Brothers, 1886.

Inskeep, Steve. *Jacksonland.* New York: Penguin, 2015.

Jackson, Andrew. *Correspondence of Andrew Jackson.* Edited by John Spencer Bassett. 7 vols. Washington, DC: Carnegie Institution, 1926–35.

_______. *The Papers of Andrew Jackson.* Edited by Sam B. Smth and Harriet Chappell Owsley. 13 vols. Knoxville: University of Tennessee Press, 1980–2009.

James, Marquis. *The Life of Andrew Jackson.* Indianapolis: Bobbs-Merrill Company, 1933.

_______. "Napoleon, Junior." *American Legion Monthly,* vol. 3, no. 4 (October 1927), pp. 14–17.

James, William. *A Full and Correct Account of the Military Occurrences of the Late War Between Great Britain and the United States of America.* Vol. 2. London, 1818.

Kanon, Tom. *Tennesseans at War, 1812–1815.* Tuscaloosa: University of Alabama Press, 2014.

Kouwenhoven, John Atlee, and Lawton M. Patten. "New Light on 'The Star Spangled Banner.'" *Musical Quarterly,* vol. 23, no. 2 (April 1937), pp. 198–300.

Lafitte, Jean. *The Journal of Jean Lafitte.* New York: Vantage Press, 1958.

Landry, Stuart Omer. *Side Lights on the Battle of New Orleans.* New Orleans: Pelican, 1965.

Langguth, A. J. *Union 1812: The American Who Fought the Second War of Independence.* New York: Simon & Schuster, 2006.

Latimer, Jon. *1812: War with America.* Cambridge, MA: Belknap Press of Harvard University Press, 2007.

Latour, Arsène Lacarrière. *Historical Memoir of the War in West Florida and Louisiana in 1814–15: With an Atlas.* 1816. Reprint edited by Gene A. Smith. Gainesville: University Press of Florida, 1999.

_______. *Historical Memoir of the War in West Florida and Louisiana in 1814–15: With an Atlas.* 1816. Reprint, with an introduction by Jane Lucas de Grummond. Gainesville: University Press of Florida, 1964.

Lossing, Benson J. *Pictorial Field-Book of the War of 1812.* New York: Harper & Brothers, 1868.

McClellan, Edwin N. "The Navy at the Battle of New Orleans." *Proceedings of the United States Naval Institute*, vol. 50 (December 1924), pp. 2041–60.

Mahon, John K. "British Command Decisions Relative to the Battle of New Orleans." *Louisiana History: The Journal of the Louisiana Historical Association,* vol. 6, no. 1 (winter 1965), pp. 53–76.

_______. *The War of 1812.* Gainesville: University of Florida Press, 1972.

Martin, François-Xavier. *The History of Louisiana from the Earliest Period*. 2 vols. New Orleans: Lyman & Beardslee, 1827–29.

Morazan, Ronald R. *Biographical Sketches of the Veterans of the Battalion of Orleans, 1814–1815*. Baton Rouge, LA: Legacy Publishing Company, 1979.

Morriss, Roger. *Cockburn and the British Navy in Transition: Admiral Sir George Cockburn, 1772–1853*. Exeter, UK: University of Exeter Press, 1997.

Nolte, Vincent. *Fifty Years in Both Hemispheres; or, Reminiscences of the Life of a Former Merchant*. New York: Redfield, 1854.

Owsley, Frank Lawrence, Jr. "Jackson's Capture of Pensacola." *Alabama Review*, vol. 19, July 1966, pp. 175–85.

_______. "The Role of the South in the British Grand Strategy in the War of 1812." *Tennessee Historical Quarterly*, vol. 31, no. 1 (spring 1972), pp. 22–38.

_______. *Struggle for the Gulf Borderland: The Creek War and the Battle of New Orleans, 1812–1815*. Gainesville: University Press of Florida, 1981.

Pack, James. *The Man Who Burned the White House: Admiral Sir George Cockburn, 1772–1853*. Annapolis, MD: Naval Institute Press, 1987.

Parton, James. *Life of Andrew Jackson*. 3 vols. New York: Mason Brothers, 1861.

Patterson, Benton Rain. *The Generals: Andrew Jackson, Sir Edward Pakenham, and the Road to the Battle of New Orleans*. New York: New York University Press, 2005.

Pickett, Albert James. *History of Alabama, and Incidentally of Georgia and Mississippi, from the Earliest Period*. 2 vols. Charleston, SC: Walker and James, 1851.

Powell, Lawrence N. *The Accidental City: Improvising New Orleans*. Cambridge, MA: Harvard University Press, 2012.

Prentice, George D. *The Biography of Henry Clay.* New York: J. J. Philips, 1831.

Reid, John, and John Henry Eaton. *The Life of Andrew Jackson, Major-General in the Service of the United States.* Philadelphia: M. Carey and Son, 1817.

Reilly, Robin. *The British at the Gates.* New York: G. P. Putnam's Sons, 1974.

Remini, Robert V. *Andrew Jackson and His Indian Wars.* New York: Viking, 2001.

________. *Andrew Jackson and the Course of American Democracy, 1833–1845.* New York: Harper & Row, 1984.

________. *Andrew Jackson and the Course of American Empire, 1767–1821.* New York: Harper & Row, 1977.

________. *The Battle of New Orleans.* New York: Viking, 1999.

Roosevelt, Theodore. *The Naval War of 1812.* G. P. Putnam's Sons, 1889.

Royall, Anne. *Letters from Alabama on Various Subjects.* Washington, 1830.

Smith, Gene A. "Arsène Lacarrière Latour: Immigrant, Patiot-Historian, and Foreign Agent." In *The Human Tradition in Antebellum America,* edited by Michael A. Morrison. Wilmington, DE: Scholarly Resources, 2000.

Smith, Harry. *The Autobiography of Lieutenant-General Sir Harry Smith.* Vol 1. London: John Murray, 1902.

Smith, Z. F. *The Battle of New Orleans.* Louisville, KY: K. P. Morton, 1904.

Stagg, J. C. A. *Mr. Madison's War.* Princeton, NJ: Princeton University Press, 1983.

Surtees, William. *Twenty-Five Years in the Rifle Brigade.* Edinburgh: William Blackwood, 1833.

Tatum, Howell. "Major H. Tatum's Journal While Acting Topographical Engineer (1814) to General Jackson, Commanding 7th Military District." In *Smith College Studies in History,* vol. 7, edited by John Spencer Bassett and Sidney Bradshaw Fay. Northampton, MA: Department of History of Smith College, 1922.

Thomson, John Lewis. *Historical Sketches of the Late War, Between the United States and Great Britain.* 4th ed. Philadelphia: Thomas Desilver, 1817.

Updyke, Frank A. *The Diplomacy of the War of 1812.* Baltimore: Johns Hopkins Press, 1915.

Vogel, Steve. *Through the Perilous Fight: Six Weeks That Saved the Nation.* New York: Random House, 2013.

Walker, Alexander. *Jackson and New Orleans.* New York: J. C. Derby, 1856.

Wellington, Field Marshal Arthur Wellesley, Duke of. *Supplementary Despatches, Correspondence, and Memoranda.* Vol. 10. London: John Murray, 1863.

Windship, John Cravath May. "Letters from Louisiana, 1813–1814." Edited by Everett S. Brown. *Mississippi Valley Historical Review,* vol. 11, no. 4 (March 1925), pp. 570–79.

Woodward, Thomas S. *Woodward's Reminiscences of the Creek, or Muscogee Indians.* 1859. Reprint, Tuscaloosa: Alabama Book Store, 1939.

INDEX

Brian Kilmeade and **Don Yeager** are the coauthors of *George Washington's Secret Six* and *Thomas Jefferson and the Tripoli Pirates*, both *New York Times* bestsellers. Kilmeade cohosts Fox News Channel's morning show *Fox & Friends* and hosts *The Brian Kilmeade Show* on Fox News Radio. He lives on Long Island. Yeager has written or co-written twenty-six books and lives in Florida.

It's easy to get regular updates and highlights from ***The Brian Kilmeade Show***, plus occasional special offers. Just visit **www.BrianKilmeade.com** and put your e-mail address in the box on the right. Or, if you prefer, send an e-mail to **subscribe@briankilmeade.com.**

You can also stay in touch with Brian on social media:

- Facebook (facebook.com/kilmeade)
- Twitter (@kilmeade)
- Instagram (@kilmeade)

To invite Brian to speak to your group or organization, please e-mail **speak@briankilmeade.com.** For media requests, please e-mail **media@briankilmeade.com.**

“Freedom is not free, never has been, and never will be. Kilmeade and Yaeger have done a wonderful job in reminding us all of the cost. Great read.”

—General Tommy Franks (U.S. Army, retired)

“Fast paced, factual, entertaining . . . and important!”

—Michael Hayden, former director of the National Security Agency and the Central Intelligence Agency

“We would not have won the Revolution and secured our freedom were it not for the leadership of George Washington and the courage of the spies he set in motion. *George Washington’s Secret Six* is a gripping and informative read.”

—Congressman Peter King, former chairman of the Counterterrorism and Intelligence Subcommittee, House of Representatives Committee on Homeland Security

*Now with a new afterword containing never-before-seen research on the identity of the spy ring’s most secret member, Agent 355

THE SECRET BEHIND THE SECRET*

Praise for *George Washington's Secret Six*

"A rollicking read by Kilmeade and Yaeger, acknowledging a long-overdue debt to six American heroes." —Karl Rove

"It would have been an honor to have served with Robert Townsend and the rest of the Culper spies in any of the deep-cover intelligence operations I spearheaded over twenty-seven years."

—Wayne Simmons, coauthor of *The Natanz Directive*; CIA–Outside Paramilitary Special Operations

"The greatest true spy story in American history. . . . The spies . . . seem to have stepped from the pages of Robert Ludlum rather than a history book. . . . Anyone who wants to know how a handful of dedicated American patriots managed to defeat the greatest empire on earth needs to read this book."

—Arthur Herman, Pulitzer Prize finalist; author of the *New York Times* bestseller *How the Scots Invented the Modern World* and *Freedom's Forge: How American Business Produced Victory in World War II*

"A fast paced, meticulously researched espionage thriller . . . This is not your daddy's history class. This is more likely the precursor of a Hollywood blockbuster with spies, sex, betrayal, and murder all unfolding in a true story important to understanding how the American Revolution was won. Why couldn't my high school teachers have taught this one?"

—Doug Wead, historian and *New York Times* bestselling author

"*George Washington's Secret Six* is about patriots, by patriots, and for patriots. A compelling story of unsung heroes and war in the shadows during our Revolution, this superbly done book is as much a pleasure to read as it is illuminating (to include a fine, very human portrayal of Washington). Very strongly recommended as a gift for those who love history—and for Americans of all ages who need to learn more about our nation's past and the amazing courage that paid for our country's freedom."

—Ralph Peters, author of *Cain at Gettysburg* and *Hell or Richmond*

"James Bond is a rank amateur compared to the heroic efforts of the Culper Ring. Brian Kilmeade and Don Yaeger's work demonstrates why the story of the 'Secret Six' should be anything but a secret in American history."

—Harvey Mackay, author of *Swim with the Sharks Without Being Eaten Alive*

SENTINEL

GEORGE WASHINGTON'S SECRET SIX

Brian Kilmeade cohosts Fox News Channel's morning show *Fox & Friends* and hosts the nationally syndicated radio show *The Brian Kilmeade Show*. He is the author of five books, and he lives on Long Island.

Don Yaeger has written or cowritten twenty-five books, including nine *New York Times* bestsellers. He lives in Tallahassee, Florida.

They are the coauthors of the *New York Times* bestseller *Thomas Jefferson and the Tripoli Pirates*.

This book is dedicated to my Fantastic Five—wife, Dawn; son, Bryan; daughters, Kirstyn and Kaitlyn; and my incredible mom—who have heard me talk about this story for years, spent countless hours researching it, and urged me to write this book. Finally, it's done.

—B.K.

Tiffany: You are a pro's pro, one of the best writers I've ever worked with. I'm honored you're on my team.

—D.Y.

BRIAN KILMEADE

AND DON YAEGER

GEORGE WASHINGTON'S SECRET SIX

THE SPY RING THAT SAVED THE AMERICAN REVOLUTION

SENTINEL

SENTINEL
Published by the Penguin Group
Penguin Group (USA) LLC
375 Hudson Street
New York, New York 10014

USA | Canada | UK | Ireland | Australia | New Zealand | India | South Africa | China
penguin.com
A Penguin Random House Company

First published in the United States of America by Sentinel,
a member of Penguin Group (USA) LLC, 2013
This paperback edition with a new afterword published 2014

Illustration credits
Collection of the New-York Historical Society: Insert page 2, bottom: no. 1940.16; page 6, top: no. 87315d; page 6, bottom: no. 45397; page 7, top: no. 87312d; page 7, bottom: no. 87311d.
Credits for other illustrations appear adjacent to the respective images.

THE LIBRARY OF CONGRESS HAS CATALOGED THE HARDCOVER EDITION AS FOLLOWS:
Kilmeade, Brian.
George Washington's secret six: the spy ring that saved the American Revolution / Brian Kilmeade and Don Yaeger.
pages cm
Includes bibliographical references and index.
ISBN 978-1-59523-103-1 (hc.)
ISBN 978-1-59523-110-9 (pbk.)
1. United States—History—Revolution, 1775–1783—Secret service.
2. New York (State)—History—Revolution, 1775–1783—Secret service.
3. Spies—United States—History—18th century.
4. Spies—New York (State)—History—18th century.
5. Washington, George, 1732–1799—Friends and associates.
6. Townsend, Robert, 1753–1838. I. Yaeger, Don. II. Title.
E279.K55 2013
973.4'1092—dc23
2013032285

Printed in the United States of America
24th Printing

Set in Bulmer MT Std
Designed by Spring Hoteling

Washington did not really outfight the British,
he simply outspied us!

MAJOR GEORGE BECKWITH,
BRITISH INTELLIGENCE OFFICER 1782–1783

CONTENTS

AUTHORS' NOTE

Much of the dialogue contained in this book is fictional, but it is based on conversations that did take place and, wherever possible, incorporates actual phrases used by the speaker.

PREFACE

How do you discover the identity of a spy—someone whose main concern is remaining anonymous—who has been dead for nearly a century? That was the mission of Morton Pennypacker, Long Island's premier historian, during the 1920s. He knew the Americans would not have won the Revolutionary War without the Culper Spy Ring, but he didn't know the identity of the ring's most valuable member.

The spies' contributions included uncovering a British counterfeiting scheme, preventing an ambush of French reinforcements, smuggling a British naval codebook to Yorktown, and (most important) preventing Benedict Arnold from carrying out one of the greatest acts of treachery in American history: his plan to surrender West Point to the enemy.

Although these events were recorded as part of Revolutionary War history, none of them were attributed to any individual or group. No plaques attested to the brave work of the men and women responsible for alerting George Washington to the plots; no statues were erected in their honor. The six members of the Culper Spy Ring had served Washington under one condition: their names and activities were never to be revealed. Washington kept his promise, but he also kept their letters.

By the 1920s, the passing years had revealed the identities of most of the spies, but two—including that of the ring's chief spy—were still in question. Pennypacker, a relentless, solemn archivist, made it his personal mission to identify the principal spy, the unknown man who fed George Washington crucial information about the British presence in New York City and helped turn the tide of the Revolutionary War. He needed a name to finally solve the mystery of the man Washington had lauded in his letters but never met. Pennypacker believed that if he could give a name to the man known only by the pseudonym "Culper Junior," then this citizen-spy and all those who served in the ring with him could ascend to their rightful, prominent place alongside Paul Revere, Patrick Henry, Betsy Ross, and the rest of America's most famous Patriots.

Pennypacker was no stranger to intricate historical detective work, but for years his efforts brought him no closer to solving the mystery. And then a phone call in the summer of 1929 changed everything.

Whenever the telephone rang at Morton Pennypacker's house, the call was almost always about the history of New York, not a social event—and this particular call was no exception.

"We've found some Townsend family papers," a voice crackled on the other end of the line. "Do you have any interest in sifting through them?"

A few days later, the yellowed sheets of paper were piled high on his desk. Pennypacker handled each one gingerly, as if it were made of spun gold. Anything with the name Townsend dating to the eighteenth century was considered historically significant by Long Island historians. The Townsend family had been on American soil since the sixteen hundreds, and a prominent family in Oyster Bay, Long Island, since before the Revolution. Any scraps of ledgers or old bills would help create a more complete picture of the family's history, and Pennypacker was eager to see what new details he might learn.

Townsend papers were fairly ordinary finds, but something about these particular discoveries intrigued Pennypacker. They were not just isolated receipts or bills of sale; they were letters and account books dated during the Revolutionary War and immediately afterward. The handwriting seemed oddly familiar. Pennypacker adjusted his glasses to get a closer look at the distinct way the fourth son of Samuel Townsend, Robert, had hooked his *D*'s and arched his *C*'s. It almost reminded him of—!

Pennypacker rushed to the archives where he stored several letters of espionage that had been signed by members of Washington's secret service during the war. He took a sample from the stack of Robert Townsend's papers next to him and placed it side by side with the Culper Junior letters, peering through a magnifying glass until he was convinced he had a match. Was he holding in his hands clear proof of the identity of the New York spy Washington trusted with his secrets? The reserved, bookish Robert Townsend—perhaps the most private of all the Townsend brothers of his generation—was the daring and courageous Culper Junior!

Of course, Pennypacker needed a professional confirmation of his hunch, so he sent the samples to the nation's leading handwriting analyst. Just a few weeks later, he received a reply. There was no doubt: Oyster Bay, the home of President Teddy Roosevelt, had another hero to celebrate.

With Townsend's identity confirmed, the pieces of the Culper puzzle began to fall into place. The previously disconnected spies now formed a coherent ring, with Townsend at its center. Under the command of Major Benjamin Tallmadge, these five men and one unidentified woman—Robert Townsend, Abraham Woodhull, Austin Roe, Caleb Brewster, James Rivington, and Agent 355—never received the acclaim they deserved in their lifetimes. Together, these men and one woman who had no formal training in the art of espionage, living in Oyster Bay, Setauket, and Manhattan, broke the back of the British military and helped defeat the most powerful fighting force on earth.

One agent remains unidentified: a woman mentioned in the Culper Ring's correspondence by the specific code number 355, "lady." The pages that follow present a compilation of the various activities associated with 355, what history tells us about her probable contributions to the efforts of the Culper Ring, and what resulted from her work. Though her name cannot be verified, and many details about her life are unclear, her presence and her courage undoubtedly made a difference. She represents all covert agents—those men and women whose true identities are never revealed and whose stories are never told, but who offer their service and their lives on behalf of their country. To each of them, we owe an inexpressible debt.

This book recounts the methods, the bravery, the cunning, the near misses, and the incredible successes of the Culper Ring, which helped to save our nation and shape our future. Most of all, this is a story about ordinary citizens doing extraordinary things, people whose fears and hopes and lives were not much different from our own, and how they changed the course of history. Their humility stopped them from seeking fame or fortune because their love of country sparked their exploits.

All Americans owe a tremendous debt of gratitude to George Washington's secret six. This book is written to honor them and the groundwork they laid for our future of freedom.

Introduction

SEPTEMBER 1776

He was twenty-one years old and knew that in a matter of moments he would die. His request for a clergyman—refused. His request for a Bible—refused. After writing a letter or two to his family, this Yale grad uttered, with dignity, the famous statement "I only regret that I have but one life to lose for my country."

A noose was placed around his neck, and the ladder he had climbed was ripped away. On September 22, 1776, on the island of Manhattan in an area now located at Sixty-Sixth Street and Third Avenue, Captain Nathan Hale was hanged for being a spy. He had volunteered to go behind enemy lines on Long Island for George Washington, and the British would claim that he was caught with sketches of British fortifications and memos of their troop movements. Without a trial, he was sentenced to death. The message sent to all New Yorkers was clear: You spy, you die.

CHAPTER 1

Hold New York, Win the War

New York, without exaggeration, is the pivot on which the entire Revolutionary War turns.

—John Adams

The execution of Nathan Hale on September 22, 1776, was the lowest point in a month of low points for General George Washington. First, the British had taken New York City and Long Island—the cornerstones of Washington's strategy because of their valuable geographic and economic positions at the heart of the North American colonies. Now, Washington's attempt at building an intelligence network to recoup that loss had failed spectacularly. Just two months after the fledgling country's declaration of independence, there seemed to be no future for the new nation.

And yet there had been so much hope just a season ago, in spring. After successfully sending the British packing from Boston in March after a prolonged siege, Washington had begun ordering troops toward New York City, whose harbor was of tremendous tactical—and psychological—importance. If the Patriots could hold that other great port of the Northeast, victory might be within reach.

As Washington left Massachusetts on April 4, 1776, to begin his own march southward to rejoin his men, the cheerful reports sent back by the advance parties were confirmed: Farmers and tradesmen were greeting the American troops as they passed through rural villages, pressing gifts of food and drink on the soldiers who had displayed such courage and pluck fighting the redcoats.

"Enjoy this bacon," urged local butchers, heaving slabs of salted meat onto the supply wagons.

"Fresh milk!" announced the housewives who scrambled out of their cottages wielding buckets and dippers.

Gaggles of little boys wearing homespun blue jackets gathered to parade in front of the men as they traversed through town—one child held up a twig as if playing a fife; another pretended to beat a drum in a marching rhythm; the rest chanted the popular refrain "Join or die!" as they reveled in the Patriotic fervor and holiday atmosphere.

Even the sophisticated city crowd, usually much more reserved in their displays of celebration than the country folk, had cheered in the streets as Washington crossed into Providence, Rhode Island. In roadside taverns and stylish urban coffeehouses across Connecticut, toasts were raised to the unlikely homegrown heroes and their quiet but imposing leader. As word spread up the Hudson Valley that the Continental Army was on the move, settlers who now considered themselves Americans, rather than Dutch or German or British subjects, had whispered prayers for the protection and advancement of the cause of independence.

Throughout his nine-day journey spanning four states and nearly three hundred miles of forest roads soggy with springtime mud, Washington had seen increasing hope among the people. There were dissenting voices—those whose closed shutters and drawn shades as the Continental Army passed bespoke their loyalty to King George III and the motherland. But it was clear that there was a sense of growing excitement that this wild, untested experiment in personal freedom and individual rights just might prove more powerful than the most disciplined and well-equipped fighting force on earth.

Despite the buoyant spirits of the people, Washington's own hope was kept in check by a sober view of facts. While the Patriots had enjoyed some early victories in Massachusetts, these wins came at a high cost when compared with their tactical significance. The Battle of Bunker Hill in June 1775, however, had gone to the British, though with heavy loss of life and limb on both sides. The Siege of Boston, which ended the following March, had been a win for the Patriots, but their success was due more to the position and strength of the American fortifications than any great offensive maneuvers to rout the enemy. In the end, the British gave up on the city, leaving voluntarily rather than fleeing in an all-out retreat. General William Howe, commander in chief of the British army in North America, had his sights set on a much bigger and more agreeable prize than belligerent Boston.

New York, tenuously held by a few American troops, was desired by both sides. In the north, the Americans had secured Boston for the moment. To the south, the action had not yet reached a critical point, though its time was coming. Right now, the most pressing concern was in the middle states, where Philadelphia and New York lay vulnerable. Philadelphia was the largest city in the colonies at the time and held great symbolic status as a seat of innovation, boasting one of the first hospitals and public libraries, as well as hosting the meetings of the Continental Congress. Capturing the seat of the fledgling nation's government would be a great victory for the British. And New York City was the linchpin—if the British won it they could bring the colonies to their knees.

As the second-most-populous city in the colonies, New York was their northern economic hub. But even more significant was New York's location and situation—right in the center of Britain's North

American settlements and home to both a large deep-water harbor and access to the Hudson River. The army that held New York City and its waterways had a strategic advantage not only in controlling the import and export of foodstuffs and dry goods (which, in turn, affected the economic stability of the region) but also in securing a key foothold for transporting troops up and down the coast.

Maintaining control of New York would give the American fighting corps and the colonial populace a tremendous boost in confidence. Failing to capture and hold New York City and New York Harbor would certainly be an embarrassment to the British army and navy, but they would survive the blow. For the Americans, however, losing the region would be a tragedy, destroying morale, cutting off trade, and drastically lowering the odds that the Patriots would win the war.

New York's strategic significance, from a trade perspective, was not lost on General Howe. The loss in Massachusetts was a disappointment, but Boston was not the ultimate prize for the British. Howe wanted to choke off the Revolution by isolating the northern colonies from the southern ones. If the political radicals in the somewhat geographically clustered northern cities were segregated from their counterparts in the more spread-out south, they could not cross-pollinate ideologies, and the various factions might be more easily eliminated. It was a classic case of divide and conquer, with New York City as the essential element in creating the chasm.

After regrouping in Halifax, Nova Scotia, following their defeat in Boston, the British set out for New York. On June 29, 1776, three British ships sailed into lower New York Harbor, with General Howe aboard one of them. Both sides knew a battle was imminent.

As Washington marched south in anticipation of Howe's attack, he must have nursed the hope that the Continental Army's muscle and moxie were enough to outfight the British and hold Manhattan. Being a seasoned fighter and a brilliant strategist, he would have understood, perhaps better than anyone else in North America at the time, that control of New York City was essential for the cause of liberty—and that keeping the city would be a daunting task.

Washington and his men arrived in New York in mid-April 1776 and settled in Manhattan. That summer news arrived that both cheered and sobered them. Fifty-six delegates had convened in the midst of stifling July heat in Philadelphia to form the Second Continental Congress, and had forged the Declaration of Independence. If ever there was a point of no return, this was it.

Knowing the attack on New York would not be long delayed, Washington made a short trip to New Jersey and Pennsylvania to meet with his generals. They discussed New York's defenses and supplies—all while trying to anticipate the exact mode of attack. The British, meanwhile, began amassing troops on undefended Staten Island in advance of storming the American positions just across the water in Brooklyn and Manhattan.

As August dragged on, tensions mounted. A copy of the July fourth declaration had been put before the Crown, which meant that King George finally understood the seriousness of the colonists' determination to fight. No longer would King George order his generals to show restraint in their efforts to squelch the rebels or maintain that a mere show of force would be enough to subdue the Revolution. He would not hold back. He would not show mercy. Of this Washington felt sure, and the weight of the "lives, fortunes, and sacred honor" pledged in the name of freedom rested heavily upon his shoulders.

Across the river from Washington, General Henry Clinton had arrived to help lead the attack upon the American positions in New York. As August waned, the British ships loomed large in the harbor, the growing number of redcoats on Staten Island intimidating the sparse American troops.

Faced with an impending attack, Washington sighed one August day as he surveyed the undisciplined, ragtag army at his command in lower Manhattan; his aide-de-camp shifted nervously behind him.

The general cleared his throat. "General Howe is rumored to have more than thirty thousand men in the Royal Navy assembled offshore, and twenty thousand men amassed on Staten Island. And we have . . . ?"

His aide was reluctant to reply: "Ten thousand."

If the number was a blow to Washington, he did not show it. Ever the stoic, he refused to allow this dismal news to throw him into despair. Washington was famed as a man who never lost his nerve in battle. The sound of musket fire, the crash of cannonballs, the smell of smoke—none of that seemed to shake his calm, measured way of surveying the chaos and keeping his wits about him as he led his men forward.

But despite Washington's steely nerve, the Americans were in grave trouble. Even substantial numbers of troops meant little without proper training and equipment, and Washington's men lacked both. Washington had the utmost confidence in his officers, but to say that the rank and file of the Continental Army was rough around the edges was an understatement. City men who had never before wielded a rifle stood with country folk who had never had a day of formal schooling. Hardy homesteaders struggled to cooperate with young men of landed wealth who had never known a moment of discomfort or hunger in their lives. Old men lined up with boys who had lied about their age to join the rebels in pursuit of adventure. They came from all over the country: from as far north as the mountains of New Hampshire and as far south as the swamps of Georgia. Many of Washington's men had never before been more than fifty miles from the place of their birth, let alone met anyone with such a strange accent as could be found in the hills of Virginia or the Puritan settlements of Massachusetts. They were all on the side of liberty, but there the unity ended.

Most were brave, to be sure, and loyal—perhaps to a fault. And they were all passionate about their liberty. Washington knew he had the hearts of his men, but whether the passion of an undisciplined few could hold New York against the meticulously trained British forces was another question.

"Hang together or we all hang separately," Washington mused, reciting one of the familiar mantras of the Patriot cause, as he caught a few strains of a bawdy pub song led by the Marylanders sitting around a campfire. All possible preparations against the British onslaught had been made, and he and his men would have to trust it would be enough.

Knowing that an attack was imminent, Washington had made the strategic decision to divide his men into five groups. One had already crossed the harbor to Long Island, and another was stationed in northern Manhattan to fend off a British encroachment from that direction. The other three groups were situated to defend the lower end of Manhattan. There were several land routes the British might take, but Washington felt confident that all but the least likely and somewhat untraveled route, through Jamaica Pass, were secure. And now . . . they waited.

BETRAYAL AT JAMAICA PASS

The battle was swift and devastating.

Tipped off by someone—whether a spy within Washington's own ranks or a disgruntled Loyalist in New York was unclear—the British learned that Jamaica Pass was guarded by only five men and set out in that direction.

William Howard Jr., a young Patriot who ran a tavern with his father near Jamaica Pass, Long Island, woke about two hours after midnight on the morning of August 27 to a British soldier standing beside his bed. The soldier ordered him to get up, dress, and go downstairs. He quickly obeyed and found his father cornered by three redcoats pointing their muskets with fixed bayonets at him. A glance out the window revealed that a whole fighting unit stood at the ready upon the grounds.

General Howe waited for the two men in the barroom. Sipping a glass of commandeered liquor, he attempted, rather absurdly, to make small talk with the terrified father and son before finally getting to the point. "I must have some one of you to show me over the Rockaway Path around the pass," he remarked, setting down his empty glass.

"We belong to the other side, General," the father replied, "and can't serve you against our duty."

Howe's reply was kind but curt. "That is all very well; stick to your country or stick to your principles when you are free to do so. But tonight, Howard, you are my prisoner, and must guide my men over the hill."

The senior Howard began to protest, but Howe cut him off: "You have no alternative. If you refuse you will be shot."

Shaking, and unaware of just how damaging their compliance would prove, the Howards directed General Howe safely up the winding footpath. Behind them marched ten thousand men through the vulnerable pass, arriving at the other side in time to effectively flank the Patriot general Nathan Woodhull and his men, who were occupied with the frontal assault waged against their defenses in Manhattan when daylight came. As the battle continued throughout the day, Washington recognized his miscalculation that the full contingent of British troops would storm Manhattan—the redcoats were also bringing heavy force to bear on Brooklyn. Washington shifted more men and matériel to Brooklyn, but it was too late for the Americans to recover and hold their ground. By day's end, Brooklyn and the surrounding area was largely in British hands, with the retreating Patriots trapped in Brooklyn Heights. Manhattan alone still held, but Washington was sure it was only a matter of time until the British overtook it, too.

Washington's troops were decimated. All told, the Americans had lost more than 300 men that day, in addition to nearly 700 wounded and 1,000 captured. The British (and their German mercenaries, the Hessians) had lost a mere 64 men, with 31 reported as missing, and 293 wounded.

A MIRACLE IN THE MIST

Things could not have gone more badly for the Continental Army, and both sides knew it. And it wasn't over, though the cannons had ceased to fire. The fighting had taken Washington across the East River, but now he was essentially trapped in Brooklyn Heights, surrounded by the British and with no way to escape. If his troops pursued a retreat by land, they would walk directly into the British camps and be either shot on sight or captured and hanged for treason. If they took to the water to escape to Patriot-held Manhattan, they would be sitting ducks as the British fired cannonballs into the rowboats. Then again, that was likely too messy—the British prided themselves on their extreme pragmatism. No, they would probably take the more gentlemanly route of allowing their marksmen to pick off the retreating Americans one by one.

Just like that, the Revolution was all but over. Washington must have reeled at the turn of events. Maybe it was inevitable; after all, who were the colonists to think they had a chance against the mighty king of England and an empire that encircled the globe? Washington had been entrusted with the hopes, dreams, lives, and futures of every American Patriot—and he was standing on the brink of failure.

The Americans needed to get out and get out fast. If the bedraggled and punch-drunk Patriot soldiers could somehow manage to escape, they could regroup with the friendly troops waiting in American-controlled territory. It was a big "if."

"We have no other options?" Washington asked the officers assembled with him at his makeshift headquarters in Brooklyn Heights.

There was a pause as each man looked around the table with raised eyebrows, as if asking his comrades, "Have *you* got any miracles to spare?"

But Washington already knew the answer. Unless he could somehow ferry nine thousand men undetected across New York Harbor, currently patrolled by the might of the Royal Navy, he would be forced to surrender or ask his men to die in a siege from which there was no foreseeable escape. And with the betrayal regarding their vulnerability at Jamaica Pass, and no individual able to convey intelligence from the British positions, there was no way to anticipate what the redcoats' next move might be.

Washington was near despair, but he was also a man of faith. No one knows what prayers passed his lips during those tense two days as he faced almost certain defeat. As night fell on the evening of August 29, he peered over New York Harbor and knew he had no other hope. Escape by water was the only chance—and even that would take a miracle. Ordering a hasty retreat, Washington oversaw the efforts to ferry his army and their possessions—every man, beast, cannon, and rifle—safely across the water under the cover of darkness. To his relief, the British sentinels failed to spot the shadowy silhouettes of the escaping soldiers. But as the sky began to lighten, there were still men to move—and it was then that Washington's prayers proved effective. A thick fog began to roll in, like the benevolent breath of God, providing cover and protection until every last soldier and piece of equipment reached safety on the other side. Washington's boots were the last to leave the Brooklyn Heights side of the harbor, and the last to alight in Manhattan, which the Patriots still held.

By the time the fog had fully lifted and the British realized what had happened, the Americans were already out of the reach of British cannons. They were down, but not out—though just barely. Washington knew it would be only a matter of days before General Howe ordered an attack on the remaining American fortifications in Manhattan, which would surely fall.

Moving north to Connecticut, Washington and his men rejoiced in their escape, though the all-but-complete loss of New York was a serious blow. Gone was the optimism created by the Boston victory. Troop morale was low. Backed into a corner, Washington now realized what every small child comes to recognize when faced with the brute strength of a school-yard bully: He could not defeat his foe with manpower, arms, or any other show of force. He would have to beat the British in a battle of wits.

CHAPTER 2

The Need for a Spy Ring

As if the loss of most of New York weren't bad enough, Washington's autumn was about to get worse. While the defeat at the Battle of Brooklyn had been a blow, the retreat had gone better than planned. Washington's next endeavor would not be so fortunate, ending instead in disaster.

The few American troops still holding Manhattan were hanging on by a thread, and Washington was desperate to strengthen their position. To do so, he would need a spy to collect information on British plans. Espionage was not a new activity to Washington. Having fought in the French and Indian War and served as a spy himself, he understood the roots of the present conflict—an insight that would frame his use of an intelligence network in the Revolution.

THE FRENCH AND INDIAN WAR

Two decades earlier, in 1754, the British army (consisting of both soldiers from the motherland and local colonial militias) had launched a war in North America against the French army and native tribes who were attacking British citizens in regions granted in previous treaties to the British government. For the next nine years, the continent was embroiled in battles to control the various outposts and forts sprinkled across the wilderness regions of the Ohio River and Appalachian Mountains.

The previous year, Washington, just twenty-one years old, volunteered to engage with the French soldiers and learn whatever he could about their intentions and fortifications through leading conversations, as well as whatever was carelessly shared over wine bottles. As it did throughout his life, Washington's temperate nature had served him well on that mission; he maintained his sobriety and clearheadedness so that he could report back to his superiors that the French had no intentions of quitting the country without a fight.

This conflict, in which Washington came of age, was part of the international unrest rooted in ancient rivalries and grudges resurrected by modern ambitions. But world attitudes had changed following the Treaty of Paris in 1763, and Washington's role would change, too. France's claims to its overseas colonies were devastated. Britain gained several of France's North American colonies along the northern Atlantic and in the Caribbean, as well as the Florida territory held by Spain. People suddenly found themselves subject to a new crown and a new flag—sometimes even those of a former enemy. For the American colonists, who had long been subjects of the king of England (despite their Dutch, German, Irish, Scottish, Welsh, or West African ancestry) and necessarily viewed his enemies as their own, the expulsion of the French and Spanish from bordering regions lifted much of their fear of invasion and need for protection. Now they could focus more on their own interests. Recognizing that their rights and freedoms were being neither defended nor advanced by the king they had faithfully served, they began to rebel against the very government they had once relied upon for security.

ACTS OF AGGRESSION

In 1764, the British Parliament determined that the cost of the French and Indian War had been too high. Troops remained stationed in the colonies, adding to the financial strain, so additional revenues were needed to pay for their presence, as well as to tighten trade restrictions on the colonies. Over the next few years, Parliament voted to levy a series of taxes against the American colonists. The Sugar Act and the Currency Act restricted trade and the issuance of colonial money. Then Parliament expanded its reach in 1765 with the Stamp Act, which required that all printed matter—newspapers, legal contracts, pamphlets—must be produced with paper from London and embossed with a seal of verification.

This action was, in itself, not unreasonable—the colonists could be expected to help pay for their own defense. But the independent-minded colonists reacted angrily because of the act's broader implications. All English citizens were supposed to be afforded the right of representation in Parliament, but there were no members of Parliament for the American colonies to agree to the taxation and insist that it be reasonable. The cry of "no taxation without representation" was sounded, and a Stamp Act Congress convened in New York City in October 1765 to protest the measure. The Stamp Act was eventually repealed, but others followed in its wake as King George continued to expand the power and grasp of the Crown, while simultaneously diminishing the rights of his colonial subjects.

In March 1770, the so-called Boston Massacre illustrated just how high tensions were running. British soldiers fired into a crowd of protesting Americans, killing five and wounding six. After the grassroots Sons of Liberty staged their famous Boston Tea Party in December 1773, dumping 342 chests of tea into Boston Harbor, London responded the following spring with harsh laws designed to make an example of Massachusetts as a warning to the other colonies not to challenge the Crown's authority.

The warning was heard loud and clear, but it did not quell the fires of rebellion as Parliament had hoped. In fact, it had the opposite effect. In response to the Intolerable Acts, as the laws had been dubbed by the Americans, the First Continental Congress met in Philadelphia in September and October of 1774. Fifty-six men representing twelve of the thirteen colonies (Georgia opted not to attend) voted to unite in a series of boycotts against British goods; prominent Patriots, including Thomas Jefferson, Patrick Henry, and Henry Lee, were among the outspoken dissenters. They also resolved to send a petition of their grievances to King George in a last effort to prevent an escalation of hostilities.

The petition went unanswered. In April 1775, combat broke out between colonists and British troops at Lexington and Concord in Massachusetts; the following month, the Second Continental Congress convened to prepare for a full-scale war. Among the delegates from Virginia was the tall, soft-spoken surveyor, farmer, and former spy widely regarded for his valor in battle and exemplary leadership in the militia during the previous war: George Washington.

HOW TO WIN A WAR

Following his brief stint as a spy, Washington had led thousands of troops into battle, riding tall and remaining calm through even the heaviest bombardment. Later myths grew up around Washington—that he was spoken of in native prophesies as a man favored by the gods, that no arrows could touch him. If not actually invincible, he was at least regarded as unflappable by his peers, a sober-minded man of vision, wisdom, humility, and experience. For these reasons Washington was asked to serve as the commander in chief of the Continental Army. Now, two decades after his first spying mission, he would be engaged in a battle of his own to drive from that same land the British government he had once faithfully served. Who could have imagined such an outcome? But life was a strange pageant; he understood that well enough. And Washington knew that espionage would play a more important role in this new war.

In traditional wars that pitted monarch against monarch, there was a mutual respect for the authority of the crown even if there was a deep hatred for the person who wore it or the land claims he or she recognized. In those battles, it was all about might; the armies fought until someone was finally overpowered. Or, as had happened so often in new territories, one army fought with weapons, manpower, disease—whatever they had—until the other population was simply eradicated. Washington quickly realized that this revolution was different. King George respected no one and recognized no authority, certainly not whatever makeshift government the colonies could cobble together. His increasingly oppressive laws and his silence in the face of organized protests had made that clear. Yet the king would not seek to completely decimate the population of the colonies; dead subjects cannot pay taxes.

No, this war would be different from any other that had come before it. Of that Washington felt sure. It would not be a fight to the death, nor could it be simply a clash of armies. If the Americans wanted to emerge victorious from this conflict, they would not try to overpower their enemy; they would simply refuse to back down or go away. They didn't need to be conquering heroes—they just needed to survive.

As New York slipped from his grasp, Washington saw that the Patriots would need to outmaneuver, not overpower, the enemy. And, by learning the enemy's secrets, spies would play a crucial role in undermining British attacks through anticipating the redcoats' next moves. It would be the only way to counter the superior numbers, training, supplies, and equipment of the British army and navy. This was especially true in the more populous cities, where the enemy had stationed large pockets of troops. There was little hope of defeating the British in head-to-head combat unless their battle plans and their weaknesses were already known.

Unfortunately for the rough-hewn Patriot army, spying required far more accuracy and delicacy than simply aiming a cannon, and it also took more time. Unlike waging a traditional battle, wherein two armies took to a field and fired at each other for several hours or days until one side declared victory, gathering useful intelligence might take weeks or months before combat even began. Developing the sophistication and buying the time necessary to grow an effective spy ring would be difficult—especially in the locations where it mattered most.

Recognizing the difficulty of setting up a good espionage network, Washington began converting his wartime strategy from relying on nonexistent combat strength to placing his trust in intelligence gathering even before the catastrophic loss of New York was complete. To begin, he needed one good man.

NATHAN HALE STEPS FORWARD

Captain Nathan Hale felt his heart leap when he learned of General Washington's request that September. The general needed a man to venture behind enemy lines disguised as a Loyalist. He would make casual inquiries and investigations into the troop movements and supply stores and report back to Washington. His work would inform the general's plans to take back New York City, its harbor, and the neighboring areas.

Lieutenant Colonel Thomas Knowlton had assembled a select group of officers to inform them of the need. Each was brave, each was trustworthy, and each was silent as he stood before them asking for a volunteer. Finally, twenty-one-year-old Nathan Hale stepped forward.

"Are you a native of Long Island?" Colonel Knowlton questioned the eager young man as they met in Knowlton's makeshift office to discuss the particulars of the mission.

"No, sir. Coventry, Connecticut, and from there to Yale College."

"Then you must have visited Long Island as a boy?"

"No, sir. I have never been, though I do have some distant cousins there." Hale neglected to add that those cousins were Loyalists, rightly assuming such information would give no boost to his petition.

"Have you even a passing familiarity with the land? Perhaps from studying its geography or the surveyors' charts?"

"Well, sir, my good friend from college, Lieutenant Benjamin Tallmadge, often urged me to visit his family there during the summer and sometimes showed me on maps where his home was located and which were the best coves for watching the ships come in."

"Nothing more?"

"No, sir."

The colonel shifted in his camp chair. This interview was growing uncomfortable. "How did you occupy your time at Yale?"

"With my studies, astronomy, debates—and theatricals, sir."

Theatricals. Well, that was something, Knowlton thought. At least Hale would have some ability to assume a role and play it convincingly. Then again, he also knew that college plays tended to be either overwrought classical dramas of the Greeks and Romans or else hilarious farces featuring boisterous young actors more interested in laughing as their friends donned ladies' dresses and wigs than in conveying any part of an intelligible story.

"I see that your unit of the Connecticut militia participated in the victorious Siege of Boston last year; am I correct to assume, then, that you are a seasoned soldier acquainted with the deprivations of supplies and the stress of battle?"

Hale blinked rapidly and color rose in his face. "No, sir. I was a schoolmaster in New London and my teaching contract did not end until that July. The siege was already over by the time I was released from my obligations. I have been involved in some small actions, but nothing of much significance. However"—he fumbled in his pocket and drew out a letter—"Lieutenant Tallmadge took it upon himself to write to me last summer when I was preparing to leave the school and join up with the Seventh Connecticut Regiment, and his words . . . well, they inspired me, sir."

The older man eyed Hale warily. That Tallmadge was a rising star in the Continental Army was undeniable, but Tallmadge's own shrewdness and ability did not automatically transfer to his idealistic young friend. "What did he say that could have possibly stirred your soul so much that you would volunteer to be the lone operative in a dangerous mission?"

"With your permission, sir?" Hale held up the letter.

Knowlton nodded.

" 'I am informed that you are honored by the Assembly with a Lieutenant's commission,' " Hale began reading in a clear, strong voice that both surprised and impressed his lone audience member. Maybe the young man had been a promising thespian on the Yale stage after all. " 'I think the more extensive Service would be my choice. Our holy Religion, the honour of our God, a glorious country, & a happy constitution is what we have to defend. Some indeed may say there are others who may supply your place. True there are men who would gladly accept such a proposal but are we certain that they would be likely to answer just as good an end? . . . We all should be ready to step forth in the common cause.' "

The taper on the wax candle atop Knowlton's desk sputtered a little as tiny flecks of ash fell onto the wood; otherwise, the room was silent. He weighed the conflicting thoughts in his mind. Hale certainly seemed intelligent, if wet behind the ears, and his conviction was undeniable and moving—inspiring, even. True, he knew nothing of Long Island, but a quick study on local geography and customs would be sufficient. Besides, who else had stepped up? There were no other volunteers as far as he knew, and Washington needed his man as quickly as possible. "You truly believe you can do this?"

"I have no doubt, sir, that I am the right man."

"And you have no concerns about espionage being a breach of honor?"

Hale took a deep breath, then voiced a sentiment he had clearly been mulling for some time: "I wish to be useful, and every kind of service necessary to the public good becomes honorable by being necessary. If the exigencies of my country demand a peculiar service, its claims to the performance of that service are imperious."

Knowlton hid a smile at the earnestness of this prepared speech but had to admire Hale's seriousness. "How soon can you travel, Lieutenant?"

Hale grinned. "Right away, sir."

"I shall inform General Washington of the fact, and of your eagerness to undertake the task at hand." Colonel Knowlton rose to his feet, closing the interview. "Speak to no one of our meeting. You will be called upon in due time if needed. You are dismissed."

With a sharp salute, Hale turned on his heel and strode buoyantly out the door.

AN ARMY OF ONE

Washington immediately approved Hale's assignment. On September 12, the young man was ferried across the water from Stamford, Connecticut, to Long Island. He would pose as a schoolmaster looking for work, a cover that would give him an excuse to meet leading townsmen and ask questions about the area.

But the move was too late. As September advanced, so had the British troops, capturing the lower end of Manhattan on September 15, just three days after Hale landed. The defeat had been inevitable and Washington was prepared for the blow, but the timing could not have been worse.

Hale had little chance to establish his identity, let alone transmit any helpful intelligence to Washington, before the attack came and changed the entire purpose of his mission. Instead of gathering clues for how the Americans might defend their last stronghold, he now had to equip them with the knowledge of how they might win back the city. Washington feared the fledgling spy would not be able to adapt.

Not that Washington hadn't been impressed with Hale. Quite the opposite, in fact. The passion, boldness, and just a touch of cockiness that Hale had demonstrated seemed to Washington to perfectly encapsulate the Patriot movement. But just as many questioned the wisdom of the Americans' challenge to the British Crown, Washington, too, found himself wondering whether Hale's fervor, while certainly admirable, was not also a little naive. Did he really know what he was getting into? Then again, did any of them? The Americans had yanked the lion's mane, and now Hale had walked into one of its lairs.

Washington felt keenly the responsibility for Hale's safety, having had the final say on whether or not the mission would go forward. There was no way of knowing how the young man was coping, and this concerned Washington even more. Where was he staying? With whom was he speaking? Had he stumbled into any situations that might put him in harm's way—more so than the mission itself, that is? Every time he heard the rapid hooves of a post-rider's horse, he had to fight the urge to run out and seize the letters from the courier's hands. Just as much as he craved the information Hale would be sending, Washington wanted the assurance that the young lieutenant still maintained his cover and felt confident in his ability to quietly exit Long Island when the right moment came.

Long Island was enemy territory. Its farmland crawled with soldiers determined to hold on to their slice of land and eager to arrest anyone who might threaten their prospects of gaining more. Because the British were so firmly entrenched in their prize real estate, it was a perfect holding pen for the British army awaiting the next offensive strike, and the troops poured in. By the time Hale landed, the island was full of redcoats armed and itching for a fight with anyone who had even a whiff of Patriot sentiments about him.

But just as potentially damning to Hale's mission was the civilian population. While a few Patriots suffered through the occupation, the sympathies of most Long Islanders lay with King George. Even if a farmer was a Patriot, with a British military officer taking quarter in his house he was very likely to shout "God save the king!" if it kept his children safe and his fields unscathed. For this reason alone, Washington worried that a seemingly trustworthy contact might be tempted to report a suspected spy, whether out of true loyalty to the Crown or in the hopes of procuring some additional protection for his own family and property.

Any number of innocent situations could blow Hale's cover to a suspicious local: an ignorance of the proximity of one town to the next, the mispronunciation of a word peculiar to that region, a slip of the tongue that betrayed him as a mainlander. The flimsy nature of Hale's cover story might easily be blown as well—what school would be looking for a teacher this far into September? Perhaps he might be spotted by an old friend and hailed with a familiarity that would be impossible to deny. A Loyalist relative might do the same thing, but with less innocent intentions. Or maybe even Hale's own Patriotic zeal would do him in, were he unable to remain silent in the face of insults to his cause or so trusting that he shared his true feelings with someone masquerading as a sympathetic ear.

A week passed with no disaster, and Washington breathed a sigh of relief. While the danger was still intense, he hoped Hale had established a solid cover and was out of direct suspicion. Unfortunately, his relief was premature.

FAILURE

On September 21, Washington spent most of the day studying maps and potential battle plans and, in the evening, writing a few letters.

He had no way of knowing that at the tip of the peninsula, Nathan Hale was, at that very moment, being arrested, charged with spying, and sentenced to "be hanged by the neck until dead" the following morning.

As if to highlight Hale's lonely experience on Long Island, no one can say with certainty exactly where he was detected and captured, or even what activities he was engaged in before that fateful event. Somehow he made his way westward to Brooklyn, then crossed over into lower Manhattan, though no records show exactly when or how. Perhaps he only made that crossing later, as a prisoner. By some reports, he was recognized by some Loyalist cousins and reported to the British; by other reports, he mistook a British boat as the ferry sent to return him to safety; by still others, he was lulled into a false sense of security and shared the details of his plans with some Loyalist locals at a tavern and they turned him in. Whatever the case, he was captured, tried, and hanged all in the span of roughly twelve hours.

Shortly after Hale's body ceased to swing like a pendulum in the Park of Artillery, Captain John Montresor of His Majesty's army set out for the American camp under a flag of truce. He was granted an audience with a young Patriot captain and aide to General Washington named Alexander Hamilton to explain the purpose of his visit and inform the Americans of the execution of Lieutenant Hale. The visit was not only a formal courtesy but also a thinly veiled warning that their sad little attempt at espionage had been an embarrassing failure.

The news cut Washington deeply. Casualties were an unavoidable part of the ugly business of war, but had the general not known the futility of the effort even before sending Hale on his mission? Had he not immediately detected a dozen problems with the plan? Did he not sense, deep down, that it had been doomed from the start when one brave but untried young man had taken all of the responsibility upon himself? Hale's death was a tragedy for its own sake, for the fact that Washington now had no agent to feed him the information he desperately needed from Long Island, and because of how unnecessary it was. Had there only been a more knowledgeable, less conspicuous ring in place whose members could not only gather the necessary information but also protect one another even as they operated in anonymity, things might have gone very differently.

Hale's attempt to gather and convey information had been an utter failure, but he had given his beloved general something just as valuable: the recognition that Washington needed more than just one brave man on Long Island; he needed an entire network.

A TURN AT TRENTON

As the autumn of 1776 progressed to winter, General George Washington found himself marching from New York to New Jersey to Pennsylvania in a series of disheartening campaigns. His troops were demoralized and the civilian population even more so, as many who were formerly enthusiastic supporters of the Patriotic cause took oaths of fidelity to the king or else simply quietly withdrew their support for liberty. In October, Washington met up with reinforcements, but found their number a mere half of the five thousand troops he had anticipated. Supplies were low and he could no longer count on the local populace to show their support by selling food and other necessary supplies to the Continental Army. The British troops, on the other hand, were well supplied and their numbers bolstered by the Hessians, German mercenaries with a reputation for being boulders of men and unflappable in battle.

Just before the celebration of Christmas, Washington was eyeing a return to New Jersey. He had to regain control of the mid-Atlantic after the disappointing autumn or lose the war, so he began to formulate a plan to attack the Hessian encampment at Trenton—a daring raid requiring yet another treacherous ferrying of men and supplies across water. Braving large masses of ice and winter winds that could easily overturn the small boats, his men would cross the river and capture the city in an attempt to break a stronghold of British control in the region.

"We are in a very disaffected part of the Provence," Washington wrote to his brothers John and Samuel in two telling and very nearly verbatim letters. Samuel's version, dated December 18, 1776, reads:

> *And between you and me, I think our Affairs are in a very bad situation; not so much from the apprehension of Genl. Howe's Army, as from the defection of New York, Jerseys, and Pennsylvania. In short, the Conduct of the Jerseys has been most Infamous. Instead of turning out to defend their Country and affording aid to our Army, they are making their submissions as fast as they can. If the Jerseys had given us any support, we might have made a stand at Hackensack and after that at Brunswick, but the few Militia that were in Arms, disbanded themselves or slunk off in such a manner upon the appearance of danger as to leave us quite unsupported and to make the best shifts we could without them and left the poor remains of our Army to make the best we could of it.*
>
> *I have no doubt but that General Howe will still make an attempt upon Philadelphia this Winter. I see nothing to oppose him a fortnight hence, as the time of all the Troops, except those of Virginia (reduced almost to nothing,) and Smallwood's Regiment of Maryland, (equally as bad) will expire in less than that time. In a word my dear Sir, if every nerve is not strain'd to recruit the New Army with all possible expedition, I think the game is pretty near up. . . .*

> *You can form no Idea of the perplexity of my Situation. No Man, I believe, ever had a greater choice of difficulties and less means to extricate himself from them. However under a full persuasion of the justice of our Cause I cannot but think the prospect will brighten, although for a wise purpose it is, at present hid under a cloud entertain an Idea that it will finally sink tho' it may remain for some time under a Cloud.*

Washington had smiled a little, in spite of himself, as he closed the letter with greetings sent to his sister-in-law and her children. Yes, the past few months had been bleak and the future looked like it would be very much the same, but Washington clung to that shred of hope with which he had reassured his brother. Though the Patriot cause was cloaked by a cloud, his cautious optimism was rooted in something more solid than just a desperate hope that another miracle may yet come to his aid. Washington had a secret.

John Honeyman, a Scots-Irish immigrant who had served the British Crown faithfully during the French and Indian War, was now plying his trade as a weaver and butcher in Trenton, supplying the Hessian troops and making his allegiance to the Crown common knowledge. While wandering dangerously close to the American lines one day, Honeyman had been captured and questioned by none other than General Washington himself. A few days later, shortly after Washington had written to his brothers, Honeyman escaped back to Trenton under the cover of some small disturbance in the camp. Once again behind Hessian lines, he insisted upon an audience with Colonel Johann Rall, informing him of what he had observed while held by the Americans.

"There will be no attack," Honeyman told Rall. "The American troops are so disheartened and so bedraggled, they have no plans of advancing any time soon."

The big German laughed at the thought of the upstart colonials wasting away as they tried to put on a brave show: "Wir werden fröhliches Weihnachten schließlich haben!" (We will have a merry Christmas, after all!)

Colonel Rall dismissed the trusted tradesman with a hearty slap on the back, and went to inform his subordinates that they could stand down and commence with the Christmas celebrations. Someone had procured quite a few casks of ale, and they were all eager to toast the birth of the Christ child in roaring fashion even as the church tolled the bells marking Christmas Eve. Meanwhile, Honeyman quickly and quietly gathered his family and retreated eastward to New Brunswick, New Jersey . . . and Washington prepared to strike.

It had all been a beautifully orchestrated setup, from Honeyman's position in Trenton to his capture, escape, and meeting with Rall. He had been a dedicated British soldier twenty years ago, but now he was Washington's man. Learning from Hale's death, the general had reached out to Honeyman earlier that fall, counting on his outstanding credentials from the previous war, unshakable bravery, and unsuspicious occupation to enable him to operate undetected. Sure enough, Honeyman casually questioned and carefully counted the men about the city and offered a full report of it back to Washington from his jail cell following his "capture." Washington, having personally arranged for the means by which Honeyman could escape, had then asked his agent to plant the false story in Rall's ear before spiriting himself and his family out of harm's way when the attack came on the unsuspecting Hessians.

It was a perfect plan that went off without a hitch. Honeyman played his part beautifully, and the Hessian troops, all fighting massive hangovers from their raucous Christmas revelries, were caught completely off guard when the Patriots launched their attack in the wee hours of December 26. The victory was swift, decisive, and crucial for the American cause.

Washington's espionage success further buoyed him and the

troops. But the loss of Long Island and Manhattan still weighed heavily on the general's mind. He didn't think the war could be won without recapturing them and, like Trenton, they could not be taken without good, reliable intelligence. Honeyman's efforts at Trenton had proved the value of a well-placed spy and taught two good lessons: Washington's spies would have to blend in as Honeyman had (and Hale had not), and they would have to be absolutely convincing in their roles.

Washington would need a collection of agents—a ring of common men and women with unquestionable fidelity and unassuming identities. His first task would be to enlist two key individuals: (1) an officer familiar with the territory and well acquainted with the local families and customs, who could orchestrate the whole enterprise but remain close to Washington's side, and (2) an agent on the ground who could recruit the other members, preferably a person who was well connected but had largely kept his political opinions to himself throughout the conflict thus far—a man who would not raise suspicions but would rather die than surrender his God-given liberties.

CHAPTER 3

Launching the Ring

In February 1777, Washington wrote to Nathaniel Sackett, a New York merchant, supplier to the Continental Army, and Patriot activist. The short letter got to the heart of the matter immediately. He offered Sackett fifty dollars a month—a generous sum from the cash-strapped American government—to establish a network of spies to learn "the earliest and best intelligence of the designs of the enemy." Sackett's efforts, while initially fruitful, collapsed a few months later in a series of unfortunate mishaps and failed missions that yielded few results of the impact Washington was seeking. Finding the right man to lead the New York ring was proving harder than planned.

In the fall of 1777, a year after Nathan Hale's death, Washington still had no New York spy ring, mostly because the general's attentions were diverted again from New York to Philadelphia, which the British had recently captured. For the next few months, Washington devoted most of his attention to regaining the City of Brotherly Love and placed the New York intelligence efforts on hold indefinitely.

A MISSION

As 1777 turned into 1778, the tide of the war changed. When Benjamin Franklin's negotiations in France finally culminated in Louis XVI's commitment to support the American cause in February 1778, the British strategy had to change. Despite a devastating winter at Valley Forge, the Americans were no longer fighting alone, scraping out victories from sheer luck, pluck, and whatever good fortune Providence threw their way. By June 1778, orders were issued for the British army in Philadelphia to abandon the city and set their sights on strengthening their all-important hold on New York.

Washington and his men prepared to follow suit, packing up the ragtag army to leave Valley Forge. The logistics of moving an army were all-consuming, but Washington was preoccupied with an even more important task—the time had come to focus his full attention on forming his spy network, and nothing would distract him now.

Washington tapped Brigadier General Charles Scott, a rustic man from central Virginia, to serve as his chief of intelligence. It was a logical appointment; Scott was experienced and able, with an impressive record in command. He had distinguished himself as a scout during the French and Indian War and had served alongside Washington for the duration of the Pennsylvania campaign. But despite Scott's capabilities and qualifications, he was abrasive and unimaginative. Even worse, his knowledge of the topography and waterways of Manhattan and Long Island was severely limited.

Quickly recognizing that Scott's efforts could easily go the same way as Nathan Hale's and Nathaniel Sackett's, Washington scrambled to find another man to head up the actual infiltration of New York. He needed someone who knew not only the city and the various routes into and out of it but also enough trusted locals to recruit as spies. The candidate would also need to be nearly inexhaustible if he were to devote the time, strategy, and energy necessary to make the ring successful.

Fortunately for Washington, one of the rising young stars of the Continental Army fit the bill exactly. Benjamin Tallmadge, a gallant young major whose curls always seemed to be escaping beneath his sharp dragoon helmet, was still rather green, but his keenness of mind was apparent to everyone who met him, and he knew how to earn the respect and faith of his men despite the occasional misstep. Besides, his demonstrated courage, his imagination, and, most important, his background made him the perfect candidate.

A RISING STAR

Major Benjamin Tallmadge was a rather unlikely military man. He was born on February 25, 1754, the second son of the Reverend Benjamin and Susannah Smith Tallmadge, in a parsonage in Setauket, a hamlet in the region of Brookhaven, Suffolk County, Long Island. The son and grandson of a minister, young Benjamin seemed destined for the pulpit rather than the trenches.

Benjamin Junior was an extremely bright, precocious child. One of his father's duties as parson was to instruct the young men of the village who were hoping to attend college, preparing them for the rigorous entrance exams by supplying them with the requisite knowledge of Latin, Greek, theology, and rhetoric. Energetic and enthusiastic about anything that seemed remotely challenging, young Benjamin was eager to join his father's classes and thrived under increasingly difficult curricula. By the age of twelve or thirteen, he had proved so proficient that he was admitted to Yale by the college president, but the Reverend Tallmadge felt his son was too young. At his father's bidding, Benjamin waited until he was fifteen to enroll. In the meantime, Susannah died, leaving the Tallmadge men alone in the parsonage. The sadness in the house following her passing was oppressive, and Benjamin found that leaving was something of a relief.

He was well prepared for college life. "Being so well versed in the Latin and Greek languages, I had not much occasion to study during the first two years of my collegiate life," Tallmadge later admitted, "which I have always thought had a tendency to make me idle." But his time was not wasted. He quickly became popular among his classmates, including Nathan Hale, who found Tallmadge's intelligence, energy, and good nature fascinating.

Playhouses were very rare in the colonies at the time, and public opinion considered theater somewhere between frivolous and downright sinful. This irresistible combination of novelty and potential scandal made theatricals a favorite pastime among college students. Tallmadge and Hale were often at the center of these productions, and frequented several other clubs that explored the various disciplines future schoolmasters should master: astronomy, geometry, history, debate, and natural sciences. These subjects were also covered in classes, but this was the Age of Enlightenment and the pursuit of knowledge was all the rage—even among fun-loving young men.

Benjamin graduated from Yale in 1773 with a distinguished academic record, despite his somewhat lackadaisical freshman and sophomore years, and a severe bout of measles that marked part of his junior and senior years; he was even invited by the college president to speak at the commencement ceremony. Upon graduation, the position of superintendent of the high school in Wethersfield, Connecticut, was offered to him, and Tallmadge seized the opportunity to impart his enthusiasm for study to a younger generation. There, he served faithfully for three years, though his ambitions drew him toward the legal profession and he began to seriously consider studying law.

But in the spring of 1775, "the shot heard 'round the world" rang out at Lexington, Massachusetts, followed by a skirmish at Concord a few hours later. That one day, April 19, would mark an indelible change in the course of history, and Benjamin Tallmadge, like many other young men of his time, was swept up in Patriotic fervor as the War of Independence officially began. The bloody battle at Bunker

Hill raged shortly afterward in June, and Tallmadge took advantage of his school's summer holiday to ride the one hundred miles to Boston to learn of the latest news firsthand. He met with some Connecticut friends who had been involved in the combat, and their stories of heroism and zeal began to shift Tallmadge's goal from fighting injustice in the courtroom to fighting tyranny on the battlefield.

He began the fall term at Wethersfield seriously weighing various courses for his future. With the arrival of 1776, the Continental Congress gave approval for the colonies to actively expand their fighting brigades. Captain John Chester, one of friends with whom Tallmadge had visited the previous summer, was elevated to the rank of colonel, and invited Tallmadge to join his regiment as a commissioned officer. Thus, Lieutenant Benjamin Tallmadge, his commission signed by Governor Jonathan Trumbull, took his leave of the school at the end of the term and officially became a member of Connecticut's Continental Line on June 20, 1776.

It was a move that astonished Benjamin's father and his second wife, the former Miss Zipporah Strong. As his unit marched toward Manhattan, Lieutenant Tallmadge gained leave to venture across the water to Long Island to see his family. His pious father was shocked to learn that both Benjamin and his older son, William, had enlisted, but he granted his blessing at Benjamin's request.

Now a soldier, Tallmadge continued to distinguish himself with his boundless energy and uncanny knack for winning people over, but the art of war didn't come easily to the new recruit. With August came the fateful Battle of Brooklyn and the betrayal of Brigadier General Nathaniel Woodhull and his branch of the Long Island militia at Jamaica Pass. The battle was Tallmadge's first taste of war, and it shook him.

"This was the first time in my life that I had witnessed the awful scene of a battle, when man was engaged to destroy his fellow-man," Tallmadge wrote more than fifty years later. "I well remember my sensations on the occasion, for they were solemn beyond description, and very hardly could I bring my mind to be willing to attempt the life of a fellow-creature."

Their father's blessing proved fruitful for Benjamin but not for his brother William. At the same time that Benjamin was experiencing such a conflict of conscience at the horror of killing, William was being hauled off as a prisoner, captured in battle by the British. In the desperate weeks that followed, Benjamin's good nature and dogged determination failed him for perhaps the first time in his life. Together with some influential friends, he made repeated attempts to have provisions delivered to William in the British prison ship where he was being held, but all efforts were rebuffed, all food parcels and blankets denied. William starved to death at some point in the autumn of 1776, and his body was either thrown over the side of the ship into cold New York Harbor or buried in an unmarked grave on the shore.

Nathan Hale's death, coinciding with William's desperate plight, was a difficult blow. Tallmadge's conscience shouted that he would have been a far better man for the job than poor Hale, who had never even set foot on Long Island. But the opportunity had not been offered to Tallmadge and he had precious little time to dwell on the tragedy. His unit continued to march with General Washington, engaging in the Battle of White Plains on October 28, when Benjamin himself was very nearly captured by Hessian troops as he was ushering his men across the river.

In mid-December 1776, Benjamin Tallmadge was appointed captain of the Second Continental Light Dragoons by General George Washington himself, who had admired the young man's abilities and conduct, not to mention his loyalty. The appointment was signed in the unmistakable hand of John Hancock, and Tallmadge accepted it willingly. He devoted the first third of 1777 to training men and horses for reconnaissance, scouting missions, and light raids ahead of the more heavily armed cavalry and artillery brigades, a job, Tallmadge later wrote, that he enjoyed thoroughly: "My own troop was composed entirely of *dapple gray horses,* which, with black straps and black bear-skin holster-covers, looked superb. I have no hesitation in acknowledging that I was very proud of this command."

Tallmadge continued his dedicated and distinguished service, and a promotion to major followed in April 1777. At the end of that year, something happened that would change his career. After an attack on his troops, Tallmadge received word of an unusual nature. As he described it, "a *country girl* had gone into Philadelphia; with eggs, instructed to obtain some information respecting the enemy." Arrangements were made that she should meet Tallmadge at the Rising Sun Tavern, where she quickly passed on all information about troop numbers and supply counts that she had been able to gather, likely from another sympathetic contact inside the city.

But the Rising Sun was not an ideal place for cover, as it was clearly visible from the British lines, and Tallmadge was spotted and identified entering the establishment. While the girl was still offering her report, the alarm was sounded that an armed British guard was fast approaching; Tallmadge dashed outside, swung the girl up behind him on his horse, and the two took off at full speed, streaking toward Germantown, a little more than three miles away, with the British in close pursuit. Once in the safety of town, the girl dismounted and disappeared, and Tallmadge began to make his way back to his unit.

But the experience of the young citizen-spy stayed with him. "During the whole ride," he recorded in his memoirs, "although there was considerable firing of pistols, and not a little wheeling and charging, she remained unmoved, and never once complained for fear after she mounted my horse. I was delighted with this transaction, and received many compliments from those who became acquainted with it."

Bravery and resolve from the most unlikely corners could still be counted on to rise to the challenge and take on whatever mission was necessary for the sake of freedom. The safety of those souls was also a sacred trust. That much was clear to Tallmadge, and soon he would not only have another chance to see such courage in action but also be a willing player.

During that brutal winter of 1777 and into January 1778, Tallmadge stayed close to General Washington at Valley Forge; in such cramped and miserable quarters, the young officer impressed his commander. He was still somewhat untested and not always as far-sighted as more seasoned officers, but it was clear that both his input and his unsinkable enthusiasm were valued by both subordinates and superiors.

When Washington tapped him to act as spymaster on Long Island, Tallmadge acted quickly. He knew right away whom he would approach to be his man on the ground.

CHAPTER 4

Crossing the Sound

Growing up, Abraham Woodhull had been a neighbor of Tallmadge's, and he shared many of the young officer's ideals, but that's where their resemblance ended. By all accounts, Woodhull was no bright-eyed, optimistic, jolly-young-man-turned-soldier who ran eagerly into the welcoming arms of the American cause. His sentiments lay with liberty, but as a confirmed bachelor and self-proclaimed old man before the age of thirty, he put such a premium on personal autonomy that he avoided official military service, where he would have been subject to the orders of superiors.

Abraham was his parents' third son, raised under the shadow of a prominent and celebrated family (which included the ill-fated General Nathan Woodhull, a cousin) to be neither the heir nor the spare to the paternal estate. While his older brothers, Richard V and Adam, were groomed to step into the role of American gentlemen, young Abraham was released to the freedom of the outdoors. It was a dismissal he neither minded nor resented, as he found the tedium of schoolwork uninspiring. While his brothers were laboring over passages of classical rhetoric, Abraham gained an intimate knowledge of the landscape of Long Island, connecting every topographical feature with its owner.

The Woodhull girls, Susannah and Mary, doted on their baby brother, and Abraham was equally fond of them. When Mary married Amos Underhill and moved with him to Manhattan, Abraham made a habit of visiting them. Sometimes he traversed Long Island and then crossed the East River to Manhattan, and other times he caught a ride with a longshoreman rowing across Long Island Sound to Connecticut and then traveled southward to the city. He enjoyed these trips, but the family was soon to face difficult times. In 1768, at the age of twenty-one, Adam died; six years later, at the age of thirty, Richard V died. And so, in 1774, Abraham found himself suddenly and unexpectedly in position to inherit the Woodhull family's homestead.

It was a windfall he had neither hoped for when it was out of reach nor relished now that it was his. He had never considered himself cut from the same fabric as the rest of the prominent landowners, and had gone to some pains to distinguish himself from their upright and uptight behavior. Abraham Woodhull was proud of being the black sheep of his straitlaced family, and he assumed the burden of familial duty with reluctance; it smacked of Old World thinking. If he was to reject King George's authority on the basis that the monarch had simply been born into his position, why could he not also reject his own family's expectations for him to pick up the mantle of Woodhull respectability simply because he was the sole surviving son-of-a-son-of-a-son-of-a-son-of-a-son?

OCCUPIED NEW YORK

When war erupted the following year, Woodhull's journeys to Manhattan by both the northern and the southern routes became more perilous, though he continued to visit his sister whenever he could. By 1777, New York had fallen from quite a height of Patriotic fervor. Manhattan and its surrounding areas had always leaned Loyalist, but in the early years of the conflict, there was still a significant Patriot population. When the newly penned Declaration of Independence was read publicly the summer before, the reaction had been wildly enthusiastic. Rowdy Patriots tore down a statue of King George in spontaneous protest and melted its four thousand pounds of lead for bullets. General George Washington, while appreciating the mettle (and resourcefulness) demonstrated, chastised some of his own officers involved in what he viewed as an undignified and disrespectful act.

After the British proved victorious at the Battle of Brooklyn and then with the fall of Manhattan, in August and September of 1776, respectively, there was a demographic shift as many Patriots left the city for more like-minded locales and Loyalists flooded into the city that was viewed as a safe haven for those who sided with the Crown. The fire that raged through a significant portion of the city following the Americans' retreat also contributed to the change in population. More than one Patriot lost his home or business to the fire. It might have been worth staying and rebuilding had the conquering army been a sympathetic one, but the loss of shelter, livelihood, *and* political power was too much for many people to bear all at once.

What destruction and politics didn't drive out, filth did. Nicholas Cresswell, an Englishman visiting New York, recorded his disgust with the state of the city following the winter thaw in the spring of 1777. He complained about the sheer number of people crowded into the city's confines, "almost like herrings in a barrel, most of them very dirty and not a small number sick of some disease, the Itch, Pox, Fever, or Flux." He further opined, "If any author had an inclination to write a treatise upon stinks and ill smells, he never could meet with more subject matter than in New York."

For those well-to-do Loyalists who stayed in the city because it was their home, the general squalor was of little concern; there was still a sparkling social scene full of dinner parties and balls, providing a glittering mask of denial. After all, such was urban life, and

New York was certainly large enough to absorb whatever elements came its way. The British officers stationed there enjoyed the high life, only occasionally interrupted by the necessary evil of having to earn their pay by leading troops into battle. When the tents were struck and the cannon smoke cleared, they went back to living it up in the ballrooms, coffeehouses, and taverns of Manhattan.

The common foot soldiers stationed there were hardly enjoying the same privileges as their commissioned leadership, but they, too, had the benefits of steady pay and the automatic authority conferred by their uniforms. Life for civilians who were less well-off was harder, as they competed for what resources were left over after the troops were supplied.

For those Patriots who remained behind when the American troops withdrew, life became a kind of fragile maze; it could be successfully navigated if one trod carefully, but a wrong turn or false move could leave one isolated and alone, and a single errant step could cause an irreparable crack. The physical fighting between armies had subsided, but that did not mean peace had filled the vacuum.

Yet despite the disease, stink, vice, and every other undesirable trait with which the city was plagued, New York was still the most desirable piece of real estate on the North American continent. As the geographical heart of the English eastern seaboard, it was strategically significant from both a naval and an economic perspective. And it was still solidly outside of General Washington's grasp—but not out of reach of Abraham Woodhull. Whether or not he was transporting goods back and forth between Manhattan and Long Island without official British sanction was, by his own estimation, no one's business but his own. After all, it was *his* neck on the line if he was caught.

SMUGGLING

Woodhull was infinitely practical and took pride in his pragmatism. What use did a farmer have for frivolity? Unlike a merchant, whose profitability hinged on the art of accurately reading and predicting the social whims of the spending public, a farmer depended on the hard science of nature for his livelihood. But sometimes those worlds intersected—a farmer with a shrewd business sense could capitalize on the tastes and trends of the general population by trading his produce for luxury goods that he could sell for a hefty profit while never having to indulge in the trappings of fashionability himself. What could be more practical than that?

Urbane, bustling New York imported exotic and high-end merchandise from around the globe; such trade was the basis of much of its economy. But its cobblestone streets and tightly packed homes and businesses left little earth for gardens, let alone large-scale farming. And yet the population needed to eat. North of the city, working farms dotted the Hudson Valley, but those areas were largely in Patriot hands. British soldiers closely monitored every road in and out of Manhattan, and farmers who brought in wagons of meats, grains, cheeses, and vegetables for sale in the city were likely to face taxes or even confiscation of part of their goods. Still, it was good business, even if some losses had to be factored in as part of the game.

The farmers and fishermen on Long Island devised ways to get around the British taxes. Some took the ferry that ran between Brooklyn and Manhattan, carrying bundles of food disguised as ordinary goods of little interest to the authorities; others found their own means of transport. One or two men could cross the Sound due west to largely Patriot Connecticut, then travel by foot or else row south to Manhattan with a well-stocked whaleboat. After quickly and easily unloading their goods at high prices to city residents hungry for fresh, wholesome produce, they would fill the skiff up with tea, spices, foreign wines, and trinkets not available on Long Island that they could buy cheaply in the city. Some of these capitalists traded for their own gratification (or that of their families); others, like Woodhull, found they could sell the goods at exaggerated prices to the isolated and luxury-starved residents of Long Island. It was a simple case of supply and demand. Luxury goods were wanted and Woodhull was happy to supply them—in return for silver.

But it was also risky business. The Sound was patrolled by the formidable British navy and, even though smuggling was accepted as common practice, an example was sometimes made of violators. Men who were caught could face anything from a stern warning to a heavy fine to imprisonment. Those who were not caught could expect to live rather comfortably.

Woodhull found himself favoring the lower-risk route of the Brooklyn ferry as he once again began making his regular trips from his home in Setauket to visit his sister Mary and her husband, Amos Underhill, at their Manhattan boardinghouse. This family connection gave him a warm meal and a roof over his head for the night, possibly a built-in clientele (if not among boarders then among neighbors) for his smuggled goods, and, most important, a plausible reason to be headed for the city with regularity. New York was not in a state of siege, and private citizens could travel with some degree of freedom, but regulations were certainly tightened and the occupying army was always on the lookout for suspicious activity that might belie smuggling or even espionage. Of the former, Woodhull was certainly guilty; he had little thought of the latter yet.

Woodhull held his political cards close to the vest; he knew what happened to the families of outspoken dissenters. Even if he chafed under a sense of inherited obligation, he still felt the weight of responsibility to care for his aging parents and his sister Susannah. He quickly squelched any burgeoning sense of Patriotic duty that tried to take root in his mind or in his heart. He couldn't leave to join the army, even if his personality had been better suited for military service. Not with both of his brothers now dead.

No, his place was in Setauket, even if it meant having to endure the inconvenience of the redcoats' watchful eyes on all trade and commerce.

ISLAND LIFE

While New Yorkers were facing their own uncertain future, their friends and relations across the Sound were finding their lives even more disrupted. The soaring population, crime, and demand on resources may not have been anything new to Manhattan residents, but for Long Islanders, it was quite a change from their idyllic existence prior to the war.

In the second half of the eighteenth century, Long Island was still largely rural and wooded, with the town green in front of the church often the only open area for acres in any direction, save for a few cleared patches for crops and pasturelands. Even the shorelines were dense with trees. Combined with the rugged topography of the land itself, that meant sweeping vistas of the sea were not nearly as common as boggy inlets that overlooked more forests or were situated at the foot of small, hilly farms. Fresh produce, meats, cheese, milk, and eggs from these small estates all fetched high prices in the city, though the trade was tightly regulated by the British.

The farmers were supposed to be fairly compensated for whatever goods were procured for the occupying soldiers, but this was not always the case. Instead of cash, locals were often given promissory notes that later proved worthless; sometimes boisterous troops simply helped themselves to a farmer's livestock or orchard, or to a tavern keeper's ale. Even more concerning was the wanton disregard for land rights. The British disassembled fences and barns for the sake of lumber, which cost the owner time and money for repair and replacement and also threatened the future viability of the farm by allowing animals to get loose or exposing plowing equipment to the elements. If the landowner objected to being so grossly misused by the British, he was told to take his complaints to the officer in charge. Disciplinary measures and restitution were never guaranteed—consequences varied according to the moral character of the presiding officer.

All around the British-occupied areas of New York and New Jersey, reports of attacks upon local women by both individual soldiers and groups of the garrisoned troops were made with startling regularity as early as the summer of 1776. Many cases were handled with a casual nonchalance as simply part of the collateral damage of war. On August 5, 1776, Lord Rawdon, a cavalry officer stationed on Staten Island, wrote a rather cavalier letter to his good friend Francis Hastings, tenth Earl of Huntingdon, back home in England, in which Rawdon declared:

> *The fair nymphs of this isle are in wonderful tribulation, as the fresh meat our men have got here has made them as riotous as satyrs. A girl cannot step into the bushes to pluck a rose without running the most imminent risk of being ravished, and they are so little accustomed to these vigorous methods that they don't bear them with the proper resignation, and of consequence we have most entertaining courts-martial every day.*

In the city, there was already a growing industry catering to the carnal urges of the occupying troops. As Woodhull's sister Mary surely discovered, running a reputable boardinghouse in Manhattan was a growing challenge as the demand grew for rooms that offered more than just a cot, a basin for washing, and a hot meal. But on the more provincial Staten Island and on Long Island there were not nearly as many opportunities for paid pleasure—so women found themselves afraid for their safety even as upper- and middle-class families were often required to open their houses for quartering soldiers. With many men away fighting on either side, or being held as political prisoners, wives and daughters left behind to tend to a house full of strange men with muskets found themselves in a precarious situation. Even if most officers conducted themselves as befitted an

English gentleman, there was a nervous tension, a constant fear and distrust that settled over each town where the king's men made themselves at home.

Woodhull had noticed it in the eyes of the men and women he passed on the street each day—that fear and weariness of a war that was still relatively young. Many islanders expressed little or no opinion as they went about their daily lives, but there were some who seemed to speak to one another through glances:

"Did we not welcome the king's army like loyal subjects? Is this how we are to be repaid?"

"Must we go without so they can live in abundance?"

"They attack our farms and our daughters, and yet we are forced to keep silent or be branded a traitor."

"I am subject to King George with my land, my money, and my fidelity but—by God!—I am not subject to his men and certainly not under my own roof!"

AN INTERVIEW

How exactly Tallmadge and Woodhull reconnected and concocted the first phase of their plan is not exactly clear. It is almost certain that Tallmadge intercepted his old neighbor and family friend in Connecticut, as the risk of setting foot in occupied New York City or Long Island would have been too great. Most of Connecticut was still solidly in American hands in August 1778, providing a good meeting point for the two men.

Under heavy cover, whether at a local watering hole or within the home of a well-vetted government official with proven allegiances, Tallmadge informed Woodhull of his charge from Washington. He was to install a ring of spies to convey information from Manhattan either directly over the border to Connecticut or, perhaps more safely, across the Sound to Long Island and from there to the more rural areas of Connecticut—and thus much farther from British inspectors who might possibly intercept the intelligence. There, Tallmadge could receive and analyze the sensitive information before spiriting it away to wherever Washington happened to be encamped at the time, which was almost always within just a few days' ride of New York City.

"You're saying I'd have license to work as I see fit—hire the men I want and carry out . . . the business the way I think it ought to go?" Woodhull asked gruffly.

"Completely," Tallmadge assured him. "General Washington wants the work carried out by men who know the land, the water, and the people—a local man, in other words."

"Who else knows about this? I don't want my name and my business put out there to anyone I don't know and trust."

"Everything would be guarded with the utmost confidence," Tallmadge promised. "Only General Washington and I need know about your involvement." Woodhull seemed twitchy, nervous—and not without cause. Tallmadge therefore felt there was no need to mention Brigadier General Scott, the spymaster for the Continental Army and a man with whom Tallmadge rarely saw eye-to-eye, as his hope was to bypass Scott as much as possible anyway.

Woodhull turned the proposition over carefully in his mind. "But why me, of all the folks on Long Island you could have chosen? What are you to do if I decline your offer?"

Tallmadge looked Woodhull in the eye. "You have a good estate with a good farm and a good income. Now, I know your sister Susannah is still living at home, but there are no wife and no children waiting at home for you whose welfare may cause you to check your daring. You know the countryside, the best places to pick up gossip, which roads to use. I've been away some years but you've stayed on at home, building a life and building relationships. I know things have been difficult since the British landed and I don't envy what you have had to endure watching the redcoats loot and burn the places you love most. You know (God forbid!) the escape routes. But, most important, I know that no matter what mask you may wear in public right now, you believe that this war must be won for the sake of human dignity. And New York must be had if that is to happen."

There was a moment of silence before Woodhull spoke. "But it's not just me. What about the others you want me to enlist? What makes you think they can be relied upon to carry out their jobs? To stay silent rather than panic the first time a lobsterback comes too near?"

"I assume you would recruit only men you knew to be of stalwart disposition and courage commensurate to the task."

"So I must ask my closest friends to gamble their own fortunes and lives?"

"We went over that already and took those concerns into account." Tallmadge leaned forward. "Abraham, we've known each other for a long time. Our families have known each other for a long time. If you believe that"—he paused and checked his words—"those handful of names we've discussed can be trusted with a mission this important in pursuit of a cause so sacred, then so do I. I have the fullest faith in you to dispatch your duty as well as you and your assistants are able."

"And you promise I won't have any dandified officers from Charleston or Boston or God knows where else landing on my sliver of land and trying to tell me about how things should work?" Woodhull insisted.

Tallmadge raised an eyebrow. "Isn't that exactly the sort of thing that started this war in the first place?"

NEW IDENTITIES

A few days later, on the afternoon of August 25, Major Tallmadge met with his commander in chief at his current encampment in White Plains, New York. The aim of this two-man congress was to allow Tallmadge to recount the meeting in Connecticut and assuage

Washington's concern on several fronts—whether Woodhull could be trusted, whether he was a skilled enough judge of character to recruit loyal men, and whether his primary aim was patriotism or profit. The other issue of utmost importance was the creation of pseudonyms. The stakes were far too high for Tallmadge and Woodhull to use their real names, especially in any kind of correspondence. In Tallmadge's case, an intercepted letter would make him an even higher-value target should the British learn he was now dabbling in espionage. In Woodhull's case, living in the midst of the enemy, identification meant immediate arrest likely followed by a trip to the gallows.

The general and the major discussed the best approach to the assignment of names—at once specific enough to be clearly and instantly identifiable to the intended recipient, yet not so unusual as to obviously be a fake name nor so common that an innocent individual who happened to bear the same name might be hunted down by the enemy. Thus, Tallmadge was dubbed "John Bolton," a mild and unassuming moniker with a surname that was among the oldest in the colonies. The genesis of Woodhull's name was a little more creative. Charles Scott's initials were inverted as a nod to his position as chief spymaster for the Continental Army, and Tallmadge selected "Samuel" for a first name, probably in honor of his younger brother, Samuel Tallmadge, who had done some courier work for Patriot efforts on Long Island. The last name, it has been suggested, became an adaptation of "Culpeper," the county in Virginia that bordered the western edge of Washington's boyhood home of Stafford County, and the region in which he did some of his early work as a surveyor. Thus, "Samuel Culper" was born.

Pseudonyms were in place. Courier routes were set. Specifics as to the type of information Washington sought were established. The groundwork was laid for the ring to begin its work. The first two cogs, Tallmadge and Woodhull, were in place to begin turning the wheel that would steadily roll out the defeat of the British in New

York. They would not disappear into their new identities and leave their old lives behind. Instead, their spy names would serve as their passports into a double life—Tallmadge as an intelligence officer with a closely guarded secret and a covert post in Connecticut where he would retrieve the latest news, and Woodhull as a man who must go unnoticed in the den while seeking ways to overthrow the lions.

CHAPTER 5

The Ring Springs into Action

Woodhull had his sights set on Caleb Brewster as a fellow spy from the beginning. He had to admire the audacity of the brash longshoreman who was a bull of a man—physically huge and imposing—and was using his intimidating size and tremendous athletic skill to make himself a regular nuisance to the British. Ever the daredevil, he taunted them from his whaler laden with smuggled goods and then amazingly evaded capture. Just as Woodhull knew the landscape, Brewster knew the coves and the waterways, slipping out of reach of the British by ducking into one or another until the patrol gave up trying to catch him red-handed.

But that had always been Brewster's way. Back in June 1775, some local men had circulated a document declaring their determination to fight British oppression, swearing that they would never "become slaves." Despite his usual caution, Woodhull had signed it, as had one of Benjamin Tallmadge's brothers. So, too, had Caleb Brewster. Remembering Brewster's signature and observing the man's high spirits and taste for adventure, Woodhull knew that Brewster would be an easy convert to the mission.

What Woodhull did not know was that Brewster had already embraced the thrill of espionage. The young man had been in correspondence with General Washington since July 1778—several weeks before Tallmadge had recruited Woodhull to manage the ring—reporting on the state of the British warships in New York Harbor, as well as troop movements and naval preparations around Long Island. His reports revealed little new information and were somewhat out-of-date by the time they reached Washington, but the gesture proved to the commander in chief that there were Patriots ready and willing to spy and that a well-organized ring of secret agents could yield real intelligence.

While taking care not to be overheard, Woodhull was probably rather direct in his proposal to Brewster. The man's vigor and fearlessness in openly defying the British navy on the Sound left little doubt about which way his sentiments lay. Already hooked on the adrenaline rush of espionage, Brewster was an easy sell. He enthusiastically agreed to ferry messages to Connecticut and even offered to add his own observations to the reports headed to Tallmadge.

Woodhull supposed that his old friend Austin Roe, however, might prove somewhat more difficult to recruit. Roe was friends with Brewster, and while he was jovial and spirited as well, Roe was also comfortably situated, married, firmly established in his business, and took no joy in evading arrest in a rowboat for sport. But unlike Woodhull, who could find ready buyers for his produce in the city even if he alienated his Loyalist neighbors, or Brewster, who could find work as a longshoreman at any dock that needed the hands, Roe was a tavern keeper. His livelihood was entirely dependent upon the loyal patronage of local folks and the occasional traveler who passed his way and needed a room for the night. Should the spies' work be discovered, they could all expect something far worse than a loss of employment. But suspicions have a way of becoming whispers in small towns, and rumors about Roe's activities could hurt his business even after the war.

Despite initial concerns, Roe was pleased by the mission and eager to offer his service in any way he could. Now a team of three, Woodhull, Brewster, and Roe devised a plan by which their intelligence would make its way across land and water to reach General Washington. Woodhull would operate from Amos Underhill's boardinghouse in Manhattan, a location unlikely to arouse suspicion because of Woodhull's family connection and because he already made fairly regular visits. The information he gathered would leave the city in one of two ways. Either Roe would make the trip into the city on the pretense of purchasing provisions for his business, or else Woodhull himself would travel back to Setauket, where he would leave the papers at Roe's tavern or a predetermined location in a field near Roe's house so the two men would not be seen together. This "dead-drop" method was less likely to raise suspicions but presented a much higher risk of a stranger's stumbling upon the papers before they had been picked up, so the men rarely employed it. The two families were known to be old friends—Roe's father had purchased the building he used for his home and business from the Woodhulls back in 1759—so nothing would seem out of place even if the two men were to be seen together carrying letters for the folks at home or visiting in the city. But Roe and Woodhull took care to ensure that the patterns of their meetings would not become too predictable and seem shady to nosy locals or eagle-eyed British soldiers.

Caleb Brewster, whose family lived just yards away from Roe, would wait for an opportunity to retrieve the papers from Roe. He would then dash across the water when the British navy had their backs turned. On the Connecticut side of the Sound, Tallmadge would be waiting for Brewster to dock and pass off the letters, which Tallmadge would then hand-deliver to the general.

The whole process took approximately two weeks from beginning to end and offered several advantages over the more traditional method of a solitary spy slipping in to gather intelligence and then slipping back out again. Local men were less likely to raise suspicions than an outsider who suddenly appeared in the town, skulked about for a few days, and then disappeared again. Using existing routines also allowed for a longer-term observance that could note changes in patterns and procedures of the troops. And, of course, if one man attracted suspicion, the seemingly convoluted method of passing off information from one member to another would make it much more difficult for the enemy to intercept sensitive documents. The intervening step of entrusting the papers to Roe was a brilliant one. It minimized the connection between Woodhull's frequent trips to and extended stays in the city and Brewster's regular dashes across the water and allowed the men to avoid apparent contact. But the proximity of Brewster's home to Roe's made their familiarity far more natural.

Even as the Culper Ring took shape, Tallmadge's superior, Brigadier General Scott, still clung to the more conventional methods of dispatching spies. He had sent at least five men on separate scouting missions to Long Island, hoping to check their reports against one another for accuracy. He believed that even if one man was caught the others would not be compromised because each mission was conducted independently of the others. What Scott had failed to plan for was the capture of three of his five spies when their presence and suspicious behavior tipped off the British that all was not as it seemed.

Washington preferred this traditional approach at first, but it soon became clear that Scott's method cost lives, and Washington's conscience would not allow him to keep paying that high price. Battles demanded sacrifice, but Washington could not stand to see any more spies go the way of Nathan Hale—and all for nothing. Soon after his Long Island spies were caught, Scott took a furlough and returned home to Virginia to sort out some personal business. Washington appointed Tallmadge as his replacement. At the tender age of twenty-four, Benjamin Tallmadge became the chief of intelligence, the role that would define his career and ultimately help secure the nascent country's future.

REPORTS BEGIN

Almost immediately, Woodhull revealed himself to be a remarkably acute observer, as well as an extremely nervous operative. On November 23, 1778, Woodhull as Culper wrote to General Washington with a precise count of troops at various towns on Long Island, as well as a request for reimbursement for his expenses: "My business is expensive; so dangerous traveling that I am obliged to give my assistants high wages, but am as sparing as possible."

Washington was impressed with the detailed information he received and spoke with Tallmadge about arranging a face-to-face meeting with his brave new ringleader—a suggestion that rattled Woodhull no small amount. He thought he had made it abundantly clear to Tallmadge that he did not want his association with spying activities to be openly acknowledged in any public way. Of course, the general knew about the ring, but Woodhull felt that his personal appearance before Washington was unnecessary and would raise questions. Because he rarely traveled beyond the city, his neighbors might ask uncomfortable questions. Local friends or relatives in Washington's camp might look askance at his presence there. Besides these objections, it is also likely that Woodhull resisted out of a sense of inferiority; later letters contain apologies for his simple and unschooled writing and his lack of a private fortune with which to bankroll the work. Even though his family held a sizable farm, they were land rich and cash poor, and Woodhull had received a practical education on growing sustainable crops rather than a classical one. Thus, a meeting with an esteemed "gentleman farmer," an archetypal figure of both British and American mythology and of whom Washington was the ideal, would only highlight Woodhull's own shortcomings of learning, culture, and person.

The proposed meeting was abandoned, but Woodhull's hackles remained raised. The more he thought about it, the more he became unnerved by the whole matter—and this agitation was not improved by a slight adjustment made to the delivery route just five weeks later, in January 1779. Instead of Tallmadge personally delivering the letters to General Washington's hand, he was now going to pass them off to General Israel Putnam, who would then carry them and other dispatches from Danbury, Connecticut, to the commander in chief. Even though Putnam, a hero of Bunker Hill, knew nothing of the true identity of "Culper'" it was nerve-racking for Woodhull, who feared any involvement of strangers.

Austin Roe also made a move that rankled Woodhull even further; he hired a young man named Jonas Hawkins as an occasional courier, both to dilute suspicion and to get letters into Tallmadge's hands more quickly, because Hawkins could carry information at times when Roe's business prevented him from traveling. Even if Hawkins was not privy to the full extent of the operation, another person now knew at least part of the secret, and this worried Woodhull. But the changes nearly halved the amount of time it took for Woodhull's intelligence to reach Washington, from two weeks to only one. Woodhull couldn't argue against the improvement.

Despite his fraying nerves, Woodhull persisted with his meticulous scouting reports on Manhattan, detailing where British troops were situated and how strong their positions were. He also added a note of personal concern for the rapidly deteriorating state of affairs on Long Island. "I cannot bear the thoughts of the war continuing another year, as could wish to see an end of this great distress. Were I to undertake to give an account of the sad destruction that the enemy makes within these lines I should fail. They have no regard to age, sex, whig or tory," he lamented.

Caleb Brewster supplemented the reports with his own reporting on shipbuilding activities and the particular ships in each Long Island inlet and harbor. "I have returned from the Island this day," Brewster wrote:

> *Genl. Erskine [quartermaster general of the British army] remains yet at Southampton. He has been reinforced to the number of 2500. They have three redoubts at South and East Hampton and are heaving up works at Canoe Place at a narrow pass before you get into South Hampton. They are building a number of flat bottom boats. There went a number of carpenters down last week to South Hampton. It is thought by the inhabitants that they will cross over to New London after the Continental Frigates. Col. Hewlet [of the Third Battalion, DeLancey's brigade] remains yet on Lloyd's Neck with 350, wood cutters included. Col. Simcoe [of the Queen's Raiders] remains at Oyster bay with 300 Foot and Light Horse. There is no troops from Oyster Bay till you come to Jamaica. There is one Regt. of Highlanders and some at Flushing and Newtown, the numbers I cannot tell, but not a regiment at both places.*

Together, these reports began to create a rich and detailed picture of New York's defenses, as well as provide important clues about the enemy's future strategy.

A SECRET WEAPON

As the spring of 1779 crept into New York, Woodhull was near panic, obsessed with the fear that he was on the verge of being found out and arrested. He was certain that the British were suspicious of his frequent trips to Manhattan, perhaps even shadowing him to learn his whereabouts and activities in the city, and noting any patterns of behavior following his return from each trip. There was one promising development, however, which gave Woodhull a sense of relief: the long-awaited arrival of a particular concoction intended to give him an added layer of security. Washington had obtained a supply of invisible ink and issued Woodhull a vial of the precious substance for the writing of the Culper reports.

The practice of writing with disappearing inks was nothing new. For centuries people had been communicating surreptitiously through natural and chemically manipulated inks that became visible when exposed to heat, light, or acid. A message written in onion juice, for example, dried on paper without a trace but became readable when held to a candle. Secret correspondence in the British military often had a subtle *F* or *A* in the corner indicating to the recipient whether the paper should be exposed to fire or acid to reveal its message.

But the usefulness of these devices was limited because they were all so well known. Washington wanted something innovative and unknown to the British, and he received just such a solution from none other than John Jay, the statesman and spymaster of the Hudson Valley.

Sir James Jay, John Jay's older brother, had traveled to England in 1762 in an effort to raise funds for King's College in New York. In 1763, he was knighted by King George and remained in England for a time before returning to America just as hostilities were heating up between the colonists and the mother country. Though his political views would shift during the war, Sir James initially sided with the Patriots and used his knowledge of chemistry to develop an ink that became visible only through the application of a specific "sympathetic stain." Both the ink and the reagent required a complicated recipe and special workshop, making them valuable commodities that were also extremely difficult to manufacture in any great quantity. The younger Jay brother took it upon himself to learn the painstaking process so he could personally make them for General Washington's use.

When Washington received his first batch of the ink, he was

delighted with the effect. It was, in a way, an unbreakable code, impervious to any of the usual means of discovery. Even if the British suspected a white-ink message in any particular letter, they had no way of revealing it unless they, too, were in possession of the related formula. Because the recipe was Jay's unique creation, it was nearly impossible for them to decipher these dispatches.

That small vial of ink must have seemed like the Holy Grail to the increasingly nervous Woodhull—a precious chalice that held a mystical liquid that could save his life. He had been waiting for its arrival for months, ever since the ink's existence was first mentioned to him, aware of how sparing he must be with its use and yet eager to entrust all of his gathered reports to its protection. He would never fully relax as long as he was living a double life, that much was clear, but he did find great comfort in possessing that ink. He could hardly wait to get started writing back to Washington all that he was witnessing as New York began to thaw from another long winter.

A CRISIS POINT

Just a few days before receiving the long-awaited white ink, Woodhull had composed a letter on April 10, 1779, that reveals something of the concern he was feeling for the security of his missive. "*Sir.* No. 10," the letter begins, using a crude code to disguise the name of the intended recipient. Immediately, he launched into an apology, stating:

> *Whenever I sit down I always feel and know my Inability to write a good Letter. As my calling in life never required it—Nor led to consider how necessary a qualification it was for a man—and much less did I think it would ever fall to my lot to serve in such publick and important business as this, and my letters perused by one of the worthiest men on earth. But I trust he will overlook any imperfections he*

> *may discover in the dress of my words, and rest assured that I indevour to collect and covey the most accurate and explicit intelligence that I possibly can; and hope it may be of some service toward alleviating the misery of our distressed Country, nothing but that could have induced me to undertake it.*

It was clear to all involved that Woodhull was suffering from severely strained nerves and might soon quit the whole business were he not reassured as to the value of his information and the confidence the other members of the ring had in his ability to obtain it in total security. Tallmadge therefore undertook a dangerous trip with Brewster back across Long Island Sound to Woodhull's home in Setauket in order to offer him this support in person, as well as to give him payment for his expenses and pains. However, as if to underscore the fact that Woodhull's fears were rooted in reality rather than paranoia, several British officers unexpectedly took up quarter in Woodhull's home at that same time, forcing Tallmadge to keep cover and only see his friend briefly before returning to Connecticut.

It was a perfect storm of worry for Woodhull: One of the most wanted men in the Continental Army had shown up on his land even as there were British troops making themselves at home under his roof. One or the other would have been quite enough to push him to the brink of nervous exhaustion; the two occurring simultaneously was sufficient to tip him over the edge.

One evening, Woodhull sat at his writing desk, composing a letter to Washington from his small supply of invisible ink, acutely aware of the presence of British soldiers in the neighboring chamber. Glancing repeatedly at the door as he hurried to finish his report, he sat ready to cover his work and divert attention should he be interrupted. The old house was quiet, which was a comfort and allowed him to breathe a little easier than he might have otherwise.

Suddenly, the door flew open and two figures barged into the room. Woodhull leapt up, attempting to sweep all his papers to his chest in the process, and overturned the table. It fell to the ground with a crash, scattering its contents and smashing the vial of ink upon the wooden floor. But where Woodhull expected to hear the roar of discovery from a British officer, he instead heard the giggles of teenage girls. Two cousins, who had observed the twitchy depression from which Woodhull was suffering, had taken it into their heads to surprise him in such a manner as to make him laugh. The joke had the opposite effect. "Such an excessive fright and so great a turbulence of passions so wrought on poor Culper that he has hardly been in tolerable health since," Tallmadge wrote to Washington, recounting the event as Woodhull had told it to him. Woodhull apparently managed to salvage some of the ink, since his next letter to the general was composed in the stain, but his supply was severely compromised, as was what little peace of mind he had remaining.

Things only continued to worsen for Woodhull. Just a few days later, while in Huntington (about twenty miles away), he was held up by highwaymen who took all the money he was carrying but were unaware that he was in possession of papers that would have proved even more valuable if turned over to the British. Woodhull, according to Tallmadge, "was glad to escape with his life." It had been a coincidence, with Woodhull simply another random victim of the crime wave that had seemingly taken over Long Island, but what happened next was no coincidence at all. His worst fears were confirmed: Woodhull had become a target.

MANHUNT

John Wolsey was just one of many privateers operating in Long Island Sound. Privateers made their living through a combination of smuggling and theft on the water. Akin to piracy in many ways, privateering was a popular profession at the time for residents on both sides of the Sound. That spring, Wolsey, a Connecticut man who made the trip to and from Long Island quite regularly, found himself in British custody. Fearing for his life, he was desperate to secure leniency.

How he happened to know anything about the doings of Abraham Woodhull is unclear. Perhaps someone at Roe's tavern had caught on to the scheme and spoke a little too freely when ale loosened his tongue. Perhaps Wolsey noticed that Woodhull traveled to see his sister in Manhattan more often than fraternal duty might otherwise call for, and that Caleb Brewster seemed always to be passing by Wolsey's own boat on urgent business a day or two after Woodhull's return. Whatever the case, Wolsey named Woodhull as a person of interest, and his betrayal seemed a credible enough threat to rouse Lieutenant Colonel John Simcoe, a British cavalry officer, from his comfortable lodging in Oyster Bay and to send him over the nearly fifty miles of road eastward to Setauket. With a handful of the Queen's Rangers in tow, Simcoe intended to arrest Woodhull on suspicion of espionage.

Simcoe's men surrounded the Woodhull house, muskets poised and sabers at their sides, and Simcoe pounded on the door, demanding that Woodhull be handed over. Richard, Abraham's elderly father who had already lost his two older sons to untimely deaths, must have felt an overwhelming sense of relief that he could report honestly that Abraham was away in the city and not at home. The soldiers searched the house and interrogated the family, but it was quickly evident that the old man had been telling the truth. This was not the outcome Simcoe had desired—he knew that Woodhull would catch wind of his presence before he arrived home and would dispose of any incriminating evidence. Furious that the opportunity to catch a suspected spy red-handed had been squandered, Simcoe ordered the suspect's father beaten in his stead. The rangers fell upon Richard, bludgeoning him while the rest of the family looked on in horror. Once the old man lay crumpled on the ground, the troops rode off. Simcoe was confident that Abraham, upon his return, would interpret the message loud and clear: "This is what happens to the families of spies."

The attack came as a shock to Woodhull. It was terrible to watch his father struggle feebly to recover from the attack even as the summer came on quickly and the heat and flies only seemed to intensify his suffering. Abraham Woodhull realized that though his absence had saved his life, he could no longer afford the suspicion brought on by his frequent trips to New York, and said as much to Tallmadge, who was forced to explain to General Washington what his spies were enduring back home. Washington heard the story with compassion, and wrote back to Tallmadge promising "more of the liquid Culper writes for" and assuring him that "should suspicions of him rise so high as to render it unsafe to continue in New York I should wish him by all means to employ some person of whose attachments and abilities he entertains the best opinion, to act in his place." Woodhull eagerly took him up on that offer.

Meanwhile, back in his cozy quarters in Oyster Bay, Colonel Simcoe had little notion of the tangled web he'd woven—that the man he'd tried in vain to arrest was, at that same moment, recruiting to his cause another man who already also deeply hated Simcoe for his own personal reasons.

CHAPTER 6

Townsend Joins the Fight

Espionage was, by no means, a gentleman's game in the eighteenth century. In a world ruled by honor, a career of deception and duplicity carried little of the allure and intrigue that it would come to enjoy among later generations. Spies were everywhere, but the general rule was that one gathered intelligence for the sake of bragging rights later on, for the money it paid out now, for the glamorous life brought by proximity to those in power, or for sheer ideological fanaticism.

Mild-mannered, bookish Robert Townsend fit none of those molds. He was no braggart, had no sumptuous tastes or mercenary tendencies, and while he harbored certain tightly held beliefs, he was no zealot. He was a quiet boy from a prominent Long Island family with a history of independent thinking that he had inherited. A peaceable man, he did his best to stay out of the war—until an event forced him to take a stand.

THE TOWNSENDS OF OYSTER BAY

Like their Setauket neighbors, the Tallmadges and the Woodhulls, the Townsends were a proud and ancient family by American standards. The fourth generation of Townsends born in America included Samuel Townsend, an outspoken and intrepid man who in 1738, at the age of twenty-one, had purchased six acres of land in the heart of Oyster Bay, near to the water and on the road to the mill. The property, which he christened the Homestead, included a small house of practical design: two rooms built atop two other rooms, with a central chimney to distribute heat throughout. Over the next several years, Samuel hired local builders to expand the structure to a total of eight rooms in the saltbox style. When the renovation and expansion were complete, he moved in, opened a general store, and married a local girl. It was at the Homestead that he and his wife, Sarah, began to cultivate both a fairly sizable orchard as well as a sizable family. There were eight children in that fifth generation of Townsends: four sons, a daughter, another son, and two more daughters. Samuel also acquired a fleet of four ships that traversed the Atlantic—east, north, and south—which, in turn, kept his shop well stocked and allowed him to trade in just about anything from fabric to rum, molasses, spices, sugar, and snuff.

Besides his small fleet and well-provisioned shop, which was the most prominent in Oyster Bay, Samuel was also well known for his political views, which were often at odds with those in power. In 1758, about halfway through the French and Indian War, he had fired off a strongly worded letter to the New York General Assembly on the subject of the treatment of prisoners. Townsend found fault with the way enemy combatants were being sheltered and provided for by the colonial arm of the British Crown and wasted no words informing the assemblymen of such. He was arrested and brought before the assembly to justify his conduct of insulting them so openly. Several days under lock and key and a stiff fine left him promising no further outbursts—a promise that lasted for a while. As the local schoolmaster noted in his journal, in the weeks following, Samuel "has been as still as a mouse in a cheese."

He took on the role of town clerk and when talk of independence began to circulate, Samuel was generally considered one of those who favored a break with the Crown, even though he seemed to consider himself middle of the road on the issue. His stances and politicking gradually got the better of him and again landed him in hot water with the local authorities more than once. His children, in the meantime, were growing into successful adults, their business connections largely unsullied by their father's reputation as a rabble-rouser and a Patriot.

ODD MAN OUT

Solomon Townsend was, by all accounts, the consummate oldest son. He was just as eager a merchant as his father and, after a short apprenticeship, assumed the captaincy of one of his father's ships. After proving himself for several years with voyages to Canada, Portugal, and the Azores, he took over a European trading route on a three-rigged ship for the Buchanan family, staunch Loyalists related to the Townsends by marriage.

The second son, Samuel Junior, began working in North Carolina as part of the flax trade, but died in 1773 at the age of twenty-three or twenty-four. As the third Townsend son, William, was employed elsewhere when Samuel Junior passed away, the fourth son, Robert, went south to briefly take his brother's place before returning to New York.

Born on November 25, 1753, Robert was in many ways out of place in the Townsend family—as dark and lean as Solomon was blond and broad, and as shy and reserved as William (nicknamed the "flower of the family") was gallant and flirtatious. His desire was not for adventure or prestige; of a much more bookish disposition than his father or brothers, he preferred to work quietly behind the scenes, managing the ledgers and accounts and inspecting incoming shipments—anything that kept him out of the limelight and the ribaldry that the other Townsend men shared with their sailors and clients. Not that Robert resented their quick wit and hearty laughter; in fact, he rather admired the spirit the rest of his family brought to life. But as the fourth son quickly followed by a long-awaited daughter, he had learned almost from infancy that he had no hope of being heard over his clamorous brothers or coddled as his mother's darling, so he separated himself by being the quiet one of such a rowdy bunch.

Old Samuel probably wondered how Robert maintained subdued habits as he watched his young son with his loping gait stride past a rough-and-tumble wrestling match on the family's front lawn. The Townsend family tree was peppered with Quakers, though Samuel had married a daughter of prominent Episcopalians, which, along with his taste for luxury goods and the occasional bit of ostentatious accessorizing, put him largely on the outs with the Friends among his relatives. But Robert seemed to have inherited all the Quaker tendencies of somber dress, quiet habit, and humble bearing that Samuel had rejected, and they suited him well. Robert's nature made him fastidious and gave him an eye for detail—traits essential for success in the merchant trade.

"Still," Samuel thought to himself, "the boy could use a little less rigidity in his life."

There was likely no small source of amusement in the Townsend family when Samuel secured the terms of Robert's apprenticeship in Manhattan with Templeton & Stewart, a merchant house in the unfortunately named "Holy Ground" district, a disreputable part of town. The blocks around Barclay, Church, and Vesey Streets were not more dangerous than any other slum in the city, but they were morally treacherous. The district's proximity to the docks meant it was prime real estate for both profit-conscious merchants who wanted to be near their ships returning from voyages and for ladies of pleasure who wanted to be near randy sailors returning from months at sea.

Surrounded by brothels, whores, and their clientele, straitlaced Robert distinguished himself at his work and navigated the seedy streets without a whiff of scandal about him in what was almost certainly a very lonely time for the young man. He marked the close of his teenage years in the firm's employment, dealing with almost every other commodity than the one being plied in the streets and cathouses around it.

CHOOSING ALLEGIANCES

Robert was not quite twenty-two when the first shots were fired at Lexington and Concord. For all of his differences from the rest of his family, he shared something of his father's Patriotic fervor. The battlefields in Massachusetts seemed far away, though, and many people expected the conflict to resolve itself before formal combat ever crossed the borders of New York State. By the following summer, however, it was clear that such assumptions were wrong. The Declaration of Independence was signed in July, war was moving inevitably closer to home, and all men of fighting age in the mid-Atlantic region were forced to make the difficult decision of whether to enlist—and on what side.

On August 22, 1776, British troops began pouring onto Long Island while the Americans hunkered down in their positions in Manhattan and in the area of Brooklyn, hoping to protect the mainland of New York City. The record of proceedings from the Provincial Congress for the state of New York show that on Saturday, August 24, 1776, among other motions adopted was the unanimous resolution that "*Robert Townsend* be a Commissary to supply the Brigade with provisions till such time as *Genl Washington* shall give further orders for that purpose." A footnote further identifies the young man named as "Son of *Samuel Townsend,* the member for

Queens County." According to the following morning's records, Samuel Senior made further recommendations for the purchasing process by which the newly appointed commissary should supply provisions to Brigadier General Nathaniel Woodhull and the Queens County militia.

So began Robert Townsend's whirlwind tenure in the Continental Army. Fighting broke out across Long Island and Manhattan in the early morning hours of the twenty-seventh, just days after Robert's appointment had been confirmed. The Queens County militia, guarding the ill-fated Jamaica Pass, suffered greatly in battle; their beloved Brigadier General Woodhull was mortally wounded. Robert's service did not last much beyond the Battle of Brooklyn, nor did his father's career as a leader for the Patriot cause on Long Island. Samuel was arrested in early September (though he avoided an unpleasant imprisonment when Thomas Buchanan, of the same family for which Solomon was working, vouched for his character). A few days later, on September 10, Samuel was called into court to swear his allegiance to the Crown. He humbly complied and rather meekly returned to the Homestead.

By the end of 1776, nearly thirteen hundred other men from Queens County had taken that same vow of loyalty, though how many did so under duress is unknowable. Robert followed his father's example and took the distasteful pledge, too. He left Oyster Bay soon afterward and returned to his quiet life as a merchant in Manhattan, running a modest dry goods shop near the Fly Market in lower Manhattan while the city cleaned up from the great fire that had ravaged it following the retreat of the Americans.

New York was now solidly in British hands, but it mattered little to Robert. His unobtrusive personality and lack of any distinguishing battlefield heroics during his brief service were perhaps his greatest allies in allowing him to continue to work and prosper in the midst of the enemy. But every man has a breaking point—a moment when he has seen one atrocity too many, weathered one insult too many, stayed still for one day too long—and he knows he must act or hate himself for keeping silent.

For Robert Townsend, that moment arrived in the fall of 1778. As Abraham Woodhull and his initial ring were beginning their intelligence war against the British in Manhattan and Long Island, the occupying armies were settling in quite comfortably in various private residences including the Homestead, Robert Townsend's beloved home, in Oyster Bay.

Lieutenant Colonel John Simcoe, the man who had ordered the beating of Woodhull's father, decided that the Townsend family's house fit his purposes quite nicely and proceeded to set up his headquarters in the main part of the home, sequestering the family to just a few back rooms and the shop. At Simcoe's orders, British troops destroyed the orchard, of which old Samuel had been so proud, to feed British fires and help build a fort. Wood from all over town, including churches and private structures, was commandeered for this effort in a move that was very much in keeping with Simcoe's reputation as a heartless combatant. The town operated as if under martial law, with roughly 470 enemy soldiers quartering there, including Hessian brute squads that roamed the streets to make sure residents stayed indoors at night. There were public lashings for those who displeased the soldiers and little recourse for those who brought complaints. The town was quickly descending into a simmering chaos, and any lingering Loyalist feelings among the good people of Oyster Bay were rapidly evaporating.

Old Samuel Townsend's history of outspoken political opinions was well known to the whole community and likely the cause of his "special" treatment from the Queen's Rangers. That his house was one of the more comfortably situated and furnished dwellings in the town was a bonus.

When Robert returned home in November 1778 to visit his family, he was no doubt shocked by his father's defeated appearance and posture.

"What has happened to you, Father?" Robert cried upon approaching the house.

Samuel shook his head. There were too many soldiers around to dare voice any dissatisfaction with the current state of things. "I have been given the honor of playing host to His Majesty's troops," he said, somewhat shakily. "Who could have imagined our humble Homestead would be put to such a purpose as this?"

Tales of hardships and abuses, recounted in hushed tones and with sideways glances, seasoned Robert's meals during his time at home. He burned with anger as he learned of the wanton liberties taken with neighbors' properties and lives, but he could only stare in mute fury as he observed how the soldiers, including Colonel Simcoe himself, flirted openly with his sisters under their father's own roof.

At the conclusion of his visit, Robert returned to his shop in Manhattan, but he was haunted by what he had seen. The crime, the squalor—these were the unfortunate accessories of city life. Or so he had assumed. But now he had seen that Oyster Bay and countless other towns that dotted Long Island were not immune to the collateral damage of war. Rumors continued to reach him during the spring of atrocities committed by Simcoe and others against unarmed citizens, including the wounds inflicted upon old Richard Woodhull. But what could anyone do? The Townsend family stood as much of a chance of evicting Simcoe from their property as they did of expelling the whole enemy encampment from Long Island. There was no other option. They were in British-held territory, so British laws stood and protesters fell—or hanged.

The feelings of frustration and helplessness weighed heavily upon Robert. Each day, British soldiers and common New York citizens alike came into his shop to purchase everyday items such as buttons and paper. He knew he would do his family no favors if he took up arms against this army—they would only be labeled as having ties to a belligerent. Besides, Robert was not a fighting man and his previous service had been focused on supply tents, not trenches; his soul was not the sort to be stirred by marching feet keeping time to a fife tune and drumbeat.

Robert admired the way that his older brother Solomon had found his own way to steer his allegiances. Still sailing for the Loyalist Buchanan family, in 1777 Solomon had carried supplies for the British army to Montreal ahead of the invasion of northern New York. But in the spring of 1778, roughly eight months before Simcoe had commandeered the Townsend family home for his own uses, Solomon had made a calculated move. He left his employment with the Buchanans and had managed to visit with none other than Benjamin Franklin in France. Obtaining a letter from Franklin vouching for his patriotism and fidelity to the American cause, Solomon then boarded an American warship and traveled back across the Atlantic to relaunch his career at home, sailing and trading under the protection of the Continental Army and supplying its troops with much-needed provisions. Robert, meanwhile, was left shaken by his visit home later that fall, and felt the weight of inaction as he walked the streets of occupied New York under the British flag and did business with His Majesty's troops for such trifles as ribbons and sugar.

Despite his internal struggles in the months following his return to Manhattan from his trip home to Oyster Bay, Townsend was almost certainly surprised and was not easily won over when Woodhull made his proposal to work as a spy just as a hot, dusty summer was beginning in 1779. He was debating his own role in the struggle for independence, that much was true. But he was not like his brothers, so brashly fearless and ready for any adventure; he was Robert, the quiet one (some might even say the timid one) of the Townsend boys. His was the name all the relations and neighbors forgot when speaking of his family, and he was perfectly content that things should stay that way.

CULPER JUNIOR

It is possible that the notion of spying had already crossed Robert Townsend's mind before Abraham Woodhull darkened the door of his shop in the late spring of 1779. It may have already been clear to Townsend that he was privy to scraps of conversation between soldiers in his own shop, to noting the flow of supplies and men into and out of the harbor as he inspected his own shipments on the docks, to observing the habits and patterns of the higher-ranking officers who graced James Rivington's posh new coffeehouse just down the street. It must have been clear to Townsend that his position in the city gave him access to potentially valuable information. But even if such a fancy had introduced itself to his mind, it does not mean it was a welcome thought or one that he relished. And even if he had been eager to undertake such an effort, he would have had no channel for it, no clearly defined plan for how to get such information into the hands of those to whom it meant something—until he found himself across the table from the old acquaintance who offered him a new mission and a new name: Samuel Culper Jr.

"I have disclosed every secret to you and laid before you every instruction that has been handed to me," Woodhull said, leaning back in his chair after the long conversation. "I have told you the whole business."

Townsend looked at his friend skeptically. Despite their nearness in age, they had never been especially close—both geography and temperament had kept them at a distance from each other. But everyone on Long Island, it seemed, was related to everyone else if you went back a generation or two. Townsend knew their families were connected somehow, and they trusted each other because of it. Even more important than blood ties, though, were ideological ones. Townsend understood that Woodhull had a heart for the cause of liberty, despite his gruff exterior; his trust in Townsend, considering him worthy of such an undertaking, was moving.

Townsend looked across the table to where Woodhull watched him, his face eager for a decision. He had laid out the nature of the mission—every risk, fright, and sleepless night it had brought him—in painful detail. Townsend knew that if he agreed to join the silent fight by taking over the observations in Manhattan, it would wear him down as much as it had Woodhull. Though they were different in personality (Woodhull somewhat cantankerous and Townsend merely reserved), Townsend suspected they were quite alike in their desire to simply be left in peace. A double life would only erode whatever sense of calm he had managed to create for himself, but he also suspected that denying a chance to fight back would erode his conscience.

He was frightened—frightened of all the unthinkable possibilities if he were ever found out, frightened that he already knew too much, frightened of what would happen if he sat by and did nothing.

Townsend reached across the table and shook Woodhull's hand. It was not without trepidation, but it was a handshake nonetheless.

The two men talked long into the night, discussing every eventuality, every risk, and every pressing reason why those risks didn't ultimately matter. Woodhull would add a "Senior" to his code name, and Townsend could become "Culper Junior." No one need ever know—nor even have the means to discover—the real man behind the intelligence reports.

Woodhull's earlier desire for anonymity now paled in comparison to Townsend's insistence that no one other than Woodhull and the courier, not even General Washington, should be aware of his involvement. Townsend was leery even of the courier knowing his face but relented on the point out of necessity.

Townsend did not accept the assignment with enthusiasm. However, despite his fear and reluctance, he was also Samuel Townsend's son. Though he might not share his father's fiery boldness, he was no less a man of brave conviction. With that conviction hardened by his father's mistreatment by Simcoe and his men, he was ready to join the ring. Woodhull wrote to Washington on June 20:

My success hath exceeded my most sanguine expectations. I have communicated my business to an intimate friend. . . . It was with great difficulty I gained his complyance, checked by fear. He is a person that hath the interest of our Country at heart and of good reputation, character and family as any of my acquaintance. I am under the most solomn obligations never to disclose his name to any but the Post, who unavoidably must know it. I have reason to think his advantages for serving you and abilities are far superior to mine.

WASHINGTON'S ORDERS

General Washington was delighted with the proposal and, together with Tallmadge, drafted a detailed list of guidelines and directives for his new agent in New York. The full document, included below, offers an intimate perspective on Washington's philosophies regarding spying, and the specific mission of Culper Junior:

INSTRUCTIONS.

C—— Junr, to remain in the City, to collect all the useful information he can—to do this he should mix as much as possible among the officers and Refugees, visit the Coffee Houses, and all public places. He is to pay particular attention to the movements by land and water in and about the city especially. How their transports are secured against attempt to destroy them—whether by armed vessels upon the flanks, or by chains, Booms, or any contrivances to keep off fire Rafts.

The number of men destined for the defence of the City and Environs, endeavoring to designate the particular corps, and where each is posted.

To be particular in describing the place where the works cross the Island in the Rear of the City—how many Redoubts are upon the line from River to River, how many Cannon in each, and of what weight and whether the Redoubts are closed or open next the city.

Whether there are any Works upon the Island of New York between those near the City and the works at Fort Knyphausen or Washington, and if any, whereabouts and of what kind.

To be very particular to find out whether any works are thrown up on Harlem River, near Harlem Town, and whether Horn's Hook is fortifyed. If so, how many men are kept at each place, and what number and what sized Cannon are in those works.

To enquire whether they have dug Pits within and in front of the lines and Works in general, three or four feet deep, in which sharp pointed stakes are fixed. These are intended to receive and wound men who attempt a surprise at night.

The state of the provisions, Forage and Fuel to be attended to, as also the Health and Spirits of the Army, Navy and City.

These are the principal matters to be observed within the Island and about the City of New York. Many more may occur to a person of C—— Junr's penetration which he will note and communicate.

C—— Senior's station to be upon Long Island to receive and transmit the intelligence of C—— Junior.

As it is imagined that the only post of consequence which the enemy will attempt to hold upon Long Island in case of attack will be at Brooklyn, I would recommend that some inhabitant in the neighborhood of that place, and seemingly in the interest of the enemy, should be procured, who might probably gain daily admission into the Garrison by carrying on marketing, and from him intelligence might be gained every day or two of what was passing within, as the strength of the Garrison, the number and size of the Cannon, &c.

Proper persons to be procured at convenient distances along the Sound from Brooklyn to Newtown whose business it shall be to observe and report what is passing upon the water, as whether any Vessels or Boats with troops are moving, their number and which way they seem bound.

There can be scarcely any need of recommending the greatest Caution and secrecy in a Business so critical and dangerous. The following seem to be the best general rules:

To intrust none but the persons fixed upon to transact the Business.

To deliver the dispatches to none upon our side but those who shall be pitched upon for the purpose of receiving them and to transmit them and any intelligence that may be obtained to no one but the Commander-in-Chief.

Washington thought Brooklyn was the one place on Long Island that the British would regard as indispensable. Because the Culper Ring's route of conveying messages passed directly from Manhattan to Brooklyn, before continuing on to Setauket and across the Sound to Connecticut, the courier would have an excellent opportunity to observe military activity in Brooklyn and could add any relevant information to the letter he was carrying from Townsend. In short, the route seemed as close to an ideal arrangement as Washington could hope for at the time.

SHOPKEEPER AND REPORTER

Robert Townsend's career as a spy began in that summer of 1779. His fears of the courier knowing his identity proved largely needless—Woodhull himself (at least at first) seems to have been the primary person who retrieved Townsend's reports to begin their circuitous route to General Washington. Woodhull's name appears in the ledger of Townsend's store several times during that season: July 18, August 15, and August 31. And they certainly saw each other more often than that. A letter to Tallmadge from Woodhull on July 9 reveals that the pair had recently met, and in a letter to Washington dated July 15, Townsend wrote: "I saw S. C. [Samuel Culper] Senr. a few days ago, and informed him of the arrival of 10 sail of vessels from the West Indies, with Rum, &c. and a small fleet from Halifax, but no Troops."

In fact, Townsend's detailed reports on naval activities were far more precise than any Woodhull had been able to provide, but Townsend's difficulties with obtaining good troop counts for the army reveal how seriously he took his work. "I am sorry that I cannot give you an exact account of the situation of the troops," he penned on August 6:

> *You may think that I have not taken sufficient pains to obtain it. I assure you that I have, and find it more difficult than I expected. It is some measure owing to my not having got into a regular line of getting intelligence. To depend upon common reports would not do. I saw and conversed with two officers of different corps from Kings-bridge from neither of whom I could obtain an account of the situation of the army there. I was afraid of being too particular.*

Townsend needed a way to move more freely about the city, making inquiries and giving people a reason to trust him. In other words, he needed a cover story, and he found one just down the street in the coffeehouse and print shop of an English expatriate named James Rivington. A printer and a bookseller by trade, Rivington had left England in 1760 over some unpleasantness (most likely having to do with losing his share of his father's business in horse racing), sailed to America, and opened up a printing shop first in Philadelphia and then later in New York City. In 1773, he started publishing his own newspaper as a neutral press with the tagline "Open and Uninfluenced," but eventually it began to promote (as did so many newspapers of the era) a very specific and forceful worldview. In Rivington's case, it was loyalty to King George, a stance that got him hung in effigy by the Sons of Liberty and mocked openly in Patriot writings—gestures that seemed to greatly amuse him.

Townsend had always had a knack for writing; for all of his natural reserve in speaking, he could be very expressive with a pen, and his meticulous, detailed-oriented nature that had served him well inspecting cargo ships also lent itself to composing interesting letters. Recognizing a perfect cover opportunity, he applied for a job at Rivington's paper to write the occasional column of local interest. Rivington recognized the quiet shopkeeper from down the street and was happy to take him up on his offer to contribute to the *Royal Gazette*'s offerings.

It was a stroke of brilliance on Townsend's part. He now had the perfect excuse for asking questions, jotting down details, and querying various movements of troops and matériel into, out of, and around the city. What was more, Rivington's Tory politics would help deflect any suspicion that Townsend might be harboring Patriotic sentiments.

Townsend found himself quite busy as he adjusted to the work of three jobs: shopkeeper, journalist, and undercover agent. As a solitary man with no family and few friends to distract him, he may have found the new duties a nerve-racking but interesting distraction. His association with Rivington likely introduced new acquaintances to his circle as well, as the prosperous set flocked to the coffeehouse to be seen in such esteemed company as the British officers. If Townsend's plain, dark clothes set him apart from the fashionable gentlemen and ladies who discussed politics and soirees, military strategy and dinner parties, no one seemed to mind too much.

Townsend might even have caught sight of a familiar face or two among the coffee-sipping patrons. He might have spotted an old acquaintance from Oyster Bay, or the nephew of a neighbor, or a member of a prominent Long Island family such as the Floyds, or perhaps even one of his own distant cousins. There was no reason for him to fear such recognitions, should they occur, however. His shop was situated just a few yards away and had been for several years, so it was completely natural for him to be found at the coffeehouse, making the acquaintance of all who came through.

MAJOR JOHN ANDRÉ

Another, more sinister figure was establishing himself at Rivington's coffeehouse at the same time as Townsend. The British had wasted no time in developing their own counterspy network. In the spring of 1779, General Henry Clinton had appointed the dashing young major John André as his chief intelligence officer. The major had impressed the general with his wit and savvy when the general arrived in Philadelphia in the early months of 1778. Now, a little over a year after they first became acquainted, Clinton entrusted André with the task of managing the espionage efforts in the colonies, with a specific eye on New York. André and Clinton were well aware that Washington was desperate to retake New York and had to be sending spies there. Eager to intercept Patriot agents, the new intelligence officer set up his headquarters in Manhattan.

André was one of those individuals who thrive wherever planted.

He'd always been a rather worldly man; his father was from Geneva and his mother from Paris, and they had raised him in London, educating him with high hopes for a future in diplomacy. He was fluent in several languages, including English, French, German, and Italian, was a gifted artist, and often composed comical verses much to the amusement of his comrades. He was also famed as a party planner and a social coordinator, having directed and painted many of the sets for a celebratory theatrical event in honor of General Howe's return to England from Philadelphia. He had been the toast of that city during the occupation, and was rumored to have offered more than just brotherly love to several ladies therein. Among those who were thought to have fancied him was Peggy Shippen, a sparkling teenager from a prominent Loyalist family, who was renowned as much for her graciousness as for her beauty.

By the summer of 1779, André had moved on to New York and Shippen had recently married a widower named Benedict Arnold, a general in the Continental Army who had gotten to know her when the Americans reclaimed the city the previous year. It was an unlikely alliance given Arnold's employment and her family's politics, but one that seemed to delight bride and groom alike. André, for his part, considered New York a step up from Philadelphia, as it was the closest thing America had to offer, in terms of bustle and variety, to his hometown of London. He quickly became a fixture on the social scene, charming all company with his gallant manners and jovial personality, and spending many languid afternoons sipping coffee and trading ideas at Rivington's shop.

André found yet another advantage to his patronage of Rivington's establishment: He now had a willing publisher for his poems. Rivington was happy to publish any doggerel the dashing young Major André sent his way, as even the silly rhymes of such a popular figure were sure to sell papers among the Loyalist set in Manhattan. So it was that the counterspy unwittingly published his poetry next to the columns of his biggest target.

THE LADY

It was probably through his newspaper work that Townsend first made the acquaintance of a young female socialite, of whom he informed Woodhull. In his letter dated August 15, 1779, Woodhull recorded that there was a specific "[lady] of my acquaintance" so situated as to "out wit them all." Her sudden appearance in his letters following the recruitment of Townsend, as well as the fact that Townsend's ledger shows he and Woodhull met that same day, hints at the fact that she may have been introduced to the ring by Townsend himself. That she was already in Woodhull's acquaintance indicates that her name, at least, was already known to him prior to that day, perhaps indicating that she or her family were originally from Long Island. But her apparent presence in Manhattan of late meant that she was somehow uniquely positioned to collect important secrets in a cunning and charming manner that would leave those she had duped completely unaware that they had just been "outwitted" by a secret agent.

But just who was this mysterious woman so perfectly poised to steal such vital secrets? Woodhull was careful not to record her name, offering only a number—355—in the code that was to define the Culper Ring.

CHAPTER 7

Creating a Code

Even as Robert Townsend was settling into his new role, something happened that highlighted the precarious nature of the world in which he now lived. On July 2, 1779, British raiders had attacked Major Tallmadge's camp at dawn, killing ten men and capturing eight, plus a dozen horses. Those losses were devastating, but in the aftermath Tallmadge made a discovery that proved unsettling and was potentially threatening to the Patriots' intelligence operations. One of the horses the British had stolen was his own, which still bore its saddlebags and some of Tallmadge's personal papers—including some money earmarked for Woodhull and a letter from Washington that specifically named George Higday, a resident of Manhattan "who I am told hath given signal proofs of his attachment to us, and at the same time stands well with the enemy."

Eleven days later, Higday was arrested at his home and confessed to having met with General Washington to discuss the possibility of spying, but claimed that he never carried out any such activity because the payment had been in fake bills. There is no record of any punishment carried out against Higday; he was probably deemed harmless and sufficiently terrified not to be tempted into any covert actions in the future, so the matter was dropped. But Washington had now seen the dangers of using real names in correspondence and, again, felt the weight of the responsibility he had to guard the lives of those risking themselves for their shared cause.

Beyond Higday's fate, there was another, even more immediate concern to the Culpers. On June 13, Washington had written to Tallmadge in regular ink and mentioned having a particular, special "liquid." What was further, he referred to "C——r," a common form of address for the day when a name was well known between two correspondents. The letter was intercepted and landed in the hands of the British *prior* to the July second raid, alerting them to the definite presence of an American spy in New York—one with whom Tallmadge was in close contact. The British had no way of knowing if C——r was a code name or a proper one, but they didn't care. They were after bigger fish than just a spy; they wanted the spymaster himself, and the seized letter pointed straight to his camp.

Though Tallmadge had been fortunate enough to escape capture, he knew that damage had been done. If the ring were to survive, the spies would have to disguise information to protect it from prying eyes while keeping it understandable to those who depended upon the contents of the letters.

Alarmed by the two close calls, Tallmadge turned to the development of a code with a new sense of urgency. The ring had already begun to use a few numerical substitutions in their letters: for example, 10 stood for New York and 20 for Setauket, so that the recipient would know the source of the information contained in the reports. Two additional numbers, 30 and 40, were used to designate Jonas Hawkins and Austin Roe as post riders delivering the messages to their next destination. Tallmadge realized how essential it was that a more complete lexicon be developed and that every member or associate of the ring have a number rather than just a code name. In a style of cryptography developed originally by the French, Tallmadge selected a book and got to work. Making a list from 1 to 763, he pored over his copy of *Entick's Spelling Dictionary,* the 1777 London edition, and assigned each pertinent word, location, or name a numeric code. He became 721, Woodhull as Culper Senior 722, Townsend as Culper Junior 723, Roe 724, and Brewster 725. General Washington was 711 and his British counterpart, General Clinton, was 712. Numbers were often represented by letters, so that the year "1779," for example, might read as "ennq." If a word needed to be made plural, or put in the past or future tense, a "flourish" would be written on top of it to designate the change.

The new system was not foolproof and required some adjustments on the part of the users, but Woodhull and Tallmadge were able to use it to correspond comfortably within a few weeks, though with a lingering sense of concern for what damage had been done by the intercepted message in June. In his same letter that mentioned the "[lady] of my acquaintance," Woodhull opened:

> *729 29 15th 1779*
>
> Sir. *Dqpeu Beyocpu agreeable to 28 met 723 not far from 727 & received a 356, but on his return was under the necessity to destroy the same, or be detected. . . . Thers been no augmentation by 592 of 680 or 347 forces, and everything very quiet. Every 356 is opened at the entrance of 727 and every 371 is searched, that for the future every 356 must be 691 with the 286 received. They have some 345 of the route our 356 takes. I judge it was mentioned in the 356 taken or they would not be so 660.*

Translated, and with a few creative grammatical adjustments required by the reader, the letter conveyed the following message:

Setauket August 15th 1779

Sir. *Jonas Hawkins agreeable to appointment. Met Culper Junior not far from New York & received a letter, but on his return was under the necessity to destroy the same, or be detected. . . . [There's] been no augmentation by ship of war or land forces, and everything very quiet. Every letter is opened at the entrance of New York and every man is searched, that for the future every letter must be write [written] with the ink received. They have some know [knowledge] of the route our letter takes. I judge it was mentioned in the letter taken or they would not be so vigilant.*

AGENT 355

Tallmadge's code contained a quirk that both reflects its time and offers up clues to a mystery. There are different codes to designate "man" (371) and "gentleman" (237), and "woman" (701) and "lady" (355); thus, there was a kind of commentary upon the social situation of a subject embedded within the code itself. Any mature adult might be referred to with the generic term "man" or "woman," according to the subject's sex; however, a "gentleman" in the American colonies was nearly always considered a man who owned land or a considerable amount of property, and was respected as a person of character in his local community. A woman might be referred to as a "lady" if she was of a well-to-do family, or was an accomplished young woman (that is, either literate and educated, or proficient in the arts of domestic leisure such as music, painting, and needlework). In other words, a man or a woman would generally only be referred to as a gentleman or a lady if he or she were of certain means and social standing. Social standing directly affected the quality of information a person could acquire: a washerwoman or a coachman might have been in a position to overhear some kinds of private conversations, whereas an established gentleman or lady might have been introduced to different types of gossip in a dining room, so Tallmadge's differentiation was strategic.

In the case of 355 (the "lady" of the Culpers' acquaintance), her code indicates that she was of some degree of social prominence. Was she Anna Smith Strong, the wife of Judge Selah Strong, a fierce Patriot who was first detained on a British prison ship in New York Harbor, then fled to Connecticut after his release? Local legend has it that Mrs. Strong, who remained behind to manage the house and family when her husband went into exile, used to hang laundry in specific patterns on her line. The Strong estate, situated on a high bluff, would be visible to anyone passing by boat across the Devil's Belt portion of Long Island Sound. The hanging clothes would appear as just that—wet clothes drying in the sun—to the untrained eye, but to Caleb Brewster, the arrangement of garments and their colors signified different counts of ships and troops, or in which cove it was safe for him to dock his boat, depending on which version of the story one hears. He would then be able to compile this information and pass it on with the Culper letters from New York when he rowed back across the water to meet Tallmadge or his courier in Connecticut.

While Anna Smith Strong might have played a satellite role in the ring—she was certainly an acquaintance of many of its members—assisting Woodhull, Roe, or Brewster at some point, there is no actual evidence that either she or her laundry ever served their country by gathering or passing along intelligence. It seems quite unlikely that the fortyish housewife, mother, and spouse of a well-known Patriot rabble-rouser would have ventured from Long Island to Manhattan to attend parties where she would have rubbed elbows with the Loyalist elite and gained the trust of high-ranking British officers.

A much more likely contender would be a young woman living a fashionable life in New York. Though of pro-American sentiments herself, she almost certainly would have been attached to a prominent Loyalist family, either as a freethinking daughter or a cousin or a niece who was staying in the city with her Tory relations. It is therefore possible that 355 was part of the glittering, giggling cluster of coquettes who flocked about Major André as he moved around the city, enjoying the finest food, wine, and company New York had to offer. Some of New York's brighter blooms were demure and others played coy, but, just as had been the case in Philadelphia, a few found themselves admitted into André's private chambers and his confidence, too.

BEYOND LETTERS

Despite the white ink and the coded communications, Washington knew that the British were growing more suspicious of the mail and that the tiniest details could attract scrutiny. Writing from his headquarters at West Point, New York, Washington sent Tallmadge a letter advising the major on this matter and also suggesting that Townsend not sacrifice his current employment in order to operate full-time as a spy. His cover story, as it stood, protected him far better and allowed him more freedom to gather information than he would have if he focused solely on intelligence gathering. The letter reveals much of General Washington's thought process concerning espionage, especially in regard to protecting his valued source.

> *Head-Quarters, West Point,*
>
> *24 September, 1779.*
>
> Sir,
>
> *It is not my opinion that Culper Junior should be advised to give up his present employment. I would imagine that with a little industry he will be able to carry on his intelligence with greater security to himself and greater advantages to us, under cover of*

his usual business, than if he were to dedicate himself wholly to the giving of information. It may afford him opportunities of collecting intelligence that he could not obtain so well in any other manner. It prevents also those suspicions which would become natural should he throw himself out of the line of his present employment. He may rest assured of every proper attention being paid to his services. One thing appears to me deserving of his particular consideration, as it will not only render his communications less exposed to detection, but relieve the fears of such persons as may be entrusted with its conveyance to the second link in the chain, and of course very much facilitate the object we have in view; I mean, that he should occasionally write his information on the blank leaves of a pamphlet, on the first, second, and other pages of a common pocket book, or on the blank leaves at each end of registers, almanacks, or any new publication or book of small value. He should be determined in the choice of these books principally by the goodness of the blank paper, as the ink is not easily legible unless it is on paper of a good quality. Having settled a plan of this kind with his friend, he may forward them without risk of search or the scrutiny of the enemy, as this is chiefly directed against paper made up in the form of letters.

I would add a further hint on this subject. Even letters may be made more subservient to this communication, than they have yet been. He may write a familiar letter on domestic affairs, or on some little matters of business, to his friend at Setauket or elsewhere, interlining with the stain his secret intelligence,

> *or writing it on the opposite blank side of the letter. But that his friend may know how to distinguish these from letters addressed solely to himself, he may always leave such as contain secret information without date or place (dating it with the stain), or fold them up in a particular manner, which may be concerted between the parties. This last appears to be the best mark of the two, and may be the signal of their being designated for me. The first mentioned mode, however, or that of the books, appears to me the one least liable to detection. I am, &c.*

Washington, it seems, was an advocate of the practice of hiding messages in plain view. If a letter appeared suspicious or was treated with the utmost caution and concern, it was more likely to tip off British inspectors. By instead passing along the highly sensitive information disguised as dull letters on day-to-day family news or hidden in a book, the vehicle by which the message was being sent would probably not warrant a second glance. Only the intended recipient would know, alerted by an otherwise meaningless clue such as a specific fold, that there was anything more to the item than what met the eye.

With Rivington's print shop operating just down the street, and as someone who enjoyed an established relationship with the owner, Townsend had no shortage of books available for sending messages the way Washington had put forward. But Townsend, using his invisible ink, seems to have preferred an alternative means of his own design: When the courier (usually Woodhull or Roe, judging from his store's ledger) arrived to pick up the goods he had purchased to bring back to Long Island, among them would be a packet of blank writing paper. Concealed within those loose leaves was a seemingly blank sheet that contained the invisible letter to be rendered readable once it reached its destination and the stain was applied. Clear communication as to how many sheets into the stack the significant paper would be placed was essential to avoid wasting precious reagent in an attempt to discern which sheet contained the message, but all in all it worked extremely well as an innocuous way to smuggle reports out of the city.

With these new security measures in place, and Culper Junior and 355 firmly established in their roles in New York, the ring could now begin to forward intelligence more swiftly, safely, and in greater detail than before, though the risk of detection and capture remained. The life of a spy always requires looking over one's shoulder, but now Washington's operatives could enjoy at least a little more freedom to speak about their observances and advisements without needing to censor their words in case a letter fell into the wrong hands.

The added security was just in time, too, with André's arrival in the city. There were plots afoot—plans of deceit, treason, and betrayal—and the only hope the Americans had to survive them was to be prepared. Washington knew that New York City was of the utmost strategic importance from a military perspective, but even he could not anticipate how crucial the intelligence collected there would be in saving the cause for liberty. And neither side, American nor British, could yet imagine just how deep the treachery reached within its own ranks.

CHAPTER 8

Mounting Tensions and Double-Dealings

Suspicions and tensions were beginning to rise even as the summer of 1779 reached its peak, and all the agents were feeling the stress. Washington sent "all the white Ink I now have (indeed all that there is any prospect of getting soon)" with a trusted colonel, along with the desperate instructions:

> *You will send these to C——r, Junr., as soon as possible, and I beg that no mention may ever be made of your having received such liquids from me or any one else. In all cases and at all times this procedure and circumspection is necessary, but it is indispensably so now as I am informed that Govr. Tryon [British governor of New York] has a preparation of the same acid or something similar to it, which may lead to a detection if it is ever known that a matter of this sort has passed from me.*

Just four days later, Townsend prepared another letter for General Washington, closing with several lines that pointed to the increased danger he was also observing. "The times now are extreamly difficult," he wrote. "Guard boats are kept out every night in the North and East Rivers to prevent any boats from passing, & I am informed that some persons have been searched on Long Island; therefore, whenever you think that my intelligence is of no service, beg you will notify me."

Indeed, letters were now being searched with regularity as they left the city. Jonas Hawkins, the ring's sometime courier, twice believed he was in danger of being found out and destroyed the missives he was carrying from Townsend, much to the older man's annoyance.

On September 11, 1779, Woodhull acted as courier in place of Hawkins and wrote to explain what had happened to the letters from Culper Junior that had never made it to Washington as a result of Hawkins's fear. "The bearer thought himself in danger. I believe it was merely imaginary," Woodhull penned. "From timidity and the situation of affairs at the time, he did to choose to come to N.Yk; I therefore met him at a place quite out of danger on Long-Island. I then made an appointment . . . at wch. time he came, I wrote it, and took it over the Ferry that he might run no hazard from the Inspector of Letters there."

Townsend had never felt confident in Hawkins, having resented that his identity necessarily should be known by a boy he considered too immature for such serious work. For all of Townsend's natural reserve, his reaction was almost certainly far from calm.

"He should have never been entrusted with such a task!" Townsend stormed to Woodhull when he learned of the destruction of his second letter.

"We needed another courier," Woodhull tried to explain.

"But why am I risking my life gathering information day after day if my letters are to be destroyed before they reach the general?"

Woodhull shook his head. "The boy simply panicked."

"But one who panics—or even looks nervous—before the inspectors is bound to bring extra scrutiny upon himself. And if he is searched and anything suspicious is found upon him, where will be the first place the British turn?" He paused, looking to Woodhull for an answer, but Woodhull just scraped at a bit of candle wax on the table. "They'll look to any of his known associates, and to the last place he did business which, inevitably, will bring them to my shop," Townsend finished, flatly.

"We are, all of us, on edge," Woodhull said quietly.

"And we are, all of us, endangered by that boy's want of good sense and composure." Townsend banged his fist upon the table with such force it caused the candles to jump.

"I cannot always be coming here to retrieve your information myself. That will raise suspicions, too," Woodhull insisted. "Besides, General Washington desires the information even more quickly than we have been supplying it. If you wait until I am able to make the trip, it will only delay the relay of news."

"Then we get another man," Townsend said, sighing and sinking into the straight-backed chair. "This time one who knows how to keep his wits about him."

"But you were the one who insisted that your identity not be disclosed to anyone else. So what are we to do?"

Townsend dropped his head into his hands. The two friends discussed several scenarios, weighing the risks and benefits of each. Finally, they thought of Amos Underhill, Woodhull's brother-in-law and the proprietor of the boardinghouse where Woodhull stayed on his frequent trips to Manhattan.

"He needs provisions as much as anyone else. Why could he not frequent my shop for goods and pick up the reports at the same time?" Townsend mused.

Woodhull considered this. "I'd still have to travel into the city to retrieve them, unless Amos could be convinced to come across the water sometimes."

"But it would lessen your visits to my shop, and give us fewer opportunities to be spotted together. And he need not know the exact nature of our business together unless you deem it absolutely necessary."

"It's a gloomy thing to toast on," Woodhull remarked. "But I agree that it's a far better thing than to have young Hawkins destroy any more of your letters or, worse, be driven to madness and confess all. Give me a bit of time to present the matter to Amos and make proper arrangements. Until then, I will continue to serve as courier."

One can hardly blame Hawkins for his trepidation; the threats were growing and the whole Culper Ring felt the squeeze. The pressure continued to mount as autumn approached. Besides fearing British searches, the couriers also faced dangers from increasingly active privateers. In his letter dated November 1, 1779, Tallmadge wrote to General Washington of the growing hazards faced by members of the ring, including the once-fearless Caleb Brewster: "The boat that crosses for dispatches from C—— has been chased quite across the Sound by those plunderers, perhaps for the sake of being the more secret in their Villany, while our crew has suspected them to be the Enemy. Indeed if some stop cannot be put to such nefarious practices C—— will not risque, nor 725 [Brewster] go over for dispatches."

By the end of November, Amos Underhill's name began to appear regularly in Townsend's ledger. Hawkins, meanwhile, seems also to have questioned his involvement and quietly removed himself from the ring. Underhill's appearance could not have been better timed, as Woodhull's nerves were again getting the best of him. Woodhull had been questioned by a party of British troops while en route to meet up with Townsend at a safe house on Long Island, but apparently he kept his wits about him, because he was released without having to succumb to a more thorough search; Townsend, however, did not show. Woodhull waited at the rendezvous point the next day as well, but there was no sign of Culper Junior. The excuse for his absence does not appear in any of Townsend's letters, but as he was quite condemning in his correspondence of others who failed to make appointments, it was undoubtedly a serious matter beyond simply a lack of courage. The slip brought Woodhull nearly to a breaking point, prompting him to tell Tallmadge afterward that he had endured "a full year's anxiety, which no one can scarcely have an idea of, but those that experience. Not long since, there was not even the breadth of your finger betwixt me and death."

Woodhull's complaint was not unwarranted. The residents of Long Island were bracing for an even greater number of troops to be quartered there during the coming winter than they had endured the winter before; they also continued to absorb Loyalist refugees from all over the eastern seaboard. "The inhabitants of this Island at present live a miserable life, which you may readily judge when having the refuse of three kingdoms and thirteen States amongst them. Plundering and rapine increaseth at no small rate," Woodhull wrote in the same letter to Tallmadge. "I am tired of this business, it gives me a deal of trouble, especially when disappointments happen. Could not consent to be any longer an assistant if I was not almost an Enthusiast for our success."

But there was a covert storm brewing in New York—one that Townsend was in the process of uncovering and confirming—that threatened the Americans not through bloodshed or siege, but through their pocketbooks. And if it was on account of uncovering this business that Townsend was unable to meet up with Woodhull, he might very well be excused by reason of the magnitude of the plot he thwarted.

STRIKING A MINT

The British were highly skilled counterfeiters, and one of their favorite ways to attack the Americans was by depreciating colonial currency. At the most basic level, a worthless currency made it difficult for the Continental Army to purchase rations and rendered the soldiers' pay quite literally not worth the paper it was printed on. On a grander scale, having a wildly inflated currency made it nearly impossible for American diplomats overseas to secure credit with foreign banks—a severe problem in both the short and long terms. Without financial backing, the Americans could not bankroll the food, men, horses, war ships, and weapons needed to win the Revolution. If, against all odds, they were successful in their split from the British Crown, the new nation would need credit to rebuild its infrastructure—a concern the British did not have to contend with, because the war was an ocean away from London.

Recognizing the vulnerability of the American currency, the British ran counterfeiting operations aboard British ships and onshore where possible. Distribution of counterfeit bills was an open secret in the early years of the war, with advertisements even running in newspapers for travelers headed to other colonies to carry with them fake bills of their current location to their new destination. Aware of the danger, Woodhull himself even insisted on being paid in the king's currency—a request Washington honored without question.

The Continental Congress had made some efforts to combat the counterfeiting but saw limited success. Eventually, they developed a special paper of a very precise quality and thickness that would be used to produce the bulk of the money minted in Philadelphia and, it was hoped, would be extremely difficult to replicate. This would allow the government much greater control as to the amount in circulation, which would, in turn, control inflation.

What Townsend learned, however, and wrote about with urgency to Washington on November 27, 1779, was that "several reams of the paper made for the last emissions struck by Congress have been procured from Philadelphia." The one safeguard upon which the Americans were counting to protect their currency had been breached. Somehow, whether through negligence or a double agent, the paper and possibly even the printer plates had made their way to

New York, where the British could use them to churn out perfect counterfeits. Distribution in New York would drive down prices and sink the economy of the colonies right in the heart of their main trading hub. General Clinton, Major André, and their colleagues based in New York would meanwhile be feasting and dining on the unmatched power of sterling currency as the city—and the entire fledgling nation—crumbled around them.

Though the attempts to destroy the war effort through counterfeit bills were neither new nor secret, the magnitude of this particular plot and the fact that the worthless bills would be undetectable before it was too late made this intelligence of no small significance. With word from the Culpers delivered swiftly, Washington was able to alert Congress to the scheme. The resulting action—a cancellation of all colonial bills a few months later in March 1780—was drastic and potentially devastating in itself, but far less destructive to the American economy and morale than a sneak attack on its currency would have been.

Just how had Townsend uncovered such a plan? He may have happened upon some gossip by lucky coincidence, but the certainty with which Townsend outlined the plan for Tallmadge and Washington indicates that he had a much more intimate knowledge of the scheme than just hearsay. His source? The newest member of the ring.

THE MANY LIVES OF JAMES RIVINGTON: THE LAST PIECE

James Rivington, that same enterprising printer, newspaper editor, and coffeehouse owner with whom both Townsend and André had a friendship, was something of an American success story—though his path was far from typical. Whatever misfortunes he had suffered in England, his businesses were thriving in the New World and he was a master of spotting new opportunities. By the middle of the 1770s, his New York–based newspaper was being read at least as far south as

Baltimore. When the sparks of revolution became the full-fledged flames of war in 1775, however, Rivington's shop was looted and burned by the Sons of Liberty, with some of his presses and typefaces being melted down for ammunition. He moved his family back to England for their own safety, then returned to New York in 1777, where he opened his businesses near Townsend's shop.

While Rivington was away, his surviving presses were busy serving the king without him. On June 26, 1776, a counterfeiter named Israel Young testified to having heard from a trusted source that a ship in New York waters, the *Duchess of Gordon,* had been the site of a counterfeiting workshop. What was more, Young recounted, the work was overseen by none other than New York's colonial governor, William Tryon. Young swore that he heard from his source that he "had also seen Governour Tryon often, and that the Governour would talk very free with them; that they had on board a number of Rivington's types and one of his printers." The source "received a letter which he said was from the Governour, and also some water-work money, which he said they counterfeited on board the *Duchess,* and he himself had seen them printing it off; that they had a chest of it."

Whether it was with Rivington's knowledge at the time or not, his name was thus linked with the counterfeiting trade and he undoubtedly drank free in British circles afterward for having such a reputation. Any rumors of counterfeiting schemes circulating among the British officer corps of New York would have certainly been considered of interest to Rivington, and he may have even been consulted as to the best way to carry out the endeavor. With Townsend in his employ and frequenting the coffeehouse, word of the plan could have easily slipped out either accidentally or as a matter of interest to the curious part-time reporter.

Or it might have been very deliberately shared.

As it turns out, there was much more to James Rivington, "Printer to the King's Most Excellent Majesty," than met the eye. At some point following his return to America from England at the end of 1777, it seems that his loyalties shifted. It remains unclear whether he was driven by a change of heart toward the American cause, a desire for monetary gain, or simply frustration at the Crown's objections and prohibitions to his printing criticisms of the leadership of General Howe in the autumn of 1778. But what is certain is that Rivington secretly threw in his lot with the Americans and began to work alongside Robert Townsend gathering information and conveying it outside the city to General Washington's waiting hands.

Rivington's name was the last to appear among the Culper code monikers, 726, indicating that Townsend had recruited him soon after his own engagement, probably by the late summer of 1779, when the code was developed. The code first lists the spies' names, concluding with Rivington as 726, then seamlessly moves on from personal names to place-names, with New York designated as 727. How so cautious and reserved a man as Townsend was able to establish a confidence with an avowedly Tory propagandist is hard to imagine. Once the connection was made, however, Rivington's mischievous nature must have delighted in the irony of his recruitment. This was the same man, after all, who found great amusement in seeing himself hung in effigy and who happily reprinted damning letters about his character from Patriot circulars in his own newspaper.

His unconventional sense of humor aside, Rivington proved a valuable asset to Townsend's work. Taking advantage of his profession, he provided books for the spies' use. Sometimes the books' bindings hid slips of paper holding intelligence Rivington himself had gleaned from his Loyalist guests and friends.

Several years later, William Hooper, a North Carolina lawyer who had signed the Declaration of Independence, wrote to his friend and future Supreme Court justice James Iredell:

> *It has come out as there is now no longer any reason to conceal it that Rivington has been very useful to*

> *Gen Washington by furnishing him with intelligence. The unusual confidence which the British placed in him owing in a great measure to his liberal abuse of the Americans gave him ample opportunities to obtain information which he has bountifully communicated to our friends.*

The British were being played, and from the least likely of corners. But they remained oblivious to the double-dealings in their midst. The parties went on. The coffeehouse debates continued as the officers went about surrounded by their circles of admirers. Major André's silly love poems were composed and published in Rivington's *Royal Gazette.* The wine and the words flowed freely as they bantered about their plans. The army was in garrison—comfortable, amused, and completely oblivious to the fact that any shopkeeper, newspaperman, or charming lady in their midst was listening, remembering, and plotting.

CHAPTER 9

Washington Demands More

Now Washington had tasted victory; his agents had outsmarted the enemy in their own territory. It could be done. By revealing the counterfeiting plot, the Culper Ring had proved that New York was not some insurmountable fortress; they had penetrated its vault of secrets successfully and unmasked an entire plot before it could be played out to its catastrophic end. Best of all, the enemy had no way of knowing at what stage the plan may have been leaked or tracing back any breaches of secrecy. Washington's informants, therefore, were relatively safe from detection and could continue their activities without too much concern for their welfare.

Even so, there was much more afoot—of that Washington was certain. Now that one plan had been foiled another would soon be hatched, probably with more speed this time to minimize the risk of leaks. Some delicacy must be sacrificed for the sake of urgency, but could he make his most trusted, most valued, and most secretive ring understand that? He pored over the maps as he would before a battle; perhaps there was a way to convey messages across the Hudson River or via Staten Island? He wrote as much to Tallmadge, urging him to talk to Culper Senior about such an option, hoping to impress upon the ring the importance of timely reports.

The Culpers, meanwhile, were enjoying something of a reprieve from the oppressive worries that had plagued them of late. Colonel Simcoe had left his reluctant hosts, the Townsends, and led the Queen's Rangers back to the mainland in an effort to capture George Washington. They had failed, and Simcoe was now being held prisoner by the Americans. Woodhull, no doubt voicing the sentiments of numerous people, concluded his letter to Tallmadge on December 12, 1779: "Were I now in the State of New Jersey without fear of Law or Gospel, [I] would certainly kill Col. Simcoe, for his usage to me." In that same message, he included a blank sheet containing a stain letter from Townsend with whom he wrote he planned to celebrate Christmas.

Holiday leisure was a luxury the commander in chief could ill afford as the fate of the entire Revolution rested heavily upon his shoulders. Even as Woodhull wrote that his "fears are much abated," Washington felt a growing sense of urgency to see the cracks in New York's armor exploited even more aggressively. Matters in the southern colonies showed signs of deteriorating come spring, which meant that his attention and resources would be even more divided and strained. If the British were plotting any offensive maneuvers from the city, he wanted to be prepared.

Washington must have communicated his urgency to the ring, because Amos Underhill visited Townsend's shop with increased frequency starting in mid-January 1780, appearing in his ledger four times in just over three weeks. But the smuggled messages were not meeting the pressing demands Washington was facing. Events were accelerating rapidly, and the laborious means of conveying the letters out of occupied New York and Long Island, into Connecticut, and overland to Washington's camp were too slow. Instead of providing new information, the Culper Ring's intelligence was now providing verification of facts the general had already learned. "His accounts are intelligent, clear, and satisfactory, consequently would be valuable, but owing to the circuitous route through which they are transmitted I can derive no immediate or important advantage from them," Washington wrote Tallmadge on February 5. "And (as I rely upon his intelligence) the only satisfaction I derive from it, is, that other accts. are either confirmed or corrected by his, after they have been some time received."

He was not unsympathetic to the tremendous challenges his ring faced—most specifically, the risks Culper Junior, who lived and worked in the heart of the British operations, endured every day. "I am sensible of the delicacy of his situation, and the necessity of caution," Washington added to his letter, as if realizing the harsh tone of his criticism in the preceding lines directed to his favorite spy. He went on to suggest that he may be able to provide Culper Junior with more direct possibilities for moving the letters out of New York, though he acknowledged the risks involved in expanding the ring beyond its current members: "I have hitherto forborn and am yet unwilling to mention, persons to him as the vehicles of conveyance lest they should not prove so trustworthy and prudent as we could wish."

A few weeks later, Woodhull found himself writing back to Washington, informing the general of detailed ship movements, as well as warning him of even more potential risk from greatly increased scrutiny and enemy presence in Setauket: "Two regts. is to be stationed in this Town. If it should take place it will I fear entirely ruin our correspondence. To prevent which I shall give you early intelligence of their motions from time to time, that you may be prepared to give them a fatal blow at the beginning, or we shall be totally ruined."

The reprieve Woodhull's emotions had enjoyed in December had proved all too brief. It was March now, which meant increased activity could be anticipated with the spring thaw. But the winter of 1779–80, known as "the Hard Winter," proved to be one of the coldest recorded seasons of the eighteenth century in North America, and refused to let up. The weather took a turn for the worse, with tumultuous spring storms thwarting several efforts to convey letters to Washington explaining that the Culpers had taken seriously his concerns regarding the speed of their reports. Under increased pressure to perform, Woodhull once again let his nerves get the best of him as he attempted to count and recount the blank sheets of paper that had come to him as part of his last batch of goods from Townsend. Somehow, the number never seemed to come up right and the same sheet was never landed upon twice. Worried about sending a worthless paper rather than the one that contained the message written in the stain, Woodhull finally threw up his hands and dashed off a note: "*Sir.* Inclosed you have a blank—Something fearful not sending the right and have inclosed three."

THE MESSENGER DEBACLE

Meanwhile, Townsend looked for new couriers who could carry messages northward across the Hudson as the general had requested instead of across the Sound and through Connecticut. Rather than choose an outsider, he turned to a family member, a cousin named James Townsend, who was only sixteen or seventeen years old at the time. The young man had no idea as to the exact nature of the letters with which he was entrusted; he only knew that they contained sensitive information that was important to his grave, somber cousin—and that they would land him in prison if his mission was found out.

Armed with just enough ignorance to be safe, just enough knowledge to be cautious, and just enough bravery to be dangerous, James set off under the assumed identity of a Loyalist visiting relatives outside the city. His travels progressed smoothly until he stopped at the home of the Deausenberry family. He expected they would be sympathetic to giving him rest and shelter, as they were ardent Patriots in an otherwise Tory-dominated area, but James seems to have played his part as a Loyalist too convincingly. The Deausenberry daughters, young women about his own age, suspected that he might even be a Tory spy. In the hopes of causing him to spill his story, they pretended to be Loyalists, too, much to James's surprise. Confused by their switch, the boy feigned intoxication in the hopes of covering his tracks and convincing the family he was harmless, but it was too tangled of a web to escape by that point.

"Oh, I was within two miles of New York City the day before yesterday," he slurred, "carrying a number of stockings to my uncle and brother. I planned to join up with the British while I was there."

"Why ever didn't you?" one of the young ladies inquired.

"They told me I should come over here and recruit several more lads to join up with me so we could meet up with the British together when they head up the river in a week, as they are expected to do."

"And is that what you are endeavoring to do at present?"

"I've persuaded many a good fellow to enlist," James pushed on. "Very frequently over the course of the last summer I've been backward and forward to and from New York, having piloted several companies of British soldiers. I've carried in and brought out many valuable articles."

The young ladies affected appropriate reactions of admiration, which only emboldened James further. "Once I was taken upon by the damned rebels who left me confined and chained down, flat on my back in the Provost three weeks." The game was too fun, too delicious an opportunity for a red-blooded young man to resist embellishing his story, especially when he could do so with a clean conscience, believing it to be necessary to save both his life and his mission. He continued: "Finally, I made my escape by breaking out—"

With a roar, John Deausenberry, the elder brother of the two ladies, leapt from his hiding place and pounced upon James, declaring him a prisoner. A terrified James was immediately carted off to the

American army camp nearby, where he was searched thoroughly, and John Deausenberry gave a full and detailed deposition on the matter. To the great disappointment of both the Deausenberrys and the soldiers, nothing of interest was found on James, though they did commandeer the two sheets of paper he was carrying that contained a groan-worthy poem called "The Lady's Dress" on a page folded in a peculiar manner and signed with a nearly illegible "S.T." The soldiers sent the letters on to headquarters, and James was held in Patriot custody.

Poor James's mission was not a complete debacle, because the papers did reach Washington. The general recognized the unusual manner of folding (his own suggestion from the September 24, 1779, letter) and knew the initials "S.T." indicated that stain was to be applied. The handwriting, too, was a giveaway that the papers had come from none other than Culper Junior. As Washington dabbed the stain between the lines of the poem (which humorously describes the elegance of a healthy-looking lady's apparel until a husband realizes his wife is half the size she appears once her hoops and many layers have been removed) Townsend's message began to appear. Unfortunately, it was almost completely unreadable and, before he even reached the end, Washington resolved to waste no more of his precious stain in an attempt to develop something that was inscrutable.

Even more frustrating to the general was that his personal involvement was required to secure James's freedom. Washington was furious that so much unnecessary attention had been drawn to covert operations, wasting resources and time on what proved to be an unfruitful mission. More than a little of the general's precious focus had to be diverted from strategy and planning to handling the matter with delicacy before James was finally released to slink back to New York with his tail between his legs. Tallmadge was briefed on the situation and he, in turn, made sure that Woodhull understood the depth of Washington's displeasure. That message, it seems, was received directly and not at all softened in tone.

TUMULTUOUS SPRING

Admittedly, Townsend's papers had reached their destination, but the whole embarrassing incident did nothing to boost anyone's confidence in the New York spies' ability to speed up the transmission of their intelligence. It even threatened a fissure within the ring itself; Woodhull was left making apologies and excuses for what he considered to be Robert Townsend's profound lack of judgment in recruiting James, while Townsend insisted that as the prime information gatherer it had been incumbent upon him to at least attempt a different mode of communication. The disagreement was sharp, and in the end proved nearly fatal to the ring. Woodhull wrote to Tallmadge on May 4, 1780, "I have had an interview with C. Junr. and am sorry to find he declines serving any longer."

Washington had had enough. New York continued to taunt him and no intelligence he had received of late offered any hope that he might be able to wage an attack soon. The ring's failure was no real fault of their own, and Washington knew there had been no lack of effort to meet his increasingly urgent requests, but the results were discouraging all the same. When the general learned that Culper Junior—the link in the ring whose intelligence he had once valued above that of all other agents in the employ of the Continental Army—wanted to withdraw, he decided the entire endeavor would be pointless without him. In frustration, he determined to start from scratch and build a new network.

From his headquarters in Morristown, New Jersey, he wrote to Tallmadge on May 19: "As C. Junior has totally declined and C. Senior seems to wish to do it, I think the intercourse may be dropped. . . . I am endeavoring to open a communication with New York across Staten Island, but who are the agents in the City, I do not know." A few other spies were acting independently in the city, among them a tailor named Hercules Mulligan, who picked up gossip while measuring English soldiers for uniforms and suits, as well as Daniel

Diehel, a man of Woodhull's acquaintance. No one compared to the finely tuned and proven Culper Ring, but they were almost all Long Islanders, and could operate most safely in their own environs. Their familiarity with the people and waterways had kept them from discovery thus far. If Washington thought a diversion of route to Staten Island was necessary to speed the delivery of the messages, then he must find spies who could navigate that island instead. It was just that simple. As far as he was concerned, the Culper business was finished, even if it had concluded on a somewhat sour note.

This news wounded Woodhull deeply. He replied to Tallmadge on June 10 in a tone that reads almost like that of a jilted lover trying to maintain dignity after an affair:

> *I am happy to find that 711 [Washington] is about to establish a more advantageous channel of intelligence than heretofore. I perceive that the former he intimates hath been of little service. Sorry we have been at so much cost and trouble for little or no purpose. He also mentions of my backwardness to serve. He certainly hath been misinformed. You are sensible I have been indefatigable, and have done it from a principal of duty rather than from any mercenary end—and as hinted heretofore, if at any time theres need you may rely on my faithful endeavours. I perceive there's no mention made of any money to discharge the remaining debts, which hath increased since I saw you, owing to your direction to continue the correspondence regular until I received your answer from 711.*

It is no wonder that the Culper communications had proved so disappointing to General Washington in the spring of 1780. The difficulties of delivering the messages in a timely fashion given the geographical constraints and weather were real, but the other reality was that there was little reliable information to be sent. General Clinton had left the city for South Carolina, taking the key decision makers with him. Even if the spies had been at the top of their game, they still would have had little news for Washington.

Agent 355 found herself in an especially difficult position. Only camp women and wives traveled with officers on the move—no respectable single woman would ever follow the soldiers, and certainly not a lady of her social standing. In the absence of the officers, whatever intelligence she was gleaning from whispered conversations with André, or from plots carelessly (or cockily) mentioned in passing, completely dried up. Townsend, for his part, could continue to chat with soldiers in his shop or make his inquiries at the docks and around the city as he inspected cargo ships for their wares or interviewed people for his newspaper column. Rivington could continue passing on bits of gossip he collected as a newspaperman and coffeehouse owner. But 355 could only await the return of her sources and the revival of her set before she could impart any further information.

Clinton's absence was short-lived. Charleston fell much the same way Manhattan had, and Clinton felt no need to stay to put down the backwoods colonists still causing trouble in the Appalachians. He would leave that to his officers and return to the metropolitan delights of New York: mistresses, theaters, balls, and the satisfaction of being the toast of one of the largest cities on the continent.

There was another reason why General Clinton hastened back to the glittering pleasures of New York in June 1780. Rumor had reached his ears that a fleet of French ships carrying troops was bound for North America. As complacent as he was, this new development troubled him. With the assistance of the French, the Americans might be able to take back New York—or even win the war without the city.

CHAPTER 10

The French Connection

General Washington could not hold a grudge for long. After cooling off for several weeks and realizing that no real harm had been done by the misadventures of James Townsend, he began to reconsider his decision. Slow but credible intelligence was better than fast but muddled—or no intelligence at all. Washington had grown accustomed to his reliable and detailed reports from the Culper Ring; those messages provided him with a sense that *something* was happening to advance the Patriot cause in New York, even if he was powerless to lead the charge to recapture the city.

Meanwhile, the same rumor that Clinton had heard grew to a buzz. A fleet of French ships was crossing the Atlantic at that very moment, coming to give the Americans a much-needed boost of men, might, and morale. If the British intercepted them it would be devastating.

Washington did not know where the French would land. He did not know whether the British knew, and, if they did know, how General Clinton was planning to ambush the fleet. Even great men make mistakes, and Washington knew he had committed a grave one in ending the spy ring. Never before, he realized, had he needed eyes and ears in New York so urgently. It had taken a long time to win over France, and the Americans could not afford to squander their new ally's good favor.

LOUIS XVI'S SECRET WAR

After centuries of warfare and uneasy truces both on home soil and in colonies abroad, the French wanted nothing more than to see the British defeated in the New World. Not only would it be beneficial for French claims in North America, but the humiliation heaped on King George for his loss to a bunch of upstart colonials was too delicious an opportunity for Louis XVI to ignore. The defeat of Britain in the American colonies would mean good things for France, and Louis was astute enough to realize that such a defeat would not be possible without outside assistance.

What was there to lose by offering help to the rebels? The British hated the French anyway, and the feeling was mutual, so French involvement would not poison any wells that were not already amply tainted. And what could be a more convenient means of deflating the British than supporting a war fought on someone else's soil, displacing someone else's population and destroying someone else's infrastructure?

As early as 1776, the fictitious Roderigue Hortalez & Company trading house had smuggled French money and provisions into the colonies. The company bolstered the American cause prior to the formal declaration of independence from Britain, and continued to supply the colonists' needs until the French and Americans finalized a treaty. After Benjamin Franklin secured the Franco-American alliance in February 1778, the company had no need to operate undercover.

That is not to say French involvement had been invisible before the treaty was signed. A number of French military officers joined the American cause; most notable was the Marquis de Lafayette, who had been serving with General Washington since 1777. Admiral Jean-Baptiste-Charles-Henri-Hector d'Estaing navigated a fleet of ships up from the West Indies to Rhode Island in 1778, where they engaged with the British in an attack on Newport. D'Estaing's expedition disappointed Washington: Not only was the battle something of a draw, but the fleet declined to attack the British navy stationed around New York. Unable to save Savannah, Georgia, from siege in September and October 1779, the fleet eventually sailed back to France, taking with it Washington's high hopes for a decisive naval engagement that would shift the momentum in his favor.

In the spring of 1780, word spread that another fleet had launched on April 6 from the port city of Brest. Code-named the Expédition Particulière (the British called it "Special Expedition"), the fleet was in charge of transporting more than six thousand troops under the command of Count Jean-Baptiste Donatien de Vimeur de Rochambeau. Both sides knew it had the potential to sway the outcome of the war.

That a large French fleet was sailing to the aid of the American cause was no secret in Europe; the extensive preparations for such a venture could scarcely be kept under wraps. But when and where the ships would land was a guessing game for both the Americans and the British. News of French plans had to travel by ship via almost exactly the same route as the fleet itself, making it nearly impossible to know ahead of time the destination of the reinforcements.

Washington had received intelligence that the fleet would be arriving soon and heading for Newport, Rhode Island. What he could not be sure of was whether the British knew the same thing or had only rumors and suspicions from which to operate. If the British were ignorant of the specifics, the Americans might have the element of surprise on their side. If the British had advance knowledge, they could move troops to engage the French as soon as they disembarked or even to prevent their landing in the first place.

By June, the British were in full-on preparation mode, making their best guesses and shoring up the areas they suspected to be the most vulnerable. In Woodhull's letter of June 10—the same in which he wrote with some offense toward Washington's revocation of the Culpers' duties—he also alerted Tallmadge to the flurry of activity on Long Island. "You speak with some assurance that the French is hourly expected to our assistance—hope they may not fail us. . . . Ther's a grand movement on foot in N.York. The troops are called from Lloyd's Neck and is said from every other distant post, and an embargo laid on all ships and small Sloops. It is suspected they are a going to quite N.York, or are going to make some diversion up the river, or are afraid of the French. But I cannot but think the former is likely to take place. For I believe their whole design is to the Southward."

RACE TO NEW YORK

On July 11—and, unbeknownst to Washington, less than twenty-four hours after the French ships dropped anchor in Narragansett Bay, Rhode Island—Washington sent an urgent letter to Tallmadge, asking him to reorganize the Culper Ring. "As we may every moment expect the arrival of the French Fleet a revival of correspondence with the Culpers will be of very great importance," he scrawled, continuing:

> *If the younger cannot be engaged again, you will endeavor to prevail upon the older to give you information of the movements and position of the enemy upon Long Island—as whether they are all confined to the port at Brooklyn or whether they have any detached posts and where, and what is their strength at those posts—in short desire him to inform you of*

> *whatever comes under his notice and what seems worthy of communication.*

Tallmadge received the letter on July 14 and immediately replied to the general that he would set out the next morning to find Brewster, who was still regularly crossing Long Island Sound to Connecticut for trading and taunting purposes. He also made a delicate suggestion to Washington: "I would at the same time hint that by Cr's last letter, we are something in arrears to him, and in order to enable him to prosecute the business, it may be necessary to afford him a small supply of money."

Once located, Brewster eagerly set off to find Woodhull, who, unfortunately, was ill with a fever and could not travel (he might have been suffering from a nervous illness as well). Instead, Austin Roe leapt upon a horse and headed straight for New York to alert Townsend, an exhausting fifty-five-mile trip one way. Washington knew by now that the landing had occurred, and he realized that General Clinton would know, too. Townsend's mission was to spy out the British response to the fleet's arrival.

Roe waited in Manhattan four days while Townsend (and very likely Agent 355) made inquiries and gathered as much information as possible from their acquaintances among the British officers. Townsend then recorded the findings in invisible ink between the lines of an order form for goods from his store, and included a fake note apologizing that the merchandise was not available at the time but would be forwarded when it arrived. Roe carried the note back with him—a simple cover story as to why he was carrying papers but no merchandise, in case he should be searched—and gave the sensitive letter to Woodhull. Woodhull passed it on to Brewster that same night to row across the Sound, adding pressing directions: "The enclosed requires your immediate departure this day by all means let not an hour pass: for this day must not be lost. You have news of the greatest consequence perhaps that ever happened to your country."

Woodhull also submitted a summary of what he had heard as an adjunct to Townsend's findings, writing that the report

> *also assures of the arrival of Admiral Graves with six ships of the line and is joined by three more out of New York, also one of 50 and two of 40 guns and has sailed for Rhode Island and is supposed they will be there before this can possibly reach you. Also 8000 Troops are this day embarking at Whitestone for the before mentioned port. I am told for certain that the French have only seven sail of the line. I greatly fear their destination.*

Understanding the urgency, Woodhull decided to eliminate Tallmadge from the chain of communication, crossing his code name, John Bolton, off the address of one letter before handing the dispatch to Brewster, who rushed it straight to Washington's headquarters. Alexander Hamilton, Washington's closest aide, received the report on the afternoon of July 21.

Unflappable as ever, Washington received the information calmly and carefully considered the possibilities. He desperately wanted to capture New York City, and with Clinton leading most of the British troops stationed there northward to engage the French, this could be his best opportunity. But Washington also knew better than to act rashly. He called together several of his top officers, and they discussed the likelihood of a successful attack; the prevailing sentiment was that it would be unwise. Even with Clinton and a large number of his men gone, the city was still well fortified and the battle would end as a siege, giving Clinton time to return with his soldiers and engage the Americans. Regretfully, Washington was forced to agree with his counselors and admit that he must reject his ambitions to recapture the city, but the brilliant strategist realized he could still capitalize on Manhattan's vulnerability.

A DIRTY BUSINESS

Washington was always conscious that even as he had spies working behind the scenes, so must the British. Every move required a risk whose cost he must calculate. Each maneuver he planned that had the potential to outsmart the enemy could be countered by the British to the detriment of his own forces. Planting a little strategic information was the best way to protect his army against counterintelligence.

Satisfied with the decision not to attack New York, Washington dismissed his officers—and then hurriedly began drawing up plans and penning correspondence signaling a full-fledged attack upon Manhattan as soon as Clinton's forces were clear of the city and too near to Newport to be easily recalled. The parcel was dispatched with a courier who hastily left camp with very specific instructions on where and when to deliver the documents. Then Washington waited.

A few hours later, a man stumbled up to a British outpost with a bundle of papers. He told the soldiers he had found the bundle lying by the side of the road and assumed it had tumbled out of the poorly secured saddlebags of a rider traveling at breakneck speed. However it got there wasn't important, the British immediately concluded. A quick glance revealed battle plans for a pending attack on New York and letters outlining the strategy coming from the hand of Washington himself. The soldiers roused their senior officers, who quickly decided that Clinton and his troops must be recalled. Defeating the newly arrived French troops was important, but holding New York was doubly so.

Flares signaled the message to Clinton, and the British ships did an about-face to sail back to New York Harbor, where Clinton ordered his troops to brace the city for an attack that could come at any time. The whole city held its breath, every citizen straining to hear the first sound of cannon fire breaking the silence of the countryside as the Americans advanced.

They waited. And while they waited, the French disembarked

and moved to an area of safety to await their marching orders with no interference from the British, no naval attacks upon their ships, and no ground offensives from Clinton's army. Washington's gamble had paid off beautifully.

George Washington, whom generations of schoolchildren would later know as a man who "could not tell a lie," couldn't help but be pleased. Even if the victory was bittersweet, because his first choice would have been to recapture New York, he had been able to secure, through his design of a fake attack, the safe arrival of the French reinforcements, which would shore up his prospects for a more successful assault at New York or elsewhere in the future. By intentionally planting misinformation, he achieved on a grand scale what he had accomplished in a smaller way with John Honeyman at Trenton in December 1776.

As for the Culpers, the ring was securely back in Washington's good graces. The quality of their information and the prudence they exercised in delivering it had enabled him to both understand the plans of the British and take decisive action by choosing not to risk an attack on New York. The ring had more than proved its worth, but the war was not yet won.

CHAPTER 11

Benedict and Peggy

Even as the Americans were congratulating themselves on the success of their counterintelligence, a traitor was building his own network within their midst. In the early summer of 1780, just as the Culper Ring was entering its hiatus and Clinton and André were settling back into New York after their foray to South Carolina, Major General Benedict Arnold was working to get his hands on a new command. Though he had been living the high life in Philadelphia, some recent unpleasantness had wounded his ego, and he had found himself in an all-too-familiar position: humiliated, angry, and desperate to prove his worth. He was about to show the world just how important he really was. If the Americans couldn't see his value, the British would.

Arnold had been a man with something to prove right from the start. Despite his current rank of major general in the Continental Army, he was profoundly insecure and carried a chip on his shoulder from a lifetime of feeling perpetually slighted by fate. Given the paternal name of "Benedict" after an older brother bearing the same name died in childhood, Arnold started out life living in the shadow of someone else, and no matter his later successes, he always seemed plagued by insecurities and a sense of somehow always falling short.

Unable to attend Yale due to his father's financial woes brought on by alcoholism and poor health, Arnold was forced to learn a trade instead. He apprenticed with two of his maternal uncles in their apothecary and mercantile shop but longed for something greater. In 1755, at the age of fourteen, he begged to be allowed to join the colonial militia that was in service of the king of England in the French and Indian War. His mother forbade him to do so, but two years later he enlisted anyway, only to leave the militia the following year, allegedly deserting.

However he came to be separated from his first term of military service, he proved to have a strong business sense and by his early twenties was running a successful pharmacy and bookshop in New Haven, Connecticut. Eventually he was able to purchase partial ownership in a small fleet of merchant ships and occasionally sailed on trading ventures to the Caribbean. With the increase of British taxation, starting with the Sugar Act in 1764 and the Stamp Act the next year, Arnold felt the pinch but followed the example of many American merchants who simply ignored the laws they viewed as unwarranted and unjust from a government that taxed its colonial citizens without granting them representation in Parliament.

In 1767, he married Margaret Mansfield, a hardworking and prudent woman who proved a valuable partner to him, thanks in large part to her family's solid standing in New Haven, where her father served as sheriff. Arnold began to fall on financial hard times and accumulated some substantial debts, but he continued in his trading business even as his outrage over the political climate in the colonies increased. On March 5, 1770, British soldiers fired into a crowd of protesters in Boston, killing five civilians and wounding six. The Boston Massacre infuriated Arnold. He had been in the West Indies at the time, so the news did not reach him until more than a month after the fact, but it stirred in him a profound sense of action and responsibility. "Good God," he wrote on June 9. "Are the Americans all asleep & tamely giving up their glorious liberties or, are they all turned philosophers, that they don't take immediate vengeance on such miscreants; I am afraid of the latter."

In March 1775, Arnold joined the Connecticut militia as a captain and just two months later received a colonel's commission in the Massachusetts Committee of Safety after he offered plans for attacking the British outpost at Fort Ticonderoga in northern New York. The mission was a success and Arnold garnered accolades for his performance, but he resigned his commission after a disagreement with another militia leader. He then set out to return home to serve in Connecticut. Bad news seemed to have a way of reaching Arnold whenever he was traveling, and he was on the road when he learned his wife had died.

Over the next few years, Arnold was involved in a number of key American victories and distinguished himself as an insightful strategist and able officer. But his talents were not nearly so celebrated as Arnold believed was his due. His advice was often heeded, though he was not sought out as a leader; he was passed over for command and promotion several times, which deeply wounded his ego. He became a polarizing figure, either loved or loathed by his comrades in arms. Those who argued in his favor pointed to his keen understanding of strategy and shrewd assessments of the enemy's vulnerabilities. Those who argued against him pointed to his quick temper, his growing pessimism toward the success of the American war effort, and his apparent motivation by personal glory and gain. Colonel John Brown, one of Arnold's rivals, prophetically wrote of him in 1777: "Money is this man's God, and to get enough of it he would sacrifice his country."

After distinguishing himself in the Battles of Saratoga in the fall of 1777, Arnold believed he had finally shamed his critics and detractors who were standing in the way of the meteoric rise he so desperately desired. His valor in combat was undeniable—even though he had acted in direct defiance of an order from his superior officer, with whom he had a personal dispute. He had been severely wounded in his left leg but refused to allow an amputation; instead, he had it set to heal, but the job was poorly done. As a result, Arnold walked with a limp for the rest of his life.

In June 1778, as the Americans were reestablishing their presence in Philadelphia—and roughly two months before Woodhull began spying in New York as Culper Senior—Washington appointed Arnold the military commander of Philadelphia. Arnold quickly realized that this new position would allow him to engage in a variety of business deals to restore his finances, which were still plagued by his numerous debts back home in New Haven. He was not particularly popular among many citizens of Philadelphia, however, and complaints were soon raised that not all of his ventures were legitimate. One vocal critic was Allen McLane, a highly respected and distinguished soldier from Delaware, who had been among the first Americans to enter Philadelphia when the British left; McLane voiced his concerns to General Washington but was reprimanded for challenging such a high-ranking officer. When Arnold learned about the complaints, he was angry that so many citizens and fellow soldiers questioned his integrity, particularly because his position was one of public service to a war-torn city. Was he not an officer of the Continental Army who was fighting for the liberty and freedom of all Americans?

This upturn in his fortunes pleased Arnold, and he lived well in Philadelphia, even under the shadow of accusations that his gains were ill gotten. Like his British predecessors, he enjoyed rich furnishings and luxurious dinners and entertainments. He even mingled with

Philadelphia's society belles, one of whom, Peggy Shippen, especially caught his attention.

PEGGY

As the youngest surviving child born into a politically prominent family, Margaret "Peggy" Shippen grew up a pampered, spoiled darling of her parents and blossomed into one of the stars of Philadelphia's social scene. Under her father's supervision, she received an excellent education, even dabbling in political theory, which was highly unusual for a young woman of her time but later made her a delight at dinner parties and a favorite conversant among the military officers quartered in the city.

The Shippens were devout Loyalists living in the midst of what was, in many ways, the heart of the American cause. Philadelphia had hosted the First Continental Congress in 1774, which convened in response to the Intolerable Acts imposed as punishment on the colonists by the British Parliament after the Boston Tea Party. In May 1775, the Second Continental Congress was called, and again the delegates met in Philadelphia. The city played host to several of the delegates' meetings over the next six years, including their most famous, in 1776, which resulted in the Declaration of Independence, all while the Shippens—and many other residents who considered themselves loyal to King George—looked on in disapproval.

When the British marched on Philadelphia in September 1777 and captured it easily, the Shippens and their friends welcomed them. The winter that followed, while miserable for the Americans encamped outside the city at Valley Forge, was rather delightful for the British soldiers stationed in town. Galas and dinners were hosted in honor of the officers, who were the centerpiece of the social scene. Major John André, the dashing British poet-spy who would later be published by Rivington in New York, was one of the most sought after, and he attracted a bevy of female followers wherever he went.

Seventeen-year-old Peggy was among André's admirers, and history hints that her attentions might have been returned. Members of the leisure class understood that flirtation was a lovely game when both parties engaged in it merely for sport; so when the British decided to abandon Philadelphia nine months later in order to shore up their defenses in New York, there were probably very few tears shed on Peggy Shippen's pillow. The dapper André had marched away, but nature, armies, and young hearts all abhor a vacuum, and the American troops who were now pouring into the city promised their own diversions and charms for the young lady.

AN UNLIKELY UNION

Peggy Shippen found her life little changed with the arrival of the Continental Army. Her family still had wealth and prestige, and the most significant alteration to the social scene was simply the color of the officers' jackets. Despite her family's political allegiances, Peggy soon found herself enamored with the widowed Patriot general Benedict Arnold, even though he was nearly twenty years her senior. For his part, he was flattered by the attentions of the young and vivacious woman who remained one of the most prominent ladies in Philadelphia.

Just what the attraction was on Peggy's side is unclear. Arnold had position and prestige, but he also had some fairly substantial debts, a military career that might be in peril due to his wounded leg, a short temper, and deep-seated insecurities. Perhaps this was precisely what made Arnold's Samson the perfect catch for Peggy's Delilah. Peggy was a woman with a mind of her own, and she may have realized just how much power she could wield over such a husband. He would, in essence, be her slave, bending himself to her will out of fear that she might cuckold him if she didn't get her way. If there was one thing Arnold craved, it was admiration, and Peggy knew he thought that a beautiful young wife on his arm would win him the envy of his rivals.

Whatever the case, she captured his notice and his heart, and the two were married the following April, in 1779. Arnold's life had never been better: His finances were improving, both through his own investments and through the fortune of his pretty new wife. He was finally garnering the kind of respect and authority he felt he deserved. Still, he was bitter because other American officers seemed to be more popular and loved by their men. Just one month after his marriage to Peggy, an indignant Arnold wrote to General Washington regarding the charges against his business practices in Philadelphia: "If your Excellency thinks me criminal, for Heaven's sake let me be immediately tried, and, if found guilty, executed. I want no favor; I ask only for justice. . . . Having made every sacrifice of fortune and blood, and become a cripple in the service of my country, I little expected to meet the ungrateful returns I have received from my countrymen."

CHANGE OF HEART

While Arnold was reveling in his newfound prominence and respect, Peggy was throwing grand parties that helped to raise her husband's social profile—and his debts. The Arnolds enjoyed an extravagant lifestyle in Philadelphia, living well beyond their means, which may have contributed to Benedict's wandering eye in terms of his Patriotic allegiances.

Despite his initial zeal for taking up arms against the tyranny of King George, Arnold had long been losing faith in the Americans' chances at success, and the company he was keeping in Philadelphia did little to change his mind. Now it seemed he had his chance to throw in his lot with both sides and (if he played it right) emerge from the war a victor, no matter which army prevailed. In May 1779,

Arnold made overtures to General Clinton in New York, by way of a Loyalist merchant in Philadelphia, as to whether he could be of service. The British did not immediately jump at his offer; after all, how often does a high-ranking enemy officer voluntarily offer to spy? Suspicions were rampant, but the proposal seemed legitimate and, if Arnold could prove himself trustworthy to the king, his intelligence would be an invaluable source of information about American strategies, plans, and plots. To test Arnold's proposal by degrees, Major John André, the newly appointed chief of intelligence for the British army, contacted Arnold—a connection aided, no doubt, by André's previous acquaintance with Arnold's new wife.

The correspondence between the two men often involved Peggy. Even as she acted as a messenger between Philadelphia girls and their British lovers who were now stationed in New York, secretly carrying letters and parcels back and forth, she would now also act as a courier between André's agent and her own husband. Her conduct on the first count was an open secret, which provided an excellent cover for her more nefarious role.

Arnold used a method similar to that of the Culpers when communicating with André: invisible ink and a book-based code. He based his code on two books: William Blackstone's *Commentaries on the Laws of England* and Nathan Bailey's *An Universal Etymological English Dictionary*. Each word was denoted by three numbers separated by a period. The first was the page number, the second was the line, and the third was the position of the word, starting from the left margin, in that line. For example, 172.8.7s stood for "troops": page 172, line 8, seventh word in. The *s* at the end simply made it plural. Like the communications of the Culpers and other spies of the era, the letters of Arnold and André were often disguised as ordinary notes about family matters or inconsequential gossip addressed to or written by Peggy. In between the lines, written in some form of invisible ink, were the real messages.

Despite the similarities in technique between the two spy rings, the Culpers were operating with several advantages. First, they had an added layer of security: Not every member or satellite was aware of the identities of the others in the ring. Arnold and André and their various go-betweens knew the names of everyone with whom they were dealing, which meant a higher risk of detection should someone be caught. Second, Arnold and André could communicate only with each other, but the Culpers had developed a more complex network that allowed Woodhull, Brewster, or Roe to add intelligence en route to General Washington, confirming or correcting the initial reports, and making the information more detailed when it finally reached its intended destination.

Third, the Culpers were able to operate in a wider social circle because the members were citizens from all walks of life. Townsend gathered information from soldiers around the city and sailors at the dock; Agent 355 charmed strategic details out of high-ranking officers at soirees; Rivington repeated gossip and plans overheard in his shop; Woodhull enhanced these reports with his own observations of troop activities on Long Island and recounted what shop owners were saying or if there was an uptick in lumber sales and ship repairs; Roe learned whatever news was shared when tongues loosened in his tavern; and from the water Brewster spied on British naval movements. The Arnolds and André were limited to the upper tier of Loyalist social circles for their intelligence.

EVERY MAN HAS HIS PRICE

Arnold's double-dealings had to be sidelined in the autumn of 1779 when suspicions fell on a number of Loyalists still residing and working in Philadelphia. Because Arnold had married into one of the most prominent Tory families, he, too, found himself forced to prove his allegiance to the Continental Army and the American cause.

Further complicating matters and frustrating Arnold was the fact that he faced a court-martial for some of his business dealings in the city. Never mind that the trial had initially been his idea when the concerns were first raised; he had hoped that just such an event would be an excellent opportunity to publicly shame his critics and exonerate himself. Now, it just seemed to add to his stress by bringing his actions under close scrutiny—an uncomfortable prospect for anyone leading a double life.

The hearing went forward, however, and Arnold conducted himself brilliantly. On January 26, 1780, he was found guilty of two minor charges; the rest were dropped. It was a tremendous moral victory for Arnold, and he wasted no time or expense in spreading the word that he had prevailed over his detractors. To make his happiness complete, six weeks later Peggy gave birth to their first child, a boy named Edward Shippen Arnold, after the baby's maternal grandfather.

The celebration was soon dampened, however, when the Continental Congress conducted a kind of self-audit and ruled in April that Arnold owed the government more than one thousand pounds for undocumented expenses from the unsuccessful invasion of Quebec he helped to lead in 1775. The records showed a substantial sum tied to Arnold for which there was no accounting or receipts; according to practice, the amount due was his own responsibility.

The investigation humiliated Arnold—and also put him in a financial bind. Shortly after the audit, he struck up a correspondence once again with the British. General Clinton was especially interested in expanding his grasp on New York beyond the boundaries of Long Island and Manhattan, and was eyeing the Hudson Valley as a means of controlling the land north of the Hudson River as well as the harbor. He would handsomely reward Arnold for his assistance, but Arnold and Peggy were still locked in Patriot Philadelphia, which wasn't nearly so rich a grounds for the intelligence Clinton and André desired. Despite his willingness to sell what he knew, the damage that Arnold was able to inflict upon the American cause was somewhat limited by his current capacity and location. Clinton wanted to see his spy situated somewhere much more significant for the Crown's goals of reestablishing authority over as much land, population, and key transportation and resource channels as possible, and he urged Arnold to seek new opportunities and a new command.

For the past year, Arnold had found life in Philadelphia quite to his liking, but now he was fed up. The bill from Congress for the invasion of Quebec was as humiliating as it was beyond his ability to pay. He had heard that the command at Fort West Point was available, and it seemed the perfect solution to his various woes. While he may not have relished the thought of moving to a remote outpost, the thought of being in absolute authority in his own fort away from Philadelphia must have appealed to his pride. He could quit the city, assume control of the strategic fort, and at precisely the right time turn it over to the British. He would then collect his reward and enjoy a life of leisure as the man who had made the king's victory over the rebellion possible. Away in New York, General Clinton, too, recognized the potential of West Point; it was situated fifty-five miles north of Manhattan, on a sharp turn of the Hudson River. From there, it was possible to control the access of ships to the rest of the river, thereby limiting or opening the movement of troops, supplies, and goods for trade. It was, in many ways, the key to the rest of the state. Through Major André, he urged Arnold to press his case for the command of the fort.

Washington resisted the petition at first. Arnold had resigned his position in Philadelphia after the Quebec payment insult, and despite his acquittal on all but two minor charges resulting from the court-martial, his conduct in those matters had still been disappointing. Washington had personally written a strongly worded letter to Arnold chastising him for such behavior not long after the verdict was handed down, despite which Arnold had commenced with his very public celebrations of the outcome. Still, West Point needed an experienced man at its helm, and much of Arnold's combat and strategy experience had been in upstate New York. Washington mulled over the matter even as Arnold and several of his allies lobbied heavily for the appointment.

With a permanent departure from Philadelphia on his mind, Arnold set off for New Haven in order to settle his affairs in that city, as well as to begin quietly transferring his cash assets to London banks. He deliberately routed his travels so that he could stop and inspect West Point on the way under the guise of wanting to get a sense of the state of the fort to better prepare for taking command. He secretly sent off whatever information he was able to gather to André with the implied promise that much more would follow should their plan succeed and he be given control in the coming months. Initially, the price he named for his treachery was ten thousand pounds, in addition to his out-of-pocket costs and losses (which makes Woodhull's occasional requests to General Washington for fifty pounds to reimburse members of the Culper Ring seem humble, paltry, even laughable). But Arnold knew the British had the money and he was certain they would pay as much for the information as for the sheer satisfaction of humiliating the Americans.

Just a few weeks later, however, whether from discovering that his debts in Connecticut were far worse than he had anticipated, from finding Peggy's influence greatly diminished with his geographical separation from her, or simply from losing heart, Arnold suddenly grew panicked, even paranoid. In a letter to André dated July 11, 1780, he complained that he was not being trusted and hinted that he would put a stop to the whole deal unless things changed to his satisfaction. The next day, he wrote again, this time doubling his price to twenty thousand pounds, overtly offering to surrender the fort, and insisting that a portion of the reward be tendered as a down payment for his services.

In all fairness, Arnold's anxiety was not unfounded. He was, in fact, being spied upon by order of General Clinton because the British did not consider him altogether trustworthy; after all, if he changed his loyalties once, what was to stop him from playing the turncoat again? But his course was set and he was determined to carry it out, certain that he would emerge as victor in the end.

CHAPTER 12

Negotiations and Treachery

Benedict Arnold's treason was well under way when the French fleet arrived in Newport during the summer of 1780. Observing that Washington was actively working on several covert plans to outmaneuver the British, Arnold tried just as actively to undo them in secret. Fortunately for Washington, the deep secrecy surrounding the Culpers kept the ring out of Arnold's reach, but the success of the spies' tip and Washington's ruse had alerted Benedict Arnold. He knew he would need to infiltrate or stop the ring were his betrayal to be successful. Little did he know that members of the very ring he was attempting to ensnare were removed from him by just a few degrees of separation.

At the end of July, with the French troops safely disembarked in Rhode Island, Washington prepared to ride out to meet them and proposed that Arnold lead a raid against some of Clinton's troops stationed around New York at the same time. Arnold pleaded to be excused from such exertion, using the same reasoning he had back in March to remove himself from other action: An injury had left him with a stiff ankle, and his doctors had recommended that he not take command of an army until it healed. Conceding to Arnold's requests and complaints, Washington kept him off the battlefield and diverted him instead to the less physically demanding post as commander of West Point, exactly as Arnold had hoped. On August 3, 1780, Benedict Arnold found himself the most powerful man on the Hudson.

He wasted no time in capitalizing on his new position. Almost immediately he began repairing the fort and stocking it with as many provisions as possible. If he was going to turn West Point over to the British, he might as well win points with his new commanders by outfitting it on the American dime first; he even consulted a French engineer fighting alongside the Americans, Major Chevalier de Villefranche. "Major Villefranche has surveyed the works at West Point, and informs me that there is a vast deal to do to complete them," Arnold wrote Washington on August 8. "That large quantities of materials, such as timber, plank, boards, stone, &c., will be wanted. Part of the materials are at different places near this post; but I do not find that there are any teams or forage in the department, and, at present there is no prospect of any being furnished."

Even more urgently, Arnold began to inquire about the names and addresses of Patriot spies he claimed might be of importance to him in defending the fort against any planned attacks by the British. Of particular interest to Arnold was the ring operating in New York, upon whom Washington had relied so heavily in the recent incident with the French fleet as well as in previous matters of significant intelligence, such as troop movements on Long Island and the foiled counterfeiting plan. The commander in chief declined the request out of both honor and necessity; he did not know the identity of most of his spies by design and he had sworn to uphold the secrecy of those he did know. Lafayette responded to Arnold's request in a similar manner.

Disappointed that he was not able to ensnare the Culpers, which would have delighted General Clinton no end, Arnold nevertheless pursued whatever prey he could. On August 5, Arnold wrote a letter to Major General Robert Howe of the Continental Army, begging for this same information about a few operatives in Howe's employ in such an eloquent and reasonable manner that his motives seemed quite aboveboard. "As the safety of this Post and garrison in a great measure depends on having good intelligence of the movements and designs of the enemy," he penned, "and as you have been fortunate in the agents you have employed for that purpose, I must request, with their permission, to be informed who they are, as I wish to employ them, for the same purpose. I will engage upon them to make no discovery of them to any person breathing."

Howe replied nine days later in a manner that shows he was clearly distressed by his spies' response at the time, though it must have seemed a tremendous blessing only a few weeks later when Arnold's true nature was revealed:

> *The two most intelligent and confidential I got to undertake with difficulty, and they did it with the greatest reluctance and not without my pledging in the most solemn manner my honor not to inform any person upon earth of their names, or of their acting in the capacity of emisarys, they are persons of character and property, who cannot without utter ruin get out of the enemy's power, and yet devoted to America, have agreed to serve in a way they do not like, but which is the only way they can at present serve her in. I have written to them and urged them to let me give their address to you, but . . . they in the most positive terms refused; and it is not without great persuasion and difficulty that they are prevailed*

> *upon to continue their acting even for me; this makes me fear they will not consent to it tho I sincerely wish they may. I cannot indeed blame this caution, as their life and the ruin of their families must be the certain consequence should any accident happen to them.*

Howe did manage to persuade one operative in his employ to correspond with Arnold, though this was under an assumed name. "He will mark the letters Private, and you must injoin your family not to open any letters so marked," Howe warned in the closing of his message.

Arnold's response was gracious, if disappointed. He had clearly anticipated obtaining specific details about the various covert operatives at work in and around New York that he could pass on to André via Peggy, but had learned almost nothing. He pledged his honor to Howe that he would not expose the one man who had agreed to send information to Arnold, nor reveal his name should he accidentally discover it. In a culture where a man's honor was considered quite sacred, these sentiments seem especially crass given Arnold's intention, but, to his credit, he was not entirely disingenuous. "I will take proper precautions that no gentlemen of my family open any letters addressed to me as Private," he added. Peggy, after all, was not a gentleman.

A WOLF IN SILK AND LACE

Peggy Arnold was not the only woman with a secret connected to Benedict Arnold. The whirl of celebration that had died down with the absence of the British top brass from New York now began anew, and Agent 355 found herself once again in the company of New York's wealthiest Loyalists and most powerful British officers. The gossip was generally unchanged. Many of the well-to-do families of the

Northeast were casually connected through intermarriage or business associations of one kind or another. More than one family loyal to King George had a cousin or two serving under General George Washington, nor was it unheard of that a family with one political allegiance should suddenly find itself related to one of the opposite persuasion when members from each decided to wed.

Therefore, it didn't seem unusual at all that the Arnolds' names should come up in conversation that summer. Benedict's family was established just across the border in Connecticut, and the former Miss Shippen—whose own family was extremely well connected—had been acquainted with many of the officers now in New York. Benedict Arnold's name might have even been something of a joke, at first, among the British. Here was an overly eager merchant-turned-major general who seemed desperate for praise and for cash—and was willing to go to great lengths for either one. His price changed even as his emotional investment did, and his letters were at once full of self-importance and a kind of panicked need for validation. The officers who despised him may have ridiculed him over their drinks within 355's hearing.

By September, however, the snickering would have ceased. Arnold had assumed the command he and General Clinton had both so desperately wanted for him, and no time had been wasted in accepting his terms of surrender. Only a few things were needed now to bring the whole plan to fruition. First, an opportunity to familiarize the British with the plans of the fort so that they could exploit its vulnerabilities and storm it as swiftly as possible and, second, time to get the necessary men and weapons in place to ensure that any resistance the Patriots offered was futile.

No plans of such a sensitive nature were explicitly discussed in social settings like dinner parties, but certain phrases, pointed glances, and delicious insinuations that something was coming would have abounded among the most senior officers. Red-faced brass chortled, slapping each other on the back and toasting their port glasses to the

Hudson River or to West Point itself. When Major André let drop in conversation that he was going north for a few days, anyone who was simply mingling for company, conversation, and culinary delights would have assumed he was attending to routine business. To someone with a more serious mission than simply seeing and being seen, however, something seemed amiss in these veiled hints. What exactly was afoot was unclear, but the lady whose job it was to "out wit them all" would have reported what she had observed.

TWO WOLVES IN MERCHANTS' SHIRTSLEEVES

While his name was being bandied around New York's most exclusive circles during his first weeks of command, Arnold was quite busy sending letters. Besides writing to Washington about his desire to increase the provisions and make improvements at the fort and composing letters about his need to learn the identity of spies, Arnold also found the time to send a letter to an American outpost, informing its members that a certain merchant from the city by the name of John Anderson might be passing their way and begging their assistance in helping him to secure safe passage to West Point. Additionally, Arnold was also carrying on his correspondence with André so as to arrange the meeting outside the city that would finalize their negotiations and plans for the handing over of the fort.

When the long-anticipated meeting finally took place, André was to pose as a prosperous businessman, Arnold as his patron. In keeping with their cover, the men wrote their letters not in the numbered code or invisible ink of their previous exchanges, but very much in the role of a client and a vendor making plans to carry out a large transaction—which, in many ways, they were, though the roles were reversed.

Townsend, meanwhile, found that when he left his shop to observe the goings-on around Manhattan that September he could not help but notice the uptick in preparations along the docks. The British were clearly fitting ships for some kind of engagement, though Townsend could not be sure if this was merely a response to the arrival of the French fleet and the fear that a naval battle might be brewing, or if it was with some other specific aim. Even the soldiers and sailors with whom he conversed seemed uncertain as to their orders. It seemed unlikely that significant troop movements would be following so closely on the heels of the intentional misinformation regarding Washington's supposed plans to attack the city and the unanticipated recall of troops. Then again, the blow to Clinton's pride that incident had delivered may have prompted him to plan an aggressive response simply to prove he would not be made the fool.

The increase of activity in mid-September was definitely new, though, after a relatively quiet August. Woodhull had written to Tallmadge on September 1: "In regard of the state of affairs in general he [Culper Junior] assured the express they remained as heretofore or as when wrote you last, nothing new, everything appeared to be at a stand, and the enemy much embarissed expecting an attack." Despite the calm in the city in August, troops had continued to shift around Long Island, and Woodhull had even mentioned that a British spy had crossed the Sound to Connecticut—a man who was "positively an agent for the enemy. He hath been a long time serviceable in that way, and this is his second embassy. I know it to be true and have lately had a perfect knowledge of his conduct for this three years past, and have been solicited by his friend as an assistant."

It was worth noting, but hardly earthshaking news. Spies were everywhere, and both sides knew it. That this operative tried to convert Woodhull to his side while clearly unaware as to Woodhull's true loyalties is both comical and a testimony to the convincing role Woodhull was playing as a man of profound apathy. His secret letters, however, reveal just how deep his passions truly ran. Four days later, Woodhull wrote again to Tallmadge to inform him of a movement of troops away from Setauket, which left the town much more vulnerable to an American invasion to reclaim it: "For God's sake attack them, you'll certainly be successful, if you are secret about it. . . . Setauket is exceedingly distressed. Pray offer some relief."

No prospect could have delighted Tallmadge more than the possibility of liberating his hometown, and he wrote to Washington to propose just such a raid: "The enclosed Dispatches from Culper have this moment come to hand. . . . C. writes with great sollicitude for troops to be sent from this side to attack those lying at Setauket. I need not repeat to your Excellency how exceedingly happy I should be to assist in such an Expedition, should it be thot. advisable." To Tallmadge's disappointment, Washington did not approve the plan, and he would have to wait several more months before he could wage battle on Long Island.

As the warm weather faded, Townsend continued to submit reports written in invisible ink, which now fell almost exclusively on Tallmadge to reveal and decipher. The job had previously belonged to Washington's aide-de-camp Alexander Hamilton, while Tallmadge was in charge of making sense of the general intelligence and summary reports Woodhull, Roe, and Brewster compiled. But recently Tallmadge had been tasked with the white-ink letters—perhaps after Washington recognized the urgency of the information conveyed about the French troops—and Tallmadge found himself even more impressed now with the quality and accuracy of Townsend's reports than he had been before.

None of them knew, however, just quite what they were in the midst of in September 1780. The reports from the city, the strange behaviors, the activity with the ships—Tallmadge couldn't put his finger on it, but his instincts told him something was not right. He felt as if he had nearly all the elements in front of him, almost all the clues gathered, but he was not sure what he was looking at or what the picture was that he needed to assemble. That he had letters on his desk from his merchant-spy in New York regarding an officer from New York venturing toward West Point seemed wholly unconnected. Despite all the hints he received from 355, Woodhull, and Townsend, Tallmadge didn't connect the dots until it was almost too late.

CHAPTER 13

The Deal Is Done

On the afternoon of Sunday, September 10, 1780, Benedict Arnold stepped onto a barge under the auspices of meeting with his long-awaited merchant friend from New York, John Anderson. If the general seemed nervous or anxious, the bargemen took no notice. They, too, were probably on alert for British gunboats patrolling the waters of the lower Hudson River and were not especially delighted with the thought of traveling southward toward enemy territory. They followed the river several miles, then let Arnold off on the shore to stay the night at the home of a friend who lived near the river. The next morning, the crew sailed the approximately twenty miles remaining, to Dobbs Ferry, where the meeting was to take place.

As the barge approached, a barrage of British gunfire opened up on the little vessel, which quickly retreated upriver a safe distance. Arnold, who had not anticipated this attack, ordered the crew to land the barge on the west bank of the river, where he could safely await Anderson's arrival at a small outpost of American troops. The merchant never appeared, and Arnold, forced to declare the meeting a failure, returned to West Point. André, it turns out, had been in the vicinity, but the vigilant gunboats had made crossing the river quite perilous in risking both his life and recognition by some of his own soldiers. He returned to New York to arrange a second attempt at meeting with his coconspirator.

Colonel Simcoe, the cold-blooded leader of the Queen's Rangers who had occupied the Townsend Homestead in Oyster Bay, had some time past been ransomed from his prison in New Jersey and was once again commanding his men on raids. André had promised him the privilege of being present for the surrender of the fort, but Simcoe now received word that the rangers were being ordered to ride south toward Chesapeake Bay and wrote to André greatly worried that this sudden change would cause him to miss out on the fun. "Rely upon it your alarms are vain," André wrote the day after his missed rendezvous with Arnold. He added, tantalizingly, "I should have been happy to have seen you and have hinted that apparent arrangements are not always real ones, but I beg you to seek no explanation."

On September 15, Arnold penned a letter to "John Anderson" recounting the failed meeting and attempting to set up another opportunity "on Wednesday the 20th instant" at the same location. ("Instant" was a form of eighteenth-century shorthand meaning "of the current month.") He may have regarded their missing each other as a bad omen, and was certainly feeling agitated and exposed. "The foregoing letter was written to caution you not to mention your business to Colonel Sheldon, or any other person," he warned, clearly concerned that André might play his part as a Patriot merchant too convincingly by chatting with the leader of the Light Dragoons as he passed through their patrol area. "I have no confidant. I have made one too many already." The letter, which he signed "Gustavus" as he had several of this series of messages, was directed toward New York, and Arnold returned his attention to making his preparations.

He had been quite eager to learn the itinerary of General

Washington, a fact that Alexander Hamilton later noted may have been an attempt to secure the commander in chief's capture along with the fort. In fact, Arnold's letters indicate that he was anticipating Washington's arrival at West Point in a matter of days with the intent of the general's staying Saturday night at the fort. The main focus of the plan, however, was to secure the handover; Arnold, after all, was acting more from a sense of monetary gain than from any deep-seated political zeal regarding who would ultimately win the conflict.

JOHN ANDERSON SETS FORTH

The evening of Monday, September 18, witnessed an elaborate dinner party at the home of a well-to-do New York Loyalist. Though it was hosted in honor of General Clinton and his closest officers, special attention was paid to Major André, and it seems to actually have been something of an unofficial send-off for the young man, as he was about to embark upon a mission that, they hoped, would result in one of the greatest victories for the British since the war began.

The next day André set out northward with the goal of reaching HMS *Vulture,* a fourteen-gun sloop docked near Teller's Point, by evening. Because it was a British ship, he arrived not as "John Anderson, Patriot merchant" but as himself, bearing letters from General Clinton that needed to be hand-delivered farther up-country. The crew was ignorant as to the true nature of André's visit, likely because of their proximity to West Point. Should any sailor let a casual word slip while onshore, the whole deal would be ruined. André boarded the *Vulture* for the night and awaited a message from Arnold for their meeting the next day. None came.

On Thursday, September 21, Arnold received a letter complaining that boats from West Point had fired upon a small vessel traveling to shore under the flag of truce, which was a violation of the terms of war. "Fortunately none of my people were hurt, but the treacherous intentions of those who fired are not vindicated from that circumstance," Captain Sutherland had written. The note was signed by both the captain and a certain "John Anderson." André's likely explanation to Sutherland for the pseudonym was that they could expect an attack should the Americans know that André himself was currently on board; the real reason, of course, was to alert Arnold to his presence on the ship.

André also wrote a letter back to his command, stating:

> *As the tide was favorable on my arrival at the sloop yesterday, I determined to be myself the bearer of your Excellency's letters as far as the Vulture. I have suffered for it, having caught a very bad cold, and had so violent a return of a disorder in my stomach which had attacked me a few days ago, that Captain Sutherland and Colonel Robinson [Beverly Robinson, at whose home Arnold was staying] insist on my remaining on board till I am better. I hope tomorrow to get down again.*

He also included a private message intended just for General Clinton's eyes: "Nobody has appeared. This is the second expedition I have made without an ostensible reason, and Col. Robinson both times of the party. A third would infallibly fire suspicions. I have therefore thought it best to remain here on plea of sickness, as my enclosed letter will feign, and try further expedients."

That same night, Arnold ordered some boatmen to row to the *Vulture* under a flag of truce, and to bring back with them a certain gentleman on board. Arnold could not approach the *Vulture* himself without arousing suspicion, given his rank and current assignment. In his stead, he sent Joshua Hett Smith, a local resident whom he charged with managing the retrieval. One of the rowers, a seasoned old hand, complained when ordered to muffle the oars to disguise their sound, lest a patrol boat find them. "If the business is of a fair and upright nature, as you assure us it is, I see no necessity for any disguise or to seize the veil of night to execute what might be as well transacted in broad daylight," he grumbled to the general.

Arnold responded by ordering the crew to carry out their plans as he had charged them, coolly reminding them, "I have the command of the militia of the county for sixty miles around West Point by the order of Congress."

The party set out with no further objections and approached the *Vulture* with the truce flag hoisted. Smith climbed aboard and, after explaining his task and showing his passes to the officers in charge, Anderson was introduced and agreed to accompany Smith back to shore for the meeting. "Very little conversation passed between Mr. Anderson and myself," Smith later recalled, "excepting trivial remarks about the tide, the weather, and matters of no concern. Mr. Anderson, from his youthful appearance and the softness of his manners, did not seem to me to be qualified for a business of such moment." But Smith conveyed him back to shore anyway, trusting that General Arnold knew best.

After introducing the two men—both of whom were dressed in blue coats—Smith was ordered to return to the boat to wait with the crew. This annoyed him somewhat, as he felt he had earned the right to be present for the discussion, given his efforts in bringing the meeting about, but he did as he was told. Some time later, Arnold and his friend returned and the order was given to bring Anderson back to the *Vulture,* but Smith objected. The men were tired and could not possibly make the trip back to the ship and to shore once again before sunrise, when they were sure to be spotted. He proposed that if the cover of darkness was, indeed, so very important to Arnold that they had best wait until the following evening to venture out again. Arnold conceded the point and Smith opened his home to them for the remainder of the night.

By morning, it was clear that the rowboat would have had an

even more strenuous voyage than previously anticipated. The *Vulture* was sailing southward, having been fired upon by American guns. André was very anxious about the situation because the longer he remained off the ship and in American territory, the greater his risk of capture. Arnold persuaded him to take advantage of the day, however, and the two rode out, presumably to inspect some of the routes to West Point and plan for the best possible approach by foot soldiers supplementing the attack from the river.

But as evening drew near, it was evident that André would have no hope of sailing back to New York on the damaged *Vulture* and would need to return to the city by land instead. "I wish I was on board," he said with a heavy sigh, looking in the direction of the ship, but he set out toward White Plains on horseback with Smith and a servant accompanying him for the first part of the journey to help him navigate the unfamiliar territory. Smith stopped at several waypoints to converse with the Patriot soldiers stationed along the route, but André kept to himself so that witnesses later recalled little other than that a man with a round, floppy hat and cape fastened tightly around his neck was a member of the riding party. Smith was well known to many of the American militiamen in the area and respected among them because, as one man later noted, "I had heard it frequently mentioned that [American] General [Robert] Howe used to employ Mr. Smith in getting intelligence." Other American officers held Smith in contempt; at least one suspected him of being a double agent and a few weeks prior had challenged Arnold on his association with the man.

Whatever the nature of Smith's character and his later claimed ignorance, he guided André easily through the American territory. Some of the men advised Smith against riding any farther that night, given the patrols in the area. Even if friendly, they might give him some trouble before checking for his pass signed by Arnold granting him safe passage; however, the militiamen were most concerned about the Cow Boys, a group of British marauders who made criminal mischief for residents in the area, stealing food supplies or robbing travelers. André would have been quite safe in their company, had they known his true identity—but he could not reveal himself as a British officer without tipping off Smith to the whole business. Reluctantly, André agreed that they should find shelter and resume their travels by daylight. Securing lodging at a nearby house, the men retired to rest, but, as Smith noted, "I was often disturbed with the restless motions, and uneasiness of mind exhibited by my bed-fellow, who on observing the first approach of day, summoned my servant to prepare the horses for our departure."

As the three men neared the bridge over the Croton River, which feeds into the Hudson River and provided the swiftest means through the remainder of the American territory back into the British-held districts approaching New York City, a profound change came over André. Shedding his anxiety and gloom, he began to be much more like the charming, cheerful wit so beloved by his comrades. "He appeared in the morning as if he had not slept an hour during the night; he at first was much dejected, but a pleasing change took place in his countenance when summoned to mount his horse," Smith remembered.

> *I observed that the nearer we approached the bridge, the more his countenance brightened into a cheerful serenity, and he became very affable; in short, I now found him highly entertaining. . . . He descanted on the richness of the scenery around us, and particularly admired, from every eminence, the grandeur of the Highland mountains, bathing their summits in the clouds from their seeming watery base at the north extremity of Haverstraw Bay. The pleasantry of converse, and mildness of the weather, so insensibly beguiled the time that we at length found ourselves at the bridge before I thought we had got half*

> *way; and I now had reason to think my fellow-traveller a very different person from the character I had at first formed of him.*

André seemed quite touched by the well-intentioned company of Smith and his servant, and as he prepared to cross over the river and leave his new friends to head home, he promised to return the saddle and bridle that he had borrowed from Smith or send payment for them, and he made an offer of "a valuable gold watch in remembrance of him, as a keep sake, which I refused." And with that final gesture of generosity and amiability, André directed his horse over the bridge in the direction of what he hoped would be a safe passage back to the city.

BETRAYAL IN BOOTS

On that same morning of September 23, three American militiamen, John Paulding, Isaac Van Wart, and David Williams, were guarding the road in a kind of no-man's-land en route to the city. So far, the watch had been dull, with only familiar local faces passing by. But when they spotted a stranger making his way down the road, one of the members of the party whispered, "There comes a gentleman-like looking man, who appears to be well dressed, and has boots on, who you had better step out and stop if you don't know him."

Paulding stepped forward and raised his firelock at the stranger. "Stand!" he demanded. "Where are you going?"

"I am a British officer out of the country, on particular business, and I hope you won't detain me a minute!" André said, flashing the gold watch he had previously offered to Smith either to make a play on words or else to prove his claim, as only a high-ranking gentleman could afford such a timepiece.

"Dismount," Paulding ordered, not amused.

"My God, I must do anything to get 'along,'" he said, laughing and pulling out the pass from General Benedict Arnold that granted him safe passage. Then, climbing down from the horse, he replied more seriously, "Gentlemen you had best let me go, or you will bring yourselves in trouble, for, by your stopping of me you will detain the General's business. I'm to go to Dobb's Ferry to meet a person there."

It was a difficult situation for the three men. Did they dare hold up a man with a pass from a general in order to search him? Did they dare not to?

Finally, Paulding spoke again. "I hope you will not be offended. There are many bad people going along the road, and I do not know but perhaps you might be one. Have you any letters about you?"

André replied coolly, "No."

Sensing something was amiss, the men searched his clothes but found nothing hidden. Then Paulding ordered André to remove his boots. He removed one rather reluctantly and in a slightly awkward manner. Rather than feel around in the boot itself, Paulding reached out and grasped André's foot, where he felt paper in his stocking. "Pull off the other boot," Paulding ordered. With three firearms pointed at his head, André had no choice but to comply. Paulding regarded the papers briefly, then announced to Van Wart and Williams, "This is a spy."

Williams winked at his friends. "What would you give us to let you go?"

"Any sum of money."

"Would you give us your horse, saddle, bridle, watch—and a hundred guineas?"

"Yes," André responded. "I will direct it to any place even if it is to this very spot, so that you can get it."

"Would you give us more?" Williams goaded, clearly enjoying the gentleman's distress.

"I'll give you any quantity of dry goods or any sum of money, and bring it to any place you might pitch upon so that you might get it."

"No, by God!" Paulding roared. "If you would give us ten thousand guineas, you should not stir a step."

The three militiamen marched their prisoner to a nearby American camp at North Castle to turn him over to Lieutenant Colonel John Jameson. Along the way, the younger two men questioned him, still not clear as to his identity but hoping to have a little fun at his expense. André's sophisticated sensibilities finally had enough of the backwoods banter. "I beg you would ask me none till we come to some officers and then I will reveal the whole," he pleaded. He was turned over to Jameson's custody, and the three militiamen went on their way to resume guarding the road.

JAMESON'S MISTAKE

Colonel Jameson was mortified by the situation in which he now found himself. Three overeager men had just delivered to his camp a man bearing a pass from General Arnold; perhaps they were so excited at the prospect of having captured a British officer that they were blind to the fact that the pass should have automatically granted him safe passage, no questions asked—certainly arrest or detention was not necessary.

The commandeered papers had been forwarded on for Washington's inspection—rushed on Jameson's special orders—but now Jameson was faced with the matter of what to do with the man currently in his custody. He certainly spoke like a rational, genteel man, not a panicked spy caught in a snare, and his simple request was to be escorted back to West Point, where General Arnold would explain everything and set the matter straight. It seemed logical to Jameson, so he hurried to make the arrangements to carry it out, lest he find himself on the receiving end of one of Arnold's infamous angry outbursts.

Benjamin Tallmadge, meanwhile, had just returned to North Castle that evening from a daylong scouting mission. He heard talk of the newly apprehended prisoner named John Anderson brought in that morning; something seemed strange about the story but so much had of late that it was hard to pinpoint what was so unsettling. As Tallmadge sat reviewing the letters that had accumulated in his absence, as well as those he had put aside before he left, he happened to spot a note from General Arnold sent some days previous, informing him of a certain man named John Anderson who might pass Tallmadge's way: "I have to request that you will give him an escort of two Horse to bring him on this way to this place, and send an express to me that I may meet him." Suddenly, it all made sense—the prisoner, the strange reports he was receiving from the Culpers in New York, and Arnold's odd behavior.

Tallmadge rushed to Jameson and demanded to see the prisoner, but the colonel informed him it was impossible: John Anderson was gone from North Castle on Jameson's orders, escorted by a lieutenant with a letter explaining the situation, through the open country back to General Arnold at West Point.

CHAPTER 14

Another Spy at the Gallows

Major Benjamin Tallmadge respected the chain of command and he respected his senior officers, but in this instance he knew that his commanding officer had made a perilous mistake. Colonel Jameson had sensed that something was amiss, because he had rushed the papers found on the prisoner to Washington for examination, but fear of displeasing Arnold had clouded his better judgment, prompting him to return the prisoner to Arnold as he requested. Chagrined, Jameson was willing to listen to his subordinate's suggestions.

Tallmadge was a spymaster and much more savvy about the backhanded operations of intelligence gathering than Jameson. Hearing a full account of the story, he recognized the seemingly disparate pieces and concluded that a major betrayal was at hand. His first thought was to suggest a daring mission designed to entrap all the involved parties. He proposed the scheme to Jameson, who found the plan much too bold. Tallmadge later wrote to a friend and historian: "[I] did not fail to state the glaring inconsistency of their conduct to Lt. Col. Jameson in a private and most friendly manner. He appeared greatly agitated, more especially when I suggested to him a plan which I wished to pursue, offering to take the entire responsibility on myself, and which, as he deemed it too perilous to permit, I will not further disclose."

With his first suggestion rejected, Tallmadge immediately pursued the next best way of intercepting the prisoner and returning him to their custody. Jameson remained hesitant, afraid of upsetting General Arnold, but Tallmadge finally managed to persuade him to rescind his order and bring André back to North Castle while they awaited word from Washington. Oddly enough, Jameson still insisted on informing Arnold of the turn of events. "Strange as it may seem," Tallmadge wrote, "Lt. Col. J. would persist in his purpose of sending his letter to Gen. Arnold—The letter did go on, and was the first information that Arch Traitor received that his plot was blown up. The Officer returned [to Jameson's camp] with his prisoner early the next morning."

Jameson's decision to alert Arnold to the matter, while shocking in retrospect, was quite understandable, given Arnold's reputation. For one thing, Arnold was widely trusted by many officers of the Continental Army; even those who held him in contempt would generally not have anticipated that his imprudence could go so far as to commit treason. Tallmadge noted later that Jameson, in writing to Arnold about the matter, "expressed great confidence in him as I believe was the case thro' the army. Until the papers were found on Anderson, I had no suspicion of his lack of patriotism or political integrity." For another, Arnold was widely feared, and Jameson was willing to take extreme steps to protect himself from the man's wrath for not following his directives. Had Tallmadge not been as acutely attuned to subtle clues and not been actively trying to piece together the Culper Ring's reports, he, too, might have fallen under Arnold's spell and failed to realize who John Anderson was.

Even now, Tallmadge kept the spies in mind and realized that more than just the fate of Fort West Point was at stake. The surrender of the fort had to be stopped at all costs, but in a somewhat delicate way. André would not have broadcast his travel plans beyond a select circle, and the collapse of his plan could endanger the spies who had helped unravel the plot. If word reached the British that there was a mole in André's inner circle, Agent 355 and any of her associates—like Townsend—could be quickly unmasked. The entire ring would collapse, and the gallows would become a little more crowded. Tallmadge would have to act swiftly but carefully.

THE PRIZE OF WEST POINT

General Washington was riding toward West Point on the evening of Sunday, September 24. He had been visiting Hartford, Connecticut, and his schedule had changed slightly from his original plan to arrive on Saturday. Still, he imagined Arnold would be happy to see him, just as he was eager to see what improvements Arnold had put into effect at the fort, now that he had been in command nearly two months.

Washington intended to arrive late that evening but found himself detained out of politeness with a friend, and decided to lodge at a nearby inn for the night and finish his journey in the morning. Very early the next day, Washington sent Alexander Hamilton ahead with the baggage for the last fifteen miles to announce their arrival to Arnold and suggest that Washington breakfast with him before touring the fort.

To Washington's surprise, when he arrived at West Point not long after Hamilton, Arnold was not waiting for him. Instead, as Washington would later recall:

> *Soon after he [Hamilton] arrived at Arnold's headquarters, a letter was delivered to Arnold which threw him into the greatest confusion. He told Colonel Hamilton that something required his immediate attendance at the garrison which was on*

> *the opposite side of the river to his quarters; and immediately ordered a horse, to take him to the river; and the barge which he kept to cross, to be ready; and desired Major Franks, his Aid, to inform me when I should arrive that he was gone over the river and would return immediately.*

It was a strange reception for his commander in chief, but Arnold was, admittedly, something of a strange man. Washington decided not to stand on ceremony, but simply went about his day as he would have had Arnold been present as planned. He had breakfast, then rode down to the river to view the fortifications of the garrison and anticipated, not unreasonably, that he would encounter Arnold in the process. When Arnold still failed to materialize, however, Washington began to ask the men standing guard where their commander was; none could tell him. Washington was puzzled. "The impropriety of his conduct when he knew I was to be there, struck me very forcibly, and my mind misgave me; but I had not the least idea of the real cause," he remembered.

After about two hours of inspecting the fort and inquiring after its officer in charge, Washington returned to Arnold's headquarters, where Hamilton was waiting with a parcel that had just arrived. The courier seemed in great concern that General Washington review the contents of the package immediately, as he had been traveling hard many hours to find him, under the strict orders that he should "ride night and day" until he reached the general. Having headed straight for Connecticut using the same route Washington had taken to get there, the unfortunate courier did not realize that Washington had taken a different road back. Thus, the rider had been frantically chasing the general from New York to Connecticut and back again in order to deliver the papers he carried, freshly plucked from the boot of a man going by the name of John Anderson.

Something was terribly, terribly wrong: First Arnold's absence and now this? Washington felt his concern grow as he reached for the packet, which explained the whole matter. Alarmed, Washington ordered Hamilton to mount his horse and gallop to a post on the river about eight miles below, hoping he could stop Arnold's barge. Hamilton pushed his horse to its limit, but he was too late. Benedict Arnold had escaped.

ARNOLD'S ESCAPE

When Alexander Hamilton had ridden up to the gates of West Point that morning, Arnold knew that General Washington would be following just an hour or two behind. He had been anticipating this visit for several days, though it is impossible to guess what Arnold's feelings might have been now that the commander in chief was about to enter through the very gates Arnold planned to swing open to the enemy upon their approach. For all he knew, André had made it safely back to New York and the British had a small fleet of ships sailing up the Hudson and several regiments of soldiers marching through the New York forests even now to storm the fort. If everything had gone according to plan—and Arnold had no reason to think it had not—the entire course of the war might be changed by the end of the day.

Arnold had little time to mull over his plan, because a lieutenant arrived very shortly after Hamilton, carrying a letter from Lieutenant Colonel Jameson explaining that a gentleman by the name of Anderson who was carrying passes issued by Arnold had been captured and had now been returned to confinement while some odd papers and plans found on him were sent to Washington via an express rider. It was all a wicked plan by the British, Jameson concluded, to besmirch Benedict Arnold's good name and to cause division in the ranks by undermining the Continental Army's confidence in him. He just felt Arnold should be made aware of the slanderous efforts being made against him by the enemy.

The jig was up. Arnold's worst fears had all been realized: The Americans were aware (or soon would be) of the depth of his treachery, but the British had yet to do anything to capture the fort and, without the plans, likely never would be able to do so. Thus, he was a traitor to one group, but hardly the hero he had anticipated becoming to the other. Now he would be nothing more than a failed turncoat—if he was even able to escape with his life, that is.

Making hasty apologies to Hamilton and to his own aide, who were both waiting for Washington's arrival and the tour to begin, Arnold dashed off toward the water full of empty promises to return promptly, just as soon as he sorted out some urgent matter across the river. He called for his bargemen to row him as swiftly as possible downstream toward where HMS *Vulture* had recently retreated, explaining to the confused men at the oars that they would receive two gallons of rum apiece if they did their job quickly, as he would need to turn around very shortly to meet General Washington for his much anticipated visit. They exerted themselves admirably. The barge reached the *Vulture* under a flag of truce, which kept them from being fired upon and allowed Arnold to board in safety. His loyal crew was also taken aboard, where Arnold promptly informed them that they were now prisoners of the British army.

Peggy and baby Edward, meanwhile, were left behind at West Point—entrusted to what Arnold knew would be the merciful and benevolent judgment of General Washington.

ANDRÉ'S FATE

After being intercepted on his way to West Point, John André (whose true identity was not yet known by his captors) was taken to Salem, Connecticut, where Colonel Elisha Sheldon, commanding officer of Tallmadge's own Second Light Dragoons, was headquartered. André seemed to have given Jameson little trouble, but upon being transferred to Sheldon's supervision at Salem on September 24,

Tallmadge noted that "it was manifest that his agitation and anxiety increased."

Later that afternoon, André made a simple request of his guards: "May I be furnished with pen, ink, and paper?"

The request was approved, and André seated himself at a table to compose an honest, forthright, and gentlemanly note to General Washington that confirmed Tallmadge's suspicions and greatest fears. "In this letter," Tallmadge recalled, "he disclosed his Character to be Major John André, Adjutant Genl. to the British Army. When I had perused the letter, which he handed to me to read, my agitation was extreme, and my emotions wholly indescribable."

Though he had no reason to imagine that Arnold would ever turn traitor, Tallmadge had never counted himself among his fans, either. "With Arnold's character I became acquainted while I was a member of Yale College and he residing in New Haven, and I well remember that I was impressed with the belief that he was not a man of integrity," he would later pen. "The revolutionary war was coming on soon after I left college, and Arnold engaged in it with so much zeal . . . we all seemed, as if by common consent, to forget his knavish tricks."

Arnold's backhanded, cowardly character contrasted sharply with that of his coconspirator, André, who comported himself with dignity by all accounts, and treated his captors with respect and even friendliness. Tallmadge could not have helped seeing something of himself reflected back in the person of André. They were both young men—twenty-six and thirty, respectively—entrusted with similar roles of secrecy and responsibility by their countries. Both men had risen to their ranks through hard work, keen intelligence, and personal affability rather than simply through purchasing a commission, as was often the case. They were popular, likable young officers with promising careers ahead of them, and both had gallant manners and a sense of honor that would otherwise seem incongruous with the low opinion of spies in their day.

But this was wartime, and there must be winners and losers. André had been caught and captured at the same game that Tallmadge was playing; they both knew the rules, the rewards, the risks—and they both knew the penalties.

On October 25, Washington wrote to Jameson regarding the treatment of the high-profile prisoner, noting, "I would not wish Mr. André to be treated with insult; but he . . . is to be most closely and narrowly watched." Then, following his sign-off, Washington added one line as if he were unsure that the seriousness of his message had truly been understood and he wished to underscore this imperative: "André must not escape." Two days later he wrote to Major General Nathanael Greene a similar caution, stating, "I would wish the room for Mr. André to be a decent one, and that he may be treated with civility; but that he may be so guarded as to preclude a possibility of his escaping, which he will certainly attempt to effect, if it shall seem practicable in the most distant degree."

In the tense days that followed, a prisoner exchange was proposed, as was often the case when high-ranking officers were captured. Washington was agreeable only if the prisoner surrendered was Arnold; Clinton would not agree to these terms, so Washington proceeded as he would with any common spy (though, admittedly, perhaps with a little more ceremony given the particular nature of this case). There is every indication that he regretted what came next, but he also knew that it was necessary to demonstrate to the British that his military was to be taken seriously and was operating within its rights as an independent entity not subject to the wishes of the king or his subordinates.

Washington granted André a trial, in which several of the top officers among the Continental Army and its allies were speedily assembled to hear arguments. André maintained that because he had been trapped behind enemy lines and was captured there, he was technically not a spy scouting the territory in the uniform of his service but was, instead, a prisoner of war. All such prisoners, he reasoned, can be expected to at least consider making an escape dressed in civilian clothes. The plea failed to persuade the tribunal, but no one (including André, presumably) had expected it would. He was sentenced to death by hanging on September 29.

That same day, André penned a letter to General Clinton, absolving his commander of any guilt he might feel for the mission on which he had sent André. The circumstances had simply been unfortunate and had not gone according to their carefully laid-out plan:

> *Under these Circumstances I have obtained General Washington's permission to send you this Letter, the object of which is to remove from your Breast any Suspicion that I could imagine that I was bound by your Excellencys Orders to expose myself to what has happened. The Events of coming within an Enemys posts and of Changing my dress which led me to my present Situation were contrary to my own Intentions as they were to your Orders; and the circuitous route which I took to return was imposed (perhaps unavoidably) without alternative upon me.*
>
> *I am perfectly and tranquil in mind and prepared for any Fate to which an honest Zeal for my Kings Service may have devoted me.*
>
> *In addressing myself to your Excellency on this Occasion, the force of all my Obligations to you and of the Attachment and Gratitude I bear you, recurrs to me. With all the Warmth of my heart I give you thanks for your Excellencys profuse kindness to me, and I send you the most earnest Wishes for your Welfare which a faithfull affectionate and respectfull Attendant can frame.*
>
> *I have a Mother and Three Sisters. . . . It is needless to be more explicit on this Subject; I am*

persuaded of your Excellencys Goodness. I receive the greatest Attention from his Excellency General Washington and from every person under whose charge I happened to be placed. I have the honor to be with the most respectfull Attachment,

Your Excellencys Most obedient
and most humble Servant,
John André Adj Gen

The sentence was to be carried out on October 2, just over a week after André's capture. By all accounts, he comported himself with dignity and propriety, stoically recognizing his sad fate as simply one of the unfortunate perils of war. On only one count did he offer up any resistance: manner of execution. André requested to die by firing squad, as the English considered this the proper form by which to carry out execution orders for a high-ranking officer. His request—perhaps in remembrance of Nathan Hale's own unceremonious death—was denied. André was hanged on the appointed day in Tappan, New York, and his body buried under the gallows, where it remained for more than forty years, until it was disinterred and returned to England to be buried with military honors at Westminster Abbey.

BACK IN MANHATTAN

News of Arnold's betrayal, as well as André's capture and execution, sent shock waves through all of the colonies, but nowhere was the impact more keenly felt than in New York City. Even Robert Townsend found himself deeply moved by the death of one of the very men on whom he had spied. "I never felt more sensibly for the death of a person whom I knew only by sight, and had heard converse, than I did for Major André," Townsend wrote to Tallmadge about two weeks after the event. "He was a most amiable character. General Clinton was inconsolable for some days; and the army in general and inhabitants were much exasperated, and think that George Washington must have been destitute of feeling, or he would have saved him. I believe General Washington felt sincerely for him, and would have saved him if it could have been done with propriety." Even Washington himself later reflected that André was "more unfortunate than criminal."

No one had any such praise for Arnold. In his same letter to Tallmadge, Townsend expressed his opinion of the turncoat, probably based on reports of the man's character provided by Agent 355: "I was not much surprised at his [Arnold's] conduct, for it was no more than I expected of him."

Now safely tucked away on a ship in New York, Benedict Arnold was enjoying the luxuries of high living, including the knowledge that his wife and infant son were safe from retribution. He had written to Washington asking if he would guarantee their secure passage to him, and Washington had agreed, not believing it proper to visit the sins of the father upon the head of the child. With Arnold's true loyalties now exposed and his body, mind, and energies openly aligned with the British, he could pose no further threat to American forts or forces under his command.

But Arnold was not finished sowing chaos for the Culper Ring. As Tallmadge had feared, his capture spelled danger for the secret six.

Route of George Washington's Culper Spy Ring

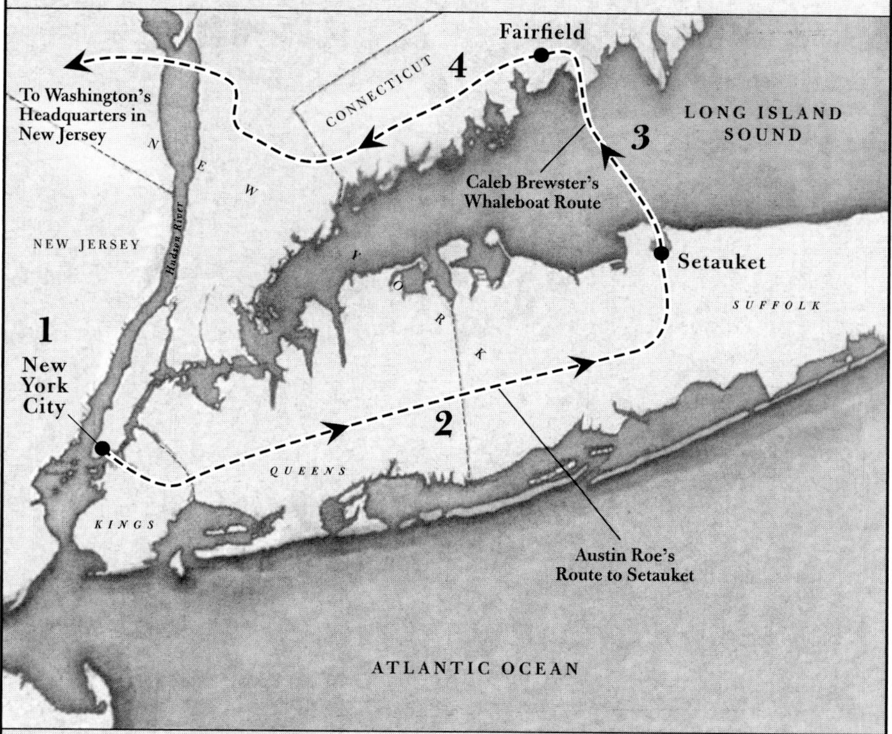

1. Robert Townsend and James Rivington gathered information in Manhattan.

2. Austin Roe and Abraham Woodhull received Townsend's intelligence in Manhattan and made the dangerous journey to Setauket, where they met Caleb Brewster in a cove off Long Island Sound.

3. Brewster and his men rowed across the sound between or around the British ships to Connecticut, where they handed off the letters to Benjamin Tallmadge.

4. Tallmadge then couriered the information to George Washington.

The secret six's intelligence route allowed them to transmit top-secret information from Manhattan through enemy territory to George Washington in about two weeks.

Benjamin Tallmadge, who fought side by side with George Washington, was tasked with forming the Culper Ring. His leadership and knowledge of Long Island made him indispensable.

Collection of the Litchfield Historical Society, Litchfield, Connecticut, a gratis copy of the work deposited in the society's library

Robert Townsend did not have the bravado of his older brother or his father, but his quieter heroic qualities made him the perfect spy leader—Culper Junior. True to his unassuming character, he seems never to have commissioned a painting of himself. This one rough sketch depicting him in his forties is known.

Courtesy of the Friends of Raynham Hall, Inc.

Collection of the New-York Historical Society

James Rivington was the respected publisher of the *Rivington Gazette*, a loyalist newspaper. What the British didn't know was that he was also a spy for George Washington. With the help of Robert Townsend, he interviewed British officers about their military exploits and took their inside intelligence directly to Washington. Rivington's biggest contribution was acquiring the redcoats' battle plan for Yorktown. The colonists would beat Lord Cornwallis in that battle and win the war in the process.

Courtesy Kurt Knapp Photography

Austin Roe's tavern still stands today, though it was moved from its original location. From here, Roe made the fifty-five-mile journey to Manhattan, passing through occupied Manhattan and Long Island to reach Robert Townsend.

Courtesy Kurt Knapp Photography

The first man to sign on to the spying mission was Abraham Woodhull, known as Culper Senior. His detailed logbook enabled historians to put together many of his movements during the ring's years of operation. (Woodhull never wanted to be paid for spying but did want to be reimbursed for his expenses, one of the reasons his log entries were so detailed and accurate.) After the war, he became a respected judge but never spoke about his days in the Culper Ring. No portrait of Abraham Woodhull exists today, but his grave reflects his eminent position as a judge and his anonymity as a spy.

As the war heated up, the cover for the secret six grew deeper. First they used invisible ink, then code numbers, and finally they used both, writing in invisible ink between the lines in books using the code number system. This page from one of the few codebooks invented by and issued to the secret six demonstrates how the spies replaced places and people with numbers.

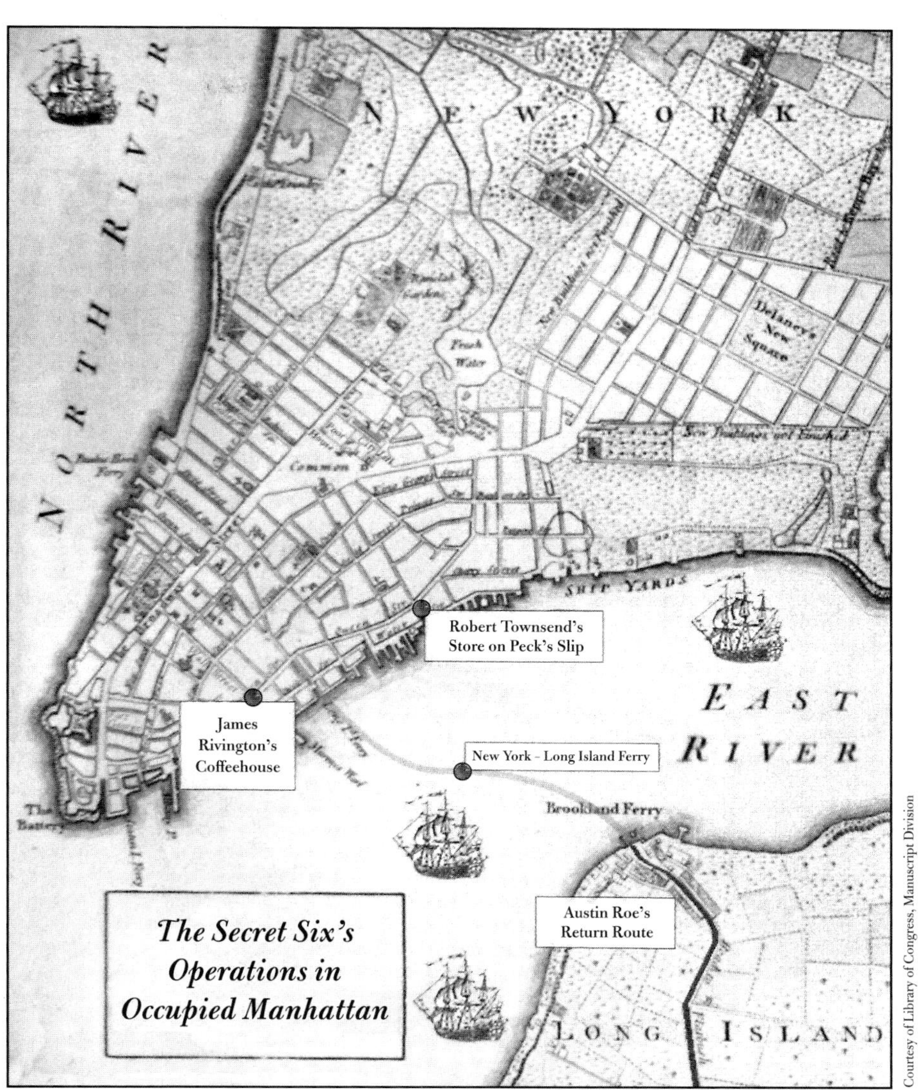

Robert Townsend's business, Templeton & Stewart, was just a few blocks from Rivington's *Gazette* office, with the Long Island ferry dock located conveniently between the two.

Major John André, a charismatic ladies' man, ran a British spy ring and ultimately lost his life because of it. After his capture, he tried to negotiate a prisoner swap for himself, but General Washington had only one deal in mind: a swap of André for Benedict Arnold. After that was rejected, André was hanged on October 2, 1780.

Collection of the New-York Historical Society

Benedict Arnold is known for being a traitor but before that was best characterized as a respected battlefield general. His expectation that the colonists would lose the war and his bitterness over his belief that Congress owed him money together prompted him to secretly join the British. Had he succeeded in handing over West Point to the redcoats, Washington would have lost the Hudson River and most certainly the war. The Culpers tipped off Washington to Arnold's traitorous ways and thwarted the plot.

Collection of the New-York Historical Society

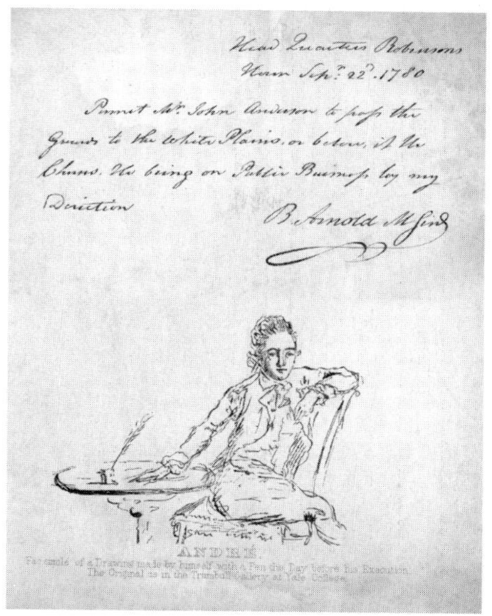

Head Quarters Robinsons House Sep.r 22d 1780

Permit Mr. John Anderson to pass the Guards to the White Plains, or below, if He Chuses. He being on Public Business by my Direction

B. Arnold M Genl

Collection of the New-York Historical Society

In addition to West Point, Arnold hoped to deliver George Washington into British hands as well. He sent important intelligence back to Manhattan with Major John André, who was code named John Anderson. The note shown here ultimately cost André his life when Patriots intercepted him and found it in his boot. André himself later drew the self-portrait below the note on the day before his execution.

Collection of the New-York Historical Society

In 1783, George Washington and his army returned to New York City in victory. He would return as president seven years later and would govern the country from Manhattan. Major Tallmadge asked the general to delay his entry so that he could secure members of the ring, because many thought they were loyal to the king and they could be harmed unless protected.

Courtesy Kurt Knapp Photography

Robert Townsend's grave, located on the edge of the Townsend family burial site up against a fence, is startlingly nondescript. Townsend wouldn't have wanted it any other way: an unassuming man, he lived and died without revealing his key role as one of George Washington's most successful and essential spies.

CHAPTER 15

The Ring in Peril

Although Arnold was exposed, the plot to surrender West Point was shattered, and André was dead, the danger to the Culper Ring was still very much alive. "I am happy to think that Arnold does not know my name. However, no person has been taken up on his information," Townsend noted in a letter to Tallmadge. Clearly, Townsend was anticipating what all of the covert operatives must have been dreading—that Arnold would disclose the identities of any spies known to him in order to keep himself in the good graces of the British.

This fear was not paranoia; something similar was certainly happening on the American side, where many of Arnold's comrades and confidants, including the shady Joshua Hett Smith, were being arrested and interrogated to learn who may have been in cahoots with the general and who had merely been manipulated unwittingly. The links of the Culper chain and every independent spy in New York—perhaps in the whole of the colonies—were all on edge, well aware that they would be the target of Arnold's wrath if he had any indication of their identities, and that he was likely to seek revenge on anyone he—or the British—suspected might have had knowledge of any part of the failed plot.

Tallmadge was keenly aware of their concern, and wrote to Washington on October 11:

> *The conduct of Arnold, since his arrival at N.Y. has been such, that though he knows not a single link in the chain of my correspondence, still those who have assisted us in this way, are at present too apprehensive of Danger to give their immediate usual intelligence. I hope as the tumult subsides matters will go on in their old channels.*
>
> *Culper, Junr. has requested an interview with me on Long Island on the 13th inst[ant], but in the present situation of affairs I believe it would be rather imprudent.*

Washington understood the perilous state of all the members of the Culper Ring, and judged Tallmadge's avoidance of a covert visit to Long Island at this particular point in time as quite wise. "I think you were right in declining an interview at this time, as the enemy would act with more than common rigor just now should an officer be taken under circumstances the least suspicious," he wrote back, though he added, "I should be exceedingly glad to hear from C. Junior."

On October 15, Washington wrote to the president of the Continental Congress (at that time, Samuel Huntington of Connecticut), informing him of several matters and noting with regard to Culper Junior: "Unluckily, the person in whom I have the greatest confidence is afraid to take any measures for communicating with me just at this time, as he is apprehensive that Arnold may possibly have some knowledge of the connection, and may have him watched. But as he is assured, that Arnold has not the most distant hint of him, I expect soon to hear from him as usual."

Townsend's return to spying was not as swift as Washington

seems to have hoped, however. Woodhull sent a letter dated October 26, in which he explained: "I have this day returned from New York, and am sorry to informe you that the present commotions and watchfullness of the Enemy at New York hath resolved C. Jur. for the present time to quit writing and retire into the country for a time.—Most certainly the enemy are very severe, and the spirits of our friends very low." In an interesting show of steeling his nerves, despite his earlier anxieties—perhaps because he recognized how much safer he was in comparison to the spies who had worked closely with the British officers in New York—Woodhull volunteered his services while Townsend was on hiatus. A few weeks later, he wrote again, "Depend my endeavours shall continue, as I hope never to lose sight of our cause, truly sensible our all is at stake."

A TURN OF AFFAIRS

General Clinton exhibited more humanity than had Arnold, and promptly released the unfortunate bargemen who had rowed Arnold to the *Vulture*. But that was the last piece of good news to reach the Americans' ears for some time. Just as the confusion of the Arnold betrayal began to dissipate, a blow was struck that threw all covert agents into a state of fear once again.

Woodhull wrote to Tallmadge, on November 12, of some disturbing news: "Several of our dear friends were imprisoned, in particular one that hath been ever serviceable to this correspondence. This step so dejected the spirits of C. Junr. that he resolved to leave New York for a time." The letter goes on to add that Austin Roe had returned from New York and that Brewster had been pursued and narrowly escaped capture while crossing the Sound. There is no indication that Rivington was ever suspected or his newspaper operations suspended, and the ring's satellite members who had functioned as couriers all seemed to be safe. The person imprisoned was someone who was known to Townsend and who enjoyed very close ties to him, making it likely that the "ever serviceable" friend apprehended was none other than Agent 355. Whether she was traced by Arnold or caught because of general suspicion, the lady's capture shattered the morale of the other five spies.

What could Agent 355 expect to face in a wartime prison? Because no separate women's prison for combatants existed, Agent 355 would have been held in the primary confinement facility at the time—HMS *Jersey,* anchored in Wallabout Bay, near Brooklyn. Prison ships, often called "death ships" for their deplorable conditions, were routinely used by the British during the war, and the *Jersey* had a reputation for being the worst of the worst, earning the nickname "Hell." Disease and vermin ran rampant among the starving prisoners. The bodies of inmates who died might not be recovered for a week or more, left to rot in the cramped, airless hulls in which the unfortunate passengers were forced to spend twenty-four hours a day. By the end of the war, approximately eight thousand people were estimated to have died aboard prison ships in New York alone.

It is no wonder, then, that Robert Townsend sank into such a deep depression. As Woodhull noted, he temporarily closed his store in Manhattan and returned to Long Island for several weeks to check on the safety of those with whom he had worked, to remove himself (as much as possible) from harm's way, and to try to nurse his spirits back to health even as he mourned the capture and imprisonment of such a brave and faithful friend.

And, as it turns out, the members of the Culper Ring were not the only spies upon whom Arnold had set his sights. A letter to Benjamin Tallmadge on October 25 revealed that Arnold had hopes of persuading the American spymaster himself to follow in his traitorous footsteps:

> *As I know you to be a man of sense, I am convinced you are by this time fully of opinion that the real*

> *interest and happiness of America consists of a re-union with Great Britain. To effect which happy purpose I have taken a commission in the British Army, and invite you to join me with as many men as you can bring over with you. If you think proper to embrace my offer, you shall have the same rank you now hold, in the Cavalry I am about to raise. I shall make use of no arguments to convince you, or to induce you to take a step which I think right. Your own good sense will suggest everything I can say on the subject.*

Inexplicably, however, the letter did not reach Tallmadge for three months. "I am equally a stranger to the channel through which it was conveyed, the reason why it was so long on its way, or the motives which induced the Traitor to address himself thus particularly to me," Tallmadge wrote to Washington on January 28, 1781. "I have determined to treat the Author with the contempt his conduct merits, by not answering his letter, unless Your Excellency should advise a different Measure."

KIDNAPPING ARNOLD

Even as Townsend was crushed by the news of the capture of fellow agents in the city, on the other side of the matter Arnold found himself somewhat dejected rather quickly as well. Despite his highest hopes and delusions of grandeur, none of his efforts had led to anything particularly fruitful. Even the suspected Patriot spies rounded up in the aftermath of his fleeing to the British failed to yield any more names of coconspirators, which left all of his efforts only half realized and hardly worth the excitement they raised. As a result, he was only paid a total of £6,315 and an annual pension of £360 rather than the full £20,000 on which he had been counting. He was somewhat mollified, however, by receiving a commission in the British army as a brigadier general, which carried with it a fairly respectable salary.

Washington had not given up hope of capturing Arnold. Using the Culper Ring to kidnap the traitor was out of the question—too many of the spies were vulnerable to being known to Arnold, and they were already in enough danger. Instead, Washington commissioned several new spies to make an attempt, explicitly instructing them to bring Arnold back alive to stand trial.

Working covertly with Major Henry Lee—the same Henry Lee who had spoken out against the Intolerable Acts of 1774—Washington devised a daring plan that would require the young officer to operate in complete secrecy and to disavow any involvement on the general's part. A sergeant named John Champe volunteered to carry out a dangerous mission, the particular details of which he learned only after stepping forward. "[Champe] was about twenty three or twenty four years of age," Lee later recalled in his *Memoirs of the War in the Southern Department of the United States,* and "rather above the common size, full of bone and muscle, with a saturnine countenance, grave thoughtful and taciturne, of tried courage and inflexible perseverance." In short, he was large, strong, serious, and stubborn—the perfect man for such a difficult job.

His mission was to desert from Lee's Second Partisan Corps and join the British in New York City as a defector. If he implied that he had been inspired by Arnold's actions, he stood a chance of meeting Arnold and gaining his confidence. Once ingratiated with Arnold, he was to study his routines and habits and discover the most efficient means of kidnapping him with the help of a handful of operatives in and around Manhattan. The men would then smuggle the traitor out of the city and back into American-held territory in New Jersey, where Washington could take custody of Arnold.

Champe and his associates needed to be extremely careful, however, for Washington did not want to give the British any reason to believe that the Americans had simply sent in thugs to finish off Arnold as revenge. The general wrote to Lee on October 20: "No circumstance whatever shall obtain my consent to his being put to death. The idea which would accompany such an event would be that Ruffians had been hired to assassinate him. My aim is to make a public example of him, and this should be strongly impressed upon those who are employed to bring him off."

The plan worked beautifully. Champe managed to successfully desert, though the extreme secrecy of the plan meant that Lee's unsuspecting men gave chase and nearly captured Champe to bring him back for punishment. Nevertheless, he made it to the shore not far from two British ships and dove into the water, swimming madly toward them. After he was taken aboard and questioned, the British brought him into the city, where General Clinton, upon interviewing him, deemed his desire to join the British genuine, introduced him to Arnold, and placed him in the force Arnold now commanded.

Over the next few weeks he formed a plan to capture Arnold during his evening walk. However, Champe never turned up on the evening of December 21, when he was scheduled to bring an unconscious Arnold to a small boat waiting in the river. A few days later, it was learned that Arnold's unit (in which Champe was now serving as part of his cover) had been unexpectedly shipped off to Virginia the day before. What had begun as a promising attempt to purchase additional safety for the Culpers by removing a dangerous enemy ended in disappointment.

SMALL VICTORIES

Despite the clever plotting of Washington and Lee and the valiant efforts of John Champe, Benedict Arnold was still at large, which meant the Culper Ring was still at risk—and one of them was still imprisoned. The pressure was felt by every member, but the spy at the center of the ring suffered the most.

Evidence of Townsend's continued anxiety and despondency throughout the fall and winter of 1780–81 shows up in the account book from his store. Whereas he had previously been quite prompt in recording his business transactions, the entries suddenly appear far more sporadic. Between November 1779 and July 1780, he updated his accounts every three to five days at first, then slowed down to every seven to nine days. During those eight months, he was almost predictable in his reckonings, with the exception of February–March 1780, when he twice lapsed thirteen days between entries. During the summer of 1780, his entries began to have much larger spans between them. He made no entries for September, just one in October (on the seventh), and then nothing again until December 2. The next time he seems to have cracked open his ledger after that was nearly four months later, on March 29, 1781.

Townsend's spying activities largely ceased during the season of his withdrawal from business, but Washington took advantage of that time to shift his focus temporarily from Manhattan to the surrounding areas. Thanks in part to the reports still coming in from Woodhull on Long Island, Washington began to reconsider Tallmadge's earlier proposals to storm certain vulnerable locations on the island.

On November 21, 1780, Tallmadge (now a colonel in the Continental Army) led a contingency of eighty men selected from his Second Dragoons—along with Caleb Brewster, who is listed as a captain in the operation—from Fairfield, Connecticut, across Long Island Sound in whaleboats to the town of Mount Sinai, roughly six miles from Tallmadge's native Setauket. Battling rain and high winds, they marched roughly twenty miles through the night of the twenty-second, straight across the island to Mastic, on the southern shore, and attacked Fort St. George on the morning of November 23. Constructed and fortified the previous year by staunch Loyalists and named for the patron saint of England, the fort had a large stockpile of supplies and provisions, including an ample supply of hay upon which British soldiers in the area depended to feed their livestock. After a brief fight against the well-armed residents, Tallmadge's men were able to seize control, destroy the stockpile, burn the hay, and take the fort's inhabitants prisoner—all with suffering only one injury on their side. The prisoners were marched back across the island to the boats that were waiting under guard, and the whole company crossed the Sound again for Connecticut.

Washington was pleased by the efforts and applauded Tallmadge in a personal letter. Woodhull, too, sent his congratulations, writing on November 28, "The burning the forage is agreeable to me and must hurt the enemy much."

It was not a major battle from a strategic standpoint, but it delivered an important morale boost to the Patriots and provided a psychological victory over the British by proving that New York and Long Island had not been forgotten, nor were they invincible.

CHAPTER 16

The Beginning of the End

With the death of André, the British found themselves without a spymaster at a time when such an officer was particularly important. Things were heating up in the south again, particularly in Virginia, where Arnold (with poor Champe in tow) had sailed with fifteen hundred troops in December 1780. Clinton found his attentions drawn to the Chesapeake even as the raid at Fort St. George had proved that New York could not be left unattended. A man was named to fill André's vacancy and manage intelligence for the commander of the British troops on American soil.

Major Oliver DeLancey was in his early thirties—a New York City native whose family was among the earliest Jewish settlers in the American colonies. He had been educated in England but returned home soon after the war began in order to organize a Loyalist regiment in New York. He may not have had the same level of star appeal that André enjoyed, but he was brilliant, able, and now operating in his native territory, which gave him a distinct advantage in understanding the people, customs, and terrain. He immediately set about to reorganize the British intelligence system, unifying codes and bringing a number of disparate and independent elements together so that information could more easily be shared, analyzed, and acted upon.

The Culper Ring, in the meantime, stayed busy (if not active in spying) as the calendar turned from 1780 to 1781. Late in the winter, Caleb Brewster captured a British boat and eight prisoners, including two officers. Townsend resumed his business and reopened his shop in the city in March. Woodhull tried to persuade him to start gathering intelligence again, but Townsend believed that the British had dispatched a spy of their own in New York who was actively trying to root out the sources and paths of the Culpers' information and insisted on lying low. The matter was dropped until the end of April, when Tallmadge could finally report the pending resurrection of the ring's activities, with a few adjustments made to their former routine. "The plan which he [Woodhull] has consented to adopt, on certain conditions, is for him to remain for the most part on Long Island and C. Junr. whom he thinks might be engaged again, to reside constantly at New York," he wrote to Washington on the twenty-fifth. "That some confidential person must of course be employed to carry dispatches as it would cause suspicions which might lead to detection if either of the Culpers should be frequently passing from New York to Setauket, &c. they being men of some considerable note."

Washington preferred a more timely delivery of intelligence, but he agreed to this arrangement. The Culpers' reports were essential to the continued success of the Americans, even if they did take a few days longer to arrive. The general had learned from his earlier mistake; vital information received a few days late was infinitely preferable to no information at all. He quickly replied to Tallmadge:

> *The great object of information you are very well acquainted with—such as, Arrivals, Embarkations, Preparations for Movements, alterations of Positions, situation*

of Posts, Fortifications, Garrisons, strength or weakness of each, distributions and strength of Corps, and in general every thing which can be interesting and important for us to know. Besides these, upon a smaller scale, which are necessary to be reported: and that whatever intelligence is communicated ought to be not in general terms, but in detail, and with the greatest precision.

At present I am anxious to know (for the reports have been very numerous vague and uncertain) whether another embarkation is preparing, and if so to what amount, and where destined. What the present force of the Enemy is; particularly on Long Island, in New York and at King's Bridge. What Corps are at the latter place, how strong, and where posted exactly—and indeed what the situation, prospect, and designs of the enemy are, so far as they can be penetrated into.

Washington's instructions are vast in their scope and display the extreme confidence he had in his most valuable ring to obtain precisely the breadth and depth of intelligence he required. He took pains in the same letter to note that he was "engaging in behalf of the United States a liberal reward for the services of the C——s, (of whose fidelity and ability I entertain a high opinion) it is certainly but reasonable, from patriotism and every other principle, that their exertions should be proportionately great, to subserve essentially the interest of the Public."

Despite Washington's praise, Townsend adamantly refused to put pen to paper. He had seen how André had been done in by the discovery of papers and plans—hard and damning evidence he could not deny or talk his way out of. He would be happy to convey orally whatever information he had observed, Townsend explained to Woodhull when they met in the city in early May, but the risk of trying to smuggle written documents out of Manhattan was far too great. Woodhull could not deny the truth of those concerns, especially now that Oliver DeLancey was asserting his authority with new ideas for uncovering plots in their midst.

In his May 19 letter to Tallmadge, Woodhull noted that, on the way back to Long Island from visiting Townsend, "the enemy must have got some hint of me for when passing at Brooklyn Ferry was strictly examined and told some vilian supported a correspondence from this place." The letter also included intelligence Austin Roe had obtained verbally from Townsend on his last visit to the city, but they all knew their visits could not be so frequent as to raise suspicions. Woodhull and Townsend worked exhaustively to recruit a new member for the ring, one who was not already under the watchful eyes of British operatives and could operate freely in Manhattan and smuggle out detailed written reports. "When at New York myself, together with Culper Junior [we] almost racked our invention to point out a proper person and made several attempts but failed—no person will write," Woodhull lamented.

SECRET SIX DELIVER YORKTOWN TO WASHINGTON

General Washington remained hopeful that the next major military engagement would be focused on retaking New York, but he was depending heavily on the French navy—specifically, the large fleet under the command of Admiral François-Joseph-Paul de Grasse, which was currently in the Caribbean—because the success of the mission would rely in large part upon the men, supplies, and ships that the French could provide to shore up the inadequately manned and provisioned American forces. This meant that Washington's plans were at the mercy of the French leaders who ordered the admiral to sail. So when word reached the general that the fleet would be sailing in August 1781 to Yorktown, Virginia, and not to New York, he was disappointed but knew he could not afford to squander such an opportunity—especially because he had a secret weapon.

By leaving a small contingency of twenty-five hundred men north of New York and ordering another unit to fake preparations for storming Staten Island, Washington gambled that the feints would frustrate General Clinton and leave him unsure of whether or not he could afford to send reinforcements to help out Lieutenant General Charles Cornwallis, one of Britain's most esteemed and feared generals, at Yorktown. Meanwhile, Washington led his troops on a miserable, sweaty summer march southward to the malarial swamps of eastern Virginia.

At roughly the same time, Allen McLane—the same McLane who had harbored suspicions against Benedict Arnold in Philadelphia in 1778—had been ordered to Long Island to gather any information he could regarding the preparations of the British ships set to bring relief and, presumably, to meet with the agents already working there who could provide him with a fuller picture before he slipped back out to rejoin Washington's troops as they made camp at Yorktown. McLane had special instructions to learn as many of the British navy's code signals as possible, so that the French fleet could decipher what the enemy ships were communicating to one another during naval engagements. It was a nearly impossible task, because ships in harbor are unlikely to use distress codes or signals for attack, so McLane was left to try any desperate or accidental manner he could devise to piece together the secret system—an ineffective (not to mention dangerous) approach.

Fortunately, while on Long Island, McLane was put into contact with James Rivington. The printer and coffeehouse owner was still operating his presses and still fraternizing with the British in Manhattan despite the dangers to spies, and his persistence had paid off. Whether someone had left a copy in Rivington's coffeehouse or the British had commissioned him to print additional copies is not clear, but somehow he managed to procure a copy of the entire British naval codebook. Rivington passed it on to McLane, who rushed it to Washington.

Both McLane and the codebook made it safely off Long Island

and down to Virginia by the end of the summer, and Washington was able to transport the book to Admiral de Grasse's custody by mid-September. In French hands, it was a more effective resource than the Americans could have dared hope for, and its loss was more devastating than the British could have imagined.

The siege of Yorktown was a roaring success, thanks in no small part to de Grasse's ability to anticipate nearly every movement of the British fleet. Paralyzed by indecision for fear of leaving New York vulnerable to attack, and despite continued assurances to Cornwallis that he would send reinforcements, General Clinton failed to deliver any of the promised troops to Virginia. Trapped by both land and sea, Cornwallis was unable to muster the power to break through in either direction. He could not attack; he could not retreat. A white flag was the only option. He surrendered on October 19.

The defeat at Yorktown was an embarrassment to the entire British military and caused a tremendous spat between Clinton and Cornwallis that became a public scandal back in Britain. Cornwallis set sail on the same ship that carried Benedict Arnold and his family to London in January 1782; once on English soil he was able to perform some measure of damage control by speaking critically of Clinton's leadership. Clinton submitted his resignation as the commander in chief for North America and departed for England in mid-May. In 1783, he published a book narrating his account of the 1781 campaign in North America, in which he wrote that Cornwallis's failings ultimately led to the defeat at Yorktown.

To military leaders on both sides, however, the events at Yorktown made it clear that the conflict was reaching its natural end. The Americans had stood their ground and doggedly fought for every inch of land they deemed rightfully their own; the British government was finally recognizing that superior military muscle was not enough to make the determined Patriot army back down when they had powerful allies on their side. On March 28, 1782, word reached New York from London that the House of Commons had voted to end all offensive strikes in the American colonies, though that by no means signified the end of military occupation or exercises. At the same time, a more moderate prime minister was coming to power backed by a Parliament that generally opposed the war. An end to the hostilities seemed inevitable, but matters were far from settled.

Savannah, Charleston, and New York still remained strongholds of the British army, and Washington was forced to decide, in the critical weeks following Yorktown, if he should continue to march southward and eliminate those threats before refocusing his energies and resources northward on New York. In the end, he decided to divide his forces, sending some to strengthen the beleaguered troops in the Carolinas and Georgia but returning with the majority of his troops to the Hudson Valley, just above the city. He was sure that the British were not going to allow New York to fall without a fight.

CHANGING TIDES IN NEW YORK

Unrest was erupting throughout the city. The pockets of Patriot dissidents who had dug in their heels and stayed during the long duration of the war now grew bolder while Loyalists who had been certain of coming out of the war on the winning side felt betrayed by the Crown. Broadsides and other printed matter began to appear posted on walls and clutched in citizens' hands. New Yorkers vented discontentment with various politicians, with the king, with the war in general. Rumors of peace negotiations between the two delegations began to trickle in via packet ships, and all wondered what the terms of peace might be. Sir Guy Carleton assumed the role of commander in chief from Clinton in May 1782, which only added to the feelings of uncertainty, transition, and unrest even as the British government seemed to turn away from all interest in a continued investment in the American conflict.

The British officers garrisoned in New York feared an uprising from within by emboldened Patriots almost as much as they feared an external attack from the Continental Army. Both out of desperation and as a show of power, the British military began enacting impressment measures around the city, pulling civilians out of their ordinary lives to serve in temporary guard duties for king and country, as Carleton's tight command of the city made Clinton's authority seem paltry. Woodhull remarked on this trend when he wrote to Tallmadge on July 5:

> *Their design appears only to act on the defensive and be as little expense to the Crown as possible. God grant their time may be short for we have much reason to fear within their lines that Carlton's finger will be heavier than Clinton's Thigh. Carlton's called a Tyrant at New York by the inhabitants in general and makes them do Soldiers duty in the city without distinction. The first Gentlemen in the City stand at Officer's doors Soldier like.*

Robert Townsend may have been one of these unwilling temporary recruits. Family tradition held that years later a British uniform was found stored with his belongings; when questioned about it, he reluctantly spoke of having been impressed into standing watch at the officers' headquarters in New York.

In July 1782, the British left Savannah. There was no doubt that the war would soon be officially over, with the Americans emerging victorious; all but the most ardent and desperate Tories recognized that only the formal terms of a peace treaty needed to be established before the remaining enemy troops would be forced to leave the soil of the sovereign, independent United States of America.

Loyalists now had a difficult choice to make: Did they stay and rebuild their lives, or did they emigrate back to Europe or northward to Canada? There was some hope, at first, that any lands and property formerly in Tory hands would be returned if they had been seized during the war; however, most people recognized that such a measure would be difficult to carry out and, in some cases, might actually pose a threat to the new nation, especially if large tracts of acreage ended up back in the hands of those who remained loyal to the king and wished to revive hostilities. Besides, the reasoning was "To the victors go the spoils"—even if that seemed unfortunate and unjust. The majority of Loyalists, like the majority of Patriots (and the revolutionary agnostics), were humble men and women of modest means: small landowners, tenant farmers, laborers in the cities, fishermen and longshoremen along the coasts, hunters and traders in the frontiers of the Appalachians. Any property they possessed likely had not been, nor would be, threatened by seizure. In deciding where to live out the remainder of their days, they had to take into consideration the inclinations of their neighbors and their own consciences; it would not be a pleasant thing to be forever regarded as "the neighbor who fought against our government." Some of the wealthiest citizens had already booked passage back to England; now the common folk began to do the same.

Each packet ship that arrived in New York Harbor carried more news from England and less hope that King George would prevail, or that those subjects who had professed fidelity to him would receive any kind of reward for their loyalty and faith in the most powerful military on earth.

TOWNSEND'S LAST LETTER

As Robert Townsend rode into Westchester County, New York, he could not have helped but admire the beauty of the foliage and the crispness in the September air. Nearly six years to the day after Nathan Hale's hanging, here was another spy carrying his reports on New York directly to Benjamin Tallmadge, and from Tallmadge's hand they would reach Washington.

It was an unlikely meeting in several ways. Not long ago, the ride west from New York City to Westchester would have been barred by sentries and checkpoints. It was still heavily guarded, that was true—the British did not want to let go of New York until absolutely required to do so, and they knew Washington was prowling outside, ready to pounce at his first opportunity—but one could now pass more safely into American-held territory without having to traverse the same tricky no-man's-land that had ensnared André.

It was also an unlikely meeting because Townsend had firmly declined to commit anything to writing back in May. But now he could see the shaky position of the city and knew that Washington needed the best intelligence he could offer in order to calculate the next—and maybe final—move of the war. Townsend shouldered the responsibility of delivering the latest report himself, figuring that at this late point in the war with all that had already transpired, if he was arrested and tried as a spy he would have only himself to blame.

Finally, the meeting was unlikely because Townsend was carrying news that the war was nearly over. Despite the British hold on New York, the Americans were in position to secure their independence, thanks in no small part to the Culper Ring.

The message Townsend delivered to Tallmadge, with the date September 19, 1782, written across the top, is the final surviving letter from Culper Junior's hand. The news painted a city in upheaval:

> *The last packet [ship], so far from bringing better news to the loyalists, has indeed brought the clearest and unequivocal Proofs that the independence of America is unconditionally to be acknowledged, nor will there be any conditions insisted on for those who joined the King's Standard.*
>
> *It is said that an Expedition is now forming at N.Y. and by many conjectured to be against the French Fleet &c. at Boston; a number of British Troops were embarking when I left the city on the*

> *14th and 15th inst[ant]. But I conversed fully with one of Carleton's Aides on this subject, who told me that I might depend they were bound to the W. Indies or Halifax. For my own part I have no expectation that they think of any offensive movements. The above gentleman, with whom I am most intimately connected, informed me that it is now under consideration to send all the B. Troops to the West Indies.*
>
> *. . . It is a fact that a fleet is going to Charlestown to bring off that Garrison.*
>
> *. . . Sir Guy himself says that he thinks it not improbable that the next Packet may bring orders for an evacuation of N. York.*
>
> *A fleet is getting ready to sail for the Bay of Fundy about the first of October to transport a large number of Refugees to that Quarter. The Aide above referred to informs us that he thinks it probable he shall go there himself. Indeed, I never saw such general distress and dissatisfaction in my life as is painted in the countenance of every Tory at N.Y.*
>
> *The Beef Contractors had orders a few days past to cease purchasing any more for the Navy and from the appearance of things the whole fleet are getting ready for a movement.*
>
> *I am myself uncertain when the Troops will leave N.Y. but I must confess I rather believe if the King's Magazines can be removed, that they will leave us this fall.*

Unfortunately for Washington, Townsend's prediction of a British evacuation before the end of 1782 proved a little too optimistic. In Paris, where John Adams, Benjamin Franklin, John Jay, and Henry Laurens were representing the American government, negotiations were dragging on with no sign of resolution. Even after Charleston was abandoned to the Americans on December 14 and South Carolina could boast its freedom from the Crown, Sir Guy Carleton stayed planted firmly and stubbornly in New York with no plans to move until ordered to do so by King George himself. The toll on life and property that would result from an attack on New York no longer seemed worth the risk to Washington, but he could not celebrate victory (nor could any of the citizens) until a binding treaty had been ratified and New York—and America—had rid itself of foreign occupation.

CHAPTER 17
Retaking New York at Last

The year 1783 dawned full of promise. On February 3, the government of Great Britain formally acknowledged the independence of what were once its American colonies as the United States of America. The following day it agreed to halt all military involvement. In April, a preliminary peace treaty was ratified, and in July tracts of land in Canada were opened to Loyalists seeking a new life and a region was designated for former slaves who had fought for Britain. Crowded ships bound for Nova Scotia and New Brunswick sailed northward from New York Harbor. But still, the British army remained firmly and fixedly in Manhattan.

North of the city, near his encampment in Newburgh, Washington was struggling to subdue a rising insurrection against the back wages owed and promises of land that had been offered to Patriot soldiers but which Congress had failed so far to deliver. Combat may have reached an end, but the enemy still would not leave and the daunting task of rebuilding the country while paying down the debts of war loomed as challenges still to be faced.

Woodhull, meanwhile, continued to send the occasional report from Long Island, though there was nothing of great urgency or importance anymore. The Culpers had done their duty, and done it well. A note dated July 5, 1783, was accompanied by a final balance record that Woodhull submitted to Tallmadge, at the major's request: "I only kept the most simple account that I possibly could, for fear it should betray me, but I trust it is a just one—and I do assure you I have been as frugal as possibly could. I desire you would explain to the Genl. the circumstances that attended this lengthy correspondence that he may be satisfied that we have not been extravagant." Woodhull then concluded the letter in a way that clearly reflected the present optimistic mood on Long Island: "Wishing you health and happiness, I am your very humble servant, Sam[l]. Culper."

After five years, four major plots thwarted, countless misgivings and close calls, and untold sleepless nights, the Culper correspondence came to an end. The ring had operated effectively from the very heart of the enemy's headquarters and had never been successfully infiltrated, uncovered, or unmasked, despite numerous efforts in that vein. The loss of Agent 355 was a tragedy, but it was also remarkable that the casualties were not much higher given how close the Culpers were to the enemy in Manhattan and the daring movements and maneuvers of the agents on Long Island. While the spies had not been able to deliver Manhattan to Washington before the war's end, they had been his eyes and ears there, enabling him to beat the British even without holding the city. The Culper Ring was a success.

All that remained now between Washington and his spies was the settling of some small monetary debts; the larger debts—the intangible kind that helped to protect a fledgling nation—could never be fully repaid, nor did the remaining members of the Culper Ring seek out such payment. A return to an open, honest, and simple life in an independent nation founded on their native soil would be reward enough. And so they hoped, and prayed, and waited for the

British to depart from New York at long last, even as the aftermath of war swirled around them.

PEACE RAGES

The British delegation finally signed the Treaty of Paris in September, and Washington's troops were at the ready to ride into Manhattan as the last redcoat left the city. Colonel Tallmadge, however, was concerned for the safety of his spies who had lived and worked as Loyalists during the occupation and might now find themselves threatened by their newly empowered Patriot neighbors who had no inkling of their true sentiments and bravery. How could Townsend erase the fact that he had run a store that served British soldiers, worked for a Loyalist newspaper, frequented the coffeehouse popular among the officers, and kept company with those who had penetrated the inner circles of the top brass in the city?

To anyone on the outside, Robert Townsend had not only enjoyed a rather cushy life during the war but also profited from it. This would hardly sit well with those who had suffered the loss of life, limb, and property for the sake of American independence, and Colonel Tallmadge was fearful that some vengeful Patriot might come looking for his pound of flesh. He was desperate to seek out his spies and contract bodyguards to ensure their personal welfare, send them underground, create for them yet another false identity elsewhere in the city, or even spirit them out of New York for a time until passions cooled.

Tallmadge wrote in his memoirs of these concerns:

> *As little doubt could be entertained but that peace would soon follow, I found it necessary to take some steps to insure the safety of several persons within the enemy's lines, who had served us faithfully and with*

> *intelligence during the war. As some of these were considered to be of the Tory character . . . I suggested to Gen. Washington the propriety of my being permitted to go to New York, under the cover of a flag. This he very readily granted, and I proceeded to New York, where I was surrounded by British troops, tories, cowboys, and traitors.*

The whole experience of crossing into Manhattan must have been rather surreal for Tallmadge, as he enjoyed the unusual privilege of dining with General Carleton himself, and noted that "by the officers of the army and navy I was treated with great respect and attention." He added, "It was not a little amusing to see how men, tories and refugees, who a little before uttered nothing but the terms, *rebels and traitors to their King,* against all the officers of the American army, would now come around me while in New York, and beg my protection against the dreaded rage of their countrymen."

Despite the various distractions, the bids for his attention, and his high-profile status, Tallmadge was able to meet quietly and safely with Townsend and the others he was seeking out to ensure their security when the British finally evacuated the city. "While at New York I saw and secured all who had been friendly to us through the war, and especially our emissaries," he wrote. Then he rode north again to Newburgh to wait for Washington's next orders:

> *Having accomplished all my business in New York, I returned again to the army, and made my report to the Commander-in-Chief. The troops now began to be impatient to return to their respective homes, and those that were destined for that purpose, to take possession of the city. Gen. Washington now dismissed the greater part of the army in so*

> *judicious a way, that no unpleasant circumstances occurred.*

The troops broke camp and returned home, their service completed and their dreams for liberty realized. Only those soldiers appointed to ride into New York with Washington stayed on, eager and grateful to be part of that historic moment.

FINALLY BACK IN NEW YORK

At noon on Tuesday, November 25, 1783—coincidentally, the same date as Robert Townsend's thirtieth birthday—Washington rode into Manhattan, with Benjamin Tallmadge among the officers at his side. A contingent rode ahead, scanning the streets as the last of the British officers boarded their ships; Washington followed with his officers and troops spanning eight across. In the previous days and hours leading up to that moment, some joyful Patriots had hoisted American flags over their homes only to have them torn down; in a few cases, they came to blows with the redcoat enforcers. But now the citizens of New York, no longer subject to British law or British soldiers, waved flags freely as Washington rode forward. Church bells tolled not in warning but in celebration, and the shouts after each firing of the cannons were triumphant rather than terrified. Some people even crowded at the water's edge, waving at the ships set for departure and laughingly bidding the defeated soldiers on board a lovely trip home. "So perfect was the order of march, that entire tranquility prevailed, and nothing occurred to mar the general joy," Tallmadge wrote.

> *Every countenance seemed to express the triumph of republican principles over the military despotism which had so long pervaded this now happy*

> *city. Most of the refugees had embarked for Nova Scotia, and the few who remained, were too insignificant to be noticed in the crowd. It was indeed a joyful day to the officers and soldiers of our army, and to all the friends of American independence, while the troops of the enemy, still in our waters, and the host of tories and refugees, were sorely mortified. The joy of meeting friends, who had long been separated by the cruel rigors of war, cannot be described.*

The next nine days were filled with celebrations and visitations as Washington toured the city. As his step-grandson, George Washington Parke Custis, would later record, the general even made a special stop at the shop of James Rivington, much to the surprise of many of the officers in his company, who considered Rivington a Loyalist scoundrel whose continued presence in the newly freed New York seemed an affront to all Patriots. But Washington seemed purposeful, even determined, as he excused himself to speak privately with Rivington about (so he claimed) certain books that the printer intended to order from London. The two men disappeared briefly, then came back to the front room, where Washington prepared to take his leave.

"Your Excellency may rely upon my especial attention being given to the agricultural works," Rivington said as he escorted the party to the door, voicing the sentiments most dear to the tired general's heart at that moment, "which, on their arrival, will be immediately forwarded to Mount Vernon, where I trust they will contribute to your gratification amid the shades of domestic retirement."

At noon on December 4, Washington met with his officers in Fraunces Tavern, just a few blocks from Rivington's establishment and the Fly Market, where Robert Townsend had operated his shop and carried out his spying duties. "The time now drew near when the Commander-in-Chief intended to leave this part of the country for his beloved retreat at Mount Vernon," Tallmadge recorded in his memoirs, adding that "it was made known to the officers then in New York, that Gen. Washington intended to commence his journey on that day."

Entering the room promptly at twelve o'clock, Washington seated himself and enjoyed a light lunch before raising his glass of wine; speaking in a voice heavy with emotion, he told them: "With a heart full of love and gratitude I now take leave of you. I most devoutly wish that your latter days may be as prosperous and happy as your former ones have been glorious and honorable."

Following the toast, Washington paused before adding, "[I] shall feel obliged if each of you will come and take me by the hand." One by one, the officers silently came forward to embrace the general.

"The *simple thought* that we were then about to part from the man who had conducted us through a long and bloody war . . . and that we should see his face no more in this world, seemed to me utterly insupportable," Tallmadge wrote. A solemn procession marched Washington to the docks, where he would begin his journey home to Virginia. He was a tired man who earnestly believed his life of public service was over, and that the next generation would be those called upon to lead the country through the coming years. Tallmadge narrated the scene with a note of finality:

> *We all followed in mournful silence to the wharf, where a prodigious crowd had assembled to witness the departure of the man who, under God, had been the great agent in establishing the glory and independence of these United States. As soon as he was seated, the barge put off into the river, and when out in the stream, our great and beloved General waived his hat, and bid us a silent adieu.*

"We the People"

Not long after General Washington's departure for civilian life, his brothers in arms followed suit. "In a few days," Tallmadge recorded, "all the officers who had assembled at New York to participate in the foregoing heart-rending scene, departed to their several places of abode, to commence anew their avocations for life." They could, at long last, enjoy the future for which they had all so gallantly fought.

Tallmadge, too, returned home to a memorable celebration he described in rather poetic terms in his memoirs:

> *Having for seven years been banished from the home of my father, at Brookhaven, in Suffolk county, on Long Island, I determined to visit the place of my nativity. . . . Being principally Whigs, and now emancipated from their late severe bondage, the people had determined that they would celebrate the occasion by some public demonstration of their joy. They therefore concluded to have public notice given, that on a day near at hand, they would have an ox roasted whole on the public green, to partake of which all were invited to attend. I remember well, that after a most joyful meeting with my former friends (many of whom I had not seen since the war commenced), I was appointed master of ceremonies for the occasion. When the ox was well roasted, the noble animal on his spit was removed to a proper place, and after a blessing from the God of Battles had been invoked by my honored father, I began to carve, dissect, and distribute to the multitude around me. The aged and the young, the male and the female, rejoiced to receive a portion, which, from the novelty of the scene, and being in commemoration of so great an event, obtained a particular zest. All was harmony and joy, for all seemed to be of one mind.*

> *A Tory could not have lived in that atmosphere one minute. . . . The joy of the Whig population through the island was literally unbounded.*

Tallmadge then set out to ride eastward across Long Island to visit friends and survey the land. As he rode from town to town, he was quite delighted to find that the Patriotic fervor had not been lost by those citizens who had endured much suffering under the rule of the British and the political dominance of the Loyalists: "Private hospitality and public honor were most liberally bestowed on any man who had served in the revolutionary army."

As picturesque as Tallmadge's transition back to civilian life was, his former commander George Washington would not have long to enjoy his own "shades of domestic retirement," as James Rivington had wished for him. Despite making every effort to remain out of the public eye, on April 30, 1789, Washington once again found himself in New York City, the capital of the new nation. This time, however, his hand was resting not upon his sword but upon a Bible as he was sworn in to the office of president of the United States. He had not wanted the position and had only accepted reluctantly when he was finally persuaded that his leadership would help unify the former colonies of the infant nation that were still struggling on wobbling legs toward complete self-governance free of foreign presence or occupation. Washington also declined all other titles and honoraria other than the simple and direct address of "Mr. President."

A DISAPPOINTING VISIT

The following year, Washington made a tour of Long Island to meet the people and examine the damage done to land and property during the British occupation. But he also had it in mind to privately visit with and thank the individuals who had risked so much to gather intelligence and smuggle it to him.

He approached Setauket on April 22, 1790, and made a stop at "the House of a Capt. Roe, which is tolerably dect. with obliging people in it." Whether those obliging people with whom he passed several pleasant hours included the rest of the Setauket Culpers—Benjamin Tallmadge, Abraham Woodhull, and Caleb Brewster—or if he was even aware that he was lodging under the roof of one of those very spies he had journeyed to thank, Washington did not say. His knowledge of the ring members' true identities was, after all, quite limited by design. He had not wanted to know more than he needed to in order to protect them, and several of the members (Townsend in particular) had been insistent that Washington never learn their names. The following day he took his leave of Roe's tavern and continued westward, where his tour took him to Oyster Bay. His brief notes make no mention of a meeting with Robert Townsend or any member of his family, despite the senior Samuel's numerous run-ins with the law and his suffering as Colonel Simcoe's reluctant landlord. Had Washington been aware of the debt of gratitude that he owed to a certain native son of this town, his stay surely would not have been so brief. Instead, he made his visit, paid his respects to the brave citizens of the town, and rode on, having never met the man he so earnestly sought to thank.

By the time the president crossed the ferry back to Manhattan at sundown on April 24, he had completed his circuit around the part of the island wherein lived the ring of spies who had served him so faithfully and carried out their weighty task with such dedication and courage. He had sincerely hoped to have some time with the mysterious Culper Junior, who had risked his life, health, and well-being for so long, passing in and out of the lion's mouth every day, seeking to still the monarch's roar within American borders. But no matter the greetings sent the general's way and the invitations extended, Townsend never stepped out of the shadows to meet with his commander in chief. It was a great honor, to be sure, but not one that Townsend sought. He did not want praise or celebration; the greatest reward Washington could give him was simply a return to a quiet and unassuming life as a man subject to no king but God.

Those few who knew the Culpers' secret kept it close, and all Washington could do was carry in his heart the gratitude he had for the sacrifices of his brave spies, which were no less meaningful for having been made in city streets and country back roads as on a battlefield. For these men and women, too, had given their all to "establish Justice, insure domestic Tranquility, provide for the common defence, promote the general Welfare, and secure the Blessings of Liberty to ourselves and our Posterity."

CHAPTER 18

Life After the Ring

With the end of the war and the start of the American republic, the Culpers could return to their lives as ordinary citizens. While a few were not shy about their role in the war effort and enjoyed a bit of notoriety for their daring adventures, most did what all good spies do: They carried on in obscurity as ordinary and unassuming people whose neighbors never knew they had led double lives. Their stories were packed away like pressed flowers in the pages of a book—quietly waiting, undetected for years—to reward some curious reader decades later with the intricacy and beauty of their design. There were whispers, rumors, and legends, of course—but no one pursued them, happy to leave well enough alone when the desired outcome of liberty had been reached, though at a high and terrible cost.

Caleb Brewster, after his years of excitement rowing back and forth across Long Island Sound in his whaleboat and engaging in hard-fought skirmishes, found that the second part of his life was much quieter than the first, though he was never far from the sea. He married Anne Lewis of Fairfield, Connecticut, in 1784, and moved to a farm at Black Rock, southwest of Bridgeport, where the couple had several children. Brewster passed away at his farm on February 13, 1827, and for all of his prodigious feats of bravery and skill during the war, his headstone notes his eventual rank of captain and then sums up his service simply: "He was a brave and active officer of the Revolution."

James Rivington had a less tranquil retirement. According to George Washington Parke Custis, during the private meeting between Washington and Rivington in the bookshop, the officers in the front room could distinctly hear a bag of gold coins being handed to the bookseller for his spying services during the war. Custis, however, was not actually present for the events and had a habit of occasionally embellishing stories in accordance with his own imagination. Whether gold really changed hands during this meeting or not remains unclear. But what is certain is that Rivington and his shop received special protection in the days and weeks following the British evacuation; there would be no burning and looting as had occurred at the hands of the Sons of Liberty in 1775. Later correspondence of Washington's confidants defended Rivington against libel. He remained in New York, though his newspaper business suffered because of his reputation as a staunch enemy of the new republic. He was eventually forced to close his shop, but with eight children to support back in England, several bad investments, and a personal taste for the high life, his financial situation deteriorated until he was forced to serve time in debtors' prison. He died in New York, where he had spent thirty-six of his seventy-eight years of life, on July 4, 1802.

Austin Roe, like Caleb Brewster, achieved the rank of captain and carried that title proudly for the rest of his life. He and his wife, the former Catherine Jones, had eight children; in 1798, the family moved from Setauket, on the north shore of Long Island, to Patchogue, almost exactly opposite on the southern shore, and opened a hotel. Unlike many of the other Culpers, Roe enjoyed sharing stories of his spying adventures with locals and patrons at his inn, though he was careful to protect the privacy of his fellow ring members. He passed away on November 29, 1830, at the age of eighty-one.

Benjamin Tallmadge married Mary Floyd, daughter of Major General William Floyd, a signer of the Declaration of Independence. The couple moved to Connecticut, where they had seven children; in 1792, Tallmadge was appointed postmaster for the town of Litchfield. He would later serve sixteen years in the House of Representatives (1801–17). Interestingly, in January 1817, one of the final matters Tallmadge undertook as a congressman before leaving office was to campaign against granting a pension to the three men (John Paulding, Isaac Van Wart, and David Williams) who first captured John André. According to a popular weekly circular of the time, Tallmadge argued that the men were hardly heroes, despite their public image, but were, in fact, "of that class of people who passed between both armies, as often in one camp as in the other." His objection was rooted in the fact that "when Major André's boots were taken off by them, it was to search for plunder, and not to detect treason. . . . If André could have given to these men the amount they demanded for his release, he never would have been hung for a spy, nor in captivity." Tallmadge died on March 7, 1835. He was eighty-one years old.

Robert Townsend never spoke of his service, never applied for a pension, never corrected those who assumed he had done nothing but tend his shop during the war, and never, it seems, recovered emotionally from the blow of Agent 355's capture and imprisonment. After the war he grew even more reserved and reclusive. Dr. Peter Townsend, the son of his brother Solomon, took a particular interest in his somber, silent uncle Robert and often asked him about his service during the war, but the older man was tight-lipped and shared very little. Townsend kept to himself, staying near his brothers and their families but never marrying himself, though he may have fathered a child with his French-Canadian housekeeper in the years following the war. The child—a large, blond, blue-eyed boy who resembled all the Townsend men except the slender, dark Robert—was named Robert Townsend Jr. by his mother, Mary. There was some suspicion that another Townsend brother, the flirtatious William, the "flower of the family," who happened at that time to share a house with Robert, was actually the father. But Robert, having no other children, took responsibility for the boy's education and welfare; his will includes bequests for his supposed son, several nephews, and a niece. Townsend developed strong abolitionist beliefs and staunchly opposed any type of slave ownership; later in life he worked on behalf of some former slaves of his father's to help them gain their freedom. The man once known as Culper Junior died exactly three years after Benjamin Tallmadge, on March 7, 1838, at the age of eighty-four.

Abraham Woodhull married Mary Smith in 1781. He spent the rest of his life in Setauket, where he raised three children and served in roles of authority in the Suffolk County government. He never spoke much about his role in the spy ring. Mary died before Abraham; Lydia Terry became his second wife in his final years. He passed away on January 23, 1826, and was buried in the Setauket Presbyterian Church graveyard. In 1936, the Mayflower Chapter of the Daughters of the American Revolution erected the following marker near his simple headstone:

> *Friend and confidant of George Washington, Head of the Long Island Secret Service During the American Revolution he operated under the alias Samuel Culper, Sr. To him and his associates have been credited a large share of the success of the Army of the Revolution. Born in Setauket Oct. 7, 1750 in the original Woodhull homestead, son of Richard W. & Margaret Smith. Fifth generation from Richard Woodhull, the original grantee of a large portion of Brookhaven Town. He was a Presbyterian, occupying a "Pew of Authority" in the old church and doing*

much toward the building of the new church. He was a man of integrity punctual and precise in his business relations. He freed his slaves long before they were legally free. He filled numerous important positions being Magistrate in Setauket many years, Judge of the Court of Common Pleas 1793–1799, First Judge of Suffolk Co. from 1799–1810.

Agent 355, whose name and whose fate have both been lost to time, might have escaped imprisonment and gone on to live a long and happy life. Or she might have passed away somewhere in the dark, disease-infested hull of HMS *Jersey*. When the British left New York in November 1783, they abandoned the *Jersey* in the harbor, with several thousand starving prisoners still on board.

It is extremely difficult to learn much at all about the lives and deaths of those unlucky enough to have been captured. After the surrender of the British, the former colonists sought to piece together their shattered lives and homes; many records were lost, destroyed, or simply filed away without any thought to their deeper significance. Thousands of individuals were missing from battlefields, prison camps, and prison ships; thousands more were untraceable due to emigration, desertion, or simply westward movement into the newly opened territories beyond the Appalachians. In the mid-nineteenth century, as the generation who lived during the Revolution was passing away, historians made some efforts to reconstruct lists of inmates' names by interviewing survivors of the *Jersey*. Though quite rare (and, since they were recalled several decades after the fact, not wholly reliable accounts), women's names do appear on some of these lists; none have yet been proved to be that of Agent 355.

For generations, the only Revolutionary War spy immortalized in history books was the brave but ultimately unsuccessful Nathan Hale. Tales of the Culper Ring were relegated to local legend or mystery (who was Culper Junior?). Learning the true identity of Washington's most consistent and valuable spy in the one city the general valued most was a pursuit undertaken by several prominent researchers, who analyzed the oral traditions and followed up on hunches. Townsend was always among those considered likely contenders, but the spy could not be unmasked until the "wagon full" of his letters was found in 1929 and given over to the care of Morton Pennypacker, who compared the writing with that of surviving Culper letters. At last a much more complete story of the ring could be told.

This momentous discovery was made during a dark and uncertain time in American history. The Great Depression threatened the very fabric of the nation, then all eyes were focused on the upheaval in Europe and the creeping threat in the Pacific. The United States was poised at the brink of its next great chapter and was not concerned with rewriting history. Despite Pennypacker's efforts to shine a light on these provincial heroes of Long Island, Manhattan, and coastal Connecticut, the Culpers once again sank into obscurity. But even if their story was not known across the nation, the fruits of their labors, their letters, and their lives were—and continue to be—felt from sea to shining sea in the freedoms and independence all American citizens enjoy.

Epilogue

We knew the story of the Culper Ring was important. We knew it was a story whose characters and events should be standard fare in history classes across the country. But what we didn't know was how relevant it still proves today within the intelligence community of the United States.

In February 2012, we were granted access to CIA Headquarters in Langley, Virginia, where we met with the agency's chief historian.

Outside the building is a statue honoring Nathan Hale's courage and patriotism; inside the building are exhibits on various spying operations of the past. But nowhere did we find homage to the Culper Ring—until we sat down for our meeting.

We were stunned to learn that the history of the ring is taught as part of the introductory training for new agents. Whether suggested by Washington or Tallmadge, or simply figured out, through bravery and intelligence, on their own, the methods used by these citizen-spies—the dead drops, the well-crafted backstories, the compartmentalizing of intelligence, the secret encrypted code—are many of the same methods still used today by secret agents the world over.

And like the courageous men and women of our modern covert services, the Culpers worked in profound secrecy. They never sought credit, never received accolades, and never revealed the risks they took or the sacrifices they made to serve our country. Under the unblinking leadership of Benjamin Tallmadge, Washington's secret six served a newborn nation against a military that was considered to be unbeatable. The observation of Major George Beckwith bears repeating: "Washington did not really outfight the British, he simply outspied us!"

In this book, we have included photographs of some of the places, portraits, and humble graves that bear silent testimony to our nation's first and most accomplished ring of clandestine operatives.

There are no statues of these brave souls, whose feats should earn them a place of honor alongside the heroes of the Revolution. It is our sincerest hope that Robert Townsend, Abraham Woodhull, Caleb Brewster, Austin Roe, James Rivington, and Agent 355 will be given their rightful place in American history. Their extraordinary heroism and patriotism, unknown to their contemporaries, should not be forgotten. George Washington wouldn't have wanted it any other way—after all, he preserved their letters among his belongings, and it is because of him that we know their story.

AFTERWORD TO THE PAPERBACK EDITION

Who Was Agent 355?

The greatest mystery surrounding the Culper Ring is the identity of Agent 355, the "lady who would outwit them all." Woodhull wrote of her but left no hints to her name. Robert Townsend deeply mourned her capture, closing his store for several weeks and falling into a deep depression, but he maintained secrecy even in his sorrow. No matter the pressure, the Culper Ring's protection of the sixth spy's name was watertight.

Since *George Washington's Secret Six* was first published in November 2013, we have received dozens of letters proposing theories of 355's identity. Readers told us of family lore connecting their relatives to 355. Some historians proposed names of women they believed may have been 355, while others argued that 355 was a composite of several women. Still others insisted that there was no 355 at all—that the line in Woodhull's letter was just a passing reference to a woman who had useful information but was not formally connected to the ring.

Inspired by readers' enthusiasm and by our own conviction that Agent 355 should not go unrecognized, we decided to dig deeper into our leads. After several false starts, we found seven women whose stories line up at least partially with our understanding of 355's story. Each of the seven candidates has evidence in her favor: she had proximity to known members of the Culper Ring, she had access to British information, she was known to have participated in espionage, or there is written or oral tradition testifying to her involvement. Yet each also has arguments against her: she wasn't present in New York for the entire war, her connections to the ring are tenuous or circumstantial at best, or her loyalties are questionable. Until further clues come to light, the mystery will remain, but in the meantime we present the seven most promising women our research has uncovered and leave it up to the readers to make up their own minds.

ANNA SMITH STRONG

The most enduring name in the running is Anna Smith Strong, a candidate whom we initially dismissed. However, several local legends tie her to the Culper Ring, so we decided to give her a closer look.

Anna was the daughter of New York's Chief Justice of the Supreme Court, and she was the wife of Selah Strong, a Patriot judge from Long Island who was imprisoned by the British in 1778. While some traditions state that Selah was held aboard one of New York's infamous prison ships, an article in Rivington's *Gazette* indicates that Strong was actually held in one of the "sugar house" prisons established by the British in Manhattan's sugar warehouses. Either way, he easily could have been known to members of the Culper Ring.

A tremendously resourceful and determined woman, Anna brought her husband's plight to the attention of her friends and family, hoping someone might be able to help secure his freedom.

Ultimately, her resilience paid off, and Judge Strong was released and allowed to travel to American-controlled Connecticut. Meanwhile, Anna remained on Long Island, maintaining the family's estate so that the British troops could not declare it abandoned and confiscate it, which would have left her family destitute.

Eventually, enemy soldiers commandeered the Strong's home, but Anna and her children were permitted to reside in a small cottage on their land where they remained until the British left Long Island and the home was restored to them. Selah, too, was able to return to his wife and children following the cessation of hostilities.

The oral traditions linking Anna to the Culper Ring are at least a century old and revolve around rumors that she used the sheets on her clothesline to signal to Caleb Brewster in which cove he could safely land his whaleboat. The elevation and position of the Strongs' home make the story seem likely, as it offered a clear view of Long Island Sound. From there, anyone could easily track the movement of British patrol boats—exactly what the Culpers would have wanted to do.

Anna's bravery and dogged determination in the face of British oppression demonstrate she had the mettle for espionage. She also had a strong motive to bring about the defeat of the army that had torn apart her family. Add to that her location on Long Island, and she fits Agent 355's profile well.

Motive and location aside, however, there are several arguments against Anna's role as 355. First, the Strong family was determined to keep its land and property safe from the Crown's claims, which is why Anna and her children remained on Long Island rather than joining Selah in his exile in Connecticut. Anna probably would have avoided doing anything to threaten her already-tenuous legal status in British-occupied New York, as being caught spying (at best) would have landed her in prison and (at worst) would have seen her executed. Either way, her arrest would have left her children parentless, unless Selah could have convinced British authorities to safely transport them to American-controlled territory, and the family's possessions would have been lost because they no longer retained a foothold on the land.

For similar reasons, Anna probably would have avoided the social scene (and thus the potential gossip) of New York or any other town outside her immediate area. Had she ventured far from home, the British could have seized her land and brought all her efforts to naught. Thus, her pool of information would have been limited to the region that Woodhull, Roe, and Brewster already covered for the Culpers.

Finally, since her husband was already a known dissident working actively against the British, the Strong family was under close observation by the Crown. If she knew that she was being watched, it is unlikely (though, admittedly, not impossible) that she would have risked drawing attention to herself by changing where or how she hung her laundry or carried out any other household tasks. It is possible that she was brave (or foolish) enough to ignore these dangers and spy against the British, but such recklessness would have been surprising for the Culpers.

SALLY TOWNSEND

Another woman linked to the Culper Ring through popular oral tradition is Sally Townsend, the younger sister of Robert and the object of Colonel Simcoe's affections during his stay at Raynham Hall.

Born in 1760, Sally was eighteen when the Queen's Rangers took up residence in her family's Oyster Bay home in 1778. With their older brothers settled in homes of their own, only the Townsend daughters, Sally and Phebe, were left behind to help their parents serve the soldiers who had invited themselves to set up headquarters under the family's roof. Both girls quickly became favorites among the young men, with Sally capturing the attention and the heart of the Colonel, who wrote a lengthy, thirteen-stanza poem in her honor, beginning:

Fairest Maid, where all is fair
Beauty's pride and Nature's care;
To you my heart I must resign
O choose me for your Valentine!

Given Simcoe's affection for her and her proximity to the British troops in her home, Sally would have had every chance to learn British plans. There is a tradition, in fact, that Sally was about to serve the troops a plate of donuts when she overhead Simcoe discussing the plans to take over West Point thanks to Benedict Arnold's treachery. The story has it that she rushed to get word to her brother in Manhattan immediately so that he could alert Tallmadge and General Washington.

Unfortunately, it is unlikely that the incident with the donuts ever took place, since the tale does not seem to have come into existence until more than a century after the alleged events. The timeline is also off; the Rangers left the Townsend home in the spring of 1779, and the betrayal at West Point did not occur until September of the following year—and there is no record that Simcoe ever made an effort to correspond with Sally after his troops left Raynham Hall.

Further, while her father and brothers were Patriots, there is no reason to believe that Sally objected to the presence of British soldiers in the house. Instead, it seems that both she and Phebe enjoyed the situation, and Sally may have returned Simcoe's affection. She kept Simcoe's valentine until the day she died, and there is a window etching made by one of the soldiers in the original glass of the house that reads, "To the adorable Miss Sally Sarah Townsend." Simcoe and his Rangers left Raynham Hall after their six-month stay, and Sally, who never married, died in 1842, at the age of 82. If she did love the British officer, it's doubtful she would have worked against him.

MARY UNDERHILL

Mary Woodhull Underhill, the older sister of Abraham Woodhull, is another Culper sister linked to the ring. Married shortly before the war started, she and her husband moved to New York City to operate a boarding house on Queen Street in downtown Manhattan, which they maintained during the course of the war.

As Abraham Woodhull's sister, Mary could easily have held the trust of the ring. Her brother often stayed at the Underhills' boarding house, as did Austin Roe and Caleb Brewster on occasion, so Mary would have known the Culpers well and would have had opportunities to pass on information. Her husband, Amos, is said to have functioned as a satellite member of the ring—most likely acting as a courier—so Mary's involvement with the ring seems even more plausible.

However, the case against Mary is threefold. First, an emotional objection: Abraham Woodhull's letters often mentioned his fear of being caught, and it is hard to picture a man so anxious about his own spying recruiting his family to join him in such a dangerous task. Involving Mary would have increased the possibility of suspicion falling upon the family—especially following the severe beating that Colonel Simcoe inflicted upon Abraham and Mary's father, Richard Woodhull, in the spring of 1779. Then again, if Amos was already a spy, this objection is weak.

Second, there is a practical objection. The Underhills made their living by running a boarding house that would have provided temporary shelter for travelers or visitors to the city, not to soldiers who were stationed there. While it may have seemed a prime location to hear gossip and rumors, the boarding house was probably not frequented by soldiers or locals who were the more likely sources of useful information about the goings-on in the city.

Finally, while there are indications that Amos may have been involved with some minor operations during the early months of the ring's existence, there is no indication that Woodhull nor Townsend ever fully initiated Amos or Mary into the ring (after all, Amos doesn't have a covert name or numeric assignment in the code). And if Mary Woodhull Underhill was indeed Agent 355, why would it have been Townsend rather than Woodhull who would have been the most distraught following what seems to have been her capture after the Arnold affair was unmasked? Mary could have been 355, but there are too many questions about her involvement to know for sure.

BETTY FLOYD

Robert Townsend's distant cousin Elizabeth Floyd was born in August 1758 on Long Island. Little is known of her other than that she was a niece of William Floyd, a signer of the Declaration of Independence, but her familial ties to Townsend coupled with the possibility that she may have died aboard a British prison ship brought her name to our attention.

Though the official record books for the British prison ship HMS *Jersey* have been lost, in 1888 the Brooklyn Historical Society compiled a list of prisoners based upon prisoners' diaries, family lore, and some loosely kept records from the British War Department. Of the eight thousand names listed, only about two dozen belong to women or are androgynous, and a "Betty Floyd" appeared among them. She was listed as having died aboard the prison ship, making her a likely match for Agent 355. (The other names have proven untraceable or are connected with women who appear to be wholly unaffiliated with the Culpers.)

Unfortunately, the case for Betty is inconclusive. First, it is possible that the "Betty" listed in the prison ship records is an error. Some versions of the *Jersey* prisoner list have only a "Barry" or "Berry" Floyd, and no "Betty" or any other derivatives of "Elizabeth" paired with the same last name. And since the lists were compiled more than a century after the events occurred, their reliability as historical documents is questionable.

Even if a Betty Floyd did die on the *Jersey*, we cannot conclusively link her to the Culpers. "Elizabeth Floyd" was a quite common name at the time, and there were several women with that name living on Long Island and in New York City during the revolution, making a positive identification of the right Betty difficult. Further, the most likely Elizabeth Floyd we could find (the one who came from a Patriot family and had family connections to Robert Townsend) died in 1820 at the age of 62, which means that she could not be the same woman who died aboard a British prison ship in New York Harbor.

We can't find records of a woman named Elizabeth or Betty Floyd living in New York City or on Long Island who died at the time when the *Jersey* was being used as a prison ship. It's possible that an unknown and undocumented Betty was indeed 355 and died on the ship, but if that is the case, her story is lost to time.

PEGGY SHIPPEN ARNOLD

One surprising name as a possible Agent 355 is Peggy Shippen Arnold, Benedict Arnold's second wife. Despite her marriage to the traitor, she was a socialite with strong Loyalist connections and a close relationship with John André. Considering her friendship with British officers, the deep secrecy surrounding her identity as 355 would be understandable.

Though Peggy came from a Loyalist family, her father, Edward Shippen, IV, held moderate views and occasionally took the Patriots' side in the years leading up to the Revolution. On September 10, 1765, in the midst of the Stamp Act controversy, Edward wrote to his father in England: "I think the Act an oppressive one, and I wish a Scheme for Repeal of it could be fallen on[.]" Five weeks later, on October 17, he wrote about the recent arrival of a baby boy, noting: "On the 9th Inst. Peggy [Edward's wife and Peggy's mother] presented me with a son, born just in time enough to breath [sic] about three weeks the Air of Freedom; for after the first of November we may call ourselves the Slaves of England."

Edward's moderate views seem to have persisted at least through the years just before the outbreak of war. George Washington was even a dinner guest at the Shippen family table in late September 1774 during the First Continental Congress in Philadelphia. The future Mrs. Arnold, who was fifteen at the time, later wrote that "nobody in America could revere his character more than I did." In the end, however, having been educated in Britain and retaining strong ties to his family there, Edward remained true to King George and fixed himself as a solid Loyalist.

Peggy's early inclinations to the American cause might seem negated by her later stance, but there is more to the story, according to her family. From the mid-nineteenth through the early twentieth century, the Shippen family argued that Peggy was innocent of treason, claiming Washington was impressed by her hysterical response to the news of her husband's treachery and had believed in her innocence. As evidence, they pointed out that Washington made special provisions for Peggy's safe passage back to her father's home, an unlikely course of action if he considered her a traitor.

The family also argued that Aaron Burr, whose memoirs are the main source for the stories of Peggy's actions following the discovery of her husband's treason, was a tainted witness. A rather dubious figure in American history, Burr is famous for having killed Secretary of the Treasury Alexander Hamilton in an ill-fated duel and was a famed ladies' man. The Shippens argued that Peggy had scorned his advances when he escorted her to the family's home in Philadelphia following Arnold's defection and that Burr made the accusations as retribution.

If this revisionist account is true and it clears Peggy's name, her position with the British army supports arguments that she was an American spy. The letters and parcels she conveyed between British soldiers and their sweethearts could have been cover for her spying activities with the Culpers. She was known and respected by André and could have learned of his movements and intentions. Her marriage to a respected (if unpopular) senior officer in the Continental Army would have given the Culpers and even General Washington himself every reason to trust her. Her social position, acquaintances, and allegiances through marriage gave her the perfect cover to convey sensitive information to Tallmadge and, from him, to Washington.

We'd love nothing more than to reveal that the wife of Benedict Arnold secretly worked against his schemes, but the evidence against Peggy still seems insurmountable. A number of letters between Benedict Arnold, John André, and General Henry Clinton indicate that the planned betrayal was well known to all the players, including Peggy. And letters between Benedict and Peggy indicate that Peggy was the more powerful member of the couple; Arnold would have done just about anything to please her. If Peggy was truly a Patriot, it is highly unlikely that Arnold—who always seemed to fear that she would leave him for someone younger, more powerful, or richer—would have switched sides and risked alienating her.

The Shippen family's accusations of Burr came years after Peggy's death, and there is no other evidence that Burr made any kind of a "pass" at Peggy or that he lied about her behavior and confession. In fact, Burr was loyal to the Shippen family, having stayed with Peggy's parents for a few months during his childhood after the death of his own parents, and he always spoke of their kind treatment of him in grateful and glowing terms. Unless new information comes to light, Peggy's name remains tainted, and her role as 355 seems highly unlikely.

SARAH HORTON TOWNSEND

One of the most intriguing possible identities of Agent 355 is Sarah Horton Townsend, the wife of Robert Townsend's cousin Samuel.

Records indicate that Samuel and Sarah lived in Norwich, NY, but it is unclear whether those records refer to the Norwich in Chenango County, some 215 miles from Oyster Bay, or the village of East Norwich, a mere four miles south of Oyster Bay. If it is the latter, which seems more likely because of their family ties, Samuel and Sarah would have been perfectly situated to help the Culpers.

During the war, Samuel served as a captain in the Continental Army. He was taken captive by the British during the late spring or summer of 1782 and held in Provost Prison, on the site of what is now City Hall Park in downtown Manhattan. By that time, the couple had a daughter named Sarah (born in December 1779), and in early August 1782 Samuel wrote to his wife with longing for his young family even as he voiced frustration at the delays in securing his release:

> *Hope my friends in the country have not forgot me. I would not wish to entertain a thought but they will use their endeavors to procure my exchange, but must confess I am at a loss for the reason that that has not been done before this time. I have repeatedly been informed that there are a number of prisoners at West Point, Peekskill, and Poughkeepsie, for whom, possibly, I could have been exchanged before this time, if properly attended to. My best respects to all friends . . . and beg that they would, without delay, apply in my behalf to their Excellencies General Washington and Governor Clinton, which I have no doubt will have the desired effect. However, as the fortune of war brought me here, I hope you will make yourself as easy as possible under present difficulties, as I am determined patiently to wait the wished-for day when I may enjoy the happiness of being present with my family.*

Though Samuel's capture and imprisonment is about a year and a half too late to be one of the arrests following the Culpers's unmasking of Arnold, his release raises the possibility of a different connection to the ring. Not only did George Washington orchestrate Townsend's release, but also a letter written by Townsend to his wife was preserved among Washington's papers at his headquarters in Newburgh, New York. Washington's attention to Townsend's case indicates that Sarah had an avenue directly to the commander-in-chief's ear. If she was indeed spying for Washington, Tallmadge might have been willing to bring her petition on her husband's behalf before Washington, who would have owed debt of gratitude for her work and intervened accordingly.

Sarah has proximity, a connection to the Culpers, and a service from Washington in her favor, but there is one factor that weighs against her: She would have been five months pregnant in mid-August of 1779 when Woodhull made mention of the enigmatic "lady." Five months into their pregnancies, many middle- and upper-class women in the eighteenth century were preparing to enter into what was commonly referred to as their "confinement"—a period before they gave birth when they would not attend any social gatherings nor be seen in public at all, if it could be avoided. Sarah's pregnancy probably would have removed her from most sources of sensitive information, making it difficult for her to help the Culpers. She may have found a way to glean information from other women, but the danger of doing so makes her role as a spy seem unlikely.

ELIZABETH BURGIN

The woman with the most compelling story is Elizabeth Burgin (or "Bergin" in some records). A widow with three young children in British-occupied New York, she devoted much of her time ministering to the needs of the American prisoners languishing in the squalor of the prison ships in New York Harbor. Most of the prisoners' food, blankets, clothing, or medicine had to be privately supplied by family members, religious figures, or benevolent patrons, and Burgin helped to provide these supplies. But that is not all she did.

Unbeknownst to the British, Burgin worked with a man named George Higday to help smuggle prisoners off the ships to freedom. No one knows exactly how the escapes were planned and carried out, and since the prison hulks were generally treated as floating rubbish bins where people were forgotten, there was no systematic record keeping to alert the British to the dwindling number of prisoners. All told, Higday and Burgin succeeded in smuggling more than two hundred American prisoners to safety before their activities were discovered.

In a letter dated June 27, 1779, George Washington wrote to Benjamin Tallmadge about the possibility of incorporating George Higday into the Culper Ring. Unfortunately, this letter, which mentioned Higday by name and was written in regular (rather than invisible) ink, was captured along with Tallmadge's horse by the British on July 2. Higday's house was raided on July 13 and his wife (probably in the hopes of obtaining a lighter sentence for her husband) offered up the name "Elizabeth Burgin" as a possible spy and confirmed prisoner smuggler. When the British followed up on the tip and found that a large number of Americans were missing from the prison hulks, they set out to bring Elizabeth in for questioning on July 17—but she was nowhere to be found. Major General James Pattinson announced a £200 reward for her capture, but by then she had managed to flee from Manhattan to Long Island.

It is not known where she stayed on Long Island, but she remained in hiding there for four to six weeks with some trusted and sympathetic friends who were familiar with the work she and Higday had accomplished. By early September she had made her way across the sound to Connecticut in a whaleboat piloted by a man named William Sherridon, who followed a route that Caleb Brewster had used. "I made my escape with him, we being chased by two boats halfway to the Sound, then got to New England," she later wrote.

From Connecticut, she made her way to newly-liberated Philadelphia and began two petitions. The first was to the British to allow her re-admittance to New York to retrieve her children, who had been presumably left in the care of friends as she fled. This was swiftly granted, and in late September or early October she traveled under a flag of truce to New York City to pick up her children, and the reunited family then traveled back to Philadelphia together. They were forced to abandon all their property and belongings, which meant that the Burgins arrived in Philadelphia nearly destitute—but with their lives.

It was then that Elizabeth Burgin launched her other petition: She appealed to lawmakers for a pension to help support her family, as she was not eligible for either a soldier's pension (as she had never served) or the war widows' pension. On November 19, 1779 she wrote to the commander-in-chief directly, outlining both her service to the country and her family's need. Five weeks later, on Christmas Day, Washington gave orders to the ration master in Philadelphia that Elizabeth and her children should be allowed to draw upon the stores for supplies, which greatly relieved the family's distress but still left her a refugee with a bounty on her head and with three children to support in a time and place that did not look kindly on women working outside the home.

In July 1781, she wrote another letter explaining that she was encountering difficulties in receiving the rations for which Washington had approved her. She asked for a job as a seamstress for the Continental Army to help support herself and her children; instead, the following month, Congress approved a measure that would grant her a pension for life in the total of $53.30 per year. She was one of a very small number of women granted a pension from the government, and records indicate that she continued to receive the annuity through at least 1787, though nothing is known of her life or death beyond that point.

The evidence in favor of Burgin as Agent 355 is, as with all other contenders, circumstantial, at best. However, several facts make a compelling case for her being 355.

First and foremost, there is a clear connection between Burgin and Higday, and between Higday and the Culpers. Additionally, Burgin's work liberating more than two hundred prisoners establishes her identity as a risk-taker and wildly successful covert agent; surely a little spying work would be a small danger after what she had already accomplished.

Also of significance is the timeline of events. Burgin fled Manhattan on or around July 17, 1779, and stayed on Long Island for at least a month. The letter in which Woodhull writes about 355 in such glowing terms, bragging that she will "outwit them all" is dated August 15, 1779—during the period in which Burgin was known to be hiding on Long Island and possibly making the acquaintance of members of the Culper Ring.

Finally, it is important to note that the news regarding the stolen currency plates and paper in Philadelphia that were intended to be used in a forgery ring in New York (as recounted in chapter 9) came out in late November of 1779—not long after Burgin and her family were settled in Philadelphia. Perhaps it was she who first caught wind of the story of the theft and alerted the Culpers to be on the lookout for any news that might indicate the intended destination and plans for the stolen goods.

There are some obstacles to establishing Burgin's identity as the female member of the Culper Ring, however. There is no evidence that Burgin ever returned to New York after she retrieved her children in the fall of 1779, and any information regarding the situation in Manhattan and the troops stationed there (especially John André) in 1780 would almost certainly have come from a resident of the city rather than someone living elsewhere. This absence of evidence does not prove that she was not in New York or did not have some other means of accessing sensitive information, but it makes her case inconclusive.

THE MYSTERY PERSISTS

It is a testimony to the effectiveness of the Culpers as covert agents that so few clues exist as to Agent 355's identity. Each candidate we have found fits one or two parts of the puzzle (e.g., a relationship with André or with one of the Culpers; a proven history of covert activity) but falls short in another aspect (e.g., she is not known to have been in New York at the right times; she would not have had the social connections required to gain the information). Further, there is no evidence that any of our possible candidates, besides the enigmatic Betty Floyd, were ever captured by the British.

Who was Agent 355? There are several possible conclusions. We may be missing information about one of the women profiled that would prove she was 355. Another woman, completely unknown at this point, may have been the spy. Or, 355 may not have existed as an individual—several women may have operated under the code name. The one conclusion that is *not* possible is that 355 does not matter. Even if she did not exist as one person, several women risked their lives to serve, and one unknown friend of the ring *was* imprisoned following the unmasking of Arnold's treachery. That heroism deserves to be honored.

We care about 355's story not only because we enjoy a good mystery but also because we still believe she was a real, living and breathing woman who sacrificed her safety—and maybe even her life—for the sake of our country. We want to learn not just who she was but what she did—and what happened to her as a result. Our research remains inconclusive, but we're hopeful that one day another Morton Pennypacker will find a new cache of letters revealing the identity of the six's most secret spy. Only when we know can we pay her the honor she deserves.

ACKNOWLEDGMENTS

There are so many great people responsible for the completion of this book. I urge you to read what follows and take note of them all. First, I must thank my longtime friend Bruce Stegner, whom I informed of this ring in 1988; he held on to the concept and has relentlessly researched the secret six ever since, unwavering in the belief that this story just had to be told to a larger audience. And thanks to our respective families—Renee, Rebecca, Olivia, and Julia Stegner; my wife, Dawn, Bryan, Kirstyn, and Kaitlyn Kilmeade; and Jeanette, Will, and Madeleine Yaeger—for indulging our excitement about the story and mirroring our enthusiasm as every aspect of the ring was brought to light and life.

Thanks to the brilliant Tiffany Yecke Brooks, without whom we could not have researched and written this project. Tiffany has worked with Don for years but absolutely fell into her sweet spot on this book, because it combined her passion for historical research with creative writing. She kept both of us on task.

Roger Ailes, who allows me to work at the most patriotic company in America, is due a tremendous amount of thanks. He underlined the need for all of us to know our history and recognize the incredible bravery and selflessness of the first generations of Americans, which are demonstrated in the story of the six brave individuals who made up America's first spy ring.

Of course, this book could not have been written without the guidance of all-star Fox VP Bill Shine, a Long Islander who is endlessly supportive and understands the significance of the story because it happened in his backyard. We also owe a salute to Diane Brandi, who was the first to hear the book pitch; without her guidance and support the project would never gotten done.

I must also salute my *Fox & Friends* cohosts, Steve Doocy, Gretchen Carlson, and Alisyn Camerota, who have heard me talk about this story for years and could not have been more supportive. Thanks for stepping up to help me during her free time go to Alyson Mansfield, executive producer of *Kilmeade & Friends.* I also can't say enough for the producing team on *Fox & Friends,* led by Lauren Petterson and Jennifer Rauchet, for their faith in the project before they read even a word on paper.

To Bob Barnett, who believed in the project so much that he wisely navigated us to the Sentinel imprint of the Penguin Group to see it through—thank you. We are in awe of his perpetually sunny, upbeat approach to life and humbled by his loyalty to us even as he handles the most famous and powerful people in the world.

Don and I were truly thrilled and moved to know that Adrian Zackheim, president and publisher of Sentinel, would be editing the book, and it flowered under his skilled eye. And what can we say about Bria Sandford that would be sufficient thanks for her role, except that she is a true professional in every way, thrives on making deadlines happen, is endlessly patient, and is extremely bright? To say that she was kind of important to this project would be like saying that LeBron James is kind of important to the Miami Heat.

Over the twenty-plus years that I have spent learning about this story, many passionate people and organizations have shared with me their hard-earned knowledge and research of the ring and these historical figures. I fear I might leave someone out, but here it goes nonetheless.

Steve Russell Boerner of the East Hampton Library Long Island Collection offered patience and insight that were critical in so many ways to the success of the book. Gina Piastuck and Frank Sorrentino from the collection brought Morton Pennypacker back to life, and thanks to Frank's rapid translation of the Woodhull-Townsend logs, we were able to break much new ground on this story. Thanks to Andrea Meyer and John Burke for thier work on Agent 355. And the good people at Black Rock history in Connecticut were a great resource for our Caleb Brewster research.

The invaluable John Tsunis not only gave us a conference room at his Holiday Inn to hold a major secret six summit with historians from around Long Island but also introduced me to Gloria Rocchio and the Ward Melville Heritage Organization. Gloria shed light on many aspects of this story and has been a stalwart in supporting the legacy of the ring and preserving Long Island history. She has been not only a great help but also a great friend. Michael Colucci and Deborah Boudreau, also part of the Ward Melville group, were a tremendous source of assistance and encouragement.

We could not have seen this project through without the cooperation and help of the people of the Raynham Hall Museum in Oyster Bay. Claire Bellerjeau, Townsend family historian, is one of the most knowledgeable people you will meet on the era and the ring; her knowledge and enthusiasm were essential in making Robert Townsend and the rest of his family come alive on these pages. Collections manager Nicole Menchise and executive director Harriet Gerard Clark could not have been more helpful or insightful. They allowed us to walk the house as Robert Townsend did centuries ago, fueling our motivation to spread this story to millions more.

I could not imagine carrying out this project without Barbara Russell, town of Brookhaven historian. She not only educated me about the Setauket spies of 1780 but also brought me to the locations as they stand today. Elizabeth Kahn Kaplan helped me not only with the story but also, as curator of the Three Village Historical Society's exhibit, got my family excited with her tremendous knowledge and passion. If you truly want to understand how special this revolutionary spy story is, just spend a few minutes with Bev Tyler. He has an awe-inspiring depth of knowledge on the topic and played a key role in acquiring many of the sketches and maps you see in the book.

Special thanks are due, too, to Matt Arthur, Living History Program coordinator at Tryon Palace Historic Sites and Gardens in New Bern, North Carolina, and to Rebecca Reimer Arthur, lecturer in history at Liberty University, for sharing their tremendous knowledge of the era and genealogical investigations during the early stages of writing this book.

If there was one trip that galvanized our belief that this was a book that should be written, it was the journey we took to CIA Headquarters in Langley, Virginia. When we heard the CIA's historians and agents talk so movingly about the success of this ring and its methods, we knew that our interest and awe were justified. At their request I will not list their names, but I would like to acknowledge the CIA Office of Public Affairs and the CIA's historical staff.

Finally, I'd like to thank the CIA Officers Memorial Foundation (www.ciamemorialfoundation.org), the Armed Forces Foundation (www.armedforcesfoundation.org), and the Wounded Warrior Project (www.woundedwarriorproject.org) for their support for today's generation of fighters and spies, which needs support more than ever before.

SELECTED SOURCES

Allen, Thomas B., and Cheryl Harness. *George Washington, Spymaster: How America Outspied the British and Won the Revolutionary War.* Washington, D.C.: National Geographic, 2004.

A highly accessible book, this is a great starting point for adults and older children alike who are interested in the spying activities under Washington's command during the Revolution. It is the result of solid research and offers a good overview of espionage activities throughout the war.

Bakeless, John Edwin. *Turncoats, Traitors, and Heroes.* New York: Da Capo, 1998.

This work provides a look at the unfortunate incident of Nathan Hale, the saga of Benedict Arnold's treachery, and many other covert operations in the American theater during the war, including the incredible adventure of John Champe and his attempt to kidnap Arnold back for the Patriots.

Baker, William S. "Itinerary of General Washington from June 15, 1775, to December 23, 1783." *The Pennsylvania Magazine of History and Biography* 15, no. 1 (1891): 41–87. http://jstor.org.

Crary, Catherine Snell. "The Tory and the Spy: The Double Life of James Rivington," *The William and Mary Quarterly*, 3rd ser., 16, no. 1 (January 1959): 61–72. Accessed online March 22, 2013.

This article pulls together a number of primary sources that shed light on Rivington's spying activities, including his contribution to the victory at Yorktown, that were previously discounted as apocryphal, and therefore unreliable, by many historians.

Fernow, Brian, ed. *Documents Relating to the Colonial History of the State of New York*. Vol. 15. *State Archives*, vol. 1. Albany, NY: Weed, Parsons and Company, 1887.

"George Washington and the Culper Spy Ring." Stony Brook University Libraries. http://guides.library.stonybrook.edu/culper-spy-ring.

Kerber, Linda K. *Women of the Republic: Intellect and Ideology in Revolutionary America*. Chapel Hill: University of North Carolina Press, 1997.

Macy, Harry, Jr. "Robert Townsend, Jr., of New York City." *The New York Genealogical and Biographical Record* 126 (1995): 25–34, 108–12, 192–98.

Perhaps more than any other single source, this article shed light on the physical appearance and relationships of the Townsend family and also offered an in-depth look at Robert Townsend and his interaction with the child named Robert Townsend Jr. after the war.

Nagy, John A. *Invisible Ink: Spycraft of the American Revolution*. Yardley, PA: Westholme, 2010.

Nagy has compiled a searching and fascinating examination of various techniques used by spies throughout the American colonies and abroad to communicate covertly. His exploration of the history of invisible ink prior to the Culper stain's development by Sir James Jay, as well as the use of that particular formula, was tremendously helpful for this book.

——. *Spies in the Continental Capital: Espionage Across Pennsylvania During the American Revolution*. Yardley, PA: Westholme, 2011.

***New York Gazette & Weekly*. Templeton & Stewart. April 25, 1774. Mercury issue 1174, p. 2.**

——. Templeton & Stewart. August 15, 1774. Mercury issue 1192, p. 4.

——. Templeton & Stewart. February 27, 1775. Mercury issue 1220, p. 3.

Norton, Mary Beth. *Liberty's Daughters: The Revolutionary Experience of American Women, 1750–1800*. Ithaca, NY: Cornell University Press, 1996.

A fascinating compilation of primary sources, this book offers valuable insight into the challenges and perils of women living in war-torn areas during the Revolution, including the lighthearted letter from Lord Rawdon about the outbreak of sexual assaults against ladies in British-occupied Staten Island.

Paul, Joel Richard. *Unlikely Allies: How a Merchant, a Playwright, and a Spy Saved the American Revolution*. New York: Riverhead, 2009.

A detailed account of the covert activities of the French government via the fabricated Roderigue Hortalez & Company, Paul's research offers a dynamic and intriguing reconstruction of the events leading up to, and resulting from, the smuggling efforts.

Pennypacker, Morton. ***General Washington's Spies.*** **Walnut Creek, CA: Aegean Park, 1999.**

Pennypacker's 1939 publication of the Culper letters includes a narrative of many of the events involving the ring, as they were known at the time, as well as both transcripts and photographs of many of the original letters exchanged between several of the ring's members, Tallmadge, and Washington. It was absolutely invaluable not only to the composition of this book but also to understanding the Culper story in general.

——. ***Two Spies: Nathan Hale and Robert Townsend.*** **Boston and New York: Houghton Mifflin, 1930.**

Pierce, Kara. "A Revolutionary Masquerade: The Chronicles of James Rivington." Binghamton University. n.d. http://wwwz.binghampton.edu/history/esources/journal-of-history/chronicles-of-james-rivington.html.

Pierce's article offers a fascinating look into the personal life of James Rivington as well as his spying activities during the war and was an important resource in helping to reconstruct Rivington's mysterious character.

Pierce, Susan M. ***The History of Raynham Hall.*** **Thesis, Columbia University, 1986.**

This thesis study provided many helpful details about the architectural history of the Townsend family homestead and its position in colonial Oyster Bay.

Rose, Alexander. *Washington's Spies: The Story of America's First Spy Ring.* New York: Bantam, 2006.

Rose undertook a tremendous depth of research to complete his book, and it served as an excellent starting point in quite a few places for our own investigation into the matter. Especially helpful was his engagement with disparate primary sources that together formed a fuller picture of the Culper Ring's activities and accomplishments.

Ross, Peter. "A Few Revolutionary Heroes—General Woodhull—Colonel Tallmadge—General Parsons—Colonel Meigs." *A History of Long Island, from Its Earliest Settlement to the Present Time.* New York and Chicago: Lewis, 1902.

Schecter, Barnet. *The Battle for New York: The City at the Heart of the American Revolution.* New York: Walker, 2002.

This book proved especially important in helping us to understand the vital importance of New York City to the overall outcome of the war and allowed us to better grasp the significance of its political, strategic, and symbolic impact. It also helped us explain the high regard that Washington had for his spy network within the city.

Tallmadge, Benjamin. *Memoir of Colonel Benjamin Tallmadge Prepared by Himself at the Request of His Children.* New York: Thomas Holman, 1858. Reprint, New York: New York Times, 1968.

Most of the accounts of Tallmadge's activities and emotions come directly from his own pen in the memoirs he originally wrote in the final years of his life and first published for widespread distribution in 1858. Rarely is an author so lucky as to have the impressions and reflections of a historical figure in his original words. This is an especially valuable resource for any student of the American Revolution or Washington's spycraft.

Townsend, Robert. "Account Book of Robert Townsend, Merchant, of Oyster Bay Township, N.Y., and New York, N.Y., Begun November 23, 1779, and Continued to March 29, 1781." Transcription. East Hampton Library, Long Island Collection, East Hampton, NY.

The firsthand information revealed in this document was extremely helpful in understanding more about how Townsend operated first in Oyster Bay and later in Manhattan. Both the detailed entries and the periods of inactivity reveal a great deal about Townsend's patterns of behavior, possible emotional struggles, and business habits in managing his shop and his daily life.

Woodhull, Mary Gould, and Francis Bowes Stevens. *Woodhull Genealogy: The Woodhull Family in England and America*. Philadelphia: H. T. Coates, 1904.

INDEX